Praise for John-Peter Pham's
*Heirs of the Fisherman: Behind the Scenes
of Papal Death and Succession*

"While it looks to the future, *Heirs of the Fisherman* offers a grand historical sweep of significant elections past. Pham explains how conclaves developed and the forces that shaped their present, and still evolving, form. He writes with clarity and verve. . . . Makes history come alive in a way that illumines the present. . . . For those interested in understanding the conclave, Pham's book will be invaluable."

—Ann Rodgers, *America*

"A timely reference for those handicapping the race for the next pope—and contemplating the future of Catholicism. . . . Pham's study may well be the last word—for now—on the arcane and controversial ways popes have been selected in the past. . . . Of broader interest, however, is his reckoning of the challenges the next pope will face, especially since talk of such conditional matters is very nearly taboo in Vatican circles. . . . Students of the papacy will find this an invaluable reference."

—*Kirkus Reviews* (starred review)

"Those who are interested in understanding an event that is usually a milestone in religious and even in secular history will find no better resource in the English language."

—Ladislas Orsy, Professor of Canon Law at
Georgetown University Law Center

"Pham's exhaustive approach and informed view will appeal to anyone interested in more than a cursory treatment of this fascinating subject. . . . this book could easily be required reading for papal observers and journalists reporting on the election."

—*Publishers Weekly*

"A lucid and useful book . . . Pham's long and detailed account of the historical intricacies of one pope succeeding another, going back two millennia, makes clear what a profoundly human institution the papacy is."

—James Carroll, *Washington Post Book World*

"A former Vatican diplomat and frequent writer on religious and public affairs, Pham here offers a veritable reference encyclopedia in disguise. . . . In a readable and objective fashion, Pham . . . shows how the tremendous struggle among popes, monarchs, and others, especially over investiture, eventually gave way in the 1100s as the electoral mechanism of the conclave developed. Such complex history often necessitates leaping back and forth in time, and Pham makes high drama of particular moments with clarity and frankness. As the likelihood of a new pontiff draws closer, this book is all the more timely."

—*Library Journal* (starred review)

"Both interesting and pleasurable to read."

—*thepopeblog.com*

"The Papacy is an extraordinary institution that has outlived nations and empires, and might yet flourish long after our present world order has faded into legend. All the more important, then, that we understand the complexities of papal power and the papal succession. *Heirs of the Fisherman* is a mine of information on these subjects, offering a lucid and helpful analysis of the process of papal elections, with some important thoughts on how papal power stands in the modern world."

—Philip Jenkins, author of
The New Anti-Catholicism and
The Next Christendom

"This UPSTAIRS/DOWNSTAIRS look at the papacy and papal succession reveals the institution itself to be Western history's most successful irony. Dr. Pham writes as a privileged observer of this long-running ballet as the dancers wait in the wings for its next act . . . "

—Paul E. Dinter, author of
*The Other Side of the Altar:
One Man's Life in the Catholic Priesthood*

"This very readable book masterfully brings together the history of papal elections, the present procedures, and insightful prognostication of what might happen in the election of a new pope. Pham skillfully uses history, objective analysis, anecdotes, and an insider's knowledge in this lively exposition. The most complete one-volume explanation of papal elections in the past and present."

—Charles E. Curran, author of the forthcoming
The Moral Theology of Pope John Paul II

HEIRS OF THE FISHERMAN

Behind the Scenes of Papal Death and Succession

JOHN-PETER PHAM

OXFORD
UNIVERSITY PRESS

OXFORD

UNIVERSITY PRESS

Oxford University Press, Inc., publishes works that
further Oxford University's objective of excellence
in research, scholarship, and education.

Oxford   New York
Auckland   Cape Town   Dar es Salaam   Hong Kong   Karachi
Kuala Lumpur   Madrid   Melbourne   Mexico City   Nairobi
New Delhi   Shanghai   Taipei   Toronto

With offices in
Argentina   Austria   Brazil   Chile   Czech Republic   France   Greece
Guatemala   Hungary   Italy   Japan   Poland   Portugal   Singapore
South Korea   Switzerland   Thailand   Turkey   Ukraine   Vietnam

Copyright © 2004 by John-Peter Pham

First published by Oxford University Press, Inc., 2004
198 Madison Avenue, New York, NY 10016
www.oup.com

First issued as an Oxford University Press paperback, 2006
ISBN-13: 978-0-19-530561-6
ISBN-10: 0-19-530561-2

Oxford is a registered trademark of Oxford University Press

The Library of Congress has cataloged the cloth edition as follows:
Pham, John-Peter.
Heirs of the Fisherman : behind the scenes of papal death and succession
/ John-Peter Pham.
p. cm.
Includes bibliographical references and index.
ISBN-13: 978-0-19-517834-0   ISBN-10: 0-19-517834-3
1. Popes—Election—History. I. Title.
BX1805.P45   2004
262'.13—dc22
200400726

Printed in the United States of America
on acid-free paper

FOR FAITHFUL FRIENDS

*De amicitia omnes ad unum idem sentiunt . . . sine amicitia vitam esse nullam,
si modo velint aliqua ex parte liberaliter vivere.*

Cicero, *Laelius de amicitia*, xxiii, 86.

CONTENTS

PREFACE

THE ORIGINAL EDITION OF THIS BOOK was written as Pope John Paul II celebrated his twenty-fifth anniversary on the papal throne. By the time it came off the presses in late 2004, the pontiff's steady decline had become painfully evident. On April 2, 2005, after having enjoyed the second longest reign of any of the 261 successors of St. Peter, John Paul passed into history. But, as chronicled in these pages, the Church he had led into the new millennium continued as it always had along its pilgrim way, calling forth another heir to the fisherman from Galilee, forging another link in the Western world's oldest dynasty, as the 115 cardinals elected their dean, Joseph Ratzinger, as Pope Benedict XVI. Even as Benedict begins writing his own chapter in the millennial history of the papacy, his advanced age—he turned seventy-eight just two days before his election—means that it may be a brief, if dramatic, one. Thus the story of papal death and succession will continue to be a timely one.

The text of the present volume remains substantially unchanged from the original except for the introduction and the last chapter, both of which now take into account the death of John Paul II and the election of his successor, and some editing in the appendices to bring various persons and figures up to date. An eighth appendix contains my annotated translation of the published text of the last will and testament of Pope John Paul.

Once again, I have incurred many debts that require discharge. Jordan Bucher, my publicist at Oxford University Press, and Janet Smith, of the James Madison University Office of Media Relations, earned my gratitude for the patience and skill with which they handled the hundreds of members of the press who literally besieged me with calls and emails in the days from the final agony of John Paul II through the installation of Benedict XVI. I might add, they also handled a tired and increasingly irascible author quite deftly as well, buying him respite when necessary and steering him through a maze of television, radio, telephone, and email interviews. Likewise, Soo Chu Yee provided a harbor of tranquility amidst the storm. For all the others, I renew the dedication of the original edition as well as the heartfelt sentiments captured by its Ciceronian epigram.

PREFACE TO THE ORIGINAL EDITION

ON JUNE 29, 1944, on the occasion of the Feast of the Apostles Peter and Paul, founders and patron saints of the Church of Rome, the future Pope Paul VI, then Monsignor Giovanni Battista Montini, *sostituto*[1] of the Secretariat of State, addressed an assembly of the Palatine Guard that gathered in St. Peter's Basilica in the Vatican. The shadow of the German occupation of the Eternal City had just passed, and the reigning pontiff, Pope Pius XII (1939–1958), had been hailed as *"Defensor Civitatis"* ("Defender of the City") by the delirious crowds when Rome was liberated three weeks earlier. Against the backdrop of these dramatic events, the prelate allowed himself the luxury of rhetorical eloquence:

> Recall the words of Jesus who said to Peter: *"Super hanc petram aedificabo Ecclésiam meam . . .* On this rock I will build my Church." Jesus conceived of Saint Peter as an architect on whose construction an immense development would be centered, a human edifice that would outlast the centuries and embrace the whole earth. Space and time have no bounds. The words of Jesus have been fulfilled. The Roman Empire fell and the Church rebuilt and created Europe and its civilization, despite crises like the medieval and the Protestant. And now, in the midst of this modern crisis in which sees the collapse of empires, in a war that is perhaps headed to the exhaustion and the ruin of both sides, the Church stands firm and potent.

If the future pope's words strike a smug triumphal tone, coming as they did from a prelate who was then considered the closest confidant of Pius XII, the sentiments he expressed were not that different from those of General Charles de Gaulle, himself no pious sentimentalist. By coincidence, the day following Montini's sermon, the French leader was received at the papal court. In his memoirs, de Gaulle dedicated two pages to the encounter with the pope and described the papacy and its incumbent in terms of the eternity of Rome: "Like Rome, which, from the heights of its serenity, keeps watch as, century after century, the constant flow of men and events washes up against its walls, so too the Church, firm but compassionate, keeps vigil over the ebbs and flows of the war . . . His information and reflections do not permit [the pope] to ignore the drama that convulses the world. His lucid thought is fixed on the consequences of the unleashing on the world of the communist and nationalist ideologies . . . His conviction is that only faith, hope, and Christian charity—even if they be forced underground everywhere and for a long time to come—will overcome these menaces."[2]

Half a century later, with the Iron Curtain gone and the Communist ideology consigned to the dustbin of history, the American weekly *Time* designated the incumbent pontiff as its "Man of the Year" for 1994, explaining its choice in these terms: "Pope John Paul II has, among many other things, the world's bulliest pulpit. Few of his predecessors over the past 2,000 years have spoken from it as often and as forcefully as he. When he talks, it is not only to his flock of nearly a billion; he expects the world to listen. And the flock and the world listen, not always liking what they hear . . . People who see him—and countless millions have—do not forget him. His appearances generate an electricity unmatched by anyone else on earth."[3] Not bad for the heir of a Galilean fisherman who abandoned his nets and boat on the seashore in response to an itinerant first-century Jewish preacher's call and promise: "Come, follow me, and I will make you fishers of men" (Matthew 4:19).

Fishers of men though they have been, each in his own time, the heirs of the fisherman—there have been, according to the legitimate order of succession, 261 heirs to the mantle of Simon, son of John, called Peter[4]—have been men, subject to all the grandeur and all the misery that is the human condition. Some were saints, others little better than bandits. Some were beloved, others execrated. Descending from Peter, the line of succession passes through the great and the mediocre, the benevolent and the malevolent, the blessed and the unfortunate, including in its singular embrace Leo I, hailed as "the Great," whose memory is venerated even in the Eastern Churches that broke communion with the Roman See; Formosus, who knew peace neither in life nor in death—his corpse was exhumed and mutilated by his successor, Stephen VI; Boniface VI, who ascended to the papal office after having been twice defrocked for gross immorality; Gregory VII, who humiliated an emperor and exalted the papal office; Innocent III, in whose pontificate the papal monarchy reached its medieval zenith; Alexander VI, the Borgia pontiff who helped to hasten the Protestant Reformation by the corruption and sensuality of his life; John XXIII, the beloved "good pope," who opened the Church to the modern world; and John Paul II, the present bishop of Rome, who contributed immensely to the collapse of the Soviet empire and whose ecclesiastical legacy remains to be determined.

And although—at least in the minds of believers—the office that these popes have held in succession to the "Prince of the Apostles" who, as "Vicar of Christ," was to "strengthen [his] brethren" (Luke 22:32), is of divine origin, how these men have been raised to that office is a very human affair. While the faithful may console themselves with the confidence that the infinite makes itself evident through the instrumentality of the finite, traditional Catholic theology nonetheless insists on the freedom of the human individual and his or her will. And human individuals, as well as humankind in general, are prone to be conditioned by the times and circumstances in which they find themselves. As the Second Vatican Council, in its "Pastoral Constitution on the Church in the Modern World," proclaimed majestically: "The joys and the hopes, the griefs and the anxieties of the men of this age, especially those who are poor or in any way afflicted, these are the joys and hopes, the griefs and anxieties of the followers of Christ. Indeed, nothing genuinely human fails to raise an echo in their hearts. For theirs is a community composed of men. United in Christ, they are led by the Holy Spirit in their journey to the Kingdom of their Father and they have welcomed the news of salvation which is meant for every man. That is why this community realizes that it is truly linked with mankind and its history by the deepest of bonds" (Gaudium et spes, 1).

Consequently, not only is the story of papal death and succession a very human story, but it is one that, now more than ever before, is of interest to all members of the human family, whether Catholic or non-Catholic, believer or not. The telling of this story, long veiled from profane eyes, is the object of the present book. Strictly speaking, this work constitutes a narrative set in a theological and historical context, rather than a proper history. Proper histories require primary sources, which, due in part to the strictures of secrecy surrounding papal succession that will be discussed subsequently, are simply unavailable. Nonetheless, the insular community of the Vatican is not without its oral traditions, and a rich lore is faithfully handed down to initiates, in whose company I was included for a number of years. In lifting the veil a little and opening this behind-the-scenes world to those on the outside, it is my hope that this rich history, replete with all its lessons, might serve not only as an introduction to the pageantry of the Catholic Church but also as an invitation for a wider public discussion, not just of the rituals and personalities that will surround the next sede vacante[5] but of the succession process itself.

The writing of any book, even one where only an individual's name appears as its author, is nevertheless a profoundly social enterprise, involving the contributions and support of many people. This is even more so in a case like my own, where the work in question was nurtured over many yeas and its final writing owed itself to a set of circumstances that mark the closing of a chapter in its author's life. Hence, I have incurred many debts that I must discharge.

Monsignor Charles Burns of the Vatican Archives, professor of ecclesiastical and diplomatic history at Pontifical Ecclesiastical Academy, encouraged a young student's passion for the past, giving it an analytical framework within the ebb and flow of modern politics and international relations. That love of history was nurtured by the treasure trove of lore that I acquired from long hours of conversation with the late Bishop Petrus Canisius Johannes van Lierde, vicar general of His Holiness for the Vatican under Popes Pius XII, John XXIII, Paul VI, John Paul I, and John Paul II, during the three years I was privileged to serve as his aide. The late Cardinal François-Xavier Nguyên van Thuân, president of the Pontifical Council for Justice and Peace and himself *papabile* at one point, provided me with a window into contemporary dynamics and a vision of a possible future for the Church and also honored me with the commission to edit and translate his two autobiographical works. Of course, these individuals and other priest friends are not in any way responsible for the interpretations and viewpoints that are entirely my own.

My agent, John F. Thornton of the Spieler Agency, showed great faith in this book as well as considerable patience with its author; I am indebted to him. I also want to thank Elda Rotor, senior editor at Oxford University Press, for her thoughtful editorial suggestions, and her assistant, Cybele Tom, for her help, especially after Elda went on maternity leave, embracing a far greater bundle of joy than my voluminous manuscript. I am likewise indebted to the peer reviewers who read the manuscript; the detailed comment that they provided with exceptional generosity proved invaluable. I am lucky to have had India Cooper as a copy editor: Her proficiency with her craft much improved the finished text. I am also grateful to the production and marketing staffs of Oxford University Press, many of whom an author never meets, but whose contributions are indispensable to the final product.

I have many others to whom I owe thanks, not only for helping me with this book but also for having walked with me on my journey thus far, occasionally even picking me up and dragging me along. Particularly to those who have remained faithful throughout the twists and turns of the road traveled, I will never be able to fully repay the debt. I can only offer the dedication of this volume and make the words of Cicero quoted therein my own, for without these friends life would indeed lose its meaning.

HEIRS OF THE FISHERMAN

JOHN PAUL II CROSSES A THRESHOLD

ON THE MORNING OF APRIL 8, 2005, Cardinal Joseph Ratzinger, dean of the College of Cardinals,[1] stood on the steps of St. Peter's Basilica and looked out on the vast crowd that had gathered between the arms of Bernini's colonnade to pay their final respects to the man whose body lay before the outdoor altar, sealed inside a simple cypress coffin adorned with a simple cross and the letter *M* for Mary.[2] The cardinal's thoughts no doubt went back to another, happier, celebration in the same *piazza* less than two years earlier. On October 16, 2003, Pope John Paul II had celebrated the silver anniversary of his election to the Throne of St. Peter, thus reaching a milestone that only two of the successors to the Prince of the Apostles achieved. Of these two predecessors, Blessed Pius IX (1846–1878), who reigned thirty-one years, seven months, and three weeks, and Leo XIII (1878–1903), who reigned twenty-five years and five months, only the former had enjoyed a longer tenure on the papal throne than John Paul. At the beginning of the Mass that the pope celebrated on the steps of St. Peter's Basilica before an assembly of the faithful estimated in the hundreds of thousands—a prodigious congregation that was easily dwarfed by the current one—Ratzinger saluted the pontiff on behalf of his confrères, the men who would now be called upon to elect John Paul's successor:

> In these twenty-five years as Vicar of Jesus Christ in the apostolic succession, you have tirelessly traveled the world, not only to bring to men and women the Gospel of the love of God made flesh in Jesus Christ, beyond all geographical boundaries; you have also crossed the continents of the spirit, often far from one another and set against each other, to bring strangers close, to make the distant friends, and to make room in the world for the peace of Christ. You have spoken to young and old, to the rich and the poor, the powerful and the humble—after the example of Jesus Christ—and you have always shown special love for the poor and defenseless,

bringing to all a spark of God's truth and love. You have proclaimed God's will fearlessly, even when it was in opposition to what people thought and desired. Like the Apostle Paul, you can say that you have never sought to flatter with words nor to be honored by mankind, but have watched over God's children as a mother. Like Paul, you too felt drawn to people and wanted to help them share not only in the Gospel but also in your own life. You have undergone criticism and insults, arousing, however, gratitude and love, and causing the walls of hatred and unfamiliarity to crumble.

While certainly not everyone—not even among his cardinals, although they would rarely, if ever, be wont to admit that there was dissension among their ranks—agreed with the ecclesiastical, much less the political, stances that John Paul II took during his more than two and a half decades in the papal office, the presence of the throngs spilling from St. Peter's Square onto the Via della Conciliazione and neighboring streets to now bid him adieu testified to the formidable moral and religious strength of both the Roman Catholic Church and its central institution, the papacy, even in the postmodern twenty-first century that finds Christianity's language of sin and redemption unintelligible. Whether they found him godly or holier-than-thou, the great and mighty of the world acknowledged that John Paul was a global player, a political force to be reckoned with. None of the world leaders present at the exequies would have thought of sneering and asking, as Joseph Stalin did when he asked French foreign minister Pierre Laval, "The Pope! How many divisions has *he* got?"[3] Stalin's empire has since fallen, in no small part due to the contributions of the pope from Poland, whose funeral was now attended by an unprecedented 190 extraordinary delegations of state (the U.S. delegation was led by President George W. Bush himself, the first sitting American president to attend a papal funeral, joined by two former presidents, his father, George H. W. Bush, and Bill Clinton) as well as representatives of numerous international organizations. Indicative of the legacy of the deceased pontiff, a large number of non-Catholic churches and denominations and even non-Christian religions sent high-ranking official representatives, whose number included the Ecumenical Patriarch, Bartholomew I of Constantinople; the Archbishop of Canterbury, Dr. Rowan Williams; Dr. Samuel Kobia, secretary-general of the World Council of Churches; the Chief Rabbi of Rome, Riccardo Di Segni; and Rabbi Israel Singer, president of the governing board of the World Jewish Congress. A funeral it was—in fact, the largest in human history—but it was also a triumphalistic reminder that, despite the vicissitudes of history, the Roman pontiff remains the most influential religious leader on the world stage, one whose comings and goings are of interest not just to members of his flock but to the whole world.

The Achievements of a Pontificate

During his pontificate John Paul II promulgated an extraordinarily voluminous corpus of official documents, in addition to being the first pontiff to publish personal theological and religious works while in office since the ill-fated John XXII (1316–1334), whose opinions on the beatific vision were condemned as heretical by the theologians of his time.[4] John Paul's official documents included fourteen encyclicals, from *Redemptor hominis* (1979),[5] on Jesus Christ as the redeemer of man, through *Ecclesia de Eucharistia* (2003), on the importance of the Eucharist in the life of the Church; thirteen apostolic constitutions from *Sapientia Christiana* (1979), which reorganized ecclesiastical faculties and universities, through *Universi Dominici gregis* (1996), which regulates the vacancy of the Apostolic See and the election of the Roman pontiff, and *Ecclesia in Urbe* (1998) which reorganized the pastoral government of the Vicariate of Rome; twenty-six apostolic letters *motu proprio*, from *Egregia virtutis* (1980), which proclaimed SS. Cyril and Methodius, the apostles to the Slavs, as co-patrons of Europe alongside the father of Western monasticism, St. Benedict, through *Misericordia Dei* (2002), which reaffirmed traditional disciplines regarding the sacrament of penance; fifteen apostolic exhortations, from *Catechesi tradendae* (1979), on catechism in the contemporary Church, through *Pastores gregis* on the ministry of bishops in the Church, which the pope promulgated on the date of the twenty-fifth anniversary of his election to the papacy; and numerous apostolic letters, including *Ordinatio sacerdotalis* (1994), which reaffirmed the reservation of the priesthood to men, *Tertio millennio adveniente* (1994), which prepared for the jubilee of the year 2000, and *Rosarium Virginis Mariae* (2002), which instituted five new "luminous" mysteries to the rosary. John Paul II also promulgated the Code of Canon Law (1983) for the Western (Latin) Church, the Code of Canons of the Eastern Churches (1990) for the Eastern Rite Churches in communion with Rome, the *Catechism of the Catholic Church* (1993), the revised *editio typica* of the Roman Missal (2002), and numerous other liturgical and legal documents.

During his twenty-five years on the papal throne, John Paul II presided over an unprecedented fifty-one canonization ceremonies, proclaiming 482 new saints, 402 of them martyrs and 80 of them confessors of the faith. The new saints include one cardinal, twenty-two bishops, ninety-six diocesan priests, 116 religious men and women, and, extraordinarily, 247 lay men and women. Additionally, the pope presided over 149 beatification ceremonies, proclaiming a total of 1,338 new *beati*,[6] including Mother Teresa of Calcutta, beatified on October 19, 2003, in the midst of the pontiff's silver anniversary celebrations.

In his nine consistories, John Paul II named 233 cardinals, including the one created *in pectore*, that is, whose name has not yet been revealed. Of the 117 cardinals who, being under the age of eighty when the pope died on April 2, 114 owed their positions to John Paul (the remaining three were created by Pope Paul VI).[7] Of the total 183 effective members of the College of Cardinals, not counting the anonymous prelate reserved *in pectore*, 170 were created by John Paul II and thirteen by Paul VI. In addition to the consistories to create new cardinals, John Paul convened the college in six plenary meetings to consult on matters of major importance, such as the Vatican's financial difficulties.

Less noticeable in the press, but perhaps far more influential over the long term, was John Paul II's impact on the composition of the worldwide episcopate of the Catholic Church. As of the morning of his death—incredibly, the Curia continued to announce appointments, ostensibly made previously, even after it became clear that the dying pope had slipped into a coma—John Paul II had appointed 3,955 bishops (of whom 362 predeceased the pontiff), more than three-quarters of the members of the worldwide College of Bishops. In addition to the quinquennial *ad limina* visits and other personal encounters with individual bishops, John Paul convened fifteen meetings of the Synod of Bishops during his pontificate.

Of course, an appointment by John Paul II is not necessarily a guarantee of philosophical or political uniformity. However, most papal nominees have fallen within a narrow range of acceptable orthodoxy, and the few who have ventured abroad have been quickly recalled. On the day after the pope announced his creation as a cardinal in the consistory of October 2003, Keith Michael Patrick O'Brien, archbishop of Saint Andrews and Edinburgh, surprisingly spoke out in favor of a more open attitude toward married priests, homosexual priests, and contraception. A week later, under pressure from the Vatican and with Bible in hand, he made an extraordinary public retraction before worshippers in his Scottish cathedral: "I state that I accept and intend to defend the law on ecclesiastical celibacy as it is proposed by the magisterium of the Catholic Church; I accept and promise to defend the ecclesiastical teaching about the immorality of the homosexual act; I accept and promise to promulgate always and everywhere what the Church's magisterium teaches on contraception." Only time will tell whether the conformity extracted from O'Brien and others will perdure or whether other sentiments, long repressed, will find expression in future pontificates.

John Paul II's pontificate was characterized by extensive diplomatic activity. Full bilateral diplomatic relations at the ambassadorial level were forged or reestablished with eighty-six countries,[8] bringing to a total of 174 the number of countries⁹ maintaining diplomatic relations with the Holy See in addition to the European Union and the Sovereign Military Order of Malta. Furthermore, the Vatican maintains what are described as "diplomatic relations of a special nature" with the Russian Federation and the Palestinian Liberation Organization, with the permanent exchange of "envoys on special mission with the personal rank of ambassador" in the case of the former. During his pontificate—at least according to the official statistics released on his twenty-fifth anniversary—John Paul II had over seven hundred audiences or other meetings with heads of state and received 226 prime ministers or heads of government. Thirty-eight heads of state were received at the Vatican with the full ceremonial of a "state visit." As a result of these contacts, in addition to its token participation in multilateral international conventions, the Holy See under John Paul signed over one hundred concordats, accords, and other bilateral treaties affecting the relations of the Catholic Church with and in certain countries or territories, including the historic "Basic Agreement" with the State of Israel (1993) and the "Basic Agreement" with the Palestine Liberation Organization (2000).

A distinctive element of John Paul's papacy was his extensive travels, which have been unprecedented in the history of the papal office.[10] During his pontificate, the pope made 104 "apostolic visits," which took him to 131 countries and distinct territories.[11] In addition to visits to almost all of the parishes in his diocese of Rome, the pope also made 146 pastoral visits to dioceses and other locations within Italy—beginning with his visit to the Marian shrine of Mentorella shortly after his election in 1978 and concluding with his visit to the shrine of Our Lady of Loreto in September 2004. The pontiff also promoted the celebrations of "World Youth Days"—a total of nineteen official events in addition to two earlier gatherings before the initiative was announced in 1985—that brought him into contact with millions of young people.

Unlike many of his papal predecessors, John Paul II continued during his pontificate to exercise sacramental ministries. According to data released by the Secretariat of State during the pope's twenty-fifth anniversary celebration, up to that point, he had personally ordained 321 bishops and 2,810 priests. He has also blessed seventy-seven marriages, anointed 274 sick people, confirmed 1,581 individuals, baptized 1,378 adults and children, and even exorcised two. When at home in the Vatican, John Paul II held regular general audiences on Wednesdays, receiving some 17 million pilgrims in the more than one thousand general audiences of his pontificate—which, in addition to the millions encountered during his travels, arguably made him the historical personality who has been seen by more people in person than any other.

A Pope's Legacy

During his quarter-century as pope, John Paul racked up an impressive list of accomplishments, even if he bequeathed to his successor a not entirely unambiguous and uncontested theological and ecclesiastical legacy, as he himself admitted in an interview with Italian journalist Vittorio Messori earlier in his pontificate:

> You rightly assert that *the Pope is a mystery.* You rightly assert that he is a *sign that will be contradicted,* that he is a *challenge.* The old man Simeon said of Christ Himself that He would be "a sign that will be contradicted." You also contend that, confronted with such a truth—that is, confronted with the Pope—*one must choose;* and for many the choice is not easy. But was it so easy for Peter? Was it easy for any of his successors? Is it easy for the present Pope? To choose requires man's initiative. Christ says: "For flesh and blood has not revealed this to you, but my heavenly Father" (Mt 16:17). This choice, therefore, is not only a human initiative but also an *act of God,* who works and reveals himself through man. And in virtue of such an act of God, a person can repeat, "You are the Messiah, the Son of the living God," and then recite the entire *Creed,* which echoes the profound logic of Revelation. A man can also remind himself, as well as others, of the consequences of this logic of the faith which also display the same *splendor of the truth.* A man can do all of this even though he knows that because of it he will become "a sign that will be contradicted."[12]

History will undoubtedly record the central role that Pope John Paul II played in bringing about the downfall of Soviet Communism not only in Poland but throughout Eastern Europe and beyond. Another one of his pontificate's accomplishments was the cultivation of relatively harmonious relations between Catholicism and other Christian denominations as well as Judaism, moderate Islam, and other faiths. Under the pope's leadership, tremendous strides were made in the Vatican's often uneasy relationship with Judaism, culminating in the establishment of full diplomatic ties between the Holy See and the State of Israel in 1993 as well as John Paul's own historic pilgrimage to the Jewish state. A signal tribute to the success of John Paul's interfaith efforts was seen when international Muslim organizations joined evangelical Protestant and Mormon groups to defend the Holy See's unique status at the United Nations as a "non-member state maintaining a permanent observer mission." On the other hand, the Vatican's status at the UN had come under attack in a campaign led by feminist and pro-choice groups precisely because of the pivotal role that the pope's envoys played in coordinating an unlikely alliance of Muslim nations in the Middle East and developing countries against the attempt, led by the Clinton administration, to establish a global right to abortion at the World Population Conference in Cairo in 1994. For many, in fact, there was no clearer example of the pope's obscurantism than his adamant insistence on the inherent immorality not only of abortion but of "artificial means" of contraception, even when used by married couples and other monogamous heterosexual adults.

John Paul's papacy was a "sign of contradiction" not only outside the Catholic Church but within its walls as well. While even his harshest critic within the Church could not impeach John Paul's personal integrity, his single-minded dedication to what he perceived to be his duty, and his commitment to an almost mystical holiness of life, they nonetheless pointed to a whole catalogue of woes, including defections and apathy among younger Catholics, falling Mass attendance across the board, an aging priesthood that seems to be self-destructing, often vicious intramural conflicts between progressives and conservatives involving a host of moral and jurisdictional issues, ever-increasing rates of divorce among Catholics, alarming syncretism (the mixing of Christian beliefs and practices with those of non-Christian traditions) in Africa and Latin America, and the *de facto* paganization of once-Christian Europe. What the former senior religion correspondent of the *New York Times*, Peter Steinfels, recently observed about the Church in America—"Today the Roman Catholic Church in the United States is on the verge of either an irreversible decline or a thoroughgoing transformation"[13]—is equally applicable to the worldwide body at the time of the pontiff's passing.

The official response to these concerns usually involved pointing to impressive statistics, such as those supplied to papal diplomatic representatives on the occasion of the pope's twenty-fifth anniversary with the exhortation to "bring them to the attention of the episcopal conferences and the local press."[14] Worldwide, the Curia pointed out, the number of baptized Catholics rose from 756,533,000 in 1978 to 1,060,840,000 in 2001 (the statistics for 2002 and 2003 were then unavailable, subsequently counted 1,085,557,000 Catholic worldwide in the latter year). The most dramatic increase has been in Africa, where Church membership more than doubled from 54,759,000 (12.37 percent of the total population) in 1978 to 143,659,000 (16.77 percent of the total population) a quarter of a century later. Other members of the hierarchy pointed to the fact that the pope, who admittedly despaired of middle-aged Catholics, reposed his hope for the future in the youth. The World Youth Day phenomenon has certainly been one of the most astonishing features of John Paul's pontificate: In 1997, for example, secular France was flabbergasted to discover over a million young people flocking to the pope at the World Youth Day in Paris. The spectacle repeated itself in Rome during the Jubilee Year of 2000 and in Toronto in 2002, where an estimated eight hundred thousand youths cheered a pontiff who by then was clearly stricken by Parkinson's disease, twitching as he drooled out of the corner of his mouth. Likewise there is no denying the perseverance of the faith of millions of ordinary Catholics and a thirst for spirituality on the part of countless others unsatisfied by materialism and a desiccated postmodernity.

On the other hand, the objective observer also arrives at the inescapable conclusion that numbers are not everything. Passing displays of mass enthusiasm belie the true state of affairs: In France, for example, barely 10 percent of the young people who greeted John Paul II in 1997 have become anything approaching regular churchgoers. The increase in the number of Catholics worldwide has not been matched by a similar increase in the number of priests: When John Paul ascended the papal throne, Catholics worldwide could count on having one priest for every 1,797; twenty-five years later (the last year for which reliable statistics are available), the ratio is one priest for every 2,677 Catholics. And various crises—including, but not limited to, the clergy child abuse scandal—have taken their toll on the morale of a flock that is often dangerously polarized between ideologues of the left and the right. These tensions were only exacerbated as the increasingly ailing John Paul suffered a protracted illness, while others in the hierarchy were paralyzed as a result of the pontificate's heavy emphasis on the person of the pope and the juridical authority of the central government of the Church that is dependent upon him. In any event, John Paul's legacy to his eventual successor consisted of both high expectations and monumental challenges.

The Next Pope and the World

For all these reasons, the choice of John Paul's successor was of considerable interest to more than just Catholics, a truth of *Realpolitik* that astute statesmen—including many of the official mourners—have long understood. Despite the humiliating blows that he had dealt the papacy, Napoleon Bonaparte still recognized the worldly power inherent in the papal office. When, as First Consul, he sent François Cacault to Rome as his envoy to Pope Pius VII (1800–1823), he instructed the diplomat to "deal with the pope as if he had two hundred thousand men at his command"—the military genius denominating the pontiff's influence on world affairs in military terms. Despite the fact that social convention prevented discussing events beyond the just-ended pontificate at the pope's funeral, much attention was nonetheless riveted on the Catholic Church's search for a successor to John Paul II. The new man would have to manage a difficult balancing act, not only amid the doctrinal and moral shoals of Catholic belief but with respect to the Church's relations with the world and, as a consequence, the role that the more than one billion Catholics play within humanity.

With the overwhelming majority of his flock expected to live in Latin America, Africa, and Asia by 2025, the next Roman pontiff would be expected to be a spokesman for more equitable economic development and political empower-ment, while not antagonizing those members of his flock who still live in Eu-rope and North America with some papal version of left-wing clericalism. As theologian and sociologist Uwe Siemon-Netto had observed: "Should the next pope be any less sensitive to global social concerns than John Paul II—or should he, conversely, proclaim a social Gospel rather than preaching social responsibil-ity from the Gospel—the consequences might be catastrophic."[15] On the other hand, lacking the military forces and economic might that, in the power calcula-tions of international statecraft, underlie effective power, John Paul's successor would have only the papacy's moral authority to rely on—and it is an authority that, given the battering it has taken in recent times, would only be effective in the measure that its exercise was judicious. Consequently, the eyes of billions—some of them devout members of the Catholic faith, others less devout, others less faithful, and still others of different faiths or no faith at all—focused on the events that followed John Paul's passage into eternity.

Notwithstanding the global political and strategic import of the election of the new pope, the election—arguably the oldest electoral process by secret bal-lot in continuous use in the world—would feature a very limited franchise: Un-der the canon (church) law presently in force, it is limited to those members of the College of Cardinals who were under the age of eighty at the moment John Paul drew his last breath. While Catholic theology has traditionally held that there is a divine providence at work in the election of the Roman pontiff, the election itself would be a very human event, one conditioned by the his-torical circumstances of the moment and the basic human idiosyncrasies of the electors—a balance that the white-haired dean of the College of Cardinals, Ratzinger, understood well as he turned from the bier to survey his gathered confrères: his own motto, *Cooperatores Veritatis* ("Co-Workers of the Truth"), enshrined the conviction that humans had the freedom to cooperate in the plans of the Almighty. For all else, it sufficed to recall that in commenting on Stalin's impertinent query to Laval about the number of divisions that the pope pos-sessed, Winston Churchill noted, "Laval's answer was not reported to me; but he might certainly have mentioned a number of legions not always visible on parade."[16] Humanity thus anxiously awaited the intervention of those unseen legions in the first papal election of the twenty-first century.

Chapter One

THE POPE IS DEAD!

IN ROME THERE IS A SAYING that declares, *"Pietro non muore,"* "Peter does not die." While allegorically Peter, like his city, is eternal in the unbroken line of his successors, it is nonetheless true that Gregory, Pius, Leo, Benedict, Paul, and John Paul die. In fact, the medieval and baroque iconography of the Eternal City is full of depictions illustrating the certainty that not even the highest dignity in the world—understood to be that of the Vicar of Christ—can exempt a man from humanity's common mortality. For example, the funerary monument of Pope Alexander VII (1655–1667) in St. Peter's Basilica, a masterpiece in Sicilian jasper of Gian Lorenzo Bernini's art, contains, among its haunting figures, a skeleton brandishing a scythe and showing an hourglass to the Chigi pope,[1] as if to tell him that the hour of his death had come.

While his mortality makes him like any other man, the rituals that begin immediately upon his death markedly separate a pope from the rest of humanity, as if to remind one and all that the deceased was no mere mortal but was, in Catholic belief, the latest in an unbroken line going back to Simon, called Peter, son of John, the Galilean fisherman to whom Jesus of Nazareth, incarnate Son of God, entrusted the care of his nascent flock. The official yearbook of the Holy See, the *Annuario Pontificio,* gives the titles of the incumbent pontiff as "Bishop of Rome, Successor of St. Peter, Prince of the Apostles, Vicar of Jesus Christ, Supreme Pontiff of the Universal Church, Patriarch of the West, Archbishop and Metropolitan of the Roman Province, Primate of Italy, Sovereign of the Vatican City State." The papal titles are not merely ceremonial but have a theological and canonical significance often forgotten, even by Catholics. The incumbent pontiff combines in his person these overlapping titles, each of which gives him a special relationship to the faithful and the bishops in the corresponding territory. As bishop of Rome he is the diocesan bishop of that diocese only;

as metropolitan he has jurisdiction over the bishops and dioceses that make up the Roman Province; as primate he presides over the Italian bishops; and as patriarch he has specific oversight over the West. In the latter role, the Roman pontiff has from ancient times ruled all the Western lands where Latin was once the civilized and, until recently, the liturgical language, and where the Roman Rite (or ritual order) is now used almost exclusively and the Roman canon law obtains. To Christians in the East, particularly those belonging to the Eastern Catholic Churches, he is supreme pontiff, not patriarch. Hence there has always been a closer relation between Western bishops and the pope than between him and their Eastern brethren, just as there is a still closer relation between him and the suburban bishops of the Roman Province of which he is metropolitan. Many customs and disciplines usually thought of as "Catholic," including clerical celibacy, actually are not universal laws of the Church but are particular to the canonical legislation of the Western patriarchate.

To the impressive catalogue of titles that appears in the papal yearbook, one may add the traditional "Servant of the Servants of God," first adopted by St. Gregory I (590–604) and in general use since St. Gregory VII (1073–1085), that still heads the Latin documents that emanate from the Vatican. And, although it has not yet appeared in official documents along with his formal titles, Pope John Paul II has repeatedly referred to himself as *"Pastore Universale della Chiesa"* ("Universal Pastor of the Church"), a title very much consonant with the "pastoral" style of papal ministry he likes to project.[2]

Is the Pope Dead?

The first ritual associated with papal death and succession is the ceremony to ascertain that the incumbent pope is truly dead. While this might seem strange in an age when medical science provides the means to monitor with great precision brain, heart, and other physiological functions, it should not be forgotten that it was not that long ago when the life or death of the members of the Soviet Politburo, to cite but one example, was subject to all manner of arcane speculation by international intelligence services. And the history of the papacy is replete with examples of the capital importance, political as well as spiritual, of verifying the death of the supreme pontiff.

The history of the papacy in the early Middle Ages was marked by constantly contested papal elections wherein the various claimants were often proxies for struggles between factions of the nobility. One such rivalry was that in the eleventh century between the Frangipani family, partisans of the German Holy Roman emperor, and the Pierleoni, a family of Jewish origins that was the standard-bearer for the nobility of the Roman countryside. When Paschal II (1099–1118) died after a long pontificate spent fighting the Emperor Henry V over the question of lay investiture,[3] the papal chancellor, Cardinal Giovanni Caetani, a Benedictine monk from Monte Cassino, was elected Gelasius II in an election held at Santa Maria in Pallara on the Palatine. The new pope had no sooner been elected, and had not yet been ordained a priest or consecrated a bishop[4]—although already elderly, he was only a deacon at the time—when he was brutally attacked and imprisoned by Cencius Frangipani. Although he was released through the intervention of Pier de Leone, prefect of the city, Gelasius fled to his native Gaeta with the cardinals when the Frangipani summoned aid from Henry V. The emperor then tried to set up an antipope,[5] Gregory VIII. When Henry left the city, after occupying it for several months, Gelasius returned, only to be attacked once more by the Frangipani when he tried to celebrate Mass at the Basilica of Santa Prassede, the Lateran Basilica[6] still being occupied by the antipope. Gelasius then fled to France; he died there at the Benedictine abbey of Cluny, where he had taken refuge, just four days short of the first anniversary of his election.

When Gelasius died, the cardinals who shared his exile quickly elected Callistus II (1119–1124) to succeed him; the cardinals remaining in Rome, under pressure from the Pierleoni, ratified the decision. In 1122, Callistus managed to arrive at an honorable settlement with the emperor through the Concordat of Worms. The emperor renounced investing those elected to bishoprics and abbeys with the ring and crosier, symbols of spiritual authority. The pope, for his part, granted to Henry personally the right to preside over elections to bishoprics and abbeys in Germany, provided that the elections were free and canonical. The emperor could then invest the candidate elected with the temporal jurisdiction of his office by means of the scepter, the symbol of temporal authority. In the lands of the empire outside Germany, the election could take place without the emperor's presence and the investiture could follow within six months of the elected candidate's consecration.

When Callistus died, the majority of the cardinals, meeting in Rome under the protection of the Pierleoni family, unanimously elected Cardinal Teobaldo Boccapecci as Celestine II. He had just been proclaimed pope and clothed with the red papal mantle, and the singing of the *Te Deum* hymn of thanksgiving had commenced, when the Frangipani broke into the assembly with armed troops. After a violent struggle, during which blows were rained upon the just-proclaimed Celestine, the papal chancellor and Leo Frangipani proclaimed Cardinal Lamberto Scannabecchi of Ostia as Pope Honorius II. The injured Celestine decided that discretion was the better part of valor and quickly resigned. The Pierleoni were paid a substantial bribe to withdraw, and the traumatized cardinals proceeded to duly elect and enthrone Honorius II, who reigned until 1130.

This complicated story sets the stage for what happened as Honorius fell ill. The chancellor, Cardinal Aimeric, foreseeing the end, had the dying pontiff removed to the monastery of San Gregorio on the Caelian Hill, where, guarded by soldiers from the nearby strongholds of the Frangipani, he died on the night between February 13 and February 14, 1130. After hastily burying Honorius in a temporary grave, Aimeric and his allies among the cardinals clandestinely elected Cardinal Gregory Papareschi as Innocent II (1130–1143), enthroning him at daybreak at the Lateran. When the news got out, the rest of the cardinals refused to accept the *de facto* coup and, meeting later in the morning in the Basilica of San Marco, elected Cardinal Pietro Pierleoni as Anacletus II.

Both elections were, by the canons of the time, irregular, Innocent's perhaps more glaringly so. The result was an eight-year schism, with both claimants (Anacletus II being succeeded in 1138 by Victor IV) competing for recognition. Victor II's act of abdication, which convalidated Innocent's election, finally put an end to the dispute in May 1138. The dispute arose not only because of the rivalry between the Frangipani and Pierleoni but because the legislation concerning papal elections was still a work-in-progress. Given the difficulties in travel at the time, the accepted procedure contained no stipulations as to how many members of the Sacred College constituted a quorum. Rather, it presumed that the election would take place among those cardinals present for the funeral of the deceased pontiff (as was the case in 1119, when the minority of cardinals present at Cluny with Gelasius II when he died elected Callistus II, the majority then accepting the decision). This loophole allowed the unscrupulous chancellor Aimeric to cloak the death and hasty funeral of Honorius II in secrecy, admitting only those cardinals sympathetic to his party into the election he engineered.

The importance of having a procedure for ascertaining the actual death of the reigning pope, a procedure that developed with great ritual over the centuries, has perhaps diminished somewhat in recent years with more tranquil times and the progress of medical science. Nevertheless, papal death remains an event vested with almost singular import, rendering it a public act—one likely to be even more closely observed in the age of the twenty-four-hour news cycle.

With the exception of John Paul I, who died unexpectedly during the night in 1978 after only thirty-three days on the papal throne, all the popes of the last two centuries have breathed their last surrounded by the members of their families and household staff as well as the highest-ranking officials of papal administration, including the dean of the Sacred College of Cardinals, the cardinal secretary of state,[7] the cardinal camerlengo (or chamberlain) of the Holy Roman Church,[8] and the cardinal major penitentiary,[9] who has the faculties to impart the indulgences that even a dying pope may feel the need for. Until Paul VI did away with the corps during his post–Vatican II simplification of the papal court, the Noble

Guards, in their scarlet uniforms and plumed helmets, would assume guard around the dying pontiff. Outside the bedchamber of the pope would gather various other dignitaries, ecclesiastical and lay, whose positions, while not elevated enough to permit them direct access to the dying pontiff, were nonetheless important enough to assure them a ringside seat at the drama unfolding.

Pope Pius XII (1939–1958), whose reserved personality caused him to be rather jealous of his privacy and resentful of intrusions, tried to limit the number of those present at his final agony in the summer of 1958. Unfortunately, he was ultimately unsuccessful in preventing his passing, the first to occur in the age of mass communications, from turning into a spectacle. A Jesuit priest from Vatican Radio, Father Francesco Pellegrino, set up a radio transmitter in the adjacent room, broadcasting updates on the rapid decline of the pontiff to the expectant millions of faithful who accompanied the pope with their prayers. Pius XII's unscrupulous personal physician, the ophthamologist Riccardo Galeazzi-Lisi, sneaked a small Leica camera into the dying pontiff's bedroom and took photographs of his patient, which he then sold to the French weekly *Paris-Match*. Galeazzi-Lisi's breach of his august patient's confidence was not limited to his playing amateur paparazzo. In addition to postmortem outrages to be recounted shortly, a retrospective examination of Pius XII's medical record reveals an extensive history of medical incompetence and outright quackery that would be a malpractice attorney's dream. Galeazzi-Lisi, an oculist with rather limited training as a medical internist, was picked to be Pius's personal physician through the sort of favoritism that has traditionally been the bane of the papal administration. His brother was none other than Count Enrico Galeazzi, a longtime confidant of Cardinal Francis Joseph Spellman of New York, who was the architect of the Pontifical North American College. Over the years, Galeazzi-Lisi subjected the aging pontiff to a wild variety of strange diagnoses and even stranger treatments. When, during the summer of 1952, Pius was stricken with gastritis and the onset of kidney dysfunction, Galeazzi-Lisi diagnosed the episode as "chromic acid poisoning" from the papal toothpaste and prescribed a different dental solution. When the gastritis, not surprisingly, showed itself again the following year, and the pope suffered from recurring hiccoughs, the physician brought in a Swiss quack, Dr. Paul Niehans, to inject his patient with cellular extracts derived from the hypothalamus and adrenal glands of fetal lambs as a rejuvenation treatment. With such medical attention, it is hardly surprising that Pius XII did not live to see the advanced age that his family was famous for enjoying.

It was, no doubt, this scandalous episode that played itself out around Pius XII's last agony that inspired Pope John Paul II to specifically decree, in his apostolic constitution on the vacancy of the Apostolic See and the election of the Roman pontiff, issued in 1996 under the title entitled *Universi Dominici gregis:*

"No one is permitted to use any means whatsoever in order to photograph or film the Supreme Pontiff either on his sickbed or after death, or to record his words for subsequent reproduction. If after the Pope's death anyone should wish to take photographs of him for documentary purposes, he must ask permission from the Cardinal Camerlengo of Holy Roman Church, who will not however permit the taking of photographs of the Supreme Pontiff except attired in pontifical vestments" (n. 30).

As the end drew near, the cardinal major penitentiary would exhort the dying pontiff to use his last reserves of energy to bless his family, his collaborators, and the world—as if to indicate that a pope should die carrying out his functions as well as to profess a belief that perhaps, as the dying pontiff was headed to an encounter with God, his final blessing was somehow more efficacious than under ordinary circumstances. The cardinal major penitentiary would then, after invoking the intercession of the angels and saints for the dying pontiff, commence the ancient ritual formulary for the final commendation of a departing soul: "*Profiscere, anima christiana, de hoc mundo...*" ("Go forth, Christian soul, from this world . . .").

When the pope had drawn his last breath, the papal physician would hold a lighted candle before the lips of the deceased. After the flame ceased to flicker, he would confirm the death by checking for any indication of heartbeat or pulse, in modern times availing himself of a stethoscope. (Such was Dr. Riccardo Galeazzi-Lisi's infamy for incompetence that, on the occasion of Pope Pius XII's death in 1958, the assembled dignitaries did not credit his pronouncement that the pontiff had breathed his last. Cardinal Alfredo Ottaviani stepped forward and took the stethoscope from the physician. Having verified for himself that the end had come, the irascible head of the Holy Office then communicated the confirmation with a nod to the other prelates present.) If no signs of life presented themselves, the prelates present in the chamber then fell to their knees and began the ritual responsory: "*Subvénite, Sancti Dei; occúrrite, Angeli Domini: Suscipientes animam eius. Offerentes eam in conspectu Altissimi*" ("Come to his aid, Saints of God; race to meet him, Angels of the Lord: Receive his soul and present it in the presence of the Most High"). Then each, in order of hierarchical rank, approached the body and kissed the hand of the deceased, while the doors of the bedchamber were thrown open and the word spread of the passing of the supreme pontiff.

In the modern period, mass communications spread the information quickly, leading journalists to compete to be the first to announce the news, even before the formal announcement by the Holy See. Once again, the unscrupulous Dr. Galeazzi-Lisi attempted to profit from his position, accepting a payment from an Italian news agency to inform them of Pope Pius XII's death before the official announcement. The signal agreed upon was that the physician, after ascertaining his patient's death, would open a certain window in the papal summer palace of Castel Gandolfo while the prelates present were distracted by paying their last homage to the deceased pontiff and offering prayers of commendation for him. By coincidence, one of the prelates waiting around for the pope's death grew hot and threw the window in question, which was usually shut, open. As a result, three Italian newspapers, taking their cue from what they thought was the prearranged signal, ran black-edged special editions proclaiming the death of Pius XII on October 8, a full day before he actually died. When officials at the Vatican denied the news of the death, the editions had to be recalled.

Traditionally, as soon as the prelates had paid their last homage to the deceased pontiff, the senior chamberlain would cover the face of the deceased with a white veil. The penitentiaries of the Vatican Basilica, the priests who hear confessions in St. Peter's, would assume their ancient privilege of keeping watch over the body. Either in the private chapel of the papal apartments or on a special altar erected in the chamber of the deceased, a prelate would begin the first of the Requiem Masses to be said for the repose of the soul of the dead pope. When he finished, another would take his place; the cardinals, bishops, and other prelates closest to the deceased carried out this task in relays, as if to say that even as the deceased pope was greater than other men in life, he had greater need for prayers for his soul in death. The same thought lies behind the extended period of funerary rites, the *Novemdiales* ("nine days"), to be described shortly.

Until Paul VI simplified the rituals of the papal court—in fact, with his *motu proprio* decree *Pontificalis Domus* of March 28, 1968, he formally abolished the "Papal Court" as such, substituting for it a much-reduced "Papal Household"—the body of the deceased would be covered with a red silk cloth, the right hand, wearing the papal ring, remaining visible. At the four corners of the bed, large beeswax candles would be lit. At the foot of the bed, a bucket of holy water would be placed on a stand, its contents to be employed by visiting prelates to sprinkle the body of the deceased pontiff in blessing. The Noble Guards, the papal honor guard recruited from members of the Italian nobility, in full dress uniform, would assume position as an honor guard for their sovereign.

Shortly thereafter, a detachment of the Swiss Guards, the Holy See's traditional "mercenary" military force, would accompany the cardinal camerlengo of the Holy Roman Church (or, in his absence, the dean of the College of Cardinals) in procession to the room where the body of the pope lay. The camerlengo is a cardinal designated by the pope to administer the Holy See in the interregnum between the death of the pontiff and the election of his successor. His responsibility is to safeguard the temporal and spiritual rights of the papal office for the man ultimately elected to it. Traditionally, he bears a red-velvet-covered

scepter-like staff as a symbol of his authority. He is also entitled to coin money—
or, in the more recent practice, strike commemorative silver medallions—and
issue postage stamps bearing his coat of arms, surmounted by the papal keys
and covered by the *ombrellino*, or little canopy, signifying his office as camerlengo.
French cardinal Jean Villot, who was cardinal camerlengo in 1978, issued two
series of coins and stamps, since he served in his office following the deaths of
Paul VI and, barely a month later, that of John Paul I. The camerlengo is assisted
in his task by the Reverend Apostolic Camera (or Chamber), a council of prelates previously designated by the deceased pope.[10]

The camerlengo's first duty is to formally identify the body of the pontiff and
to ascertain his death. He is assisted by the vice-camerlengo of the Holy Roman
Church, an archbishop who will assume his regency functions once he enters
the conclave,[11] and the other prelates of the Apostolic Camera. By tradition (a
tradition not observed since John XXIII died in 1963), the camerlengo withdrew
from the papal bedchamber after the medical declaration of death and exchanged
his bright scarlet cardinal's robes for purple-red robes indicative of mourning
before returning with an honor guard detachment of Swiss Guards to carry out
his task of formal certification of death. One of the prelates would lift the veil
covering the face of the pope while the cardinal camerlengo called out to the
deceased using his baptismal name. Until John XXIII abolished the ritual in his
1962 decree *Summi pontificis electio*, the camerlengo would lightly tap the pope's
brow with a silver hammer as he called out the name. Having received no response from the pope, the camerlengo would then officially certify the death
with a brief declaration, *"Vere Papa mortuus est"* ("The Pope has truly died"), and
fall to his knees to recite Psalm 130, *De profundis* ("Out of the depths").

The camerlengo would remove the "Ring of the Fisherman"—the signet ring
used to authenticate certain papal documents, so called because, as well as bearing the name of the incumbent pope, it depicts St. Peter fishing from a boat—
from the finger of the deceased. The notary of the Apostolic Camera would draw
up a legal record of the events. The bells of St. Peter's Basilica would then toll to
broadcast the news, the other bells of the Eternal City joining in. At the deaths of
Pius XII and Paul VI, both at Castel Gandolfo, it was the bells of the humble church
of that picturesque resort village, nestled on the crater of the Alban Lake, that
tolled the news.

Pope John Paul II's apostolic constitution on vacancies in the papal office,
Universi Dominici gregis, succinctly gives only the following instructions concern-
ing the death of a pope: "As soon as he is informed of the death of the Supreme
Pontiff, the Camerlengo of Holy Roman Church must officially ascertain the
Pope's death, in the presence of the Master of Papal Liturgical Celebrations,[12] of
the Cleric Prelates of the Apostolic Camera and of the Secretary and Chancellor

of the same; the latter shall draw up the official death certificate. The Camerlengo must also place seals on the Pope's study and bedroom, making provision that the personnel who ordinarily reside in the private apartment[13] can remain there until after the burial of the Pope, at which time the entire papal apartment will be sealed; he must notify the Cardinal Vicar for Rome[14] of the Pope's death, whereupon the latter shall inform the People of Rome by a special announcement; he shall notify the Cardinal Archpriest of the Vatican Basilica; he shall take possession of the Apostolic Palace in the Vatican and, either in person or through a delegate, of the Palaces of the Lateran and of Castel Gandolfo,[15] and exercise custody and administration of the same; he shall determine, after consulting the heads of the three Orders of Cardinals,[16] all matters concerning the Pope's burial, unless during his lifetime the latter had made known his wishes in this regard; and he shall deal, in the name of and with the consent of the College of Cardinals, with all matters that circumstances suggest for safeguarding the rights of the Apostolic See and for its proper administration. During the vacancy of the Apostolic See, the Camerlengo of Holy Roman Church has the duty of safeguarding and administering the goods and temporal rights of the Holy See, with the help of the three Cardinal Assistants, having sought the views of the College of Cardinals, once only for less important matters, and on each occasion when more serious matters arise" (n. 17).

What Do Popes Die Of?

Interestingly, an autopsy has never been formally part of the certification of papal death. However, the examination of historical records reveals a variety of reasons for papal deaths over the centuries.[17]

Old age. The Psalmist declared that "the sum of our years is seventy, eighty for the strongest" (90:10). Statistics show that, at least over the course of the last two centuries, this has held true for the popes. Of the fourteen pontiffs who have sat on the Throne of Peter before John Paul II, the average age at death has been seventy-seven, the average reign being fourteen years. Of course, dying at an advanced age does not necessarily mean dying *of* old age. But some pontiffs, even in the most violent of times, did manage to die peacefully in the winter of life.

St. Agatho (678–681) is traditionally reputed to have been the longest-lived pope. A Sicilian monk who was said to already have been a centenarian when he was elected bishop of Rome, he reigned only three years before his death at the reputed age of 107. His pontificate saw an end to the Monothelite controversy over the human and divine wills of Christ with his approval of the decrees of the Third Council of Constantinople, the sixth of the Ecumenical Councils.[18] Agatho was buried in a grotto below the Vatican Basilica and eventually venerated as a saint by both the Eastern and Western Churches.

In his youth, Celestine III (1191–1198) was a student of Peter Abelard at the University of Paris. On Christmas Day 1197, feeling the weight of his ninety-two years, he offered to abdicate the papacy if the College of Cardinals would agree to elect as his successor his protégé, Cardinal Giovanni of Santa Prisca. The cardinals balked at this attempt to deprive them of their electoral franchise, and the pope died the following January 8 and was buried in the Basilica of St. John Lateran.

Gregory IX (1227–1241), known for his codification of canon law and his friendship with St. Francis of Assisi as well as for his quarrels with the Emperor Frederick II, also died in his nineties. The compilation of papal decretals he promulgated (the Liber extra) became the fundamental source for the law of the Church (i.e., canon law) until the promulgation in 1917 of a Code of Canon Law. Gregory also first established the papal Inquisition, entrusting it to the newly formed Order of Preachers, popularly known as the Dominicans, and making convicted heretics liable to the death penalty (to be applied, however—once the Inquisition determined it—by the civil authorities). On the other hand, he reopened the University of Paris in 1231. He is buried in the crypt of St. Peter's Basilica.

John XXII (1316–1334) was elected as a compromise candidate after a conclave lasting more than two years precisely because he was thought sickly and deemed by the deadlocked cardinals to be a transitional figure, being already seventy-two years old at the time of his election. Recovering almost miraculously, he reigned eighteen years before dying at the age of ninety. John enjoys the dubious distinction of being one of the few popes—and the only one in times recent enough for an accurate record to still exist—to be accused of heresy while on the papal throne. He expounded his conviction that the saints do not see God until after the day of final judgment, in contradiction to the traditional doctrine that the saints enjoy the "Beatific Vision" immediately after death. The pope expressed his view, along with his idea that devils and the souls of the damned were not yet in hell (since they obviously had to await the day of judgment for their punishment just as the saints had to await it for their reward), in a series of sermons he preached between All Saints Day (November 1, 1331) and the Feast of the Annunciation (March 25, 1332). In an age in which theological controversies were closely followed, the pope's preaching caused uproar throughout Christendom. Theologians of the University of Paris condemned it formally, and a number of cardinals planned a council to depose him for heresy. However, John fell ill and, on his deathbed, moderated his position to hold that the saints see God "as their condition allowed" and insisting that his view was a purely personal one.[19]

Gregory XII (1406–1415) died in 1417 at the age of ninety-two, but as cardinal bishop of Porto rather than as supreme pontiff, having abdicated at the Council of Constance in 1415. He was buried in the cathedral of Recanati. When his tomb was opened during the renovations of that edifice in 1623, his body was found to be perfectly preserved and was clothed again in papal vestments before being reburied.

Leo XIII (1878–1903), having celebrated his silver jubilee on the papal throne in February 1903, died peacefully the following July at the age of ninety-three.[20] He was buried in a sumptuous monument near the entrance to the sacristy of the Lateran Basilica.

Other popes, even if they did not reach such a prodigious age as these, also died peacefully after a long life.

St. Anterus (235–236) was the first of his line not to succumb to the persecutions that claimed the lives of the popes during the centuries before the Peace of Constantine. The fourth-century *Liberian Catalogue* says that he "fell asleep," implying a quiet death in his old age.

Innocent VII (1404–1406) died peacefully, aged seventy, in the midst of the Great Schism.[21]

Gregory XIII (1572–1585), great patron of the Jesuits, who gratefully named their principal university in Rome, the Pontifical Gregorian University,[22] after him, died at the age of 84. He is perhaps best known to the world for having reformed the Julian calendar, promulgating in 1572 the calendar subsequently named after him. He is buried in St. Peter's Basilica.

Urban VIII (1623–1644), having survived two attempts on his life by clerics, died peacefully at the age of seventy-six. Urban, who was born Maffeo Barberini, earned for himself the unflattering epigram "*Quod non fecerunt Barbari fecerunt Barberini*" ("What the Barbarians did not do, the Barberini did") when he took the ornamental bronze girders from the Pantheon to make armaments for his wars, melting them down after the peace to provide material for Bernini's *baldacchino* over the main altar in St. Peter's Basilica, the church where this pope was also buried.[23]

Benedict XIII (1724–1730) died at the age of eighty-one. As he aged, he was counseled to cut back on his liturgical activities to avoid unnecessary fatigue. His response was lapidary: "A pope should die with his vestments on." Originally entombed in St. Peter's Basilica, his body was subsequently moved to the Church of Santa Maria sopra Minerva, associated with his beloved Dominican order.

Gregory XVI (1831–1846), a noted reactionary who condemned freedom of conscience and of the press as well as the separation of Church and state, died peacefully at the age of eighty, even as the city of Rome seethed on the edge of revolt. A quick wit, he once explained his opposition to railroads to a French visitor by stating that they were not *"chemins de ferre"* but *"chemins d'enfer"* (the "road to hell"). He is buried in St. Peter's Basilica in a monument created by Luigi Amici.

Finally, Blessed Pius IX (1846–1878) died serenely at the age of eighty-five, after the longest pontificate in history, which saw the loss of the papacy's temporal dominion over central Italy. (While Pio Nono's passing may have been peaceful, death marked only the beginning of his travails, as will be recounted shortly.)

Illness.   Over the centuries, the illnesses of the pontiffs were kept secret— or at least as secret as they could be in an ambience as rumor-driven as the Vatican's. There is even a Vatican truism that holds that "the pope is not sick until dead." In recent years, the increasing manifestations of the physical infirmities of John Paul II have lifted the veil slightly, but the old policy of discretion still prevails. During the last years of the pontificate of Paul VI (1963–1978), one of the biggest indications that the pontiff's health was in decline was the restoration of the *sedia gestatoria*, the portable throne formerly used to bear the popes in procession, to move Pope Paul to and from functions in St. Peter's Basilica. It had been Paul VI himself who, in his pursuit of "apostolic simplicity" after the Second Vatican Council, had retired the *sedia* to a museum he created at the old papal palace next to the Lateran Basilica in Rome.

Veil of secrecy or not, surrounding papal infirmities, it is known that some popes did succumb to illness.

Virgilius's (537–555) reign was clouded by the Monophysite theological controversy that split Christianity over the nature of the divine-human relation in Christ. He was arrested during Mass and deported to Constantinople by officers acting under the orders of the Byzantine emperor Justinian, dying of gallstones at Syracuse in Sicily while en route into his exile.

Sisinnius (708), though greatly respected, was so old and crippled with gout that at the time of his election he was unable to use his hands to feed himself. He died barely twenty days after his consecration as bishop of Rome, with his only recorded ecclesiastical act as pontiff being the consecration of a bishop for Corsica.

Stephen (II) (752) suffered a stroke three days after his election and died on the fourth day. There is a dispute over whether he figures into the papal succession or not. As he was never consecrated a bishop, and consecration was deemed essential by the canons of the time, he was not reckoned a pope by any contemporary or medieval documents. In the sixteenth century, however, the theory developed that valid election was all that was required to make a man the pope. Thus the official yearbook of the Holy See, the *Annuario Pontificio*, until 1960 included him as "Stephen II" in its official list of pontiffs. Editions since 1961 have suppressed his name. Hence, all subsequent popes called Stephen have a dual numbering.

John XI (931–935) was one of the most unfit incumbents ever to sit on the Throne of Peter. The illegitimate son of Pope Sergius III (904–911) and Marozia, the female senator and all-powerful ruler of Rome at the time, he was elevated to the papacy in his early twenties. Living up to the maxim that he who lives in a glass house ought not cast stones, he ratified the Byzantine emperor Romanus I's appointment of his sixteen-year-old son Theophylact as patriarch of Constantinople, dispatching two bishops as his legates to consecrate and enthrone the boy, to the understandable shock of the Eastern Church. The contemporary chronicler Luitprand of Cremona relates delicately that John XI died from "excesses of table and bed." He was buried in the Lateran Basilica.

Gregory XI (1370–1378) was barely forty-two when he was elected to the papal throne. He definitively returned the papacy to Rome, a move that probably shortened his life, as he gradually succumbed to what appears to have been cardiac tensions, the combined stressful effects of the climate and the internecine civil disturbances. He was buried in the Church of Santa Maria Nuova, his titular church as a cardinal, now known as Santa Francesca Romana, near the Roman Forum.

Julius III (1550–1555) spent most of his pontificate, the occasional bout of serious activity excepted, in pleasurable pursuits at the luxurious Villa di Papa Guilio (Villa Guilia) he caused to be erected outside Rome's Porta del Popolo. He caused serious scandal when he became infatuated with a fifteen-year-old boy picked up on the streets, Innocenzo, whom he forced his brother to adopt and whom he then named a cardinal. Not surprisingly, his lasting contributions were in the realm of the arts; he made Michelangelo the chief architect of St. Peter's and the composer Palestrina the choirmaster of the Cappella Giulia. For years a victim of the gout, he finally died from the diet he had undertaken as a cure for appendicitis and was buried in the crypt of the Vatican Basilica.

Clement XIV (1769–1774) is best known as the pope who, under pressure from the Catholic powers, decreed the suppression of the Society of Jesus in 1773, citing the Jesuit order's difficulties with secular rulers and other religious congregations alike and the need to bring peace to the Church. His last months, however, were anything but peaceful. He caught a chill when a sudden cloudburst soaked him during the traditional Assumption Day procession in 1774 and never quite recovered. During the last weeks of his life, the ill pontiff was beset by a manic depression marked by a fear of being assassinated. When he finally died, the rapid decomposition of his body fueled speculation, proven unfounded by the subsequent autopsy, that he had been poisoned by members of the order he had suppressed. He was buried in the Basilica of the Holy Apostles.[24]

Paul VI (1963–1978) inherited the task of concluding the Vatican Council and carrying out its mandate for the renewal of the Church. Having to balance the competing tensions within the Church during the explosive 1960s and early 1970s proved an almost impossible burden for a man whose predecessor had characterized him as being a "Hamlet," despite being intellectually gifted. The icon of his difficult pontificate might well be his last public appearance, the funeral at St. John Lateran of his lifelong friend the former Italian prime minister Aldo Moro, who had been kidnapped and murdered by Red Brigade terrorists. An anguished Paul, departing from the prepared text of his discourse, took to clamoring, in the manner of the biblical Job, "Why, Lord?" Retreating afterward to the papal summer palace at Castel Gandolfo, he was stricken with arthritis and died after suffering a heart attack. Always a meticulous planner, he left specific instructions for his funeral and his burial, which required an excavation of the floor of the crypt of St. Peter's Basilica in order to lay him in the earth.

Sudden death. Popes who died of illness had, to a greater or lesser extent, some time to prepare for their end; other pontiffs have not been as fortunate. Catholic tradition, in fact, has tended to look upon sudden death as a misfortune, since the deceased would not have had the opportunity to prepare for that definitive accounting for their deeds. The traditional form of the Litany of the Saints even has an invocation against this potential calamity: *"A subitanea et improvisa morte libera nos, Dómine"* ("From a sudden and unforeseen death deliver us, O Lord").

Nicholas II (1058–1061) was a reformer who continued the long struggle to free the Church from the entanglements of lay investiture, whereby the German emperors and other secular rulers sought to assert their suzerainty over the spiritual realm. He died in Florence, presumably from shock, when he received word that a synod of German bishops close to the imperial court declared his reforms null and broke communion with him. He was buried near Stephen IX (X) in the church of San Reparata.

Hadrian IV (1154–1159), the only Englishman ever elected pope, asserted the monarchical claims of the papacy against both the Roman mobs and the Emperor Frederick I Barbarossa. Withdrawing to the stronghold of Anagni, he entered into an alliance with the Lombard cities and was preparing to pronounce a sentence of excommunication against the emperor when he died suddenly, having only the time to commend his aged mother to the charity of the Church of Canterbury before expiring. He was buried in the crypt of the Vatican Basilica. When his tomb was opened in 1607, during the reconstruction of St. Peter's, his body, clothed in black vestments, was found not to have decayed.

Gregory VIII (1187) reigned for just fifty-seven days before dying of a heart attack at Pisa while trying to mediate a dispute between that city and Genoa. Some contemporary chroniclers interpreted his sudden death as divine retribution for his having stopped en route to Pisa at a poor monastery in Lucca and ordered the opening of the tomb there of the antipope Victor IV (1159–1164), whose remains were thrown out of the church. A similar interpretation was found when the Duomo of Pisa caught fire in 1595 and Gregory's tomb and body were consumed in the conflagration.

Innocent III (1198–1216) was perhaps the most brilliant and commanding of the medieval popes. He had an exalted view of his position as Vicar of Christ, a title he preferred to the "Vicar of St. Peter" employed by his predecessors, seeing it as "set midway between God and man, below God but above man," given "not only the universal Church, but the whole world to govern" with a "plenitude of power." Innocent energetically applied himself to making this theocratic ideal a reality, reasserting control over the Papal States and forcing the monarchs of Europe to recognize his judgments. Among those he thus brought to submission was King John of England, whom he excommunicated in 1209 for refusing to accept Stephen Langton as archbishop of Canterbury. In 1213, John capitulated and paid homage to the pope, handing his English and Irish domains over to the Apostolic See as a fief. Subsequently, acting as John's overlord, Innocent declared the Magna Carta void as having been improperly extorted from a papal vassal by the barons without papal consent. A reformer, he patronized the early beginnings of both the Franciscan and Dominican orders, first commissioning the latter to first preach against the Albigensians in southern France and then sending a crusade against the heretics when his legate was murdered. The Fourth Lateran Council, which met under his guidance, confirmed previous reforms, defined the Eucharist in terms of transubstantiation, and legislated the requirement that Catholics confess at least once a year. Traveling to settle another dispute between Pisa and Genoa, he died suddenly at Perugia after complaining of indigestion and then lapsing into a fever. He was only fifty-six. Although he was buried originally in Perugia, his remains were moved to the Lateran Basilica in 1891.

Nicholas III (1277–1280) was elected pope by voting for himself after the seven cardinals who made up the conclave bickered for some six months, with three backing him and three fiercely opposing him. His price for recognizing the election of the first Habsburg emperor, Rudolf I, was Rudolf's abandonment of all imperial claims to territory in Romagna. Thus Nicholas enlarged the papal domain to the frontiers that it was to hold until the mid-nineteenth century. He carried out a restoration of St. Peter's Basilica and became the first pope to make the Vatican his residence. In the midst of his activities, he suffered a stroke and died at his new summer residence at Soriano, near Viterbo, where he was mediating a dispute between Rudolf of Habsburg and Charles of Anjou, the ruler of Sicily. His body was buried in the Orsini family chapel that he had constructed in St. Peter's Basilica. Dante, however, was not impressed by this worldly-minded pontiff, consigning him to hell in Canto XIX of *Inferno*.[25]

Martin V (1417–1431), the sole member of the powerful Colonna family to become pope, was elected after the Council of Constance, called to end the Great Schism, deposed the antipopes John XXIII and Benedict XIII and received the abdication of Gregory XII (1406–1415). Although he carried out some limited reforms, Martin dedicated himself to reasserting papal authority both within the Church and in the Papal States. He showed a toleration for Jews remarkable for his age, denouncing violent anti-Jewish preaching and legislating a ban on the baptism of Jewish children under the age of twelve. He died suddenly of apoplexy and is buried in the Lateran Basilica, where his brass effigy can still be seen.

Paul V (1605–1621) was a dedicated religious reformer. During his pontificate, he raised to the altar some of the great figures of the Catholic Counter-Reformation, canonizing Charles Borromeo and beatifying Ignatius Loyola, Francis Xavier, Philip Neri, and Teresa of Avila. He encouraged missions and even approved the use of the vernacular in the liturgy in China, a forward-looking step not to be fully implemented until the Second Vatican Council in the late twentieth century. On the other hand, he censured Galileo Galilei in 1616 for teaching the Copernican theory and had the Congregation of the Index suspend Copernicus's treatise "until corrected." The first pope who belonged completely to the Baroque age, he completed the nave, portico, and façade of St. Peter's Basilica, immortalizing his name, as well as that of his family and native city, in six-foot high bronze letters there: PAULUS V BURGHESIUS ROMANUS. During his reign, he favored his family; his largesse permitted his nephew Cardinal Scipioni to build the Villa Borghese. He suffered a stroke during a procession held to celebrate the defeat of the Bohemian Calvinists by Catholic forces under the Habsburgs at the Battle of the White Mountain and died of a second stroke shortly thereafter. He was buried in the magnificent Borghese family chapel in the Basilica of St. Mary Major.

John Paul I (1978), the "Smiling Pope" elected to succeed the sad Paul VI, reigned only a month before he died of a heart attack. A humble man, impatient with pomp and ceremony, he dispensed with the traditional papal coronation, choosing instead to be invested with the pallium, a woolen band worn by metropolitan archbishops, as a sign of his pastoral office. The confused conduct of Vatican officials during the interregnum following his death—to be discussed subsequently—as well as their refusal to permit an autopsy fueled wild speculation that he had been killed to prevent an investigation of the Institute for Religious Works (as the Vatican bank is officially known) and the demotion of important curial figures. The evidence produced, however, in volumes such as British journalist David Yallop's sensationalistic bestseller, *In God's Name*, is rather questionable and based principally on improbable presumptions.[26] He was buried simply in the crypt of the Vatican Basilica.

Accidents. If most pontiffs have died of natural causes, succumbing to old age or illness (prolonged or sudden), others have met less peaceful ends. Two popes are known to have died accidental deaths.

John XXI (1276–1277) was the only physician ever elected to the papal throne. The son of a Portuguese doctor, he studied at the University of Paris before becoming a professor of medicine at the new University of Siena. It was his medical knowledge that opened for him the path of preferment, leading eventually to his becoming the personal physician of Pope Gregory X (1271–1276), who made him a cardinal. Although as a curial prelate he participated in the governance of the Church, his principal interests remained scientific and philosophical. His essay *The Eye* was one of Western medicine's earliest treatises on ophthalmology, and he was also the author of a popular manual on curing illnesses entitled *The Poor Man's Treasury*. Upon election, owing to some confusion regarding the enumeration of the popes called John during the tenth and eleventh centuries, he adopted the style "John XXI," even though there had never been a "John XX." Even as pope, he had no intention of giving up his academic pursuits, delegating most of his responsibilities to Cardinal Giovanni Gaetano Orsini, later Pope Nicholas III, and retired to a cell he had constructed in the back of the papal palace at Viterbo to house his extensive library. The roof of the hastily built study collapsed on him, and he died a few days later from the injuries sustained and was buried in the Duomo of Viterbo. Dante placed John in the "heaven of the Sun" in Canto XII of *Paradiso*.[27]

Pius VII (1800–1823), a Benedictine monk and theologian, was elected pope in a conclave held in Venice under Austrian protection in the midst of the wars of the French Revolution. Although he tried to conciliate the opposing sides, coming to terms with revolutionary France within the limits permissible by Catholic principles, he ultimately fell out with the Emperor Napoleon, who had him arrested and carried off into exile in France. The pope's personal prestige, as well as that of the papal institution, was enhanced by his harsh captivity, which he bore with the discipline and courage of his Benedictine monastic training. After Napoleon's defeat, the magnanimous pontiff, restored to his dominions, gave refuge in Rome to the relatives of his fallen persecutor. He restored the Jesuits in 1814, despite opposition from some of the powers. Pius died as a result of complications from a broken hip, injured during a fall. As he lay dying, an accidental fire destroyed the ancient Basilica of St. Paul-outside-the-Walls on the night of July 16, 1832. News of the tragedy, however, was withheld from the pope, who died on July 20, for fear that it would add to his burdens since the Benedictine monastery there had been his home in his youth. His monument in the Vatican Basilica was the final tribute of his longtime faithful secretary of state, Cardinal Ercole Consalvi, who sold all of his own possessions to pay for it.

Martyrdom. The Church's existence during the early centuries was repeatedly menaced by local as well as general persecutions instituted by the Roman state. The lives of many of the first occupants of the papal office were, as a consequence, lost to martyrdom. The *Liber Pontificalis*, the most ancient chronicle of the bishops of Rome and the source for the dating used by the official *Annuario Pontificio* published by the Holy See, lists almost all the popes before Constantine the Great's Edict of Milan (313) as martyrs. However, a more careful study of the historical record, while in no way detracting from the challenge of the persecutions and their importance in the development of the early Church (recall Tertullian's observation that *"sanguis martyrum semen christianorum,"* "the blood of martyrs is the seed of Christians"), verifies only part of the hagiography. Nonetheless, it is reasonably certain that the following popes were martyrs:

St. Peter (died c. 64–67), the "Prince of the Apostles" whom Jesus Christ declared to be "the Rock" and to whom he entrusted the "keys of the kingdom of heaven" (Matthew 16), was the first head of the Roman Church, arriving in the imperial capital somewhere around the year 42. The importance of his preaching and death in that city to Catholicism's self-understanding is underlined in the very first paragraph of Pope John Paul II's constitution *Universi Dominici gregis*, which governs the procedure for the death of a pope and the election of his successor: "The Shepherd of the Lord's whole flock is the Bishop of the Church of Rome, where the Blessed Apostle Peter, by sovereign disposition of divine Providence, offered to Christ the supreme witness of martyrdom by the shedding of his blood."

According to tradition, Peter fled Rome at the start of the persecution that broke out after the Emperor Nero set the city on fire and, when confronted with the anger of the Roman mob, passed the blame to the nascent Christian community. As he headed south on the Via Appia, the legend has it, he encountered Jesus heading in the opposite direction. Peter questioned him in Latin, *"Quo vadis, Dómine?"* ("Where are you going, Lord?") and received the answer, "I am going to Rome to be crucified once more." Understanding these words to be both a reproach of his flight and a prophecy of his death, Peter returned to the city, where he was arrested and condemned to death. Supposedly, as a miraculous commemoration of the prodigious encounter, Jesus left his footprints impressed in a stone that can still be seen in the Church of *Quo Vadis*, near the catacombs of St. Sebastian and St. Callistus on the Appian Way. The legend inspired the great Polish author Henryk Sienkiewicz to write his novel *Quo Vadis*, which was turned into the screenplay for the Hollywood blockbuster of the same title.

In any event, Peter was crucified near the circus of Nero, on the Vatican Hill. He was hung upside down at his own request, as he did not deem himself worthy to die in the same manner as his Lord. He was buried in the nearby cemetery.

After the persecutions, the Emperor Constantine built a basilica over the tomb. Successive constructions buried the site of the apostle's burial, but excavations ordered by Pope Pius XII, the results of which were announced by Pope Paul VI, have rediscovered, under the main altar of St. Peter's Basilica, an ancient sepulcher with a chest containing the bones of a first-century man that bear signs consistent with those of the first pope's martyrdom.

St. Alexander I (c. 109–c. 116), the sixth pope, was traditionally credited with the insertion of the narrative of the Last Supper into the Christian eucharistic celebration and the introduction of the practice of blessing houses with water mixed with salt. According to ancient tradition, he was beheaded on the Via Nomentana, which leads northeast out of Rome.

St. Callistus (217–222) was the principal deacon and advisor to his predecessor, St. Zephyrinus (198/9–217). He acquired and administered the Roman Church's great cemetery, now known as the Catacombs of St. Callistus, on the Appian Way. His election as bishop of Rome was disputed by his rival, the priest St. Hippolytus, who, before finally reconciling, provoked the first schism in the papacy, becoming the first antipope. He was martyred in Trastevere, traditionally at a spot to the right of the main altar of the present-day Basilica of Santa Maria in Trastevere. His tomb, decorated with frescoes depicting his martyrdom, was discovered on the Via Aurelia by archaeologists in 1960.

St. Sixtus II (257–258) was elected just as the Emperor Valerian abandoned his earlier policy of toleration in favor of a persecution of those who refused to take part in state religious sacrifices. He advanced the Roman theological position, against the churches of North Africa and Asia Minor, that baptism, properly administered, was valid regardless of who did the ministering. Shortly after Valerian published a supplementary persecution edict, ordering the summary execution of Christian bishops, priests, and deacons, Sixtus was surprised, seated in his episcopal throne, addressing a congregation gathered for the liturgy in the cemetery of Praetextatus. He was beheaded with the four deacons attending him. Two of the remaining three deacons were caught and executed the same day, while the seventh deacon, St. Lawrence, was martyred four days later.

The long-celebrated liturgical feasts of St. Linus (c. 67–c. 78), St. Evaristus (c. 100–c. 109), St. Sixtus I (c. 116–c. 125), St. Telesphorus (c. 125–136), St. Hyginus (c. 138–142), St. Pius I (c. 142–c. 155), St. Anicetus (c. 155–c. 166), St. Soter (c. 166–c. 174), St. Eleutherius (c. 174–189), St. Victor I (189–198), St. Zephyrinus (198/9–217), St. Urban I (222–230), St. Lucius I (253–254), St. Stephen I (254–257), St. Felix I (269–274), St. Gaius (283–296), St. Marcellinus (296–304), St. Marcellus I (306–308), and St. Miltiades (311–314) were suppressed in the 1970 revision of the Roman Calendar for want of documentation on their supposed martyrdoms.

Murders and assassinations.   The Edict of Constantine, while ending the creation of martyrs by non-Christians, did not put an end to the line of martyr popes. Three popes, in fact, suffered martyrdom at the hands of fellow Christians.

St. John I (523–526) was sent by the Ostrogothic king of Italy, Theodoric, an Arian, to intercede with the Emperor Justin I for Arians in the Byzantine Empire. Although John was received triumphantly into Constantinople and given the place of honor in Hagia Sophia, his embassy failed to achieve its goals, for which Theodoric imprisoned him in Ravenna upon his return to Italy. His body was taken back to Rome and buried in St. Peter's Basilica, where he was venerated as a martyr.

St. Silverius (536–537), son of Pope St. Hormisdas (514–523), was the victim of the intrigues of his eventual successor, Vigilius (537–555), and the Byzantine general Belisarius. Vigilius succeeded in having him exiled to Anatolia after the conquest of Rome by Belisarius, only to see him returned by the Byzantine court. Vigilius then arranged to have Silverius fall into his hands, deporting the pope under guard of his own agents to the island of Palmaria in the Gulf of Gaeta, where the pontiff died of starvation.

St. Martin I (649–653) was arrested by Constans II for having defended the orthodox Christian faith against the Monothelitism favored by the emperor. Tried on trumped-up charges in Constantinople, he was flogged and deported to Chersonesus in the Crimea (near present-day Sevastopol), where he died from the combined effects of cold, starvation, and harsh treatment.[28]

Other popes, especially in that low period commonly denominated as the "Dark Ages," have died violently. However, these were not martyrs, who suffered as the classical definition had it, because of hatred for the faith, but rather the unfortunate victims of political ambition and rivalry, court intrigue, or simple mob violence.

Sabinian (604–606) had been the legate of his predecessor, St. Gregory I, in Constantinople but was recalled for not being sufficiently firm with the emperor. He nursed a grudge against Gregory that he gave evidence of in a series of verbal assaults on the memory of the deceased. His attacks did little to endear him to the Romans, who had already begun to venerate Gregory as a saint. Reversing Gregory's policy of giving away grain from the papal stores freely, Sabinian withheld the grain, selling it for profit. This made him so unpopular that a general insurrection broke out, during the course of which he was killed. He was so hated that he was buried in secret somewhere on the grounds of the Lateran complex.

John VIII (872–882) struggled valiantly to uphold the traditions of papal leadership even as Italy was torn by dissension from within and raided by Muslim fleets from without. He sanctioned the use of Slavonic in the liturgy by St. Methodius, the Apostle of the Slavs, whom he vindicated, and put an end to the

Photian Schism with the Eastern Church. He went down in history, however, as the first pope assassinated. The Annals of Fulda record that a member of his entourage poisoned him and, when he did not die fast enough, clubbed him to death. Some historians have speculated that it was John's alleged effeminate mannerisms and affectations in his personal life that gave rise to the legend of "Pope Joan," supposedly a female pope.

Stephen VI (VII) (896–897) is recalled principally for having presided over the macabre "Cadaver Synod" of January 897. At the instigation of the Emperor Lambert of Spoleto, Stephen had the decaying corpse of his predecessor, Formosus (891–896), the emperor's relentless foe, exhumed and propped up on a throne in full pontifical vestments. Stephen himself solemnly arraigned his predecessor and then proceeded to convict him of the alleged crime of coveting the papal office as well as perjury and other offenses. The acts and ordinations of Formosus were declared null, and the first three fingers of his right hand (which the late pope used to swear and bless) were hacked off. The body was then thrown into the Tiber, from where it was recovered by a saintly hermit. A few months after the travesty, the enraged supporters of Formosus, encouraged by the reports of miracles worked by the retrieved corpse and interpreting the sudden collapse of the Lateran Basilica as a divine portent, rebelled and deposed Stephen. They threw the pope into jail, where he was strangled shortly afterward.

John XIV (983–984) was archchancellor for Italy of the Emperor Otto II, who imposed his election to the papal throne. Unfortunately for the new pope, the emperor was stricken by malaria while assisting at his protégé's installation and died shortly afterward. Seizing the opportunity, the antipope Boniface VII returned from Constantinople, where he had fled with the papal treasury after murdering Benedict VI, and once more seized the papacy. Thrown into the Castel Sant'Angelo after being brutally assaulted, John died four months later from starvation (although some chroniclers report that he was poisoned).

Lucius II (1144–1145) enjoyed notable successes in his conduct of world affairs—during his brief pontificate, he received Portugal as a fief of the Holy See and settled numerous ecclesiastical disputes—but faced bitter opposition in Rome from rebellious factions that proclaimed a government independent of the papacy and set up their own senate and elected their own magistrates. Besieging the rebels, who had taken refuge in the Capitol, Lucius was hit in the head by a large stone thrown from the ramparts and died shortly thereafter in the monastery of San Gregorio, to which he had been carried. He was buried in the Lateran Basilica.

Alexander VI (1492–1503) is usually held up as the example of the nadir to which the Renaissance papacy fell, expending much of the spiritual and temporal capital of his office to advance his children, especially those born to the aristocratic Roman Vannozza Catanei—Juan, Cesare, Lucrezia, and Goffredo. Immediately upon being elected, he named Cesare, then only eighteen years old, the bishop of several dioceses, including Valencia. A year later, he named Cesare a cardinal along with Alessandro Farnese, later Pope Paul III, brother of Giulia Farnese, his current mistress. To Juan, already duke of Gandía, he gave the duchy of Benevento, which he carved out of the papal dominions. He arranged one brilliant marriage after another for Lucrezia, whom he employed as virtual regent of Rome during his absences. Goffredo was married to the granddaughter of King Ferdinand I of Naples, Alexander thus reversing the support traditionally lent to the claims to the Neapolitan throne advanced by Charles VIII of France. Alexander's most lasting legacy was probably his arbitration between Spain and Portugal in the New World, the line of demarcation he approved determining the subsequent division of Portuguese-speaking Brazil from the rest of Latin America which had a Spanish colonial legacy. Alexander and Cesare suddenly took ill after dining with Cardinal Adriano de Corneto in August 1503. Although his son survived with some difficulty, Alexander died. The death was explained as malaria, but there is every reason to believe that father and son were victims of poisoning.

Leo X (1513–1521) was the younger son of Lorenzo the Magnificent de' Medici, destined early for a career in the Church. Tonsured at seven, a cardinal at thirteen, he was pope by the time he was thirty-seven. This pleasure-loving Renaissance prince's need for funds led him to a lucrative financial arrangement with Albrecht of Brandenburg, archbishop of Magdeburg and Mainz, which entailed the sale of indulgences by Johann Tetzel that provoked Martin Luther to publish his ninety-five theses at Wittenberg. Leo's condemnation of Luther with the 1520 bull *Exsurge Domine* and his subsequent excommunication in the 1521 bull *Decet Romanum pontificem* accelerated the course of the Protestant Reformation. Interestingly, the title "Defender of the Faith" borne by England's monarchs dates from a grant by Leo to Henry VIII after the latter penned a little treatise defending the Catholic belief in the seven sacraments against Luther. Leo survived one assassination attempt, in 1517, when at least five members of the Sacred College, led by Cardinal Alfonso Petrucci, plotted to have him poisoned by the papal physician, Pietro Vercelli. Petrucci, after being degraded from the cardinal's dignity, was executed along with Vercelli, while the other plotters were demoted. Leo then thought to diminish the power of the college by enlarging its numbers, packing it with thirty-one new members. Probable, but never definitively proven because the autopsy sought by the papal master of ceremonies, París de Grassis, was never carried out, is the suspicion that Leo's death, officially ascribed to malaria, was actually due to a poison administered by the papal cupbearer, Bernabò Malaspina. The documents from the period, some of which have only recently become available to scholars, certainly lend not insignificant support to this theory.[29] He is buried in the church of Santa Maria sopra Minerva.

Leo's death brought to an end the list of pontiffs who have been victims of violent deaths. However, two popes have survived attempts on their lives in recent times.

During his 1970 voyage to Asia, Pope Paul VI was attacked in Manila by a mentally ill man wielding a bayonet. The attacker was seized by Monsignor (later Archbishop) Paul Marcinkus, an American prelate in the pope's entourage who went on to be the controversial head of the Vatican bank, and the quick reaction of Paul's secretary, Monsignor (later Archbishop) Pasquale Macchi, in grabbing the assailant's arm assured that the wound was not mortal (in fact, that the pope was even wounded was for a long time not even officially admitted).

Pope John Paul II survived at least three known attempts on his life. The first was the May 13, 1981, shooting in St. Peter's Square by the Turkish terrorist Mehmet Ali Agca, an attempt that many have long alleged to have been masterminded by Soviet bloc intelligence services. As the attempt, which seriously wounded the pontiff, took place on the anniversary of the apparition of Mary to the three shepherd children at Fatima in Portugal in 1917, the pope attributed his miraculous survival to the intercession of the Virgin. The following year, he went personally to the shrine there to pay homage to the Virgin. On that occasion, a deranged priest, formerly associated with the archconservative French archbishop Marcel Lefebvre and his Fraternity of St. Pius X, attempted to stab the pontiff but was prevented from doing so. Recently, evidence has been released that Islamic terrorists, associated with Osama bin Laden's al-Qaʻeda, plotted to assassinate John Paul during his 1995 visit to the Philippines for World Youth Day, but that attempt was foiled by Filipino security services working with American intelligence.

Overall, the record for the longest pontificate belongs to Pius IX, who was elected on June 16, 1846, and died on February 7, 1878—a reign of thirty-one years, seven months, and three weeks. John Paul II, who was elected on October 16, 1978, claims the second-place position, having exceeded in March 2004 the longstanding record of Leo XIII, who was elected on February 20, 1878, and died on July 20, 1903 – thus enjoying a pontificate of twenty-five years and five months. At the other end of the spectrum, the shortest pontificate was that of Urban VII, who was elected on September 15, 1590, and died twelve days later on September 27. He is followed by Boniface VI, who reigned for some fifteen days in April 896, and Celestine IV, who was elected on October 25, 1241, and died sixteen days later on November 10. In 1978, John Paul I was elected on August 26 and died thirty-three days later on September 28.

The Rituals of Death

After the official certification of the pope's death by the cardinal camerlengo, his body is turned over to the embalmers unless, as was the case with Pius X, the deceased pontiff expressly forbade it. By a tradition last observed in 1903, the internal organs extracted during the process were buried separately from the rest of the corpse. From Sixtus V (1585–1590) to Leo XIII (1878–1903), while the body was interred in the location determined by the deceased, the internal organs were kept in the crypt beneath the sanctuary of the Church of St. Vincent and St. Anastasius in front of the Trevi Fountain.[30] The present church, built by Louis XIV's chief minister, Cardinal Jules Mazarin, stands close to the Quirinal Palace, now the residence of the president of the Italian Republic but once home of the popes as temporal rulers of Rome. The reason for this bizarre custom of entombing the internal organs apart from the rest of the body is to be found in the old canons of the Catholic Church that stipulated that the parish priest of the parish of the deceased had the right to conduct the funeral. The Church of St. Vincent and St. Anastasius being near to the Quirinal Palace, that right with respect to a deceased pope theoretically was held by the incumbent of the little church. However, holding an as important a function as a papal funeral in that little church being unthinkable, in the typical Roman legal fashion, the parish got the internal organs, and one of the major basilicas, generally St. Peter's, got the rest of the deceased.

Even with regard to his embalming, poor Pius XII suffered once more at the hands of his personal physician, the oculist Riccardo Galeazzi-Lisi. The pontiff having expressed an aversion to the idea of having his corpse cut and his internal organs removed, his obliging physician proceeded to invent a method that he claimed would preserve the body without the need for invasive procedures. All that would be needed would be the injection into the blood vessels of some substance concocted by Dr. Galeazzi-Lisi. As proof of his alleged technique, Galeazzi-Lisi showed Pius the preserved hand, amputated from an accident victim, that the physician claimed had been treated with his experimental formula. Upon the pope's death, the physician presented himself to the dean of the Sacred College, the French cardinal Eugène Tisserant—the office of camerlengo being vacant—and obtained permission to treat the late pontiff's remains. In an uncharacteristically uncritical move, Tisserant agreed to allow the physician to spray the papal corpse with a compound of resins, oils, and other chemicals that were supposed to produce a "deoxidizing process" and prevent decay. The results were disastrous: The body decayed almost immediately, and such a stench arose that the casket had to be lined with cellophane. During the transfer of the body back to Rome, the hearse had to make repeated stops as its drivers were overcome by the odor emanating from the casket. During a stop at the Lateran Basilica for a brief service, the seals on the casket exploded loudly just as the vice-gerent of Rome, the future Cardinal Luigi Traglia, intoned the ancient prayer *In paradisum deducant te angeli* ("May the angels lead you into paradise"): The pressure from the pope's badly embalmed body had blown the seals. Once the body reached the Vatican, artists were summoned to hastily make up the deteriorating remains so that they might be laid out in state.

Once the embalmers finished their work, the body was dressed in the white papal cassock as well as the lace rochet (or surplice) and the red mozzetta, the shoulder cape of the pope.[31] A papal stole was draped over the body. Thus vested, the remains were carried by eight Noble Guards to the Sistine Chapel, escorted by cardinals and prelates in purple mourning vesture as well as the diplomatic corps in full dress uniforms, but without decorations, as a sign of mourning.

In the Sistine Chapel, under Michelangelo's fresco of the the Last Judgment, the body was placed on a catafalque covered in red silk and flanked by lit tapers. There the body lay in state until nightfall, when the canons[32] of St. Peter's Basilica came to vest it in pontifical vestments of red, as if the pope were going to celebrate Mass, placing a white miter on the head.

The following morning, a procession would form from the Sistine Chapel, descending by way of the Scala Regia, or Royal Stairs,[33] to St. Peter's Basilica. The procession would be made up of all the components of the pontifical court as if for a papal liturgy. The only difference would be that instead of bearing the pontiff triumphantly on his portable throne, it would bear his remains. Entering the basilica, the procession would be greeted by silent grief instead of the sound of the silver trumpets and the applause of the crowd. After winding its way to the Chapel of the Blessed Sacrament[34] on the right side of the basilica, the procession would deposit the remains on a catafalque erected there for the occasion.

After the deaths of Pius XII (1958) and Paul VI (1978) at Castel Gandolfo, their bodies were brought directly to St. Peter's Basilica, by-passing the lying in state in the Sistine Chapel. Pius XII's decaying body, both because of the stench it emitted[35] and because of the Roman crowds that came to mourn that son of the Eternal City, was laid in the airy central nave of the basilica rather than the smaller Chapel of the Blessed Sacrament. The remains of John XXIII were laid out in the atrium of the basilica.

Traditionally, after three days of lying in state in the Chapel of the Blessed Sacrament, the body of the deceased pope was carried in procession to the Chapel of the Canons of the Vatican Basilica,[36] on the opposite side of the basilica, where the College of Cardinals, other ecclesiastical dignitaries, the diplomatic corps accredited to the Holy See, representatives of the Catholic knightly orders (principally the Sovereign Military Order of Malta and the Equestrian Order of the

Holy Sepulchre of Jerusalem), and the Roman nobility awaited it. The procession was led by the cardinal archpriest of St. Peter's Basilica and his canons.

In the Chapel of the Canons, the body was placed inside a casket of cypress wood that, in turn, was placed inside a lead casket. The latter was, in turn, placed in a burnished pine casket. The lead casket, engraved with the late pontiff's name, titles, and dates, was to preserve his remains and to ensure their certain identification in case of exhumation. The outer pine box was to allow the pope to go to his grave, like most men, in a wooden box.

The face of the pope was veiled once more with a white silk cloth, as were his hands and feet. The whole body was then covered with a crimson silk pall. Before the caskets were sealed, the secretary for briefs to princes, a prelate whose actual function was to compose the Latin text of formal correspondence that the pontiff sent to heads of state, would pronounce a Latin discourse highlighting the achievements of the pontificate just ended. A parchment containing the text of this eulogy was rolled up in a copper tube and placed inside the casket. Also deposited within were three velvet bags containing exemplars in gold, silver, and bronze, respectively, of the annual coins minted by the deceased pope during his reign. A recent exception to this last custom occurred at the funeral of Pope John Paul I. So brief was his reign that his coins became available posthumously.

The cypress casket containing the body of the deceased pope was closed and then crossed with two cords of violet silk, which were sealed in wax with the seals of the cardinal dean, the cardinal camerlengo, and the cardinal archpriest of St. Peter's, as well as that of the Chapter of Canons of St. Peter's Basilica. It was then placed inside the lead casket, which was welded shut before being sealed in a similar manner. This was, in turn, placed inside the pine casket, the top of which was ornamented with a crucifix as well as the arms of the deceased. The triple casket was then wheeled to the confession before the main altar of St. Peter's and from there lowered into the basilica's crypt. There, the body was laid in a temporary tomb until the completion of the pope's final tomb.

John XXIII, who was given to simplifying many aspects of both his life and death, stipulated that the assembly need only remain for the sealing of the cypress casket.[37] The rest of the ceremony, including the laborious welding of the lead casket, need only be witnessed by the senior cardinal in each of the three categories of the Sacred College (cardinal bishops, cardinal priests, and cardinal deacons) and the cardinal ex-secretary of state as well as those relatives of the deceased pontiff and canons who wished to remain.[38] In 1978, the burials of Paul VI and John Paul I took place after funeral Masses celebrated in the open air on the steps of the Vatican Basilica, before the assembled masses. In Pope Paul's case, according to his expressed wishes, he went to his grave in a simple wooden box, which for the funeral was placed on the ground before the altar, an open Book of the Gospels on top of it, its pages fluttering in the wind.[39]

Nine Days of Mourning

The first of the funeral Masses of the deceased pope precedes his interment, usually scheduled between the fourth and sixth days after his death, and is traditionally presided over by the dean of the College of Cardinals. In the past this Mass was celebrated within the Vatican Basilica. However, Pope Paul VI ordered that his funeral take place outdoors on the *sagrata*, or portico steps, of St. Peter's Basilica so that as many persons who wished to attend could. This precedent, observed a month later for the funeral of Pope John Paul I, is likely to be repeated in the future. In addition to the assembled crowds, millions of others— an estimated sixty million in the case of each of the 1978 funerals—will follow the ceremonies via live television.

The funeral Mass marks the first of nine official days of mourning known as the *Novemdiales*. It is as if the Vatican protocol wanted to express that as the Roman pontiff was greater than ordinary men, once deceased he had greater need of suffrages before the judgment seat of the Almighty. Consequently, for nine consecutive days, in St. Peter's Basilica as well as the other patriarchal basilicas and other important churches of Rome, Masses are offered for the repose of the deceased. The daily principal service in the Vatican Basilica is presided over in turn, after the funeral Mass by the dean of the College of Cardinals, by the senior cardinals of the order of priests, the senior cardinal of the order of deacons, and other figures in a manner that each day expresses mourning by a different sector of the late pope's universal ministry. In 1978, one of the eucharistic celebrations of the *Novemdiales* was celebrated according to the Armenian Catholic Rite by the Armenian Catholic patriarch of Cilicia on behalf of all the Eastern Rites in communion with the Roman See.

Rest in Peace?

Even as their passage from this life is not like that of other men, so too some popes find that they do not enjoy the peace of the grave as do other mortals. The macabre fate that the remains of Pope Formosus (891–896) suffered at the hands of his successor, Stephen VI (VII) (896–897), was recounted previously. For another controversial pontiff, Alexander VI (1492–1503), death likewise brought no peace. According to the contemporary chronicler Jacopo da Volterra, when he died on August 18, 1503, whether it was from the declared malaria or the suspected poison, the Borgia pope was abandoned by his retainers, some of whom claimed to have seen seven demons in wait for the soul of the deceased. Demons or not, the body quickly decayed in a horrifying manner—further evidence, to those contemporaries who sought it, of the influence of the malevolent; proof to modern scholars of the poisoning thesis. The Venetian ambassador in Rome, Antonio Giustiniani, wrote in his dispatch home that the corpse was "the most horrible and monstrous ever seen . . . a cadaver so deformed that it no longer presented a human figure." So bad was the stench from the corpse that Johannes Burkhardt, the papal master of ceremonies under various popes and meticulous chronicler of the Renaissance papacy, cut short its lying in state after only one day (August 19) and had the body buried hastily around midnight in the Spanish Chapel of old St. Peter's Basilica, placing Alexander VI near the tomb of his uncle, Callistus III (1555–1558).

Even in his hastily prepared tomb, Alexander was not to remain in peace. Julius II (1503–1513) began the work of building a new St. Peter's, clearing away the funerary monuments of the old Constantinian basilica, including that of the two Borgias. When Sixtus V (1585–1590) decided to move the obelisk of Nero's Circus to its present location in the center of the piazza before the basilica, the Spanish Chapel had to be demolished to facilitate the transfer. The two Borgia popes were thus exhumed, their leaden caskets put in the antechamber of the construction site. At the beginning of the seventeenth century, a Valencian prelate, Monsignor Juan Bautista Vives, arranged to have the bodies entombed in the wall separating the old basilica from the new one rising around it. When the construction was nearing completion and the wall was demolished, the bodies were disinterred once more. This time, they were transferred to the Church of Our Lady of Montserrat, the national church in Rome belonging at the time to the crown of Aragon, the native land of the two Borgia pontiffs. There, the two caskets were not buried, but rather simply deposited in a corner of the sacristy. Only at the end of the nineteenth century, at the initiative of some Spanish aristocrats living in Rome, were dignified tombs prepared for Callistus and Alexander in the first chapel on the right of the church. Such was the odium attached to Alexander VI that for over two centuries, no one—neither the dukes of Gandía, directly descended from Alexander, nor the many cardinals and prelates related to the family—had bothered to expend the effort to accord a burial to his mortal remains.

One of the Borgia relations, Alexander VI's great-great-grandson through the maternal side, was Giambattista Pamphilj, who was elected Innocent X in 1644. He is best known for the haunting portrait of him painted by Diego Velázquez, now housed in Rome's Galleria Doria-Pamphilj. During Innocent's pontificate, his ambitious sister-in-law Donna Olimpia Maidalchini—to whom wagging tongues linked him in a scandalous relationship—acquired enormous influence. The pope showered her with gifts, including the palace on the Piazza Navona that presently houses the Brazilian Embassy to Italy. For the Jubilee of 1650, the pope decorated the piazza with its fountains as an additional gift to his sister-in-law. Donna Olimpia's son, Cardinal Camillo Pamphilj, obtained a dispensation from his clerical vows so that he could marry Olimpia Aldobrandini, only heiress of the house of Pope Clement VIII (1592–1605). Unfortunately, Donna Olimpia and her new daughter-in-law did not get along, hence Innocent had to construct a new palace for the couple on the Via del Corso, which residence is still the seat of the House of Doria-Pamphilj and home for their gallery. Unlike his great-great-grandfather, Innocent was to rest in peace after his death, although his passing was not that pacific: As he lay dying in 1655, his relatives pillaged the Apostolic Palace for what treasures they could find. After his death, Innocent was buried in the Church of St. Agnes on the Piazza Navona, the edifice in front of Bernini's Fountain of the Four Rivers,[40] in a magnificent tomb constructed by his nephew, the former cardinal Camillo Pamphilj, and his in-laws (the pope's sister-in-law Donna Olimpia refused to contribute, declaring herself "a poor widow"). The church, interestingly enough, remains the private property of the princely Doria-Pamphilj family.

Another pope with a less than peaceful repose was Pius IX. At the time of his death on February 7, 1878, after the longest pontificate in recorded history—except, perhaps, that of St. Peter—"Pio Nono" was the self-declared "prisoner of the Vatican," the territorial sovereignty of the papacy having been usurped by newly unified Italy, whose sovereign, Vittorio Emanuele II, he had excommunicated. The pope was temporarily buried in St. Peter's Basilica while his permanent tomb was prepared, as he willed, at the Basilica of Saint Lawrence-outside-the-Walls, close to the Campo Verano, the ancient cemetery of Rome. On the night of July 13, 1881, while the remains of the deceased pontiff were being transferred to their final resting place, the cortege was attacked at the bridge of Sant'Angelo by a mob of anticlerical Italian nationalists who, howling and shouting profanities, tried to throw the papal casket into the Tiber. Only the forceful intervention of the Italian police prevented the sacrilege, although the funerary procession broke into disorder and the cortege was still stoned and abused during its subsequent route to the opposite end of Rome.

At St. Lawrence, Pius IX was buried, although as was subsequently revealed, not in the magnificent sarcophagus labeled *"Ossa et Cineres PP. Pii IX"* ("Bones and Ashes of Pope Pius IX"). So controversial was "Pio Nono," especially in the years before the settlement of the "Roman Question" and the reconciliation between the papacy and unified Italy in 1929, that his presumed tomb became the object of attempted bombings and lesser vandalism (ironically, the most successful bombing was that carried out, albeit accidentally, by Allied bombers during the Second World War, who leveled the basilica, mistaking it for a railroad station). It was subsequently revealed that, to give the mortal remains of Pius a peaceful repose, they were never enshrined in the sumptuous funerary monument but had in fact been hidden elsewhere in the basilica complex. Interestingly, when, in anticipation of his beatification in 2000, the remains were exhumed, they were found to be incorrupt.

Chapter Two

BEFORE THERE WERE CONCLAVES

ONCE THE DECEASED POPE IS BURIED, the process of designating his successor begins in earnest. However, the present electoral process, known as the "conclave," is a fairly late development in the history of the Catholic Church. To appreciate the nature of the conclave and the reasons behind its seemingly arcane mechanisms—the subject of the next chapter—it is necessary to first review how some popes were chosen in the centuries preceding the first prototypical conclave to be recognized as such, the papal election of 1271.

Divine Designation

As previously noted, according to Catholic doctrine, St. Peter, the first bishop of Rome, was designated directly by God. After the Galilean fisherman confessed the divinity of Jesus, he was told: "Blessed are you, Simon Bar-Jona! For flesh and blood has not revealed this to you, but my Father who is in heaven. And I tell you, you are Peter, and on this rock I will build my church, and the powers of death shall not prevail against it. I will give you the keys of the kingdom of heaven, and whatever you bind on earth shall be bound in heaven, and whatever you loose on earth shall be loosed in heaven" (Matthew 16:17–19). Later, at the Last Supper, after prophesying Simon Peter's denial, the Lord also foretold his conversion: "Simon, Simon, behold, Satan demanded to have you, that he might sift you like wheat, but I have prayed for you that your faith may not fail; and when you have turned again, strengthen your brethren" (Luke 22:31–32).

After the Resurrection, as if to balance Peter's triple denial of his Lord, the Gospels record his triple profession of love and the consequent triple charge to tend to the nascent flock of believers: "When they had finished breakfast, Jesus said to Simon Peter, 'Simon, son of John, do you love me more than these?' He said to him, 'Yes, Lord; you know that I love you.' He said to him, 'Feed my lambs.' A second time he said to him, 'Simon, son of John, do you love me?' He said to him, 'Yes, Lord; you know that I love you.' He said to him, 'Tend my sheep.' He said to him the third time, 'Simon, son of John, do you love me?' Peter was grieved because he said to him the third time, 'Do you love me?' And he said to him, 'Lord, you know everything; you know that I love you.' Jesus said to him, 'Feed my sheep'" (John 21:15–17).

Catholic theology has traditionally interpreted subsequent events recorded in the New Testament, especially in the Acts of the Apostles, as confirming Peter's preeminent role in the early Christian community. It was at Peter's initiative that the primitive band of believers elected a new apostle to take the place of the traitor Judas Iscariot (cf. Acts 1:15–26). After the coming of the Holy Spirit on the feast of Pentecost, the event that has been traditionally held by Christians as the birth of the Church, it was Peter who, on behalf of the others, addressed the assembled Jews (cf. Acts 2:14–41). It was Peter who worked the first miracle officially done in the name of the Lord Jesus (cf. Acts 3:1–26). When the early believers were summoned before the Jewish priestly authorities, it was Peter who spoke in the community's name (cf. Acts 4:1–20, 5:28–41). When two members of the primitive community, Ananias and Sapphira, threatened its communitarian ethos by withholding from it, it was Peter's curse that brought divine wrath upon them (cf. Acts 5:1–10). And although it was Paul who eventually was to carry the Gospel to the nations, it was Peter who took the first steps of opening the way for Gentiles by his conversion of the centurion Cornelius and his household (cf. Acts 10:1–48).

Paul himself, after his conversion on the road to Damascus, went to Jerusalem to see Peter, whom he considered the principal witness to the Resurrection (cf. 1 Corinthians 15:5). Even when Paul had cause to quarrel with Peter, as he did at Antioch over the question of the obligatory nature of Jewish customs (cf. Galatians 2:14), he admitted that there was no authority to which he could appeal over Peter (1 Corinthians 9:5). In the end, at the Council of Jerusalem, it was Peter who, perhaps hewing a line closer to Paul's position, settled the question in the early Church (cf. Acts 15:7–11).

In any event, both the early recorded history of the Church and the uncontested—at least until the modern period—tradition posit Peter first as bishop of Antioch and then, after about the year 42, bishop of Rome, where he died during the persecution of the Emperor Nero in the circumstances recounted previously. While Peter's function in the early community as the "rock" holding the "keys of the kingdom of heaven" and "strengthening his brethren," being a sociological as well as theological necessity, continued after him, he was the only one about whom it could be said by believers that he was directly designated for the office by divine authority. His successors could, at best, claim divine design acting through human instrumentality.

Testamentary Disposition

The earliest historical sources, writing within a century of the events chronicled, agree that Peter designated his immediate successors, although they differ on how many were directly chosen by the first pope. St. Irenaeus of Lyons (c. 180), who also provided the earliest complete list of the succession of the bishops of Rome in his treatise *Adversus haereses*, stated that St. Linus (c. 68–c. 79) succeeded Peter to the head of the Roman Church, having already served as his substitute when the apostle's journeys took him away from the capital. The chronicler Hegesippus (c. 160) and the apologist Tertullian (c. 160–c. 225) also recorded a Petrine designation of Linus.

Irenaeus and Tertullian also agreed that Peter predesignated Linus's two immediate successors, St. Anacletus (c. 80–c. 92) and St. Clement (c. 92–c. 99). The sixth-century edition of *Liber Pontificalis*, a collection of biographies of the bishops of Rome, makes the same claim for St. Evaristus (c. 99–c. 108).

After Evaristus, it seems that election by the Christian community of the city became the means for designating the bishop of Rome, although the exact mechanisms of the electoral process are unknown. It also seems that some of the popes designated the candidate they would have wanted to succeed them, although the designations do not always seem to have been ratified by the electors.

The historical documentation of the period before the Peace of Constantine is rather sporadic, whereas that subsequent to the end of the persecutions is more detailed. St. Jerome, St. Paulinus of Nola, and other patristic writers record, for example, that St. Zosimus (417–418), a Greek cleric of Jewish descent, owed his election to the bishopric of Rome to being commended to the clergy of the city—who were the electors at that historical moment—by his predecessor, St. Innocent I (401–417). Innocent, in turn, had taken Zosimus under his tutelage on the recommendation of St. John Chrysostom (c. 347–407), the patriarch of Constantinople.

St. Symmachus (498–514), a Sardinian pagan who converted to Christianity and became a deacon, was elected bishop of Rome by a majority of the clergy, assembled in the Lateran Basilica, after the death of Anastasius II (496–498). However, a minority of the clergy, with the support of the majority of the Roman Senate, was dissatisfied with that outcome and, meeting at St. Mary Major, elected the archpriest of that basilica, one Lawrence. The contested election resulted in such violence that Theodoric, the Ostrogothic king of Italy, although an Arian himself, stepped in to settle the dispute, ruling in favor of Symmachus as the man chosen by the majority and consecrated a bishop first.

To prevent a repeat of a disputed election such as his own, Symmachus then summoned a synod to meet in St. Peter's Basilica on March 1, 499. The assembly, composed of seventy-two bishops from throughout Italy as well as members of the Roman clergy, gave its assent to what was eventually called the "Decree of Symmachus," the first legislative document dealing directly with the question of the designation of the bishop of Rome. The statute banned all discussion of a pope's successor during his lifetime, a provision that, interestingly enough, has remained virtually unchanged in all the subsequent legislation on the subject, including the apostolic constitution of 1996 promulgated by Pope John Paul II. The Decree of Symmachus went on to stipulate that the pope should, if possible, designate his successor. Should he die before he was able to do so, then the clergy were to choose the successor by election. Any participation by the laity was expressly prohibited. Armed with this legislation, Symmachus designated St. Hormisdas, who succeeded him in 514. When Hormisdas died in 523 without having first designated his successor, the Roman clergy elected the elderly John I (523–526), a revered intellectual and statesman. John I was a friend of the philosopher Boethius, who consulted him frequently and dedicated three treatises to him. Unfortunately, as previously recounted, John fell out with the Ostrogothic king, Theodoric, and died a martyr at Ravenna.

After John I's martyrdom, the orderly succession was broken when Theodoric, wanting a reliable pope, imposed Felix IV (526–530) on the See of Rome. Fortunately, Theodoric died shortly thereafter, and Felix was able to assert the independence of his office during the minority of the king's grandson and successor, Athalaric. When he fell ill in 529 and felt death approaching, Felix summoned the Roman clergy as well as the Senate to his sickbed and, citing the Decree of Symmachus, nominated his archdeacon, Boniface, as his successor, bestowing on him his own pallium. Felix ordered the nomination to be posted on all the churches of Rome, along with a declaration of excommunication against anyone who would disturb the peace of the Church by disputing the legitimate succession of his appointed successor.

When Felix died the following year, the majority of clergy, backed by the Senate, balked at his nomination and proceeded to elect the deacon Dioscorus as pope. A smaller group, consisting of those priests faithful to the will of the deceased pope, confirmed Boniface II. The resulting schism, however, was short-lived, for Dioscorus died twenty-two days later. The clergy who had backed the antipope then submitted to Boniface II, who forced them to sign a declaration that not only admitted their guilt and promised to never attempt a similar maneuver again but also condemned the memory of the late Dioscorus.

Boniface then proceeded to assure his own succession, convoking a synod at St. Peter's in 531. There, he promulgated a constitution that designated the deacon Vigilius as his successor and forced all the clergy present to subscribe to it under oath. The outcry that this measure provoked was such that the pope quickly retreated and, at a subsequent synod, held in the presence of the Senate, revoked the nomination of the hapless Vigilius, who nonetheless ended up eventually becoming pope after three other popes had followed Boniface in quick succession.

After Boniface II died in 532 without leaving a designated successor in place, the clergy elected Mercurius, the elderly parish priest of the Basilica of St. Clement, as bishop of Rome. Since his name was that of a pagan deity, he assumed the name John II, in honor of the martyred pope, thus becoming the first pontiff to change his name upon election to the Throne of Peter. At John II's death in 535, his archdeacon was elected pope as Agapitus I (535–536). Having been one of the clergy who balked at the notion of a pope designating his own successor, Agapitus had Boniface II's document against Dioscorus solemnly burned at St. Peter's. Interestingly enough, even then popes could be prisoners of obstructionism by the papal bureaucracy: While it was clear that Agapitus intended to rehabilitate Dioscorus, the officials of his chancery saw to it that the name of Dioscorus remained off the pontifical succession lists and on that of antipopes and other usurpers of the papal office.

After Agapitus's death while on a mission to defend orthodox Chalcedonian[1] Christology at the court of Constantinople, the son of Hormisdas, St. Silverius (536–537), acceded to the papal office through the influence of the Gothic court. Silverius, however, quickly fell victim to the frustrated ambitions of Vigilius for the papacy, as was narrated in the first chapter. Vigilius (537–555), his position depending on the goodwill of the Byzantine imperial forces, accepted the so-called Pragmatic Sanction decreed by the Emperor Justinian on August 13, 554, during the pope's visit to Constantinople. By the Pragmatic Sanction, the papal office was integrated into the political constitution of Byzantine-ruled Italy. While the popes acquired increased political and fiscal authority, their elections now had to be submitted, like that of all hierarchs of the Byzantine Empire, to an imperial ratification, the so-called *placet*. Consequently, the Decree of Symmachus, which provided for complete papal autonomy in the determination of succession, was essentially a dead letter.

The collapse of the system of popes being designated by their predecessors did not, however, preclude further attempts by certain pontiffs to influence their succession. Celestine III (1191–1198), for example, convened the cardinals on Christmas Day 1197 and, citing the toll that illness and old age had taken, expressed his willingness to abdicate the papal throne provided the cardinals first promised to elect his closest confidant, Cardinal Giovanni of Santa Prisca, as the new pope.

The cardinals rejected the attempt to deny them what had become their prerogative of election. Within a few weeks, Celestine was dead and the cardinals chose
Cardinal Lotario de' Segni, whose election Celestine wanted to preclude and who
was to become, as Innocent III, arguably the greatest of the medieval popes.

In more recent times, albeit with far greater finesse, Pope Pius XI (1922–1939)
achieved the election of his protégé, Cardinal Eugenio Pacelli, as his successor,
Pius XII (1939–1958). Pacelli's talents were recognized early by his predecessors.
Benedict XV (1914–1922) consecrated him an archbishop and sent him on delicate diplomatic missions, entrusting to him the sensitive wartime legation in
Munich (later transferred to Berlin). As apostolic nuncio in Berlin, Pacelli enjoyed the confidence of Pius XI's secretary of state, Cardinal Pietro Gasparri,
who brought him to the pontiff's attention. Recalled to Rome and made a cardinal in 1929, Pacelli became secretary of state when Gasparri, having brought the
vexatious "Roman Question" between the Holy See and the Italian government
over the loss of the papacy's temporary sovereignty over central Italy to a happy
conclusion with the Lateran Treaty, retired the following year.

It was not long before Pius XI began to appreciate the qualities of his secretary of state and set about preparing him for even greater things. He sent Cardinal Pacelli as his legate *a latere*—a rare sort of "super-envoy" of the pope who
stands as the pontiff's alter ego, international diplomatic protocol accords to a
legate *a latere* all the privileges of a sovereign—to Argentina in 1934, France in
1935 and 1937, and Hungary in 1938. Pacelli also took an extensive, albeit officially
private, trip to the United States in 1936, where he met with President Franklin
Delano Roosevelt. As Pius XI aged, his secretary of state assumed greater direction of affairs. When Pius XI was complimented on the publication, in 1937, of
his encyclical denouncing Nazism, *Mit brennender Sorge*, his response was to point
to his secretary of state and say bluntly, "The credit is his." More than one of the
cardinals who entered the conclave after Pius XI's death could recall being told
explicitly by the deceased pontiff that Eugenio Pacelli would be a magnificent
pope (*"Sarà un bel Papa"*). Whether it was his predecessor's undisguised preference for his candidacy or his own incomparable personal abilities and diplomatic
experience that swayed the electors will never be known with certainty, but
Eugenio Pacelli emerged as Pius XII after only three ballots in a one-day conclave, held on his own sixty-third birthday.

Popular Election

Although, according to the traditional account, Peter designated his first three
successors—Linus, Anacletus, and Clement—and possibly also the fourth,

Evaristus, upon the latter's death, the line of those who could claim direct apostolic designation came to an end. The selection of Evaristus's successor, St. Alexander I (c. 109–c. 116), established the model for papal succession that was to last for nearly three hundred years. Alexander was elected by the clergy and the people of the small Christian community in Rome, with bishops from nearby cities attending, both to oversee the electoral process and to consecrate as bishop the one elected.

This relatively uncomplicated process, practical in the small community of the time, where all the believers knew each other personally, did on occasion give rise to divisions, perhaps precisely because of the intimate knowledge that contenders would have of one another. When Pope St. Zephyrinus (198–217/218) died, the majority of the clergy and people elected his deacon, Callistus, as his successor. Callistus, in his youth, had been the slave of a Christian freedman, Carpophorus, who set him up in a banking venture that eventually collapsed, causing severe losses to the depositors, many of whom were Christians. Callistus fled, only to be captured and brought back. His master set him to work on a treadmill, but his creditors interceded to obtain his release, perhaps hoping that he would recover their losses. Instead, he was arrested for brawling in a synagogue on the Sabbath and sentenced by the city prefect to hard labor in the Sardinian salt mines. When Marcia, the mistress of the Emperor Commodus, obtained amnesty for Christian prisoners in the mines, Callistus's name was not on the list since his conviction was for violence rather than religious persecution. Callistus nonetheless managed to convince the authorities to release him with the other Christians and returned to Rome, where he became a deacon and, eventually, Zephyrinus's chief administrator.

When Callistus was elected to succeed Zephyrinus, Hippolytus, the leading intellectual as well as senior priest among the Roman clergy, would not accept the outcome. Although a man of vast culture—his writings are some of the best documentary evidence of liturgical and theological life in the early Roman Church—Hippolytus was a dogmatic and moral rigorist whose vision of the Church as a "communion of saints" tended to make the function of the ministers dependent on their personal sanctity. Under this last criterion, Callistus's well-known shortcomings disqualified him in Hippolytus's view. Hippolytus, with the backing of a minority of the clergy as well as the bishops of some of the neighboring cities who consecrated him, thus set himself up as a rival bishop of Rome, becoming the first official antipope in history. The unhappy schism continued through the pontificates of Callistus's successors Urban I (222–230) and Pontian (230–235). When the Emperor Maximinus Thrax began his persecution, both Hippolytus and Pontian were arrested. Before their deportation, however, the two were reconciled as Pontian abdicated and Hippolytus renounced his own claim to be bishop of Rome, advising his followers to abandon the schism. Both Pontian and Hippolytus were later hailed as saints, sharing today the same feast day, August 13, in the calendar of the Roman Catholic Church.

After the death of Pope St. Fabian (236–250), the election of his successor was postponed due to the ferocity of the persecution under the Emperor Decius. During the intervening period, the Roman Church was governed collectively by the priests who had not been arrested, with the priest Novatian acting as spokesman. When the persecution abated enough in early 251 to permit an election, the majority elected the patrician Cornelius. Resentful of being passed over after having handled affairs for more than a year, Novatian had himself consecrated bishop by three bishops from southern Italy and went into schism. Although the split was originally motivated for personal reasons, it was eventually sharpened by theological differences. Cornelius favored the readmission, after suitable penance, of Christians who had lapsed during the persecutions, while Novatian argued for their permanent exclusion. Unlike Hippolytus, Novatian was never reconciled with the Roman Church. Instead, after his teachings had been condemned and he had been excommunicated by a synod of the Roman clergy along with some sixty bishops, he created his own parallel hierarchy, which spread through the empire and beyond. Although Novatian died in 258, rigorist Novatian-inspired communities existed well into the fifth century.

Meanwhile, Pope St. Stephen I (254–257), learning a lesson from the electoral controversies preceding his accession to the papal office, decreed that henceforth the only electors would be those priests who held the title to—that is, they were the incumbents of—one of the parish churches of the city of Rome and those deacons who were responsible for the Church's charity work in one of the districts of the city. The rest of the community merely ratified the results of the election.

Stephen's legislation established the basis for the eventual College of Cardinals. To this day, with the exception of the six "cardinal bishops" who hold title to the seven dioceses surrounding Rome (the dean of the College holds the title of Ostia as well as that of the diocese he held prior to his elevation to the deanship), all members of the Sacred College are either "cardinal priests," holding title to one of the parish churches of Rome, or "cardinal deacons," holding title to one of the *diaconia* that descend from the ancient charity districts administered by the deacons of the early Roman Church. Consequently, at least in theory, the election of the bishop of Rome is still carried out by the clergy of the city.

Imperial Interventions

The Edict of Milan, issued by the Emperor Constantine the Great in 313, brought an end to the persecutions that had menaced the Church during the first three centuries of its existence and opened the way for it to become the official religion of the empire, as it eventually did at the end of the century. This change in status, however, did come at a price. As Constantine and his successors recognized the increasing importance of Christianity in Roman society, they also sought to bring it within the orbit of their political control. Throughout his reign, although he was not baptized until his last illness, Constantine repeatedly intervened in ecclesiastical affairs, even summoning the first ecumenical (or worldwide) council of the Church to meet at Nicaea to settle the dispute over the divinity of Christ that was challenged by the Alexandrian priest Arius and his followers. The Nicene Creed, orthodox Christianity's traditional profession of faith, was promulgated on the emperor's authority.[2]

Constantine's son, Constantius II, did not share his father's zeal for Nicene orthodoxy. Rather, he sought to restore peace to the empire by forcing the adherents of orthodoxy to accept an ambiguous doctrinal formulation palatable to the Arians. To this end, in late 355, he arrested and exiled Pope Liberius (352–366) and forced the Roman clergy to elect the archdeacon as Felix II, arranging to have him consecrated by three Arian bishops. However, as the majority of the laity supported the exiled pope and demonstrated for his return, the emperor became convinced that public order would only be restored by recalling Liberius, which he did in 358, with the understanding that Liberius and Felix would be "co-bishops" of Rome. The citizenry, however, refused to accept this arrangement and, shouting the slogan "One God, one Christ, one Bishop," expelled Felix from the city. When the antipope tried to stage a return, he was thrown out again. Liberius and his rival then arrived at an unofficial *modus vivendi*, whereby the former governed the city and the latter the suburbs to which he had retired, an arrangement lasting until the death of Felix in 365, when Liberius remained the undisputed bishop of Rome.

When Liberius died the following year, violent disorders broke out over the choice of his successor. One group of clergy, led by seven priests and three deacons who had been steadfastly loyal to the late pope, met in the Julian Basilica (now Santa Maria in Trastevere) and elected the deacon Ursinus, having him consecrated bishop by the visiting bishop of Tivoli. The rest of the clergy, including many former adherents of the late antipope Felix II, elected the deacon Damasus, who, during the preceding years, had switched his allegiance from Liberius to Felix and then back to Liberius. Damasus proceeded to hire a gang of thugs, who stormed the Julian Basilica and massacred those followers of Ursinus who were not able to flee. His partisans then seized the Lateran Basilica, where Damasus was consecrated bishop of Rome several days later. Damasus then sought the intervention of the city prefect, Viventius—the first time the civil authorities were called upon to intervene directly in the election of a pope—

who exiled Ursinus and two of his deacons and arrested the priests loyal to him. A year later, Ursinus returned, but as renewed rioting broke out, the Emperor Valentinian I ordered his definitive exile and expelled his followers from any churches they held.

Despite the controversial start to his tenure in the See of Rome, Damasus I, who was later acclaimed a saint, dedicated his pontificate (366–384) to promoting the primacy of the papal office, referring to Rome as "the Apostolic See" and persuading the imperial government to recognize it as both the court of first instance and the tribunal of appeal for the entire episcopate of the Western Empire. However, if the Roman See was to be so exalted, it also behooved the imperial government to pay particular attention to which incumbent would occupy it, especially since Christianity had been transformed, with the edict of the Emperor Theodosius I in 380, into the state religion of the entire Roman Empire. Such was the case with the accession of Damasus's successor, St. Siricius (384–399), whose election was the first of a bishop of Rome to be officially confirmed by an imperial rescript, that issued by the Emperor Valentinian II on February 25, 385.

The collapse of the Western Roman Empire with the deposition of the last emperor in the West, Romulus Augustulus, did not free papal elections from lay intervention. The German general Odoacer, who established himself as king in Italy, claimed the imperial prerogative to intervene in the election of the bishop of Rome. When Pope St. Simplicius (468–483) died, Odoacer dispatched his praetorian prefect, Basilius, to Rome. Basilius, in the name of his king, decreed that in papal elections, the delegates of the king would need to be consulted. Influenced by the prefect, the clergy elected Felix III (483–492), a widower with two children (from one of whom Gregory I would descend), who then received the royal *placet.*

The Ostrogothic kings who succeeded Odoacer maintained the claim to a royal *placet* in papal elections. When Anastasius II (496–498) died, the succession was disputed between Symmachus, elected by a majority of the clergy, and Lawrence, elected by a minority supported by most of the Senate. As recounted earlier, this contested election had to be settled by the Ostrogothic king Theodoric, an Arian, in favor of Symmachus, who, as previously seen, once enthroned tried, albeit without long-term success, to legislate papal succession by testamentary designation.

John II (533–535) managed to obtain from Theodoric's grandson and successor, Athalaric, a document confirming the freedom of the clergy and people of Rome in the election of their pontiff. However, the document also explicitly reserved to the ruler the right to "propose for their free consideration" a candidate of his choosing and to spend money to promote that candidate among the electors. On the death of John's successor, St. Agapitus I (535–536), the last Ostrogothic king in Italy, Theodahad, terrorized the Roman clergy into electing St. Silverius (536–537), the son of Pope St. Hormisdas, as bishop of Rome. The election was unprecedented in that Silverius was then only a subdeacon. In any event, the hapless pontiff soon fell victim to the machinations of his eventual successor, Vigilius (537–555), and the Byzantine reconquest of Italy.

Belisarius's reestablishment of a Byzantine suzerainty over the Italian peninsula marked a new phase of imperial intervention in papal succession. When word reached Constantinople that Vigilius had died, a Roman deacon in residence at the imperial court was designated pope by the Emperor Justinian without benefit of election. Not surprisingly, Pelagius I (556–561) had a hostile reception when he arrived in Rome, many of the clergy and nobility refusing to have dealings with him. His episcopal consecration had to be repeatedly postponed for want of a bishop to perform the ceremony and when it was finally carried out, only two reluctant bishops could be rounded up by the Byzantine authorities to officiate. While initially the pontiff had to rely on the exarch (imperial viceroy), Narses, for support, his efficient administration and able reform gradually won over the Romans.

After Pelagius died, his successor, John III (561–574), was forced by Narses to wait four months after his election for the imperial authorization for his consecration to arrive from Constantinople. The precedent thus established forced subsequent pontiffs to wait often extended periods of time between their elections and consecrations, during which time the papal administration remained effectively paralyzed. In the interim, ordinary affairs of the Roman Church were handled by a triumvirate consisting of the archpriest, the archdeacon, and a lay official known as the "*primicerius defensorum*," a sort of chief executive agent of the Church.

St. Gregory I (590–604), subsequently hailed as "the Great," was a deacon at the time of his unanimous election to the papacy. Genuinely reluctant and wishing to retire to the family mansion on the Caelian Hill that he had turned into a monastery, he wrote to the Emperor Maurice, not to ask for the *placet*, but to ask the emperor to withhold it. When, several months later, the imperial mandate arrived nonetheless, Gregory was consecrated on September 3, subsequently his feast day in the liturgical calendar.

Gregory's immediate successors—Sabinian (604–606), Boniface III (607), St. Boniface IV (608–615), and Adeodatus I (615–618)—each had to wait nearly a year for imperial confirmation to arrive, a considerable time penalty when one considers the length of their pontificates. Boniface V (619–625) had to wait some thirteen months after his election for the imperial sanction to arrive as the Emperor Heraclius was campaigning against the Persians in the far eastern end of the empire. However, in recompense, Boniface obtained the concession that the required *placet* could henceforth be granted by the imperial exarch at Ravenna. Thus Boniface's successor, Honorius I (625–638), was consecrated only two days after his election, the imperial mandate being issued by the exarch Isaac, who was present in Rome to oversee the election.

A Brief Respite

The decline of Byzantine power in Italy during the eighth century, culminating in the Lombard capture of Ravenna in 751 that brought the exarchate to an end, brought a respite to the papacy from the increasingly onerous interventions of the imperial authorities in the selection of incumbents to the papal office. The last Greek elected to the papacy, St. Zacharias (741–752), did not seek imperial ratification for his succession, although he did send envoys to Constantinople to announce it and to deliver synodical letters to the patriarch, the last pope to do so until Paul VI revived the custom in 1963. Perhaps the most momentous act of Zacharias's pontificate was his response, delivered in 750, to an embassy sent by Pepin III, mayor of the palace of the Frankish kingdom. It was better, the pope decided, that the royal title should belong to him who exercised effective power in the kingdom rather than to him who had none. The ruling enabled Pepin to depose King Childeric III, the last of the enfeebled Merovingian royal line, and to be elected king by the Frankish nobles assembled at Soissons in November 751. The new king's anointing by the papal legate, St. Boniface, and the role that the pope played in the transfer of sovereignty to the Carolingian dynasty were to prove significant in future relations between the papacy and the nascent Frankish empire rising to dominance in the West.

Stephen IV (V) (816–817) was the first pope elected after the reestablishment of the empire in the West under Pepin's son Charlemagne. As there was no precedent for the role of the Carolingian emperor in papal elections and the relation of the papal state to the restored imperial authority was still to be determined, he simply dispatched envoys to Charlemagne's successor, Louis the Pious, to inform him of his election and enthronement and to request a personal meeting. Stephen anointed and crowned Louis and his wife, Iremengard; the ceremony represented the first anointing of an emperor by a pope, Charlemagne having been simply crowned emperor. This act, in turn, would establish a precedent whereby later generations thought that it was necessary that an emperor receive papal anointing for the full exercise of his sovereignty.

St. Paschal I (817–824) was elected and consecrated within twenty-four hours of the death of his predecessor, Stephen, the rather unseemly haste demonstrating a fear among the Roman clergy that the new Western emperor would attempt, like his Eastern predecessors, to interfere with the papal succession. Paschal, however, was careful to announce his accession to the Emperor Louis and obtained from him a statute, the *Pactum Ludovicianum*, guaranteeing the integrity of the territorial possessions of the papacy and promising to refrain from interfering in papal elections. In exchange, the pope promised that his successors would notify the emperor of their succession to the papal office, each pontiff undertaking to renew the treaty of friendship with the Frankish monarchy.

Unfortunately, Paschal's pact with Louis, which would have assured the papacy an independence from the control of civil authorities that generations of pontiffs had sought, fell apart upon the pope's death. The Roman clergy and nobility quarreled over the succession, their disputes spilling over into disturbances. Consequently, the Frankish monarchy had to assume the role of mediator; the monk Wala, trusted counselor of the Emperor Louis and his son Lothair I, was delegated to settle the electoral dispute between the rival candidates acclaimed by the various Roman factions. The eventual choice was Eugene II (824–827), who went so far in his gratitude that he swore an oath of loyalty to the emperor and acknowledged the empire's sovereignty over the papal state. During Lothair's subsequent visit to the new pope, the monarch, with Eugene's agreement, published a "Roman Constitution" that restored the tradition, suspended since the pontificate of Stephen III, whereby the people of Rome as well as the clergy took part in papal elections. Lothair's constitution also stipulated that before being consecrated the pope-elect would be required to swear an oath of loyalty to the emperor before an imperial legate. In essence, the papacy's progress toward independence from the secular authority was arrested and a situation created that mirrored the state of things under the Byzantine exarchate.

The Papacy in the Hands of One Family

With the Carolingian imperial line coming to an end in 888 with the death of the Emperor Louis II's childless nephew, Charles the Fat, the papacy gradually fell under the domination of competing families of the Roman and Italian nobility, thus entering what was perhaps the darkest chapter in the history of the papal institution. It was also one of the most colorful in the history of papal succession.

The most famous (or infamous) of the noble families of this period was that of Theophylact and his wife, the Byzantine princess Theodora. The couple owned extensive properties on the Via Lata, today the very fashionable Via del Corso. In fact, the present-day Church of Santa Maria in Via Lata is located on the spot where Theophylact and Theodora had their palace; the Byzantine icon venerated on the main altar of the church came from their private chapel. The name of Theophylact first appears in history in the list of *optimates*, or magnates, in a document issued in 901 by the Emperor Louis III. By 906, he had been named to the position of *sacellarius*, or head of the papal chapel with the functions of chancellor, as well as that of commander of the Roman militia. Theophylact also enjoyed the title of senator, which the most powerful Romans still claimed although the legislative body of ancient Rome had long ceased to function, while his ambitious wife, Theodora, was hailed as the *"domna senatrix."*

The Theophylact clan's influence in papal Rome was due not only to their military and political power—in addition to their properties along the Via Lata as well as feudal holdings surrounding the city, they held the Castel Sant'Angelo, the fortress on the west bank of the Tiber River constructed out of the Emperor Hadrian's mausoleum that controlled the city during the medieval period—but also to the lovers the women of the family took on. Pope Sergius III (904–911), for example, was the lover of Marozia, the older of the two daughters of Theophylact and Theodora. When she was fifteen years old, Marozia bore the pontiff an infant who was destined to be the future Pope John XI (931–936). With the collusion of Sergius III, the Theophylact family's power was consolidated, its patriarch becoming effectively the financial director of the Holy See. Sergius's short-lived successors Anastasius III (911–913) and Lando (913–914), were essentially nonentities whose candidacy for the papacy was put forward by Theophylact and Theodora.

John X (914–928) was elevated to the papacy in large part because of his past as Theodora's lover, although he was already archbishop of Ravenna when he was called to the papacy (during the first millennium, bishops were usually not transferred from one see to another). During John's reign, Theophylact and his son-in-law, Marozia's husband Alberic I, duke of Spoleto, besieged the Muslim enclave at the mouth of the Garigliano River, decisively defeating the Saracen threat to mainland Italy.

After the deaths of Theodora (c. 916) and Theophylact (c. 920), the clan was headed by their daughter Marozia. Gradually, John X's relations with Marozia and her all-powerful family soured and he sought to reestablish the independence of the papacy with the aid of Hugh of Provence, king of Italy after 926, relying on his own brother Peter in the conduct of the Holy See's day-to-day affairs. Marozia, who married Guido, Marquis of Tuscany, when her first husband died in 925, organized a revolt against John and his brother, striking Peter down in the Lateran before John's eyes. John himself was deposed in May 928, being imprisoned in the Theophylact stronghold of Castel Sant'Angelo. The pope remained in the dungeon for a year before being suffocated with a pillow at Marozia's instigation in mid-929.

The next two popes, Leo VI (928) and Stephen VII (VIII) (928–931), were both elected and enthroned by the compliant Roman clergy at the behest of Marozia, now hailed "*senatrix*" and "*patricia*," while the hapless John X was still alive in prison. The best that could be said about the elderly pair was that they were stopgap appointments pending the time when Marozia's own son by Pope Sergius III was ready to succeed to the papal throne. The boy's moment came when Stephen died in 931. Although he was only in his early twenties, his mother imposed him upon the electors, who dutifully elected him bishop of Rome as John XI.

The following year, being widowed again, Marozia married Hugh of Provence, king of Italy, at a ceremony officiated by her son, even though it was uncanonical by the standards of the time since Hugh was his bride's brother-in-law. The union, however, was to prove unpopular with the Romans, who feared foreign rule, and Marozia's son by her first marriage, Alberic II, staged a successful revolt and took control of the city. Although Hugh managed to escape with his life, Alberic imprisoned both his mother (about whom nothing more is recorded) and his half-brother the pope. Alberic was to rule Rome as the self-proclaimed "Prince and Senator of all Romans" with a firm hand until he died in 954, treating his half-brother as a sort of personal slave until the pope died three years later.

For the rest of his life, Alberic II essentially appointed popes at will, compelling the electors to go through the motions of voting in his nominee for the papal office. Thus he designated, in turn, Leo VII (936–939), Stephen VIII (IX) (939–942), Marinus II (942–946), and Agapitus II (946–955). Although not all of them were unworthy incumbents, their authority was strictly limited to spiritual matters such as monastic reform. As he lay dying in August 954, Alberic was anxious that power in Rome, spiritual as well as temporal, should remain in his family. Assembling the nobility and clergy, including Pope Agapitus II, in St. Peter's, the prince made them swear that after the pope's death they would elect Alberic's bastard son, Octavian, who was designated to succeed him as prince, pontiff as well. Alberic died at the end of the month and was succeeded by the seventeen-year-old Octavian. When Agapitus died the following year, the eighteen-year-old was elected pope. He assumed the name John XII, becoming the second pontiff (the first being John II in 533) known to have changed his name upon his election to the papacy.

By most accounts, the teenaged pontiff had no interest in spiritual matters, dedicating himself instead to a life of debauchery and turning the papal palace at the Lateran into a brothel. In January 962, under pressure from a Roman populace that deplored his personal behavior, John summoned the German king Otto I to Rome and anointed him as emperor, thus inaugurating the Holy Roman Empire of the German Nation, which was to last until Napoleon forced the abdication of Francis II from that title in 1806.

The "Ottonian Privilege"

Following his coronation, the new Emperor Otto I published the so-called *Privilegium Ottonianum* (Ottonian Privilege) on February 13, 962. The decree solemnly confirmed the "Donations" of Pepin and Charlemagne and added further territories that extended papal rule to nearly two-thirds of the Italian peninsula. The emperor pledged to defend the Church's rights and possessions and to refrain from interfering in the internal affairs of Rome. The "Privilege" reaffirmed the old rules stipulating free elections to the papacy, subject to the elected candidate securing imperial ratification and obliging him to swear allegiance to the emperor.

When Otto left Rome to fight his rival Berengar II, John XII began to regret his having crowned the emperor and entered into intrigues with Berengar's son Adalbert. John even corresponded with the Magyars, inviting them to attack the emperor's rear. The enraged emperor returned to Rome and held a synod that deposed the pope, who had fled. The synod then "invited" the emperor to replace the pontiff with a more worthy successor. Although the validity of the pope's deposition was questionable given the ancient principle that the Holy See cannot be judged by an earthly power, Otto appointed a papal official of exemplary character, Leo, who was consecrated Leo VIII on December 4, 963.

John managed to stage a comeback in January 964, inflicting savage reprisals on those opponents he could find. Leo VIII, meanwhile, fled to Otto. John then held a synod quashing the edicts of the imperial synod. Otto, however, marched on Rome again, and John fled south, where he died in early May, killed by a stroke while still in his mid-twenties as he was preparing to bed a married woman.

When John XII died, the Roman electors, instead of recalling Leo VIII, applied to the emperor, then at Rieti, for leave to elect the devout and learned deacon Benedict. In spite of Otto's angry refusal, the clergy and people elected Benedict V anyway. The emperor then besieged Rome, despite the anathemas that the newly enthroned pope hurled from the walls. The starved citizenry finally handed Benedict over to Otto, who then convened a synod at the Lateran under the presidency of Leo VIII. The synod condemned Benedict as a usurper, stripping him of the pontifical robes and other papal insignia. The pastoral staff was broken over the old man's head by Leo himself. Reduced to the rank of a deacon, Benedict was exiled to Hamburg, where he outlived the reinstated Leo, who died eight months later.

After Leo's death, the papal throne remained vacant for five months while the Romans tried unsuccessfully to have Benedict reinstated. Only after word reached Rome that Benedict had died in exile did the clergy and people proceed to elect, with the agreement of the two representatives dispatched by the Emperor

Otto, John XIII (965–972). The new pope was a compromise candidate whose person was meant to reconcile the various competing factions. Although he was the emperor's choice, he was the son of Theodora the Younger and, as such, was the nephew of the *"senatrix"* Marozia, the cousin of John XI, and the uncle of John XII. His pontificate opened the way for the rise of the cadet branch of the Theophylact clan, the Crescentii, which was to figure prominently in papal politics for the next century and beyond.

Hereditary Popes

With the Emperor Otto III's unexpected death in 1002 and the resulting struggle for the imperial throne, the Crescentii, now led by John II Crescentius, once again rose to control Rome and, with the city, the papacy.

In 1012, however, the deaths of Pope Sergius IV and the patrician John II Crescentius within one week of each other led to an outbreak of violence as the rival family of the Count of Tusculum (near modern-day Frascati), Gregory I, seized power. Count Gregory was also descended from the Theophylact clan, being the grandson of Marozia and her first husband, Alberic, and thus the brother of Pope John XII. The speed and efficiency with which the Tusculan family acted has led historians to suggest that Sergius and John Crescentius may not have died naturally. Within five days of Pope Sergius's death and as John Crescentius lay dying, Count Gregory engineered the election of his second son, a young layman named Theophylact after his great-grandfather, as Benedict VIII (1012–1024). The Crescentii rallied and elected another Gregory as pontiff, but their position weakened when Benedict took possession of the Lateran and his brother Romanus, later pope himself, set about besieging Crescentian strongholds. The victorious Tusculan family then set about assuming the principal offices in the papal state. The father, Count Gregory, was named prefect of the papal army, with his oldest son, Alberic III, who was also heir to the family's feudal possessions in the Roman countryside, as his deputy. The third brother, Romanus, was given the titles "Consul, Duke, and Senator of the Romans."

The Tusculan family's ascendancy brought the papacy to a new nadir as the papal office was reduced to a private fief. When Benedict VIII died, the family succeeded in getting his younger brother Romanus, then only a layman, elected as John XIX (1024–1032). When John died, his surviving brother, Count Alberic III of Tusculum, bribed the Roman clergy into electing his son, another Theophylact, as pope. Installed as Benedict IX, the nephew of Benedict VIII and John XIX was, at the time of his succession to the papal throne, not even in orders. Although historians differ as to his age at the time—it may have been as young as ten or twelve—it quickly became evident that the new pope was brutal and dissolute.

In September 1044, a violent insurrection broke out in Rome, fueling long-simmering political resentment of his domineering family as well as popular disgust with his loose life. The pope and his family were forced to retreat across the Tiber as the Crescentii and their supporters took control of Rome. Although they did not formally depose Benedict, the Crescentii did install the bishop of their town of Sabina as Pope Sylvester III. After several months of fighting, the Tusculans managed to dislodge the Crescentii from Rome in early March 1045. Sylvester III retired to his former bishopric where he functioned as bishop under the protection of the Crescentii until his death around 1062.

Tired by the fighting and perhaps feeling insecure because of the discovery of the hostility of the populace, two months after his restoration Benedict IX deeded the papacy to his godfather, John Gratian, the archpriest of St. John at the Latin Gate, who assumed the style of "Pope Gregory VI" (1045–1046). A descendant of the wealthy Pierleoni family, Gregory was imbued with a reforming spirit and probably thought he was doing the Church a service by ridding its helm of his godson, to whom he paid an enormous sum in exchange for his abdication. Although his manner of obtaining the papal office was most irregular, even by the standards of those tumultuous times, Gregory's succession was greeted enthusiastically by many reformers, including St. Peter Damian, future doctor of the Church, who served as his apologist, and the future Pope St. Gregory VII (1073–1085), who served in his Curia. Gregory VI's tenure on the papal throne, however, proved to be short-lived. After barely eighteen months, he found himself deposed and exiled to Germany when King Henry III crossed the Alps, not only to claim the imperial crown but also to restore order to the papacy by a wholesale deposition of all claimants to the papal throne—Gregory VI, Sylvester III, and Benedict IX—and the imposition of Suidger of Bamberg as Pope Clement II (1046–1047).

Meanwhile, Benedict IX had taken his payment from his godfather, Gregory VI, and retired to the Tusculan family holdings in the Latin hill country. When the German pope, Clement II, died after only eight months in office, Benedict staged a comeback and, reentering Rome in early November 1047, ruled anew until he was expelled by imperial forces the following July. Retreating once more back into the family fief, he continued in his recalcitrance until his death in late 1056 or early 1057. Benedict went down in the histories not only as the youngest man ever to ascend the papal throne but also as the only pontiff to reign in three separate spells.

The Gregorian Reform

The disorder of the preceding period gave the Emperor Henry III the occasion to intervene in the papal succession, installing a series of German popes, beginning with the short-lived Clement II. After the imperial vassal Count Boniface of Tuscany expelled Benedict IX from the papal throne for the third and final time, the emperor had him elevate the bishop of Brixen, Poppo, who was enthroned as Pope Damasus II on July 17, 1048. When Damasus expired after less than a month in office, the emperor nominated the reform-minded bishop of Toul, Bruno of Egisheim, who ascended the papal throne as Leo IX (1049–1054). Later acclaimed a saint, Leo moved energetically to root out simony and transform the papacy. Although his pontificate was to be marred by the Great Schism with the Eastern Church, which broke out when legates acting in his name—although he was by then dead—excommunicated Patriarch Michael Cerularius of Constantinople and his followers,[3] Leo was a precursor of the reform movement that was to come.

After Leo's death in April 1054, it took protracted negotiations with Roman delegates before Henry III named the bishop of Eichstätt, Gebhard of Dollnstein-Hirshberg, to the papacy. Consequently, the papal throne had been vacant for almost a year when Gebhard was finally enthroned as Victor II (1055–1057). Although an energetic Church reformer, Victor was much preoccupied with German affairs; he fell victim to a fever and died the following July, while holding a local synod at Arezzo.

When news of Victor II's death reached Rome, the clergy and nobility, noting the minority of Henry IV and the weakness of the regency government of the Empress Agnes, proceeded to hastily elect Frederick of Lorraine, Abbot of Monte Cassino, as Stephen IX (1057–1058). The move was an overt attempt to wrest control of papal succession from the German imperial family, which had nominated the preceding four pontiffs. When Pope Stephen died less than eight months later, Count Gregory II of Tusculum entered Rome at the head of his troops and imposed John Mincius, cardinal bishop of Velletri, who was enthroned with the style "Benedict X." The Tusculans hoped that by putting forward a candidate esteemed within reforming circles they might succeed in regaining control of the papacy.

However, the cardinals fled the city, anathematizing Benedict. Assembling in Siena, the electors then chose Gerard of Burgundy, bishop of Florence, as Nicholas II (1058–1061). The new pope held a synod at Sutri, near Rome, and, in the presence of the imperial chancellor, excommunicated Benedict as an antipope. Supported by imperial troops, Nicholas then entered Rome, from where Benedict had fled, and was enthusiastically received.

At a synod convened in the Lateran Basilica on April 13, 1059, Pope Nicholas issued a decree reorganizing papal elections in conformity with the reform principles. The decree, solemnly promulgated in the papal bull *In nomine Domini*, restricted the actual voting to the College of Cardinals for the first time. The cardinal bishops would have the exclusive prerogative of proposing the candidates. They would then be joined by the cardinal priests and cardinal deacons to form the electoral college that would actually elect the new pope from among the candidates proposed. The rest of the Roman clergy and people would have their role limited to that of expressing their assent to the election. While Nicholas envisioned the election taking place in Rome, he also stipulated that the cardinal bishops could, if they deemed it opportune, hold the election elsewhere. Likewise, while the legislation expressed a preference for the election of a Roman candidate, the choice of a non-Roman candidate was permitted. There was a vague clause about the provisions of the new legislation being firm *"salvo debito honore et reverentia dilicti filii nostri Henrici"* ("save for the honor and reverence due to our beloved son Henry"). This ambiguous declaration was to be the source of conflict, as future popes argued that it was a sort of diplomatic courtesy granted to the person of Henry IV, while the pro-imperial party would envision it as codifying imperial ratification as the condition *sine qua non* of the election.

The first test of the new procedure came rather quickly, as Nicholas II died during the summer of 1061. Under the leadership of Nicholas's archdeacon, Hildebrand, the cardinals proceeded to elect the bishop of Lucca, Anselm, as Alexander II (1061–1073), without any reference to the imperial court. In response, the Empress Agnes, as regent for the young Henry IV, nominated a rival pope, Honorius II. Although the court eventually dropped Honorius, it was several years before Alexander could reign as undisputed pope.

When Alexander II died, his successor was the archdeacon Hildebrand, who had guided policy during the pontificates of both Nicholas II and Alexander II. Ironically for the man whose very name came to mark the reform movement, St. Gregory VII (1073–1085) was elected in a most irregular fashion. During the funeral procession for Alexander II, Cardinal Hugh Candidus proposed aloud the name of Hildebrand, who was immediately acclaimed pope by the people. The cardinals finding themselves in accord with the popular acclamation, the archdeacon was consecrated without any notification given or ratification sought from Henry IV.

Gregory brought to the papacy a rather high sense of the office he now occupied. According to the *Dictatus Papae*, a series of assertions he wrote on the subject, the Roman pontiff alone had the right to be called "universal." By virtue of his office, he was to be qualified as "holy." He was entitled to depose kings and emperors. No synod was legitimately gathered unless he summoned it. No legislation was exempt from his authority. The Church had never fallen into error and never would.

It is beyond the scope of the present study to enter into the complexities of the monumental struggle between Gregory VII and Henry IV over the question of lay investiture, that is, over lay interference in ecclesiastical appointments through the right to install clerics in their offices. However, the quarrel did lead Henry to convene a synod of German bishops at Worms in 1076 that declared the pope deposed. Gregory's reaction was to excommunicate Henry, suspending him from the exercise of his royal authority and releasing his subjects from their allegiance to him. When Henry realized that the pope's action gave his many opponents an opening that threatened the Hohenstaufen monarchy, he found it prudent to appear before the pope at Canossa, in northern Italy, in January 1077, dressed in penitential robes and begging absolution. The pope relented and absolved the king, and the incident entered into both history and the popular imagination of the time as the one of the signal moments of papal supremacy.

The king, however, quickly relapsed into his intransigency, causing the pope to excommunicate him again in 1080 and to recognize his rival Rudolf of Swabia as lawful king of the Germans. Henry's response to this new sentence was to convene a council of bishops at Brixen, which declared Gregory deposed and elected Guibert of Ravenna as a rival pope with the style "Clement III." When Henry took Rome in 1084, he staged an election of Clement by the Roman clergy and people, installing him in the Lateran. The approach of a Norman army under Robert Guisgard, duke of Apulia, compelled the withdrawal of the king and his antipope. Unfortunately for Gregory, the populace was so antagonized by the excessive force employed by his Norman allies that it vented its wrath on the pope, forcing him to withdraw to the south. Gregory died in Salerno in early 1085; his celebrated last words were *Dilexi iustitiam et odivi iniquitatem, propterea morior in exsilio* ("I have loved justice and hated iniquity, therefore I die in exile").

As he lay dying, Gregory feared a return of disorder with the coming papal elections and sought to avoid it by proposing three names for the consideration of the cardinal electors: Hugh of Lyons, Anselm of Lucca, and Odo (Eudes) of Ostia. However, with the confusion of the times, it was over a year before pressure from the papacy's Norman ally, Jordan of Capua, forced the cardinals to proceed to holding the election. They then elected Desiderius, Abbot of Monte Cassino, who adopted the name of Victor III. Immediately after the election, however, rioting caused the pope to withdraw to his monastery while the antipope Clement III once more occupied Rome. It was another year before Norman troops expelled the usurper and Victor III could be installed in Rome, only to die several months later, once more back at his monastery.

At Victor's death in 1087, Clement III once again occupied Rome, forcing the cardinals, after a lengthy delay, to assemble at Terracina, near Gaeta, under Norman protection. There, in mid-March 1088, they elected a Frenchman originally from Châtillon-sur-Marne, Odo (Eudes), cardinal bishop of Ostia, as Urban II (1088–1099). Urban, who was eventually beatified like his predecessor, had been one of the prelates on the original list of candidates for the papacy proposed by Gregory VII. Because of the ongoing struggle against Henry IV and his antipope Clement III, it was five years after his election before Urban could enter Rome. Even then, it took him another year to secure possession of the Lateran. Castel Sant'Angelo held out against him until shortly before he died. Despite these difficulties, Urban's pontificate was an energetic one, his most memorable achievement being the launch of the First Crusade; the crusaders finally succeeded in liberating the Holy City from the Muslims, who had occupied it since the seventh century Arab invasion, two weeks before his death.

When Urban died, his successor, Paschal II (1099–1118) was elected two weeks after his death in the first regular election under the Gregorian reform. Although, like his predecessors, he had to contend with the ever-vexatious antipope Clement III, who once more had to be expelled from Rome, the old contender finally died the following year. Paschal had few difficulties with the three successive antipopes, none of whom enjoyed much of a following, although their presence represented a continual obstacle to papal efforts to reestablish order in the Roman See.

Paschal II died and was succeeded by his chancellor, John of Gaeta, who assumed the style "Gelasius II." Gelasius was barely elected in Santa Maria in Pallara when he was set upon by a mob led by Cencius Frangipani, head of a noble pro-imperial family that had opposed the late Pope Paschal. Gelasius had hardly escaped from the Frangipani when he received word that Henry V was marching on Rome. Gelasius fled with the cardinals to his native city of Gaeta, where he was ordained a priest and consecrated a bishop. Meanwhile, in Rome, Henry installed Archbishop Maurice of Braga, who had been excommunicated by the late Pope Paschal, as antipope Gregory VIII. Gelasius then anathematized both the emperor and his antipope, sending letters throughout Europe denouncing the attack on the Holy See. When the emperor withdrew, Gelasius returned to Rome but found both the Lateran and Vatican basilicas under the control of the antipope. After being attacked once more by a Frangipani mob, Gelasius retreated to France, where he died at the abbey of Cluny a few days after the first anniversary of his election to the papacy.

After the death of Gelasius, the handful of cardinals who had followed him into exile elected Archbishop Guido of Vienne, who was related to the German, French, and English royal houses, as the new pope, the majority of the cardinals in Rome, with the Roman clergy and people, ratifying the election a month later. As Pope Callistus II (1119–1124) he finally succeeded in making peace with the emperor, concluding the famous Concordat of Worms on September 22, 1122. The agreement guaranteed the essential liberty of the Church that the reformers sought, while accommodating the honor and political interests of the empire, thus ending the long struggle between Church and empire over investiture.

In the new climate of relative ecclesiastical freedom, papal elections entered into a new phase of their history, which became the history of the conclave.

Chapter Three

THE CARDINALS
UNDER LOCK AND KEY

ONCE THE LONG CONFLICT over lay investiture was concluded, the successive popes shifted slowly, but progressively, toward a more restricted electoral mechanism capable of avoiding a repetition of the disastrous elections and contested successions of the preceding centuries. This evolution was not immediately evident, as when the pope who settled the investiture controversy, Callistus II (1119–1124), died, the events surrounding the contested succession led to a schism that lasted, in one form or another, until 1138.

Recognizing that the seemingly incessant squabbling over succession was not only diminishing the prestige of the papal office but also invited outside powers to interfere in the electoral franchise that they were jealous to safeguard, the cardinals of the period moved quickly to elect a new pope, often on the very day of the death of his predecessor. The reign of one of those thus elected, Alexander III (1159–1181), was marked by a turbulent struggle with the Emperor Frederick Barbarossa, the conclusion of which with the Peace of Venice in 1177 opened the great golden age of the medieval papacy. For the next century and a half, there were no rival claimants to the papal office and elections adhered to the norms established back in 1059 by Nicholas II: The cardinal bishops effectively picked the candidates; the other cardinals joined them to elect—albeit by a required majority of at least two-thirds as legislated by Alexander III at the Third Lateran Council in 1179 (a super-majority still in force, hardly modified over the years, to the present day); and the Roman clergy and people were informed of the election in time to acclaim the one elected.

Only one further modification was needed to effectively give this electoral regime its modern form: the introduction of keeping the electors enclosed under lock and key (the term "conclave" derives from the Latin *cum clave*, that is, "with key"). This innovation was introduced by the senator of Rome, Matteo

Rosso Orsini, following the death of Gregory IX (1227–1241). The number of electors had been reduced, by attrition and the failure of the deceased pontiff to nominate new cardinals, to a mere twelve, of whom two were being held prisoner by the Emperor Frederick II. The senator found that the remaining ten were deeply divided. To compel them to reach a decision, he had them locked up in a crumbling palace known as the Septizonium. Despite this harsh regime, it still took the nine cardinals—one of their number having died during their confinement—some sixty days to achieve the two-thirds majority required to elect Goffredo da Castiglione, the cardinal bishop of Sabina, as Celestine IV. Unfortunately, the new pope fell ill two days after his enthronement and died before the fortnight was out. Nonetheless, the precedent of the electoral conclave was established.

The election of the ill-fated Celestine's successor, eventually Innocent IV (1243–1154), was put off for some eighteen months as the surviving eight cardinals, realizing that they were hopelessly deadlocked and being none too eager to be confined once more, negotiated with the emperor for the release of their two captive colleagues. At Innocent's death in Naples a decade later, the mayor of that city, fearing that the cardinals, who had accompanied him there, would procrastinate once more, took his cue from the example set by Matteo Rosso Orsini and locked up the members of the Sacred College. Forced to hold an election then and there, the cardinals elected their dean, the cardinal bishop of Ostia, Count Rinaldo of Segni, nephew of Gregory IX and grandnephew of the great Innocent III, as Alexander IV (1254–1261). From then on, it became established practice that the cardinals were the sole electors and that they would be held in "conclave" until they performed their function and elected a pope for the Church.

The Cardinals of the Holy Roman Church

According to the Code of Canon Law promulgated by Pope John Paul II in 1983, the cardinals are defined in the following manner: "The Cardinals of the Holy Roman Church constitute a special College, whose prerogative it is to elect the Roman Pontiff in accordance with the norms of a special law. The Cardinals are also available to the Roman Pontiff, either acting collegially, when they are summoned together to deal with questions of major importance, or acting individually, that is, in the offices which they hold in assisting the Roman Pontiff especially in the daily care of the universal Church" (canon 349). The old Code of Canon Law of 1917 contained an even more concise definition: "The Cardinals of the Holy Roman Church constitute the Senate of the Roman Pontiff and assist him as counselors and collaborators in the government of the Church" (canon 230). It in the classical characterization of the College of Cardinals as the "Senate of the Roman Pontiff" that the historical significance of the cardinalate is to be found.

It should be remembered that the Roman Church has always derived many of its institutions from those of ancient Rome, whose universal ambition was, for many of the Church Fathers, a presage of the universal vocation of the Church centered in the Eternal City. Consequently, the early Church had no difficulty in accepting Roman institutions and concepts it found useful and baptizing them, as it were. One of these institutions was that of the Senate, the fundamental pillar of the Roman Republic that, despite a loss of power during the principate and then the empire, still retained a universal prestige as the deliberative body and custodian of the traditions of Rome. Thus, even in the increasingly monarchical empire, the monogram S.P.Q.R. (*Senatus Populusque Romanus*, "the Roman Senate and People") continued to designate the Roman state as a consortium of the Senate and the people.

As the Roman Church emerged from the period of the persecutions, its bishop adopted as the basis for the pastoral care of the city the existing administrative subdivisions of the civil administration, dividing the overall Christian community of the city into twenty-five smaller neighborhood community units, or parishes, each headed by a priest. The city was also divided into fourteen districts for the purposes of charitable assistance, each headed by a deacon. In addition, seven deacons, based in the Lateran Palace, where the bishop of Rome was installed by the Emperor Constantine, directly collaborated in the overall administration of the Roman Church. These clerics, the twenty-five parish priests and twenty-one deacons, became known as the "hinges" (in Latin, *cardines*) of the Roman Church's government, or "cardinals." The parish priests were designated "cardinal priests" and the deacons "cardinal deacons." By the eighth century, these cardinal priests and cardinal deacons were joined by the seven (later reduced, in the twelfth century, to six) "cardinal bishops," who headed the so-called suburbicarian dioceses, the small autonomous communities in the suburbs surrounding the Eternal City.

The popes grew to depend on the cardinals as a consultative body in the manner that the Roman emperors and their Byzantine successors continued to employ the Senate. By the reign of Eugene III (1145–1153), the cardinals constituted a formally recognized collegiate body headed by a dean, the cardinal bishop of Ostia, and a camerlengo, or chamberlain,[1] administering the goods that the college held collectively. The college was divided into three "orders," those of cardinal bishops, cardinal priests, and cardinal deacons. Over the centuries, as the power of the papacy increasingly developed in a monarchical fashion, the College of Cardinals evolved into a sort of aristocratic check on the papal monarchy, much as the Senate functioned in the Rome of the imperial period. With the reforms of Pope Nicholas II in 1059, the members of the college became the exclusive holders of the electoral franchise in the process of papal succession.

By the twelfth century, clerics who, while not members of the clergy of Rome, were nonetheless close collaborators of the pope, began to be designated cardinals by assuming the title to one of the parishes or diaconal districts. The first recorded cardinal who was not resident at the papal court in Rome was Konrad von Wittelsbach, archbishop of Mainz, the son of Duke Otto of Bavaria, who was appointed to the Sacred College by Pope Alexander III in 1163. Contemporaneous with the College of Cardinals acquiring the exclusive electoral franchise, its membership grew in prestige, until Pope Eugene IV (1431–1447) decreed in the *Non mediocri* of 1439 that cardinals would take precedence over all non-cardinal patriarchs, archbishops, and bishops, even if they were not themselves bishops or even priests.

The prestige of the College of Cardinals has always been based, at least in part, on the exclusivity of membership in it. Between the thirteenth and fifteenth centuries, its membership never exceeded thirty (meaning that not all the parishes or diaconal districts always had a titular). Pope John XXII (1316–1334) even limited its membership for a time to no more than twenty. As has been recounted above, at times papal elections were held with fewer than a dozen electors.

During the Renaissance, the need to raise funds for construction projects or, as notorious in the case of Pope Julius II (1503–1513), to wage military campaigns prompted some popes to create additional cardinals by selling the dignity. Other popes, such as Leo X (1513–1521), who created thirty-one cardinals on one memorable occasion, increased the size of the college in order to water down its concentration of power. Paul IV (1555–1559) established the maximum number of cardinals at forty, while his successor, Pius IV (1559–1565), raised that number to seventy-six. Finally, Pope Sixtus V (1585–1590), the great organizer of the central government of the Church, gave the college the structure that was to characterize it well into the late twentieth century through his bull *Postquam verus ille* of December 3, 1586. Recalling the seventy elders who assisted Moses in leading the Israelites during the exodus, Sixtus established a limit of seventy cardinals, dividing them into three orders: the six cardinal bishops (the dean of the Sacred College assuming the title of the suburbicarian diocese of Ostia in addition to the one he already held), fifty cardinal priests, and fourteen cardinal deacons.

During the following centuries, the majority of the cardinals were Italian, although the term was more ethnic and geographical rather than national until the *Risorgimento* established a unified Italian state. Pius XII (1939–1958) began the dramatic internationalization of the membership of the college, which was continued by his successor, John XXIII (1958–1963), who raised the number of cardinals to seventy-five with his very first consistory shortly after his election and raised it again to eighty-eight in 1960, and again to ninety in 1962. Paul VI (1963–1978) created twenty-seven cardinals in his consistory of 1965, thus raising the membership to 105, including four patriarchs of the Eastern Rites whom he permitted to be included in the "Senate" of the Roman Church with his *motu proprio* entitled *Ad purpuratorum Patrum.*[2] With his consistory of 1967, Paul effectively raised the number of cardinals to 120, but the number of actual electors was reduced three years later when the pope, with another *motu proprio, Ingravescentum aetatem,* disqualified those cardinals who had reached the age of eighty from participation in the conclave and the other governing institutions of the Holy See. In 1973, Paul VI fixed the limit for cardinal electors, that is, the number of cardinals below the age of eighty, at 120, a limit officially maintained by Pope John Paul II, although he has approved temporary derogations of it at several of his consistories, most recently that of October 2003. The enlargement of the membership of the college has, in recent years, necessitated the creation of new presbyteral and diaconal titles, so that many cardinals are now just as likely to find themselves titulars of churches built in the periphery of Rome to serve the post–World War II emigrants from the Italian countryside as bearers of one of the splendid ancient titles of the Roman See.

While John XXIII, with his *motu proprio* of 1962 *Cum gravissima sint* decreed that all cardinals should be consecrated bishops if they were not already bishops, and Paul VI adhered to that stipulation, it should be recalled that through most of its history, many members of the College of Cardinals were not bishops, being only ordained priests, while a few were not even ordained priests, being only ordained to the diaconate.[3] More recently, John Paul II has appointed several cardinals who were not already bishops and, for reasons of their already advanced age, excused them the necessity of episcopal ordination. Presently, there are seven such cardinals, including two Jesuit priests, former papal advance man Roberto Tucci, an Italian, and American theologian Avery Dulles, son of onetime secretary of state John Foster Dulles, who declined the episcopate. Others, including three of the four cardinals over the age of eighty during the consistory of 2003—Georges Cottier, Gustaaf Joos, and Stanislaw Nagy—opted to be ordained archbishop just prior to the consistory.

The members of the College of Cardinals voting in conclave determine the identity of the pope. In turn, it is the pope who determines the membership of the Sacred College. The official Vatican yearbook, the *Annuario Pontificio*, gives for each cardinal the date when he was "created and published" by the pope. The use of the Italian verb *creare* ("to create") is not accidental: The cardinal is raised to his rank and continues to enjoy it at the pleasure of the reigning pontiff, who can strip him of it should he wish. Such was the case of the Jesuit

Cardinal Louis Billot: created Cardinal Deacon of Santa Maria in Via Lata by Pope St. Pius X in 1911, he was forced to resign his cardinalate in 1927 for opposing Pius XI's condemnation of the right-wing French political movement Action Française. In contrast, Catholic doctrine is that while the pope appoints bishops, they receive their authority from God through the sacrament of holy orders. Thus a pope may remove a bishop and even excommunicate him—as was the case with the conservative French archbishop Marcel Lefebvre, excommunicated in 1988, for consecrating four traditionalist bishops without papal permission— but he cannot undo the bishop's consecration and the sacramental powers that derive from it.

While cardinals enjoy their office at the pleasure of the reigning pontiff, the popes often find themselves under pressure to promote certain prelates to the college either because of the expectation of certain historic sees that their incumbents wear the red hat or even less subtle political considerations. An extreme example of the latter was the unusual case of Archbishop Vincenzo Bichi, apostolic nuncio in Portugal from 1709 to 1720. The incumbents of certain posts abroad in the papal diplomatic service—historically, the nuncios in Vienna, Paris, and Madrid, and nowadays the nuncios in Washington, New York (the United Nations), and usually Paris—expected the cardinal's hat at the end of their tenures. The cardinalate was thought to reflect not only on the man to whom it was conferred but also on the importance of his mission. King João V of Portugal was determined that the papacy would grant him the great power recognition that it accorded the sovereigns of the empire, France, and Spain. When the lackluster Bichi was recalled in 1720 after an otherwise undistinguished sojourn at the Portuguese court, João demanded that Pope Clement XI (1700–1721) create the departing nuncio a cardinal. The pope refused, and in response the king not only refused to grant Bichi leave to depart, but also refused to receive his successor, Archbishop Giuseppe Firrao.

Pope Clement died shortly thereafter, leaving the matter to his successor, Innocent XIII (1721–1724), who found the king just as intransigent. The next pope, Benedict XIII (1724–1730), found a complex problem awaiting his attention when he came to office: Bichi, the recalled nuncio, was still at the Portuguese court, while Firrao, the new nuncio, was not allowed to exercise any of his functions. While Benedict would have liked to resolve the impasse by giving Bichi the hat, the cardinals in Rome argued against the move, both on the merits of Bichi's person—or rather, the lack thereof—and on the question of the precedent the appointment would set. As the deadlock continued into its eighth year, João recalled his ambassador from the papal court in 1728 and expelled Firrao, who, after waiting eight years, had never been received at court anyway, from Portugal. When the rupture in diplomatic relations did not produce the desired effect, the king decreed the expulsion of all subjects of the Papal States—including the would-be cardinal, Bichi—to quit Portugal and ordered all Portuguese subjects, clerical and lay, to leave papal territory. Furthermore, the king's subjects were forbidden to petition the Holy See, even for religious matters.

When Benedict died in 1730, the new pope, Clement XII (1730–1740), became the fourth pope involved in a quarrel with the irascible Portuguese monarch, who apparently enjoyed a longer life expectancy than the Roman pontiffs who treated with him. For the peace of the Church, Clement yielded to the persistent king and gave Bichi the red hat first sought a decade earlier, raising the hapless Giuseppe Firrao to the cardinalate in the same consistory.

Since the nomination of cardinals comes by an act of papal will, there arises the possibility of the creation of the so-called cardinals *in pectore* (Latin, "in the heart"), whose names are kept by the pope in the secrecy "of the heart," usually for reasons of political expedience. The seniority of these cardinals dates from the time the pope secretly nominated them, even if their promotion is not announced until much later. A notable recent example was the extraordinary figure of Ignatius Kung Pin-mei, the bishop of Shanghai and apostolic administrator of Nanking and Soochow, who spent over thirty years in Communist prisons for his refusal to go along with the Chinese government's creation of a "Patriotic Catholic Church" independent of the papacy. In his first consistory, on June 30, 1979, John Paul II announced the creation of a cardinal *in pectore* without revealing the identity of the nominee. The nomination was published on June 28, 1991, when the Chinese prelate, then released and living in exile in the United States, received his red hat from John Paul II to an unprecedented standing ovation by the assembly at St. Peter's. When he announced the names of the thirty cardinals to be created in the consistory of October 21, 2003, Pope John Paul stated that he had "nominated cardinal another worthy prelate whose name would be reserved *in pectore*."

Once his name is formally made public, before he receives the distinctive insignia of his rank, a new cardinal swears a solemn oath whereby, above and beyond the profession of faith and oath of loyalty that he swore upon assuming his previous ecclesiastical offices, he binds himself in a particular way to the supreme pontiff and the Church of Rome:

> I, [name and surname], Cardinal of the Holy Roman Church, promise and swear to be faithful henceforth and forever, while I live, to Christ and His Gospel, being constantly obedient to the Holy Roman Apostolic Church, to Blessed Peter in the person of the Supreme Pontiff [name of the reigning pope], and of his canonically elected Successors; to maintain communion with the Catholic Church always, in word and deed; not to reveal to anyone what is confided to me in secret, nor to divulge what may bring harm or dishonor to Holy Church; to carry out

with great diligence and fidelity those tasks to which I am called by my service to the Church, in accord with the norms of law. So help me Almighty God.

On the subject of the biretta, the distinctive square red hat of the cardinal, a curious historical relic endured until recently with regard to its conferral. The sovereigns of the Catholic nations of Austria, France, Portugal, Spain, and, after the settlement of the "Roman Question," Italy enjoyed the privilege of bestowing the biretta, in the name of the reigning pope, on their subjects who were raised to the cardinalate as well as on the apostolic nuncio, or papal ambassador, accredited to their country should his elevation come during his tenure in their capital. After the fall of the monarchies, the presidential successors of these sovereigns claimed the privilege, a claim implicitly allowed by the papacy. Thus, for example, photographs often appear in biographies of Pope John XXIII, who was named a cardinal while serving as nuncio in Paris, kneeling before the Socialist president Vincent Auriol, to receive the biretta. This custom officially ended when the last head of state to claim the privilege, Generalissimo Francisco Franco, who as Spanish chief of state exercised all the traditional prerogatives of the Spanish crown, renounced it in early 1969 at the request of Pope Paul VI, who sought, in the wake of the Second Vatican Council, to modernize the Church.

Despite the post–Vatican II simplification of both the vesture and the lifestyle of cardinals, the members of the Sacred College still retain a number of prerogatives—both in the effective governance of the Church and in its ceremonial life as well as in civil society—that make their dignity "the world's most exclusive club," as one pundit has characterized it. Cardinals still enjoy the style of "Most Reverend Eminence" (in Italian, *Eminenza Reverendissima*) and, in diplomatic protocol, rank with princes of the blood of sovereign houses. In fact, in the most recent edition of the famous *Almanac de Gotha*, the list of the members of the College of Cardinals appears in the first, most exclusive part of the directory of royalty and nobility. Thus these "Princes of the Church" show the Roman Church's centuries-long function as a channel for social mobility.

Over the course of the centuries, the membership of the Sacred College has included some of the most luminous figures and some of the most controversial characters in the long history of Catholicism. Among the cardinals who have been subsequently canonized as saints, one counts the medieval theologians Peter Damian and Bonaventure and the Catholic Reformation leaders Charles Borromeo and Robert Bellarmine. More worldly have been a long series of cardinal statesmen: Thomas Wolsey, chancellor of Henry VIII; Reginald Pole, last Catholic archbishop of Canterbury and counselor to his cousin Queen Mary; Armand Richelieu and Jules Mazarin, chief ministers of Louis XIII and Louis XIV, respectively; and Francisco Ximénez Cisneros, regent of Spain.

There have even been two cardinals who were proclaimed kings, one effective, the other a pretender. Dom Enrique of Portugal was a cardinal when his
young nephew King Dom Sebastián died at Alcazarquivir in 1578. The cardinal,
the last scion of the Royal House of Avís, was proclaimed king as Dom Enrique
II and, while retaining his cardinalate, reigned for two years before dying without legitimate issue and leaving the throne to another nephew, Philip II of Spain.
The other "cardinal king" was Henry Benedict Stuart, styled the "cardinal-
duke of York." The son of James, the "Old Pretender," and brother of Charles
Edward, the "Young Pretender" known also as "Bonnie Prince Charles," he was
the cardinal bishop of Frascati. At the death without heirs of his brother, the
cardinal was proclaimed "Henry IX" by Stuart loyalists and was considered the
last of the Stuart line when he died in 1807. In one of the paradoxical twists that
characterized the gentlemanly history of monarchical Europe, the cardinal-duke
of York received a pension from the Hanoverian "usurper," George III, after his
patrimony was seized by revolutionary France during the Napoleonic Wars. He
used part of the proceeds from this income to commission Canova to create a
monument near the baptistery of St. Peter's to the last of his line.[4]

Cardinals and Conclaves in History

The principal *raison d'être* of the College of Cardinals is, of course, the election
of a new pope on the death—or, extremely rarely and never since the late Middle
Ages, the abdication—of his predecessor. The transition to this restricted electoral college, although intended to facilitate papal succession, happened neither
automatically nor without a hesitant start.

Despite the precedent of the "conclave" enclosure to force an election, when
Clement IV died on November 29, 1268, at Viterbo, the electoral impasse reached
its extreme. Not only were the cardinals divided by personal rivalries, but they
were deadlocked by divergent attitudes to the rival claims to the papacy's Sicilian vassal kingdom put forward by the French in favor of the saintly Louis IX's
brother, Charles of Anjou, and the Hohenstaufen heirs.

As the second year threatened to turn into a third year, the exasperated people
of Viterbo rose up. Alberto of Montebono, the city's *podestà*, or magistrate, and
commander of its militia, had the roof torn off the papal palace to expose the
electors to the elements and put them on a starvation diet to encourage their
deliberations. Alberto would have demolished the entire palace complex around
the cardinals had not the noble family of the Savelli intervened and organized a
guard from their feudal levies to protect the electors. This intervention was gratefully remembered by the Holy See, which subsequently made the Savelli family

and the Chigi, who were their heirs, hereditary protectors of the conclave. The assaults on the papal palace, however, finally proved efficacious in convincing the college to arrive at a compromise. The cardinals delegated their electoral franchise to a committee of six of their number. This committee then went outside the Sacred College and elected Tedaldo Visconti, archdeacon of Liège, then on crusade at Acre with the future Edward I of England, on September 1, 1271. The conclave, the longest in papal history, had lasted two years, nine months, and two days.

The new pope, Gregory X (1271–1276), who was later beatified, proved to be a good choice. Scandalized by the long vacancy in the papal office, on July 16, 1274, he promulgated the bull *Ubi periculum*, which was designed to preclude future prolonged vacancies in the papal office by providing that the cardinals must assemble no later than ten days after the death of the pope in the place where he died. The decree stipulated that the members of the college were to be constrained to stay together, without contact with the outside world, until they elected a pope. Gregory detailed the progressively more austere conditions under which the conclave was to be observed: If after three days it had not succeeded in electing a pope, its members were to be limited to one dish of food twice a day; after five more days, the ration for the deadlocked electors was to be reduced to bread and water with a little wine. To add a further incentive for a speedy election, the electors were to receive no income from their benefices during the vacancy of the Holy See.

Encouraged, as it were, by the rigorous legislation of Gregory X, the cardinals who assembled after his untimely death at Arezzo elected Blessed Innocent V (1276) on the eleventh day after the pope's death. Unfortunately, the new pope lasted barely six months, dying on June 22, 1276. Charles of Anjou, now king of Sicily and acting in his capacity as senator of Rome, rigorously applied the rules of Gregory X at the conclave that took place in Rome. As the deliberations dragged on, Charles cut the rations so drastically and confined the electors so strictly that several were prostrated by the sweltering heat of the Roman summer. Thus, on July 11, they elected Cardinal Ottobono Fieschi as Hadrian V (1276). On the day following his election, Hadrian assembled the cardinals in the Lateran and, noting the "many intolerable and obscure provisions" of Gregory X's reform decree, declared it suspended, promising to issue new legislation. However, Hadrian took ill and died without providing anything to replace it, leading to nearly two decades during which, in the absence of both outside intervention and the strict discipline of the conclave regimen, the cardinals once again prolonged their deliberations for months at a time.

The death of Nicholas IV on April 4, 1292, led to some of the strangest episodes in papal history as well as the eventual reestablishment of Gregory X's strict legislation. At that time, the Sacred College had twelve members, who, hopelessly divided by personal and familial rivalries, could not reach the required two-thirds majority for the election of a pope. Thus the papal throne remained vacant for some twenty-seven months as the deadlocked electors met in spurts, interspersed by two periods when several frustrated electors abandoned Rome, depriving the others of a quorum, as well as an attempt by the cardinals of the Colonna family to carry out an election by themselves. The cardinals reassembled in Perugia in October 1293 but still could not arrive at a compromise. Charles II, king of Sicily and Naples and thus, nominally, a papal vassal, arrived in the city in March 1294, seeking to speed up the election by producing a short list of four names for the electors. Although the king left after failing to persuade the cardinals, the outbreak of disturbances in Rome and elsewhere in the papal state succeeded in spurring them to hasten their deliberations.

At the meeting of the Sacred College on July 5, 1294—twenty-seven months to the day after the death of the preceding pope—the dean, Cardinal Latino Malabranca, announced to his colleagues that the reputed saintly hermit Pietro del Morrone was prophesying divine retribution if they left the Church without a head any longer. Cardinal Malabranca then announced that he was voting for the hermit. By stages, the other cardinals agreed, and the college unanimously elected the eighty-five-year-old recluse as Celestine V.

Originally from Molise, the new pope had entered the Benedictine order as a teenager but eventually withdrew to a solitary life in the wilderness of the Abruzzi. Ordained a priest in Rome at some indeterminate point, he lived for several years in a cave on Mount Morrone—thus his name—before retreating in his mid-thirties to the inaccessible heights of the Maiella to escape the public curiosity that his unusual lifestyle had attracted. Nonetheless, his fame as an ascetic and miracle worker drew a number of followers, who formed a brotherhood that was eventually incorporated as a branch of the Benedictines with the successive blessings of Urban IV and Gregory X. In 1293, relinquishing the governance of the nascent community, he moved back to Mount Morrone, settling in a new cave at an elevation of some 2,100 feet.

To characterize the choice as eccentric is probably an understatement. While electing the reluctant Celestine V seemed a charismatic bold stroke, the fact was that, for all his piety and reputation for holiness, the new pope was hopelessly naive, almost ridiculously incompetent, and rather ill educated—a dangerous combination in those troubled times. As he was in the domains of Charles II at the time of his election, the Angevin monarch arranged to have him consecrated in L'Aquila, which town he entered astride a donkey in imitation of the entrance of Jesus into Jerusalem. Celestine was then maneuvered by Charles to take residence not in Rome, as the cardinals expected, but in Naples, where the king installed him in the Castel Nuovo.

It quickly became evident that when the pope was not a puppet manipulated by Charles—French nominees of the king accounted for seven of the twelve cardinals created by Celestine—he fell into confusion, assigning, for example, the same benefice to more than one applicant. About the only area in which he showed any initiative was his attempts to shower privileges on his own little congregation, to whom he tried to give several of the great Benedictine abbeys, including Monte Cassino, much to the ire of the venerable monastic order. To the resentment of the Franciscan order, he privileged the "Spirituals," dissidents who opposed the main body of Franciscans in calling for a literal observance of strict poverty.

As the season of Advent approached, Celestine proposed to hand over the government of the Church to a committee of three cardinals while he retired to his cave to fast and pray, a plan rebuffed by the Sacred College as unprecedented. After consulting the noted canon lawyer Cardinal Benedetto Caetani on the possibility of resigning—the canonist erroneously told him that there were precedents for a voluntary papal retirement—Celestine published a bull on December 10, 1294, declaring that Gregory X's conclave legislation was once again in force. Three days later, on December 13, he assembled a consistory and read out to it a formula of abdication prepared by Cardinal Caetani. Stripping off the papal insignia, he invited the cardinals to proceed to elect his successor. The College of Cardinals thus met at Castel Nuovo ten days after the abdication, allowing the interval stipulated by Gregory X's decree, and on the following day, Christmas Eve 1294, elected Cardinal Gaetani as Boniface VIII (1294–1303).[5]

Among the achievements of Boniface VIII's controversial pontificate—the last line of his 1302 bull *Unam sanctam* proclaimed that it was necessary for salvation that every creature be subject to the Roman pontiff—was his publication in 1298 of the *Liber sextus*, which formed the third part of the *Corpus of Canon Law*. Among the legislation thus codified was a provision confirming the electoral discipline decreed by Gregory X, thus consolidating the practice of the conclave.

The conclave that met at the Vatican following Gregory XI's death was the first to meet in Rome since the one following Boniface VIII's some seventy-five years earlier. Crowds of Romans, fearing that the French cardinals who constituted the majority of the electors would choose one of their own and return the papacy to Avignon, surrounded the meeting amid scenes of unprecedented uproar, at one point invading the papal palace, clamoring for "a Roman, or at least an Italian" pope. The evening before the conclave officially began, the city magistrates called on the Sacred College and warned them of the danger they faced if they ignored popular sentiment. The following morning, sixteen cardinals met in a panic-stricken session and, on the first ballot, hurriedly elected Bartolomeo Prignano, archbishop of Bari. Before the absent pope-designate—not being a member of the College, he was not present at its meeting—could be asked if he accepted the office, the mob burst in on the electors. The terrified cardinals managed to placate the angry crowd by resorting to a bit of play-acting: They dressed up their elderly Roman colleague Cardinal Tebaldeschi in the papal regalia and presented him to the mob to show them an Italian "pope." Satisfied, the mob dispersed to loot the papal palace while the cardinals fled.

Ten days later, the Italian who was elected, Bartolomeo Prignano, was duly enthroned as Urban VI (1378–1389). While the cardinals showed no reservations about their choice, collaborating with the new pope, they quickly discovered that he planned a radical reform of the Church, including the drastic simplification of their lifestyles, and went about implementing it with an almost paranoid violence. One by one all but three of the sixteen cardinals fled the papal court— the three unfortunates who did not flee were subsequently put to torture along with the visiting bishop of L'Aquila on the charge of having conspired with the runaways—and were joined by their colleagues from Avignon at Anagni. On August 2, 1378, the cardinals issued a declaration declaring Urban's election invalid, basing the claim on the argument that the tense atmosphere surrounding the conclave deprived the electors of their freedom. A week later, they issued another statement proclaiming the deposition of the pope. Moving on to Fondi, under the protection of Queen Joanna of Naples, the cardinals proceeded to elect Cardinal Robert of Geneva, son of the Count of Savoy and cousin of the king of France, as Clement VII (1378–1394) on September 20, thus inaugurating the Great Schism of the Western Church.

The dispute between Urban VI and his rival Clement VII, both elected by the same College of Cardinals, split Christendom down the middle. France, after a brief neutrality that ended when Clement moved to Avignon, along with Burgundy, Savoy, Naples, and Scotland, supported Clement, while the empire and the German princes, England, most of Italy outside Naples, and the central European states declared for Urban. The Spanish kingdoms, at least initially, remained neutral. Each of the popes (it should be noted that the *Annuario Pontificio* lists Urban and his successors as the legitimate line of pontiffs, their rivals being listed as antipopes) anathematized his rivals and his rivals' supporters. After Urban died in 1389, the twenty-nine cardinals he had created elected the Cardinal Priest of Santa Anastasia, Pietro Tomacelli, as Boniface IX (1389–1404). When Clement died in 1394, there was hope that the schism would end if the Avignon cardinals refrained from electing a successor. However, the twenty-one who assembled, after swearing an oath to work for an end to the conflict and to abdicate if and when the majority of their number determined it expedient to restore unity, elected the Cardinal Deacon of Santa Maria in Cosmedin (the church where the famous Bocca della Verità is located), the Aragonese aristocrat Pedro de Luna, who had been named a cardinal by Gregory XI shortly before the return to Rome, as Benedict XIII (1394–1417). Thus the schism was prolonged. Boniface was succeeded by Innocent VII (1404–1406), who, in turn, was succeeded by Gregory XII (1406–1415).

As the schism continued, the cardinals of both sides, with the support of an increasing number of European monarchs, sought to reach a compromise. However, neither side showed any signs of giving way. Gregory's partisans were certain of the canonical right of his succession (a point of view legitimized by subsequent official papal historiography), while Benedict's held that as the sole surviving undisputed cardinal appointed by the last uncontested pope (he was created by Gregory XI in his last consistory) he was entitled to cast the only undisputed vote—for himself. The exasperated cardinals from both obediences then met together in a joint conclave at the Duomo of Pisa on June 26, 1409, and, declaring both popes deposed, proceeded to unanimously elect yet a third claimant to the papal office, the Greco-Italian Franciscan Pietro Philarghi, as Alexander V (1409–1410). When Alexander died unexpectedly in Bologna the following spring, the cardinals who had elected him met in that city and elected one of their number, Baldassare Cossa, a former pirate, as John XXIII (1410–1415).

At this point, the German king (and later emperor), Sigismund of Luxembourg, convinced that only a general council could resolve the schism, intervened and demanded the holding of one under his protection at Constance. The council, originally convoked by a bull of John XXIII, convened on November 5, 1414. It quickly turned on him, however, especially when he tried to flee in disguise when he realized it was not inclined to automatically legitimize his position. Thus the Council of Constance deposed him on May 29, 1415, and had him entrusted to the strict custody of the Elector Ludwig III of Bavaria. Later freed and made cardinal bishop of Tusculum (Frascati) by Pope Martin V (1417–1431), John died in 1419 and is buried in a magnificent tomb, the work of Bartolomeo di Michelozzo and Donatello, in the baptistery of the Duomo in Florence.

After John XXIII's deposition, Gregory XII, the pope of the Roman obedience, communicated to the Council of Constance his willingness to abdicate provided he was allowed to formally convoke the assembly afresh as a general council. The proposal was accepted, and on July 4, 1415, his bull convoking the council was read, followed by the notice of his resignation (this date, incidentally, is the date officially given for the convening of the council by subsequent official Catholic histories). The acts of Gregory's pontificate were ratified and he was appointed cardinal bishop of Porto and legate of the March of Ancona for life, being guaranteed precedence immediately after the new pope (this last provision was rendered meaningless by the fact that he died on October 18, 1417, three weeks before the election of Martin V).

The last claimant to the papal office, the Avignon pope, Benedict XIII, re-buffed Sigismund's attempt to persuade him to abdicate honorably. Taking ref-uge in the impregnable castle of Peñiscola on the coast of Valencia in mid-1415, he was eventually abandoned by all but the most diehard of his followers. De-clared deposed by the Council of Constance on July 26, 1417, "Papa Luna" lived on until 1423, when, at the age of ninety-five and still maintaining his claims, he passed away.[6]

Interestingly, throughout the Great Schism, all sides adhered scrupulously to the dispositions of Gregory X's decree on papal succession, consolidating the institution of the conclave. The Council of Constance, after lengthy discussions, departed from it, holding a unique conclave of twenty-two cardinals and thirty representatives of the "nations" present. This "super-conclave" elected Cardinal Oddo Colonna as Martin V on November 11, 1415, thus ending the schism. After Martin's election, the exclusive electoral franchise was restored to the College of Cardinals, where it has remained since.

During the Renaissance, the strict discipline of the conclave gave way to a certain laxity, with the ambassadors of the Catholic states coming and going, lobbying the electors. As part of his reform of the government of the Church, Pope Pius IV (1559–1565) issued a decree, entitled *In eligendis*, in 1562, which he compelled all the cardinals to sign, restoring the former strict discipline to the conclave. In his decree, Pius stipulated that the Sacred College could not make any financial dispositions during the period of the *sede vacante*. He also provided for the conclave's strict enclosure, specifying for the first time that the part of the papal palace to be occupied by the electors within the conclave area be not just sealed but bricked up and ordering that the cardinals be housed in small cells, which were to be distributed by lot.

Pope Gregory XV (1621–1623) perfected the arrangements of Pius IV through two decrees, *Aeterni Patris Filius* (November 15, 1621) and *Decet Romanum pontificem* (March 12, 1622), which dictated the minutest details of papal elec-tion. Among the details prescribed by Gregory was the introduction, for the first time, of secret ballots; previously the cardinals expressed their choice openly within the confines of the conclave, much in the manner of the secret delibera-tions of a parliamentary body. And although he did not entirely exclude the possibility of election by acclamation, Gregory rendered it more difficult by ban-ning discussion of candidates among the cardinals. Until the flurry of legislation that came in the twentieth century—with the exceptions of Benedict XV (1914–1922) and John Paul I (1978), every twentieth-century pontiff tinkered with the electoral legislation—Gregory's arrangements were the unaltered basis for all subsequent papal elections.

Political Interference

While the question of papal succession has always been linked with political considerations, the combined effects of the strict election procedures imposed by Pius IV and Gregory XVI curtailed the amount direct pressure that the various nations could bring to bear on the conclave. On the other hand, the reality of the papal office, which united spiritual authority affecting the lives of millions in a still-Christian Western world and temporal authority over a large portion of an Italian peninsula that occupied a critical geopolitical position in Europe, required that the College of Cardinals take into account the concerns of at least the Catholic states. Thus evolved the curious historical institution—never officially recognized by canon law but implicitly respected by the Sacred College—of the so-called *ius exclusivae*, or "right of exclusion."

When Urban VII died in 1590, a victim of malaria caught the night after his election, after barely two weeks on the papal throne, King Philip II of Spain transmitted to the College of Cardinals, along with his condolences on the untimely death of the pontiff, a list of some fifty names that he would prefer to see *not* elected as well as seven candidates he supported. The extent to which the Spanish monarch's unprecedented public expression of preference affected the deliberations is not known, but it did represent the first recorded overt attempt to exclude the election of certain candidates by secular power with what would evolve into the exclusionary veto.

Philip II's maneuver was repeated twice by his grandson Philip III, both times directed against the potential candidacy of Cardinal Giulio Cesare Sacchetti. When Pope Urban VIII (1623–1644) died, the Spanish court expressed its objections to the election of Cardinal Sacchetti, who had been the patron of the early career of the French king's chief minister, Cardinal Jules Mazarin. In response, the French tried to block the election of the former nuncio to Spain, Cardinal Giambattista Pamphilj, but that attempt came too clumsily (and too late, in any event) to stop his election as Innocent X. Innocent's subsequent policies vindicated Philip III's trust. Portugal having broken away from Spain in 1640, Innocent refused both to recognize Dom João IV of Braganza as king and to fill any vacant sees with his nominees. When Naples revolted against the Spanish crown, he rebuffed the suggestion of the French ambassador that he avail himself of the opportunity, as the feudal overlord of the Neapolitan kingdom, to incorporate it into the papal state. After Innocent died in 1655, Philip III again excluded the candidacy of Cardinal Sacchetti, opening the way for the election of Cardinal Fabio Chigi, the late pope's secretary of state, as Alexander VII, who continued his predecessor's policy of not recognizing the monarchy of João IV of Portugal. Alexander's election had initially been excluded by the French court, but that veto was withdrawn by Cardinal Mazarin when his candidate, Cardinal Sacchetti, interceded with him for the good of the Roman Church.[7]

At the conclave following Alexander's death in 1670, the institution of the exclusionary veto acquired its definitive, albeit never officially sanctioned, form. The practice was that the principal Catholic powers—the Habsburg emperor and the kings of France and Spain—communicated to the respective cardinal protector, or cardinal procurator, of their realms a list of those members of the Sacred College who were *personae minus gratae,* or undesirable, so that, if there was a possibility of one of these becoming pope, the authorized cardinal might, before the decisive ballot, give the veto, in the name of his government, against such election. Originally this veto was given orally, although later it was occasionally communicated in writing. The declaration was made at the last moment; as the tradition developed, a government might invoke this alleged right only once at each conclave, and consequently would not wish to employ it unnecessarily. A veto made after the election was not recognized. Thus, in the election of 1670, Louis XIV imposed a French veto against the candidacy of Cardinal Scipione Pannocchieschi d'Elci, securing the election of Cardinal Giulio Rospigliosi as Pope Clement IX.

Blessed Pius IX tried, with his bull *In hac sublimi* of August 23, 1871, to forbid any interference of the secular power in papal elections, although he did not specifically abolish the "right of exclusion." The *ius exclusivae* was to be exercised one last time in the conclave of 1903 when Cardinal Jan Puzyna de Kosielsko, prince-bishop of Cracow, pronounced the exclusion of Leo XIII's secretary of state, Cardinal Mariano Rampolla del Tindaro, by the Emperor Franz Josef II of Austria-Hungary.

Following that last episode, the pope eventually elected, St. Pius X, absolutely repudiated and abolished forever the exclusionary veto. In his constitution *Commissum Nobis* of January 20, 1904, he declared that the Apostolic See had never approved the veto, though previous legislation had not succeeded in preventing it, and decreed: "Wherefore in virtue of holy obedience, under threat of the Divine judgment, and pain of excommunication *latae sententiae . . .* we prohibit the cardinals of the Holy Roman Church, all and single, and likewise the Secretary of the Sacred College of Cardinals, and all others who take part in the conclave, to receive even under the form of a simple desire the office of proposing the veto in whatever manner, either by writing or by word of mouth . . . And it is our will that this prohibition be extended . . . to all intercessions, etc. . . . by which the lay powers endeavor to intrude themselves in the election of a pontiff." Therefore, the pope threatened: "Let no man infringe this our prohibition . . . under pain of incurring the indignation of God Almighty and of his Apostles, Saints Peter and Paul." The constitution required the cardinals to swear an oath that they would "never in any way accept, under any pretext, from any civil power whatever, the office of proposing a veto of exclusion even under the form of a mere desire" and would "never lend favor to any intervention, or intercession, or any other method whatever, by which the lay powers of any grade or order may wish to interfere in the election of a pontiff."

Preparations for the Conclave

Every one of the popes of the twentieth century, with the exceptions of Benedict XV, who died prematurely after being preoccupied during most of his reign by World War I, and John Paul I, who reigned barely a month, has fine-tuned the legislation concerning the vacancy of the Apostolic See and the election of a new pope. Some of the decrees were responses to abuses that occurred in the very conclaves that elected the legislating pope—Pius X's severe censure of the exclusionary veto after the conclave of 1903 being a prime example—while others, such as the most recent, John Paul II's apostolic constitution *Universi Dominici gregis* (UDG) of February 22, 1996, represented attempts to bring practices up-to-date with modern exigencies.[8] It is beyond the scope of the present work to analyze these successive pieces of legislation for their juridical content. Rather, what follows is a description of the period of the *sede vacante* and an analysis of the electoral mechanism. Only those comparative elements that lend a certain context or understanding to the present norms will be noted.

During the *sede vacante*, the interim government of the Church is entrusted to the College of Cardinals. The authority of the college, like that of all institutions of the Church's central government, is strictly circumscribed during this period. In fact, the Code of Canon Law specifically stipulates that "when the Roman See is vacant, or completely impeded, no innovation is to be made in the governance of the universal Church. The special laws enacted for these circumstances are to be observed" (canon 335). The code also specifies that should an "ecumenical council" of all the bishops of the Catholic Church be meeting when the pope dies, that assembly "is by virtue of the law itself suspended until the new Supreme Pontiff either orders it to continue or dissolves it" (canon 340). The same applies for the periodic meetings of the Synod of Bishops, constituted by representatives of the bishops: "If the Apostolic See becomes vacant after the synod has been convened or during its celebration, the meeting of the synod, and the function entrusted in it to the members, is by virtue of the law itself suspended, until the new Pontiff decrees either that the assembly is to be dissolved or that it is to continue" (canon 340 §2). Both these provisions are meant to protect the prerogatives of the future pope as well as the exclusive electoral franchise of the cardinals from any move to transfer them to a larger, presumably less deliberative, body, as occurred during the Great Schism.

Likewise, at the death of the pope all the heads of the dicasteries, or departments, of the Roman Curia—the cardinal secretary of state, the cardinal prefects of the congregations, the cardinal or archbishop presidents of the pontifical councils—as well as all the members of those dicasteries cease to exercise their office. The only exceptions are the camerlengo of the Holy Roman Church, whose function enters into play during the interregnum, and the major penitentiary, whose faculties to absolve continue lest, as traditional Catholic theology holds, the salvation of souls be jeopardized. Likewise, for the same latter reason, the cardinal vicar general for the Diocese of Rome (who, in the name of the pope, carries out the *de facto* spiritual functions of the diocesan bishop for the city of Rome) and the cardinal archpriest of the Vatican Basilica (who presently exercises the functions of vicar general for the Vatican City State) continue with their charges. As for the administrative offices, they may only carry out ordinary activities of lesser importance, all matters of greater significance being deferred to the future pope. Should a matter arise that cannot wait, the College of Cardinals as a body may deal with it provisionally, but the final disposition is still reserved for the future pontiff.

While the exclusive electoral franchise of the College of Cardinals is defended by John Paul II in his 1996 apostolic constitution—the pope cites in the introduction to the document the linkage of the cardinals with the Church of Rome through their titles to the suburbicarian dioceses and urban parishes and diaconal stations as well as their international composition as representative of the universality of the Church—its power is carefully limited, as John Paul II affirmed: "During the vacancy of the Apostolic See, the College of Cardinals has no power or jurisdiction in matters which pertain to the Supreme Pontiff during his lifetime or in the exercise of his office; such matters are to be reserved completely and exclusively to the future Pope" (UDG 1). The cardinals are specifically prohibited from making any dispositions concerning the rights of the Apostolic See and the Roman Church and are, in fact, enjoined to defend those rights. They are also prohibited from modifying or dispensing with any laws issued by preceding popes, although they may interpret any doubtful or controverted points concerning those laws, deciding by majority vote of the cardinals present. In fact, any acts of the College of Cardinals that exceed the limits prescribed in the legislation are explicitly declared null and void in advance.

The first duty of the College of Cardinals is to see to the funeral rites for the deceased pontiff. Meanwhile, the cardinal camerlengo of the Holy Roman Church is charged with administering the goods and temporal rights of the Holy See, consulting with the college as needed. The camerlengo is a sort of "prince regent" who enjoys certain prerogatives of sovereignty, including the right to mint coinage and issue postage stamps bearing his name, title, and arms. The camerlengo is assisted in his task by the vice-camerlengo, who assumes the former's responsibilities once he is locked incommunicado inside the conclave. The camerlengo and vice-camerlengo are aided by the ancient office known as the Apostolic Camera, which consists of a College of Prelates, headed by a dean, and a lay secretary-chancellor.

During the *sede vacante* and before the opening of the electoral conclave, the College of Cardinals carries out its functions through meetings called "congregations," of which there are two types. The *general congregation* is a meeting of the entire College of Cardinals. All cardinals who are not legitimately impeded are required to attend once they are informed of the vacancy in the papal office. Those cardinals over the age of eighty, who were excluded from voting in the conclave by Pope Paul VI, are excused from this obligation. However, if they choose, they may attend the general congregation and have the right to participate and vote in its deliberations. The meetings of the general congregation, which are generally to be held in the Apostolic Palace of the Vatican, are presided over by the dean of the College of Cardinals or, in his absence, the subdean. If these dignitaries should be of an age when they no longer enjoy the right of electing the pope, the senior cardinal elector, according to the customary order of precedence, presides.

In the past, the cardinals assembled in a general congregation received delegations from the various powers who, availing themselves of the occasion of presenting their condolences upon the death of a pope, took the occasion to impress upon the electors their political preferences for the coming conclave. Contemporary chroniclers record the spectacle of royal ambassadors, led by papal guards, processing in the dozen or so carriages of their entourage and accompanied by the carriages of sympathetic colleagues and members of the Roman aristocracy—all to heighten the splendor of the monarch whose envoy was on his way to salute (and influence) the assembled princes of the Church. Among the Roman populace, the spectacle was even more appreciated for the coins thrown by the parading envoys to the crowds en route.

Under the current norms, the general congregation meetings are to be held daily, beginning with the day fixed by the camerlengo in accord with the senior cardinal of each of the three orders (cardinal bishops, cardinal priests, cardinal deacons). The general congregation meets every day, including days on which the funeral rites of the deceased pope are celebrated. At the very first general congregation, copies of the apostolic constitution are distributed to the cardinals present and the part of the decree regarding the vacancy of the Apostolic See is read aloud. The cardinals present then take an oath swearing to uphold the provisions of the law: "We, the Cardinals of Holy Roman Church, of the Order of Bishops, of Priests and of Deacons, promise, pledge and swear, as a body and individually, to observe exactly and faithfully all the norms contained in the Apostolic Constitution *Universi Dominici gregis* of the Supreme Pontiff John Paul II, and to maintain rigorous secrecy with regard to all matters in any way related to the election of the Roman Pontiff or those which, by their very nature, during the vacancy of the Apostolic See, call for the same secrecy." To this formula, each cardinal adds the personal declaration: "And I, [his first name] Cardinal [his family name], so promise, pledge and swear." Then, placing his hand on the Book of the Gospels, the individual cardinal adds: "So help me God and these Holy Gospels which I now touch with my hand."

Besides arranging for the late pope's funeral, the general congregation sees to it that a commission, made up of the cardinal camerlengo and the cardinals who had formerly held the offices of secretary of state and president of the Pontifical Commission for Vatican City State, ensures that the rooms of the Domus Sanctae Marthae, the new guest palace built within the Vatican City behind the Paul VI Audience Hall, are made ready for the lodging of the cardinal electors and that other suitable rooms are prepared for others who will assist with the conclave, as well as that all necessary arrangements are made to prepare the Sistine Chapel so that the election process can be carried out smoothly. The general congregation also approves a budget for the operation of the Holy See for the period between the death of the pope and the election of his successor, hears any messages left to it by the deceased pontiff, witnesses the destruction of the Fisherman's Ring[9] and the seal used to dispatch papal documents, casts lots for the assignment of rooms to the cardinal electors, and sets the day and hour for the beginning of the conclave. John Paul II also ordered that the assembled cardinals hear two "well-prepared meditations on the problems facing the Church at the time and the need for careful discernment in choosing the new pope," to be given by "two ecclesiastics known for their sound doctrine, wisdom and moral authority" (UDG 13).

The controversial construction of the Domus Sanctae Marthae—rumored to have cost more than $20 million and blocking the views that many older buildings outside the Vatican had enjoyed of the cupola of St. Peter's Basilica—with its 120 discreetly uniform and air-conditioned suites, removed a major source of tension from the conclave process. Previously, a section of the Vatican Palace was sealed off for the conclave and rudimentary rooms erected in the palace's halls and corridors for the use of the cardinals. While the potentially oppressive heat or chilling cold (the medieval section of the palace used lacks central heat, to say nothing of air-conditioning) contributed—as was, no doubt, intended by the arrangement—to hastening the conclave's deliberations, there was a certain cruelty to subjecting elderly gentlemen to such crude conditions, especially the lack of private (or even convenient) toilets. Thus the casting of lots for the rooms is presently more symbolic than functional.

In addition to the general congregation, there is also a *particular congregation* of cardinals. The second type is a smaller committee constituted by the camerlengo and three cardinals, one from each order (cardinal bishops, cardinal priests, cardinal deacons), chosen by lot from the cardinal electors present in Rome. With the exception of the camerlengo, who remains in office until the future pope replaces him, the other cardinals of the particular congregation, called "cardinal assistants," serve for three days, their place being taken in turn by others, also chosen from by lot, until the conclave begins. The particular congregation deals with matters of lesser importance that need not be submitted to the general congregation of cardinals. However, decisions taken by one particular congregation cannot be altered by another one; the right to do so belongs exclusively to the general congregation and requires a majority vote.

According to the present legislation, in fixing the start of the conclave, the College of Cardinals must take into account that "from the moment when the Apostolic See is lawfully vacant, the Cardinal electors who are present must wait fifteen full days for those who are absent." The cardinals may "defer, for serious reasons, the beginning of the election for a few days more. But when a maximum of twenty days have elapsed from the beginning of the vacancy of the See, all the Cardinal electors present are obliged to proceed to the election" (UDG 37). From Gregory X's electoral dispositions in 1276 through the conclave of 1922, the interval between the death of the pope and the beginning of the conclave was fixed at ten days.

Until the nineteenth century, this provision effectively limited the franchise to cardinals of the Roman Curia or Italian cardinals, when one took into account the time required for notice of the death of a pope to reach any electors and for them to undertake the journey to the Eternal City. The exception of non-curial or non-Italian cardinals participating in the conclave before the advent of faster means of travel in the nineteenth century was limited to those cardinals from far off who happened to be in Rome when the pope died, either by coincidence or design (there are historical examples, especially in the eighteenth century, of trans-Alpine cardinals setting off for Rome at the merest rumor of a pope's declining health and then camping out in the Eternal City for extended periods, leaving their dioceses without bishops). By the beginning of the twentieth century, better means of communication and travel ensured that most cardinals could arrive within the stipulated interval, the only exception being the cardinals from the Americas, who, even after the trans-Atlantic cable was laid, could still not make it in time. In 1922, Cardinal William O'Connell, archbishop of

Boston, raced across the Atlantic on a steamship, only to arrive in Rome as the announcement of Pope Pius XI's election was made. The complaints of the American cardinals led Pius XI to extend the interval to fifteen days with his *motu proprio* entitled *Cum proxime* of March 1, 1922. The present interval of a minimum of fifteen days and a maximum of twenty days was decreed by Pope Paul VI with his apostolic constitution *Romano Pontificis eligendo* of October 1, 1975, and subsequently confirmed by John Paul II.[10]

The Conclave

John Paul II's apostolic constitution reaffirms the precept, first formulated in the 1059 reform decree of Nicholas II, that the right of voting in papal elections belongs exclusively to members of the College of Cardinals: "The right to elect the Roman Pontiff belongs exclusively to the Cardinals of Holy Roman Church, with the exception of those who have reached their eightieth birthday before the day of the Roman Pontiff's death or the day when the Apostolic See becomes vacant. The maximum number of Cardinal electors must not exceed one hundred and twenty. The right of active election by any other ecclesiastical dignitary or the intervention of any lay power of whatsoever grade or order is absolutely excluded" (*UDG* 33). With the exception of the election of Martin V in 1417, when other prelates from the Council of Constance joined with the cardinals in electing a pope to end the Great Schism, and the negative interventions of the secular powers with their claim to a *ius exclusivae*, every papal election since Nicholas II has reserved the right of active vote to the College of Cardinals.

In the early 1970s, it was said that Pope Paul VI proposed adding the patriarchs of the Eastern Catholic Churches,[11] the members of the Council of the General Secretariat of the Synod of Bishops, and other bishops elected by the Synod of Bishops to the electoral college. He even entertained the idea of making the voting public. However, the radical proposals were criticized by Cardinal Giuseppe Siri, archbishop of Genoa, in a brilliant article in the theological journal *Renovatio*, which argued that the changes would empty both the College of Cardinals of its real significance and further weaken the already titular link between the election of the bishop of Rome by the clergy of the See of St. Peter. Paul was evidently swayed by Siri's arguments since the proposals did not appear in his 1975 apostolic constitution.

Paul VI did, however, succeed in promulgating one innovation: the exclusion of cardinals over the age of eighty from the conclave with his *motu proprio* of November 21, 1970, *Ingravescentem aetatem*. Officially, the change was made to spare the elderly the rigors of the conclave. However, in reality, this change was

motivated, in large part, by his concern that, in the event of his death, conservative elements in the college—conservative equated at that time with older, since
they would have been overwhelmingly nominees predating the pontificate of
Blessed John XXIII—might succeed in overturning the reforms of the Second
Vatican Council. This change met with much resentment among the ranks of
the cardinals. Two years after the change, when the aged dean of the Sacred
College, the French cardinal Eugène Tisserant, died, the cardinals implicitly re-
buked the pope by electing as their new dean the quasi-nonagenarian Cardinal
Amleto Cicognani. The final lie to the official reasons given for the change—the
motu proprio of Pope Paul VI mentioned "special solicitude" for the "natural rap-
port between advanced age and the need to disengage from important functions"—
was given when Paul died in 1978 at the age of 80 and was joined not long
thereafter by his sixty-five-year-old successor, John Paul I: Presiding regally at
both funerals was none other than the eighty-five-year-old dean of the College
of Cardinals, Carlo Confalonieri.[12]

By law, the conclave must nowadays take place within the territory of the
Vatican City, since it is to elect not only the bishop of Rome and spiritual head of
the Roman Catholic Church but also the sovereign of the tiny city-state, the last
remnant of the papacy's temporal dominions. As recounted previously, since the
Middle Ages, conclaves have taken place wherever the last pope died or at least
within the territory of the papacy, with the exception of the conclave of 1800, held
under Austrian protection on the Venetian island of San Giorgio during the revolutionary French occupation of Rome. In fact, since the 1455 conclave that elected
Callistus III, every conclave has been held inside the precincts of the Vatican
with the exception of that of 1800 and those of 1823, 1829, 1830, and 1846, which
were held in Rome's Quirinal Palace, then seat of the papal monarchy.

The term "conclave" originated in the literal enclosure under lock and key of
the electors, and, indeed, the area where the electors are lodged and where they
deliberated has traditionally been sealed off against communication with the
outside. As recently as the conclaves of 1978, the conclave area, with the exception of the principal entrance, was literally bricked up. John Paul II has relaxed
this practice somewhat with his provision for lodging the cardinals in the relative
comfort of the Domus Sanctae Marthae and housing their deliberations in the
Sistine Chapel of the Apostolic Palace. This change—the two structures are separated by the Vatican gardens as well as St. Peter's Basilica—has necessitated new
provisions for the enclosure of large parts of the Vatican City State to ensure
privacy for the electors and to prevent even those legitimately within the territory of the Vatican from approaching the cardinals as they move back and forth
between their lodgings and the Sistine Chapel. It remains to be seen how this is
carried out.

The arrangements for the security of the conclave are entrusted to the cardinal camerlengo and his three cardinal assistants *pro tempore*. Until Pope Paul VI's abolition of the papal court, this charge was in the hands of the hereditary marshal of the Holy Roman Church, *ex ufficio* governor of the Sacred Conclave: the incumbent head of the princely family of Chigi Albano della Rovere, heirs to the Savelli family that received the honor for their part in protecting the electors of the conclave of 1268–1271.

From the beginning of the conclave until its conclusion with the public announcement of the newly elected pope, the cardinal electors are forbidden to communicate, whether by writing, telephone, or any other means, with persons outside the election enclosure. In an acknowledgment of modern technological advances, the present regulations stipulate that "careful and stringent checks must be made, with the help of trustworthy individuals of proven technical ability, in order to ensure that no audiovisual equipment has been secretly installed in these areas for recording and transmission to the outside" (*UDG* 51). The penalty stipulated for an infraction of this secrecy of the conclave is an automatic excommunication, whose absolution is reserved to the future pope.

In addition to the cardinal electors, John Paul II's legislation provides for the admission of other officials within the conclave enclosure, including the archbishop secretary of the College of Cardinals, who acts as secretary of the electoral assembly; the master of papal liturgical celebrations and two masters of ceremonies, to coordinate the liturgical rites of the conclave; two religious attached to the Papal Sacristy;[13] and an ecclesiastic chosen by the cardinal dean, or whoever presides in the event of the dean being ineligible to enter the conclave, to assist him in his duties. This assistant is the only personal aide permitted to any cardinal and is the last functional relic of the entourages that cardinals of former times brought with them. To regulate the abuses that occurred in previous conclaves, St. Pius X limited the assistants to two for each cardinal, stipulating that they could be clerical or lay, and permitting a third assistant if the cardinal was infirm or otherwise in need of additional assistance. He also ruled, however, that the assistants could be neither close relatives of the cardinal nor, in the event the elector was a member of a religious order, members of the same religious community. Pius XII, obviously taking note of abuses that had occurred since Pius X's regulations, further stipulated that the cardinals were forbidden to introduce into the conclave any of the prohibited relatives or fellow members of the same order under the guise of members of the entourage of another cardinal. Paul VI simplified the entire procedure by banning personal assistants unless the medical infirmity or physical condition of an elector required it, in which case it had to be approved for the cardinal by the pre-electoral congregation. John Paul II decreed that there "must also be available a number of priests from the regular clergy for hearing confessions in the different languages, and two medical doctors for possible emergencies," as well as adequate provision "for a suitable number of persons to be available for preparing and serving meals and for housekeeping" during the conclave (*UDG* 46). All these persons must be previously approved by the camerlengo and the three cardinal assistants and are likewise bound to secrecy about what they may observe during the conclave.

Before John Paul II's changes regarding the location and enclosure of the conclave, during the election, food, medicines, and other supplies that might be needed would be passed to those inside through the *rota*, a sort of turntable invented by the Renaissance papal master of ceremonies Paris de Grassis for the second conclave of 1503, to prevent the communications that occurred between the conclavists and those on the outside during the first conclave of that year. The conclaves of the twentieth century usually had two *rote*, a more formal one that the cardinals employed and a service model for their attendants. Each *rota* consisted of a vertical panel of wood installed on a circular tray that was set in an open drum with two openings, one facing the conclave enclosure and the other facing the outside. Objects could be passed in and out of the conclave by rotating the tray once it had been ascertained that no forbidden communications were concealed. Until cooks and a kitchen area were enclosed within the conclave area beginning with the conclave of 1878, the *rota*'s most important function was the passage of meals to the cardinals.[14]

Before the conclave, in the presence of the cardinal camerlengo, or another cardinal designated by him, and of two papal masters of ceremonies, each of these officials and assistants is required to swear the following oath:

> I, [name], promise and swear that, unless I should receive a special faculty given expressly by the newly-elected Pontiff or by his successors, I will observe absolute and perpetual secrecy with all who are not part of the College of Cardinal electors concerning all matters directly or indirectly related to the ballots cast and their scrutiny for the election of the Supreme Pontiff. I likewise promise and swear to refrain from using any audio or video equipment capable of recording anything which takes place during the period of the election within Vatican City, and in particular anything which in any way, directly or indirectly, is related to the process of the election itself. I declare that I take this oath fully aware that an infraction thereof will make me subject to the spiritual and canonical penalties which the future Supreme Pontiff will see fit to adopt, in accordance with Canon 1399 of the Code of Canon Law. So help me God and these Holy Gospels which I touch with my hand."

After the funeral rites for the deceased pontiff have been celebrated according to the ritual described previously, on the appointed day—that is, between the fifteenth day and the twentieth after the death of the pope—the cardinal electors meet in the St. Peter's Basilica for the celebration of a special votive Mass *pro eligendo Papa* ("for the election of the pope") in the morning. Then, in the afternoon of the same day, the cardinals gather in the Pauline Chapel of the Apostolic Palace, dressed in their distinctive red "choral" vestments, and process from there across the Sala Regia, or Royal Hall, to the Sistine Chapel, where the election is held. The passage from the Pauline Chapel through the Sala Regia to the Sistine Chapel could not, from the artistic and iconographic point of view, be more poignant for the occasion. The Pauline Chapel contains two frescoes that are the aged Michelangelo's last works, the *Martyrdom of St. Peter* and the *Conversion of St. Paul*, serving, no doubt, to remind the electors of the two apostles who founded the Church of Rome. The Royal Hall is decorated with triumphant frescoes by Giorgio Vasari of the Christian victory at the Battle of Lepanto, when the combined fleets of the papacy, Spain, Venice, and the Knights of Malta destroyed the superior Ottoman armada and saved Western Europe from the Muslim advance. The Sistine Chapel, of course, has Michelangelo's frescoed ceiling of the history of salvation as well as the *Last Judgment*.

Once the procession has arrived in the Sistine Chapel, the cardinals will take their conclave oath:

> We, the Cardinal electors present in this election of the Supreme Pontiff promise, pledge and swear, as individuals and as a group, to observe faithfully and scrupulously the prescriptions contained in the Apostolic Constitution of the Supreme Pontiff John Paul II, *Universi Dominici gregis*, published on 22 February 1996. We likewise promise, pledge and swear that whichever of us by divine disposition is elected Roman Pontiff will commit himself faithfully to carrying out the munus Petrinum of Pastor of the Universal Church and will not fail to affirm and defend strenuously the spiritual and temporal rights and the liberty of the Holy See. In a particular way, we promise and swear to observe with the greatest fidelity and with all persons, clerical or lay, secrecy regarding everything that in any way relates to the election of the Roman Pontiff and regarding what occurs in the place of the election, directly or indirectly related to the results of the voting; we promise and swear not to break this secret in any way, either during or after the election of the new Pontiff, unless explicit authorization is granted by the same Pontiff; and never to lend support or favor to any interference, opposition or any other form of intervention, whereby secular authorities of whatever order and degree or any group of people or individuals might wish to intervene in the election of the Roman Pontiff.

Each of the cardinal electors, according to the order of precedence, will then take the oath according to the following formula: "And I, [first name] Cardinal [family name], do so promise, pledge and swear." Placing his hand on the Book of the Gospels, each cardinal then adds: "So help me God and these Holy Gospels which I touch with my hand" (*UDG* 53).

Formerly, the cardinals were seated around the Sistine Chapel on individual thrones, each covered by a canopy, symbolic of the papal sovereignty of which each cardinal was a depository. As recently as the conclave of 1963, when the newly elected pope accepted his charge, each cardinal would reach to pull a small cord that would collapse his canopy, thus leaving only the canopy over the throne of the one elected still in place, thus symbolizing that now only one of them held the sovereign power. Since then, however, due to the expansion of the College of Cardinals to a number that can no longer be accommodated in the Sistine Chapel without resorting to seating in rows, coupled with the post–Vatican II simplifications of Catholic ritual, this little custom has been abolished.

The cardinals will then listen to a chosen ecclesiastic who will deliver to them a meditation on their duties. In the past, this discourse was delivered by a prelate with the impressive title of "secretary for briefs to princes," that is, the official whose classical knowledge qualified him to compose official papal communications to sovereigns in elegant Ciceronian Latin. Many of these discourses were preserved as masterpieces of Latin epistolary style. The discourse pronounced by Monsignor Antonio Bacci at the 1958 conclave that eventually elected him delighted John XXIII so much that, after his election the pope, who was a noted connoisseur of classical learning, rewarded the prelate orator with the red hat of a cardinal. With the collapse of classical formation in the period after Vatican II, it is unlikely that such a performance will be repeated in future conclaves.[15]

After the conclusion of this final hortatory discourse, the master of papal liturgical celebrations will pronounce the ritual formula *"Extra omnes!"* ("All out!"), ordering all to leave the electors to conduct their business. In former times, this ritual expulsion of those not permitted inside the conclave enclosure was carried out to the ringing of bells and the lighting of torches, but those anachronisms have been discarded in the post–Vatican II simplifications.

Until the apostolic constitution *Universi Dominici gregis* of Pope John Paul II, there were three recognized methods for electing a pope in conclave: by acclamation (or "quasi-inspiration"), by delegated compromise, and by secret ballot. Election by acclamation occurred when all the cardinals present spontaneously acclaimed one of their number as the one chosen by God. It is the electoral method depicted in the novel *The Shoes of the Fisherman* by Morris West (later made into a movie with Anthony Quinn playing Kiril Lakota, the Ruthenian cardinal elected the first non-Italian pope). Historically, this has been a rare method; the last time it was employed was the disastrous election of Celestine V in 1294. John Paul suppressed it as "no longer an apt means of interpreting the thought of an electoral college so great in number and so diverse in origin."

Election by delegated compromise occurred when a deadlocked conclave would delegate its franchise to a committee of cardinals to negotiate, each cardinal swearing an oath to accept the results of the committee's deliberations. John Paul likewise suppressed this option, noting the "difficulty of the procedure, evident from the unwieldy accumulation of rules issued in the past, but also because by its very nature it tends to lessen the responsibility of the individual electors who, in this case, would not be required to express their choice personally" (*UDG* introduction).

Thus the sole remaining form for electing the pope is by secret ballot, with a two-thirds majority of those present and voting required for election (or two-thirds plus one if the number of electors present cannot be divided into three equal parts).[16] Each of the cardinals has a seat in the Sistine Chapel along one of the rows of convention-style tables, the elaborate thrones and individual writing desks having been abolished. Once the cardinals have taken their places, the voting begins. On the first day, only one ballot is taken. If no one is elected on that ballot, then two ballots are held in the morning and two in the afternoon on each of the successive days. The voting in each ballot is carried out in three phases.

The first phase is called the "pre-scrutiny." During this part, the master of ceremonies hands out ballot papers to the cardinals. The ballot papers are rectangular in shape and bear, printed in the upper half, the words *"Eligo in Summum Pontificem"* ("I elect as supreme pontiff"). In the lower half of the ballot papers is a space for writing in the name of the person the elector wishes to vote for (John Paul advises the cardinals to do so "as far as possible in handwriting that cannot be identified as his"). Meanwhile the junior cardinal deacon draws lots for three cardinals to act as "scrutineers," three cardinals (*infirmarii*) to collect votes from any sick cardinals who cannot make it to the Sistine Chapel to vote, and three cardinals to act as "revisers."

After the distribution of the ballot papers and before the electors begin writing, the secretary of the College of Cardinals, the master of papal liturgical celebrations, and the masters of ceremonies must leave the chapel. The junior cardinal deacon is responsible for opening and closing the door.

The second phase of the voting, called the "scrutiny" proper, then takes place. Each cardinal, in order of precedence, after having completed and folded his ballot, holds it up and carries it to the altar, on which the receptacle for receiving the ballot, covered by a plate, is placed. The three cardinals chosen to serve as scrutineers stand close by to watch the proceedings. Upon reaching the altar, each elector pronounces aloud the Latin oath: "I call as my witness Christ the Lord who will be my judge, that my vote is given to the one who before God I think should be elected" (*UDG* 66). The elector then places the ballot on the plate and tips it into the receptacle. Having done this, he bows to the altar and returns to his seat.

If a cardinal present in the Sistine Chapel is unable to go up to the altar because of infirmity, the third of the three scrutineers goes to him. The elector pronounces the same oath and hands the folded ballot to the scrutineer, who carries it to the altar for him. If any of the cardinals happens to be sick and confined to his room, the three cardinals designated by lot as the *infirmarii* go together to him carrying a box with an opening at the top through which a folded ballot can be inserted. To avoid any recriminations—needless to say, the history of the Catholic Church is replete with them—John Paul provided detailed indications as to how this procedure was to work: "Before giving the box to the *Infirmarii*, the Scrutineers open it publicly, so that the other electors can see that it is empty; they are then to lock it and place the key on the altar. The *Infirmarii*, taking the locked box and a sufficient number of ballot papers on a small tray, then go, duly accompanied, to the *Domus Sanctae Marthae* to each sick elector, who takes a ballot, writes his vote in secret, folds the ballot and, after taking the above-mentioned oath, puts it through the opening in the box. If any of the electors who are sick is unable to write, one of the three *Infirmarii* or another Cardinal elector chosen by the sick man, having taken an oath before the *Infirmarii* concerning the observance of secrecy, carries out the above procedure. The *Infirmarii* then take the box back into the Chapel, where it shall be opened by the Scrutineers after the Cardinals present have cast their votes. The Scrutineers then count the ballots in the box and, having ascertained that their number corresponds to the number of those who are sick, place them one by one on the plate and then drop them all together into the receptacle" (*UDG* 67).

It goes without saying that these procedures take a rather extended amount of time given the number of electors now involved in the papal conclave. As papal biographer George Weigel relates, during the 1978 conclave that elected him, Cardinal Karol Wojtyla, the future John Paul II, brought along academic journals to read during the scrutinies and, ironically, given his role in bringing down Communism in Eastern Europe, was reading a Marxist philosophical journal when he was elected.

After all of the votes have been collected in the receptacle on the altar of the Sistine Chapel, the first scrutineer shakes the container several times to mix the ballot papers, and the third scrutineer counts them into an empty receptacle. If the number of ballots does not correspond to the number of electors, the ballots are burned and another vote is taken. If the number does correspond, then the counting of the ballots takes place according to a very precise procedure detailed in the apostolic constitution. The scrutineers sit at a table set up in front of the altar. The first of them takes a ballot, unfolds it, notes the name of the person for whom the vote is cast, and passes the ballot to the second scrutineer, who in turn notes the name of the person voted for and passes the ballot to the third, who reads it out in a loud and clear voice, so that all the electors present can record the vote on a sheet of paper prepared for that purpose, and writes down the name read from the ballot himself. As he reads out the individual ballots, he pierces each one with a needle through the word *"Eligo"* and places it on a thread. After all the names have been read out, the ends of the thread are tied in a knot, binding the ballots together in a bundle.

When all the ballots have been opened, the scrutineers add up the sum of the votes obtained by the different names and write them down on a separate sheet of paper. They then proceed to the third phase, the "post-scrutiny." If no one has obtained two-thirds (or two-thirds plus one, depending on the number of electors present) of the votes on that ballot, the pope has not been elected; if, however, it turns out that someone has obtained the required majority of the votes, the election of the Roman pontiff has taken place. In either case, the three revisers proceed to check both the ballots and the notes made by the scrutineers, in order to ascertain that the latter have performed their task correctly. Immediately after the checking has taken place, and before the cardinal electors leave the Sistine Chapel, all the ballots are to be burned by the scrutineers with the assistance of the secretary of the conclave and the masters of ceremonies, summoned in the meantime by the junior cardinal deacon, who in the past had to do all the burning for the duration of the entire conclave. If, however, a second vote is to take place immediately, the ballots from the first vote will be burned only at the end, together with those from the second vote.

The burning of the ballots is also the traditional means of informing the those outside the conclave of the results of the voting, or at least of whether the voting has resulted in an election. They are burned in a special stove set up in the Sistine Chapel—all the conclaves since 1922 have used the same one—whose chimney is visible from St. Peter's Square below. The traditional signals are a black *sfumata*, or smoke, for no election, and a white *sfumata* for a successful election. If there is no election, the ballots are mixed with wet straw to produce black smoke. If a pope is elected, the ballots are mixed with dry straw to produce white smoke—at which signal crowds of Romans and other faithful fill the piazza to await the announcement of the name of the new pope and to receive his blessing.

This primitive method of communication via smoke signals is not foolproof: Confusing signals have been sent in the past. During the conclave of 1958, the smoke repeatedly came up white on the first day, despite the efforts of the cardinal responsible to produce a black *sfumata*. The marshal of the conclave, Prince Sigismondo Chigi Albani della Rovere, then dispatched an assistant to a fireworks factory to purchase black smoke bombs, which the prince passed into the conclave through the *rota*. Subsequently, until John XXIII was elected, the cardinal responsible for burning the ballots ignited a smoke bomb and added it to the voting papers kindled in the stove. For the conclave of 1963, Prince Sigismondo provided black flares he obtained from the Italian military. The office of the prince-marshal of the conclave having been abolished by the reforms of Paul VI, no one thought to supply "help" to the smoke signals in 1978. Consequently, the election of John Paul I was initially announced by black smoke that only later turned white. It is rumored that the cardinals resorted to chemical smoke canisters for the election of John Paul II.

John Paul II's electoral provisions stipulate that all the cardinals must hand over, along with the ballots, any notes they have made during the voting. These are to be burned together with the ballots. The only record of the voting is to be the official report that the cardinal camerlengo is charged with drafting and undersigning with the three cardinal assistants. This document is given to the new pope, who will keep it sealed in a special archive, access to which will be exclusively by permission of the reigning pontiff.[17]

If the first ballot in either the morning or afternoon session—except for the initial ballot on the afternoon of the opening of the conclave—does not result in an election, the electors proceed immediately to a second ballot with all the formalities of the first, except that they need not draw lots for new sets of scrutineers, infirmarii, or revisers, nor are they required to swear the oath anew.

In an innovation, John Paul II decreed that if after three days of voting the cardinals fail to elect a pope, a maximum one-day halt is called to the proceedings for "prayer, informal discussion among the voters, and a brief spiritual exhortation given by the senior cardinal in the order of deacons" (UDG 74). The voting then resumes for seven more ballots. If the electors still cannot arrive at an election, another pause is called for more prayer, informal discussion, and another exhortation to be given by the senior cardinal priest. After another series of seven ballots, should the electors fail to arrive at a two-thirds majority for a candidate, another pause is called for still more prayer, informal discussion, and an exhortation by the senior cardinal bishop present. Voting then resumes for another seven ballots, unless an election occurs.

At this point—theoretically, approximately ten to twelve days into the conclave (the actual timing depends on how much time the cardinals decide each halt in the voting is to be allotted, the maximum being one day)—if an election has not occurred, John Paul's constitution has introduced a radical departure from previous legislation: "The Cardinal electors shall be invited by the Camerlengo to express an opinion about the manner of proceeding. The election will then proceed in accordance with what the absolute majority of the electors decides. Nevertheless, there can be no waiving of the requirement that a valid election takes place only by an absolute majority of the votes or else by voting only on the two names which in the ballot immediately preceding have received the greatest number of votes; also in this second case only an absolute majority is required" (UDG 75). Whereas the long-standing requirement of a "super-majority" of two-thirds of the electors has tended to force the election of popes who, whatever their personal strengths and weaknesses, enjoyed at least initially a broad consensus of support within the College of Cardinals, this new provision makes it at least theoretically possible that a persistent majority, even a bare majority of 50 percent plus one, could hold together and force through a candidate opposed by nearly half the electors. While it remains to be seen what the actual consequences of this provision will be, the question is an interesting one, especially (as will be seen in the subsequent chapter) in light of fairly recent conclave history. This question is all the more interesting as the cardinal electors are now relatively younger and healthier than their predecessors—Paul VI's exclusion of those over eighty years of age combining with the general improvement in healthcare for the elderly—and, thanks to John Paul II's construction of the Domus Sanctae Marthae, will be rather comfortably housed for the duration of the conclave.

After a candidate has received the necessary majority for election—whatever number that might happen to be—under canon law a valid election is declared to have taken place. The junior cardinal deacon then summons the secretary of the College of Cardinals and the master of papal liturgical celebrations to enter the Sistine Chapel. The dean of the College of Cardinals (or the senior cardinal bishop present who has been presiding during the conclave) then approaches the one elected[18] and, in the name of the electoral college, asks him to give his consent to the election using the traditional Latin formula: "*Acceptasne electionem de te canonice facta in Summum Pontificem?*" ("Do you accept your canonical election as supreme pontiff?"). As soon as the consent is given, the dean proceeds to ask, "*Quomodo vis vocari?*" ("By what name do you wish to be called?"). The master of papal liturgical celebrations, acting as notary, draws up a document attesting to the acceptance and the choice of name, with two masters of ceremonies, summoned at that moment, serving as legal witnesses for the juridical act.

While the custom of changing one's name to indicate a new calling has a rich tradition in biblical history—one recalls Abram and his wife Sarai becoming Abraham and Sarah with the vocation to become the ancestors of all believers in the one true God, and Jacob becoming Israel, the heir to the promises made to Abraham, to say nothing of Simon becoming Peter, the rock on which the Church was founded—it was adopted relatively late in papal history with regard to the man elected bishop of Rome. The first pope to change his name on his election was John II (533–535), whose given name was Mercury and who deemed it inappropriate that the Roman pontiff should bear the name of a pagan deity. With the election of Pietro Osporci (or "Buccaporca," depending on the chronicle)—who chose to reign as Sergius IV (1009–1012) in order to avoid both the name of the Prince of the Apostles and his own rather undignified second name, which meant "pig's mouth"—the practice of the new pope adopting a new name became *de rigueur*. Subsequently, only Hadrian VI (1522–1523) and Marcellus II (1555) retained their given names.

By tradition, the choice of a name is usually indicative of the tenor that the newly elected pontiff wishes to signal concerning his pontificate.[19] Pius X is thought to have indicated his sympathies with the anti-modernist sympathies of the controversial Pius IX, as opposed to the more open policies of his immediate predecessor, Leo XIII, and proceeded to validate that speculation with his vigorous condemnations of modernism. Benedict XV chose his name, one not used for two centuries, to recall the learned Benedict XIV, who had also preceded him in the archbishopric of Bologna. Pius XII explicitly attributed his choice of name to three predecessors: Pius IX, under whom he was born; Pius X, who brought him into the service of the Secretariat of State; and Pius XI, who groomed him for the succession. John XXIII chose his name as a break with long-standing precedents and further signaled a change of course in the choice of the number employed by the notorious antipope during the Great Schism. Paul VI chose his name for the Apostle of the Gentiles and became the first modern pope to travel outside Europe during his pontificate. John Paul I, the first pope to choose a double name, explained his choice in his desire to combine the progressive and traditional qualities of his two immediate predecessors, a continuity that his successor endorsed by taking the name of John Paul II. John Paul I expounded on his choice on the crowds that gathered under his windows for the recital of the *Angelus* prayer and the papal blessing on the morrow of his election:

Yesterday morning, I went in tranquility to the Sistine Chapel to vote. I never imagined what was about to take place. When things became dangerous for me, two of my colleagues whispered words of encouragement. One of them said, "Courage, if the Lord gives a burden, he also gives the strength to carry it." And the other said, "Do not be afraid, the whole world is praying for the new pope." Then when the moment came, I accepted. As for the choice of a name, when they asked me, I had to stop and think; and my thoughts went like this: Pope John deigned to consecrate me a bishop with his own hands here in the Basilica of Saint Peter. Then, though I was unworthy, I succeeded him in the see of Saint Mark—in that Venice that still is filled with the spirit of Pope John. The gondoliers remember him, the sisters, everybody. On the other side, Pope Paul not only made me a cardinal, but, some months before that, in the *piazza* of Saint Mark, he made me blush in front of twenty thousand people, because he took off his stole and placed it on my shoulders. I was never so red-faced. Also, in the fifteen years of his pontificate, this pope showed not only me but also the whole world how he loved the Church, how he served her, and how he suffered for this Church of Christ. So I took the name John Paul. Be sure of this: I do not have the wisdom of heart of Pope John. I do not have the preparation and culture of Pope Paul. But now I stand in their place. I will try to serve the Church, and hope that you will help me with your prayers.

At the moment of his acceptance, if the man elected is already a bishop, he "is immediately Bishop of the Church of Rome, true Pope and Head of the College of Bishops. He thus acquires and can exercise full and supreme power over the universal Church" (UDG 88). The cardinals then approach the new pope to pay him homage. The conclave is then officially over as the senior cardinal deacon, sometimes called the "proto-deacon of the Holy Roman Church," announces the election to the crowd assembled in St. Peter's Square to receive the new pope's first apostolic blessing.

Chapter Four

THE CONCLAVES
OF THE TWENTIETH CENTURY

THE DISTINGUISHED ITALIAN JOURNALIST Cesare De Agostini,[1] who has followed Vatican affairs for nearly four decades, once waxed lyrical concerning the institution of the electoral conclave: "Sequestered in house arrest under the dictatorship of God and yet free to think and act according to the most profane canons, the cardinals gathered in conclave exist at the very point of tension between time and eternity." There is a great deal of truth in De Agostini's poetic imagery. To the believer, the true protagonist of the papal election is not the assembled College of Cardinals but the Holy Spirit, who expresses his mysterious will through the very human dreams, ambitions, friendships, and rivalries of the electors. But even the most fervent believer must admit that eternal Providence can manifest its designs through some very temporal machinations. As the camerlengo of the two 1978 conclaves, the French cardinal Jean Villot, admitted to his confrères in his pre-conclave address: "It will be as men, granted responsible men, but nonetheless men, that we shall be required by the office entrusted to us to proceed. The result will not be a 'miracle,' but the fruit of action and the prayers of mortal men."

While the will of God is the province of the theologian and the priest, the political and ecclesiastical maneuvers are the proper object of the historian who tries to reconstruct the history of the papal conclaves from the handful of reliable published accounts, available archival material, and the oral tradition handed down behind the Vatican's walls by such participants who, years removed from the events, have chosen to recall some of the most dramatic moments of their careers in the papal service. Aside from their narrative value, the story of the eight conclaves of the twentieth century is a privileged optic through which to examine in snapshots, as it were, the issues and personalities that shaped the history of Roman Catholicism during that period.

The Emperor's Veto and the Saint Elected Pope (1903)

After the tumultuous reign—the longest one in documented history—of Blessed
Pope Pius IX (1846–1878), which saw the loss of the papacy's temporal dominion,
the Sacred College had chosen the almost sixty-eight-year-old camerlengo, Cardinal Gioacchino Vincenzo Pecci, already fragile in health, as a stopgap appointment who was expected to have neither a long nor even an active pontificate.
Leo XIII (1878–1903), however, was to surprise his electors by outliving all but
one of them[2] and ruling the Church for over twenty-five years, during which he
published some sixty encyclicals and created 157 cardinals, of whom ninety-four
preceded him in death. In fact, Pope Leo's remarkable longevity gave rise to
much humor. The last survivor (other than Leo himself) among Pio Nono's
"creations," Cardinal Luigi Oreglia di Santo Stefano, exclaimed more than once
that instead of a "Holy Father," he and his brethren had elected an "Eternal
Father." On one occasion, when an American bishop visiting Rome for the Holy
Year of 1900 told the pope that he regretted the thought that he would no longer
have the joy of seeing the pontiff again, Leo replied to the inopportune prelate:
"Oh? Is that so? Does Your Excellency suffer from some illness?"

All jest aside, during his long pontificate Leo had succeeded, within the narrow limits that traditional teaching allowed him, in bringing the Roman Church
in general and the denizens of Vatican Hill in particular to terms with the modern age, or at least opening up a dialogue between the Church and society. In
contrast to the failed intransigence of his predecessor, his flexible diplomacy
permitted him a few triumphs, including the withdrawal by Germany of the
harsh anti-Catholic legislation of Bismarck's *Kulturkampf* and the prestige of first
being invited to successfully mediate the dispute between Germany and Spain
over the Caroline Islands, and then succeeding. Under the influence of his fourth
secretary of state (Leo outlived two of his first three), the aristocratic Sicilian
cardinal Mariano Rampolla del Tindaro, he affirmed the legitimacy of any form
of government, including republicanism, as long as it provided for the common
good. Consequently, Leo outraged Catholic royalists by his support of the
Ralliement, which attempted to reconcile traditionalist French Catholics to the
Third Republic. With respect to the "Roman Question," while he abandoned
none of the reclamations of Pio Nono, Leo adopted a less acerbic tone toward
the Italian government. Whatever the concrete successes or failures of his many
initiatives, in the final balance, after the political and spiritual isolation of Pius
IX, Leo successfully raised the international prestige of the papacy and won for
the papal office a recognition, by both Catholics and non-Catholics, that it had
not enjoyed for some centuries.

Leo XIII died at four o'clock in the afternoon of July 20, 1903. Ironically appropriate for a pontiff who had outlived so many, even as Leo lay dying, Monsi-

gnor Alessandro Volpini, secretary of the Sacred Consistorial Congregation and, consequently, *ex ufficio* secretary of the upcoming conclave, expired in the papal antechamber while waiting to witness the pope's death. Thus the first order of business for the cardinals assembled after Leo's death was to elect Archbishop Rafael Merry del Val, president of the Pontifical Academy of Noble Ecclesiastics (the elite finishing school for papal diplomats), as secretary *pro tempore* of their electoral assembly.

The conclave began on the afternoon of Friday, July 31, 1903. Of the sixty-four cardinals, only two were absent. Thus, with sixty-two electors, forty-two votes were needed to achieve the two-thirds majority required to elect a new pope.

The first ballot was held the following morning. By coincidence, it fell by lot to Rampolla to serve as the scrutineer charged with reading aloud the votes.[3] The surprise in the ballot was not so much the strong support for the much-admired Rampolla as the lack of support for Cardinal Serafino Vannutelli, whose election his own brother, Cardinal Vincenzo Vannutelli, had campaigned hard to achieve. It was later revealed by two cardinals, Domenico Ferrata and Francesco di Paola Cassetta, that the electioneering by the Vannutelli brothers had the opposite effect on the electors, who, it seemed, recalled not only the old adage that "he who would enter the conclave a pope, comes out a cardinal" but also a new satirical Italian verse, of the genre called the *"pasquinata,"*[4] then making its rounds in Rome: *"Se va Vannutelli, avremo due papi"* ("If it goes for Vannutelli, we'll have two popes").

Since, according to the rules then in force, there were only two ballots a day, one in the morning and one in the afternoon, the cardinals adjourned after the inconclusive ballot, certain that Rampolla would be Leo's heir. The Sicilian cardinal had the support of the French and Spanish cardinals as well as that of many of his fellow Italians. After Rampolla's defeat, the French cardinal François-Désiré Mathieu, a longtime veteran of the Roman Curia, would, in violation of the secrecy of the conclave, publish an account of the proceedings in the journal *Revue de Deux-Mondes* in which he lamented: "What better could we have done than to give the great Leo as his successor the intimate confidant of his thoughts, the devoted collaborator of his great projects, the minister who served him with an intelligence and self-sacrifice to which all pay homage? Where would we have found a comparable experience united with the same holiness of life?"

The German-speaking bloc at the conclave was not so enthusiastic about Rampolla's candidacy, judging him too progressive in his politics (he was behind Leo's acceptance of republicanism as well as the pope's advocacy of social justice and defense of workers) and too close to France in his diplomacy (and, hence, hostile to the interests of the German and Austria-Hungarian empires). They had initially planned to support Serafino Vannutelli, the former nuncio in Vienna, but were persuaded by Cardinal Anton Hubert Fischer, archbishop of Cologne, that Vannutelli was unelectable. Hence they had thrown their support behind Gotti.

In the second ballot of the conclave, held that Saturday afternoon, both Rampolla and Cardinal Giuseppe Melchiorre Sarto,[5] patriarch of Venice, picked up votes that fell away from other Italian candidates, including Cardinal Girolamo Maria Gotti, prefect of the Sacred Congregation for the Propagation of the Faith, who had come in second on the first ballot but now lost votes. Thus the still-inconclusive total at the end of the first day was Rampolla 29, Gotti 16, and Sarto 10, with the rest of the votes divided among minor candidates. Serafino Vannutelli was left with only one vote, presumably that of his brother Francesco.

The German and Austrian cardinals as well as their allies grew concerned, since Rampolla now lacked only thirteen votes to secure election to the papacy. The vice-chancellor of the Holy Roman Church, Cardinal Antonio Agliardi, approached the German-speaking bloc through Cardinal Georg von Kopp, prince-bishop of Breslau (now Wroclaw). Agliardi admitted that Rampolla was a "mortal enemy" of Austria and "probably not a sincere friend of Germany's." However, he pointed out that Gotti was a religious with a reputation for not being particularly affable. He recommended that the German-speakers consider the candidacy of Sarto of Venice, a decision they decided to take the next day.

The next morning, Sunday, August 2, after the ballot papers were distributed and the cardinals were writing their votes, the prince-bishop of Cracow (then part of the Austro-Hungarian Empire), Jan Puzyna Kniaz (Prince) de Kosielsko, rose and asked Oreglia di Santo Stefano, in his capacity as camerlengo of the Roman Church, for the floor. Receiving leave to speak, he took out a sheet of paper and began in a halting voice his formal declaration: "I have the honor, having been given this charge by the highest authority, to humbly ask Your Eminence, as Dean of the Sacred College of the Most Eminent Cardinals and Camerlengo of the Holy Roman Church, to receive the formal communication and to deign to transmit to and to officially notify the Sacred College in the name and by the authority of His Apostolic Majesty, Franz Josef, Emperor of Austria and King of Hungary . . ." A deathly silence fell over the assembled cardinals as Puzyna continued: "His Majesty, intending to avail himself of an ancient right and privilege, pronounces the exclusionary veto against my Most Eminent Lord Cardinal Mariano Rampolla del Tindaro."

Even in the silence of the Sistine Chapel Puzyna's frail voice could not be heard by all. And, perhaps in their shock, even those who heard did not fully understand the import of his communication. The junior cardinal deacon, Felice Cavagnis, took the sheet of paper from Puzyna and, ascending the steps of the altar, read the Polish cardinal's pronouncement in a clear voice so that all could understand. When Cavagnis finished reading and the import of the communication sank into the cardinals, Oreglia, without rising from his throne, responded: "This communication cannot be received officially or unofficially. No cardinal is to give any consideration to this 'veto' and all are to continue to vote according to their conscience." Several cardinals applauded this declaration, while the Frenchman Mathieu yelled out, *"Bravo!"*

Rampolla, the late pope's secretary of state and the target of the emperor's veto, rose with quiet dignity and spoke. "It appears that a grave attack has been made on the liberty of the Church with regard to the election of the pontiff. It is an affront to the dignity of the Sacred College by a lay power and I protest strongly." However, he continued, "with regard to my humble person, I declare that nothing could be more honorable, nothing more agreeable could have happened." As even his critics admitted afterward, it was the moment of Rampolla's greatest grandeur.

In that tense environment, the cardinals proceeded with their voting. The results were Rampolla 29, Sarto 21, and Gotti 9, with three other cardinals receiving one vote each. Rampolla had gained no additional votes despite the outpouring of sympathy following the Austrian emperor's veto. The saintly Spanish Capuchin Cardinal José de Calasanz Félix Santiago Vives y Tutó rose and suggested that the conclave proceed to elect Rampolla by acclamation, but Oreglia refused to even discuss the possibility. Thus the morning session broke up with the cardinals pausing to take stock of what had occurred. Cardinal Andrea Carlo Ferrari of Milan wrote in his journal that it was a "disgusting episode."[6] Ferrata wrote in his that it left a "great, painful impression on all." The canonist and future cardinal Pietro Gasparri observed that it was "monstrous" that the first phrase of Puzyna's Latin declaration was *"Honoro mihi duco"* ("I have the honor") instead of at least the form-saving *"Doleo"* ("I regret").

It seems that Puzyna's announcement was well planned in advance. Subsequently opened diplomatic archives show that at eight o'clock on the evening of July 20, just hours after Leo XIII died, Count Agenor Goluchowski, the Austro-Hungarian foreign minister, had telegraphed Count Szécsen de Temerin, the imperial ambassador to the Holy See: "Top secret. Decipher personally. The member of the Sacred College against whom the exclusionary veto should eventually and in the extreme case be given is Cardinal Rampolla."

Why the opposition against Rampolla? On the surface, the explanation was found in the political interests of Austria-Hungary and its German ally, interests that went against the progressive, pro-French policies of Leo's secretary of state. However, less evident—but no less real—was the concern of the Italian government, then part of the Triple Alliance with Germany and Austria-Hungary, over the Sicilian cardinal's ill-concealed hostility to the Piedmontese-dominated Italian national government, which had overthrown his native Kingdom of the Two

Sicilies in the south as well as usurping the Holy See's temporal dominions in the center of the peninsula.[7] Thus the Italian ambassador in Vienna, Costantino Nigra, had indicated to the Austrian court the discomfiture of the Italian government, which did not enjoy a veto, over Rampolla's candidacy. Consequently, the imperial veto not only served the direct political interests of the Austro-Hungarian monarchy but also accommodated the domestic interests of an allied power, Italy.

In the afternoon session, those who favored Rampolla tried to rally support for his candidacy, hoping that a delayed sympathy would carry their candidate across the threshold of forty-two votes needed for election. To that end, the French cardinal Adolphe Perraud, bishop of Autun, rose to address the conclave before the start of the fourth ballot. Given permission to speak in protest against the veto, Perraud turned his discourse into an exhortation to vote for Rampolla, who was embarrassed by the ill-conceived electioneering. In any event, Rampolla picked up only one vote, receiving a total of 30, his highest total during the conclave. Sarto, on the other hand, received 24 votes, picking up three. Gotti fell to 3 votes, while three other cardinals divided five votes among them.

The tensions mounted as the cardinals adjourned for the day, Rampolla's supporters lashing out against his opponents. At one point Mathieu publicly accused the Hungarian primate, Cardinal Kolos Ferenc Vaszary, of using the special meals brought into the conclave for him because of dietary reasons as a means of secretly communicating with agents of the imperial government on the outside. The secretary of the conclave, Archbishop Merry del Val, had to make a formal denial after inspecting the Hungarian's victuals. Sarto, meanwhile, grew nervous at the prospect of being elected and retired to his cell, where his conscience racked him.

The following morning, it was evident that a tide had turned, as an entire series of cardinals called on the patriarch of Venice to check on him. The prospect before him evidently frightened him. He told Ferrari that once they had elected a pope, he would ask the new pontiff's permission to resign both his red hat and his see and enter a monastery. His fellow cardinals thought otherwise: On the fifth ballot that Monday morning, Sarto received 27 votes, passing Rampolla, who fell to 24 votes, and Gotti, who received 6 votes, while four other cardinals received one vote each. A final vote, that of Cardinal Serafino Cretoni, prefect of the Sacred Congregation of Rites, was null: The unfortunately named prelate ("Cretoni" means "big idiot," hence some would argue "appropriately named") wrote "neminem eligo" ("I vote for no one") on his ballot papers on this and the following ballots.[8]

Sarto then rose to address a plea to the electors: "Conscience imposed upon me the obligation of telling you that I do not have the qualities required to accept the papacy. You are obliged to look to others with your thoughts and votes. I am not worthy. I am not capable. Forget about me!" The German Kopp noted that "all were struck by his fear and humility, but no one took his refusal into consideration." The American cardinal James Gibbons of Baltimore was more cynical: "It was these protests, full of humility and wisdom, that gained for him the favor of the conclave. His words caused him to be more esteemed than he would have been on the merits of his works or the basis of the testimony of those who knew him."

The dean, Oreglia, used the break at noon to send the secretary of the conclave, Merry del Val, to Sarto with orders to obtain either a formal refusal to be elected or the acceptance of the eventual will of the electors. The young archbishop found the cardinal kneeling on the marble floor, crying before the image of Our Lady of Good Counsel in the Pauline Chapel. Struck by the scene being played before him, Merry del Val forgot his mission and simply grabbed Sarto: "Eminence, take courage! The Lord will help."

The afternoon ballot brought Sarto 35 votes, Rampolla 16, and Gotti 7, while three votes were cast for two other cardinals and Cretoni continued to vote for no one. The following morning, August 4, the already foregone conclusion came to pass. On the seventh and final ballot, Sarto received 50 votes, Rampolla 10, and Gotti 2. Giuseppe Melchiorre Sarto, son of a village postman and a seamstress from Riese, was elected the supreme pontiff, assuming the style of "Pius X."

The "Stone Rejected" (1914)

As Pius X lay dying, the winds of war were sweeping across Europe. On August 1, 1914, Germany opened hostilities against Russia. On August 13, Great Britain declared war on Austria-Hungary. On the day of the pope's death, August 20, the German front, stretched out between Lorraine and Luxembourg, began to advance.

The task of organizing an electoral conclave in the midst of a war fell on the shoulders of the camerlengo (who was also the proto-deacon) of the Holy Roman Church, Cardinal Francesco Salesio Della Volpe.

Cardinals from warring nations would have to sit down pacifically with each other—humanly speaking, a difficult task, even for men of God. After the conclave, Cardinal Alessandro Lualdi, whose room was between that of the German cardinal Felix von Hartmann of Cologne and the Belgian cardinal Desiré Mercier of Mechlin (Malines), recounted a dialogue that took place between the "invader" and the "invaded" that highlighted some of the tensions. As they were moving into their quarters, Hartmann suggested politely: "Let's not talk about war." Mercier's reply was lapidary: "Let's not talk about peace."

Even getting the cardinals to the conclave was a difficult task due to the inter-ruptions in travel. Cardinal Friedrich Gustav Piffl, the archbishop of Vienna whose posthumously published diaries are the best record of the conclaves of 1914 and 1922,[9] noted that his first problem on learning of Pope Pius's death was arranging for a special train to take the six Austro-Hungarian cardinals (Piffl himself, Károly von Hornig, Kolos Ferenc Vaszary, János Csernoch, Franziskus von Sales Bauer, and Lev de Skrbensky z Hriste) at least to the border with Italy. In the end, of the sixty-five members of the Sacred College, fifty-seven made it into the conclave that opened on August 31, 1914. Faced as they were by the outbreak of war and divided among themselves along national lines, the cardinals—or at least a good number among them—were united in their agreement that the most pressing issue for the conclave was nonetheless one internal to the life of the Church: the doctrinal and disciplinary crisis of "modernism," which had been brought to a head during Pius X's pontificate by the anti-modernist campaign launched by the secretary of state, Cardinal Merry del Val, with the late pontiff's blessing.

The conflict had its origins in the pontificate of Leo XIII when the cautious opening of the Church to the world encouraged many Catholic intellectuals to employ in their studies the resources of new, more critical, approaches that had become popular during the nineteenth century. A crisis arose when various theo-logians, biblical scholars, historians, and social philosophers, influenced by their new academic insights, began to reconsider their understanding of some ele-ments of traditional Catholic teaching. In biblical studies, for example, the French priest Alfred Loisy, who after his dismissal from the Institut Catholique de Paris taught at the elite state institutions of the Ecole des Hautes Etudes and the Collège de France, questioned the historical veracity of certain Old Testament narra-tives such as the six-day creation story and the account of the Flood as well as the authorship of the Gospels. In theology, scholars like the former Anglo-Irish Jesuit George Tyrrell argued that Church teachings were better understood as dynamic, being conditioned by times and circumstances, rather than static. While never part of an organized movement, these "modernists" shared an openness to innovation and a belief that the established structures of the Church could and perhaps should be changed to better adapt to the times. These views found little sympathy in Rome, especially with Pius X, himself the product of a provin-cial seminary and distrustful of intellectuals. The pope saw the movement as a threat, not only to the authority of the papacy but to the faith and morals of the Church. A decree of the Supreme Sacred Congregation of the Holy Office, *Lamentabili sane exitu*, published on July 3, 1907, condemned some sixty-five am-biguous propositions said to be those of modernism, which Pius X branded as "the synthesis of all heresies" in his encyclical *Pascendi Dominici gregis* (Septem-ber 8, 1907). Pius imposed on the clergy an oath explicitly disavowing the tenets of modernism with the decree *Sacrorum antistitum* (September 1, 1910). The writings of modernist authors were placed on the Index of Prohibited Books, while prominent scholars who refused to be silenced, like Loisy and Tyrrell, were excommunicated.

Not content with condemning the movement and excommunicating its principal exponents, Pius and his secretary of state moved to root out any tainted with modernism. An unscrupulous and rather mediocre Italian prelate, Monsignor Umberto Benigni, was appointed undersecretary for extraordinary affairs in the Secretariat of State in 1906, a post he occupied until 1911. Benigni proceeded, with the tacit approval of Pius and Merry del Val, to establish a network of secret informers, the Sodalitium Pianum, to report suspected modernists and their alleged sympathizers to Rome. Rank had been no protection against being suspect during the campaign against modernism; both Cardinal Ferrari of Milan and Cardinal Pietro Maffi of Pisa spent long periods under investigation, the former for his defense of those he believed unjustly accused, the latter for being a scientist. Consequently many, even those who were themselves, in their personal sensibilities, anti-modernists, were convinced that the conclave presented them with an opportunity to rein in the excesses of the anti-modernist campaign and to restore some sort of balance in the life of the Church.

With fifty-seven electors present, the two-thirds majority required for election meant that thirty-eight votes were needed to choose a pope. The first ballot, taken on the morning of September 1, resulted in 12 votes each for Cardinals Maffi and Giacomo della Chiesa,[10] 9 for Cardinal Basilio Pompilj, 7 for Cardinal Merry del Val, and the rest divided among ten other cardinals. The votes sent a clear message as to the sentiments of the Sacred College. Only a small minority—witness the seven votes for Merry del Val—wanted to continue the strict course charted by the deceased pope and his chief collaborator. The contest was between Maffi, a victim of the persecution and a clear modernizer, and the subtler della Chiesa, who likewise represented change, albeit at the more moderate pace of Leo XIII and Rampolla. A Genoese aristocrat, Giacomo della Chiesa was a career diplomat, although, with the exception of the years he spent in Spain as then-Nuncio Rampolla's deputy (1883–1887), his entire service was spent in Rome. Rising through the ranks as Rampolla's protégé, he became substitute of the Secretariat of State in 1901. After Rampolla was put aside, della Chiesa still remained loyal to him, a fidelity that cost him his position in the Apostolic Palace. Exiled from the Vatican as archbishop of Bologna in 1907, he was denied the red hat that was the traditional prerogative of the incumbent of that see until just three months before the conclave. While, like Maffi's, his candidacy was seen as an implicit rebuke of the just-concluded pontificate, his diplomat background made him, in the eyes of many electors, according to Piffl's notes, a more moderate alternative. And, of course, diplomacy was also needed in a world gone to war.

Under the revised norms of Pius X, the college then proceeded immediately to a second morning ballot, which resulted in Maffi and della Chiesa obtaining 16 votes each and Pompilj 10 votes, while Merry del Val remained at 7 votes. In the afternoon, the third ballot of the conclave resulted in della Chiesa pulling ahead with 18 votes. The fourth ballot, which followed immediately, resulted in della Chiesa 21, Maffi 15, Pompilj 9, and Merry del Val 6.

That evening, Merry del Val and his supporters, realizing the hopelessness of their position, decided to switch their votes to one of the minor candidates, the Benedictine Cardinal Domenico Serafini, arguing that the election of della Chiesa would be interpreted as an affront to the memory of Pius X. The hope was that in presenting an apparently alternative candidate, they could prevent a general defection from the direction set. The tactic worked, to a certain point, on the following day, September 2. In the four ballots, Serafini, who had finished the previous day with 2 votes, went from 10 votes to 17 votes to 21 votes to 24 votes. Even as the votes for Serafini rose, it became apparent that those votes were drawn from Maffi's supporters rather than della Chiesa's: Maffi went from 13 votes to 7 votes to 2 votes to no votes, while della Chiesa went from 20 votes to 27 votes to 31 votes to 32 votes, finishing the day just six votes shy of election.

On the third day of the conclave, September 3, della Chiesa received 34 votes on the first ballot of the day. On the second ballot of the day, della Chiesa received 38 votes—the bare minimum required for election—while Serafini received 18 votes and Richelmy 1 vote. The opponents, however, were not finished. They attempted one final maneuver: As was their right, they demanded that the thirty-eight votes for della Chiesa be examined to determined if he had voted for himself—the rules at that time declaring the entire vote invalid if a man should vote for himself. So the newly elected pope was forced to wait while the scrutineers examined all the ballots and determined that his vote was not among the thirty-eight cast for him. Thus Giacomo della Chiesa, the "stone rejected" by Pius X and Merry del Val, became Benedict XV, the "great pope of the world tragedy," as the statue erected in Istanbul by Atatürk in gratitude for the pontiff's humanitarian endeavors declares.

An Electoral Compromise (1922)

Benedict XV died unexpectedly on January 22, 1922, at the early age of only sixty-seven, of influenza that developed into pneumonia. His reign had been overshadowed by the Great War. While maintaining a strict neutrality that annoyed both sides in the conflict, as each wanted him to condemn the other, the pope protested against the inhumanities of modern warfare and concentrated on alleviating suffering. On August 1, 1917, Benedict dispatched to the Allies and the Central Powers a peace proposal based on justice rather than military victory. While the initiative met with a cool reception, many of its points presaged the later "Fourteen Points" of President Woodrow Wilson of the United States of America. Unfortunately, the Holy See was not allowed to participate in the postwar peace conference, the Allies having agreed in the secret Treaty of London of 1915 to exclude the Vatican as part of the price for Italy's entrance into the war. Thus, at Benedict's death, the memory of this diplomatic isolation made the settlement of the "Roman Question" between the Holy See and Italy a priority for many of the cardinals who assembled for the conclave.[11]

Within the Church, Benedict had, with his first encyclical, *Ad beatissimi Apostolorum*, in 1914, called a halt to the bitter feud between the diehard integralists and more progressive elements, a legacy of Pius X's anti-modernist campaign. Benedict had also been a "pope of the missions"; his apostolic letter *Maximum illud* (1919) urged missionary bishops to move forward with the formation of a native clergy and reminded them to promote the welfare of the people among whom they worked rather than the imperialist interests of their own country of origin. Thus the other great concern on the minds of the cardinals was the increasing internationalization and, in fact, the very identity of the Church.

Because of the tactful discretion of the camerlengo, Cardinal Pietro Gasparri, editor of the newly promulgated Code of Canon Law and secretary of state of the late Pope Benedict, few of the cardinals gathered were aware of another concern, one with direct implications for both of the major issues that preoccupied them: the dismal financial position of the Holy See. With the loss of the Papal States, the Roman Curia had been cut off from the revenues it had derived from taxes as well as properties for over a generation. The recent world war and Benedict's relief initiatives both during and after the conflict had left the Holy See virtually bankrupt. Gasparri had to telegraph the apostolic delegate in the United States, Archbishop Giovanni Bonzano, to send any surplus funds that the delegation had on hand. When these did not suffice, Gasparri was forced to take out a loan to pay for the conclave, which became legendary for its frugality: One sole bottle of cognac was purchased and entrusted to the pharmacist; the cardinals were able to imbibe only if prescribed by a physician.

Of the fifty-nine cardinals, fifty-three entered into the conclave on the afternoon of February 2, 1922, the other six being impeded by illness, distance,[12] or, in the strange case of Lev de Skrbensky z Hriste, disappearance.[13] Thus thirty-six votes would be required to achieve the two-thirds majority necessary for election.

Given the issues that they faced, the electors had several options. The prefect of the Sacred Congregation for the Propagation of the Faith, charged with overseeing the missions, the Dutch cardinal Willem Marinus van Rossum, thought that the time had come for a non-Italian pope and went about gathering support for Rafael Merry del Val as the only non-Italian candidate who had enough Italian backing to present a realistic candidacy. Van Rossum's hope, as he confided in Piffl of Vienna who wrote everything down in his famous diaries, was that Merry del Val would garner votes both from those who saw in him a *straniero* ("foreigner," as opposed to Italian) and from those who wanted another chance at continuing the policies, apparently rejected at the previous conclave, of Pius X. Another possibility, this one signaling a continuation of the line traced out by the just-deceased Pope Benedict, was Gasparri. The youngest of the nine children of a shepherd from the Umbrian Apennines, he was a veritable font of historical and canonical knowledge combined with diplomatic experience, even if hidden behind a gruff exterior. Maffi of Pisa was both favored and rejected at the previous conclave for the same reason: his reputation for modernizing tendencies, born perhaps of his scientific interests as well as his priestly heart. In the conclave of 1922, he enjoyed the additional attribute of his well-known good relations with the House of Savoy (in 1930, it would be Maffi who was asked to preside at the marriage of the future last king of Italy, Umberto of Savoy, with Maria José of Belgium). The final cardinal seen as a possible contender was Pietro La Fontaine, patriarch of Venice, who during the anti-modernist campaign was sent about as "apostolic visitor" (as one pundit put it, the "modern euphemism for what they used to call the traveling inquisitor") to the seminaries of the western coast of Italy. As one chronicler noted, La Fontaine had the prudence to "interpret the severe directives and exigencies of orthodoxy with a sense of balanced moderation not detached from his rich humanity."

On the first ballot on the morning of Friday, February 3, the results were predictable given the field of possible candidates: Merry del Val 12, Maffi 10, Gasparri 8, La Fontaine 4, Van Rossum 4, with thirteen votes divided among five other cardinals. The only surprise was the emergence of an unexpected name: Cardinal Achille Ratti,[14] who received five votes. So new was Ratti among the cardinals that many did not know him and asked about to learn of his incredible rise in the past few years after a lifetime of obscurity amid the books of the Ambrosian and Vatican libraries. But, as events would shortly show, it was that academic life—especially one in a field like Ratti's specialty of paleography that was apparently "apolitical"—shielded from the bitter feuds of the anti-modernist controversy that rendered Ratti attractive to electors. And his mission in Poland in the aftermath of the world war and his brief episcopal ministry in his native Milan gave him both a diplomatic and pastoral finish.

The second ballot that same morning resulted in a similar pattern. However, the third and fourth ballots, taken that afternoon, revealed a clear pattern. The fourth ballot's results were: Merry del Val 14, Gasparri 11, Maffi 10, and Ratti 5.

Thus the old traditionalist faction had rallied around Merry del Val, while Gasparri seemed to be the focus of those seeking a continuation of the policies of Benedict XV.

The following day, Saturday, February 3, brought the total collapse of Merry del Val's candidacy. The four ballots of the day saw Pius X's secretary of state go from 13 votes to 7 votes to 1 vote to no votes, as his supporters transferred their votes to the "humane inquisitor" La Fontaine, whose tallies went from 7 votes to 13 votes to 22 votes to finish at 21 votes. Maffi's candidacy disappeared altogether after receiving a solitary vote in the first ballot of the morning session.

On Sunday, February 4, the morning ballots revealed that the two front-runners were at an impasse and some momentum had switched to the previously unknown Ratti. Consequently, the results of the eleventh ballot of the conclave were Ratti 24, La Fontaine 23, and six votes for two other cardinals. The twelfth ballot consolidated the contest: Ratti 27, La Fontaine 22, and four votes between the two others.

Piffl was not the only one to wonder whether Ratti and Gasparri had arrived at an understanding. Realizing that their attempt to promote La Fontaine as a substitute for Merry del Val had failed, the traditionalists made one last-ditch attempt to at least exclude Gasparri from the reins of power. One of Merry del Val's closest allies, Cardinal Gaetano De Lai, sub-dean of the Sacred College, approached Ratti that evening with an offer: "We will vote for Your Eminence if Your Eminence would promise that you will not choose Cardinal Gasparri as your secretary of state."

Ratti's response was measured but firm, indicative of his future tenor: "I hope and pray that the Holy Spirit will choose from the many worthier cardinals another Head of the Holy Church, Vicar of Our Lord. But I tell Your Eminence frankly that, if I am chosen, it will be precisely the Most Eminent Cardinal Gasparri whom I will take as my secretary of state."

"Your Eminence would commit a grave error," de Lai insisted.

"I regret that it probably it will not be the only mistake that I will make on the Throne of St. Peter, but it certainly will be the first."

This conversation was recorded in his unpublished memoirs by Gasparri, who cited both Ratti, by then Pius XI, and Monsignor Luigi Sincero, secretary of the conclave, as witnesses.[15] Gasparri the canonist did not hesitate to add that by the act of trying to strike a pact with Ratti the two cardinals (Gasparri doubted that De Lai would have acted without Merry del Val's knowledge) incurred the sentence of excommunication *latae sententiae* (that is, "automatic") stipulated in Pius X's constitution *Vacante Sede Apostolica* of 1904.

In any event, on the final ballot (the fourteenth of the conclave), Ratti received 42 votes, six more than required for election, while La Fontaine received 9 votes, Laurenti 2, and De Lai 1.

When the dean of the Sacred College, Cardinal Vincenzo Vannutelli, approached him to ask his assent to the election, Ratti paused in silence—"two very long minutes," according to Mercier—before giving his acceptance. The Hungarian primate Csernoch was to later comment, "We made Cardinal Ratti pass through the fourteen stations of the *Via Crucis* and then we left him alone on Calvary." Given the era in which Pius XI was to reign—with the rise of totalitarian states and, toward the end of his pontificate, the gathering clouds of the Second World War—more prophetic words could not have been uttered.

The Inevitable Choice (1939)

The cardinals, after a deadlock caused by the Sacred College's split between a reinvigorated traditionalist contingent that wanted a return to the strict antimodernist line of Pius X and a moderate group seeking continuity with the cautiously open policies of Benedict V, had chosen Cardinal Achille Ratti as a compromise. In so doing, their hope was that within the framework of the Church's traditions, they might have a pope whose rule would be sensitive to the pressing issues of a settlement with the Italian government in the external forum and of the strengthening within of a Church whose reach was now wider than ever. The newly elected Pius XI did not disappoint them on either count.

Immediately after giving his assent to the election and choosing the name Pius—because, he explained, he was baptized under one Pius and called to Rome under another—he unexpectedly addressed the cardinals: "I would like to add a word: I declare before the members of the Sacred College that I have it in my heart to protect and defend all the rights of the Church and all of the prerogatives of the Holy See. But having said that, I want my first blessing to go, as a token of the peace that all humanity aspires to, not only to Rome and to Italy, but also to all the Church and to the entire world. I will impart it from the external balcony of St. Peter's." With that gesture, Pius signaled the effective cessation of the cold war that had existed between the Vatican and Quirinal since the regiments of unified Italy had occupied the city of the popes. The Italian regime was not slow to respond. Long-stalled negotiations were reopened, the final rounds being conducted personally between the pope's newly reconfirmed secretary of state, Cardinal Pietro Gasparri, and the king of Italy's new prime minister, Benito Mussolini. On February 11, 1929, in the Lateran Palace, the ancient residence of the bishops of Rome, the two ministers, acting as plenipotentiaries for their respective sovereigns, signed the Lateran Treaty whereby the Holy See recognized Italy as a kingdom with Rome as its capital, while Italy indemnified the Holy See for the loss of the Papal States. The treaty also created the Vatican

City State as a neutral, independent state, united to the Holy See, with the purpose of giving a minimal territorial independence to the Roman pontiff to insure his religious and spiritual mission. At the same time, the two initialed a concordat that made Catholicism the official religion of the Italian state.

With the pope becoming very much interested in overseas missions, Pius's reign saw the number of missionaries double. Following in the footsteps of Benedict XV, Pius pressed on with the development of an indigenous Catholicism in the mission territories. In 1926, against not insignificant opposition, he personally ordained the first six native Chinese bishops, who were soon joined by the first native Japanese and Vietnamese bishops. During the same period, the number of native priests rose from approximately three thousand to more than seven thousand. Within the Church, especially in Europe, Pius continued Benedict's policy of easing the tensions arising from the debate over modernism. The first scholar-pope since Benedict XIV (1740–1758), Pius naturally sympathized were with some of the leading intellectuals who had been demoted or pushed aside during the height of the anti-modernist campaign carried out by Pius X and Merry del Val.

However, as his pontificate drew to a close, the pope found himself increasingly preoccupied with the rise of totalitarianism. His repeated attempts to negotiate with the Soviet Union failed to temper the Communist regime's fierce anti-Christian persecutions, so, in 1937, Pius issued his encyclical *Divini Redemptoris*, in which he sharply condemned "Bolshevistic and atheistic Communism, which aims at upsetting the social order and at undermining the very foundations of Christian civilization" and warned—prophetically, in the light of post–World War II events that he did not live to witness—that "those who permit themselves to be deceived into lending their aid towards the triumph of Communism in their own country will be the first to fall victims of their error." In 1933, hoping to salvage what he could from a deteriorating situation, Pius negotiated a concordat with Adolf Hitler's new National Socialist government in Germany. However, he was quickly disillusioned and, between the signing of the concordat and 1936, because of the Nazi regime's increasing repression of the Church, he addressed to it no fewer than thirty-four notes of protest. Finally, in 1937, he published the encyclical *Mit brennender Sorge*, which he had smuggled into the Third Reich and read from the pulpits of all Catholic churches. In the document, Pius took direct aim at the regime's ideology, noting that "whoever exalts race, or the people, or the State, or a particular form of State, or the depositories of power, or any other fundamental value of the human community—however necessary and honorable be their function in worldly things—whoever raises these notions above their standard value and divinizes them to an idolatrous level, distorts and perverts an order of the world planned and created by God; he is far

from the true faith in God and from the concept of life which that faith upholds."
Even as he lay dying on February 10, 1939, Pius XI was planning a discourse—never
delivered because of his death—for the following day when he planned to use
the tenth anniversary of the Lateran Pacts to renew in stronger terms the denunciation of Mussolini's Fascists that he had issued in the encyclical *Non abbiamo
bisogno* (1931) and to further denounce their Nazi allies.

Following Pius XI's death and thanks to provisions he had made for a longer
interval to permit those far off to travel to Rome, for the first time in the twentieth century all the members of the College of Cardinals were present for and
participated in the conclave that opened on Wednesday, March 1, 1939. The sixty-
two cardinals who processed into the Sistine Chapel that afternoon had one pre-
occupation in mind: the Second World War that was threatening to break out at
any moment. They also knew that only one among them seemed to possess the
diplomatic knowledge and experience that would be needed to face the challenges that the war would bring: the camerlengo of the Holy Roman Church,
Cardinal Eugenio Pacelli,[16] who had served as secretary of state to the late Pope
Pius XI after the retirement of the great Pietro Gasparri.

Especially in his later years, Pope Pius XI had made no secret of his desire that
his secretary of state should follow him on the Throne of St. Peter. Unlike his
predecessors, Pius XI sent his secretary of state abroad repeatedly: as papal legate
a latere[17] to the International Eucharistic Congress in Buenos Aires (1934), the
jubilee celebrations at Lourdes (1935), the consecration of the Basilica of St.
Thérèse at Lisieux (1937), and the International Eucharistic Congress in Budapest
(1938). Pacelli was also dispatched on an extended trip to the United States, during which he met with President Franklin Delano Roosevelt and cemented his
relations with the then-Bishop Francis Spellman, who played host. Pius did not
hide the reason for these travels, explaining to a group of cardinals, "I send him
about so that the world can get to know him and he can get to know the world."
Toward the end, Pius was even more explicit. While posing for a photograph
with the five cardinals he created in his last consistory on December 13, 1937, Pius
pointed to Pacelli and told them, "*Sarà un bel papa!*" ("He'll make a good pope!").

Despite his experience and the evident favor of the late pontiff, Pacelli's candidacy did face some hurdles. He had been the secretary of state of the deceased
pope, and no secretary of state had been elected since 1667, when Alexander
VII's secretary of state, Giulio Rospigliosi, was elected Clement IX. He was
camerlengo of the Holy Roman Church, and, with the exception of Gioacchino
Vincenzo Pecci, elected Leo XIII in 1878, no camerlengo, after being "prince regent" of the Church during the *sede vacante,* had ever been called to fill the see.
Both of these hurdles, while apparently minor, were significant institutional
checks that served to preserve an already conservative institution from total os-

sification. By definition, the secretary of state and the camerlengo are among a deceased pope's closest confidants. Hence their election to the papacy would be an almost certain continuation of the previous reign's policies. In both cases in which one of these officials had succeeded, it was because they were thought to be so old or frail that they would serve as transitional figures. Pacelli, in contrast, was just shy of his sixty-third birthday. Furthermore, he was a native Roman, and no Roman had been elected since Emilio Altieri was elected Clement X in 1670.

In any event, while these considerations may have weighed in under ordinary circumstances, the circumstances surrounding the conclave of 1939 were anything but ordinary. The thirty-five Italians and twenty-seven non-Italians who gathered under Michelangelo's *Last Judgment* had two preoccupations in the forefront of their minds: to prevent the Church from returning to the catacombs in the wake of the totalitarian ascendancy and, in the measure possible, to avert the impending war.

Of course, precisely because of that apparently inevitable world war, the great powers were not indifferent to the outcome of the conclave. While he was always careful to protect the neutrality of both the papacy and the newly founded Vatican City State, Pius XI, with his ideals of peace and justice and his denunciations of racism, had clearly sympathized with the democracies against the dictatorships. Consequently, on the very day of the pope's death, the French foreign minister, Georges Bonnet, suggested to the British ambassador in Paris, Sir Eric Phipps, that the two countries should cooperate to secure the election of a pope who would continue the deceased pontiff's policies. In contrast, the Italian government and its German ally desired the very opposite: if they could not realistically expect a pro-Fascist pontiff, at the very least they hoped for a neutral, non-political, perhaps an otherworldly man who would not condescend to muddle in the mess of international politics.

The British minister to the Holy See, Sir d'Arcy Osborne, later the last duke of Leeds, and his French colleague, François Charles-Roux, settled on the late pope's secretary of state, Cardinal Eugenio Pacelli, as their candidate. Charles-Roux, thought by many to be the most influential ambassador accredited to the Vatican, saw the six French cardinals one by one as they came to Rome, as well as Canadian cardinal Jean-Marie-Roderigue Villeneuve of Québec and the Syrian patriarch Ignace-Gabriel I Tappouni, both of whom counted as French on account of their education and culture, and the Spanish Cardinal Francisco de Asís Vidal i Barraquer, archbishop of Tarragona, who, exiled from Spain by Generalissimo Francisco Franco for his Catalonian nationalism and his refusal to sign the pro-Nationalist joint letter of the Spanish episcopate during the civil war, was a refugee in France. Osborne called upon the only British cardinal, Arthur Hinsley of Westminster. All of these cardinals—with the exceptions of the French curialist Eugène Tisserant, who thought Pacelli was indecisive and favored Cardinal Luigi Maglione, the former nuncio in Paris, and Hinsley, who was embarrassed that his government was approaching him in the matter—were reportedly amenable to the suggestions of the two ambassadors.

The Italian ambassador to the Holy See, Bonifacio Pignatti, likewise consulted with his German colleague, Diego von Bergen, doyen of the diplomatic corps accredited to the papal court and a Prussian aristocrat of the old school. Bergen's sympathies for the Nazi regime were lukewarm at best, but he remained nonetheless a German patriot. Ironically, he arrived at the same conclusion as his British and French counterparts, albeit for entirely different motives, and looked favorably on the candidacy of the secretary of state, reasoning that Pacelli, who had served as nuncio in Germany for twelve years, and who spoke perfect German and surrounded himself with German aides and housekeepers, would at least be sympathetic to German—if not necessarily Nazi—interests. While the Third Reich's rather unpleasant recent dealings with the Church in Germany and Austria made it difficult for its ambassador to lobby the four German cardinals (including Theodor Innitzer of Vienna), Bergen was convinced that the prelates would nonetheless favor Pacelli, who, as nuncio, had procured the promotion of the three Germans to their archiepiscopal sees.

When the cardinals gathered the morning following their enclosure, Thursday, March 2, the votes quickly went to Pacelli.[18] By the second ballot, he had 41 votes, one short of election.

As the cardinals broke for lunch, there was no doubt as to the results that their afternoon voting would bring—if there were ever any doubt about the results of the conclave. The story is told that Dalla Costa was so certain that the Sacred College would finish its work within a day that he complained aloud about the inconvenience of having to move inside the Vatican for the one night that the cardinals would be sequestered and, when leaving his lodgings at the Collegio Pio Latino to make his way to the conclave, gave orders that his room be heated and ready for his return the following evening. Even the lay officers of the conclave, who were not privy to the voting, entertained no doubts. When the hereditary marshal of the Holy Roman Church and *ex ufficio* governor of the Conclave, Prince Ludovico Chigi Albano della Rovere,[19] returned to the precincts of the Apostolic Palace to supervise the entrance of the masters of ceremonies into the conclave enclosure, it was noted that he had changed his velvet robes, appropriate for the period of the *sede vacante*, for formal attire appropriate to calling on a new pope.

As the cardinals filed back toward the Sistine Chapel, Pacelli turned to speak with Boston's Cardinal William O'Connell and, missing a step, tripped and fell down. Observing the scene, Paris's Cardinal Jean Verdier, a noted wit, exclaimed,

"*Vicarius Christi in terra!*"—a Latin pun that could mean either "the Vicar of Christ on Earth," one of the papal titles, or "the Vicar of Christ on the ground," a reference to Pacelli's prone state. The French prelate's prophetic pun was soon confirmed by his confrères: On the first ballot of the afternoon (the third of the conclave), taken shortly after four o'clock, Pacelli received 48 votes, six more than needed for election.[20]

The aristocratic dean of the Sacred College approached to ask Pacelli if he would accept the office that he seemed preordained for. The day of his election was, by coincidence or providence, his sixty-third birthday. Accepting, the new pontiff added, "*Domine Iesu, miserere me!*" ("Lord Jesus, have mercy on me!"). The conclave had taken only one day, a feat not seen since the conclave of 1534 elected Cardinal Alessandro Farnese as Paul III. While the conclusion of the electoral assembly seemed easy, the coming years would not be as facile. As Verdier predicted in an interview before entering the conclave, the times were such that "the new pope will have to be either a hero or a saint." And perhaps both.

The Surprise Choice (1958)

The fifty-one cardinals who entered the conclave on the afternoon of Saturday, October 25, 1958, were very conscious of a sense of absence, and not only that of Pope Pius XII, who had died on October 9. The hand of providence seemed to lean heavy on the college, as one by one its numbers had been whittled down; death seemed disposed to carry off cardinals up to the moment the conclave doors were shut. In fact, just one hour before the opening of the conclave, Cardinal Edward Mooney of Detroit, one of the first Americans to play a significant role in papal diplomacy, was found dead in his guest room at the Pontifical North American College on the Janiculum Hill. Eight days earlier, on October 17, Cardinal Celso Costantini, chancellor of the Holy Roman Church, had died. With more than a decade's worth of experience as a diplomat and missionary bishop in China, he was convinced of the need to recognize the increasing importance of the young churches of Africa and Asia and had made it no secret that he planned to push for the election of a non-Italian pope.

Death had also claimed some of the late pope's most illustrious creations before they ever had a chance to enter a conclave. Cardinal Adam Sapieha, the archbishop of Cracow who had the time to nurture the priestly vocation of a young university student named Karol Wojtyla[21] even as he was preoccupied with standing up to the Nazi occupation—even the new Russian occupiers treated him with deference as the "uncrowned king of Poland"—had died in 1951. Also missing was another resister to German occupation, Cardinal Jan de Jong of

Utrecht, who died in 1955; during the War, he led the Dutch bishops in their courageous protest of the Nazi deportations. Likewise absent was Cardinal Jules-Géraud Saliège of Toulouse, who died in 1956 and to whose memory a forest on the road from Tel Aviv to Jerusalem was planted by a grateful State of Israel.

The three aristocratic German cardinals who had stood up to Hitler had also died, the war years having taken their toll: Cardinal Clemens August von Galen, the "Lion of Münster," had died in 1946, only thirty-three days after receiving the red hat; Cardinal Konrad von Preysing Lichtenegg-Moos of Berlin had died in 1950; and Cardinal Michael von Faulhaber of Munich and Freising had died in 1952.

In addition, the assembled cardinals felt the absence—for the first time in conclave history since the Middle Ages—of two members of the Sacred College who were imprisoned. The prince-primate of Hungary, Cardinal József Mindzenty, was a *de facto* prisoner who had taken refuge in the United States legation in Budapest after the Hungarian Revolution of 1956, before it was crushed by Soviet tanks, had sprung him from his prison cell. The Communist regime in Hungary had rebuffed an American diplomatic request to grant the cardinal a guarantee of safe passage to the conclave. The archbishop of Zagreb, Cardinal Alojzije Stepinac, condemned to sixteen years of imprisonment by the Tito regime after a 1946 show trial, was confined in his native village of Krásic. He was to die in 1960—given his relatively young age, the suspicion quickly fell on the regime—never having received his red hat.

And, of course, the greatest void was that left by the death of Pope Pius XII. Taking on the international political role his electors had wanted him to play, up to the outbreak of hostilities on September 1, 1939, he strove to avert the war by diplomatic means. Even after the start of the conflict, he worked to try to keep Italy out of it. Succeeding at neither endeavor, he remained strictly neutral, in adherence to both his interpretation of the Lateran Treaty and his conception of the Church's role, although he did repeatedly call for peace based on the natural-law principles of justice. Throughout the Second World War, Pius directed, through the Pontifical Aid Commission, a vast relief program. When the Germans occupied Rome in 1943, he made Vatican City and the various extraterritorial papal holdings established by the Lateran Treaty asylums for political refugees and Jews. He tried to have Rome declared an open city, and when the capital was liberated on June 4, 1944, he was hailed as "Defender of the City."

On the other hand, Pius was criticized for failing to speak out forcefully against the Nazi regime, especially regarding the atrocities it committed against Jews and other persecuted groups. However, his defenders have pointed out that the pope did issue unmistakable, albeit generalized, condemnations of racist crimes, citing, for example, his Christmas address of 1942, and noted the assistance that he gave either personally or through his agents to large numbers of individual

Jews, including the chief rabbi of Rome, Israel Zolli, who, after the war, converted to Catholicism and took the pope's baptismal name of Eugenio.[22] Nonetheless, perhaps because he was convinced that explicit protests would only lead to harsher reprisals—such was certainly the case in the Netherlands after the Dutch bishops protested—and perhaps because he was used to the veiled language of the Roman Curia and the fine-tuned nuances of diplomacy, he never issued that public condemnation of the Holocaust that would have spared his memory the controversy that continues to surround it.

Pius did not allow the war to distract him from his doctrinal and ecclesiastical office. Even as the German army occupied Rome in 1943, he published two major encyclicals: *Mystici corporis*, on the nature of the Church in terms of the mystical body of Christ, and *Divino afflante Spiritu*, permitting the use of modern historical methods in the interpretation of the Scriptures. In 1950, he defined the dogma of Mary's bodily assumption into heaven. Beginning in 1951, he reformed the entire liturgy of Holy Week. He internationalized the College of Cardinals, reducing the Italian contingent to barely a third of the college's total composition: Of the fifty-one cardinals who entered the conclave after his death, only seventeen were Italian. On the other hand, he also diminished the role of the Sacred College in the governance of the Church, concentrating increasingly greater decision-making authority in his own person. After Cardinal Maglione's death in 1944, he did not appoint a replacement, choosing instead to act as his own secretary of state with the aid of two *monsignori*, Domenico Tardini and Giovanni Battista Montini.[23]

The first pope to widely use radio and television, Pius, with his ascetic figure, became for millions the embodiment of the Roman papacy. However, as he grew older, his solitary inclination left him increasingly isolated. As a result, the last years of his pontificate were not as productive as the earlier ones, and there were even occasional displays of a most eccentric variety. After the proclamation of the dogma of the assumption on November 1, 1950, for example, Pius had Cardinal Federico Tedeschini, the archpriest of the Vatican Basilica, announce that both before and after the event, the pope had been privileged to witness the "miracle of the sun" no fewer than four times, specifically on October 30 and 31, and then again on November 1 and 8. The cardinal told the astonished assembly that it was "just like at Fatima" in 1917, omitting the detail that whereas some seventy thousand claimed to have seen some sort of phenomenon during the Marian apparition in Portugal, this time only the pontiff witnessed anything unusual. Such displays, as well as the increasing influence of Pius XII's longtime housekeeper, the German nun Mother Pasqualina Lehnert, dubbed "*la papessa*," diminished the pope's standing, at least within the circle of the Vatican.

With fifty-one cardinals present, the conclave of 1958 would require thirty-four votes to elect a pope. After such a long pontificate, and with the absence of some who would be looked toward for guidance even if they themselves were not contenders, the conclave was predicted to be a difficult one. Before entering the conclave, Cardinal Giuseppe Pizzardo told the Italian daily *L'Unità* that "there will be many ballots." Cardinal Gaetano Cicognani told the same newspaper that he expected to be inside "for a long time." On this pessimistic note, the cardinals were led into the Sistine Chapel for what would prove to be the most pivotal conclave of the century by their white-bearded dean, the French cardinal Eugène Tisserant.

Unlike his predecessor, who had indicated his secretary of state as his designated successor, Pius XII did not indicate any clear preference. For many years, it was thought that Giovanni Battista Montini was the pope's favorite, but whether under pressure from Montini's rivals in the Curia or because of a personal falling-out with his longtime aide, Pius had packed him off to Milan as its archbishop, withholding the cardinalate that was the quasi *ex ufficio* prerogative of the successors of St. Ambrose and St. Charles Borromeo. Thus Montini did not participate in the conclave. Others thought that Pius had given the nod to the archbishop of Genoa, Cardinal Giuseppe Siri, but at only fifty-two years of age, he was judged too young by many cardinals. In fact, referring to Siri, another Italian cardinal, Pietro Ciriaci, adapted Luigi Oreglia's famous witticism about Leo XIII—"We would end up with an Eternal Father," he commented of Siri's possible election, "not a Holy Father"—and went so far as to suggest that perhaps the electors ought to choose an elderly transitional figure to give the Genoese prelate time to age enough to be elected. Still others suggested that Pius had expressed a preference for the pro-secretary of the Supreme Sacred Congregation of the Holy Office, Cardinal Alfredo Ottaviani. However, while the late pope's theological and ecclesiological affinities were close to those of the brusque Roman prelate, a worthy heir to the predecessors in his office who bore the style of "grand inquisitors," Pius could hardly have thought that Ottaviani had even a remote possibility given the amount of the controversy the cardinal's disciplinary measures aroused around the world. Those silenced, at least for a time, under orders from Ottaviani's Holy Office included the American Jesuit John Courtney Murray, later the architect of the Second Vatican Council's Declaration on Religious Liberty, as well as the future cardinals Henri de Lubac and Yves-Marie Congar.

In this situation, where the members of the Sacred College arrived in conclave having no clear consensus on the future direction of the Church, much less agreement on the candidate to lead in whatever direction, the first ballot on the morning of Sunday, October 26, threw votes at a group of older—hence pre-

sumably transitional—figures.[24] It seems the nearly seventy-seven-year-old patriarch of Venice, Cardinal Angelo Roncalli,[25] and the sixty-three-year-old Rome-
based patriarch of the Armenian Catholics, Grégoire-Pierre XV Agagianian,
received approximately 20 votes each, while a smattering of votes went to other
figures, including the dean of the college, Tisserant; the archbishop of Bologna,
Cardinal Giacomo Lercaro; and the former nuncio in Vichy France, Cardinal
Valerio Valeri. Surprisingly, for the first time since the Middle Ages, a few votes
went to a prelate who was not even a member of the Sacred College: the archbishop of Milan, Giovanni Battista Montini, apparently from non-Italian cardinals
as a symbolic protest against the curial faction that was seen as opposed to him.

By the end of the first day, after four ballots, it was evident that Agagianian's
candidacy had stalled, if it ever was a candidacy. In fact, it was said that the Armenian patriarch could have been elected by the conclave had he chosen to seek
the papacy. His many years of service in Rome made him a familiar figure with
whom the curial faction, small but powerful, especially in the final years of Pius
XII's pontificate, was comfortable: It was said that he was *"più Romano d'un
romano"* ("more Roman than a Roman"). On the other hand, the fact that
Agagianian was a non-Italian appealed to the non-Italian majority in the Sacred
College. The late pope had clearly shown him favor: Agagianian had been the
first cardinal named during Pius's pontificate. However, Agagianian was himself
not entirely comfortable, personally and ecclesiologically, with the prospect of
an Eastern Rite hierarch like himself ascending to head the Roman Church. Had
his longtime friend the just-deceased chancellor Celso Costantini lived, the latter
might have persuaded him as well as serving as his promoter in the conclave.
Nonetheless, it is remarkable that the Armenian cardinal continued to receive
the consistent support of a large bloc of votes (around eighteen) until the end of
the conclave—not enough to elect him, but enough to block anyone else from
being elected and permitting him to serve as a "grand elector," or arbiter of the
conclusion.

Meanwhile, some cardinals, mainly associated with the curial faction or sympathetic to its policies, considered Roncalli, the other large vote-getter during
the first day's balloting, an inadequate figure to succeed to the legacy of the
great Pius. However, faced with the fact that Siri was too young and Elia Dalla
Costa of Florence was too old, this group agreed during the evening to support
the candidacy of Cardinal Benedetto Aloisi Masella, the newly elected
camerlengo, during the following day's voting. The failure of the Aloisi Masella
candidacy, however, is emblematic of the role that apparently small factors can
play in a closed environment like that of the conclave. According to the subsequent accounts of Tisserant and Cicognani as well as a number of non-cardinals
present in the conclave, Aloisi Masella acquired an eccentricity during the *sede*

vacante that annoyed a number of electors. One of the prerogatives of the camerlengo during the *sede vacante,* aside from the well-known right—of particular interest to philatelists and numismatists—to issue postage stamps and mint coins bearing his coat of arms, is to carry a scepter covered in red velvet as a sign of his office as "prince regent" of the Church. Evidently, Aloisi Masella grew quite attached to this token of his office and carried his scepter everywhere, even having a stool set next to his seat in the cardinals' dining room so that he could set down the bauble while he ate. Equally evident, it seems, was the annoyance this caused among his confrères, traditionally jealous of their equality as sovereign electors.

The eyes of all turned to take a second look at the patriarch of Venice, the only remaining viable candidate. It seems that Roncalli himself was aware of what would transpire the following day. Cardinal Maurilio Fossati of Turin, whose room was adjacent to Roncalli's, subsequently related that the Venetian patriarch stopped in and asked to borrow his copy of the official yearbook of the Holy See, the *Annuario Pontificio.* When the volume was later returned, Fossati found a scrap of paper, in Roncalli's handwriting, making notes on the various popes named John.

On Tuesday, October 28, on the first afternoon ballot (the eleventh of the conclave), Angelo Roncalli received 38 votes and accepted the election shortly before five o'clock in the afternoon. Then came the first of many surprises from the newly elected pontiff: *"Mi chiamerò Giovanni . . .* I will call myself John," he declared, speaking in Italian rather than the Latin of protocol. "This name is dear to me because it is the name of my father. It is the name of the patron saint of the humble parish where I was baptized . . . and almost all who bore that name had a brief pontificate." Brief it would be indeed, but momentous.

The Demands of the Council (1963)

The eighty cardinals—the entire Sacred College was present except for József Mindszenty, who remained shut up in his asylum at the American legation in Budapest, and the ailing ninety-year-old Carlos María de la Torre—who processed into the Sistine Chapel on June 19, 1963, were keenly aware of the pressure that was being brought to bear upon them by events set in motion by the late pope. Just eight months before, on October 11, 1962, more than two thousand cardinals, patriarchs, archbishops, bishops, and abbots—the largest assembly of hierarchs in the history of the Church—had filled St. Peter's Basilica for the opening of the Second Vatican Council, called by the late Pope John XXIII to be a new Pentecost, a means of regenerating the Church by bringing its teaching, discipline, and organization up-to-date and opening a way for the hoped-for reunion of the Churches of Christendom. In his allocution opening the assembly, optimistically entitled *Gaudet Mater Ecclesia* ("Mother Church Rejoices"), John outlined his vision: "Our duty is not just to guard this treasure [of the Church's doctrine], as though it were some museum-piece and we the curators, but earnestly and fearlessly to dedicate ourselves to the work that needs to be done in this modern age of ours, pursuing the path which the Church has followed for almost twenty centuries . . . What is needed, and what everyone imbued with a truly Christian, Catholic and apostolic spirit craves today, is that this doctrine shall be more widely known, more deeply understood, and more penetrating in its effects on the moral lives of humanity. What is needed is that this certain and immutable doctrine, to which the faithful owe obedience, be studied afresh and reformulated in contemporary terms. For this deposit of faith, or truths which are contained in our time-honored teaching is one thing; the manner in which these truths are set forth is something else . . . For with the opening of this Council a new day is dawning on the Church, bathing her in radiant splendor. It is yet the dawn, but the sun in its rising has already set our hearts aglow. All around is the fragrance of holiness and joy."

John's council, the calling of which he attributed to a sudden inspiration of the Holy Spirit, had provoked reactions running the entire spectrum from horror to euphoria. All these emotions, both expectations and fears, were now concentrated on the conclave. In a dispassionate interview given to the veteran Italian journalist and Vatican insider Benny Lai, Cardinal Pietro Ciriaci summed up the situation: "No one is in a position to suspend the Council; even Ottaviani, were he elected, would be forced to bring it to a conclusion . . . The challenge is to find the right man as pontiff who will keep the Council within reasonable limits. Find the man and we will have the solution to the puzzle."

The late pope had given indications, albeit not as blatantly as Pius XI had done with Eugenio Pacelli, that he saw in Giovanni Battista Montini his heir apparent. Barely a month after his own election to the papal throne, John XXIII gave Montini the cardinal's red hat long denied him during the last years of Pius XII's pontificate, when the Milanese archbishop had been a victim of that old Roman maneuver of *promoveatur ut amoveatur* ("let him be promoted so that he might be removed"), listing him first among the twenty-three cardinals he created in the consistory of December 15, 1958. In fact, John was overheard telling Montini before a crowd of well-wishers from Milan that "if you had received your red hat when you should have, I would not be here." And, like Pius XI with his designated successor, John encouraged the archbishop of Milan to travel abroad. Thus Montini traveled to the United States (1960), where he received an honorary doctorate from the University of Notre Dame, Ireland (1961), and Africa (1962).

As John's confidant, Montini played a significant role in the Central Preparatory Commission as well as the technical-organizational committee planning for the Vatican Council, even though he spoke only twice during the first session of the assembly. Thus, Montini brought to the conclave a reputation for possessing a fine intellect (the ninety crates of books that followed him when he was exiled from the Vatican in 1954 had become legendary), influential correspondents and protégés throughout the Italian and European cultural and political scene (his years as national chaplain of the Federation of Italian Catholic University Students [FUCI] made him the mentor of an entire generation of Italian political and cultural leaders, and he had for years maintained an active correspondence with a number of leading European intellectuals, including Jean Guitton and Jacques Maritain), and the experience of a fruitful episcopal ministry in the largest diocese in Europe (he did much to rebuild his war-battered see as well as to reach out to disaffected working classes), along with his unparalleled knowledge of diplomacy and the Roman Curia (not only from his years there under Pius XI and Pius XII, but from his many sources who kept him, even when he was in Milan, incredibly well informed on the goings-on in the Vatican). On the other hand, his years in Rome had also procured Montini a host of enemies, who had succeeded in exiling him during Pius XII's declining years and who continued to view him with a certain suspicion, especially for his French-influenced intellectualism.

Others, enthusiastic for the winds of change that John had allowed to sweep away what seemed to be centuries of hieratic stiffness, looked to the archbishop of Bologna, Cardinal Giacomo Lercaro. Appointed to a run a see teeming with social problems—on the political map of postwar Italy, Bologna was a solid red stronghold where the Communist Party regularly received a higher percentage of the vote than anywhere else in Europe outside the Iron Curtain—Lercaro managed to temper the anti-clerical vehemence with his open arms and heart. He turned his palatial residence into a community home where he lived, family style, with runaways from broken homes, sheltering and educating them out of his own pocket. He often walked through the city, speaking with people about their business. When one interlocutor lamented to him that industrial Bologna had little in the way of park space wherein to escape the summer heat, he threw open the grounds of the diocesan seminary. One of the most familiar and beloved figures on the Italian ecclesiastical scene, he was nonetheless viewed as too unpredictable by many prelates.

Faced with a choice between Montini (judged "strange in his head") and Lercaro (deemed "strange in his deeds"), the stalwarts of the Roman Curia, among whom were some of the prelates who were the least enthusiastic about Pope John's council, cast about for a candidate they could present to the electors, even as they recognized, as Ciriaci dispassionately noted, that the convocation of the Vatican Council limited the scope of what they could hope to accomplish.[26] Despite the entreaties of Ottaviani, the Armenian Agagianian refused once more to enter the lists as a candidate. A close ally of the curial faction, the other elector from the Eastern Churches, Ignace-Gabriel I Tappouni, the eighty-four-year-old patriarch of Antioch of the Syrians, then approached Giuseppe Siri of Genoa, entreating him to allow his candidacy to be promoted, telling him, "Either you accept, or it will be a disaster." Siri, however, did not think the moment opportune and refused. He did, however, agree that what was needed was a *"papa di difesa"* (a "defensive pope") to restore order to a theological field that he judged had been allowed to run amuck. Twice rebuffed, the conservative faction turned to the former nuncio to Spain, Cardinal Ildebrando Antoniutti.

The voting began on the morning of Thursday, June 20, the cardinals being summoned—a sign of the times?—not by the traditional bells but by an electrical alarm. With eighty cardinals present, fifty-four votes would be required to reach the two-thirds majority (John XXIII having abolished Pius XII's "two-thirds plus one") to elect. On the first ballot, Montini received the votes of thirty cardinals, while Antoniutti and Lercaro each received those of about twenty. A few votes also went to the pro-vicar general of Rome, Cardinal Luigi Traglia. The second ballot produced an identical result, causing the cardinals to wonder if they were facing a long, deadlocked conclave. However, after the midday break, the third ballot of the day showed a shift as Montini received close to fifty votes, the supporters of Lercaro switching their votes to the archbishop of Milan. It was a significant shift, but insufficient to elect, as some thirty cardinals continued to vote for Antoniutti or some other conservative candidate on this and on the subsequent fourth ballot. Thus the first day of voting ending with Montini clearly the choice of a majority of the electors, albeit an insufficient one, but firmly opposed by a not insignificant minority.

John XXIII's friend of some sixty years, Cardinal Gustavo Testa, a corpulent septuagenarian obviously overcome by the prospects of an electoral deadlock, stood up and, in violation of the ban on discussions during the voting, loudly berated his confrères for turning the conclave into a travesty that threatened to squander the goodwill that the late pope had accumulated for the Church in the eyes of the world. Siri tried to shout him down, crying to the dean that the outburst was an intolerable violation of the rules. At this point, Montini gave a display of the tormented indecision that was, in the eyes of many observers, to characterize him in the future. Not wishing to be the cause of discord and deadlock, he rose to announce the withdrawal of his candidacy. However, sensing the Milanese prelate's intentions, John XXIII's successor as patriarch of Venice, Cardinal Giovanni Urbani, who as the second cardinal created by the late pope sat next to Montini, the first "creation," seized him by the arm and pulled him back into his throne, hissing loudly enough to be heard by several other cardinals, "*Eminenza, Lei stia zitto!*" ("Eminence, keep your mouth shut!").

That evening, against his own wishes but at the persistent urging of his supporters, Montini paid calls on several of those opposed to his candidacy who might be persuaded otherwise, including the late pope's secretary of state, Cardinal Amleto Giovanni Cicognani. According to Montini's former student and longtime friend, the seven-time Italian prime minister Giulio Andreotti,[27] the archbishop of Milan promised Cicognani to reconfirm him in his office if the latter would support his candidacy for the papacy.

Consequently, the following morning, June 21, on the second ballot (the sixth of the conclave), the deadlock was finally broken when Ottaviani and several of his closest allies decided that, with the council having been called, the election of a progressive was inevitable. Deeming Montini as the "least dangerous" of the progressives—and one whose curial experience, if not his intellectual habits, would predispose him at least to caution—they switched and cast their votes for the cardinal from Milan, giving him fifty-seven votes, just three more than needed for election.

His acceptance of the election, presaging things to come, was more anguished than that typically demonstrated by newly elected popes. Addressing the Almighty, he lamented: "My election indicates two things: my insignificance and your freedom, mercy, and power, which did not fail despite my unfaithfulness, misery, and capacity to betray you." As the cardinals approached him to pay homage, the new Pope Paul VI spoke to each one with the humble sincerity that was to characterize the style of his pontificate. To Lercaro, he said: "See, Eminence, how life is! This should have been you here!"[28] He addressed the failed curial candidate Antoniutti and asked him to "be a brother and a friend to me." Antoniutti responded, "I will always be deferent to the pope." Paul told Siri, "I need Your Eminence's help. Stay close!" To which the Genoese cardinal replied obliquely, "As always, I am most faithful." Following the apostolic blessing *Urbi et Orbi* to the crowds gathered in St. Peter's Square, Paul returned to the conclave and, refusing the special place prepared for him, took his lunch at the seat he had occupied as a cardinal. While some greeted these acts with optimistic enthusiasm, others were less sanguine. The bearded dean of the Sacred College, Tisserant, commented, "Not all were favorable to Montini, but they convinced themselves that it was impossible to do otherwise."

Looking for "God's Candidate" (1978)

The 111 cardinals—fifteen others were excluded for reasons of age,[29] while three others were too ill to attend—who entered the conclave on August 25, 1978, constituted the largest electoral assembly convened for the election of a Roman pontiff since perhaps the days of the early Church, when all the members of the small Christian community of Rome gathered to take part in electing their bishop.

Their increased numbers, as well as the ferocious heat of the Roman summer, made their enclosure all the more difficult, although it was not without its twists of humor. Siri told his biographer Benny Lai that he took a half-bottle of cognac into the conclave: "Do you know why? I did it in the previous conclaves and believe me it was needed." The Genoese cardinal would have done well to take along a bottle of oxygen as well, as the heat made some of the temporary rooms unbearable. Cardinal Silvio Oddi invoked his authority as a member of the oversight committee to have workmen break down the conclave seals on his window, which had caused his room to become "an asphyxiation chamber." The increase in the number of cardinals also meant that what were once suites became one-room cells. The Belgian primate, Cardinal Leo-Jozef Suenens, assigned by lot to Room 88, had to walk through Room 86, assigned to Cardinal Léon-Etienne Duval, archbishop of Algiers. Between the two of them, Suenens and Duval had a shower that was shared by the two cardinals from the adjoining suite, Raúl Silva Henríquez of Santiago de Chile and Juan Landázuri Ricketts of Lima. In the Sistine Chapel, so many were the electors that the traditional arrangement of thrones along the walls for the cardinals was no longer possible. Instead, the electors sat at convention-style tables set up in rows, each man having exactly three feet of table space—hardly conducive to maintaining the secrecy of their ballots. Two veteran Vatican correspondents, Philippe Levillain and François-Charles Uginet, no doubt echoing the views of the French cardinals they interviewed, reported that the arrangements "imposed on the electors appear to be due either to thoughtlessness or utter sadism."

In any event, the physical pressures on the cardinal electors were mild compared to the moral pressure that they felt. The eyes of the world were literally upon them in a manner that their predecessors of earlier conclaves could not have imagined. The procession into the Sistine Chapel—led by the camerlengo, Cardinal Jean Villot, since the dean, Carlo Confalonieri, who had presided majestically at the recent papal funeral, was too old to have the right to vote—was televised live into the homes of millions. And, with the sense of empowerment unleashed by the Second Vatican Council, those millions voiced their desires. On his way to the conclave, British cardinal Basil Hume was handed a leaflet headlined "We want a Catholic Pope." The bemused prelate commented, "Perhaps they think we're here to elect a Protestant?"

Humor aside, however, the task facing the electors was as daunting as the changes that had taken place in the Church and the world since the last conclave. On the morrow of his election, Paul VI had pledged himself to continuing the recessed Vatican Council, begun by his predecessor. He opened the second session of the council on September 29, 1963, by introducing several momentous innovations, including admitting laymen as auditors and relaxing the confidentiality of the proceedings to permit more journalistic coverage. When he closed the session on December 4, he promulgated the council's Constitution on the Liturgy, *Sacrosanctum concilium*, that was to set in motion the complete modernization of the worship and ceremonial of the Catholic Church, as well as its Decree on Mass Media. During the break, he made, on January 4–6, 1964, an unprecedented pilgrimage to the Holy Land, where he met with the Ecumenical Patriarch Athenagoras I, spiritual leader of the world's Orthodox Christians. Before he opened the third session of Vatican II on September 14, 1964, Paul VI announced the even more unprecedented admission of women, both lay and religious, into the council as auditors. On closing that session on November 21, he promulgated the Dogmatic Constitution of the Church *Lumen Gentium*, with an explanatory note attached defining the collegiality of bishops (i.e., the doctrine that they form a college that acts in concert with but not independently of the its head, the pope) and the Decree on the Eastern Catholic Churches *Orientalium Ecclesiarum*. Despite the reservations of some council fathers, acting on the petition of the Polish bishops who were supported by the Vietnamese bishops, he also proclaimed the Virgin Mary as "Mother of the Church." During this break, he flew to Bombay on December 2–5 for the International Eucharistic Congress, thus becoming the first pope to travel outside Europe during his papacy in a millennium. During the final session of the council, September 14–December 8, 1965, Paul traveled to the United Nations in New York to plead for peace on October 4. The day before the session closed, December 7, a joint declaration by Paul VI and the Ecumenical Patriarch Athenagoras I was read, annulling the mutual anathemas of 1054. The following day, in bringing the Vatican Council to its conclusion, he solemnly confirmed its sixteen documents.

Unlike his predecessor's confident address opening the council, Paul VI's closing message had an almost plaintive tone, perhaps an augury of what was to come: "You will hear shortly, at the end of this holy Mass, a reading of some messages which, at the conclusion of its work, the ecumenical council is addressing to various categories of persons, intending to consider in them the countless forms in which human life finds expression. And you will also hear the reading of our official decree in which we declare terminated and closed the Second Vatican Ecumenical Council. This is a moment, a brief moment of greetings. Then, our voice will be silent . . . This greeting is, before all, universal . . . Just as the sound of the bell goes out through the skies, reaching each one within the radius of its sound waves, so at this moment does our greeting go out to each and every one of you. To those who receive it and to those who do not, it resounds pleadingly in the ear of every man. From this Catholic center of Rome, no one, in principle, is unreachable; in principle, all men can and must be reached. For the Catholic Church, no one is a stranger, no one is excluded, no one is far away. Every one to whom our greeting is addressed is one who is called, who is invited and who, in a certain sense, is present. This is the language of the heart of one who loves. Every loved one is present! And we, especially at this moment, in virtue of our universal pastoral and apostolic mandate, we love all, all men."

In the wake of the council, it nonetheless fell to Paul to implement its decisions while steering a middle course between the extremes that threatened schism, although his moderation—to which, admittedly, one would have to add his propensity to be indecisive, agonizing over each detail—satisfied neither progressives nor conservatives. The former hailed his promotion of liturgical reform, with its introduction of worship in the vernacular and revision of the rites, as well as his commitment to social justice, reflected in his 1965 encyclical *Populorum progressio*, while the latter approved of his reaffirmation of priestly celibacy in the 1967 encyclical *Sacerdotalis coelibatus* and his condemnation of artificial methods of birth control in the 1968 encyclical *Humanae vitae*. The latter was a particular disappointment to the expectations of many both within and without the Church, not the least because the pontifical commission Paul himself had appointed to review the matter had reported in favor of contraception under certain circumstances. In fact, the furor caused by *Humanae vitae* profoundly shook the pope, who, perhaps for the first time, realized the extent to which the climate had changed. In this regard, he became increasingly torn between his progressive intellectual vision and his worry that innovations might undermine the integrity of the Church's doctrine. In his final years, many detected that he became more withdrawn, his pronouncements emphasizing the mysterious dimension of faith and the otherworldliness of the Church, while ignoring the day-to-day struggles between traditionalists and progressives for ascendancy.

With 111 cardinals present, seventy-five votes were needed to elect (Paul VI having restored the electoral majority to two-thirds plus one). Seventy-five votes to indicate the "man of God" who was needed not only to keep the competing factions within the Church from tearing the institution apart but also to inject new energy into a body that seemed to have grown tired and withdrawn with the aging Paul VI. In their quest, the cardinals met with each other in a number of informal caucuses, often on linguistical bases. For example, the German cardinals—Joseph Schröffer of the Congregation for Catholic Education, Joseph Höffner of Cologne, Alfred Bengsch of Berlin, and Joseph Ratzinger of Munich and Freising—met several times in Schröffer's Vatican apartment with their Austrian confrère, Franz König of Vienna, as well as the two Brazilian cardinals of Germanic descent, Paulo Evaristo Arns of São Paulo and Aloisio Lorscheider of Fortaleza.

On the morning of Saturday, August 26, according to the notes left by Cardinal Mario Casariego of Guatemala, the first ballot brought Siri—this time the not unwilling candidate of the conservative faction—25 votes, followed by a relatively unknown name, that of the patriarch of Venice, Cardinal Albino Luciani,[30] who received 23 votes. There was a smattering of votes for a dozen other candidates, including 4 for Cardinal Karol Wojtyla of Cracow. The second ballot brought Siri a few more votes, while the support for Luciani remained stable.

During the midday break, several of the leaders of the progressive faction—Benny Lai named the Belgian Suenens as well Cardinal Bernardus Johannes Alfrink of Utrecht and Cardinal Franz König of Vienna—met in the larger room of Cardinal Vicente Enrique y Tarancón of Madrid-Alcalá. Realizing that it was apparent that the choice was between Siri and Luciani, with the former seemingly in the ascendancy, the progressives decided to throw their support behind Luciani for fear of what a Siri pontificate might be like. The word quickly spread at lunch. During the post-prandial strolls, Joseph-Albert Malula of Zaire came across Luciani and embraced him. The Venetian patriarch, appreciating the likely consequence of the maneuvering going on among the cardinals, was visibly nervous and muttered in Latin, *"Tempestas magna est super me"* ("A great storm is overshadowing me").

On the first ballot of the afternoon (the third of the conclave), Luciani's candidacy surged forward, receiving almost seventy votes. On the following ballot, a veritable landslide swept the patriarch of Venice well over the required majority. As the prefect of the Papal Household, the future Cardinal Jacques Martin,[31] described it, "it was the finger of God." Cardinal Hume described the new pope as "God's candidate."

If so, providence seemed to have sweeping changes in mind, as the newly elected pope quickly demonstrated. He became the first pope to choose a double name, John Paul, to express his desire to combine the progressive and traditional, earthy and mystical, qualities of his two predecessors, John XXIII and Paul VI. And, despite Paul's radical reform of the Church's liturgy as well as his simplification of the papal court, the late pope had left in his 1975 decree reforming papal elections, *Romano Pontifici eligendo*, provision that "the new pope shall be crowned by the Cardinal Proto-Deacon." Instead, John Paul I dispensed with the tiara and simply "inaugurated" his pontificate with a Mass celebrated in St. Peter's Square on September 3, during which he was invested with the pallium, the narrow band of wool worn around the shoulders by metropolitan archbishops within their provinces as a sign of their jurisdiction and by the pope as a sign of his universal jurisdiction.

The day after his election, John Paul addressed the Sunday crowd gathered in St. Peter's Square from his window, telling them, "I do not have the wisdom of heart of Pope John. I do not have the preparation and culture of Pope Paul. But now I stand in their place. I will try to serve the Church, and I hope that you will help me with your prayers."

Another Conclave (1978)

Barely a month after they had taken their leave of the smiling "man of God" they had elected by an unprecedented landslide, John Paul I, 111 cardinals—the same electors as in the previous conclave save for Luciani, now dead, whose place was taken by the American curialist John Wright, now sufficiently recovered—filed somberly into the Sistine Chapel on the afternoon of Saturday, October 14, 1978. The shock they felt was palpable, made all the more painful by the rumors of foul play that were fanned by the decision, made in haste by the camerlengo in consultation with a small circle of curial officials, not to break with tradition by authorizing an autopsy. The European tabloids created a sensational account whereby the pope had planned to clean up the Curia, beginning with the controversial Institute for the Works of Religion (IOR, the "Vatican bank"), demote certain curial figures, and revise the teachings of *Humanae vitae* regarding birth control.[32] While it is impossible, even for his electors, to speculate what policies John Paul I would have pursued had he lived, they knew they would be hard pressed to find another man whose captivating personal charisma would generate the same spontaneous outburst of hope and enthusiasm, which they knew was needed if the Church was to have any chance of entering the new millennium as still a force in the modern world. As Joseph Ratzinger later observed: "Personally, I am totally convinced that [John Paul I] was a saint, because of his great goodness, simplicity, humanity, and great courage. He had the courage to say things with great clarity, even if he had to go against current opinions." The German cardinal admitted that the pope's death left the members of the college "somewhat depressed" because "the fact that Providence would say no to our choice was really a very hard blow." However, the "unexpected death also opened the doors to an unexpected choice."

There were only three Italian cardinals—Italian because the electors were still thinking the tradition of not having elected a non-Italian since the difficult pontificate of the Dutch Hadrian VI (1522–1523)—who were serious contenders. One was the conservative Giuseppe Siri of Genoa, who had been Albino Luciani's only serious rival in the August conclave and whose reputed doctrinal temperament, in the words of one curial prelate, had helped the Holy Spirit to shepherd the votes to the mild patriarch of Venice. As the electors knew from the photocopied newspaper article that had been anonymously delivered to each of their lodgings that morning—complete with translation into the major European languages for those not reading Italian—Siri made no secret of his views. In a remarkably wide-ranging interview with journalist Gianni Licheri, published in the *Gazzetta del popolo*, the Genoese prelate respectfully but clearly criticized both John XXIII and Paul VI, characterizing the upheavals caused by the Second Vatican Council as a "disaster" and lamenting a lack of firm doctrinal discipline in the Church. It was later learned that the interview had been granted on condition that it not be published until the cardinals were in conclave, a promise that was not honored by the newspaper's editors.[33] While giving such an interview was an amazing gaffe on Siri's part, it was not clear whether it would affect his standing within the electoral assembly: In his more than twenty-five years in the college, he had never sought to mask his views, which were well known to his confrères. Long before it became fashionable for cardinals and other prelates to publish their theological analyses, Siri had published a book-length jeremiad, entitled *Gethsemane: Reflections on the Contemporary Theological Movement*,[34] questioning the orthodoxy of many of the most influential post–Vatican II theologians.

Siri was the senior cardinal priest of the college, having been created by Pius XII in 1953. The other Italian contender was the newest cardinal priest, Giovanni Benelli, archbishop of Florence and formerly Paul VI's all-powerful *sostituto*, who was elevated to the college by Pope Paul in a special consistory on June 27, 1977, held for his benefit, with Joseph Ratzinger, Bernardin Gantin, and Mario Luigi Ciappi thrown in essentially for the sake of appearances. Although Benelli, despite his relative youth at only fifty-seven years of age, was esteemed and would enjoy the support of a number of progressive non-Italian cardinals—a pre-conclave meeting at his old alma mater, the Pontifical French Seminary, convened by Cardinals François Marty of Paris and Paul Gouyon of Rennes and attended by a dozen other cardinals, including Salvatore Pappalardo of Palermo, Giovanni Colombo of Milan, Hyacinthe Thiandoum of Dakar, the Brazilian Franciscans Aloisi Lorscheider and Paulo Evaristo Arns, and Leo-Josef Suenens of Mechlin-Brussels, had agreed to vote for him—memory of his tenure as substitute of the Secretariat of State would turn ensure a strong opposition, especially from the curial cardinals.

There was talk of a compromise candidacy, putting the seventy-six-year-old Giovanni Colombo of Milan forward as a moderate Italian who had pastoral experience and was old enough to serve as a transitional figure. However, the experience of John XXIII, who was supposedly a transitional pope, had rendered the concept of a transitional figure meaningless to the electors of 1978. And, in any event, Colombo made it clear that he would refuse to accept even if elected and that he was supporting Benelli.

One person who thought of another compromise candidate was the aristocratic Cardinal Maximilien de Fürstenberg, one-time rector of the Pontifical

Belgian College. Walking past his former student Cardinal Karol Wojtyla of Cracow, who later recounted the incident, the Belgian cardinal leaned over to his Polish colleague and whispered in Latin, paraphrasing John 11:28, "*Deus adest, et vocat te*" ("God is near, and he calls you").[35] Others, however, were not quite sure. Vienna's Franz König later related that, entering the conclave, he had turned to the Polish primate, Cardinal Stefan Wyszyński, and broached the subject of a non-Italian pope with him: "Perhaps Poland can provide us with a candidate." Wyszyński turned in surprise: "You want *me* to come to Rome?" When König explained that he was referring to the other Polish cardinal, Wyszyński was skeptical: "*Him?* He's too young."

The first ballot of the conclave, taken on the morning of Sunday, October 15, not only showed that the electors were disposed to look for another Italian pope if one could be found but also confirmed the pre-conclave speculation that there were two contenders. Siri and Benelli received approximately thirty votes each, while the rest of the votes went to a smattering of other cardinals. On the second ballot, which followed immediately after the first, Benelli surprised everyone by surging ahead, almost doubling the number of votes he received, while Siri held steady.

Benelli's critics in the Roman Curia rallied with the traditionalists at the midday break, however, and in the first ballot after the recess Benelli fell back to 42 votes, while Siri received 60 votes. On the fourth ballot, Siri received 70 votes, just five short of the majority required for election, while Benelli's position eroded, a number of the non-Italian progressives who had been voting for him apparently transferred their votes to others, including Wojtyla, who received 5 votes.

As the electors adjourned their deliberations for the evening, the election of Siri on the morrow seemed inevitable. The Polish primate Wyszyński even congratulated Siri's secretary, Monsignor Mario Grone, telling him that he would soon be the papal secretary.[36] The problem, however, was picking up the few votes needed for election. Both Giulio Andreotti and Benny Lai later reported that, despite the strenuous lobbying efforts of his supporters, the Genoese archbishop could not pick up any additional support without giving the other cardinals some guarantees for the future. The price for election suggested by several uncommitted cardinals was the recall of Benelli from his Florentine exile and his appointment as secretary of state—the understanding being that the younger, more progressively inclined former substitute would moderate any excesses of orthodox zeal on the part of the older, traditionalist Siri. Siri, however, refused to make any promises and sent interlocutors packing with a stern reminder of the canons against such electoral pacts.

Consequently, on the first ballot of the following morning (the fifth of the conclave), Siri lost some ground, with a few votes going to the reluctant Colombo and several to the distinguished Dutch ecumenist Cardinal Johannes Willebrands, while Wojtyla picked up several votes for a total of 11. On the following ballot, both Siri and Benelli fell below forty votes, while Wojtyla continued to pick up several votes.

During the midday break, König, supported by the Polish-American cardinal John Krol of Philadelphia, made the rounds of the non-Italians, talking up the candidacy of the archbishop of Cracow. One of those approached, Mario Casariego of Guatemala, was hard of hearing. When Wojtyla's canvassers spoke to him during the customary postprandial strolls, Casariego ingenuously asked in the not too discreet voice of a man with poor hearing, "Who is this Cardinal *Bottiglia?*" Wojtyla, walking by, overheard the conversation. Later, when Casariego approached him to pay his homage, the newly elected pope smiled and whispered to him, "Now you know who *Bottiglia* is!"

The canvass had its effect as, in the first afternoon ballot (the seventh of the conclave), Wojtyla pulled ahead of the two faltering Italian rivals, although the sources differ on exactly how many he received: the estimates vary from 47 votes (Andreotti) to 73 votes (Lai). In any event, the momentum had swung. On the eighth and final ballot of the conclave, Wojtyla swept well past the seventy-five votes needed for election. According to the sources of the Italian weekly *Panorama*, he received 104 votes, while Cardinal Casariego reported 99 votes—in any event, a veritable landslide. Thus Karol Wojtyla was elected the 261st successor of St. Peter and, in homage to his predecessor, assumed the style "John Paul II."

The Lessons of History

The eight conclaves of the twentieth century are not simply an interesting historical excursus, perhaps a privileged optic through which to survey the life of the Roman Church during the period. The chronicle of these electoral assemblies also serves to illustrate some of the different factors—aside from any questions of providence, which are beyond the scope of a historical study—that come into play in determining the outcome of a conclave.

Political considerations do play a part, albeit not necessarily the predominant part. While the *ius exclusivae,* the right of the exclusionary veto, asserted by the Austrian emperor in the conclave of 1903 was never formalized and, in fact, was rejected by the conclave by its repudiation of the veto against Cardinal Rampolla del Tindaro and subsequently prohibited by Pope Pius X under pain of excommunication, it remains a fact that the electors subsequently turned away from Rampolla and elected someone else. This turn of events illustrates the reality that the electors, sovereign and free though they may be in theory, are nonetheless bound by political considerations in their choice. They could then and cannot now make their decision in a vacuum without taking into account the views of the international political community, especially of those governments or institutions that represent significant Catholic populations. Not only did the Emperor Franz Josef rule a large predominantly Catholic population, his government was an important financial benefactor of the Church, within the Habsburg lands and abroad as well.

In the modern context, while there are perhaps no Catholic sovereigns with so clear a stake in the outcome of a conclave as the Habsburg monarchy, the continued political role of the Holy See on the world stage makes the election of a new pope a matter of political, as well as religious, interest to the international community.[37] Hence it should be expected that the cardinals will weigh political considerations in their deliberations—excluding, for example, from consideration the prospective candidacy of any of their confrères who hail from politically controversial nations, like the United States—and that political actors will take an interest in the proceedings. In this sense, it is both unrealistic and hypocritical for certain prelates to claim a political role, while rejecting political influence: One cannot have it both ways. Also, it should be noted that the political influences on a conclave will more likely be along the lines of the *ius exclusivae*: While they may act to exclude a contender, they are unlikely to tip the scales in favor of one.

Religious concerns can trump temporal concerns, no matter how pressing the latter may be. While political considerations do indeed influence the conclave—the electoral assembly might even be defined as the culminating drama of ecclesiastical politics—the politics may be ecclesiastical rather than temporal in scope. During the conclave of 1914, for example, while the world teetered on the edge of the Great War, the predominant concern of the electors was not the imminent conflict on the battlefields of Europe but that within the walls of the Church wrought by the modernist crisis. While Giacomo della Chiesa's diplomatic experience certainly put him in good stead, it was his reputation as a theological moderate that earned him election as Benedict XV.

With the increased number of cardinals participating in the conclave, there is a greater probability of swings in momentum sweeping the electoral assembly. As sociologists have noted, the larger the group, the greater the likelihood of a bandwagon effect occurring. The two conclaves of 1978 are examples of this phenomenon. In neither conclave was the outcome predictable; rather, other circumstances caused a certain momentum to swing toward an unexpected candidate, and the enthusiasm of the electors carried it from there. In this context, timing will be everything. The likelihood of extended deadlocks of the sort that occurred in previous eras is much diminished by not only the enlargement of the College of Cardinals but also its internationalization.

The reverse side of this phenomenon is that the influence of the individual elector, especially the one who is not habitually in the centers of power, will in fact be diminished with respect to that of organized groups or individuals. One would be hard pressed to imagine the scene of Cardinal Mario Casariego mistaking—because he did not know him—the name of the candidate he was being asked to vote for in the second conclave of 1978 happening in an earlier age. If anything, one can easily see it repeating itself with the addition of prelates from far-off regions who have little regular contact with their confrères. In many respects, the equality of the electoral franchise within the College of Cardinals, coupled with the expansion of its membership, risks turning the venerable body into the ecclesiastical equivalent of the United Nations General Assembly: All are theoretically equal, but some enjoy greater "equality" than others.

Electoral procedures and dynamics are subject to change. The procedures that will be employed at the next conclave will be new: they were promulgated by John Paul II in his 1996 apostolic constitution *Universi Dominici gregis.* The fact is that the electoral procedures have been changed by every pope during the past century, except for the short-lived John Paul I—and they have been changed even more radically by popes in previous historical periods. And these changes, each conditioned by specific historical and ecclesiastical circumstances, have influenced future outcomes each time. Hence, it is to be expected that there will be further changes in the future. After all, the Spirit is said to blow where he will.

Chapter Five

THOU ART PETER!

UNLESS THE NEWLY ELECTED POPE should determine otherwise, the conclave officially ends immediately after he assents to his election. According to Pope John Paul II's apostolic constitution governing papal elections, "from that moment the new pope can be approached by the Substitute of the Secretariat of State, the Secretary for Relations with States, the Prefect of the Papal Household and by anyone else needing to discuss with him matters of importance at the time" (UDG 91). Before dealing with business, however, the new pope is traditionally led to the altar of the Sistine Chapel, where, below the grandiose panorama of Michelangelo's *Last Judgment*, he kneels down in prayer, perhaps contemplating the burdens of the office now placed on his shoulders.

First Ceremonies

Following the few moments of prayer allowed to him, the new pontiff is swept up in a whirl of ceremonies. He is led into the sacristy of the Sistine Chapel to be vested in vestments. The small sacristy attached to the left of the Sistine Chapel is known in Italian as the *sala delle lacrime* ("room of tears") because of the emotions that often overtake the only man who ever vests there. In the simple room, where recent restoration has brought to light the frescoed arms of Pope Alexander VI (1492–1503), three white[1] simars (Italian *zimarra*, or papal cassocks)—large, medium, and small—have been prepared by the exclusive clerical tailor Annibale Gammarelli, whose ancestors have dressed popes and their courts for over two centuries. At times, such as in the case of the conclave of 1914 when Cardinal Giacomo della Chiesa was elected Benedict XV (1914–1922), all three options proved to be inadequate. Benedict XV was so physically diminutive that even the smallest of the three *zimarre* was too large. Consequently, the smallest papal cassock had to be quickly pinned and stitched up so that the new pope could appear vested in papal robes. At other times, Signor Gammarelli's predecessors seemed to have bet on the outcome. In the conclave of 1963, so certain was the papal tailor—and he was surely not alone in his speculation—that the electors would choose Cardinal Giovanni Battista Montini as the successor to Blessed Pope John XXIII (1958–1963) that, in addition to the traditional three fits, a fourth cassock, cut to Cardinal Montini's exact measurements, was prepared. Thus the newly elected Paul VI (1963–1978) was vested in a perfect fit. Poor John XXIII, in contrast, found that even the largest cassock would not button up properly around his enormous girth: The papal tailor had to resort to taking the center seam of the back apart, buttoning the rotund pontiff up in front, and improvising closure for the open back until a made-to-measure robe could be produced hastily.

The white papal cassock is trimmed with white hand-knotted silk buttons and white watered-silk (moiré) cuffs. At the waist is a white watered-silk sash whose ends are gold-fringed. The ends of the sash will eventually be decorated with the embroidered coat of arms of the pontiff. Over the cassock, the new pope puts on the *rochetto*, or rochet, traditionally a tight-sleeved linen overgarment, decorated with handmade lace, that reaches down to the knees. The rochet is also worn by cardinals, bishops, and other prelates over their choral robes.[2] Over the rochet, the pope puts on the mozzetta, or buttoned shoulder cape, of an imperial ("papal") red hue.[3] Over his shoulders is placed the red papal stole, embroidered in gold with the papal tiara and keys as well as the images of the two Apostles of Rome, St. Peter and St. Paul. Literally topping off the outfit is the white watered-silk papal *zucchetto*, or skullcap.[4]

Once the new pope is properly vested, he is led back into the Sistine Chapel, where a throne has been prepared for him on the steps of the altar. The dean of the College of Cardinals, or the senior cardinal bishop who has presided over the conclave, presents the pontiff with the papal signet ring, the so-called Fisherman's Ring, and pays him homage. The other cardinals, in their respective order of precedence, then come one by one to pay him homage and to pledge to him their obedience. The newly elected pontiff gives to each the kiss of peace. When all the cardinals present have approached and been greeted by the pope, the assembly together makes "an act of thanksgiving to God," traditionally by chanting the centuries-old hymn of praise, the *Te Deum*.[5]

After the singing of the hymn, the senior cardinal deacon announces the election and identity of the new pope to the crowds that have assembled in St. Peter's Square since the white smoke signal went up after the election. A procession thus forms to move from the Sistine Chapel, led by a cross, past the Pauline Chapel to the Hall of Benedictions, the throne room running the full length above the atrium of the Vatican Basilica. A tapestry bearing the papal arms is draped over the external balcony. The cross appears first, followed by various clerics. The senior cardinal deacon then appears to make his announcement to the silenced crowd. The formula he uses to make his proclamation in Latin is by now hallowed by centuries of use: "*Nuntio vobis gaudium magnum: Habemus Papam*" ("I announce to you a great joy: We have a pope"). The tension is palpable as the cardinal proceeds: "... *Eminentissimum ac Reverendissimum Dominium ... Sanctae Romanae Ecclesiae Cardinalem ... qui sibi nomen imposuit ...*" ("... the Most Eminent and Reverend Lord ... Cardinal ... who has taken on himself the name of ..."), inserting the name of the cardinal elected and the name he has chosen for his pontificate. At times the name is that of the cardinal who was the favorite of the Roman crowds and is greeted with immediate applause. When Cardinal Eugenio Pacelli was elected Pius XII (1939–1958), the assembled masses of his native Rome—he was the first native Roman to be elected since Cardinal Pietro Francesco Orsini was elected Benedict XIII (1724–1730)—went wild; some, remembering that the day was the new pope's birthday, even burst into song. In contrast, there was a momentary hesitation before the applause when, in the second conclave of 1978, the cardinal proto-deacon, Pericle Felici, announced the election of Cardinal Karol Wojtyla. News footage of the event recorded audible comments from the confused Romans such as "*È cinese? È africano?*" ("Is he Chinese? An African?"). As the only "Charles" known to the Italians was the eighty-five-year-old dean of the College of Cardinals, Carlo Confalonieri, one spectator, thinking the aged prelate had been elected, was recorded by the cameras as he gasped, "*Sono mati!*" ("They're crazy!").

The newly elected pontiff then appears on the balcony,[6] accompanied by the master of papal liturgical celebrations and other masters of ceremonies. Usually, he proceeds to give his first apostolic blessing *Urbi et Orbi* ("to the City [of Rome] and the world"), intoning, "*Sit nomen Domini benedictum*" ("Blessed be the name of the Lord"). The crowd responds, "*Nunc et usque in saeculum*" ("Now and forever"). The pope continues the dialogue with the crowd responding: "*Adiutórium nostrum in nómine Dómini ... Qui fecit caelum et terram*" ("Our help is in the name of the Lord ... Who made heaven and earth"). The new pope then imparts his blessing: "*Benedictio Dei Omnipotentis, Patris, et Filii, et Spiritus Sancti descéndat super vos et máneat semper*" ("May the blessing of Almighty God, the Father, and the Son, and the Holy Spirit, descend upon you and remain forever"). Traditionally, the pope gives the blessing tracing three crosses—one for each Person of the Trinity—with his right hand, the ring and pinky fingers being doubled over. Some popes then address impromptu remarks to the crowd. This was the case after the second conclave of 1978 when Pope John Paul II, brushing aside the remonstrations of the papal master of ceremonies, the future Cardinal Virgilio Noè, addressed the crowd in Italian before giving his blessing:

Sia lodato Gesù Cristo! Carissimi fratelli e sorelle, siamo ancora tutti addolorati dopo la morte del nostro amatissimo Papa Giovanni Paolo I. Ed ecco che gli Eminentissimi Cardinali hanno chiamato un nuovo vescovo di Roma. Lo hanno chiamato da un paese lontano . . . lontano, ma sempre così vicino per la comunione nella fede e nella tradizione cristiana. Ho avuto paura nel ricevere questa nomina, ma l'ho fatto nello spirito dell'ubbidienza verso Nostro Signore Gesù Cristo e nella fiducia totale verso la sua Madre, la Madonna Santissima. Non so se posso bene spiegarmi nella vostra . . . nostra lingua italiana. Se mi sbaglio mi correggerete. E così mi presento a voi tutti, per confessare la nostra fede comune, la nostra speranza, la nostra fiducia nella Madre di Cristo e della Chiesa, e anche per incominciare di nuovo su questa strada della storia e della Chiesa, con l'aiuto di Dio e con l'aiuto degli uomini. (Praised be Jesus Christ! Dearest brothers and sisters, we are all still saddened by the death of our most beloved Pope John Paul I. And behold, the Most Eminent Cardinals have called a new Bishop of Rome. They have summoned him from a faraway country . . . faraway, but always very close by through the communion in faith and Christian tradition. I was afraid to receive this nomination, but I accepted in the spirit of obedience to Our Lord Jesus Christ and trust entirely in his Mother, the Most Holy Madonna. I do not know if I can express myself well in your . . . *our* Italian language. If I make a mistake, you will have to correct me. And so I present myself to all of you, by professing our common faith, our hope, our trust in the Mother of Christ and of the Church, and to begin anew on the road of history and of the Church, with the help of God and men.)

From Coronation to Inauguration

At one time, within a short period after his election, the new pope would be crowned with the most distinctive of the symbols of his office, the *triregno*, or tiara. Of uncertain origin, the tiara, in its final evolution, consisted of a white beehive-shaped headdress with three gold and jeweled crowns. Two gold-fringed ribbons, known as *infulae*, hang from the back. The entire piece is surmounted by a cross and orb. While the headdress is of ancient usage, related to that of the miter used by all bishops, the crowns were added later. The first crown appeared as an ornament at the bottom of the headdress of the bishops of Rome when they assumed a temporal sovereignty. The second crown was added by Boniface VIII (1294–1303) in 1298, to represent his spiritual dominion. At some later date, most likely during the Avignon period of the papacy and perhaps by Clement V (1305–1314), a third crown was added. Consequently, the classic explanation for the three crowns has been threefold: (1) the pope's universal episcopate, his supreme jurisdiction, and his temporal power; (2) the pope's authority over the Church militant (on earth), the Church penitent (in purgatory), and the Church triumphant (in heaven); and (3) the three "offices" of the pope as priest, prophet, and ruler.

The tiara is still employed heraldically, along with the crossed "keys of the kingdom," in the papal coat of arms. The tiara and keys are also used as the emblem of the offices of the Roman Curia, the diplomatic representations of the Holy See, and the Vatican City State, indicating their dependence upon the pope.

The new pope was crowned with the tiara by the cardinal proto-deacon, or senior cardinal deacon, in a simple ceremony at the end of the coronation Mass.[7] The pope would be seated on the throne, the papal anthem, the *Hymnus Pontificius* composed by Charles Gounod, would be played, and, after a prayer by the dean of the College of Cardinals, the cardinal proto-deacon would place the tiara on the pope's head while intoning the formula: *"Accipe tiaram tribus coronis ornatum et scias te esse patrem principum et regum, rectorem orbis in terra, vicarium Salvatoris Nostri Iesu Christi, cui est honor et gloria in saecula saeculorum"* ("Receive this tiara adorned with three crowns and know yourself to be the father of princes and kings, ruler of the world on earth, and vicar of our Savior Jesus Christ, to whom be honor and glory unto the ages of ages").

However, Paul VI was the last pope to actually wear the tiara as part of his vesture. While Pope Paul's 1975 apostolic constitution *Romano Pontifici eligendo* contemplated the pope's coronation with the tiara of his successors by the senior cardinal deacon, as was the tradition, John Paul I dispensed with the coronation and simply received from the same cardinal the pallium as a sign of his having assumed the metropolitan authority over the Diocese of Rome and the consequent universal jurisdiction that derives from the Roman See. During the ceremony, the pope received the pallium with the simple prayer composed for the occasion and recited by the senior cardinal deacon: "Blessed be God, Who has chosen you as Shepherd of the Universal Church, entrusting you with this apostolic ministry. May you shine brilliantly during long years of earthly life, until, when called by our Lord, you are vested with immortality as you enter His celestial kingdom. Amen."

John Paul II followed the practice of his immediate predecessor, concelebrating with the cardinals who had elected him a Mass of "Solemn Inauguration of Ministry as Universal Pastor of the Church." During the Mass, the cardinals repeated, this time under the eyes of the public, their homage to the new pope and received the kiss of peace. Like his predecessor, John Paul II dispensed with the coronation with the tiara, although he invoked the image of that triple crown in his homily: "In the past, one placed on the head of the pope the tiara of three crowns to express, by that symbol, that the entire hierarchical order of the Church, all of her 'sacred power,' is exercised for no other end than that of service, service that has for its purpose but one end: that the People of God participate in the threefold mission of Christ and remains always under the authority of the Lord, which has its origins not in the power of this world, but that coming from the heavenly Father and from the mystery of the Cross and the Resurrection."

The new apostolic constitution *Universi Dominici gregis* speaks of a "solemn inauguration" of the pontificate without specifying the form that it would take. However, it is highly unlikely that a future pope would revive the coronation.

Peter's Heir

Crowned or uncrowned, the man is now "Bishop of Rome, Successor of St. Peter, Prince of the Apostles, Vicar of Jesus Christ, Supreme Pontiff of the Universal Church, Patriarch of the West, Archbishop and Metropolitan of the Roman Province, Primate of Italy, Sovereign of the Vatican City State," the spiritual leader of over one billion Catholics throughout the world. And even if his modern flock does not obey the Roman pontiff as readily or uncritically as their forebears, they still look to him to "confirm their faith." In short, he is Peter's heir, inheritor not only of unseen spiritual riches in which the faithful repose their trust but also of an unparalleled historical patrimony in this world. As the Protestant Lord Macaulay, reviewing Leopold von Ranke's monumental history of the papacy, wrote eloquently over a century and a half ago:

> There is not, and there never was on this earth, a work of human policy so well deserving of examination as the Roman Catholic Church. The history of that Church joins together the two great ages of human civilisation. No other institution is left standing which carries the mind back to the times when the smoke of sacrifice rose from the Pantheon, and when camelopards and tigers bounded in the Flavian amphitheatre. The proudest royal houses are but of yesterday, when compared with the line of the Supreme Pontiffs. That line we trace back in an unbroken series, from the Pope who crowned Napoleon in the nineteenth century to the Pope who crowned Pepin in the eighth; and far beyond the time of Pepin the august dynasty extends, till it is lost in the twilight of fable. The republic of Venice came next in antiquity. But the republic of Venice was modern when compared with the Papacy; and the republic of Venice is gone, and the Papacy remains. The Papacy remains, not in decay, not a mere antique, but full of life and youthful vigour. The Catholic Church is still sending forth to the farthest ends of the world missionaries as zealous as those who landed in Kent with Augustin, and still confronting hostile kings with the same spirit with which she confronted Attila. The number of her children is greater than in any former age. Her acquisitions in the New World have more than compensated for what she has lost in the Old. Her spiritual ascendency extends over the vast countries which lie between the plains of the Missouri and Cape Horn, countries which a century hence may not improbably contain a population as large as that which now inhabits Europe. The members of her communion are certainly not fewer than a hundred and fifty millions; and it will be difficult to show that all other Christian sects united amount

to a hundred and twenty millions. Nor do we see any sign which indicates that the term of her long dominion is approaching. She saw the commencement of all the governments and of all the ecclesiastical establishments that now exist in the world; and we feel no assurance that she is not destined to see the end of them all. She was great and respected before the Saxon had set foot on Britain, before the Frank had passed the Rhine, when Grecian eloquence still flourished at Antioch, when idols were still worshipped in the temple of Mecca. And she may still exist in undiminished vigour when some traveller from New Zealand shall, in the midst of a vast solitude, take his stand on a broken arch of London Bridge to sketch the ruins of St. Paul's.[8]

Chapter Six

FROM THE LAST CONCLAVE
TO THE NEXT

ONE OF THE PARADOXES OF MODERN TECHNOLOGY is that no one truly knows when the next conclave will take place. For over a decade, for example, improved camera technology and ever-faster telecommunications combined to transmit to the entire world in real-time graphic images of Pope John Paul II's physical infirmities, even as contemporaneous advances in medical science increased the likelihood that the octogenarian pontiff might continue even longer despite the progress of his Parkinson's disease and other illnesses. Consequently, while speculating about papal death and succession has been a popular spectator sport for as long as there has been a Christendom, its futility has never been more apparent than it proved to be during John Paul's long pontificate. As the pope's faithful secretary of over three decades, Archbishop Stanisław Dziwisz noted rather acidly about speculation about John Paul's illness during the papal twenty-fifth anniversary festivities, "Some journalists who in recent years have spoken and written a lot about the pope's health are already in heaven."[1]

Nonetheless, it is clear in the early months of 2005 that there would be a conclave sooner rather than later, even as curial officials insisted that the Church "keeps watch, knowing neither the day nor the hour" (Matthew 25:13). The progressive deterioration of John Paul's health and his repeated hospitalization—despite some *opera buffa* attempts by some of the pontiff's closest collaborators to minimize the gravity of situation[2]—transformed what had been discreet speculation by a small circle of *aficionados* into a global media phenomenon.

By the time Holy Week arrived, it was clear that John Paul II was undergoing his own Calvary and that this time for the pope—who had already survived both an assassin's bullet and a battle with cancer—there would be no resurrection, at least in this world. One by one, the pope's traditional Paschal appointments were canceled and various cardinals delegated to preside at the major liturgical celebrations. Meanwhile, in their thousands, pilgrims who had come to the Eternal City for the holy days gathered in St. Peter's Square to pray under the windows of the papal apartment where the pontiff lay on his simple wooden bed. The indomitable 84-year-old rallied sufficiently to appear at his window to greet the crowds on Easter morning and again the following Wednesday, although he appeared visibly frustrated that he was physically unable to utter the words of blessing. By the end of Easter Week, John Paul was slipping in and out of consciousness. On Friday, as a multitude gathered in St. Peter's Square to pray for him, he is said to have uttered, "You have come to me, and I thank you." The following day, if his spokesmen were to be believed, he uttered his last words, pleading with a hoarse voice in Polish, "Let me go to the house of the Father." John Paul's closest friends and collaborators surrounded him, among them—Archbishop Dziwisz; the pope's other secretary, Monsignor Mieczysław Mokrzycki; Cardinal Marian Jaworski, archbishop of Lviv of the Latins and once a fellow curate with the young Karol Wojtyła in Cracow; Archbishop Stanisław Ryłko, secretary of the Pontifical Council for the Laity and another longtime papal protégé from the Cracow days; Father Tadeusz Styczeń, who had succeeded the pontiff in the chair of ethics at the Catholic University of Lublin; and three Polish Handmaidens of the Sacred Heart of Jesus who had for many years looked after domestic arrangements in the papal apartment, led by their superior, Sister Tobiana Sobótka—as well as a team of three physicians. John Paul breathed his last at 9:37 PM on Saturday, April 2, 2005.

A Time for Electors and "Grand Electors"

At half past nine o'clock on the following morning—coincidentally the Feast of Divine Mercy, an observance promulgated by John Paul based on the visions of a Polish nun who lived in the early twentieth century—the Camerlengo of the Holy Roman Church, Cardinal Eduardo Martínez Somalo, assisted by the Vice Camerlengo, Archbishop Paolo Sardi, and the prelates of the Reverend Apostolic Camera, led by their dean, Monsignor Karel Kasteel, officially certified the death of the pontiff.[3] The formalities observed, Cardinal Joseph Ratzinger, acting in his capacity as *primus inter pares* of the College of Cardinals, convoked his brethren to gather to mourn the deceased pontiff and to carry out their centuries old prerogative to choose his successor.

For several reasons, the College of Cardinals that gathered in response to Ratzinger's summons was unlike any of its predecessors. At the time of John Paul II's passing, there were 183 cardinals (not counting the prelate named *in pectore*, whose appointment lapsed when the pontiff died without making public his name), less than two-thirds of whom, some 117, still enjoyed the right to vote in the conclave. John Paul's 1996 apostolic constitution *Universi Dominici gregis*, in confirming Pope Paul VI's *motu proprio* of 1973, *Ingravescentem aetatem*, stipulated that "those Cardinals who celebrate their eightieth birthday before the day when the Apostolic See becomes vacant do not take part in the election." The official reason given by Pope Paul for removing the electoral franchise from the older cardinals was that "it seems to us that the good of the Church demands that the increasing burden of age should be taken into consideration also for the illustrious office of the cardinalate. . . . It is in fact a particularly important office which demands great prudence, both for its unique connection with our supreme office at the service of the whole Church and because of the high importance that it has for the Church when the Apostolic See falls vacant."

The implied causal relationship between old age and diminishing prudence and ability to carry out important functions was belied in 1978 when the eighty-year-old Paul VI died and was followed in quick succession by the sixty-five-year-old John Paul I: Presiding majestically at both their funerals was the eighty-five-year-old dean of the College of Cardinals, Carlo Confalonieri. Furthermore, Confalonieri's vast experience—he attended his first conclave in 1922, when he was the private secretary to Cardinal Achille Ratti of Milan, who was elected Pope Pius XI—proved crucial in the general congregations of cardinals that had to decide several questions following the unexpected death of John Paul I. Rather it was understood from the beginning that Paul's true intention was an ill-concealed political maneuver to prevent older cardinals, many of whom had been appointed in earlier pontificates and were less sympathetic to the reforms that he had instituted in the wake of the Second Vatican Council, from forming a large enough bloc of electors to overturn his reform legacy.

The irony of Paul VI's provision was that its confirmation by John Paul II meant that the Polish pope appointed all the electors in the conclave save for the two Pauline creations still under the age of eighty and participating:[4] Joseph Ratzinger, dean of the College of Cardinals, and William Wakefield Baum, retired major penitentiary and onetime archbishop of Washington, D.C. Hence the next conclave would be determined by the appointees of the just-deceased pontiff in a proportion not seen since Leo XIII's death in 1903, when all the cardinals were his creations save for their dean, Luigi Oreglia di Santo Stefano.

The 115 effective electors hailed from fifty-four different countries: Argentina, Australia, Austria, Belgium, Bolivia, Bosnia-Herzegovina, Brazil, Cameroon, Canada, Chile, Colombia, the Democratic Republic of Congo, Dominican Republic, Côte d'Ivoire, Croatia, Cuba, the Czech Republic, Ecuador, France, Germany, Ghana, Great Britain, Guatemala, Honduras, Hungary, India, Indonesia, Ireland, Italy, Japan, Latvia, Lithuania, Madagascar, Mexico, the Netherlands, New

Zealand, Nicaragua, Nigeria, Peru, the Philippines, Poland, Portugal, Slovakia, South Africa, Spain, Sudan, Switzerland, Syria, Tanzania, Thailand, Uganda, Ukraine, the United States of America, and Vietnam. While the contemporary internationalization of the college—as well as its enlargement from its reduced ranks at the death of Pius XII in 1958—is a reflection of the growth of the Church throughout the world, that expansion did not come without a price. Unlike previous conclaves, especially the ones where the curial cardinals were either a majority or a significant minority, most of the cardinals who gathered in April 2005 had not spent any considerable time with each other; some had not even met many of their brethren.

This lack of personal acquaintance with their confrères was compounded by the inability of many of the cardinals to communicate with each other directly, especially with the *de facto* disappearance of Latin from the life of the Roman Church.[5] During the two conclaves of 1978, the cardinals—who at that time were of an age where they had been trained in Latin—had already tended to segregate themselves into national or linguistic groups within their common dining room. Several participants in those conclaves noted the contrast with earlier conclaves, when, despite rivalries and other disagreements, the electors tablehopped and socialized in Latin, albeit with wildly differing accents. Now, with even that minimum common language gone,[6] the cardinals tended to group themselves almost entirely by linguistic affinity and, in the meetings of the general congregations which were conducted largely in Italian, several cardinals appeared at quite a lost to follow the proceedings.[7]

In this context, the role of the so-called grand electors was all the more important in the conclave. The only way that such a diverse body will arrive at anything approaching the two-thirds majority required for election on the early ballots[8] will be if enough of the cardinals follow the lead of their more influential colleagues. Traditionally, the "grand electors" were not themselves so much candidates for the papal office, although a failed candidate may retain enough support to turn himself into a "grand elector" or a "grand elector" might emerge as a consensus candidate. However the usual historical pattern has been that the subtle influence and indications given by the "grand electors" help determine the choice of their peers. For example, during the conclaves of 1978, Giovanni Benelli, archbishop of Florence, and Giuseppe Siri, archbishop of Genoa, were the "grand electors" for their progressive and traditionalist brethren, respectively. The "grand electors" who emerged following the death of John Paul II included:

Joseph Ratzinger. Ratzinger's theological influence was pervasive throughout John Paul II's pontificate: since 1981, he had been prefect of the Congregation for the Doctrine of the Faith (CDF) and president of the Pontifical Biblical Commission and the International Theological Commission. During his tenure at its head, the CDF had a higher profile than its predecessor dicasteries have enjoyed in centuries, not only investigating doctrinal errors but promoting a positive theological vision and—according to a number of critics—formulating new theological dogmas. Ratzinger commanded a considerable following among the cardinals created by John Paul II and loyal to the theological trail that the pope and his doctrinal chief have blazed. Furthermore, as dean of the College of Cardinals since 2002, Ratzinger would also preside over the general congregations and all other meetings of the cardinals between the death of John Paul II and the election of his successor. That and his prerogative of presiding at the funeral services for the pope—a role that would include giving the deceased pontiff's eulogy as well as addressing his brethren on several occasions—gave him unequaled opportunities to send subtle signals to the electors as well as to the world at large. Ratzinger, however, was not considered *papabile*, a serious contender for the papacy, by most Vatican observers given the almost visceral reaction that mention of his name elicited in some quarters.

Angelo Sodano. The cardinal secretary of state is the effective prime minister of the papal government. In late 2002, when Sodano reached his seventy-fifth birthday, Pope John Paul II publicly confirmed him in office despite the retirement age. While many cardinals would look to him for political guidance at the conclave in deference to his close collaboration with the pope, Sodano's familial political ties—both his father and his brother were prominent parliamentarians in the scandal-tainted Italian Christian Democratic Party—as well as his age precluded his consideration as a candidate for the papacy by many handicappers. In any event, Sodano is generally considered to lack the broad geopolitical vision, brilliant insights, and diplomatic aplomb of his predecessor, Cardinal Agostino Casaroli, who was the architect of the Vatican's *Ostpolitik* of simultaneous *rapprochement* with the Communist bloc during the 1970s and increasing support for civil society opposition to totalitarianism in the 1980s. In contrast to Casaroli's full-fledged participation in the 1975 Conference of Security and Cooperation in Europe in Helsinki alongside the representatives of thirty-four states, including the United States and the Soviet Union, Sodano's frantic diplomatic efforts failed to secure even mention of the continent's Christian heritage in the recent constitutional treaty for the European Union.

Giovanni Battista Re. From 1989 to 2000, as *sostituto* of the Secretariat of State, Re was the *de facto* "minister of the interior" for the Church. Since 2000, he had been prefect of the Congregation of Bishops, where he had been secretary previously. In his new position, the cardinal presides over the dicastery charged with nominating and supervising the work of bishops for all the dioceses that do not fall, as "mission territories," under the jurisdiction of the Congregation for the Evangelization of Peoples (formerly the Congregation for the

Propagation of the Faith) or under the jurisdiction of the Congregation for the Eastern Churches by reason of their belonging to one of the Eastern Rites or being in those territories historically pertaining to them. Consequently, he exercised an enormous influence over the bishops of the Americas and Europe. His influence was consolidated by his contemporaneous position as president of the Pontifical Commission for Latin America. Were it not for some ill-concealed tensions with Sodano, Re might have entered the lists as one of the *papabile*.

Crescenzio Sepe. The relatively young—he was born in 1943—prefect of the Congregation for the Evangelization of Peoples is charged with overseeing the work of bishops and other missionaries in the countries of the developing world where the Catholic presence is either relatively new or, even if long-standing, tenuous for reasons of size or economy. Thus almost all of Africa and Asia as well as large sections of Latin America fall under his purview. Many of the cardinals from these countries would come calling on Sepe during the *sede vacante*, some in order to avail themselves of the occasion to deal with various administrative matters regarding the Church in their home countries, others—especially those from the very poorest countries, where the Church is almost completely dependent on Sepe's dicastery for funding—to draw the allowances to support their sojourns in the Eternal City. In either case, the Italian prelate could count on using these visits to express his preferences to his visitors, passing on impressions that would undoubtedly be confirmed by news coverage provided by Mario Agnès, a longtime friend whom Sepe, then head of the Secretariat of State's information office, installed as editor of the official Vatican newspaper *L'Osservatore Romano*. Given his relative youth and diplomatic experience—as well as the unbridled ambition that has characterized him throughout his career—Sepe was thought to be nurturing hopes of emergence from the conclave as the new secretary of state, especially if he could deliver Third World votes to the eventual pontiff.

Camillo Ruini. The Cardinal Vicar of Rome since 1991, Ruini was also president of the Italian Episcopal Conference (CEI) for an unprecedented three terms when John Paul died. Although their numbers are much reduced in contrast to previous years, the Italian cardinals still constituted a significant contingent and would, no doubt, look to their president for guidance. In his capacity as president of the CEI—with its substantial bureaucracy and international presence as a non-governmental aid agency, albeit one whose revenues derive heavily from funds collected by the Italian government through its *otto per mila* check-off on fiscal declarations—Ruini also had extensive dealings with members of the college coming from developing countries. Although Ruini is close to the Roman Curia by reason of his physical proximity, his role has been pastoral, attending to the spiritual needs of the pope's diocese—a fact that enhanced his standing with the majority of cardinals, who would be coming to the conclave from pastoral ministry in the dioceses of the world. In the last years of John Paul's pontificate, Ruini spent his summer holidays in England trying to learn English, perhaps recognizing that his lack of cosmopolitan culture and languages is the factor weighing against his being considered *papabile*.

Eduardo Martínez Somalo. Despite having a lower profile than many of his predecessors in the office of camerlengo, Martínez Somalo, a Spaniard who served in the diplomatic service of the Holy See before being created a cardinal by Pope John Paul II in 1988, was expected to quickly acquire influence because of the role that his office would require him to play during the *sede vacante*. His influence was expected to be particularly strong with cardinals who were either new to the college or who were not frequent visitors to Rome and who would, consequently, look to his office for guidance. Within the College of Cardinals, his influence was strongest with those members who share his conservative worldview and his affinity with Opus Dei (his sister is a numerary, or celibate lay member, and his nephew is a priest of the prelature).

Darío Castrillón Hoyos. Although he would, no doubt, have preferred to see himself as a candidate, the role of the prefect of the Congregation for the Clergy during the *sede vacante* would be that of a "grand elector." A diocesan bishop in Colombia for nearly three decades before John Paul II brought him into the Curia in 1998, Castrillón Hoyos had a vast experience of the Church in Latin America: In addition to his pastoral experience, he was secretary general of the Latin American Episcopal Council (CELAM) from 1983 to 1987 and its president from 1987 to 1991. Since 2000, as president of the Pontifical Commission *Ecclesia Dei*, the dicastery charged with facilitating the reconciliation with the Roman Church of traditionalist followers of the late French archbishop Marcel Lefebvre, who was excommunicated in 1988 for consecrating four bishops without papal mandate and thus inaugurating the first schism in the Catholic Church in over a century, Castrillón Hoyos had also developed a constituency among traditionalist sympathizers.

Carlo Maria Martini. The retired archbishop of Milan, Martini was once thought of as one of the *papabili*. However, age had diminished his electoral prospects, as had the bad taste that his seemingly open campaigning for the job left in the mouths of many of his confrères.[9] However, his breadth of intellect— a Jesuit, he was successively a professor of biblical studies, rector of the Pontifical Biblical Institute, and rector of the Pontifical Gregorian University before being elevated to the see of Milan in 1979—and the forthrightness with which he has enunciated his liberal views commands respect from many, even those who disagree with him.

Karl Lehmann. The only "grand elector" who did not reside in Rome or its environs, Lehmann is the bishop of Mainz. Since 1987, he had been president of the German Episcopal Conference, which, thanks to the generosity of German Catholics as well as the financial provisions dating back to the concordat signed by the Holy See with the nascent Nazi regime in 1933, is one of the wealthiest in the world. Consequently, the German bishops—and, *par excellence,* their president—enjoy enormous reserves of gratitude from cardinals and other bishops in poorer countries. Lehmann is an academic by training, holding doctorates in philosophy and theology. Before being appointed to his own chair in ecumenical and dogmatic theology at the Universities of Mainz and Freiburg, he served as the assistant to the influential Jesuit theologian Karl Rahner, a fact that he would count on to give himself enormous standing among the members of the College of Cardinals with progressive sympathies.

In the Shadow of John Paul II

The "grand electors"—indeed, all the electors—confronted an entirely changed electoral system that bore the personal imprint of Pope John Paul II. In his quarter of a century on the papal throne, John Paul held nine consistories, creating over 230 cardinals,[10] of whom 117 were still eligible to participate in the conclave following the pope's death and 115 ultimately did so.

However, the Polish pontiff's influence extended beyond the nomination of presumably like-minded prelates to the electoral college. Since the inception of the College of Cardinals, the requirement of a two-thirds (or two-thirds plus one) majority for election to the papal office ensured that the candidate eventually chosen would be a consensus figure—or, at the very least, not a divisive one, vehemently opposed by more than a third of the electors. *Universi Dominici gregis* subtly altered this constitutional system, stipulating that after three days of voting, if no one has been elected, a brief pause will take place, after which seven more ballots will be taken. If there is still no result, another break in the voting occurs—to allow for prayer and reflection—followed by seven more ballots. If no one is elected, then, after another pause, seven more ballots are taken. If the conclave is still deadlocked, a simple majority could decide to drop the two-thirds-plus-one requirement for majority and proceed to vote on the two names that in the ballot immediately preceding have received the greatest number of votes. In this last case, only a simple majority is required.

Theoretically, therefore, after as little as a week—the actual time elapsed depends on the length of the breaks taken, which may be up to one full day—a determined majority of the College of Cardinals could elect its candidate over the equally determined opposition of a significant minority. And, unlike previous conclaves, instead of being sealed inside the relatively cramped quarters of the Apostolic Palace, the cardinals would be lodged in the comfort of a spacious new building inside the Vatican, the Domus Sanctae Marthae, built with the conclave in mind, and bused the short distance to the Sistine Chapel to vote. Hence the physical discomforts that might have deterred a group of elderly men from holding out doggedly had been eliminated.

While no one could predict whether or not such an event would happen, some recalled that during the second conclave of 1978, seventy-five votes (out of 111 cardinals present) were required to elect a pope. The archconservative Cardinal Giuseppe Siri of Genoa, his journalistic indiscretions notwithstanding, received sixty votes on the third ballot and seventy votes on the fourth ballot—in both cases a majority of the electors. However, the fierce opposition of the thirty to forty electors who rallied around Paul VI's *delfino*,[11] the progressive Cardinal Giovanni Benelli of Florence, blocked the former's ascendancy, leading the college to consider other possibilities. Under the new rules, Siri's supporters would only have had to wait out the required intervals in their air-conditioned suites in the Domus Sanctae Marthae until the apostolic constitution permitted them to lower the bar, which they had more than enough votes to do.

In addition to shaping the way his successor would be chosen, Pope John Paul II bequeathed to the College of Cardinals an enormous personal legacy, discussed at the beginning of this book, which its members had to confront in their deliberations. While time alone will sort out John Paul's theological and ecclesiastical legacy—the enormous corpus of official documents alone will defy many a scholar in years to come—the cardinals who assembled after the camerlengo certified the pontiff's death were not afforded that luxury. The eyes of the world—literally in this age of instantaneous global communications and mass access to media—were upon them as they gathered to commend the pontiff to the mercies of his God and held their congregations, or preliminary deliberations, in the Apostolic Palace. While many pundits predicted that the divisions between curial and pastoral, conservative and progressive—hidden beneath the surface, but present, during the long twilight of John Paul's pontificate—would emerge, in the time-honored tradition of the Roman Church and in the spirit of *romanità* that pervades the central corridors of the Vatican, they took great pains to demonstrate a unified front to the outside world, despite their internal divisions. However, this required them to look—and quickly at that—for a candidate who, while ideally capable with grappling with John Paul's legacy at a later moment, might be immediately presentable to the world as the face of continuity of the Roman Church as well as an equal match to expectations created by the Polish pontiff's unique and dynamic personal traits.

In this respect, John Paul II left the cardinals with a difficult task. Irrespective of one's opinions regarding his theological and ecclesiastical orientation, honesty forces one to admit that he was one of the most humanly gifted men ever to occupy the Throne of Peter. The cinematic good looks he enjoyed before the illnesses of his last years took their toll, combined with the charismatic expressions and spontaneous gestures he employed in public, struck an immediate chord with the masses. In an age driven less by reverence for the sacred than adulation of the visual, it would be nearly impossible for the cardinals to contemplate electing a thoroughly unimpressive—and rather socially timid—pope like Benedict XV (1914–1922), although he was quite intellectually and diplomatically accomplished.

John Paul's hectic schedule of public audiences and international travels, even as his age and physical infirmities eventually made these appearances arduous, also raised expectations of the visibility of the incumbent of the papal office. His successor would be hard pressed to curtail the demands on his time and presence. Consequently, the man elected in the conclave would have to possess the physical stamina required to run this course. Paul VI, who, despite his intellectual precociousness, was cursed with poor health—from infancy, he suffered annual bouts of various respiratory infections—and who had a known history of depression and exhaustion (in 1935, while a middle-level official in the Secretariat of State, he suffered a breakdown that required six months of complete rest)[12] would face a skeptical electorate in today's College of Cardinals.

However, the young John Paul II was not only physically impressive: Behind his benign appearance was a formidable intellect. He was a gifted linguist with earned doctorates in theology and modern philosophy; his pre-papal scholarly writings alone total over 1,600 pages and include such erudite essays as "Evaluations on the Possibility of Building Up the Christ Ethic on the Foundations of the System of Max Scheler."[13] In a Church where, as in the world around them, men and women place a greater premium on personal merit than position, the cardinals would have to search for a candidate who evinces a credible intellectual ability to grasp the issues that concern believers and non-believers, rather than merely relying on the authority of his sacred office. In such circumstances, the choice of a pope who, like Pius X (1903–1914), was less than au courant on the principal intellectual currents of his day, or who, like the same pontiff, was less than linguistically gifted—to put it charitably—would be unthinkable.

Pope John Paul also brought to his office of pasturing a global flock in the age of mass media the linguistic ability to communicate with large segments of the faithful. While it is often forgotten, the pope is head of the Catholic Church by virtue of being the bishop of Rome—and not the other way around. John Paul II showed his appreciation of this datum when, immediately after this election and even before he imparted his blessing, he spoke to the crowd that gathered in St.

Peter's Square in fluent Italian. At the very least, any serious candidate for the papal office, should he not be an Italian, would be expected to be fluent in that language. In addition, given the demographics of the Catholic faithful as well as necessities of a global pulpit, the cardinals would look at a prospective candidate's fluency in English, French, and Spanish, as well as the Latin that remains the official language of the Roman Church, even if its liturgical use has diminished considerably in the period after the Second Vatican Council. A familiarity with German would be an additional plus since most of the theological development in the post–Vatican II Catholicism originates in a Teutonic setting, both progressive (e.g., Karl Rahner, Bernhard Häring) and more conservative (e.g., Hans Urs von Balthasar, Leo Scheffczyk).

John Paul II came to the papacy with nearly two decades of experience in the day-to-day running of a major archdiocese—and under the considerable strain of having to do so behind the Iron Curtain. However, unlike many diocesan bishops, he also had considerable experience of both Rome and the world: He had participated in all four sessions of the Second Vatican Council as well as in the subsequent Synods of Bishops, he had preached the Lenten retreat for Pope Paul VI and the Roman Curia in 1977, and he had traveled the world extensively. Hence, John Paul was not entirely unprepared to have the government of the Church thrust into his hands. The majority of the cardinals entering the conclave come out of pastoral backgrounds in the dioceses of the world and were more comfortable with someone who has shared some of their experiences. At the same time, they were well aware that a novice cannot be enthroned in the Apostolic Palace without the central administration of the Church grinding into gridlock as the various curial factions and ambitious Roman prelates run circles around the newcomer. Memories are long on Vatican Hill, and many will recall that the last total outsider elected to the papacy—John Paul I's thirty-three-day reign being too short to evaluate—was Pius X, and remember the results of that pontificate in the crises like the witch hunts for "modernism" and the rupture with France.

In short, the electors came to Rome realizing that they faced an incredible challenge to find the right candidate who could simultaneously satisfy the immediate popular and political expectations, balance the contradictory internal forces within the Church in the intermediate, and still, over the long term, enunciate the essentials of the message that they believe was entrusted to the Prince of the Apostles and his brethren.

The Search for the *Papabili*

Almost immediately after John Paul II's death it quickly became evident that the popular reaction exceeded anything even the most obsequious curial official could have imagined. Literally millions of people—including an estimated one million of the deceased pontiff's fellow Poles, many of whom traveled more than two days over whatever conveyance they could find—poured into Rome to pay their final respects as the body lay in state in St. Peter's Basilica. So many pilgrims gathered for the outdoor funeral in St. Peter's Square on Friday, April 8, that not only was the Via della Conciliazione packed but so were most of the surrounding streets. Italian civil defense officials estimated the crowd at over two million people, making it the largest funeral in human history. In addition to the ordinary faithful, there was an unprecedented representation of the world's great and powerful, including no fewer than ten reigning sovereigns and three crown princes, seventy-four republican heads of state or government—including the presidents of nations as disparate as Afghanistan, France, Germany, Iran, Israel, Taiwan, the United States, and Zimbabwe[14]—and the secretary-general of the United Nations.

However it was perhaps not so much the counsels of the mighty that the gathering electors took to heart so much as the spontaneous cries and placards of humble mourners proclaiming *"Santo subito!"* ("Saint immediately!") that called for the deceased pontiff to be raised to the glory of the altars. While some members of the College of Cardinals hastened to pander to the sentiment of the crowds by relating fantastic stories of the late pope's alleged thaumaturgic abilities—Cardinal Francesco Marchisano, archpriest of the Vatican Basilica, told one astonished congregation of mourners about a previously unmentioned healing of a throat condition that had left him unable to speak after John Paul touched the affected area—most, while mourning the lost of their leader, were also preoccupied with identifying who among them might be *papabile* now that they were not only free to indulge such speculations but were positively commanded to do so by their electoral charge.

In Vatican circles, openly aspiring to the papacy is usually adjudged to be fatal to one's career, but it seemed that to even be considered *papabile* while Pope John Paul II continued to reign proved to be a literal death sentence. Until 2002, most observers listed as the top *papabili* two non-Italians whom the pontiff had brought into the central administration of the Church after distinguished careers in pastoral work in the Third World: the Brazilian cardinal Lucas Moreira Neves and the Vietnamese cardinal François-Xavier Nguyên van Thuân. Neves was born into a modest family descended from African slaves. Joining the Dominican order, he carried an extensive pastoral ministry to students, intellectuals, and artists, until he was appointed a bishop. Brought to Rome by Paul VI in 1974, he then spent over a decade in the central administration of the Church before John Paul II sent him back home as archbishop of São Salvador da Bahia and primate of Brazil in 1987, elevating him to the cardinalate the following year. Given the cardinal's conservative doctrinal and political views, the move was widely interpreted as placing additional pressure on the progressive wing of the Latin American Church. In 1998, he returned to Rome as head of the powerful Congregation for Bishops. In the conclave, Neves would have represented the choice of the conservative bloc.

The apparent contrast between Neves and Nguyên van Thuân could not have been starker. In contrast to his Brazilian confrère's humble origins, Nguyên van Thuân was born into one of Vietnam's oldest and most prominent Catholic families. Although the family numbered among its ancestors several martyrs from the period of the anti-Christian persecutions, by the time young François-Xavier Nguyên van Thuân was born in the then imperial capital of Huê, the family's status was unassailable. His uncles included the Vietnamese nationalist leader Ngo dinh Diem, who became the first president of the Republic of Vietnam, and Pierre-Martin Ngo dinh Thuc, first archbishop of Huê. After advanced studies in Rome, he was successively a seminary professor and rector and vicar general of his native diocese, before being appointed bishop of Nha Trang at the age of thirty-eight. The eight years of his episcopate in Nha Trang were marked with an energetic implementation of the Second Vatican Council's reforms and a dynamic evangelization program. In 1975, as South Vietnam was collapsing under the Communist North Vietnamese invasion, Paul VI promoted him to be coadjutor archbishop of Saigon. The Communist regime refused to allow him to occupy his see and, instead, jailed him, first in the so-called re-education camps and then for nine years in isolation in an underground cell. Released from his imprisonment in 1988, he was still prevented from assuming his archbishopric and detained under house arrest in the north of the country. In 1991, he was expelled by the regime as a *persona non grata* and took up residence in Rome. In 1994, Pope John Paul II appointed him vice-president of the Pontifical Council for Justice and Peace, promoting him to the presidency in 1998. In this capacity, he traveled extensively promoting the Church's social doctrine, particularly advocating the link between the political and the socioeconomic in human rights, as well as preaching a simple spirituality.[15] John Paul II chose him to preach the Lenten retreat for the cardinals and bishops of the Roman Curia during the Jubilee Year 2000. Nguyên van Thuân's unassuming demeanor and simple lifestyle masked both a sharp mind—he spoke nearly a dozen languages fluently—and an open theological vision that combined his personal taste for traditional devotional piety with progressive views on the Church's outreach to the world. In the conclave, he would have received support both from cardinals who admired his heroic sufferings and from those who hold the view that doctrinal orthodoxy has been overemphasized in recent years at the expense of evangelization.

By a strange providence, both Neves and Nguyên van Thuân died within a week of each other in September 2002, leaving a weakened field of candidates in the center whose previously unfamiliar names were tossed around by pundits in the now massive media coverage, including:

Dionigi Tettamanzi. Elevated to the archbishopric of Milan in 2002 in succession to the retiring Carlo Maria Martini, Tettamanzi headed Europe's largest diocese. While his scholarly writings have adhered closely to official teachings, including those on contraception and other sexual questions, Tettamanzi was reputed to have been the driving force behind John Paul II's 1993 encyclical letter *Veritatis splendor,* which condemned, in broad strokes, public theological dissent, moral relativism, and certain modern schools of ethics. Nevertheless, the cardinal had more recently also shown evidence of a greater nuance and understanding in his thought than many of his colleagues. For example, in condemning "licentious" sexual behavior, Tettamanzi explicitly expressed the understanding that the Church cannot have a separate set of criteria for judging the morality of heterosexual and homosexual activity. While hardly earthshaking, that view is more progressive than is usually expected from most of his Italian peers. On the other hand, since his appointment to Milan, Tettamanzi seemed— at least in the eyes of many—to have been openly campaigning for the papal office. Having proven his progressive *bona fides* during his earlier period in Genoa—while archbishop of the Ligurian city, he hosted the activist Sant'Egidio Community as well as welcoming the anti-globalization protesters who tried to disrupt the G8 summit—he now went out of his way to cultivate ties with the new conservative ecclesial movements within the Church that were beloved of Pope John Paul. In his first year in the Ambrosian See alone, Tettamanzi wrote a treatise in favor of the controversial canonization of the founder of Opus Dei, Monsignor Josemaría Escrivá, participated in conferences of the Communion and Liberation and the Focolare movements, and invited Catholic Action to his cathedral. On the eve of the Second Gulf War, he packed the Milan Duomo for a candlelit peace vigil. As one prelate told the Italian newsweekly *Espresso,* Tettamanzi "seem[ed] like a Christian Democrat during an election campaign— neither too far to the right nor too far to the left—a perfect centrist building a successful candidacy."[16] Ultimately, that political savvy proved to be too slick for the taste of his fellow cardinals.

Severino Poletto. The archbishop of Turin enjoyed a particularly close relationship to the influential cardinal secretary of state, Angelo Sodano, having served as bishop of the latter's hometown of Asti from 1989 to 1999, when he was promoted to his present see. While not particularly distinguished or well known—his career before being elevated, in 1980, to the episcopate of his small home diocese of Fossano was spent almost entirely in pastoral ministries—he had a long career in pastoral ministry and was one of the few Italians of the right age and experience entering the conclave, so his name surfaced in many discussions.

Angelo Scola. Created a cardinal by Pope John Paul II in the pontiff's last consistory, in October 2003, the patriarch of Venice came to the meetings of the cardinals already enjoying a certain international renown within theological circles, mostly for his nearly two decades of editorial work with the influential Italian edition of the theological review *Communio*, co-founded by Joseph Ratzinger and Hans Urs von Balthasar. Other than his brief stint in the early 1990s as bishop of Grosseto, Scola's career until his appointment to Venice in 2002 had been almost entirely academic, having taught, at various intervals, political philosophy, fundamental moral theology, Christian anthropology, and contemporary Christology. His scholarly work overall was judged to be more synthetic than original, his best-known work being a brief introduction to the thought of Balthasar.[17] Although he was an experienced Italian of approximately the right age and centrist orientation, Scola's possible candidacy raised some concerns in the mind of electors. A native of the Archdiocese of Milan, Scola was ordained a priest for the Diocese of Teramo in the Marches—although he never served there—for reasons that have never been adequately explained. The fact alone would not have been remarked upon had it not been for the lengths that Scola went to hide it in the mid-1990s. He was also an active collaborator with the Communion and Liberation movement, which unnerved many more theologically progressive confrères.

Francis Arinze. The Nigerian cardinal prefect of the Congregation for Divine Worship and the Discipline of the Sacraments was well known to his confrères, having been a fixture in the Roman Curia throughout almost John Paul II's entire pontificate. The son of an Ibo chieftain, he was baptized at the age of nine by Cyprian Michael Iwene Tansi, a Nigerian monk of the Cistercian order who was beatified by Pope John Paul II in 1998—in part as a result of Arinze's lobbying. While he was highly regarded for both his intellect—his pioneering dissertation, *Ibo Sacrifice as an Introduction to the Catechesis of Holy Mass*, anticipated later developments in inculturation and contextualization of the Christian message—and his personal piety, Vatican insiders had long remarked about Arinze's lack of administrative capacity, to put it charitably. Progressive in certain matters such as inculturation, Arinze also excited some conservatives— including those who have followed his frequent appearances on the Eternal Word Television Network cable broadcasts of the reactionary Mother Angelica—with his traditional doctrinal stances. He defined himself closely with John Paul II and had even been quoted as saying: "Where does Rome stand? There I stand." As a consequence, his views on issues such as homosexuality and academic freedom were certainly not to the liking of Western liberals. Arinze's emergence as a possible *papabile* caused some excitement in the media, but the only real chance he stood would have been if a deadlocked electoral college solved its dilemma by choosing form over substance.

Christoph Schönborn. Although he was, in many respects, arguably the most qualified candidate for the papal office, his young age—born in 1945, he was the second youngest member of the College of Cardinals—essentially disqualified the archbishop of Vienna unless the electors had been willing to break with their historical preference to follow long pontificates with shorter ones in order to give the Church a pause to take stock of the legacy. Of course, the momentum of John XXIII's pontificate should have shattered traditional notions of the utility of "transitional papacies." Schönborn's status as the only nobleman in the college was also something of a handicap given the democratic mores espoused by the post–Vatican II Church, at least with respect to the institutional hostility that has developed against the aristocrats who formerly filled the papal court.[18] All of this aside, Schönborn is a gifted scholar and theologian—in addition to numerous academic publications, he served as secretary of the commission that prepared the *Catechism of the Catholic Church*—and a man with a wide culture. A Dominican friar, he also enjoys a reputation for personal piety. His effective leadership of the Church in Austria after he assumed the See of Vienna from his disgraced predecessor, Cardinal Hans Hermann Groër, speaks well of his pastoral qualities. Even if he did not fare well in the conclave after John Paul's death, he may be *papabile* in the next conclave.

The lack of obvious frontrunners—to say nothing of any inspired qualities— among this group of five possible *papabili* or among other names mentioned in the popular press, left the electors at a loss as they gathered to bid their final farewell to John Paul II.

Benedictus Qui Venit in Nomine Domini

During the *sede vacante*, the period of vacancy between the death of one pope and the election of his successor, the Holy See is in a juridical state of suspended animation, as it were. The apostolic constitution *Universi Dominici gregis* stipulates that "the government of the Church is entrusted to the College of Cardinals solely for the dispatch of ordinary business and of matters that cannot be postponed and for the preparation of everything necessary for the election of the new Pope" (n. 2). Within these limits, the members of the College carry out their charge through meetings called "general congregations," which must be attended by all cardinals who are not otherwise impeded once they have been notified of the death of the pontiff, where decisions are made by majority vote. The legislation gives the presidency of these congregations to the dean of the College of Cardinals, a position which, since the 2002 retirement to his native Benin of Cardinal Bernardin Gantin, had been held by Cardinal Joseph Ratzinger.

Thus it was that in April 2005, the prefect of the Congregation for the Doctrine of the Faith found himself presiding over meetings and ceremonies that were the focus of unprecedented global media coverage during those days. While Ratzinger had certainly been the focus of not inconsiderable controversy during John Paul II's papacy as the deceased pontiff's theological enforcer for nearly a quarter of a century, cracking down on theologians and others who strayed beyond the bounds of what Rome viewed as doctrinal orthodoxy, he was generally regarded as shy and retiring by those who knew him. A professional academic theologian before Pope Paul VI summoned him from his university chair and appointed him archbishop of Munich in 1977, elevating him just three months later to the cardinalate, Ratzinger lived frugally just outside St. Peter's Square in a modest apartment just over a major bus stop and generally walked across the square to work. His chief diversions, other than his books, were his piano—he favored Mozart—and his occasional forays to a nearby restaurant that served Germanic fare, the Cantina Tirolese. Although he may have perhaps grown accustomed over the years to controversy that surrounded the discharge of his official duties, he nonetheless never seemed to have bothered to adapt his message to the fashions of the day, continuing to speak with the freedom of a tenured scholar. Just one day before John Paul died, Ratzinger traveled to the ancient Benedictine Monastery of St. Scholastica in Subiaco to honor a speaking engagement he had accepted some time earlier. In his lecture, entitled "Europe's Crisis of Culture," the German cardinal lamented that "in Europe a culture has developed that constitutes the absolutely most radical contradiction not only of Christianity, but of the religious and moral traditions of humanity." After criticizing a series of social and political developments—including the twin failures of the European Union's Constitutional Charter to mention God and to acknowledge the Christian roots of the continent's culture—he concluded:

> Above all, that of which we are in need at this moment in history are men who, through an enlightened and lived faith, render God credible in this world. The negative testimony of Christians who speak about God and live against him, has darkened God's image and opened the door to disbelief. We need men who have their gaze directed to God, to understand true humanity. We need men whose intellects are enlightened by the light of God, and whose hearts God opens, so that their intellects can speak to the intellects of others, and so that their hearts are able to open up to the hearts of others. Only through men who have been touched by God, can God come near to men. We need men like Benedict of Norcia, who at a time of dissipation and decadence, plunged into the most profound solitude, succeeding, after all the purifications he had to suffer, to ascend again to the light, to return and to found Montecassino, the city on the mountain that, with so many ruins, gathered together the forces from which a new world was formed.

As one of the dean's responsibilities was to preside at the deceased pope's funeral, many speculated that he might use the occasion to rally those cardinals who shared his worldview by sending messages in his homily about the qualities requisite for a successor of a pontiff that some were already hailing as "John Paul the Great." Instead, he surprised many on that windy Friday morning by delivering less a theological *tour de force*—which would have perhaps gone right over the heads if not directly in and out of the ears of the hundreds of thousands who crammed the *piazza*—and more of an impassioned *cris de coeur* for his friend who had been the world's pope:

> None of us can ever forget how in that last Easter Sunday of his life, the Holy Father, marked by suffering, came once more to the window of the Apostolic Palace and one last time gave his blessing *Urbi et Orbi*. We can be sure that our beloved Pope is standing today at the window of the Father's house, that he sees us and blesses us. Yes, bless us, Holy Father. We entrust your dear soul to the Mother of God, your Mother, who guided you each day and who will guide you now to the eternal glory of her Son, our Lord Jesus Christ. Amen!

Perhaps it was listening to this message and perhaps for the first time hearing what they perceived to be the soul of a pastor rather than the voice of a school-master, the cardinals seated in a semi-circle around Ratzinger began to wonder if he might not be the *papabile* for whom they were looking, that perhaps there was more to him than the fearsome reputation he had both within and without the Church. And whether intentionally or not, Ratzinger the "grand elector" slowly became Ratzinger the candidate as the indomitable dean continued over the course of the days leading up to the April 18 opening of the conclave to strike all the right chords, constantly reminding his confrères both of the legacy of the deceased pontiff that was now entrusted to them and of the challenges that it—and the Church—faced.

On the very morning of the conclave, as the 115 electors gathered in St. Peter's Basilica to concelebrate the Mass "for the election of the Roman Pontiff, their dean made clear what he thought their duty was. Choosing as his point of departure the second verse of the sixty-first chapter of the book of the prophet Isaiah— "to proclaim the year of the Lord's favor, and the day of vengeance of our God"—Ratzinger sketched out a panorama of the dangers that he saw confronting the Church and the world:

> How many winds of doctrine we have known in these last decades, how many ideological currents, how many fashions of thought? The small boat of thought of many Christians has often remained agitated by the waves, tossed from one extreme to the other: from Marxism to liberalism, to libertinism; from collectivism to

radical individualism; from atheism to a vague religious mysticism; from agnosticism to syncretism, etc.

Every day new sects are born and we see realized what St. Paul says on the deception of men, on the cunning that tends to lead into error (cf. Ephesians 4:14). To have a clear faith, according to the creed of the Church, is often labeled as fundamentalism. While relativism, that is, allowing oneself to be carried about with every wind of "doctrine," seems to be the only attitude that is fashionable. A dictatorship of relativism is being constituted that recognizes nothing as absolute and which only leaves the "I" and its whims as the ultimate measure.

However, rather than end on a note of pessimism, he offered his brethren both a challenge and what, under the circumstances, both he and they were disposed to see as a hope:

We have another measure: the Son of God, true man. He is the measure of true humanism. "Adult" is not a faith that follows the waves in fashion and the latest novelty. Adult and mature is a faith profoundly rooted in friendship with Christ. This friendship opens us to all that is good and gives us the measure to discern between what is true and what is false, between deceit and truth.

We must mature in this adult faith; we must lead the flock of Christ to this faith. And this faith, the only faith, creates unity and takes place in charity. St. Paul offers us a beautiful phrase, in opposition to the continual ups and downs of those who are like children tossed by the waves, to bring about truth in charity, as fundamental formula of Christian existence. Truth and charity coincide in Christ. In the measure that we come close to Christ, also in our life, truth and charity are fused. Charity without truth would be blind; truth without charity would be like "a clanging cymbal" (1 Corinthians 13:1).

By the time he concluded by exhorting the electors to "ask our Lord insistently that, after the great gift of Pope John Paul II, he will again give us a pastor according to his heart, a pastor who will lead us to knowledge of Christ, to his love, to true joy," many of them had already concluded that their dean was precisely that pastor to whom they should entrust John Paul's legacy.

In fact, enough of them signaled that conviction on the first ballot that very afternoon—47 of them, according to the notes that one cardinal subsequently leaked to an Italian journalist and generally confirmed by other cardinals—that Ratzinger, quickly surpassed the rest of the field of more than thirty prelates who received votes. On the following morning, when the second ballot was taken, the dean's candidacy surged forward to 65 votes. In the conclave's third ballot, which followed immediately, Ratzinger received 72 votes, just five shy of the two-thirds majority of needed for election to the papal office and, in any event, a clear majority. Given the late John Paul II's tinkering with the electoral conven-

tions discussed earlier in this book, the rest of the conclave—including a progressive group that had tried unsuccessfully to rally opposition to Ratzinger
around either the retired archbishop of Milan, Cardinal Carlo Maria Martini, or
the archbishop of Buenos Aires, Jorge Mario Bergoglio—gave in to the inevitable and, after the midday break for lunch and the obligatory Mediterranean
siesta, threw their support behind the majority consensus.[19]

Ratzinger himself, speaking to a group of pilgrims from his native Germany,
subsequently related his experience of the conclave:

> As the voting process gradually showed me that the guillotine, so to speak, was to
> fall on me, my head began to spin. I was convinced that I had done my life's work
> and that I could hope to end my days in tranquility. With profound conviction I
> said to the Lord: "Do not do this to me! You have younger and more talented
> people who are able to face this great task with a completely different kind of
> approach and strength." Then I was deeply touched by a brief letter that had been
> written to me by one of my fellow members of the College of Cardinals. He
> reminded me that on the occasion of the mass for John Paul II, I had centered the
> homily, using the Gospel as my point of departure, on what the Lord said to Peter
> at the lake of Gennesaret: follow me! I had explained how Karol Wojtyla had
> always received anew this call from the Lord, and how he had always needed to
> renounce much and say simply: "Yes, I will follow you, even if you lead me where
> I would not have wished to go." This cardinal wrote to me: "If the Lord now says
> to you 'follow me,' remember what you preached. Do not refuse! Be obedient,
> just as you spoke of our great pope who has returned to the house of the Father."
> This moved me deeply. The ways of the Lord are not comfortable, but we are not
> created for comfort, but for great things, for the sake of the good. So, in the end,
> I could do nothing other than say yes.

Barely twenty-four hours after the cardinals had entered their enclosure, white
smoke arose from the chimney of the Sistine Chapel to announce the election of
the 262nd successor to St. Peter. A short while later, the protodeacon of the Holy
Roman Church, Chilean Cardinal Jorge Arturo Medina Estévez emerged on the
center balcony of St. Peter's Basilica and, in a break with tradition, addressed the
massive crowd in the square as his "dearest brothers and sisters" in Italian, Spanish,
French, German and English—each language eliciting cheers from the international assembly—before continuing with the traditional announcement in Latin:

> *Annuntio vobis gaudium magnum; habemus Papam: Eminentissimum ac*
> *Reverendissimum Dominum, Dominum Josephum Sanctae Romanae Ecclesiae*
> *Cardinalem Ratzinger qui sibi nomen imposuit Benedictum XVI . . .* I announce
> to you a great joy; We have a Pope: The most eminent and most reverend Lord,
> Lord Joseph, Cardinal of the Holy Roman Church Ratzinger, who takes to him-
> self the name Benedict XVI.

In his first words to the enthused crowds, the new pontiff was characteristically self-effacing: "After the great Pope John Paul II, the Cardinals have elected me, a simple and humble laborer in the vineyard of the Lord." However, in the choice of his name, the new pope also sent a signal of his ambitions, noticed by those who looked up the lecture he had given on the eve of John Paul's passing: "We need men like Benedict of Norcia, who at a time of dissipation and decadence, plunged into the most profound solitude, succeeding, after all the purifications he had to suffer, to ascend again to the light, to return and to found Montecassino, the city on the mountain that, with so many ruins, gathered together the forces from which a new world was formed."

Towards the Future

On the very morrow of his election, Benedict XVI again faced the electors who had thrust him on the papal throne and addressed them—in Latin no less—assuring them that "it is on this path, taken by my Venerable Predecessors, that I also intend to set out, with the sole concern of proclaiming the living presence of Christ to the whole world" and pledging to "have before my eyes in particular the testimony of Pope John Paul II" who left "a Church that is more courageous, freer, more youthful." What was not mentioned were the questions that John Paul II, despite his impressive list of accomplishments, did not bequeath his successor as settled.

Hierarchical communion. One of the most important contributions of Catholic social doctrine to modern political discourse has been the articulation of the principle of *subsidiarity*. Although the concept has a long history in the natural law tradition, it was first given its modern formulation in Pope Pius XI's 1931 encyclical letter on the social order, *Quadragesimo anno,* and reiterated by each one of his successors, including John Paul II, who defined it concisely in his 1991 social encyclical, *Centesimus annus*: "A community of a higher order should not interfere in the internal life of a community of a lower order, depriving the latter of its functions, but rather should support it in case of need and help to coordinate its activity with the activities of the rest of society, always with a view to the common good" (n. 48). The theological understanding is that just as the Creator entrusted some of the exercise of authority to mortal creatures, each according to his or her nature and capacity, so too this mode of governance ought to be followed in social life.

While the magisterium is replete with examples of how this principle ought to be applied to sociopolitical institutions—the *Catechism of the Catholic Church,* for example, declares that it "is opposed to all forms of collectivism sets limits for state intervention . . . aims at harmonizing the relationships between individuals and societies . . . tends toward the establishment of true international order" (n. 1885)—it has been uniquely silent about its application to the social institution that is the Church itself. If anything, modern advances in communications have facilitated a centralization of decision making unprecedented in the history of the Church as the reigning pope and his closest collaborators in the Roman Curia have availed themselves of the possibilities of reaching into every aspect of the life of local churches. This phenomenon has been observed and much debated by eminent theologians, who, depending on their viewpoint, see it either as a grace or a curse. In either case, there has been an undeniable increase in effective government from the center.

So noticeable is the phenomenon that some bishops have even spoken out on the subject, as retired San Francisco archbishop John R. Quinn did in a critical 1996 lecture at Campion Hall, Oxford, which was subsequently published in book form.[20] Those who share Quinn's views as well as those who differ with them, like the Jesuit theologian Avery Dulles, later a cardinal,[21] differ on the fundamental tension built into the Second Vatican Council's formulation of the principle of *collegiality,* or shared responsibility, between the pope and bishops contained in the Dogmatic Constitution on the Church *Lumen Gentium:*

> This collegial union is apparent also in the mutual relations of the individual bishops with particular churches and with the universal Church. The Roman Pontiff, as the successor of Peter, is the perpetual and visible principle and foundation of unity of both the bishops and of the faithful. The individual bishops, however, are the visible principle and foundation of unity in their particular churches, fashioned after the model of the universal Church, in and from which churches comes into being the one and only Catholic Church. For this reason the individual bishops represent each his own church, but all of them together and with the Pope represent the entire Church in the bond of peace, love and unity. The individual bishops, who are placed in charge of particular churches, exercise their pastoral government over the portion of the People of God committed to their care, and not over other churches nor over the universal Church. But each of them, as a member of the episcopal college and legitimate successor of the apostles, is obliged by Christ's institution and command to be solicitous for the whole Church, and this solicitude, though it is not exercised by an act of jurisdiction, contributes greatly to the advantage of the universal Church. For it is the duty of all bishops to promote and to safeguard the unity of faith and the discipline common to the whole Church, to instruct the faithful to love for the whole mystical body of Christ, especially for its poor and sorrowing members and for those who are suffering persecution for justice's sake, and finally to promote every activity that is of interest to the whole Church, especially that the faith may take increase and the light of full truth appear to all men. And this also is important, that by governing well

their own church as a portion of the universal Church, they themselves are effectively contributing to the welfare of the whole Mystical Body, which is also the body of the churches. (n. 23)

How this hierarchical communion, eloquently described in theory by the council, is to be achieved in concrete remains one of the major issues that Pope Benedict will have to contend with. While some institutions have been established since Vatican II, most noticeably the worldwide Synod of Bishops and the national conferences of bishops, they have proven less than fully satisfactory. The meetings of the Synod of Bishops have often been described, even by the synod's defenders, as little better than expensive, orchestrated kaffeeklatsches. While, on the day after his election, Benedict was almost constrained to confirm his predecessor's summoning of an Ordinary Assembly of the Synod of Bishops, slated for October 2005 with the rather prolix theme of "The Eucharist, Source and Summit of the Life and Mission of the Church," it remains to be seen if he can or will reinvigorate the institution. Likewise, the national bishops' conferences have often degenerated into bureaucracies that have only added another layer to the Church's administrative structure—an observation made rather pointedly by Cardinal Ratzinger when he was prefect of the Congregation for the Doctrine of the Faith.

Less noticed than the tensions between papal authority and that of the bishops—but no less real—has been the concentration of power in the hands of local bishops at the expense of collaboration with their priests, especially with the post–Vatican II disappearance of some of the older institutional checks on the exercise of power by bishops. And, as recent struggles in the aftermath of the 2002 clergy sexual abuse scandals showed, a similar tension has emerged between some members of the clergy and the laity. In short, Benedict will face the incredible task of trying to satisfy demands for greater subsidiarity in decision making and power sharing while maintaining the fundamental unity of the Roman Church.

Vocations. Even prescinding from the questions of hierarchical communion, the Church, as a global institution, requires significant manpower to carry out its mission.[22] The decline, in both relative and, in some cases, absolute terms, of the numbers of priests as well as of men and women belonging to religious orders has not been without its impact on the Church's ability to meet the ritual and catechetical religious needs of its members, as well as its capacity to undertake missions aimed at addressing social needs.

The decline in numbers is particularly noticeable in the developed countries that were long the strongholds of the institutional Church. And while a number of parallel social phenomena, no doubt, share causal responsibility, the decline since the Second Vatican Council has been dramatic. The year their bishops entered the council halls, Catholics in the United States, for example, were supporting some 4,955 candidates for the priesthood in graduate theological studies, 3,304 seminarians in college-level philosophical studies, and more than 16,572 "minor seminarians" in seminary programs at the high school and junior college levels. These numbers seemed to bode well for the continued growth of a Church where every 711 Catholics were served by a priest. But even before the council adjourned, the bottom had fallen out in the United States. By 1998, enrollment in the theologates, the graduate-level seminaries leading directly to priestly ordination, were down to 3,158 students, of whom 2,359 were candidates aspiring to the diocesan priesthood and 799 were candidates for religious communities. Declines in the enrollment levels at college and high school seminaries are even more dramatic. In 1967–1968, the first year for which national statistics were systematically kept, there were 13,401 college and 15,823 high school seminarians in America. The corresponding figures for 1997–1998 were 1,516 and 853. While part of the decline is attributable to the development of new trends and models in priestly formation, the collapse is nonetheless significant.[23]

Even as the trends have stabilized somewhat in recent years, it remains true that the clergy are an aging population. While the minimum age under canon law for priestly ordination is twenty-five, fewer than 13 percent of seminary students are presently under that age, while 30 percent are between twenty-five and twenty-nine, 25 percent between thirty and thirty-four, and 15 percent between thirty-five and thirty-nine, and an unprecedented 17 percent are over the age of forty. In contrast, less than twenty years ago, a 1986 study found that over 70 percent of seminary students were under the age of thirty. In the year 2000, the average age of diocesan priests in active ministry in the United States was fifty-nine, while the average age of priests who were members of religious orders was sixty-three. Almost 45 percent of priests in the United States are older than fifty-five, while barely 5 percent are under thirty-four. Between 1995 and 1999, there were 1,247 ordinations of diocesan priests in the United States. During the same period, there were 2,654 deaths and resignations from the priesthood.

The comparable figures from other countries show similar trends. With the exception of Poland, the number of priests has declined in almost every European country over the last three decades. A study released in 1992, the year that Pope John Paul II published his apostolic exhortation on priestly vocations and formation, *Pastores dabo vobis*, found that fully one-third of the parishes in Europe were without a resident priest. And while there have been significant positive trends in the number of priestly vocations in developing countries, the growth has not kept pace with the Church's expansion. Consequently, in sub-Saharan Africa, the faithful went from one priest for every 3,251 Catholics in

1978 to one for every 4,500 at the present moment. Meanwhile, the Church in
Latin America, once considered a solidly Catholic territory, must contend not
only with the increased activities of Protestant evangelical churches and new
sects but also with a ratio of over 7,000 members of the faithful to each priest.

Nor is the challenge one of quantity alone. A qualitative problem has arisen
that has yet to be addressed by many Church leaders. As one cynic has put it, the
crisis in vocations has led many bishops and religious superiors to go from the
selective Biblical model of "many are called, few are chosen" (Matthew 22:14) to
the pragmatic one of "few are called, all are chosen." In a 1972 report, *The Theological Formation of Future Priests*, the Vatican's Sacred Congregation for Catholic Education concluded:

> The priests of tomorrow will also have to exercise their ministry among people
> who are more adult, more critical, and better informed, immersed in a world of
> ideological pluralism where Christianity is exposed to many interpretations and
> suspicions common to a culture becoming ever more alien to the faith. It will be
> impossible for priests to serve the faith and the ecclesial community effectively with-
> out sound theological formation begun in the seminary and carried on beyond.

John Paul II took up this point in *Pastores dabo vobis* when he urged seminaries "to oppose firmly the tendency to play down the seriousness of studies and
the commitment to them" (n. 56). Notwithstanding the pontiff's counsel, such
research as has been conducted on the subject has shown that at a time when the
educational level of the Catholic laity in the developed world has gone up, the
academic and pastoral preparation of their remaining priests have declined.[24]
Pope Benedict's initial response to this has included the ordering of a visitation
of each of the 229 seminaries in the United States to ascertain the doctrinal
orthodoxy of their teaching.

Clergy scandals. If declining numbers in its ranks and inferior educational
preparation of new recruits were not bad enough—to say nothing of doctrinal
conservatives' concerns about the purity of their training—the Catholic clergy
have been rocked by revelations of literally thousands of cases of alleged sexual
misconduct, including the abuse of minors. In this respect the last decade of the
twentieth century has not been kind to the Church in the United States. The
year 1990 saw the resignation of an archbishop after his relationship with a woman
was uncovered. The year 1995 saw the first death of a bishop known to have died
from complications of AIDS. The year 1999 saw the resignation of another bishop
amid sordid allegations of embezzlement, misappropriation of funds, and the
alleged sexual "enslavement" of a priest.

However, all of this was but a prelude to what the noted priest commentator
Richard John Neuhaus called "the Great Lenten Humiliation of 2002."[25] Begin-

ning with a Pulitzer Prize–winning investigative series in the *Boston Globe* on a seemingly routine pattern of the Boston archdiocese's covering up allegations of the sexual abuse of minors by priests, the scandal grew into a media firestorm as revelations began hitting in diocese after diocese across the United States. Before the attention of the press was diverted by world events, dozens of American bishops were hit by lawsuits and subpoenas, and five bishops, including the cardinal archbishop of Boston, were forced to resign.

Pope John Paul II had to summon the American cardinals as well as the president of the National Conference of Catholic Bishops to an extraordinary meeting at the Vatican. Later, meeting in Dallas, Texas, under an unprecedented glare of protesters and media coverage, the American bishops were cowed into adopting a retroactive policy of "zero tolerance" for sexual offenders that, once applied, resulted in yet another blow to the morale of the clergy since it did nothing to punish the bishops and chancery officials who, even more grievously, protected—or at least remained willfully ignorant—of serial abusers. The only ecclesiastical "casualty" of scandal seems to be the hapless Cardinal Bernard Francis Law, former archbishop of Boston, who resigned under intense public pressure (although the prelate was subsequently "rehabilitated" by John Paul II and appointed archpriest of the Basilica of St. Mary Major in Rome, in which role he presided—not without controversy—at one of the official *Novemdiales* Masses following the pontiff's death). No other bishop, even ones with records more grievous than the Boston prelate's, have been forced out. More worrying is the fact that almost no attention has been paid to the "middle management"— the vicars general, chancellors, and other diocesan officials—who were often even more directly involved in the failure to deal with the abuse than the bishops. It is from the very ranks of this middle tier of diocesan hierarchies that the next generation of bishops will be drawn.

While the Church in the United States has been the focus of the media's attention, similar scandals have rocked local churches in other countries. In 1995, amid accusations that he had sexually abused minors, the cardinal archbishop of Vienna resigned the pastoral government of his diocese, although he refused to admit guilt. The following year, however, when an internal Church investigation verified the charges, he was asked by John Paul II to leave the country and refrain from the exercise of any of his ecclesiastical prerogatives. In 2002, while the scandal was causing upheaval in the American church, the archbishop of Poznan, Poland, a former chamberlain in the Vatican of Pope John Paul II, was forced to resign after allegations of misconduct with seminarians.

Despite the uncovering of abuses worldwide, some ranking churchmen persisted in blaming the media for exaggerating the sexual scandals. In an interview with Reuters on the eve of the celebration of Pope John Paul II's silver jubilee in the papacy, no less a figure than the pontiff's secretary of state, Cardinal Angelo Sodano, insisted that "the scandals in the United States received disproportionate attention from the media" and, incredibly, refused to dismiss the notion that the whole affair was a plot to discredit the Church: "We don't have evidence of this, but I know that many people have thought this."

Pope Benedict will not only need to deal with sexual abuse scandals—both those present and those that have yet to be uncovered—but he will need to confront the root causes of the problem with a commitment to forthright diagnosis and treatment. Catholic thinkers have differed in their analyses of the problem, some attributing it to obligatory clerical celibacy,[26] others to lack of fidelity to the Church's discipline. Whether one explanation or the other is correct—or both, for that matter—forceful action will be expected. Of course, Benedict knows all of this: As prefect of the Congregation for the Doctrine of the Faith, it was his responsibility to oversee the dismissal from the clerical state of priests found to have committed the abuses. How this experience will inform his subsequent action remains to be seen.

Laity. Aside from the harm caused to individual victims, the sexual abuse scandal has affected both the identity and morale of the clergy as well as the trust of members of the laity in the clerical leadership. The Second Vatican Council's decree on the laity, *Apostolicam actuositatem,* declared that "the laity likewise share in the priestly, prophetic, and royal office of Christ and therefore have their own share in the mission of the whole people of God in the Church and in the world" (n. 2). However, as the recent disputes over how to deal with the clergy sexual abuse scandals showed, there remains a gap between the ideal and the actual in terms of how to share responsibilities within the Church between the clergy and the laity.

Former Oklahoma governor Frank Keating, who was appointed by the American bishops to chair the advisory panel overseeing the new National Office of Child and Youth Protection, resigned after only a year, angrily comparing the prelates to "La Cosa Nostra" and declaring: "I have seen an underside that I never knew existed. I have not had my faith questioned, but I certainly have concluded that a number of serious officials in my faith have very clay feet. That is disappointing and educational, but it's a fact." While most Catholics would probably not go as far as the hard-hitting politician, the confidence of many members of the faithful in their pastors will need to be strengthened during Benedict's pontificate if the breach is not to become irreparable.

Contraception. Perhaps no other point of the Church's moral teaching elicits such visceral reactions, pro and con, from rank-and-file Catholics as its ban on contraception. While the Catholic theological doctrine on the subject dates at least back as far as the third century,[27] it was only in 1931 that, partly in response to the decision of the Anglican bishops meeting in their Lambeth Conference the preceding year to allow contraception, Pope Pius XI explicitly condemned it in his encyclical *Casti connubii*:

> First consideration is due to the offspring, which many have the boldness to call the disagreeable burden of matrimony and which they say is to be carefully avoided by married people not through virtuous continence (which Christian law permits in matrimony when both parties consent) but by frustrating the marriage act. Some justify this criminal abuse on the ground that they are weary of children and wish to gratify their desires without their consequent burden. Others say that they cannot on the one hand remain continent nor on the other can they have children because of the difficulties whether on the part of the mother or on the part of family circumstances.
>
> But no reason, however grave, may be put forward by which anything intrinsically against nature may become conformable to nature and morally good. Since, therefore, the conjugal act is destined primarily by nature for the begetting of children, those who in exercising it deliberately frustrate its natural power and purpose sin against nature and commit a deed which is shameful and intrinsically vicious.
>
> Small wonder, therefore, if Holy Writ bears witness that the Divine Majesty regards with greatest detestation this horrible crime and at times has punished it with death. As St. Augustine notes, "Intercourse even with one's legitimate wife is unlawful and wicked where the conception of the offspring is prevented. Onan, the son of Judah, did this and the Lord killed him for it."
>
> Since, therefore, openly departing from the uninterrupted Christian tradition some recently have judged it possible solemnly to declare another doctrine regarding this question, the Catholic Church, to whom God has entrusted the defense of the integrity and purity of morals, standing erect in the midst of the moral ruin which surrounds her, in order that she may preserve the chastity of the nuptial union from being defiled by this foul stain, raises her voice in token of her divine ambassadorship and through Our mouth proclaims anew: any use whatsoever of matrimony exercised in such a way that the act is deliberately frustrated in its natural power to generate life is an offense against the law of God and of nature, and those who indulge in such are branded with the guilt of a grave sin. (n. 53–56)

In early 1963, Pope John XXIII was persuaded by the Belgian primate, Cardinal Leo-Jozef Suenens, to establish a special papal commission to review the question of contraception in the light of new medical science as well as theological reflection. The commission consisted of two physicians, an economist, an expert on demographics, and two priests, one of whom was a papal diplomat while the other was a sociologist by training. This commission, however, did not have a chance to report its findings before the pontiff died.

During subsequent sessions of Vatican II, a number of bishops tried to open a discussion of the ban within the council, but the subject was removed from the table by Pope Paul VI, who shortly after his election entrusted the study of the question to the special commission, whose membership he expanded by adding nine appointees to join the original six nominated by his predecessor. In 1965, as the council drew to a close, Paul expanded the commission to fifty-eight members. As is well known, the pope rejected the conclusion of the majority of the commission in his encyclical *Humanae vitae*, published June 25, 1968. In his letter, Paul VI reaffirmed the line taken by Pius XI and confirmed by Pius XII:

> Therefore We base Our words on the first principles of a human and Christian doctrine of marriage when We are obliged once more to declare that the direct interruption of the generative process already begun and, above all, all direct abortion, even for therapeutic reasons, are to be absolutely excluded as lawful means of regulating the number of children. Equally to be condemned, as the magisterium of the Church has affirmed on many occasions, is direct sterilization, whether of the man or of the woman, whether permanent or temporary.
>
> Similarly excluded is any action which either before, at the moment of, or after sexual intercourse, is specifically intended to prevent procreation—whether as an end or as a means.
>
> Neither is it valid to argue, as a justification for sexual intercourse which is deliberately contraceptive, that a lesser evil is to be preferred to a greater one, or that such intercourse would merge with procreative acts of past and future to form a single entity, and so be qualified by exactly the same moral goodness as these. Though it is true that sometimes it is lawful to tolerate a lesser moral evil in order to avoid a greater evil or in order to promote a greater good, it is never lawful, even for the gravest reasons, to do evil that good may come of it—In other words, to intend directly something which of its very nature contradicts the moral order, and which must therefore be judged unworthy of man, even though the intention is to protect or promote the welfare of an individual, of a family or of society in general. Consequently, it is a serious error to think that a whole married life of otherwise normal relations can justify sexual intercourse which is deliberately contraceptive and so intrinsically wrong.
>
> The teaching of the Church regarding the proper regulation of birth is a promulgation of the law of God Himself. (n. 10, 14, 20)

Paul's teaching, despite its repeated confirmation by John Paul II, has been a constant source of division. On the theological and ecclesiastical-political levels, both the doctrine's defenders[28] and its critics[29] agree that it is the proxy for a whole host of issues in the post–Vatican II Church. And, on the existential level, as the Dutch theologian Edward Schillebeeckx has noted, "Nowhere is the discrepancy between the official teaching of the Catholic Church and the actual convictions of many believers so great as in the domain of sexuality and marriage. Yet nowhere do faith and life touch each other so closely as in this domain." Whether Benedict XVI will continue to defend the traditional teaching is not in doubt, but his record indicates that he may not do so with the same passion as his predecessor—unlike Karol Wojtyła, Joseph Ratzinger fought different battles in the late 1960s. Nonetheless, the Church's stance on contraception—and the resentment it foments among both Catholics and non-Catholics—will remain an issue he will find impossible to duck as pope.

Women. Even though women serving in the Church's ministries as professed religious outnumber male priests and religious by two to one, the Catholic Church and the Eastern Orthodox Churches remain the only two principal branches of Christianity not to recognize the possibility of their ordination. In the apostolic letter *Ordinatio sacerdotalis* that he published from his hospital bed on May 22, 1994,[30] Pope John Paul II declared:

> Although the teaching that priestly ordination is to be reserved to men alone has been preserved by the constant and universal Tradition of the Church and firmly taught by the Magisterium in its more recent documents, at the present time in some places it is nonetheless considered still open to debate, or the Church's judgment that women are not to be admitted to ordination is considered to have a merely disciplinary force.
>
> Wherefore, in order that all doubt may be removed regarding a matter of great importance, a matter which pertains to the Church's divine constitution itself, in virtue of my ministry of confirming the brethren (cf. Luke 22:32) I declare that the Church has no authority whatsoever to confer priestly ordination on women and that this judgment is to be definitively held by all the Church's faithful. (n. 4)

The following year, in response to some lingering doubts as to the status of this teaching, the Congregation for the Doctrine of the Faith issued an official clarification, dated October 28, 1995, and signed by its then prefect, declaring:

> This teaching requires definitive assent, since, founded on the written Word of God, and from the beginning constantly preserved and applied in the Tradition of the Church, it has been set forth infallibly by the ordinary and universal Magisterium (cf. Second Vatican Council, Dogmatic Constitution on the Church *Lumen Gentium* 25, 2). Thus, in the present circumstances, the Roman Pontiff, exercising his proper office of confirming the brethren (cf. Luke 22:32), has handed on this same teaching by a formal declaration, explicitly stating what is to be held always, everywhere, and by all, as belonging to the deposit of the faith.

While this teaching arouses little controversy in many parts of the Church, including Latin America and the African and Asian countries, which have seen the largest growth in numbers of faithful in recent years, it is a sore point in

Europe and North America, where many members—men as well as women—resent what they perceive to be sexual discrimination. Although any change in the teaching is unlikely in the near future—especially when one considers that the long-sought reunion of the Eastern Orthodox Churches with the Roman See would be irreparably jeopardized by any innovations perceived by the Easterners as "unilateral"—during Benedict's pontificate Rome will have to address with sensitivity the demands of women for greater recognition while simultaneously balancing this concern with its solicitude for the Eastern Churches and the cultural prejudices of non-Western societies.

Divorce (and remarriage). Historically, of all the Christian denominations, the Catholic Church has hewed the strictest line with regard to the indissolubility of marriage, opposing—as evidenced recently in Chile—even the introduction of *civil* divorce. The *Catechism of the Catholic Church*, while conceding that "this unequivocal insistence on the indissolubility of the marriage bond may have left some perplexed and could seem to be a demand impossible to realize" (n. 1615), reaffirms that "the marriage bond has been established by God himself in such a way that a marriage concluded and consummated between baptized persons can never be dissolved. This bond, which results from the free human act of the spouses and their consummation of the marriage, is a reality, henceforth irrevocable, and gives rise to a covenant guaranteed by God's fidelity. The Church does not have the power to contravene this disposition of divine wisdom" (n. 1640). The Church's adherence to this understanding has not been without its costs: The schism of the Church of England from the communion of the Roman See resulted directly from Henry VIII's inability to obtain the dissolution of his marriage with Catherine of Aragon from Pope Clement VII (1523–1534).

In more contemporary times, the divorce rate among Catholics mirrors that of the general population, and the Church has, especially in the decades since the Second Vatican Council, struggled to deal with the phenomenon. The traditional approach has been primarily juridical: Canon law asserts that the Church "after an examination of the situation by the competent ecclesiastical tribunal, can declare the nullity of a marriage, i.e., that the marriage never existed. In this case the contracting parties are free to marry, provided the natural obligations of a previous union are discharged" (*Catechism of the Catholic Church,* n. 1629). This canonical process, coming in the wake of the tragedy of a failed marriage, can often be traumatizing and intrusive. For example, the ecclesiastical tribunal in one United States diocese requires the Catholic seeking an "annulment" of his or her marriage to respond in writing to no fewer than 107 essay questions that probe everything from the petitioner's relationship with his or her former spouse to his or her sexual history to the civil issues related to the divorce. However, without the juridical determination that the collapsed marriage was null and void, the Catholic cannot remarry within the Church. And should he or she remarry outside the Church, he or she, while not exactly excommunicated, is excluded from the sacraments, including receiving communion. In fact, a declaration of the Pontifical Council for Legislative Texts, the office of the Roman Curia responsible for official interpretations of church law, dated June 24, 2000, determined that divorced Catholics who had remarried without obtaining an annulment fell into the category of "those who obstinately persist in manifest grave sin" who should be refused communion. Even if they were to "repent" and agree to refrain from sexual relations with their new spouses, "while their condition as persons who are divorced and remarried is per se manifest, they will be able to receive Eucharistic Communion only *remoto scandalo*," that is, only if "scandal" can be averted.

Two responses have been generally adapted as a result of this strict line from Rome. In some dioceses, especially in the United States, the process for the ecclesiastical trial of the validity of marriages has become virtually automated, with nearly all the petitions for declarations of nullity being granted, often over the well-founded objections of one of the former spouses. The latter was the case after the divorce between Massachusetts congressman Joseph Kennedy and Sheila Rauch Kennedy, who later wrote a devastating account of her experience with the ecclesiastical tribunal in the Archdiocese of Boston, *Shattered Faith: A Woman's Struggle to Stop the Catholic Church from Annulling Her Marriage.*[31] In fact, while American Catholics account for barely 5 percent of the world's Catholics, their ecclesiastical tribunals grant more than 75 percent of annulments in any given year, two-thirds of which are granted on specious "psychological reasons" culled from the essays petitioners are asked to write.[32] The whole process, which at times resembles an assembly line, rather than strengthening the Church's doctrinal stance on marriage, turns it into a farce—an impression reinforced when one considers that the ecclesiastical tribunal of the Diocese of Rome employed more than twenty-five judges to decide fewer than two hundred cases a year, while the tribunal for the Archdiocese of Chicago had two dozen officials handling almost fifteen hundred.[33] Not surprisingly, Cardinal Vincenzo Fagiolo, when he was president of the Pontifical Council for Legislative Texts, called the American annulment process "a grave scandal."[34]

At the opposite end of the spectrum are the ecclesiastical tribunals in more conservative dioceses of the United States and those of almost all the rest of the Catholic world, which adhere to the traditional doctrine and law. In these places, however, while the Church's coherence is preserved, Catholics whose marriages have failed, often through no fault of their own—such as after spousal abuse or abandonment—have little hope for a recourse.

Between these two extremes, Pope Benedict will need to draw on the resources of the Catholic tradition—contrary to both the official line and general
perceptions, the history of Catholic theology reveals a less than monolithic position on marriage and divorce—and the spirit of the Gospels to find a balance
that provides real compassion and hope to many Catholics. Otherwise, both the
lack of understanding and the farcical nature of the annulment process will further undermine the Church's credibility on moral matters.

Ecumenism. The Second Vatican Council, while reaffirming that the "one
Church of Christ…constituted and organized in the world as a society, subsists
in the Catholic Church, which is governed by the successor of Peter and by the
Bishops in communion with him," acknowledged that "many elements of sanc-
tification and of truth are found outside of its visible structure" (Dogmatic Constitution on the Church *Lumen Gentium*, n. 8). Consequently, the council urged
"all the Catholic faithful to recognize the signs of the times and to take an active
and intelligent part in the work of ecumenism" to restore the unity willed by the
Church's founder (Decree on Ecumenism *Unitatis Redintegratio*, n. 4).

While in the heady days following the council many Christians, Catholic and
non-Catholic alike, saw unity as only around the corner, the realities of centuries of division as well as continuing evolution have led to increasing complications that it will be the task of the next Roman pontiff to attempt to reconcile.
The tone of dialogue between the different Christian denominations has vastly
improved in its cordiality and even affection in the ensuing decades, but theological trends and ecclesiastical developments have widened, rather than nar-
rowed, gaps. With regard to Rome's relations with the Anglican Communion
and other Christian denominations arising from the Reformation, differences on
a variety of moral issues—including the ordination of women and homosexuals
and other issues that likewise divide many rank-and-file Catholics from their
hierarchy—have been added to the earlier theological strains. Many observers
often forget that, as facile as compromises might appear with regard to more
progressive tendencies that characterize contemporary Western Christianity, the
theological self-understanding of the Catholic Church places a higher premium
on restoring unity with the Eastern Orthodox Churches; the Vatican Council
declared that "these Churches, although separated from us, yet possess true sacraments and above all, by apostolic succession, the priesthood and the Eucharist, whereby they are linked with us in closest intimacy" (*Unitatis redintegratio*,
n. 15). However, any accommodation of progressives in the West would further retard union with the East. The Vatican acknowledged as much when it
suspended—officially for "consultations" and "reassessment"—the ongoing An-
glican-Roman Catholic International Consultation (ARCIC) in the wake of the
consecration of the openly gay V. Gene Robinson as bishop of New Hampshire

in the Episcopal Church of the United States. On the other hand, most Roman Catholics share greater *cultural* affinities with Western Christians than with their Eastern Orthodox counterparts, any *theological* bonds notwithstanding. Consequently, Benedict inherited a complex balancing act, one to which he pledged his commitment during the Mass he concelebrated with his electors the day after his election:

> The current Successor of Peter feels himself to be personally implicated in this question and is disposed to do all in his power to promote the fundamental cause of ecumenism. In the wake of his predecessors, he is fully determined to cultivate any initiative that may seem appropriate to promote contact and agreement with representatives of the various Churches and ecclesial communities.

Nonetheless, given his theological vision and ecclesiological sensibilities, many observers expect Benedict to dedicate his most energetic efforts to pursuing dialogue with the Eastern Orthodox and Ancient Orthodox Churches. In fact, many of the initial gestures of the new pontificate—including the pope's decision to surmount his papal coat of arms with a bishop's miter rather than a traditional tiara, his adoption of a pallium not used in nearly a thousand years, and his pilgrimage to take custody of the icon of Mary *Salus Populi Romani* in St. Mary Major—were carefully choreographed to evoke the spirit of the first millennium when Rome and its sister churches in the East were in communion.

Church and state. Throughout its history, the Catholic Church has been involved in relations with states. Alone of all the world's religious leaders, the Roman pontiff maintains diplomatic standing in the international community as a sovereign. Presently, the Holy See maintains bilateral diplomatic relations at the ambassadorial level with 174 countries[35] as well as with the European Union and the Sovereign Military Order of Malta, in addition to what is described as "diplomatic relations of a special nature" with the Russian Federation and the Palestinian Liberation Organization, with the permanent exchange of "envoys on special mission with the personal rank of ambassador" in the case of the former. As previously noted, the expansion of the Holy See's international diplomatic presence was one of the significant hallmarks of John Paul II's papacy.

During the first part of the pontificate of John Paul II, the Holy See used these diplomatic ties to assure, insofar as possible, the survival of the Church in Communist countries and, eventually, to contribute to the downfall of the Soviet empire. At the same time, the Vatican's diplomats were often involved, usually in tandem with local Church officials, in assisting the transition to democracy in a number of authoritarian states outside the Iron Curtain. This role continues in a number of countries. For example, it was not by accident that, following the peaceful overthrow of Filipino president Joseph Estrada on January 20, 2001, that his successor, President Gloria Macapagal Arroyo, was sworn in at a Catholic shrine with the apostolic nuncio, Archbishop Antonio Franco, and Manila's Cardinal Sin clearly seen standing behind her. During more recent years, this diplomatic access has been used at multilateral assemblies to stitch together coalitions with the widest assortment of countries on issues such as reproductive rights and women. An example was the alliance of the Holy See, smaller developing countries, and Islamic states at the 1994 United Nations Conference in Cairo on Population and Development.

On the other hand, although papal diplomats would be quick to deny the accusation, the almost single-minded pursuit of diplomatic relations with any country willing to receive a papal envoy has—in part due to the conventions of the diplomatic craft—resulted in less, rather than more, freedom for the Church's emissaries on the world stage, even if it has meant a few alliances of convenience at certain international conferences. During the early years of the Cold War, for example, when diplomatic ties had been broken between the Holy See and all the states of the Communist bloc with the exception of Tito's Yugoslavia, papal envoys were in the forefront of the moral campaign against the totalitarian regimes behind the Iron Curtain. In contrast, the establishment of diplomatic relations with many Islamic states has served to blunt criticism of the pernicious influence of militants, even if few papal diplomats would go as far as Cardinal Roger Etchegaray in his slavish accommodation to Iraqi dictator Saddam Hussein on the eve of the Second Gulf War.

Within some countries, notably the United States, the contribution of the Catholic Church to engendering mass movements against legal abortion can hardly be underestimated. In July 2003, the Holy See published a document on delineating the Church's opposition to the legal recognition of homosexual unions, no doubt with the hope of encouraging a popular movement similar to the one that was organized for the pro-life cause. In other countries, such as Germany, relying on old treaties and concordats, the Church continues to enjoy a close financial relationship with the state.

Nor have the Roman Church's interventions been limited to issues of personal morality. During the pontificate of John Paul II, the Holy See took positions against capital punishment and the use of military force—including the two Gulf Wars and the conflict in the former Yugoslavia—which are difficult to reconcile with traditional Catholic theology's acceptance of the death penalty and the "just war" theory, as witnessed by the writings of the Fathers and the medieval synthesis of St. Thomas Aquinas. In fact, the exaltation of a desire for peace—apparently understood as the absence of armed conflict rather than as the tranquillitas ordinis (the "tranquility of order") espoused by St. Augustine—compromised the Holy See's moral witness against tyranny and terrorism and undermined its credibility with many observers during the period between the terrorist attacks of September 11, 2001, and the beginning of Operation Iraqi Freedom in 2003.[36]

How these entanglements—diplomatic, political, and financial—evolve in increasingly pluralistic global societies will be questions that Pope Benedict will have to begin to formulate a response to. While he has not yet indicated how he will proceed in this regard as pontiff—he has retained, at least temporarily, his predecessor's secretary of state—in one Lenten conference that he gave in 1997, he warned against the temptations of political power:

> The Christian Roman Empire sought very early on to make of the faith a political factor in the unity of the empire. The kingdom of Christ was to have assumed the configuration of a political kingdom, and of such a kingdom's splendor. The weakness of the faith, the earthly fragility of Jesus Christ, was to be sustained by a political or military power. Down through the centuries, this temptation to ensure the faith's survival by power has re-emerged in many different forms, and always the faith has been threatened with suffocation in the embrace of power. The struggle for the freedom of the Church, the struggle so that the kingdom of Jesus is not assimilated into a political form, must be waged in every century. In fact, the price of faith's union with political power is always paid in the end when faith is placed at the service of power and must bow to the latter's criteria.

Islam. Although it did figure prominently in the deliberations of the College of Cardinals—historically intramural issues have always played the predominant role in conclaves—the electors could not entirely ignore the looming shadow of Islam, knowing that certainly whoever emerged from their deliberations would have to contend with the fact that Islam is Christianity's most powerful rival for the hearts and souls of millions of Africans and Asians—and, increasingly, for those of Europeans and Americans. While during the pontificate of John Paul II the diplomatic emissaries of the Holy See have occasionally struck political alliances with Islamist clerics and states—the United Nations International Conference on Population and Development in Cairo in 1994, when the two sides united in opposition to the proposed reproductive programs that included a right to abortion, being the most memorable instance—the future of such marriages of convenience is doubtful, especially as the two missionary faiths meet in increasingly hostile conditions in the developing world as well as in the traditionally Catholic lands of Europe.

Vatican II laid down the basis for Catholicism's dialogue with Islam when it declared:

> The Church regards with esteem also the Moslems. They adore the one God, living and subsisting in Himself; merciful and all-powerful, the Creator of heaven and earth, who has spoken to men; they take pains to submit wholeheartedly to

even His inscrutable decrees, just as Abraham, with whom the faith of Islam takes pleasure in linking itself, submitted to God. Though they do not acknowledge Jesus as God, they revere Him as a prophet. They also honor Mary, His virgin Mother; at times they even call on her with devotion. In addition, they await the day of judgment when God will render their deserts to all those who have been raised up from the dead. Finally, they value the moral life and worship God especially through prayer, almsgiving and fasting. (Declaration on the Relation of the Church with Non-Christian Religions *Nostra Aetate,* n. 3)

Faithful to this mandate, John Paul II adroitly avoided characterizing the conflict between militant Islamists and the West as a part of a global struggle between Islam and Christianity. In fact, not only did his pontificate see the unprecedented expansion of the Vatican's diplomatic relations with Islamic states, but he cultivated the concept of the "Abrahamic religions," a family of faiths embracing Judaism, Christianity, and Islam, braving criticism from traditionalists within the Church who accused him of religious relativism in blurring the uniqueness of the Godhead of Judaism and Christianity—including the then Cardinal Ratzinger who argued that while Judeo-Christianity and Islam have many elements in common, "there is a profound difference in the foundations of the two realities"—as well as from human rights advocates who charged that the Vatican routinely soft-pedals on the question of religious persecution of minorities, including Catholics, in some Islamic states in order to maintain its international alliances. Whether, in the current global context of the West's "war against terror" and Europe's struggles to cope with a growing—and restive—Muslim population, Benedict XVI will be able to maintain (assuming that he is even interested in doing so) his predecessor's course will have significant geopolitical consequences.

Theological pluralism. While Pope John Paul II won admiration for his outreach to believers of other faiths—the Assisi prayers of peace with other Christian as well as Jewish, Muslim, Buddhist, Hindu, and other religious leaders being a case in point—the legacy of his pontificate with regard to differences within the Church is more mixed. The unintended centralization of authority in the Church in the years since the Second Vatican Council has not been without its effects on Catholic theological inquiry. The theologians whose renowned— or notorious, depending on one's doctrinal point of view—works have been formally censured by the Congregation for the Doctrine of the Faith during the pontificate of John Paul II include Jacques Pohier (1979), Edward Schillebeeckx (1979, 1980, 1984), Hans Küng (1980), Georges de Nantes (1980), Leonardo Boff (1985), Charles Curran (1986), André Guindon (1992), Tissa Balasuriya (1997), Anthony De Mello (posthumously, 1998), Reinhard Messner (2000), Jacques Dupuis (2001), and Marciano Vidal (2001). Others, including the eminent moral theologian Bernhard Häring, were subjected to lengthy investigations and, although ultimately not censured, were never officially cleared.[37] In all these cases except for that of Pohier, Joseph Ratzinger presided as the prefect of the congregation.

On the other hand, with an extraordinary decree promulgated on July 1, 2001, the Congregation, with the same Cardinal Ratzinger at its head, moved to remove any remaining stigma from the memory of Italian philosopher and theologian, Antonio Rosmini Serbati (1797–1855), whose works had been on the Index of Prohibited Books and forty of whose alleged propositions were posthumously condemned by the Sacred Congregation of the Holy Office in 1887.

While some of the theologians censured in recent years clearly went well beyond the pale of mainstream Catholic theology, the overall effect of the doctrinal investigations, if not reaching the level of "inquisition" that some critics have alarmingly decried, cannot but be chilling on the theological enterprise. Consequently, many Catholics will be looking to the former CDF prefect to strike the balance between pluralism and unity, perhaps in the spirit of St. Augustine's dictum of unity in the essentials, liberty in all else, and charity in all matters.

The changing face of Catholicism. Ultimately, the single most dramatic challenge that will face the next pontiff may be the one that has received the least attention in both the ecclesiastical and popular press: how the changing demographics of the Roman Church may ultimately transform its structure and dynamics. The Anglo-French writer Hilaire Belloc once declared, "The Church is Europe; Europe is the Church."[38] Although many churchmen have been slow to appreciate the fact, Belloc's triumphal boast has not been true for over a generation. Europeans and North Americans presently make up only one-third of the world's Catholics. By 2025—that is, conceivably by the end of the next pontificate—that proportion will slip even further to barely one-fourth.[39] As Philip Jenkins has observed:

> By 2025, Africans and Latin Americans will make up about 60 percent of Catholics, and that number should reach 66 percent by 2050. European and Euro-American Catholics will by that point be a small fragment of a church dominated by Filipinos and Mexicans, Vietnamese and Congolese (although of course, the North still provides a hugely disproportionate share of Church finances). The twentieth century was clearly the last in which Whites dominated the Catholic Church: Europe simply is *not* The Church. Latin America may be.[40]

This shift in population centers has been reflected in the composition of the Catholic hierarchy, including the membership of the College of Cardinals. It should be recalled that it was only in 1960 that the first black African, Laurent Rugambwa of Tanzania, was admitted to the college, by Pope John XXIII. In contrast, in the most recent consistory, of the thirty new cardinals (not counting the cardinal created *in pectore*) appointed by Pope John Paul II, three each hailed from Africa, Asia, and Latin America, while four of the new Europeans nominated to the college were already ineligible to vote due to their advanced age. In the next conclave, half of the cardinals eligible to vote will come from developing nations.

A fact that many have been slow to appreciate is that these numbers represent not just a demographic shift but also one that might well have seismic repercussions for an array of ecclesiastical and theological issues. As author Bruce Bawer, an Episcopalian, has observed, "Liberal Catholics in the U.S. and Europe fault John Paul II for being out of touch with his Church; but they're the ones, alas, who are out of touch."[41] Bawer should know: Many members of his own denomination, the generally theologically progressive American branch of the Anglican Communion, had a rude awakening at the Lambeth Conference of 1998 when the worldwide assembly of the bishops of that communion—a now overwhelmingly African and Asian institution of which the Episcopal Church forms but 3 percent—resoundingly approved a resolution reaffirming traditional marriage and "rejecting homosexual practice as incompatible with Scripture." In late 2003, after consecration of the openly gay V. Gene Robinson as bishop of the Episcopal Diocese of New Hampshire, a number of national churches in the Anglican Communion—including those of Nigeria, Kenya, Zambia, Central Africa, Uganda, and South Asia—either cut ties or declared states of "impaired communion" with the U.S. church.

Progressive Catholics in Europe and North America may soon find themselves in similar straits with their co-religious. In Africa, for example, with the exception of the question of clerical celibacy, which is often honored there in the breach at best (including by some bishops), most of the disciplinary and doctrinal stances that vex Western Catholics—including the ordination of women, the ban on contraception, the role of the laity, and academic freedom for theologians—hardly register with the vast majority of the churchgoers. If anything, the newer and growing churches of the developing world have manifested a penchant for theological fundamentalism—perhaps even obscurantism—that is almost alien to the experience of the Church in Europe and North America. In fact, if the Vatican has appeared in recent years to have been deaf to the demands of its relatively stagnant and aging European and North American flocks, it might well be because it has been attentive to the dynamic younger flocks in Africa, Asia, and Latin America. Whether Benedict XVI is, as some pundits have suggested, the last European pope remains to be seen.[42] What is certain, however, is that the last conclave may well be the last one where some of the issues raised above will figure prominently and the first where a whole series of new concerns will come to the fore.

For nearly two millennia, the Church has declared in its creed that it believes itself to be "*unam, sanctam, cathólicam, et apostólicam ecclésiam*" ("one, holy, catholic, and apostolic Church"). With over one billion members on every continent,[43] representing every race, culture, and tongue, and embracing every social class and economic stratum from the king of Spain to the anonymous Filipina guest worker in a Gulf sheikdom, the Church's claim to universality (the term "catholic" is derived from the Greek *katholikos*, meaning "throughout the whole, universal") is not in dispute. Nor is its apostolic character, with its claim for unbroken succession from Jesus Christ through his disciples, particularly from St. Peter to the reigning pontiff. The challenge for Pope Benedict XVI, now enthroned as the 262nd heir to the Fisherman, however, will be similar to that faced by his predecessors: To maintain and preserve a rapidly changing Church's unity while seeking to renew its holiness.

Appendix 1

THE SUCCESSION OF THE POPES[1]

St. PETER from Bethsaida in Galilee, Prince of the Apostles, who received from JESUS CHRIST the supreme pontifical authority to transmit to his successors; after first residing in Antioch, as noted in the chronicle dating from the year 354, he lived in Rome for twenty-five years, suffering martyrdom in either the year 64 or 67 of the present era.

St. LINUS, from Tuscia, 68–79.

St. ANACLETUS or CLETUS, Roman, 80–92.

St. CLEMENT, Roman, 92–99 (or 68–76).

St. EVARISTUS, Greek, 99 or 96–108.

St. ALEXANDER I, Roman, 108 or 109–116 or 119.

St. TELESPHORUS, Greek, 127 or 128–137 or 138.

St. HYGINUS, Greek, 138–142 or 149.

St. PIUS I, from Aquileia, 142 or 146–157 or 161.

St. ANICETUS, from Emessa (Syria), 150 or 157–153 or 168.

St. SOTER, from Fondi (Campania), 162 or 168–170 or 177.

St. ELEUTHERIUS, from Nicopolis (Epirus), 171 or 177–185 or 193.

---

[1]The list of the succession of popes given conforms to the one published in the most recent (2004) edition of the official yearbook of the Holy See, the *Annuario Pontificio*. The source given for data for the first seven centuries is the definitive edition of *Liber Pontificalis*, edited by L. Duchesne and published in Paris between 1886 and 1892. The names and dates of the principal antipopes are given in brackets. It should be noted that the liturgical and hagiographical books of the Church of Rome consider as martyrs all popes before Sylvester I (314–335) and as saints those from Sylvester I to Felix IV (526–530), except for Liberius (352–366) and Anastasius II (496–498). Subsequent to this period, those popes designated "saint" or "blessed" either have been the subjects of formal canonization proceedings or at least had their respective cults approved.

St. Victor I, African, 186 or 189–197 or 201.

St. Zephyrinus, Roman, 198–217 or 218.

St. Callistus I, Roman, 218–222.

  [St. Hippolytus, Roman, 217–235.][2]

St. Urban I, Roman, 222–230.

St. Pontian, Roman, July 21, 230–September 28, 235.

St. Antherus, Greek, November 21, 230–January 3, 236.

St. Fabian, Roman, . . . 236–January 20, 250.

St. Cornelius, Roman, March 6 or 13, 251–June . . . , 253.

  [Novatian, Roman, 251.]

St. Lucius I, Roman, June or July . . . , 253–March 5, 254.

St. Stephen I, Roman, March 12, 254–August 2, 257.

St. Sixtus II, Greek, August 30, 257–August 6, 258.

St. Dionysius, from parts unknown, July 22, 259–December 26, 268.

St. Felix I, Roman, January 5, 269–December 30, 274.

St. Eutychian, from Luni, January 4, 275–December 7, 283.

St. Caius, from Dalmatia, December 17, 283–April 22, 296.

St. Marcellinus, Roman, June 30, 296–October 25, 304.

St. Marcellus I, Roman, 306[3]–January 16, 309.[4]

St. Eusebius, Greek, April 18, 309–August 17, 309.[5]

St. Miltiades or Melchiades, African, July 2, 311–January 10, 314.

St. Sylvester I, Roman, January 31, 314–December 31, 335.

St. Mark, Roman, January 18, 336–October 7, 336.

St. Julius I, Roman, February 6, 337–April 12, 352.

Liberius, Roman, May 17, 352–September 24, 366.

  [Felix II,[6] Roman, . . . 355–November 22, 365.]

St. Damasus I, Roman, October 1, 366–December 11, 384.

  [Ursinus, September 24, 366–. . . 367.]

---

[2]Exiled with St. Pontian to Sardinia, he died there, reconciled to the Church.
[3]The year might have been 307 or 308.
[4]The year might have been 308 or 310.
[5]The year might have been 308 or 310.
[6]For some time, this antipope was confused with St. Felix the Martyr of Rome and, consequently, appeared in some chronicles as "St. Felix II." Consequently, Pope Felix III and Pope Felix IV as well as the antipope Felix V should have borne the designations II, III, and IV, respectively.

St. Siricius, Roman, December 15 or 22 or 29, 384–November 26, 399.

St. Anastasius I, Roman, November 27, 399–December 19, 401.

St. Innocent I, from Albano, December 22, 401–March 12, 417.

St. Zosimus, Greek, March 18, 417–December 26, 418.

Boniface I, Roman, December 28; December 29, 418–September 4, 422.[7]

   [Eulalius, December 27; December 29, 418–April 3, 419.]

St. Celestine I, from Campania, September 10, 422–July 27, 432.

St. Sixtus III, Roman, July 31, 432–August 19, 440.

St. Leo I, *the Great*, from Tuscia, September 29, 440–November 10, 461.

St. Hilarus, Sardinian, November 19, 461–February 29, 468.

St. Simplicius, from Tivoli, March 3, 468–March 10, 483.

St. Felix III (II), March 13, 483–February 25 or March 1, 492.

St. Gelasius I, African, March 1, 492–November 21, 496.

Anastasius II, Roman, November 24, 496–November 19, 498.

St. Symmachus, Sardinian, November 22, 498–July 19, 514.

   [Lawrence, November 22, 498– . . . 499; . . . 502– . . . 506.]

St. Hormisdas, from Frosinone, July 20, 514–August 6, 523.

St. John I, from Tuscia, Martyr, August 13, 523–May 18, 526.

St. Felix IV (III), from Sannio, July 12, 526–September 20 or 22, 530.

Boniface II, Roman, September 20 or 22, 530–October 17, 532.

   [Dioscorus,[8] from Alexandria, September 20 or 22, 530–October 14, 530.]

---

[7]From Boniface I onward, where the separate dates of both the pope's election as Roman pontiff and his ordination as a bishop and/or coronation are known, both dates are given. It should be noted that until the Middle Ages, a man elected to the papal office was not considered to have the fullness of authority (*plenitudine potestatis*) until his episcopal consecration. In earlier times, the new pope could exercise none of the powers of his office until the consecration, which often required imperial approval. Later canon law considered the papacy beginning with the acceptance of the election. The most recent legislation on the subject, Pope John Paul II's apostolic constitution *Universi Dominici gregis*, attempts to settle the question for practical purposes by ordering that, in the event the man elected pope is not a bishop, he be ordained one immediately before news of the election is announced.

[8]Although the subsequent chronicles have acknowledged Boniface II as the legitimate pope in succession to St. Felix IV (III) and labeled Dioscorus as an antipope, historically speaking, it could be argued that Dioscorus was the legitimate pope for the twenty-two days he lived between the assertion of his claim and his unexpected death and that Boniface II was only legitimately the pontiff after his rival's death. It certainly is without a doubt that the election of Dioscorus was canonical, being made by a large majority of the clergy, whereas Boniface owed his election to a minority party and the testamentary designation of his predecessor.

JOHN II,[9] Roman, *Mercurius*, December 31, 532; January 2, 533–May 8, 535.

St. AGAPITUS, Roman, May 13, 535–April 22, 536.

St. SILVERIUS, from Frosinone, Martyr, June 8, 536–... 537.[10]

VIGILIUS,[11] Roman, March 29, 537–June 7, 555.

PELAGIUS I, Roman, April 16, 556–March 4, 561.

JOHN III, Roman, *Catalinus*, July 17, 561–July 13, 574.

BENEDICT I, Roman, June 2, 575–July 30, 579.

PELAGIUS II, Roman, November 26, 579–February 7, 590.

St. GREGORY I, *the Great*, Roman, September 3, 590–March 12, 604.

SABINIAN, from Blera in Tuscia, March . . . ; September 13, 604–February 22, 606.

BONIFACE III, Roman, February 19, 607–November 10, 607.

St. BONIFACE IV, from the territory of the Marsi, August 25, 608–May 8, 615.

St. DEUSDEDIT or Adeodatus I, Roman, October 19, 615–November 8, 618.

BONIFACE V, from Naples, December 23, 619–October 23, 625.

HONORIUS I, from Campania, October 27, 625–October 12, 638.

SEVERINUS, Roman, October . . . , 638; May 28, 640–August 2, 640.

JOHN IV, from Dalmatia, August . . . ; December 24, 640–October 12, 642.

THEODORE I, from Jerusalem, October 12; November 24, 642–May 14, 649.

St. MARTIN I, from Todi, Martyr, July 5, 649–September 16, 655.

St. EUGENE I,[12] Roman, August 10, 654–June 2, 657.

St. VITALIAN, from Segni, July 30, 657–January 27, 672.

ADEODATUS II, Roman, April 11, 672–July 16, 676.

DONUS, Roman, November 2, 676–April 11, 678.

St. AGATHO, Sicilian, June 27, 678–January 10, 681.

St. LEO II, Sicilian, January . . . , 681; August 17, 682–July 3, 683.

St. BENEDICT II, Roman, June 26, 684–May 8, 685.

---

[9]John II was the first pope to exchange his given name (that of the pagan divinity Mercury) for another style upon his election to the papal throne.

[10]Violently deposed in March, he abdicated and died several months later.

[11]Installed by Belisarius on March 29, 537, Vigilius became legitimate with the subsequent abdication of St. Silverius and recognition by the Roman clergy. The *Annuario Pontificio* asserts that the recognition "validated the defects with his election."

[12]When St. Martin I was arrested and deported on June 17, 653, St. Eugene I was elected and ordained his successor without apparent objection from him. However, some chroniclers only accept Eugene's legitimacy from the date of Martin's death. See Chapter 1, note 28.

JOHN V, Syrian, July 23, 685–August 2, 686.

CONON, from unknown parts, October 23, 686–September 21, 687.

   [THEODORE, . . . 687.]

   [PASCHAL, . . . 687.]

St. SERGIUS I, Syrian, December 15, 687–September 7, 701.

JOHN VI, Greek, October 30, 701–January 11, 705.

JOHN VII, Greek, March 1, 705–October 18, 707.

SISINNIUS, Syrian, January 15, 708–February 4, 708.

CONSTANTINE, Syrian, March 25, 708–April 9, 715.

St. GREGORY II, Roman, May 19, 715–February 11, 731.

St. GREGORY III, Syrian, March 18, 731–September 28, 741.

St. ZACHARIAS, Greek, December 3, 741–March 15, 752.

STEPHEN II (III),[13] Roman, March 26, 752–April 16, 757.

St. PAUL I, Roman, April . . . ; May 29, 757–June 28, 767.

   [CONSTANTINE, from Nepi, June 28; July 5, 767–July 30, 768.]

   [PHILIP, July 31, 768.][14]

STEPHEN III (IV), Sicilian, August 1; August 7, 768–January 24, 772.

HADRIAN I, Roman, February 1; February 9, 772–December 25, 795.

St. LEO III, Roman, December 26; December 27, 795–June 12, 816.

STEPHEN IV (V), Roman, June 22, 816–January 24, 817.

St. PASCHAL I, Roman, January 25, 817–February or May . . . , 824.

EUGENE II, Roman, February or May . . . , 824–August . . . , 827.

VALENTINE, Roman, August . . . , 827–September . . . , 827.

GREGORY IV, Roman, September . . . , 827; March 29, 828–January 25, 844.

   [JOHN, January 25, 844.]

SERGIUS II, Roman, January 25, 844–January 27, 847.

---

[13]At the death of St. Zacharias, the elderly Roman priest Stephen was elected on March 22 or 23, 757, but died four days later without being consecrated a bishop. This Stephen was not reckoned a pope by the *Liber Pontificalis* or any medieval document, since the canon law of the time deemed episcopal ordination essential to the papal office. Only since the sixteenth century did the practice of considering him a pope become general, based on the different notion that valid election was all that was required for a man to be pope. Thus the editions of the *Annuario Pontificio* through 1961 included him as "Stephen II," while editions since 1961 have dropped him. Hence all subsequent pontiffs with the name Stephen"are given a dual numbering.

[14]Installed as antipope, he abandoned the pretense and returned to his monastery on the same day.

St. Leo IV, Roman, January . . . ; April 10, 847–July 17, 855.

Benedict III, Roman, July . . . ; September 29, 855–April 17, 858.

[Anastasius, *the Librarian*, September 21–24, 855; died c. 878.]

St. Nicholas I, *the Great*, Roman, April 24, 858–November 13, 867.

Hadrian II, Roman, December 14, 867–November or December . . . , 872.

John VIII, Roman, December 14, 872–December 16, 882.

Marinus I, from Gallese, December . . . , 882–May 15, 884.

St. Hadrian III, Roman, May 17, 884–August or September . . . , 885.[15]

Stephen V (VI), Roman, September . . . , 885–September 14, 891.

Formosus, Bishop of Porto, October 6, 891–April 4, 896.

Boniface VI, Roman, April 11, 896–April 16, 896.

Stephen VI (VII), Roman, May or June . . . , 896–July or August . . . , 897.

Romanus, from Gallese, July or August . . . , 897–November . . . , 897.

Theodore II, Roman, December . . . , 897–December . . . , 897 or January . . . , 989.

John IX, from Tivoli, December . . . , 897 or January . . . , 898–January or May . . . , 900.

Benedict IV, Roman, January or May . . . , 900–July . . . , 903.

Leo V, from Ardea, July . . . , 903–September . . . , 903.

[Christopher, Roman, September . . . , 903–January . . . , 904.]

Sergius III, Roman, January 29, 904–April 14, 911.

Anastasius III, Roman, June or September . . . , 911–July or August . . . , 913.

Lando, from Sabina, July or November . . . , 913–March . . . , 914.

John X, from Tossignano (near Imola), March or April . . . , 914–May or June . . . , 928.

Leo VI, Roman, May or June . . . , 928–December . . . , 928 or January . . . , 929.

Stephen VII (VIII), Roman, January . . . , 929–February . . . , 931.

John XI, Roman, March . . . , 931–January . . . , 936.

Leo VII, Roman, January . . . , 936–July 13, 939.

Stephen VIII (IX), Roman, July 14, 939–October . . . , 942.

Marinus II, Roman, October 30; November . . . , 942–May . . . , 946.

Agapitus II, Roman, May 10, 946–December . . . , 955.

John XII, *Octavian of the Counts of Tusculum*, December 16, 955–May 14, 964.

Leo VIII,[16] Roman, December 4; December 6, 963–March . . . , 965.

---

[15]His cult was confirmed by Pope Leo XIII on June 2, 1891.

[16]Leo VIII was elected by the Roman council held in St. Peter's Basilica by the Emperor Otto I after the assembly had deposed that same day, December 4, 963, John XII, who died the following May 14. Scholars have been divided over the validity of the deposition and the legitimacy of Leo's pontificate.

BENEDICT V,[17] Roman, May . . . , 964–July 4, 964 or 965.

JOHN XIII, Roman, October 1, 965–September 6, 972.

BENEDICT VI, Roman, December . . . , 972; January 19, 973–July . . . , 974.

   [BONIFACE VII, Roman, *Francone*, June . . . ,974–July . . . , 974; August . . . , 984–July 20, 985.]

BENEDICT VII, Roman, October . . . , 974–July 10, 983.

JOHN XIV, from Pavia, *Peter*, November or December . . . , 983–August 20, 984.

JOHN XV, Roman, August . . . , 985–March 996.

GREGORY V, from Saxony, *Bruno of the Dukes of Carinthia*, May 3, 996–February or March . . . , 999.

   [JOHN XVI,[18] from Rossano, *John Filagato*, February or March . . . , 997–May . . . , 998.]

SYLVESTER II, from Aquitaine, *Gerbert*, April 2, 999–May 12, 1003.

JOHN XVII, Roman, *Siccone*, May 16, 1003–November 6, 1003.

JOHN XVIII, Roman, *Fasano*, December 25, 1003–June or July . . . , 1009.

SERGIUS IV, Roman, *Pietro*, July 31, 1009–May 12, 1012.

BENEDICT VIII, *Theophylact of the Counts of Tusculum*, May 18, 1012–April 9, 1024.

   [GREGORY, May . . . –December . . . , 1012.]

JOHN XIX, *Romano of the Counts of Tusculum*, April 19, 1024–... 1032.

BENEDICT IX, *Theophylact of the Counts of Tusculum*, August or September . . . , 1032–September . . . , 1032.

SYLVESTER III, Roman, *Giovanni*, January 13 or 20, 1045–March . . . , 1045.

BENEDICT IX (for the second time), March 10, 1045–May 1, 1045.

GREGORY VI, Roman, *Giovanni Graziano*, May 1, 1045–December 20, 1046.

CLEMENT II, from Saxony, *Suidger of the Lords Morsleben von Horneburg*, January 24, 1046–October 9, 1047.

BENEDICT IX (for the third time), October . . . , 1047–July . . . , 1048.[19]

DAMASUS II, from Tyrol, *Poppo*, July 17, 1048–August 9, 1048.

---

[17]If Leo VIII was legitimately installed as pope, then Benedict V, who was deposed in another synod on June 23, 964, under Leo VIII and the Emperor Otto I, should be numbered among the antipopes. The *Annuario Pontificio* itself seems to be of two mutually contradictory minds, listing both as popes.

[18]Due to a chronicler's error, accepted at the time as truth, the numeration of the popes named John skipped two numbers.

[19]The pontificate of Benedict was interrupted first by the intrusion of Sylvester III, then by Benedict's resignation and succession by Gregory VI; finally Benedict IX returned to the papacy a third time after the death of Clement II.

St. LEO IX, from Alsace, *Bruno of the Counts of Egisheim*, February 2; February 12, 1049–April 19, 1054.

VICTOR II, Swabian, *Gebhard of the Counts of Dollnstein–Hirschberg*, April 13, 1055–July 28, 1057.

STEPHEN IX (X), from Lorraine, *Frederick of the Dukes of Lorraine*, August 2; August 3, 1057–March 29, 1058.

[BENEDICT X, Roman, *Giovanni*, April 5, 1058–January . . . , 1059.]

NICHOLAS II, from Burgundy, *Gerard*, December . . . , 1058; January 24, 1059–July 27, 1061.

ALEXANDER II, from Baggio (Milan), *Anselmo*, September 30; October 1, 1061–April 21, 1073.

[Honorius II, from near Verona, *Cadalo*, October 28, 1061–May 31, 1064; died 1071 or 1072.]

St. GREGORY VII, from Tuscia, *Hildebrand*, April 22; June 30, 1073–May 25, 1085.

[CLEMENT III, from Parma, *Guibert*, June 25, 1080; March 24, 1084–September 8, 1100.]

Blessed VICTOR III, from Benevento, *Daufer (Desiderius)*, May 24, 1086; May 9, 1087–September 16, 1087.[20]

Blessed URBAN II, from Châtillon-sur-Marne, *Odo (Eudes) de Lagery*, March 12, 1088–July 29, 1099.[21]

PASCHAL II, from Bleda or Galeata (near Ravenna), *Raniero*, August 13; August 14, 1099–January 21, 1118.

[THEODORIC, Bishop of Albano, . . . 1100; died 1102.]

[ALBERT, Bishop of Sabina, . . . 1101.]

[Sylvester IV, Roman, *Maginulfo*, November 18, 1105–April 12 or 13, 1111.]

GELASIUS II, from Gaeta, *Giovanni Caetani*, January 24; March 10, 1118–January 28, 1119.]

[GREGORY VIII, from France, *Maurice Burdinus*, March 10, 1118–April 22, 1121.]

CALLISTUS II, *Guido of Burgundy*, February 2; February 9, 1119–December 13 or 14, 1124.

HONORIUS II, from Fiagnano (near Imola), *Lamberto Scannabecchi*, December 15; December 21, 1124–February 13 or 14, 1130.

[CELESTINE II, Roman, *Tebaldo Buccapecus*, December . . . , 1124.]

INNOCENT II, Roman, *Gregorio Papareschi*, February 14; February 23, 1130–April 24, 1143.

[ANACLETUS II, Roman, *Pietro Pierleoni*, February 14; February 23, 1130–September 24, 1138.]

[VICTOR IV, from Ceccano, *Gregorio*, March . . . , 1138–May 29, 1138.]

CELESTINE II, from Città di Castello, *Guido*, September 26; October 3, 1143–March 8, 1144.

---

[20]His cult was confirmed July 23, 1887.

[21]His cult was confirmed July 14, 1881.

Lucius II, from Bologna, *Gerardo*, March 12, 1144–February 15, 1145.

Blessed Eugene III, from Pisa, *Bernardo*, February 15; February 18, 1145–July 8, 1153.[22]

Anastasius IV, from Abbot's Langley (Hertfordshire), *Nicholas Breakspear*, December 4; December 5, 1154–September 1, 1159.

Alexander III, from Siena, *Rolando Bandinelli*, September 7; September 20, 1159–August 30, 1181.

[Victor IV,[23] *Octavian of the Lords of Monticelli (near Tivoli)*, September 7; October 4, 1159–April 20, 1164.]

[Paschal III, *Guido of Crema*, April 22; April 26, 1164–September 20, 1168.]

[Callistus III, *Giovanni, Abbot of Strumi (Austria)*, September . . . , 1168–August 29, 1178.][24]

[Innocent III, from Sezze, *Lando*, September 29, 1179–January . . . , 1180.]

Lucius III, from Lucca, *Ubaldo Allucingoli*, September 1; September 6, 1181–November 25, 1185.

Urban III, from Milan, *Uberto Crivelli*, November 25; December 1, 1185–October 20, 1187.

Gregory VIII, from Benevento, *Alberto di Morra*, October 21; October 25, 1187–December 17, 1187.

Clement III, Roman, *Paolo Scolari*, December 19; December 20, 1187–March . . . , 1191.

Celestine III, Roman, *Giacinto Bobone*, April 10; April 14, 1191–January 8, 1198.

Innocent III, from Gavignano (near Rome), *Lotario of the Counts of Segni*, January 8; February 22, 1198–July 16, 1216.

Honorius III, Roman, *Cencio*, July 18; July 24, 1216–March 18, 1227.

Gregory IX, from Agnani, *Ugolino of the Counts of Segni*, March 19; March 21, 1227–August 22, 1241.

Celestine IV, from Milan, *Goffredo of Castiglione*, October 25; October 28, 1241–November 10, 1241.

Innocent IV, from Lavagna (near Genoa), *Sinibaldo Fieschi*, June 25; June 28, 1243–December 7, 1254.

Alexander IV, from Ienne (near Rome), *Rinaldo of the Lords of Ienne*, December 12; December 20, 1254–May 25, 1261.

Urban IV, from Troyes, *Jacques Pantaléon*, August 29; September 4, 1261–October 2, 1264.

---

[22]His cult was confirmed October 3, 1872.

[23]Should have been styled "Victor V," but perhaps Octavian of Monticelli did not take into account the previous antipope Victor IV, who submitted to Innocent II after only two months.

[24]Date of his submission to Alexander III.

CLEMENT IV, from Saint-Gilles-sur-Rhône (southern France), *Guide Foulques*, February 5; February 22, 1265–November 29, 1268.

Blessed GREGORY X, from Piacenza, *Tedaldo Visconti*, September 1, 1271; March 27, 1272–January 10, 1276.[25]

Blessed INNOCENT V, from Savoy, *Pierre de Tarentaise*, January 21; February 22, 1276–June 22, 1276.[26]

HADRIAN V, from Genoa, *Ottobono Fieschi*, July 11, 1276–August 18, 1276.

JOHN XXI,[27] from Lisbon, *Pedro Julião or Petrus Hispanus*, September 16; September 20, 1276– May 20, 1277.

NICHOLAS III, Roman, *Giovanni Gaetano Orsini*, November 25; December 26, 1276–August 22, 1280.

MARTIN IV,[28] from France, *Simon de Brie (or of Brion or of Mainpincien)*, February 22; March 23, 1281–March 29, 1285.

HONORIUS IV, Roman, *Giacomo Savelli*, April 2; May 20, 1285–April 3, 1287.

NICHOLAS IV, from Lisciano (near Ascoli Piceno), *Girolamo*, February 22, 1288–April 4, 1292.

St. CELESTINE V, from Molise, *Pietro del Morrone*, July 5; August 29, 1294–December 13, 1294; died May 19, 1296.[29]

BONIFACE VIII, from Agnani, *Benedetto Caetani*, December 24, 1294; January 23, 1295–October 11, 1303.

Blessed BENEDICT XI, from Treviso, *Niccolò di Boccasio*, October 22; October 27, 1303–July 7, 1304.[30]

CLEMENT V, from Villandraut (near Gironde), *Bertrand de Got*, June 5; November 14, 1305–April 20, 1314.

JOHN XXII, from Cahors, *Jacques Duèse*, August 7; September 5, 1316–December 4, 1334.

[NICHOLAS V, from Corvaro (near Rieti), *Pietro Rinalducci or Rainalducci*, May 12; May 22, 1328–August 25, 1330; died October 16, 1333.]

BENEDICT XII, from Saverdun (southern France), *Jacques Fournier*, December 20, 1334; January 8, 1335–April 25, 1342.

CLEMENT VI, from Maumont (Limousin), *Pierre Roger*, May 7; May 19, 1342–December 6, 1352.

---

[25] His cult was confirmed September 12, 1713.

[26] His cult was confirmed March 14, 1898.

[27] As noted previously, a "Pope John XX" never existed. However, the style "John XXI" was the one adopted by this pontiff.

[28] Considering Pope Marinus I (882–884) and Marinus II (942–946) as "Martin," this pontiff took the style "Martin IV."

[29] Canonized May 5, 1313.

[30] His cult was confirmed April 24, 1736.

INNOCENT VI, from Monts (Limousin), *Etienne Aubert*, December 18; December 30, 1352–September 12, 1362.

Blessed URBAN V, from Grizac (southern France), *Guillaume Grimoard*, September 28; November 6, 1362–December 19, 1370.[31]

GREGORY XI, from Rosier d'Egletons (Limousin), *Pierre Roger de Beaufort*, December 30, 1370; January 3, 1371–March 26, 1378.

URBAN VI, from Naples, *Bartolomeo Prignano*, April 8; April 18, 1378–October 15, 1389.

BONIFACE IX, from Naples, *Pietro Tomacelli*, November 2; November 9, 1389–October 1, 1404.

INNOCENT VII, from Sulmona, *Cosma Migliorati*, October 17; November 11, 1404–November 6, 1406.

GREGORY XII, Venetian, *Angel Correr*, November 30; December 19, 1406–July 4, 1415.[32]

[CLEMENT VII, from Geneva, *Robert of the Counts of Geneva*, September 20; October 31, 1378–September 16, 1394.]

[BENEDICT XIII, from Illueca (Aragon), *Pedro Martínez de Luna*, September 28; October 11, 1394–November 29, 1422 or May 23, 1423.][33]

[ALEXANDER V, from Kare (Crete), *Pietro Filargis*, June 26; July 7, 1409–May 3, 1410.]

[JOHN XXIII, from Naples, *Baldassare Cossa*, May 17; May 25, 1410–May 29, 1415.][34]

MARTIN V, from Genazzano, *Oddone Colonna*, November 11; November 21, 1417–February 20, 1431.

EUGENE IV, Venetian, *Gabriele Condulmer*, March 3; March 11, 1431–February 23, 1447.

[FELIX V, from Chambéry, *Amedeo VIII, Duke of Savoy*, November 5, 1439; July 24, 1440–April 7, 1449.][35]

NICHOLAS V, from Sarzana, *Tommaso Parentucelli*, March 6; March 19, 1447–March 24, 1455.

CALLISTUS III, from Torre del Canals near Játiva (Valencia), *Alonso Borja (Borgia)*, April 8; April 20, 1455–August 6, 1458.

PIUS II, from Corsignano (Sienna), *Enea Silvio Piccolomini*, August 19; September 3, 1458–August 14, 1464.

---

[31]His cult was confirmed March 10, 1870.

[32]The date of his abdication. He died October 18, 1417. The antipopes that follow constitute the two obediences, Avignon and Pisa.

[33]The Council of Constance deposed him on July 26, 1417, just as the Council of Pisa had done on June 5, 1409. He was succeeded in his obedience by Clement VIII (Gil Sánchez Muñoz), June 10, 1423–July 26, 1429 (died December 28, 1447), and Benedict XIV (Bernard Garnier), November 12, 1425– . . . 1430.

[34]Date of his deposition, after a forced resignation, in the Council of Constance. He died December 27, 1419.

[35]Date of his abdication. He died January 7, 1451.

PAUL II, Venetian, *Pietro Barbo*, August 30; September 16, 1464–July 26, 1471.

SIXTUS IV, from Celle (Savona), *Francesco della Rovere*, August 9; August 25, 1471–August 12, 1484.

INNOCENT VIII, Genoese, *Giovanni Battista Cibo*, August 29; September 12, 1484–July 25, 1492.

ALEXANDER VI,[36] from Játiva (Valencia), *Rodrigo de Borja (Borgia)*, August 11; August 26, 1492–August 18, 1503.

PIUS III, from Siena, *Francesco Todeschini-Piccolomini*, September 22; October 1; October 8, 1503–October 18, 1503.

JULIUS II, from Albisola (Savona), *Giuliano della Rovere*, November 1; November 26, 1503–February 21, 1513.

LEO X, Florentine, *Giovanni de' Medici*, March 11; March 19, 1513–December 1, 1521.

HADRIAN VI, from Utrecht, *Adrian Florensz*, January 9; August 31, 1522–September 14, 1523.

CLEMENT VII, Florentine, *Giulio de' Medici*, November 19; November 26, 1523–September 25, 1534.

PAUL III, from Canino (Viterbo), *Alessandro Farnese*, October 13; November 3, 1534–November 10, 1549.

JULIUS III, Roman, *Giovanni Maria Ciocchi del Monte*, February 7; February 22, 1550–March 23, 1555.

MARCELLUS II, from Montefano (Macerata), *Marcello Cervini*, April 9; April 10, 1555–May 1, 1555.

PAUL IV, from Capriglia (Avellino), *Gian Pietro Carafa*, May 23; May 26, 1555–August 18, 1559.

PIUS IV, Milanese, *Giovan Angelo Medici*, December 26, 1559; January 6, 1560–December 9, 1565.

St. PIUS V, from Bosco (Alessandria), *Antonio (Michele) Ghisleri*, January 7; January 17, 1566–May 1, 1572.[37]

GREGORY XIII, Bolognese, *Ugo Boncompagni*, May 13; May 25, 1572–April 10, 1585.

SIXTUS V, from Grottamare (Ascoli Piceno), *Felice Peretti*, April 24; May 1, 1585–August 27, 1590.

URBAN VII, Roman, *Giambattista Castagna*, September 15, 1590–September 27, 1590.

GREGORY XIV, from Somma Lombarda, *Niccolò Sfondrati*, December 5; December 8, 1590–October 16, 1591.

---

[36]He should have been styled "Alexander V," as Alexander V (1409–1410), elected by the Council of Pisa, is not considered a legitimate pope.

[37]Beatified May 1, 1672; canonized May 22, 1712.

INNOCENT IX, Bolognese, *Giovan Antonio Facchinetti,* October 29; November 3, 1591–December 30, 1591.

CLEMENT VIII, from Fano, *Ippolito Aldobrandini,* January 30; February 9, 1592–March 3, 1605.

LEO XI, Florentine, *Alessandro de' Medici,* April 1; April 10, 1605–April 27, 1605.

PAUL V, Roman, *Camillo Borghese,* May 16; May 29, 1605–January 28, 1621.

GREGORY XV, Bolognese, *Alessandro Ludovisi,* February 9; February 14, 1621–July 8, 1623.

URBAN VIII, Florentine, *Maffeo Barberini,* August 6; September 29, 1623–July 29, 1644.

INNOCENT X, Roman, *Giovanni Battisti Pamphilj,* September 15; October 4, 1644–January 7, 1655.

ALEXANDER VII, from Siena, *Fabio Chigi,* April 7; April 18, 1655–May 22, 1667.

CLEMENT IX, from Pistoia, *Giulio Rospigliosi,* June 20; June 26, 1667–December 9, 1669.

CLEMENT X, Roman, *Emilio Altieri,* April 29; May 11, 1670–July 22, 1676.

Blessed INNOCENT XI, from Como, *Benedetto Odescalchi,* September 21; October 4, 1676–August 12, 1689.[38]

ALEXANDER VIII, Venetian, *Pietro Ottoboni,* October 6; October 16, 1689–February 1, 1691.

INNOCENT XII, from Spinazzola, *Antonio Pignatelli,* July 12; July 15, 1691–September 27, 1700.

CLEMENT XI, from Urbino, *Giovanni Francesco Albani,* November 23; November 30, 1700–March 19, 1721.

INNOCENT XIII, from Poli, *Michelangelo Conti,* May 8; May 18, 1721–March 7, 1724.

BENEDICT XIII, from Gravina, *Pietro Francesco (Vincenzo Maria) Orsini,* May 29; June 4, 1724–February 21, 1730.

CLEMENT XII, Florentine, *Lorenzo Corsini,* July 12; July 16, 1730–February 6, 1740.

BENEDICT XIV, Bolognese, *Prospero Lambertini,* August 17; August 22, 1740–May 4, 1758.

CLEMENT XIII, Venetian, *Carlo Rezzonico,* July 6; July 16, 1758–February 2, 1769.

CLEMENT XIV, from Sant'Arcangelo di Romagna, *Giovanni Vincenzo Antonio (Lorenzo) Ganganelli,* May 19; May 28; June 4, 1769–September 22, 1774.

PIUS VI, from Cesena, *Giannangelo Braschi,* February 15; February 22, 1775–August 29, 1799.

PIUS VII, from Cesena, *Barnabà (Gregorio) Chiaramonti,* March 14; March 21, 1800–August 20, 1823.

LEO XII, from Monticelli di Genga (Fabriano), *Annibale della Genga,* September 28; October 5, 1823–February 10, 1829.

---

[38]Beatified October 7, 1956.

Pius VIII, from Cingoli, *Francesco Saverio Castiglioni*, March 31; April 5, 1829–November 30, 1830.

Gregory XVI, from Belluno, *Bartolomeo Alberto (Mauro) Cappellari*, February 2; February 6, 1831–June 1, 1846.

Blessed Pius IX, from Senigallia, *Giovanni Maria Mastai Ferretti*, June 16; June 21, 1846–February 7, 1878.[39]

Leo XIII, from Carpineto Romano, *Vincenzo Gioacchino Pecci*, February 20; March 3, 1878–July 20, 1903.

St. Pius X, from Riese (Treviso), *Giuseppe Melchiorre Sarto*, August 4; August 9, 1903–August 20, 1914.[40]

Benedict XV, Genoese, *Giacomo della Chiesa*, September 3; September 6, 1914–January 22, 1922.

Pius XI, from Desio (Milan), *Achille Ratti*, February 6; February 12, 1922–February 10, 1939.

Pius XII, Roman, *Eugenio Pacelli*, March 2; March 12, 1939–October 9, 1958.

Blessed John XXIII, from Sotto il Monte (Bergamo), *Angelo Giuseppe Roncalli*, October 28; November 4, 1958–June 3, 1963.[41]

Paul VI, from Concesio (Brescia), *Giovanni Battista Montini*, June 21; June 30, 1963–August 6, 1978.

John Paul I, from Forno di Canale (Belluno), *Albino Luciani*, August 26; September 3, 1978–September 28, 1978.

John Paul II, from Wadowice (Cracow), *Karol Wojtyla*, October 16; October 22, 1978—April 2, 2005.

Benedict XVI, from Marktl am Inn (Passau), *Joseph Ratzinger*, April 19; April 24, 2005—Universal Pastor of the Church.

---

[39]Beatified September 3, 2000.

[40]Beatified June 3, 1951; canonized May 29, 1954.

[41]Beatified September 3, 2000.

Appendix 2

THE APOSTOLIC CONSTITUTION
UNIVERSI DOMINICI GREGIS
ON THE VACANCY OF THE APOSTOLIC SEE
AND THE ELECTION OF THE ROMAN PONTIFF[1]

JOHN PAUL, BISHOP
SERVANT OF THE SERVANTS OF GOD
FOR PERPETUAL REMEMBRANCE

The Shepherd of the Lord's whole flock is the Bishop of the Church of Rome, where the Blessed Apostle Peter, by sovereign disposition of divine Providence, offered to Christ the supreme witness of martyrdom by the shedding of his blood. It is therefore understandable that the lawful apostolic succession in this See, with which "because of its great preeminence every Church must agree,"[2] has always been the object of particular attention.

Precisely for this reason, down the centuries the Supreme Pontiffs have deemed it their special duty, as well as their specific right, to establish fitting norms to regulate the orderly election of their Successor. Thus, also in more recent times, my Predecessors Saint Pius X,[3] Pius XI,[4] Pius XII,[5] John XXIII,[6] and lastly, Paul VI,[7] each with the intention

---

[1]The text, in the official Latin version, was published in *Acta Apostolicae Sedis* 88 (1996): 305–343. The following is an unofficial translation.

[2]Saint Irenaeus, *Adversus haereses*, III, 3, 2: SCh 211, 33.

[3]Cf. Apostolic Constitution *Vacante Sede Apostolica* (25 December 1904): *Pii X Pontificis Maximi Acta*, III (1908), 239–288.

[4]Cf. Motu Proprio *Cum proxime* (1 March 1922): AAS 14 (1922), 145–146; Apostolic Constitution *Quae Divinitus* (25 March 1935): *Acta Apostolicae Sedis* 27 (1935): 97–113.

[5]Cf. Apostolic Constitution *Vacantis Apostolicae Sedis* (8 December 1945) [in *Acta Apostolicae Sedis* 38 (1946): 65–99].

[6]Cf. Motu Proprio *Summi Pontificis electio* (5 September 1962) [in *Acta Apostolicae Sedis* 54 (1962): 632–640].

[7]Cf. Apostolic Constitution *Regimini Ecclesiae Universae* (15 August 1967) [in *Acta Apostolicae Sedis* 59 (1967): 885–928]; Motu Proprio *Ingravescentem aetatem* (21 November 1970) [in *Acta Apostolicae Sedis* 62 (1970): 810–813]; Apostolic Constitution *Romano Pontifici eligendo* (1 October 1975) [in *Acta Apostolicae Sedis* 67 (1975): 609–645].

of responding to the needs of the particular historical moment, issued wise and appropriate regulations in order to ensure the suitable preparation and orderly gathering of the electors charged, at the vacancy of the Apostolic See, with the important and weighty duty of electing the Roman Pontiff.

If I too now turn to this matter, it is certainly not because of any lack of esteem for those norms, for which I have great respect and which I intend for the most part to confirm, at least with regard to their substance and the basic principles which inspired them. What leads me to take this step is awareness of the Church's changed situation today and the need to take into consideration the general revision of Canon Law which took place, to the satisfaction of the whole Episcopate, with the publication and promulgation first of the Code of Canon Law and subsequently of the Code of Canons of the Eastern Churches. In conformity with this revision, itself inspired by the Second Vatican Ecumenical Council, I then took up the reform of the Roman Curia in the Apostolic Constitution *Pastor Bonus*.[8] Furthermore, Canon 335 of the Code of Canon Law, restated in Canon 47 of the Code of Canons of the Eastern Churches, makes clear the need to issue and constantly update the specific laws regulating the canonical provision for the Roman See, when for any reason it becomes vacant.

While keeping in mind present-day requirements, I have been careful, in formulating the new discipline, not to depart in substance from the wise and venerable tradition already established.

It is in fact an indisputable principle that the Roman Pontiff has the right to define and adapt to changing times the manner of designating the person called to assume the Petrine succession in the Roman See. This regards, first of all, the body entrusted with providing for the election of the Roman Pontiff: based on a millennial practice sanctioned by specific canonical norms and confirmed by an explicit provision of the current Code of Canon Law (Canon 349), this body is made up of the College of Cardinals of Holy Roman Church. While it is indeed a doctrine of faith that the power of the Supreme Pontiff derives directly from Christ, whose earthly Vicar he is,[9] it is also certain that this supreme power in the Church is granted to him "by means of lawful election accepted by him, together with episcopal consecration."[10] A most serious duty is thus incumbent upon the body responsible for this election. Consequently the norms which regulate its activity need to be very precise and clear, so that the election itself will take place in a most worthy manner, as befits the office of utmost responsibility which the person elected will have to assume, by divine mandate, at the moment of his assent.

Confirming therefore the norm of the current Code of Canon Law (cf. Canon 349), which reflects the millennial practice of the Church, I once more affirm that the College of electors of the Supreme Pontiff is composed solely of the Cardinals of Holy Roman

---

[8] Cf. *Acta Apostolicae Sedis* 80 (1988): 841–912.

[9] Cf. First Vatican Ecumenical Council, Dogmatic Constitution on the Church of Christ *Pastor Aeternus*, III; Second Vatican Ecumenical Council, Dogmatic Constitution on the Church *Lumen Gentium*, 18.

[10] *Code of Canon Law*, Canon 332 §1; *Code of Canons of the Eastern Churches*, Canon 44 §1.

Church. In them one finds expressed in a remarkable synthesis the two aspects which characterize the figure and office of the Roman Pontiff: *Roman*, because identified with the Bishop of the Church in Rome and thus closely linked to the clergy of this City, represented by the Cardinals of the presbyteral and diaconal titles of Rome, and to the Cardinal Bishops of the suburbicarian Sees; *Pontiff of the universal Church*, because called to represent visibly the unseen Pastor who leads his whole flock to the pastures of eternal life. The universality of the Church is clearly expressed in the very composition of the College of Cardinals, whose members come from every continent.

In the present historical circumstances, the universality of the Church is sufficiently expressed by the College of one hundred and twenty electors, made up of Cardinals coming from all parts of the world and from very different cultures. I therefore confirm that this is to be the maximum number of Cardinal electors, while at the same time indicating that it is in no way meant as a sign of less respect that the provision laid down by my predecessor Pope Paul VI has been retained, namely, that those Cardinals who celebrate their eightieth birthday before the day when the Apostolic See becomes vacant do not take part in the election.[11] The reason for this provision is the desire not to add to the weight of such venerable age the further burden of responsibility for choosing the one who will have to lead Christ's flock in ways adapted to the needs of the times. This does not however mean that the Cardinals over eighty years of age cannot take part in the preparatory meetings of the Conclave, in conformity with the norms set forth below. During the vacancy of the Apostolic See, and especially during the election of the Supreme Pontiff, they in particular should lead the People of God assembled in the Patriarchal Basilicas of Rome and in other churches in the Dioceses throughout the world, supporting the work of the electors with fervent prayers and supplications to the Holy Spirit and imploring for them the light needed to make their choice before God alone and with concern only for the "salvation of souls, which in the Church must always be the supreme law."[12]

It has been my wish to give particular attention to the age-old institution of the Conclave, the rules and procedures of which have been established and defined by the solemn ordinances of a number of my Predecessors. A careful historical examination confirms both the appropriateness of this institution, given the circumstances in which it originated and gradually took definitive shape, and its continued usefulness for the orderly, expeditious and proper functioning of the election itself, especially in times of tension and upheaval.

Precisely for this reason, while recognizing that theologians and canonists of all times agree that this institution is not of its nature necessary for the valid election of the Roman Pontiff, I confirm by this Constitution that the Conclave is to continue in its essential structure; at the same time, I have made some modifications in order to adapt

---

[11]Cf. Motu Proprio *Ingravescentem aetatem* (21 November 1970), II, 2 [in *Acta Apostolicae Sedis* 62 (1970): 811]; Apostolic Constitution *Romano Pontifici eligendo* (1 October 1975), 33 [in *Acta Apostolicae Sedis* 67 (1975): 622].

[12]*Code of Canon Law*, Canon 1752.

its procedures to present-day circumstances. Specifically, I have considered it appropriate to decree that for the whole duration of the election the living-quarters of the Cardinal electors and of those called to assist in the orderly process of the election itself are to be located in suitable places within Vatican City State. Although small, the State is large enough to ensure within its walls, with the help of the appropriate measures indicated below, the seclusion and resulting concentration that an act so vital to the whole Church requires of the electors.

At the same time, in view of the sacredness of the act of election and thus the need for it to be carried out in an appropriate setting where, on the one hand, liturgical actions can be readily combined with juridical formalities, and where, on the other, the electors can more easily dispose themselves to accept the interior movements of the Holy Spirit, I decree that the election will continue to take place in the Sistine Chapel, where everything is conducive to an awareness of the presence of God, in whose sight each person will one day be judged.

I further confirm, by my apostolic authority, the duty of maintaining the strictest secrecy with regard to everything that directly or indirectly concerns the election process itself. Here too, though, I have wished to simplify the relative norms, reducing them to their essentials, in order to avoid confusion, doubts and even eventual problems of conscience on the part of those who have taken part in the election.

Finally, I have deemed it necessary to revise the form of the election itself in the light of the present-day needs of the Church and the usages of modern society. I have thus considered it fitting not to retain election by acclamation *quasi ex inspiratione* ("as if by inspiration"), judging that it is no longer an apt means of interpreting the thought of an electoral college so great in number and so diverse in origin. It also appeared necessary to eliminate election *per compromissum* ("by [delegated] compromise"), not only because of the difficulty of the procedure, evident from the unwieldy accumulation of rules issued in the past, but also because by its very nature it tends to lessen the responsibility of the individual electors who, in this case, would not be required to express their choice personally.

After careful reflection I have therefore decided that the only form by which the electors can manifest their vote in the election of the Roman Pontiff is by secret ballot, in accordance with the rules set forth below. This form offers the greatest guarantee of clarity, straightforwardness, simplicity, transparency, and, above all, an effective and fruitful participation on the part of the Cardinals who, individually and as a group, are called to make up the assembly that elects the Successor of Peter.

With these intentions, I promulgate the present Apostolic Constitution containing the norms which, when the Roman See becomes vacant, are to be strictly followed by the Cardinals whose right and duty it is to elect the Successor of Peter, the visible Head of the whole Church and the Servant of the servants of God.

PART ONE

THE VACANCY OF THE APOSTOLIC SEE

Chapter I
The Powers of the College of Cardinals
During the Vacancy of the Apostolic See

1. During the vacancy of the Apostolic See, the College of Cardinals has no power or jurisdiction in matters which pertain to the Supreme Pontiff during his lifetime or in the exercise of his office; such matters are to be reserved completely and exclusively to the future Pope. I therefore declare null and void any act of power or jurisdiction pertaining to the Roman Pontiff during his lifetime or in the exercise of his office that the College of Cardinals might see fit to exercise, beyond the limits expressly permitted in this Constitution.

2. During the vacancy of the Apostolic See, the government of the Church is entrusted to the College of Cardinals solely for the dispatch of ordinary business and of matters that cannot be postponed (cf. No. 6), and for the preparation of everything necessary for the election of the new Pope. This task must be carried out in the ways and within the limits set down by this Constitution: consequently, those matters are to be absolutely excluded which, whether by law or by practice, come under the power of the Roman Pontiff alone or concern the norms for the election of the new Pope laid down in the present Constitution.

3. I further establish that the College of Cardinals may make no dispositions whatsoever concerning the rights of the Apostolic See and of the Roman Church, much less allow any of these rights to lapse, either directly or indirectly, even though it be to resolve disputes or to prosecute actions perpetrated against these same rights after the death or valid resignation of the Pope.[13] All the Cardinals are obliged to defend these rights.

4. During the vacancy of the Apostolic See, laws issued by the Roman Pontiffs can in no way be corrected or modified, nor can anything be added or subtracted, nor a dispensation be given even from a part of them, especially with regard to the procedures governing the election of the Supreme Pontiff. Indeed, should anything be done or even attempted against this prescription, by my supreme authority I declare it null and void.

5. Should doubts arise concerning the prescriptions contained in this Constitution, or concerning the manner of putting them into effect, I decree that all power of issuing a judgment in this regard belongs to the College of Cardinals, to which I grant the faculty of interpreting doubtful or disputed points. I also establish that should it be necessary to discuss these or other similar questions, except the act of election, it suffices that the majority of the Cardinals present should concur in the same opinion.

6. In the same way, should there be a problem that, in the view of the majority of the assembled Cardinals, cannot be postponed until another time, the College of Cardinals may act according to the majority opinion.

---

[13]Cf. *Code of Canon Law*, Canon 332 §2, *Code of Canons of the Eastern Churches*, Canon 47 §2.

Chapter II
The Congregations of the Cardinals in Preparation
for the Election of the Supreme Pontiff

7. While the See is vacant, there are two kinds of Congregations of the Cardinals: *General* Congregations, which include the whole College and are held before the beginning of the election, and *Particular* Congregations. All the Cardinals who are not legitimately impeded must attend the General Congregations, once they have been informed of the vacancy of the Apostolic See. Cardinals who, by virtue of No. 33 of this Constitution, do not enjoy the right of electing the Pope are granted the faculty of not attending these General Congregations, should they prefer.

The Particular Congregation is made up of the Cardinal Camerlengo of Holy Roman Church and three Cardinals, one from each Order, chosen by lot from among the Cardinal electors already present in Rome. The office of these Cardinals, called Assistants, ceases at the conclusion of the third full day, and their roles are taken over by others, also chosen by lot and having the same term of office, also after the election has begun.

During the time of the election, more important matters are, if necessary, dealt with by the assembly of the Cardinal electors, while ordinary affairs continue to be dealt with by the Particular Congregation of Cardinals. In the General and Particular Congregations, during the vacancy of the Apostolic See, the Cardinals are to wear the usual black cassock with piping and the red sash, with skullcap, pectoral cross and ring.

8. The Particular Congregations are to deal only with questions of lesser importance that arise on a daily basis or from time to time. But should there arise more serious questions deserving fuller examination, these must be submitted to the General Congregation. Moreover, anything decided, resolved or refused in one Particular Congregation cannot be revoked, altered or granted in another; the right to do this belongs solely to the General Congregation, and by a majority vote.

9. The General Congregations of Cardinals are to be held in the Apostolic Palace in the Vatican or, if circumstances demand it, in another place judged more suitable by the Cardinals. At these Congregations the Dean of the College presides or, should he be absent or lawfully impeded, the Vice-Dean. If one or both of these, in accordance with No. 33 of this Constitution, no longer enjoy the right of electing the Pope, the assembly of the Cardinal electors will be presided over by the senior Cardinal elector, according to the customary order of precedence.

10. Votes in the Congregations of Cardinals, when more important matters are concerned, are not to be expressed by word of mouth but in a way that ensures secrecy.

11. The General Congregations preceding the beginning of the election, which are therefore called "preparatory," are to be held daily, beginning on the day which shall be fixed by the Camerlengo of Holy Roman Church and the senior Cardinal of each of the three Orders among the electors, and including the days on which the funeral rites for the deceased Pope are celebrated. In this way the Cardinal Camerlengo can hear the opinion of the College and communicate whatever is considered necessary or appropriate, while the individual Cardinals can express their views on possible problems, ask for explanations in case of doubt and make suggestions.

12. In the first General Congregations provision is to be made for each Cardinal to have available a copy of this Constitution and at the same time to have an opportunity to raise questions about the meaning and the implementation of its norms. The part of the present Constitution regarding the vacancy of the Apostolic See should also be read aloud. At the same time the Cardinals present are to swear an oath to observe the prescriptions contained herein and to maintain secrecy. This oath, which shall also be taken by Cardinals who arrive late and subsequently take part in these Congregations, is to be read aloud by the Cardinal Dean or by whoever else presides over the College by virtue of No. 9 of this Constitution, in the presence of the other Cardinals and according to the following formula:

We, the Cardinals of Holy Roman Church, of the Order of Bishops, of Priests and of Deacons, promise, pledge and swear, as a body and individually, to observe exactly and faithfully all the norms contained in the Apostolic Constitution Universi Dominici Gregis *of the Supreme Pontiff John Paul II, and to maintain rigorous secrecy with regard to all matters in any way related to the election of the Roman Pontiff or those which, by their very nature, during the vacancy of the Apostolic See, call for the same secrecy.*

Next, each Cardinal shall add: *"And I, N. Cardinal N., so promise, pledge and swear."* And, placing his hand on the Gospels, he will add: *"So help me God and these Holy Gospels which I now touch with my hand."*

13. In one of the Congregations immediately following, the Cardinals, on the basis of a prearranged agenda, shall take the more urgent decisions regarding the beginning of the election. In other words:

a) they shall fix the day, hour and manner in which the body of the deceased Pope shall be brought to the Vatican Basilica in order to be exposed for the homage of the faithful;

b) they shall make all necessary arrangements for the funeral rites of the deceased Pope, to be celebrated for nine consecutive days, determining when they are to begin, in such a way that burial will take place, except for special reasons, between the fourth and sixth day after death;

c) they shall see to it that the Commission, made up of the Cardinal Camerlengo and the Cardinals who had formerly held the offices of Secretary of State and President of the Pontifical Commission for Vatican City State, ensures that the rooms of the *Domus Sanctae Marthae* are made ready for the suitable lodging of the Cardinal electors, that rooms suitable for those persons mentioned in No. 46 of the present Constitution are also made ready, and that all necessary arrangements are made to prepare the Sistine Chapel so that the election process can be carried out in a smooth and orderly manner and with maximum discretion, according to the provisions laid down in this Constitution;

d) they shall entrust to two ecclesiastics known for their sound doctrine, wisdom and moral authority the task of presenting to the Cardinals two well-prepared meditations on the problems facing the Church at the time and on the need for careful discernment in choosing the new Pope; at the same time, without prejudice to the provisions of No. 52 of this Constitution, they shall fix the day and the time when the first of these meditations is to be given;

e) they shall approve—at the proposal of the Administration of the Apostolic See or, within its competence, of the Government of Vatican City State—expenses incurred from the death of the Pope until the election of his successor;

f) they shall read any documents left by the deceased Pope for the College of Cardinals;

g) they shall arrange for the destruction of the Fisherman's Ring and of the lead seal with which Apostolic Letters are dispatched;

h) they shall make provision for the assignment of rooms by lot to the Cardinal electors;

i) they shall set the day and hour of the beginning of the voting process.

Chapter III
Concerning Certain Aspects During the Vacancy of the Apostolic See

14. According to the provisions of Article 6 of the Apostolic Constitution *Pastor Bonus*,[14] at the death of the Pope all the heads of the Dicasteries of the Roman Curia—the Cardinal Secretary of State and the Cardinal Prefects, the Archbishop Presidents, together with the members of those Dicasteries—cease to exercise their office. An exception is made for the Camerlengo of Holy Roman Church and the Major Penitentiary, who continue to exercise their ordinary functions, submitting to the College of Cardinals matters that would have had to be referred to the Supreme Pontiff.

Likewise, in conformity with the Apostolic Constitution *Vicariae Potestatis* (No. 2§1),[15] the Cardinal Vicar General for the Diocese of Rome continues in office during the vacancy of the Apostolic See, as does the Cardinal Archpriest of the Vatican Basilica and Vicar General for Vatican City for his jurisdiction.

15. Should the offices of Camerlengo of Holy Roman Church or of Major Penitentiary be vacant at the time of the Pope's death, or should they become vacant before the election of his successor, the College of Cardinals shall as soon as possible elect the Cardinal, or Cardinals as the case may be, who shall hold these offices until the election of the new Pope. In each of the two cases mentioned, election takes place by a secret vote of all the Cardinal electors present, with the use of ballots distributed and collected by the Masters of Ceremonies. The ballots are then opened in the presence of the Camerlengo and of the three Cardinal Assistants, if it is a matter of electing the Major Penitentiary; if it is a matter of electing the Camerlengo, they are opened in the presence of the said three Cardinals and of the Secretary of the College of Cardinals. Whoever

---

[14] Cf. *Acta Apostolicae Sedis* 80 (1988): 860.
[15] Cf. *Acta Apostolicae Sedis* 69 (1977), 9–10.

receives the greatest number of votes shall be elected and shall *ipso facto* enjoy all the relevant faculties. In the case of an equal number of votes, the Cardinal belonging to the higher Order or, if both are in the same Order, the one first created a Cardinal, shall be appointed. Until the Camerlengo is elected, his functions are carried out by the Dean of the College or, if he is absent or lawfully impeded, by the Vice-Dean or by the senior Cardinal according to the usual order of precedence, in conformity with No. 9 of this Constitution, who can without delay take the decisions that circumstances dictate.

16. If during the vacancy of the Apostolic See the Vicar General for the Diocese of Rome should die, the Vicegerent in office at the time shall also exercise the office proper to the Cardinal Vicar in addition to the ordinary vicarious jurisdiction that he already holds.[16] Should there not be a Vicegerent, the Auxiliary Bishop who is senior by appointment will carry out his functions.

17. As soon as he is informed of the death of the Supreme Pontiff, the Camerlengo of Holy Roman Church must officially ascertain the Pope's death, in the presence of the Master of Papal Liturgical Celebrations, of the Cleric Prelates of the Apostolic Camera and of the Secretary and Chancellor of the same; the latter shall draw up the official death certificate. The Camerlengo must also place seals on the Pope's study and bedroom, making provision that the personnel who ordinarily reside in the private apartment can remain there until after the burial of the Pope, at which time the entire papal apartment will be sealed; he must notify the Cardinal Vicar for Rome of the Pope's death, whereupon the latter shall inform the People of Rome by a special announcement; he shall notify the Cardinal Archpriest of the Vatican Basilica; he shall take possession of the Apostolic Palace in the Vatican and, either in person or through a delegate, of the Palaces of the Lateran and of Castel Gandolfo, and exercise custody and administration of the same; he shall determine, after consulting the heads of the three Orders of Cardinals, all matters concerning the Pope's burial, unless during his lifetime the latter had made known his wishes in this regard; and he shall deal, in the name of and with the consent of the College of Cardinals, with all matters that circumstances suggest for safeguarding the rights of the Apostolic See and for its proper administration. During the vacancy of the Apostolic See, the Camerlengo of Holy Roman Church has the duty of safeguarding and administering the goods and temporal rights of the Holy See, with the help of the three Cardinal Assistants, having sought the views of the College of Cardinals, once only for less important matters, and on each occasion when more serious matters arise.

18. The Cardinal Major Penitentiary and his Officials, during the vacancy of the Apostolic See, can carry out the duties laid down by my Predecessor Pius XI in the Apostolic Constitution *Quae Divinitus* of 25 March 1935,[17] and by myself in the Apostolic Constitution *Pastor Bonus*.[18]

---

[16]Cf. Apostolic Constitution *Vicariae Potestatis* (6 January 1977), 2 §4 [in *Acta Apostolicae Sedis* 69 (1977): 10].

[17]Cf. No. 12 [in *Acta Apostolicae Sedis* 27 (1935): 112–113].

[18]Cf. Art. 117 [in *Acta Apostolicae Sedis* 80 (1988): 905].

19. The Dean of the College of Cardinals, for his part, as soon as he has been informed of the Pope's death by either by the Cardinal Camerlengo or by the Prefect of the Papal Household, shall inform all the Cardinals and convoke them for the Congregations of the College. He shall also communicate news of the Pope's death to the Diplomatic Corps accredited to the Holy See and to the Heads of the respective Nations.

20. During the vacancy of the Apostolic See, the Substitute of the Secretariat of State, the Secretary for Relations with States and the Secretaries of the Dicasteries of the Roman Curia remain in charge of their respective offices, and are responsible to the College of Cardinals.

21. In the same way, the office and attendant powers of Papal Representatives do not lapse.

22. The Almoner of His Holiness will also continue to carry out works of charity in accordance with the criteria employed during the Pope's lifetime. He will be dependent upon the College of Cardinals until the election of the new Pope.

23. During the vacancy of the Apostolic See, all the civil power of the Supreme Pontiff concerning the government of Vatican City State belongs to the College of Cardinals, which however will be unable to issue decrees except in cases of urgent necessity and solely for the time in which the Holy See is vacant. Such decrees will be valid for the future only if the new Pope confirms them.

Chapter IV
Faculties of the Dicasteries of the Roman Curia During the Vacancy of the Apostolic See

24. During the period of vacancy, the Dicasteries of the Roman Curia, with the exception of those mentioned in No. 26 of this Constitution, have no faculty in matters which, *Sede plena* ("when the See is occupied"), they can only deal with or carry out *facto verbo cum Sanctissimo* ("by order of His Holiness") or *ex Audientia Sanctissimi* ("from an audience with His Holiness") or *vigore specialium et extraordinariarum facultatum* ("in virtue of special and extraordinary faculties") which the Roman Pontiff is accustomed to grant to the Prefects, Presidents or Secretaries of those Dicasteries.

25. The ordinary faculties proper to each Dicastery do not, however, cease at the death of the Pope. Nevertheless, I decree that the Dicasteries are only to make use of these faculties for the granting of favors of lesser importance, while more serious or controverted matters, if they can be postponed, shall be exclusively reserved to the future Pope. If such matters admit of no delay (as for example in the case of dispensations which the Supreme Pontiff usually grants *in articulo mortis* ["in danger of death"]), they can be entrusted by the College of Cardinals to the Cardinal who was Prefect until the Pope's death, or to the Archbishop who was then President, and to the other Cardinals of the same Dicastery, to whose examination the deceased Supreme Pontiff would probably have entrusted them. In such circumstances, they will be able to decide *per modum provisionis*

("provisionally"), until the election of the Pope, what they judge to be most fitting and appropriate for the preservation and defense of ecclesiastical rights and traditions.

26. The Supreme Tribunal of the Apostolic Signatura and the Tribunal of the Roman Rota, during the vacancy of the Holy See, continue to deal with cases in accordance with their proper laws, with due regard for the prescriptions of Article 18, paragraphs 1 and 3 of the Apostolic Constitution *Pastor Bonus*.[19]

Chapter V
The Funeral Rites of the Roman Pontiff

27. After the death of the Roman Pontiff, the Cardinals will celebrate the funeral rites for the repose of his soul for nine consecutive days, in accordance with the *Ordo Exsequiarum Romani Pontificis*, the norms of which, together with those of the *Ordo Rituum Conclavis*, they are to observe faithfully.

28. If burial takes place in the Vatican Basilica, the relevant official document is drawn up by the Notary of the Chapter of the Basilica or by the Canon Archivist. Subsequently, a delegate of the Cardinal Camerlengo and a delegate of the Prefect of the Papal Household shall separately draw up documents certifying that burial has taken place. The former shall do so in the presence of the members of the Apostolic Camera and the latter in the presence of the Prefect of the Papal Household.

29. If the Roman Pontiff should die outside Rome, it is the task of the College of Cardinals to make all necessary arrangements for the dignified and reverent transfer of the body to the Basilica of Saint Peter's in the Vatican.

30. No one is permitted to use any means whatsoever in order to photograph or film the Supreme Pontiff either on his sickbed or after death, or to record his words for subsequent reproduction. If after the Pope's death anyone should wish to take photographs of him for documentary purposes, he must ask permission from the Cardinal Camerlengo of Holy Roman Church, who will not however permit the taking of photographs of the Supreme Pontiff except attired in pontifical vestments.

31. After the burial of the Supreme Pontiff and during the election of the new Pope, no part of the private apartment of the Supreme Pontiff is to be lived in.

32. If the deceased Supreme Pontiff has made a will concerning his belongings, bequeathing letters and private documents, and has named an executor thereof, it is the responsibility of the latter to determine and execute, in accordance with the mandate received from the testator, matters concerning the private property and writings of the deceased Pope. The executor will give an account of his activities only to the new Supreme Pontiff.

---

[19]Cf. *Acta Apostolicae Sedis* 80 (1988): 864.

PART TWO
THE ELECTION OF THE ROMAN PONTIFF

Chapter I
The Electors of the Roman Pontiff

33. The right to elect the Roman Pontiff belongs exclusively to the Cardinals of Holy Roman Church, with the exception of those who have reached their eightieth birthday before the day of the Roman Pontiff's death or the day when the Apostolic See becomes vacant. The maximum number of Cardinal electors must not exceed one hundred and twenty. The right of active election by any other ecclesiastical dignitary or the intervention of any lay power of whatsoever grade or order is absolutely excluded.

34. If the Apostolic See should become vacant during the celebration of an Ecumenical Council or of a Synod of Bishops being held in Rome or in any other place in the world, the election of the new Pope is to be carried out solely and exclusively by the Cardinal electors indicated in No. 33, and not by the Council or the Synod of Bishops. For this reason I declare null and void acts which would in any way presume with temerity to modify the regulations concerning the election or the college of electors. Moreover, in confirmation of the provisions of Canons 340 and 347 §2 of the Code of Canon Law and of Canon 53 of the Code of Canons of the Eastern Churches in this regard, a Council or Synod of Bishops, at whatever point they have reached, must be considered immediately suspended *ipso iure*, once notification is received of the vacancy of the Apostolic See. Therefore without any delay all meetings, congregations or sessions must be interrupted, and the preparation of any decrees or canons, together with the promulgation of those already confirmed, must be suspended, under pain of nullity of the same. Neither the Council nor the Synod can continue for any reason, even though it be most serious or worthy of special mention, until the new Pope, canonically elected, orders their resumption or continuation.

35. No Cardinal elector can be excluded from active or passive voice in the election of the Supreme Pontiff, for any reason or pretext, with due regard for the provisions of No. 40 of this Constitution.

36. A Cardinal of Holy Roman Church who has been created and published before the College of Cardinals thereby has the right to elect the Pope, in accordance with the norm of No. 33 of the present Constitution, even if he has not yet received the red hat or the ring, or sworn the oath. On the other hand, Cardinals who have been canonically deposed or who with the consent of the Roman Pontiff have renounced the cardinalate do not have this right. Moreover, during the period of vacancy the College of Cardinals cannot readmit or rehabilitate them.

37. I furthermore decree that, from the moment when the Apostolic See is lawfully vacant, the Cardinal electors who are present must wait fifteen full days for those who are absent; the College of Cardinals is also granted the faculty to defer, for serious reasons, the beginning of the election for a few days more. But when a maximum of twenty days have elapsed from the beginning of the vacancy of the See, all the Cardinal electors present are obliged to proceed to the election.

38. All the Cardinal electors, convoked for the election of the new Pope by the Cardinal Dean, or by another Cardinal in his name, are required, in virtue of holy obedience, to obey the announcement of convocation and to proceed to the place designated for this purpose, unless they are hindered by sickness or by some other grave impediment, which however must be recognized as such by the College of Cardinals.

39. However, should any Cardinal electors arrive *re integra*, that is, before the new Pastor of the Church has been elected, they shall be allowed to take part in the election at the stage at which it has reached.

40. If a Cardinal with the right to vote should refuse to enter Vatican City in order to take part in the election, or subsequently, once the election has begun, should refuse to remain in order to discharge his office, without manifest reason of illness attested to under oath by doctors and confirmed by the majority of the electors, the other Cardinals shall proceed freely with the election, without waiting for him or readmitting him. If on the other hand a Cardinal elector is constrained to leave Vatican City because of illness, the election can proceed without asking for his vote; if however he desires to return to the place of the election, once his health is restored or even before, he must be readmitted.

Furthermore, if a Cardinal elector leaves Vatican City for some grave reason, acknowledged as such by the majority of the electors, he can return, in order once again to take part in the election.

Chapter II
The Place of the Election and Those Admitted to It
by Reason of Their Office

41. The Conclave for the election of the Supreme Pontiff shall take place within the territory of Vatican City, in determined areas and buildings, closed to unauthorized persons in such a way as to ensure suitable accommodation for the Cardinal electors and all those legitimately called to cooperate in the orderly functioning of the election.

42. By the time fixed for the beginning of the election of the Supreme Pontiff, all the Cardinal electors must have been assigned and must have taken up suitable lodging in the *Domus Sanctae Marthae*, recently built in Vatican City.

If reasons of health, previously confirmed by the appropriate Congregation of Cardinals, require that a Cardinal elector should have a nurse in attendance, even during the period of the election, arrangements must be made to provide suitable accommodation for the latter.

43. From the beginning of the electoral process until the public announcement that the election of the Supreme Pontiff has taken place, or in any case until the new Pope so disposes, the rooms of the *Domus Sanctae Marthae*, and in particular the Sistine Chapel and the areas reserved for liturgical celebrations are to be closed to unauthorized persons, by the authority of the Cardinal Camerlengo and with the outside assistance of

the Substitute of the Secretariat of State, in accordance with the provisions set forth in the following Numbers.

During this period, the entire territory of Vatican City and the ordinary activity of the offices located therein shall be regulated in a way that permits the election of the Supreme Pontiff to be carried out with due privacy and freedom. In particular, provision shall be made to ensure that no one approaches the Cardinal electors while they are being transported from the *Domus Sanctae Marthae* to the Apostolic Vatican Palace.

44. The Cardinal electors, from the beginning of the election until its conclusion and the public announcement of its outcome, are not to communicate—whether by writing, by telephone or by any other means of communication—with persons outside the area where the election is taking place, except in cases of proven and urgent necessity, duly acknowledged by the Particular Congregation mentioned in No. 7. It is also the competence of the Particular Congregation to recognize the necessity and urgency of any communication with their respective offices on the part of the Cardinal Major Penitentiary, the Cardinal Vicar General for the Diocese of Rome and the Cardinal Archpriest of the Vatican Basilica.

45. Anyone not indicated in No. 46 below and who, while legitimately present in Vatican City in accordance with No. 43 of this Constitution, should happen to meet one of the Cardinal electors during the time of the election, is absolutely forbidden to engage in conversation of any sort, by whatever means and for whatever reason, with that Cardinal.

46. In order to meet the personal and official needs connected with the election process, the following individuals must be available and therefore properly lodged in suitable areas within the confines mentioned in No. 43 of this Constitution: the Secretary of the College of Cardinals, who acts as Secretary of the electoral assembly; the Master of Papal Liturgical Celebrations with two Masters of Ceremonies and two Religious attached to the Papal Sacristy; and an ecclesiastic chosen by the Cardinal Dean or by the Cardinal taking his place, in order to assist him in his duties.

There must also be available a number of priests from the regular clergy for hearing confessions in the different languages, and two medical doctors for possible emergencies.

Appropriate provisions must also be made beforehand for a suitable number of persons to be available for preparing and serving meals and for housekeeping.

All the persons indicated here must receive prior approval from the Cardinal Camerlengo and the three Cardinal Assistants.

47. All the persons listed in No. 46 of this Constitution who in any way or at any time should come to learn anything from any source, directly or indirectly, regarding the election process, and in particular regarding the voting which took place in the election itself, are obliged to maintain strict secrecy with all persons extraneous to the College of Cardinal electors: accordingly, before the election begins, they shall take an oath in the form and using the formula indicated in No. 48.

48. At a suitable time before the beginning of the election, the persons indicated in No. 46 of this Constitution, having been duly warned about the meaning and extent of the oath which they are to take, shall, in the presence of the Cardinal Camerlengo or another Cardinal delegated by him, and of two Masters of Ceremonies, swear and sign the oath according to the following formula:

I, N.N., promise and swear that, unless I should receive a special faculty given expressly by the newly-elected Pontiff or by his successors, I will observe absolute and perpetual secrecy with all who are not part of the College of Cardinal electors concerning all matters directly or indirectly related to the ballots cast and their scrutiny for the election of the Supreme Pontiff.

I likewise promise and swear to refrain from using any audio or video equipment capable of recording anything which takes place during the period of the election within Vatican City, and in particular anything which in any way, directly or indirectly, is related to the process of the election itself. I declare that I take this oath fully aware that an infraction thereof will make me subject to the spiritual and canonical penalties that the future Supreme Pontiff will see fit to adopt, in accordance with Canon 1399 of the Code of Canon Law.

So help me God and these Holy Gospels which I touch with my hand.

Chapter III
The Beginning of the Election

49. When the funeral rites for the deceased Pope have been celebrated according to the prescribed ritual, and everything necessary for the regular functioning of the election has been prepared, on the appointed day—and thus on the fifteenth day after the death of the Pope or, in conformity with the provisions of No. 37 of the present Constitution, not later than the twentieth—the Cardinal electors shall meet in the Basilica of Saint Peter's in the Vatican, or elsewhere, should circumstances warrant it, in order to take part in a solemn Eucharistic celebration with the Votive Mass *Pro Eligendo Papa.*[20] This celebration should preferably take place at a suitable hour in the morning, so that in the afternoon the prescriptions of the following Numbers of this Constitution can be carried out.

50. From the Pauline Chapel of the Apostolic Palace, where they will assemble at a suitable hour in the afternoon, the Cardinal electors, in choir dress, and invoking the assistance of the Holy Spirit with the chant of the *Veni Creator*, will solemnly process to the Sistine Chapel of the Apostolic Palace, where the election will be held.

51. Retaining the essential elements of the Conclave, but modifying some less important elements which, because of changed circumstances, no longer serve their original purpose, I establish and decree by the present Constitution that the election of the Supreme Pontiff, in conformity with the prescriptions contained in the following Numbers, is to take place exclusively in the Sistine Chapel of the Apostolic Palace in the Vatican. The Sistine Chapel is therefore to remain an absolutely enclosed area until the conclusion of the election, so that total secrecy may be ensured with regard to everything said or done there in any way pertaining, directly or indirectly, to the election of the Supreme Pontiff.

[20]*Missale Romanum*, No. 4, p. 795.

It will therefore be the responsibility of the College of Cardinals, operating under the authority and responsibility of the Camerlengo, assisted by the Particular Congregation mentioned in No. 7 of the present Constitution, and with the outside assistance of the Substitute of the Secretariat of State, to make all prior arrangements for the interior of the Sistine Chapel and adjacent areas to be prepared, so that the orderly election and its privacy will be ensured.

In a special way, careful and stringent checks must be made, with the help of trustworthy individuals of proven technical ability, in order to ensure that no audiovisual equipment has been secretly installed in these areas for recording and transmission to the outside.

52. When the Cardinal electors have arrived in the Sistine Chapel, in accordance with the provisions of No. 50, and still in the presence of those who took part in the solemn procession, they shall take the oath, reading aloud the formula indicated in No. 53.

The Cardinal Dean, or the Cardinal who has precedence by order and seniority in accordance with the provisions of No. 9 of the present Constitution, will read the formula aloud; then each of the Cardinal electors, touching the Holy Gospels, will read and recite the formula, as indicated in the following Number.

When the last of the Cardinal electors has taken the oath, the Master of Papal Liturgical Celebrations will give the order *"Extra omnes"* ("everyone out") and all those not taking part in the Conclave must leave the Sistine Chapel.

The only ones to remain in the Chapel are the Master of Papal Liturgical Celebrations and the ecclesiastic previously chosen to preach to the Cardinal electors the second meditation, mentioned in No. 13 d), concerning the grave duty incumbent on them and thus on the need to act with right intention for the good of the Universal Church, *solum Deum prae oculis habentes* ("having only God before their eyes").

53. In conformity with the provisions of No. 52, the Cardinal Dean or the Cardinal who has precedence by order and seniority, will read aloud the following formula of the oath:

> *We, the Cardinal electors present in this election of the Supreme Pontiff promise, pledge and swear, as individuals and as a group, to observe faithfully and scrupulously the prescriptions contained in the Apostolic Constitution of the Supreme Pontiff John Paul II,* Universi Dominici Gregis, *published on 22 February 1996. We likewise promise, pledge and swear that whichever of us by divine disposition is elected Roman Pontiff will commit himself faithfully to carrying out the* munus Petrinum *of Pastor of the Universal Church and will not fail to affirm and defend strenuously the spiritual and temporal rights and the liberty of the Holy See. In a particular way, we promise and swear to observe with the greatest fidelity and with all persons, clerical or lay, secrecy regarding everything that in any way relates to the election of the Roman Pontiff and regarding what occurs in the place of the election, directly or indirectly related to the results of the voting; we promise and swear not to break this secret in any way, either during or after the election of the new Pontiff, unless explicit authorization is granted by the same Pontiff; and never to lend support or favor to any interference, opposition or any other form of intervention, whereby secular authorities of whatever order and degree or any group of people or individuals might wish to intervene in the election of the Roman Pontiff.*

Each of the Cardinal electors, according to the order of precedence, will then take the oath according to the following formula: *"And I, N. Cardinal N., do so promise, pledge and swear."* Placing his hand on the Gospels, he will add: *"So help me God and these Holy Gospels which I touch with my hand."*

54. When the ecclesiastic who gives the meditation has concluded, he leaves the Sistine Chapel together with the Master of Papal Liturgical Celebrations. The Cardinal electors, after reciting the prayers found in the relative *Ordo*, listen to the Cardinal Dean (or the one taking his place), who begins by asking the College of electors whether the election can begin, or whether there still remain doubts which need to be clarified concerning the norms and procedures laid down in this Constitution. It is not however permitted, even if the electors are unanimously agreed, to modify or replace any of the norms and procedures which are a substantial part of the election process, under penalty of the nullity of the same deliberation.

If, in the judgment of the majority of the electors, there is nothing to prevent the election process from beginning, it shall start immediately, in accordance with the procedures indicated in this Constitution.

Chapter IV
Observance of Secrecy on All Matters Concerning the Election

55. The Cardinal Camerlengo and the three Cardinal Assistants *pro tempore* are obliged to be especially vigilant in ensuring that there is absolutely no violation of secrecy with regard to the events occurring in the Sistine Chapel, where the voting takes place, and in the adjacent areas, before, as well as during and after the voting.

In particular, relying upon the expertise of two trustworthy technicians, they shall make every effort to preserve that secrecy by ensuring that no audiovisual equipment for recording or transmitting has been installed by anyone in the areas mentioned, and particularly in the Sistine Chapel itself, where the acts of the election are carried out.

Should any infraction whatsoever of this norm occur and be discovered, those responsible should know that they will be subject to grave penalties according to the judgment of the future Pope.

56. For the whole duration of the election, the Cardinal electors are required to refrain from written correspondence and from all conversations, including those by telephone or radio, with persons who have not been duly admitted to the buildings set aside for their use.

Such conversations shall be permitted only for the most grave and urgent reasons, confirmed by the Particular Congregation of Cardinals mentioned in No. 7.

It shall therefore be the duty of the Cardinal electors to make necessary arrangements, before the beginning of the election, for the handling of all non-deferrable official or personal business, so that there will be no need for conversations of this sort to take place.

57. The Cardinal electors are likewise to refrain from receiving or sending messages of any kind outside Vatican City; naturally it is prohibited for any person legitimately present in Vatican City to deliver such messages. It is specifically prohibited to the Cardinal electors, for the entire duration of the election, to receive newspapers or periodicals of any sort, to listen to the radio or to watch television.

58. Those who, in accordance with the prescriptions of No. 46 of the present Constitution, carry out any functions associated with the election, and who directly or indirectly could in any way violate secrecy—whether by words or writing, by signs or in any other way—are absolutely obliged to avoid this, lest they incur the penalty of excommunication *latae sententiae* ("automatically") reserved to the Apostolic See.

59. In particular, the Cardinal electors are forbidden to reveal to any other person, directly or indirectly, information about the voting and about matters discussed or decided concerning the election of the Pope in the meetings of Cardinals, both before and during the time of the election. This obligation of secrecy also applies to the Cardinals who are not electors but who take part in the General Congregations in accordance with No. 7 of the present Constitution.

60. I further order the Cardinal electors, *graviter onerata ipsorum conscientia* ("as a grave obligation of conscience"), to maintain secrecy concerning these matters also after the election of the new Pope has taken place, and I remind them that it is not licit to break the secret in any way unless a special and explicit permission has been granted by the Pope himself.

61. Finally, in order that the Cardinal electors may be protected from the indiscretion of others and from possible threats to their independence of judgment and freedom of decision, I absolutely forbid the introduction into the place of the election, under whatsoever pretext, or the use, should they have been introduced, of technical instruments of any kind for the recording, reproducing or transmitting of sound, visual images or writing.

Chapter V
The Election Procedure

62. Since the forms of election known as *per acclamationem seu inspirationem* ("by acclamation or inspiration") and *per compromissum* ("by [delegated] compromise") are abolished, the form of electing the Roman Pontiff shall henceforth be *per scrutinium* ("by voting") alone.

I therefore decree that for the valid election of the Roman Pontiff two thirds of the votes are required, calculated on the basis of the total number of electors present.

Should it be impossible to divide the number of Cardinals present into three equal parts, for the validity of the election of the Supreme Pontiff one additional vote is required.

63. The election is to begin immediately after the provisions of No. 54 of the present Constitution have been duly carried out.

Should the election begin on the afternoon of the first day, only one ballot is to be held; then, on the following days, if no one was elected on the first ballot, two ballots shall be held in the morning and two in the afternoon. The voting is to begin at a time that shall have been determined earlier, either in the preparatory Congregations or during the election period, but in accordance with the procedures laid down in Nos. 64ff of the present Constitution.

64. The voting process is carried out in three phases. The first phase, which can be called the *pre-scrutiny,* comprises: 1) the preparation and distribution of the ballot papers by the Masters of Ceremonies, who give at least two or three to each Cardinal elector; 2) the drawing by lot, from among all the Cardinal electors, of three Scrutineers, of three persons charged with collecting the votes of the sick, called for the sake of brevity *Infirmarii,* and of three Revisers; this drawing is carried out in public by the junior Cardinal Deacon, who draws out nine names, one after another, of those who shall carry out these tasks; 3) if, in the drawing of lots for the Scrutineers, *Infirmarii* and Revisers, there should come out the names of Cardinal electors who because of infirmity or other reasons are unable to carry out these tasks, the names of others who are not impeded are to be drawn in their place. The first three drawn will act as Scrutineers, the second three as *Infirmarii* and the last three as Revisers.

65. For this phase of the voting process the following norms must be observed: 1) the ballot paper must be rectangular in shape and must bear in the upper half, in print if possible, the words *Eligo in Summum Pontificem* ("I elect as Supreme Pontiff"); on the lower half there must be a space left for writing the name of the person chosen; thus the ballot is made in such a way that it can be folded in two; 2) the completion of the ballot must be done in secret by each Cardinal elector, who will write down legibly, as far as possible in handwriting that cannot be identified as his, the name of the person he chooses, taking care not to write other names as well, since this would make the ballot null; he will then fold the ballot twice; 3) during the voting, the Cardinal electors are to remain alone in the Sistine Chapel; therefore, immediately after the distribution of the ballots and before the electors begin to write, the Secretary of the College of Cardinals, the Master of Papal Liturgical Celebrations and the Masters of Ceremonies must leave the Chapel. After they have left, the junior Cardinal Deacon shall close the door, opening and closing it again each time this is necessary, as for example when the *Infirmarii* go to collect the votes of the sick and when they return to the Chapel.

66. The second phase, the *scrutiny* proper, comprises: 1) the placing of the ballots in the appropriate receptacle; 2) the mixing and counting of the ballots; 3) the opening of the votes. Each Cardinal elector, in order of precedence, having completed and folded his ballot, holds it up so that it can be seen and carries it to the altar, at which the Scrutineers stand and upon which there is placed a receptacle, covered by a plate, for receiving the ballots. Having reached the altar, the Cardinal elector says aloud the words of the following oath: *I call as my witness Christ the Lord who will be my judge, that my vote is given to the one who before God I think should be elected.* He then places the ballot on the plate, with which he drops it into the receptacle. Having done this, he bows to the altar and returns to his place.

If any of the Cardinal electors present in the Chapel is unable to go to the altar because of infirmity, the last of the Scrutineers goes to him. The infirm elector, having pronounced the above oath, hands the folded ballot to the Scrutineer, who carries it in full view to the altar and omitting the oath, places it on the plate, with which he drops it into the receptacle.

67. If there are Cardinal electors who are sick and confined to their rooms, referred to in Nos. 41ff of this Constitution, the three *Infirmarii* go to them with a box which has an opening in the top through which a folded ballot can be inserted. Before giving the box to the *Infirmarii*, the Scrutineers open it publicly, so that the other electors can see that it is empty; they are then to lock it and place the key on the altar. The *Infirmarii*, taking the locked box and a sufficient number of ballot papers on a small tray, then go, duly accompanied, to the *Domus Sanctae Marthae* to each sick elector, who takes a ballot, writes his vote in secret, folds the ballot and, after taking the above-mentioned oath, puts it through the opening in the box. If any of the electors who are sick is unable to write, one of the three *Infirmarii* or another Cardinal elector chosen by the sick man, having taken an oath before the *Infirmarii* concerning the observance of secrecy, carries out the above procedure. The *Infirmarii* then take the box back into the Chapel, where it shall be opened by the Scrutineers after the Cardinals present have cast their votes. The Scrutineers then count the ballots in the box and, having ascertained that their number corresponds to the number of those who are sick, place them one by one on the plate and then drop them all together into the receptacle. In order not to prolong the voting process unduly, the *Infirmarii* may complete their own ballots and place them in the receptacle immediately after the senior Cardinal, and then go to collect the votes of the sick in the manner indicated above while the other electors are casting their votes.

68. After all the ballots of the Cardinal electors have been placed in the receptacle, the first Scrutineer shakes it several times in order to mix them, and immediately afterwards the last Scrutineer proceeds to count them, picking them out of the urn in full view and placing them in another empty receptacle previously prepared for this purpose. If the number of ballots does not correspond to the number of electors, the ballots must all be burned and a second vote taken at once; if however their number does correspond to the number of electors, the opening of the ballots then takes place in the following manner.

69. The Scrutineers sit at a table placed in front of the altar. The first of them takes a ballot, unfolds it, notes the name of the person chosen and passes the ballot to the second Scrutineer, who in his turn notes the name of the person chosen and passes the ballot to the third, who reads it out in a loud and clear voice, so that all the electors present can record the vote on a sheet of paper prepared for that purpose. He himself writes down the name read from the ballot. If during the opening of the ballots the Scrutineers should discover two ballots folded in such a way that they appear to have been completed by one elector, if these ballots bear the same name they are counted as one vote; if however they bear two different names, neither vote will be valid; however, in neither of the two cases is the voting session annulled.

When all the ballots have been opened, the Scrutineers add up the sum of the votes obtained by the different names and write them down on a separate sheet of paper. The last Scrutineer, as he reads out the individual ballots, pierces each one with a needle through the word *"Eligo"* and places it on a thread, so that the ballots can be more securely preserved. After the names have been read out, the ends of the thread are tied in a knot, and the ballots thus joined together are placed in a receptacle or on one side of the table.

70. There then follows the third and last phase, also known as the *post-scrutiny*, which comprises: 1) the counting of the votes; 2) the checking of the same; 3) the burning of the ballots.

The Scrutineers add up all the votes that each individual has received, and if no one has obtained two thirds of the votes on that ballot, the Pope has not been elected; if however it turns out that someone has obtained two thirds of the votes, the canonically valid election of the Roman Pontiff has taken place.

In either case, that is, whether the election has occurred or not, the Revisers must proceed to check both the ballots and the notes made by the Scrutineers, in order to make sure that these latter have performed their task exactly and faithfully.

Immediately after the checking has taken place, and before the Cardinal electors leave the Sistine Chapel, all the ballots are to be burnt by the Scrutineers, with the assistance of the Secretary of the Conclave and the Masters of Ceremonies who in the meantime have been summoned by the junior Cardinal Deacon. If however a second vote is to take place immediately, the ballots from the first vote will be burned only at the end, together with those from the second vote.

71. In order that secrecy may be better observed, I order each and every Cardinal elector to hand over to the Cardinal Camerlengo or to one of the three Cardinal Assistants any notes which he may have in his possession concerning the results of each ballot. These notes are to be burnt together with the ballots.

I further lay down that at the end of the election the Cardinal Camerlengo of Holy Roman Church shall draw up a document, to be approved also by the three Cardinal Assistants, declaring the result of the voting at each session. This document is to be given to the Pope and will thereafter be kept in a designated archive, enclosed in a sealed envelope, which may be opened by no one unless the Supreme Pontiff gives explicit permission.

72. Confirming the dispositions of my Predecessors, Saint Pius X,[21] Pius XII[22] and Paul VI,[23] I decree that—except for the afternoon of the entrance into the Conclave—both in the morning and in the afternoon, after a ballot which does not result in an

---

[21]Cf. Apostolic Constitution *Vacante Sede Apostolica* (25 December 1904), 76: *Pii X Pontificis Maximi Acta*, III (1908), 280–281.

[22]Cf. Apostolic Constitution *Vacantis Apostolicae Sedis* (8 December 1945), 88 [in *Acta Apostolicae Sedis* 38 (1946): 93].

[23]Cf. Apostolic Constitution *Romano Pontifici eligendo* (1 October 1975), 74 [in *Acta Apostolicae Sedis* 67 (1975): 639].

election, the Cardinal electors shall proceed immediately to a second one, in which they are to express their vote anew. In this second ballot all the formalities of the previous one are to be observed, with the difference that the electors are not bound to take a new oath or to choose new Scrutineers, *Infirmarii* and Revisers. Everything done in this regard for the first ballot will be valid for the second one, without the need for any repetition.

73. Everything that has been laid down above concerning the voting procedures must be diligently observed by the Cardinal electors in all the ballots, which are to take place each day, in the morning and in the afternoon, after the celebration of the sacred rites or prayers laid down in the *Ordo Rituum Conclavis*.

74. In the event that the Cardinal electors find it difficult to agree on the person to be elected, after balloting has been carried out for three days in the form described above (in Nos. 62ff.) without result, voting is to be suspended for a maximum of one day in order to allow a pause for prayer, informal discussion among the voters, and a brief spiritual exhortation given by the senior Cardinal in the Order of Deacons. Voting is then resumed in the usual manner, and after seven ballots, if the election has not taken place, there is another pause for prayer, discussion and an exhortation given by the senior Cardinal in the Order of Priests. Another series of seven ballots is then held and, if there has still been no election, this is followed by a further pause for prayer, discussion and an exhortation given by the senior Cardinal in the Order of Bishops. Voting is then resumed in the usual manner and, unless the election occurs, it is to continue for seven ballots.

75. If the balloting does not result in an election, even after the provisions of No. 74 have been fulfilled, the Cardinal electors shall be invited by the Camerlengo to express an opinion about the manner of proceeding. The election will then proceed in accordance with whatever the absolute majority of the electors shall decide.

Nevertheless, there can be no waiving of the requirement that a valid election takes place only by an absolute majority of the votes or else by voting only on the two names which in the ballot immediately preceding have received the greatest number of votes; also in this second case only an absolute majority is required.

76. Should the election take place in a way other than that prescribed in the present Constitution, or should the conditions laid down here not be observed, the election is for this very reason null and void, without any need for a declaration on the matter; consequently, it confers no right on the one elected.

77. I decree that the dispositions concerning everything that precedes the election of the Roman Pontiff and the carrying out of the election itself must be observed in full, even if the vacancy of the Apostolic See should occur as a result of the resignation of the Supreme Pontiff, in accordance with the provisions of Canon 333 §2 of the Code of Canon Law and Canon 44 §2 of the Code of Canons of the Eastern Churches.

Chapter VI

Matters to be Observed or Avoided in the
Election of the Roman Pontiff

78. If—God forbid—in the election of the Roman Pontiff the crime of simony were to be perpetrated, I decree and declare that all those guilty thereof shall incur excommunication *latae sententiae* ("automatically"). At the same time I remove the nullity or invalidity of the same simoniacal provision, in order that—as was already established by my Predecessors—the validity of the election of the Roman Pontiff may not for this reason be challenged.[24]

79. Confirming the prescriptions of my Predecessors, I likewise forbid anyone, even if he is a Cardinal, during the Pope's lifetime and without having consulted him, to make plans concerning the election of his successor, or to promise votes, or to make decisions in this regard in private gatherings.

80. In the same way, I wish to confirm the provisions made by my Predecessors for the purpose of excluding any external interference in the election of the Supreme Pontiff. Therefore, in virtue of holy obedience and under pain of excommunication *latae sententiae*, I again forbid each and every Cardinal elector, present and future, as also the Secretary of the College of Cardinals and all other persons taking part in the preparation and carrying out of everything necessary for the election, to accept under any pretext whatsoever, from any civil authority whatsoever, the task of proposing the *veto* or the so-called *exclusiva*, even under the guise of a simple desire, or to reveal such either to the entire electoral body assembled together or to individual electors, in writing or by word of mouth, either directly and personally or indirectly and through others, both before the election begins and for its duration. I intend this prohibition to include all possible forms of interference, opposition and suggestion whereby secular authorities of whatever order and degree, or any individual or group, might attempt to exercise influence on the election of the Pope.

81. The Cardinal electors shall further abstain from any form of pact, agreement, promise or other commitment of any kind that could oblige them to give or deny their vote to a person or persons. If this were in fact done, even under oath, I decree that such a commitment shall be null and void and that no one shall be bound to observe it; and I hereby impose the penalty of excommunication *latae sententiae* upon those who violate this prohibition. It is not my intention however to forbid, during the period in which the See is vacant, the exchange of views concerning the election.

82. I likewise forbid the Cardinals before the election to enter into any stipulations, committing themselves of common accord to a certain course of action should one of them be elevated to the Pontificate. These promises too, should any in fact be made, even under oath, I also declare null and void.

---

[24]Cf. Saint Pius X, Apostolic Constitution *Vacante Sede Apostolica* (25 December 1904), 79: *Pii X Pontificis Maximi Acta*, III (1908), 282; Pius XII, Apostolic Constitution *Vacantis Apostolicae Sedis* (8 December 1945), 92 [in *Acta Apostolicae Sedis* 38 (1946): 94]; Paul VI, Apostolic Constitution *Romano Pontifici eligendo* (1 October 1975), 79 [in *Acta Apostolicae Sedis* 67 (1975): 641].

83. With the same insistence shown by my Predecessors, I earnestly exhort the Cardinal electors not to allow themselves to be guided, in choosing the Pope, by friendship or aversion, or to be influenced by favor or personal relationships towards anyone, or to be constrained by the interference of persons in authority or by pressure groups, by the suggestions of the mass media, or by force, fear or the pursuit of popularity. Rather, having before their eyes solely the glory of God and the good of the Church, and having prayed for divine assistance, they shall give their vote to the person, even outside the College of Cardinals, who in their judgment is most suited to govern the universal Church in a fruitful and beneficial way.

84. During the vacancy of the Apostolic See, and above all during the time of the election of the Successor of Peter, the Church is united in a very special way with her Pastors and particularly with the Cardinal electors of the Supreme Pontiff, and she asks God to grant her a new Pope as a gift of his goodness and providence. Indeed, following the example of the first Christian community spoken of in the Acts of the Apostles (cf. 1:14), the universal Church, spiritually united with Mary, the Mother of Jesus, should persevere with one heart in prayer; thus the election of the new Pope will not be something unconnected with the People of God and concerning the College of electors alone, but will be in a certain sense an act of the whole Church. I therefore lay down that in all cities and other places, at least the more important ones, as soon as news is received of the vacancy of the Apostolic See and, in particular, of the death of the Pope, and following the celebration of his solemn funeral rites, humble and persevering prayers are to be offered to the Lord (cf. *Mt* 21:22; *Mk* 11:24), that he may enlighten the electors and make them so likeminded in their task that a speedy, harmonious and fruitful election may take place, as the salvation of souls and the good of the whole People of God demand.

85. In a most earnest and heartfelt way I recommend this prayer to the venerable Cardinals who, by reason of age, no longer enjoy the right to take part in the election of the Supreme Pontiff. By virtue of the singular bond with the Apostolic See which the Cardinalate represents, let them lead the prayer of the People of God, whether gathered in the Patriarchal Basilicas of the city of Rome or in places of worship in other particular Churches, fervently imploring the assistance of Almighty God and the enlightenment of the Holy Spirit for the Cardinal electors, especially at the time of the election itself. They will thereby participate in an effective and real way in the difficult task of providing a Pastor for the universal Church.

86. I also ask the one who is elected not to refuse, for fear of its weight, the office to which he has been called, but to submit humbly to the design of the divine will. God who imposes the burden will sustain him with his hand, so that he will be able to bear it. In conferring the heavy task upon him, God will also help him to accomplish it and, in giving him the dignity, he will grant him the strength not to be overwhelmed by the weight of his office.

Chapter VII

The Acceptance and Proclamation of the New Pope
and the Beginning of His Ministry

87. When the election has canonically taken place, the junior Cardinal Deacon summons into the hall of election the Secretary of the College of Cardinals and the Master of Papal Liturgical Celebrations. The Cardinal Dean, or the Cardinal who is first in order and seniority, in the name of the whole College of electors, then asks the consent of the one elected in the following words: *"Do you accept your canonical election as Supreme Pontiff?"* And, as soon as he has received the consent, he asks him: *"By what name do you wish to be called?"* Then the Master of Papal Liturgical Celebrations, acting as notary and having as witnesses two Masters of Ceremonies, who are to be summoned at that moment, draws up a document certifying acceptance by the new Pope and the name taken by him.

88. After his acceptance, the person elected, if he has already received episcopal ordination, is immediately Bishop of the Church of Rome, true Pope and Head of the College of Bishops. He thus acquires and can exercise full and supreme power over the universal Church.

If the person elected is not already a Bishop, he shall immediately be ordained Bishop.

89. When the other formalities provided for in the *Ordo Rituum Conclavis* have been carried out, the Cardinal electors approach the newly elected Pope in the prescribed manner, in order to make an act of homage and obedience. An act of thanksgiving to God is then made, after which the senior Cardinal Deacon announces to the waiting people that the election has taken place and proclaims the name of the new Pope, who immediately thereafter imparts the Apostolic Blessing *Urbi et Orbi* from the balcony of the Vatican Basilica.

If the person elected is not already a Bishop, homage is paid to him and the announcement of his election is made only after he has been solemnly ordained Bishop.

90. If the person elected resides outside Vatican City, the norms contained in the *Ordo Rituum Conclavis* are to be observed.

If the newly-elected Supreme Pontiff is not already a Bishop, his episcopal ordination, referred to in Nos. 88 and 89 of the present Constitution, shall be carried out according to the usage of the Church by the Dean of the College of Cardinals or, in his absence, by the Subdean or, should he too be prevented from doing so, by the senior Cardinal Bishop.

91. The Conclave ends immediately after the new Supreme Pontiff assents to his election, unless he should determine otherwise. From that moment the new Pope can be approached by the Substitute of the Secretariat of State, the Secretary for Relations with States, the Prefect of the Papal Household and by anyone else needing to discuss with him matters of importance at the time.

92. After the solemn ceremony of the inauguration of the Pontificate and within an appropriate time, the Pope will take possession of the Patriarchal Archbasilica of the Lateran, according to the prescribed ritual.

Promulgation

Wherefore, after mature reflection and following the example of my Predecessors, I lay down and prescribe these norms and I order that no one shall presume to contest the present Constitution and anything contained herein for any reason whatsoever. This Constitution is to be completely observed by all, notwithstanding any disposition to the contrary, even if worthy of special mention. It is to be fully and integrally implemented and is to serve as a guide for all to whom it refers.

As determined above, I hereby declare abrogated all Constitutions and Orders issued in this regard by the Roman Pontiffs, and at the same time I declare completely null and void anything done by any person, whatever his authority, knowingly or unknowingly, in any way contrary to this Constitution.

Given in Rome, at Saint Peter's, on 22 February, the Feast of the Chair of Saint Peter, Apostle, in the year 1996, the eighteenth of my Pontificate.

IOANNES PAULUS PP. II

Appendix 3

CARDINALS PRESENTLY
ELIGIBLE TO VOTE IN A CONCLAVE[1]

NAME / POSITION / TITLE	COUNTRY	DATE OF BIRTH
—Cardinal Bishops		
ANGELO SODANO Secretary of State *Titular of the Suburbicarian Sees of Ostia* *and of Albano* *Titular "in commendam" of Santa Maria Nuova* *Dean of the College of Cardinals*	Italy	November 23, 1927
ALFONSO LÓPEZ TRUJILLO President of the Pontifical Council for the Family *Titular of the Suburbicarian See of Frascati*	Colombia	November 8, 1935

GIOVANNI BATTISTA RE
Prefect of the Congregation of Bishops
President of the Pontifical Commission for
  Latin America
Titular of the Suburbicarian See of
  Sabina-Poggia Mirteto
	Italy	January 30, 1934

[1]Under the provisions of the apostolic constitution *Universi Dominici gregis*, promulgated by Pope John Paul II on February 22, 1996, "those Cardinals who celebrate their eightieth birthday before the day when the Apostolic See becomes vacant do not take part in the election." The present list includes those members of the College of Cardinals who were eligible under this norm to participate as of December 31, 2005. The cardinals are listed according to their respective order of precedence within the college.

NAME / POSITION / TITLE	COUNTRY	DATE OF BIRTH

IGNACE MOUSSA I DAOUD   Syria   September 18, 1930
Prefect of the Congregation for the
  Oriental Churches
Patriarch Emeritus of Antioch of the Syrians

FRANCIS ARINZE   Nigeria   November 1, 1932
Prefect of the Congregation for Divine Worship
  and the Discipline of the Sacraments
Titular of the Suburbicarian See of
Velletri-Segni

—Cardinal Priests

JAIME L. SIN   Philippines   August 31, 1928
Archbishop Emeritus of Manila
Titular of Santa Maria ai Monti

WILLIAM WAKEFIELD BAUM   U.S.A.   November 21, 1926
Major Penitentiary Emeritus
Titular of Santa Croce in Via Flaminia

FRANCISZEK MACHARSKI   Poland   May 20, 1927
Archbishop of Cracow
Titular of San Giovanni a Porta Latina

MICHAEL MICHAI KITBUNCHU   Thailand   January 25, 1929
Archbishop of Bangkok
Titular of San Lorenzo in Panisperna

GODFRIED DANNEELS   Belgium   June 4, 1933
Archbishop of Mechlin-Brussels
Titular of Santa Anastasia

THOMAS STAFFORD WILLIAMS   New Zealand   March 20, 1930
Archbishop Emeritus of Wellington
Titular of Gesù Divin Maestro alla Pineta Sacchetti

CARLO MARIA MARTINI, S.J.   Italy   February 15, 1927
Archbishop Emeritus of Milan
Titular of Santa Cecilia

NAME / POSITION / TITLE	COUNTRY	DATE OF BIRTH
JEAN-MARIE LUSTIGER Archbishop Emeritus of Paris *Titular of San Luigi dei Francesi*	France	September 17, 1926
JÓZEF GLEMP Archbishop of Warsaw Primate of Poland *Titular of Santa Maria in Trastevere*	Poland	December 18, 1929
JOACHIM MEISNER Archbishop of Cologne *Titular of Santa Pudenziana*	Germany	December 25, 1933
MIGUEL OBANDO BRAVO, S.D.B. Archbishop Emeritus of Managua *Titular of San Giovanni Evangelista a Spinaceto*	Nicaragua	February 2, 1926
RICARDO J. VIDAL Archbishop of Cebu *Titular of Santi Pietro e Paolo a Via Ostiense*	Philippines	February 6, 1931
PAUL POUPARD President of the Pontifical Council of Culture *Titular of Santa Prassede*	France	August 30, 1939
FRIEDRICH WETTER Archbishop of Munich and Freising *Titular of Santo Stefano al Monte Celio*	Germany	February 20, 1928
ADRIANUS JOHANNES SIMONIS Archbishop of Utrecht *Titular of San Clemente*	Netherlands	November 26, 1931
BERNARD FRANCIS LAW Archbishop Emeritus of Boston *Titular of Santa Susanna*	U.S.A.	November 4, 1931
GIACOMO BIFFI Archbishop Emeritus of Bologna *Titular of Santi Giovanni Evangelista e Petronio*	Italy	June 13, 1928

NAME / POSITION / TITLE	COUNTRY	DATE OF BIRTH

EDUARDO MARTÍNEZ SOMALO
Prefect Emeritus of the Congregation
  for Institutes of Consecrated Life
  and Societies of Apostolic Life
Camerlengo of the Holy Roman Church
Titular of Santissimo Nome di Gesù
	Spain	March 31, 1927

MICHELE GIORDANO Archbishop of Naples *Titular of San Gioacchino ai Prati di Castello*	Italy	September 26, 1930

EDMUND CASIMIR SZOKA
President of the Pontifical Commission
  for the Vatican City State
President of the Governorate of the
  Vatican City State
Titular of Santi Andrea e Gregorio al Monte Celio
	U.S.A.	September 14, 1927

LÁSZLÓ PASKAI, O.F.M. Archbishop Emeritus of Esztergom-Budapest *Titular of Santa Teresa al Corso d'Italia*	Hungary	May 8, 1927
CHRISTIAN WIYGHAN TUMI Archbishop of Douala *Titular of Santi Martiri dell'Uganda a Poggio Ameno*	Cameroon	October 15, 1930
FRÉDÉRIC ETSOU-NZABI-BAMUNGWABI Archbishop of Kinhasa *Titular of Santa Lucia a Piazza d'Armi*	Dem. Congo	December 3, 1930
NICOLAS DE JESUS LOPEZ RODRIGUEZ Archbishop of Santo Domingo Military Ordinary for the Dominican Republic *Titular of San Pio X alla Balduina*	Dominican Rep.	October 31, 1936
ROGER MICHAEL MAHONEY Archbishop of Los Angeles *Titular of Santi Quattro Coronati*	U.S.A.	February 27, 1936

NAME / POSITION / TITLE	COUNTRY	DATE OF BIRTH
CAMILLO RUINI Vicar General of His Holiness for the Diocese of Rome Archpriest of the Patriarchal Lateran Archbasilica *Titular of Sant'Agnese fuori le Mure*	Italy	February 19, 1931
HENRI SCHWERY Bishop Emeritus of Sion *Titular of Santi Protomartiri a Via Aurelia Antica*	Switzerland	June 14, 1932
GEORG MAXIMILAN STERZINSKY Archbishop of Berlin *Titular of San Giuseppe all'Aurelio*	Germany	February 9, 1936
MILOSLAV VLK Archbishop of Prague *Titular of Santa Croce in Gerusalemme*	Czech Rep.	May 17, 1932
PETER SEIICHI SHIRAYANAGI Archbishop Emeritus of Tokyo *Titular of Sant'Emerenziana a Tor Fiorenza*	Japan	June 17, 1928
ADOLFO ANTONIO SUÁREZ RIVERA Archbishop of Monterrey *Titular of Nostra Signora di Guadalupe a Monte Mario*	Mexico	January 9, 1927
JULIUS RIYADI DARMAATMADJA, S.J. Archbishop of Jakarta Military Ordinary for Indonesia *Titular of Sacro Cuore di Maria*	Indonesia	December 20, 1934
JAIME LUCAS ORTEGA Y ALAMINO Archbishop of San Cristóbal de La Habana *Titular of Sante Aquila e Priscilla*	Cuba	October 18, 1936
EMMANUEL WAMALA Archbishop of Kampala *Titular of Sant'Ugo*	Uganda	December 15, 1926

NAME / POSITION / TITLE	COUNTRY	DATE OF BIRTH
WILLIAM HENRY KEELER Archbishop of Baltimore *Titular of Santa Maria degli Angeli*	U.S.A.	March 4, 1931
JEAN-CLAUDE TURCOTTE Archbishop of Montréal *Titular of Nostra Signora del Santissimo* *Sacramento e Santi Martiri Canadesi*	Canada	June 26, 1936
RICARDO MARÍO CARLES GORDÓ Archbishop of Barcelona *Titular of Santa Maria Consolatrice al Tiburtino*	Spain	September 24, 1926
ADAM JOSEPH MAIDA Archbishop of Detroit *Titular of Santi Vitale, Valeria, Gervasio e Protasio*	U.S.A.	March 18, 1930
VINKO PULJIC´ Archbishop of Vrhbosna (Sarajevo) *Titular of Santa Chiara a Vigna Clara*	Bosnia	September 8, 1945
JUAN SANDOVAL ÍÑIGUEZ Archbishop of Guadalajara *Titular of Nostra Signora di Guadalupe* *e San Filippo Martire in Via Aurelia*	Mexico	March 28, 1933
SALVATORE DE GIORGI Archbishop of Palermo *Titular of Santa Maria in Ara Coeli*	Italy	September 6, 1930
ANTONIO MARÍA ROUCO VARELA Archbishop of Madrid *Titular of San Lorenzo in Damaso*	Spain	August 24, 1931
ALOYSIUS MATTHEW AMBROZIC Archbishop of Toronto *Titular of Santi Marcellino e Pietro*	Canada	January 27, 1930
DIONIGI TETTAMANZI Archbishop of Milan *Titular of Santi Ambrogio e Carlo*	Italy	March 14, 1934

NAME / POSITION / TITLE	COUNTRY	DATE OF BIRTH
POLYCARP PENGO Archbishop of Dar-es-Salaam *Titular of Nostra Signora de La Salette*	Tanzania	August 5, 1944
CHRISTOPH SCHÖNBORN, O.P. Archbishop of Vienna Ordinary for Byzantine Rite Faithful in Austria *Titular of Gesù Divin Lavatore*	Austria	January 22, 1945
NORBERTO RIVERA CARRERA Archbishop of Mexico City *Titular of San Francesco d'Assisi a Ripa Grande*	Mexico	June 6, 1942
FRANCIS EUGENE GEORGE, O.M.I. Archbishop of Chicago *Titular of San Bartolomeo all'Isola*	U.S.A.	January 16, 1937
MARIAN JAWORSKI Archbishop of Lviv of the Latins *Titular of San Sisto*	Ukraine	August 21, 1926
JÁNIS PUJATS Archbishop of Riga *Titular of Santa Silvia*	Latvia	November 14, 1930
IVAN DIAS Archbishop of Bombay *Titular of Santo Spirito alla Ferratella*	India	April 14, 1936
GERALDO MAJELLA AGNELO Archbishop of São Salvador da Bahia *Titular of San Gregorio Magno alla Magliana Nuova*	Brazil	October 19, 1933
PEDRO RUBIANO SÁENZ Archbishop of Bogotá *Titular of Trasfigurazione di Nostro Signor Gesù Cristo*	Colombia	September 13, 1932
THEODORE EDGAR MCCARRICK Archbishop of Washington *Titular of Santi Nereo e Achilleo*	U.S.A.	July 7, 1930

NAME / POSITION / TITLE	COUNTRY	DATE OF BIRTH
DESMOND CONNELL Archbishop Emeritus of Dublin *Titular of San Silvestro in Capite*	Ireland	March 24, 1926
AUDRYS JUOZAS BACKIS Archbishop of Vilnius *Titular of Natività di Nostro Signore Gesù Cristo*	Lithuania	February 1, 1927
FRANCISCO JAVIER ERRÁZURIZ OSSA Archbishop of Santiago de Chile *Titular of Santa Maria della Pace*	Chile	September 5, 1933
JULIO TERRAZAS SANDOVAL, C.SS.R. Archbishop of Santa Cruz de la Sierra *Titular of San Giovanni Battista de'Rossi*	Bolivia	March 7, 1936
WILFRID FOX NAPIER, O.F.M. Archbishop of Durban Apostolic Administrator of Umzimkulu *Titular of San Francesco d'Assisi ad Acilia*	South Africa	March 8, 1941
OSCAR ANDRÉS RODRÍGUEZ MARADIAGA Archbishop of Tegucigalpa *Titular of Santa Maria della Speranza*	Honduras	December 29, 1942
BERNARD AGRÉ Archbishop of Abidjan *Titular of San Giovanni Crisostomo a Monte Sacro Alto*	Côte d'Ivoire	March 2, 1926
JUAN LUIS CIPRIANI THORNE Archbishop of Lima *Titular of San Camillo de Lellis*	Peru	December 28, 1943
CLÁUDIO HUMMES, O.F.M. Archbishop of São Paulo *Titular of San Antonio da Padova in Via Merulana*	Brazil	August 8, 1934
VARKEY VITHAYATHIL, C.SS.R. Major Archbishop of Ernakulam-Angamaly of the Syro-Malabars *Titular of San Bernardo alle Terme*	India	May 29, 1927

NAME / POSITION / TITLE	COUNTRY	DATE OF BIRTH
JORGE MARIO BERGOGLIO, S.J. Archbishop of Buenos Aires *Titular of San Roberto Bellarmino*	Argentina	December 17, 1936
JOSÉ DA CRUZ POLICARPO Patriarch of Lisbon *Titular of San Antonio in Campo Marzio*	Portugal	February 26, 1936
SEVERINO POLETTO Archbishop of Turin *Titular of San Giuseppe in Via Trionfale*	Italy	March 18, 1933
CORMAC MURPHY-O'CONNOR Archbishop of Westminster *Titular of Santa Maria sopra Minerva*	England	August 24, 1932
EDWARD MICHAEL EGAN Archbishop of New York *Titular of Santi Giovanni e Paolo*	U.S.A.	April 2, 1932
LUBOMYR HUSAR Major Archbishop of Kyiv and Halych *Titular of Santa Sofia in Via Boccea*	Ukraine	February 26, 1933
KARL LEHMANN Bishop of Mainz *Titular of San Leone I*	Germany	May 16, 1936
ANGELO SCOLA Patriarch of Venice *Titular of Santi XII Apostoli*	Italy	March 7, 1941
ANTHONY OLUBUNMI OKUGIE Archbishop of Lagos *Titular of Beata Vergine Maria del Monte Carmelo a Mostacciano*	Nigeria	June 16, 1936
BERNARD PANAFIEU Archbishop of Marseilles *Titular of San Gregorio Barbarigo alle Tre Fontane*	France	January 26, 1931

NAME / POSITION / TITLE	COUNTRY	DATE OF BIRTH
GABRIEL ZUBEIR WAKO Archbishop of Khartoum *Titular of Sant'Anastasio a Via Tiburtina*	Sudan	February 27, 1941
CARLOS AMIGO VALLEJO, O.F.M. Archbishop of Seville *Titular of Santa Maria di Monserrato* *degli Spagnoli*	Spain	August 23, 1934
JUSTIN FRANCIS RIGALI Archbishop of Philadelphia *Titular of Santa Prisca*	U.S.A.	April 19, 1935
KEITH MICHAEL PATRICK O'BRIEN Archbishop of Saint Andrews and Edinburgh *Titular of Santi Gioacchino e Anna al Tuscolano*	Scotland	March 17, 1938
EUSÉBIO OSCAR SCHEID, S.C.I. Archbishop of São Sebastião do Rio de Janeiro *Titular of Santi Bonifacio e Alessio*	Brazil	Decemher 8, 1931
ENNIO ANTONELLI Archbishop of Florence *Titular of Sant'Andrea delle Fratte*	Italy	November 18, 1936
TARCISIO BERTONE, S.D.B. Archbishop of Genoa *Titular of Santa Maria Ausiliatrice in* *Via Tuscolana*	Italy	December 2, 1934
PETER KODWO APPIAH TURKSON Archbishop of Cape Coast *Titular of San Liborio*	Ghana	October 11, 1948
TELESPHORE PLACIDUS TOPPO Archbishop of Ranchi *Titular of Sacro Cuore di Gesù agonizzante* *a Vitinia*	India	October 15, 1939
GEORGE PELL Archbishop of Sydney *Titular of Santa Maria Domenica Mazzarello*	Australia	June 8, 1941

NAME / POSITION / TITLE	COUNTRY	DATE OF BIRTH
Josip Bozanic Archbishop of Zagreb *Titular of San Girolamo dei Croati*	Croatia	March 20, 1949
Jean-Baptiste Pham minh Man Archbishop of Ho Chi Minh City (Saigon) *Titular of San Giustino*	Vietnam	1934
Rodolfo Quezada Toruño Archbishop of Guatemala Titular of San Saturnino	Guatemala	March 8, 1932
Philippe Barbarin Archbishop of Lyons *Titular of Santissima Trinità al Monte Pincio*	France	October 17, 1950
Péter Erdö Archbishop of Esztergom-Budapest Primate of Hungary *Titular of Santa Balbina*	Hungary	June 25, 1952
Marc Ouellet, P.S.S. Archbishop of Quebec *Titular of Santa Maria in Traspontina*	Canada	June 8, 1944

—Cardinal Deacons

Jorge Arturo Medina Estévez
Prefect Emeritus of the Congregation for
  Divine Worship and the Discipline of
  the Sacraments
Deacon of San Saba
Proto-Deacon of the Holy Roman Church
	Chile	December 23, 1926

Darío Castrillón Hoyos
Prefect of the Congregation for the Clergy
President of the Pontifical Commission
  Ecclesia Dei
Deacon of Santissimo Nome di Maria al
  Foro Traiano
	Colombia	July 4, 1929

NAME / POSITION / TITLE	COUNTRY	DATE OF BIRTH
JAMES FRANCIS STAFFORD Major Penitentiary *Deacon of Gesù Buon Pastore alla Montagnola*	U.S.A.	July 26, 1932
AGOSTINO CACCIAVILLAN President Emeritus of the Administration of the Patrimony of the Apostolic See *Deacon of Santi Angeli Custodi a Città Giardino*	Italy	August 14, 1926
SERGIO SEBASTIANI President of the Prefecture for the Economic Affairs of the Holy See *Deacon of Sant'Eustachio*	Italy	April 11, 1931
Zenon Grocholewski Prefect of the Congregation for Catholic Education *Deacon of San Nicola in Carcere*	Poland	October 11, 1939
JOSÉ SARAIVA MARTINS, C.M.F. Prefect of the Congregation for the Causes of Saints *Deacon of Nostra Signora del Sacro Cuore*	Portugal	January 6, 1932
CRESCENZIO SEPE Prefect of the Congregation for the Evangelization of Peoples *Deacon of Dio Padre Misericordioso*	Italy	June 2, 1943

MARIO FRANCESCO POMPEDDA
Prefect Emeritus of the Supreme Tribunal
  of the Apostolic Signatura
*Deacon of Annunciazione della Beata
  Vergine Maria a Via Ardeatina*
	Italy	April 18, 1929

WALTER KASPER President of the Pontifical Council for the Promotion of Christian Unity *Deacon of Ognissanti in Via Appia Nuova*	Germany	March 5, 1933

NAME / POSITION / TITLE	COUNTRY	DATE OF BIRTH

JEAN-LOUIS TAURAN
Librarian and Archivist of the
  Holy Roman Church
*Deacon of Sant'Apollinare alle
  Terme Neroniane-Alessandrine*
	France	April 5, 1943

RENATO RAFFAELE MARTINO President of the Pontifical Council for Justice and Peace *Deacon of San Francisco di Paola ai Monti*	Italy	November 23, 1932
FRANCESCO MARCHISANO Archpriest of the Vatican Basilica *Deacon of Santa Lucia del Gonfalone*	Italy	June 25, 1929
JULIAN HERRANZ President of the Pontifical Council for Legislative Texts *Deacon of Sant'Eugenio*	Spain	March 31, 1930
JAVIER LOZANO BARRAGÁN President of the Pontifical Council for Healthcare *Deacon of San Michele Arcangelo*	Mexico	January 26, 1933

STEPHEN FUMIO HAMAO
President of the Pontifical Council
  for the Pastoral Care of Migrants
  and Itinerants
Deacon of San Giovanni Bosco in Via Tuscolana
	Japan	March 9, 1930

ATTILIO NICORA President of the Administration of the Patrimony of the Apostolic See *Deacon of San Filippo Neri in Eurosia*	Italy	March 16, 1937

Appendix 4

BIOGRAPHICAL NOTES
ON SELECT PERSONALITIES,
HISTORICAL AND PRESENT,
APPEARING IN THE NARRATIVE

The following biographical notes cover some of the personalities, other than the popes, encountered in the narrative. For detailed biographies of the popes as well as more complete information on other figures, see the newly revised *New Catholic Encyclopedia* (Washington: Catholic University of America Press, 2002) or any of several one-volume biographical dictionaries of the popes, including Eamon Duffy, *Saints and Sinners: A History of the Popes*, rev. ed. (New Haven: Yale University Press, 2002); J.N.D. Kelly, *The Oxford Dictionary of Popes* (Oxford/New York: Oxford University Press, 1986); and Richard P. McBrien, *Lives of the Popes* (San Francisco: HarperSanFrancisco, 1997).

AGAGIANIAN, GRÉGOIRE-PIERRE **XV** (1895–1971), *cardinal*, patriarch of the Armenian Catholic Church. Agagianian was born in the then–Russian Caucasus to an Armenian family belonging to the Armenian Rite of the Catholic Church and grew up in the village of Akhaltzikhe, in the very shadows of the sacred Armenian mountain of Ararat, where tradition says the ark of Noah settled. After studies at the seminary of Tifflis in Russian Georgia and the Pontifical Urbanian Athenaeum *de Propaganda Fide*, he was ordained a priest in 1917. Following a brief period as a parish priest in Tifflis, he was called back to Rome in 1921 as vice-rector of the Pontifical Armenian College and a member of the faculty of his alma mater, the Pontifical Urbanian Athenaeum. He served as rector of the Armenian College from 1932 to 1937. In 1935, he was ordained a bishop. The Synod of Bishops of the Armenian Catholic Church elected him patriarch of Cilicia of the Armenians and head of the Armenian Catholic Church on November 30, 1937, the election receiving papal confirmation on December 13, 1937. He was created a cardinal by Pius XII in 1946 and participated in the conclaves of 1958 and 1963, being a serious (albeit unwilling) candidate for the papacy. While remaining patriarch of the Armenian Catholics, he was appointed president of the Pontifical Commission for the Revision of the Code of Oriental Canon Law in 1955 and pro-prefect of the Sacred Congregation for the Propagation of the Faith in 1958, becoming prefect in 1960. He resigned the pastoral governance of the Armenian patriarchate in 1962 to devote himself full-time to his

Roman duties, which included the co-presidency of the Second Vatican Council. As his homeland came to be under Soviet rule, he did not see some members of his family after he left for Rome in 1921 until 1962, when, at the personal intervention of Nikita Khrushchev, his sister Elisaveta was allowed to travel to see him in Rome. He resigned his prefecture in 1970.

AGLIARDI, ANTONIO (1832–1915), *cardinal.* Hailing from the village of Cologno al Serio, near Bergamo in northern Italy, he earned doctorates in canon and civil law and was ordained a priest in 1855. After service as a curial official and seminary professor, he was elevated to the archbishopric and appointed apostolic delegate to India in 1884. He became apostolic nuncio to Bavaria in 1889. Appointed apostolic nuncio to Austria-Hungary in 1893, he was created a cardinal in 1896. He served in various curial capacities until his death and participated in the conclaves of 1903 and 1914.

ALFRINK, BERNARDUS JOHANNES (1900–1987), *cardinal.* Alfrink was ordained in 1924, after studies at the Seminary of Rijsenburg, Utrecht. He pursued advanced studies at the Pontifical Biblical Institute in Rome and the Ecole Biblique in Jerusalem before returning to the Netherlands for pastoral work (1930–1933) and teaching at the Seminary of Rijensburg (1933–1945). He became a professor at the Catholic University of Nijmegen in 1945. In 1951, he was appointed coadjutor archbishop of Utrecht, becoming apostolic administrator and then succeeding to the see in 1955. In 1957, he was also appointed military vicar for the Netherlands. Created a cardinal by John XXIII in 1960, he attended the Second Vatican Council and served on its presidency. He also attended the subsequent Synods of Bishops. He resigned the pastoral governance of the Archdiocese of Utrecht in 1975, although he participated in the two conclaves of 1978.

ANDREOTTI, GIULIO (born 1919), Italian statesman. Andreotti grew up in Rome, the son of a devout Catholic family. He was to maintain that connection to the Church throughout his life. As a young university student, he became active in the Federation of Italian Catholic University Students (FUCI) and, as a protégé of FUCI's national chaplain, the then-Monsignor Giovanni Battista Montini, served as its president from 1942 to 1945. Andreotti began his political life under the tutelage of Alcide De Gasperi, a Catholic politician of the old school who waited out the Fascist period by working in the Vatican Library, where Andreotti met him while looking for a book. The two immediately hit it off, Andreotti becoming De Gasperi's right-hand man. After World War II, the two helped found a new Catholic party, the Christian Democrats, and Andreotti rose quickly to the top with his knack for details and parliamentary procedure. In 1945, De Gasperi was appointed prime minister, and Andreotti became his chief of staff in 1947. An Italian journalist once wrote, "When De Gasperi and Andreotti went to church together, De Gasperi talked to God, while Andreotti talked to the priest: Priests were known to have considerable power and could solicit votes for the Christian Democrats." He was successively minister of the interior (1953–1955), minister of finance (1955–1958), minister of the treasury (1958–1959), and minister of defense and, subsequently, minister of commerce and industry as well (1959–1966). In 1968, he became parliamentary leader of the

Christian Democrats. In February 1972, he formed his first government as prime minister and, in the volatile context of Italian politics, repeated the performance five additional times (June 1972, 1976–1978, 1978, 1989, 1991). He was also foreign minister (1983, 1987, 1988–1989). In June 1991, he was appointed a senator-for-life. Maintaining his close ties to the Vatican establishment over the decades, he edits an influential Catholic monthly *30 Giorni* ("30 Days") that is translated into several languages and has written a number of books in which he, beneath his lengthy prose, reveals a significant amount of "insider" information on the Holy See. Most relevant to the present subject is *A ogni morte di papa* (Milan: Rizzoli, 1982).

ANTONIUTTI, ILDEBRANDO (1898–1974), *cardinal*. Antoniutti was ordained in 1920, after studies at the seminary of his native archdiocese of Udine and the Pontifical Roman Seminary. After serving as secretary to the archbishop of Udine and teaching at the local seminary, he entered the diplomatic service of the Holy See in 1934 and was sent to the apostolic delegation in China. He was transferred to the nunciature in Portugal in 1934. In 1936, he was appointed apostolic delegate to Albania and elevated to the rank of archbishop. The following year, he was sent as a special papal envoy to the Nationalist government formed by General Francisco Franco during the Spanish Civil War. In 1938, he was appointed apostolic delegate to Canada. In 1953, he was supposed to be appointed apostolic nuncio to France, but the French government refused the *agrément* necessary in diplomacy for the appointment of ambassadors because of his previous ties to Spain's Franco. Consequently, he was appointed nuncio to Spain. He was created a cardinal by John XXIII in 1962. In 1963, he was appointed prefect of the Sacred Congregation for Religious, a post he resigned when he reached his seventy-fifth birthday in 1973, as required by the new dispositions. He died in a car accident near Bologna the following year.

ARINZE, FRANCIS (born 1932), *cardinal*, prefect of the Congregation for Divine Worship and the Discipline of the Sacraments. Born in Eziowelle, Nigeria, Arinze studied at the seminaries of Nuewi and Enugu before being sent to further studies at the Pontifical Urbanian University in Rome. Ordained a priest in 1958, he earned a doctorate with his pioneering dissertation, *Ibo Sacrifice as an Introduction to the Catechesis of Holy Mass*. Returning to Nigeria, he served successively as a professor at the seminary in Enugu and secretary for Catholic education in western Nigeria. He later published a study of his experience of this period under the title *Partnership in Education between Church and State in Nigeria*. After further studies at the University of London in 1963–1964, he was appointed auxiliary bishop of his native archdiocese of Onitsha in 1965. He became archbishop in 1967. Called to Rome by Pope John Paul II in 1984, he was appointed pro-president of the Secretariat for Non-Christians. In 1985, he was created a cardinal and became president of the Secretariat for Non-Christians. In 1988, his dicastery was renamed the Pontifical Council for Inter-Religious Dialogue. In 2002, he was transferred to the Congregation for Divine Worship and the Discipline of the Sacraments as prefect. Following his election, Pope Benedict XVI raised Arinze to the rank of cardinal bishop with the title to the suburbicarian see of Velletri-Segni formerly held by the pontiff himself.

ARNS, PAULO EVARISTO (born 1921), *cardinal*. Arns joined the Franciscan order and made his profession in 1943. He studied at the various Brazilian houses of study of his order as well as the Faculty of Philosophy in Curitiba, the Franciscan Institute of Theology in Petrópolis, and the University of Paris-Sorbonne, and was ordained a priest in 1945. He subsequently taught in various institutes of his religious order as well as directing the monthly review of religious *Sponsa Christi*. He was elected vice-provincial of the Franciscan province of the Immaculate Conception in 1961. He was appointed auxiliary bishop of São Paulo in 1966, and promoted to archbishop of São Paulo in 1970. He attended several of the Synods of Bishops. Paul VI created him a cardinal in 1973. He participated in the two conclaves of 1978. He resigned the pastoral governance of his archdiocese in 1998.

ATHENAGORAS I SPYROU (1886–1972), *ecumenical patriarch*. Athenagoras was born on the island of Epirus. Ordained to the diaconate at the early age of seventeen, he was assigned as archdeacon to the archbishop of Athens after graduating from the Halki Theological Academy in Constantinople. He was ordained a priest in 1910 and appointed to the Secretariat of the Holy Synod of Greece. Elected metropolitan of Corfu, he was consecrated a bishop in 1913. In 1931, the Holy Synod of the Patriarchate of Constantinople appointed him archbishop of the Greek Orthodox Church in North and South America. He was elected "archbishop of Constantinople, New Rome, and ecumenical patriarch" in 1948 and was enthroned in 1950. On December 7, 1965, Athenagoras and the Synod of the Church of Constantinople issued a joint declaration with Pope Paul VI and the Vatican Council annulling the mutual anathemas of 1054.

VON BALTHASAR, HANS URS (1905–1988), *Swiss-German theologian*. Born in Lucerne, Switzerland, to a prominent Catholic family—among his relations was the martyred Hungarian bishop Blessed Vilmos von Apor—he received a first-rate classical education at the Universities of Vienna, Berlin, and Zürich, earning his doctorate in literature for his three-volume dissertation on the history of the eschatological problem in modern German literature. Joining the Society of Jesus in 1929, he studied at the institutes of the Jesuit order at Feldkirch, Pullach, and Munich, Germany, as well as Lyon, France. He was ordained a priest in 1939 and appointed chaplain of the University of Basel. He left the Jesuits in 1950, becoming a secular priest. Although he never held an academic appointment, he was the author of 119 books, 532 articles, 114 contributions to other books, 110 translations, 29 contributions to literary anthologies, 103 forewords and afterwords to works by other authors, 93 major book reviews, and 13 complete critical editions of various writers. Balthasar was excluded from the Second Vatican Council because of his somewhat unconventional ecclesiastical career; recognition came late in his life: He received the Pope Paul VI International Prize in 1984 and the Wolfgang Amadeus Mozart Prize in 1987. On May 29, 1988, Pope John Paul II announced his creation as a cardinal, but he died on June 26, two days before receiving the red biretta in the consistory.[1]

---

[1] For more on Balthasar, see the essay by the present author, "Uniting Faith and Culture: Hans Urs von Balthasar," *Modern Age* 42, no. 2 (Spring 2000): 176–184.

BAUDRILLART, ALFRED-HENRI-MARIE (1859–1942), *cardinal*. Educated at the famed Ecole Normale Supérieure and the Institut Catholique, after joining the Oratory of St. Philip Neri and being ordained a priest in 1893, he joined the faculty of the latter, where he founded the *Revue practique d'apologetique*. For his scholarly contributions, he was elected a member of the Académie Française. He was appointed vicar general of Paris in 1908 and consecrated its auxiliary bishop in 1921, being promoted to the rank of titular archbishop in 1938. He was created a cardinal in 1935 by Pius XI and participated in the conclave of 1939.

BAUER, FRANZISKUS VON SALES (1841–1915), *cardinal*. Ordained a priest in 1863, Bauer was a seminary and university professor before being named bishop of Brno in 1882. In 1904, he was promoted to the metropolitan see of Olomouc with the title of prince-arch-bishop. In the Austrian Empire, the prince-archbishops of Olomouc were *ex ufficio* dukes of Hotzenplote and imperial senators. He was created a cardinal in 1911 and partici-pated in the conclave of 1914.

BENELLI, GIOVANNI (1921–1982), *cardinal*. Hailing from the village of Poggiole di Vernio, in the Diocese of Pistoia, Benelli was ordained a priest in 1943 after studies at the semi-nary of Pistoia and the Pontifical Gregorian University in Rome. Interestingly, although Italian, as a seminarian studying in Rome, he lodged at the Pontifical French Seminary so as to acquire and perfect a knowledge of French, then as now the principal language of papal diplomacy in international settings. Passing after ordination to the Pontifical Ecclesiastical Academy for further studies, he entered the diplomatic service of the Holy See in 1947. His first posting was as the private secretary to the then-Monsignor Giovanni Battista Montini, substitute of the Secretariat of State. Successively, he served as secre-tary of the nunciatures in Ireland (1950–1953) and France (1953–1960), auditor of the nunciature in Brazil (1960–1962), counselor of the nunciature in Spain (1962–1965), and permanent observer of the Holy See at UNESCO (1965–1966). Appointed pro-nuncio to Senegal and apostolic delegate in Western Africa in 1966, he was elevated to the rank of archbishop. The following year, he was recalled to Rome by Paul VI as substitute of the Secretariat of State. At the Vatican, he enjoyed a reputation for hard work and efficiency, although his detractors argued that he concentrated too much power in his own hands— a not too difficult feat for the seasoned substitute given Pope Paul's withdrawal in his later years and the lack of diplomatic experience on the part of his secretary of state, Cardinal Jean Villot. Eventually, Benelli's critics, especially among some older curial car-dinals, prevailed upon Paul to exile him from Rome. Remembering his own exile to Milan some two decades earlier, Paul hastily arranged a "mini-consistory" in 1977 to at least give his longtime aide the cardinal's biretta before sending him away as archbishop of Florence. He was a force to be reckoned with in the conclaves of 1978.

BENGSCH, ALFRED (1921–1979), *cardinal*. A native of Berlin, he studied at the Superior School of Philosophy and Theology at Fulda, the Archdiocesan Seminary "Bernardinum" at Neuzelle-Oder, and the Theological Faculty of Munich before he was drafted into the German army during the Second World War. Wounded and taken prisoner by the

Americans in 1944, he was eventually paroled and, after the war, finished his studies and was ordained a priest in 1950. He did pastoral work in Berlin until 1954, when he began an academic career that saw him teach at the seminary of Erfurt (1954–1956) and the Archdiocesan Seminary "Bernardinum" (1956–1959), as well as serve as the regent of the seminary of Erfurt (1959). Appointed auxiliary bishop of Berlin in 1959, he became bishop of Berlin in 1961. The following year, he was given the personal title of arch-bishop. He attended the four sessions of the Second Vatican Council. Created a cardinal by Pope Paul VI in 1967, he attended the subsequent sessions of the Synod of Bishops and participated in the two conclaves of 1978.

BILLOT, LOUIS (1846–1931), *cardinal*, last member of the College of Cardinals to resign from the body. Billot was born in the village of Sierch, near Metz. After studies at the seminaries of Metz, Bordeaux, and Blois, he was ordained a priest in 1869. That same year, he joined the Society of Jesus and made his final vows as a Jesuit in 1883. After stints of pastoral work in Paris (1875–1878) and Laval (1878–1879), he taught at the Catho-lic University of Angers (1879–1882), the Jesuit scholasticate on the island of Jersey (1882–1885), and the Pontifical Gregorian University (1885–1910). His published works, most of which originate in this period, give a dynamic interpretation to the doctrines of St. Thomas Aquinas, adapting them to modern philosophical concerns. Among his most famous works, all of which were published in Latin, were *De Verbo Incarnato* ("On the Word Incarnate," 1892), *De Ecclesiae Sacramentis* ("On the Sacraments of the Church," 1894–1895), *De Deo Uno et Trino* ("On God One and Three," 1895), and *De Ecclesia Christi* ("On the Church of Christ," 1910). He was created a cardinal by Pope St. Pius X in 1911. His serialized tract *La Providence de Dieu et le nombre infini d'hommes en dehors de la voie normale du salut* ("The Providence of God and the infinite number of men outside the normal path of salvation"),written during this period and published between 1919 and 1921, anticipated many later theologians on the question of salvation outside the Church. He lost his cardinalate in 1927 during a dispute with Pius XI over the political movement Action Française, condemned by the pope.

BONZANO, GIOVANNI (1867–1927), *cardinal*, one-time apostolic delegate to the United States. Ordained in 1890, Bonzano served as a missionary in China and then a professor at the Pontifical Urbanian Athenaeum *de Propaganda Fide* for the missions before being appointed archbishop and apostolic delegate to the United States in 1904. In 1915, dur-ing the persecutions of the Catholic Church in Mexico, he also assumed charge of the apostolic delegation there. He returned to Rome and was created a cardinal in 1922. He was the papal legate to preside at the twenty-eighth International Eucharistic Congress in Chicago in 1926.

CANOVA, ANTONIO (1757–1822), Italian artist. In addition to the tomb of Clement XIV (1769–1774) in Rome's Church of the Holy Apostles, he is known for a number of other funerary monuments, including the tomb of James Stuart, the "Old Pretender," in the Vatican Basilica.

CAPOVILLA, LORIS FRANCESCO (born 1915), *archbishop*, private secretary of Pope John XXIII. A native of Pontelengo, near Padua, Capovilla was ordained a priest in 1940. Then Cardinal Roncalli chose him to be his secretary during his tenure in the patriarchate of Venice. Following his patron to Rome, he served as Pope John's private secretary during the latter's pontificate. After John's death, Pope Paul VI appointed him bishop of Chieti and Vasti in 1967. In 1971, he was promoted to archiepiscopal rank and appointed prelate of Loreto and pontifical delegate of the Shrine of the Holy House. He retired in 1988 to John XXIII's ancestral town of Sotto il Monte and was succeeded by Paul VI's secretary, Pasquale Macchi.

CASARIEGO, MARIO (1909–1983), *cardinal*. Casariego was born in Figueras de Castropol, near Oviedo, Spain. Joining the Clerics Regular of Somasca (Somaschi Fathers) in El Salvador in 1924, he was ordained a priest in 1936, after studies at institutes of that order in Bergamo, Genoa, and San Salvador. He held various positions within his religious congregation until 1958, when he was appointed auxiliary bishop of Guatemala. He was promoted to coadjutor archbishop in 1963, succeeding to the see as archbishop the following year. He attended the Second Vatican Council. He gained notoriety when he was kidnapped by a terrorist group briefly in 1968. In 1969, Paul VI created him a cardinal. He participated in the two conclaves of 1978. His notes on the conclave were accessed by Giulio Andreotti, who published their contents.

CASAROLI, AGOSTINO (1914–1998), *cardinal*, secretary of state of Pope John Paul II. Born in Castel San Giovanni, near Piacenza, Casaroli studied at the Collegio Alberoni in Piacenza and the diocesan seminary of Bedonia before being ordained a priest in 1937. Sent to further studies in Rome, he earned a doctorate in canon law from the Pontifical Lateran Athenaeum and completed his studies at the Pontifical Academy of Noble Ecclesiastics. Entering the service of the Secretariat of State in 1940, he became undersecretary of the Sacred Congregation for Extraordinary Ecclesiastical Affairs (as the Holy See's "foreign ministry" was known at the time) in 1961. He represented the Holy See at the 1961 United Nations conference on diplomatic relations in Vienna and the 1963 UN conference on consular relations. During that time, he began a series of trips to negotiate with Communist regimes in Eastern Europe that led to the Vatican's *Ostpolitik*. In 1966, he successfully negotiated the Holy See's *modus vivendi* with the Tito regime in Yugoslavia. The following year, he was appointed secretary of the Sacred Congregation for Extraordinary Ecclesiastical Affairs and consecrated an archbishop by Pope Paul VI. He served as the Vatican's envoy at the negotiations leading to the Helsinki Accord on European Security and Cooperation in 1975. Created a cardinal by Pope John Paul II in 1979, he was appointed secretary of state. He retired in 1990 and became vice-dean of the College of Cardinals in 1993. Despite the high offices he held, Casaroli served quietly as chaplain to juvenile delinquents detained in Rome from 1943 until shortly before his death. The title of his posthumously published memoirs, *Il martirio della pazienza* ("The martyrdom of patience," 2000), aptly describes his diplomatic style.

CASSETTA, FRANCESCO DI PAOLA (1841–1919), *cardinal*. A native Roman, he studied at the Pontifical Roman Seminary, earning doctorates in theology, canon law, and civil law, and was ordained a priest in 1865, after which he held a succession of judicial offices. Consecrated bishop in 1884, he served as secret almoner to Pope Leo XIII and then as vicegerent of the Diocese of Rome. He was created a cardinal in 1899.

CASTRILLÓN HOYOS, DARÍO (born 1929), *cardinal*, prefect of the Congregation for the Clergy. Born in Medellín, Colombia, he studied at the seminaries of Antioquia and Santa Rosa de Osos before being sent to the Pontifical Gregorian University in Rome, where he earned a doctorate in canon law. Ordained a priest in 1952, he served in a variety of pastoral ministries at both the diocesan and national levels until he was appointed coadjutor bishop of Pereira in 1971. He succeeded to the see in 1976. From 1983 to 1987, he served as secretary general of the Latin American Episcopal Council (CELAM). In 1987, he was elected its president, serving in that capacity until 1991. In 1992, he was promoted to be metropolitan archbishop of Bucaramanga. He was called to Rome as proprefect of the Congregation for the Clergy in 1996, he became its prefect in 1998, when Pope John Paul II created him a cardinal. In 2000, he added the presidency of the Pontifical Commission *Ecclesia Dei* to his responsibilities.

CAVAGNIS, FELICE (1841–1906), *cardinal*. After studies at the Pontifical Roman Seminary and priestly ordination in 1863, Cavagnis enjoyed a brilliant academic career, earning doctorates in philosophy, theology, canon law, and civil law. A professor of law for many years, his three-volume *Institutiones Iuris Publici Ecclesiastici* ("Elements of Public Ecclesiastical Law") is still a point of reference a century after its publication. Leo XIII brought him into the service of the Roman Curia in a variety of offices, including that of secretary of the Congregation for Extraordinary Ecclesiastical Affairs (i.e., the foreign secretary of the Vatican), where he help rebuild the Holy See's diplomatic and political relations with the modern states. Created a cardinal in 1901, he participated in the conclave of 1903.

CIAPPI, MARIO LUIGI (1909–1996), *cardinal*. A native Florentine, Ciappi attended the seminaries of Lucca and Arezzo before joining the Order of Preachers (the Dominicans). He was ordained a priest in 1932. Earning a doctorate in theology from the Pontifical Angelicum Athenaeum, he pursued further studies at the University of Louvain and the University of Fribourg. He was a professor of theology and, subsequently, dean of the theological faculty of the Pontifical Angelicum Athenaeum from 1935 to 1955. In 1955, Pius XII appointed him master of the Sacred Palace, a title that was changed to "theologian of the Papal Household" with the reforms of Paul VI in 1968. In 1977, he was ordained an archbishop and created a cardinal by Paul VI, but continued to serve as protheologian of the Papal Household until he reached the age of eighty and retired in 1989. He participated in the two conclaves of 1978.

CICOGNANI, AMLETO GIOVANNI (1883–1973), *cardinal*, secretary of state of Pope John XXIII (1958–1963) and Pope Paul VI (1963–1978) and one-time apostolic delegate to the United States. Amleto Giovanni Cicognani was the younger brother of Cardinal Gaetano Cicognani (1881–1962) and followed in his older brother's footsteps. After studies at the seminary of his native diocese of Faenza, he was ordained a priest in 1905. Finishing further studies at the Pontifical Roman Athenaeum of Sant'Apollinare, he joined the staff of the Sacred Congregation for the Discipline of the Sacraments in 1910. He also assumed some teaching duties at the Pontifical Roman Athenaeum of Sant'Apollinare in 1921, continuing there until 1932. In 1922, he was appointed adjunct substitute of the Sacred Consistorial Congregation, in which capacity he undertook special missions to the United States in 1924 and 1931 and to Brazil in 1926. He was appointed assessor of the Sacred Congregation for the Oriental Church in 1928, adding the office of secretary of the Commission for the Codification of Oriental Canon Law the following year. Appointed apostolic delegate to the United States in 1933, he was elevated at the same time to the rank of archbishop. He remained in Washington for more than two decades because his older brother's successes blocked his own advancement: papal representatives to the United States—like those to France, Germany, Spain, and other major nations—traditionally are promoted to the Sacred College when they finish their missions; however canon 232 §3 of the 1917 Code of Canon Law then in force prohibited anyone having a brother who was a cardinal from being himself a cardinal. Gaetano Cicognani, created a cardinal by Pius XII in 1953, was still alive; thus his brother Amleto stayed put in Washington. John XXIII was persuaded to grant a dispensation to the canon and, in 1958, created Amleto a cardinal, appointing him secretary of the Sacred Congregation for the Oriental Church. In 1961, he was appointed secretary of state, president of the Pontifical Commission for the Vatican City State, and president of the Commission of Cardinals for the Administration of the Wealth of the Holy See. He participated in the conclave of 1963. The day of his election, Pope Paul VI confirmed him in all his offices. In 1968, he was also appointed president of the newly constituted Administration of the Patrimony of the Holy See. He resigned his offices in 1968, becoming the first to assume the style "emeritus secretary of state." He was elected and confirmed as dean of the College of Cardinals in 1972.

CICOGNANI, GAETANO (1881–1962), *cardinal*. Gaetano Cicognani was ordained a priest in 1904, after studies at the seminary of his native Faenza. He pursued further studies at the Pontifical Athenaeum of Sant'Apollinare and the Pontifical Academy of Noble Ecclesiastics before joining, successively, the staffs of the Tribunal of the Sacred Roman Rota and the Supreme Tribunal of the Apostolic Signatura. He entered the Secretariat of State in 1915 and was posted the following year to the nunciature in Spain, from where he went on to the nunciature in Belgium in 1920. Appointed apostolic nuncio to Bolivia in 1925, he was elevated to the archbishopric. He became nuncio to Peru in 1928. In 1935, he was transferred as nuncio to Austria. In 1938, he was sent as nuncio to the Nationalist government formed by General Francisco Franco in Spain. Pius XII created him a cardinal in 1953, appointing him prefect of the Sacred Congregation of Rites. In 1954, he was appointed pro-prefect of the Apostolic Signatura, a position he held until 1959. He participated in the conclave of 1958. For many years, until Pope John XXIII granted a dispensation from the norm at his instance, Cicognani was much exercised by canon 232 §3, which forbids anyone having a brother in the Sacred College from being a cardinal: his younger brother, Amleto Giovanni, for many years apostolic delegate in the United States, consequently could not advance.

CIRIACI, PIETRO (1885–1966), *cardinal.* A native Roman, Ciriaci attended the Pontifical Roman Seminary and the Pontifical Roman Athenaeum of Sant'Apollinare, where he earned doctorates in philosophy, theology, and canon law. Ordained a priest in 1909, he served as assistant pastor of the parish of San Rocco while teaching philosophy and fundamental theology at the Pontifical Urbanian Athenaeum *de Propaganda Fide* and his alma mater, the Pontifical Roman Athenaeum of Sant'Apollinare. Joining the staff of the Apostolic Penitentiary in 1911, he was seconded to the Sacred Congregation of the Council in 1913. He was transferred to the Sacred Congregation for Extraordinary Ecclesiastical Affairs (i.e., the Vatican "foreign ministry") in 1917 and was appointed its undersecretary in 1921. During his tenure at Extraordinary Ecclesiastical Affairs, he successfully negotiated the *modus vivendi* between the Holy See and the newly established government of Czechoslovakia. In 1928, he was appointed nuncio to Czechoslovakia and elevated to the archiepiscopal dignity. In 1934, he was transferred to the nunciature in Lisbon. Created a cardinal by Pius XII in 1953, he was appointed prefect of the Sacred Congregation of the Council the following year, a position he held until his death. In 1955, he added the presidency of the Pontifical Commission for the Authentic Interpretation of the Code of Canon Law to his responsibilities. He participated in the conclaves of 1958 and 1963.

COLOMBO, GIOVANNI (1902–1992), *cardinal.* Colombo was born in Caronno, near Milan, and studied at the seminary of Milan and the Catholic Sacred Heart University of Milan, before being ordained a priest in 1926. He taught at the seminary of Milan (1926–1937) and the Catholic Sacred Heart University of Milan (1937–1939). He was rector of the minor seminary of Milan (1939–1953) and of the major seminary (1953–1960). He was appointed auxiliary bishop to the then-archbishop of Milan, Giovanni Battista Montini, in 1960. When the latter became Pope Paul VI, he chose Colombo to succeed him, promoting him to archbishop of Milan in 1963 and creating him a cardinal in 1965. Colombo attended the Second Vatican Council and some of the subsequent Synods of Bishops. He participated in the two conclaves of 1978. He resigned the pastoral governance of the archdiocese in 1979.

CONFALONIERI, CARLO (1893–1986), *cardinal.* Confalonieri attended the minor seminary in his native town of Seveso, the seminary of Monza, and the Pontifical Gregorian University. Ordained a priest in 1916, he nonetheless served in the Italian Army during the First World War. After the war, he did pastoral work in Milan (1919–1921), until the new archbishop, Cardinal Achille Ratti, appointed him his personal secretary in 1921. He attended the conclave of 1922 as the cardinal's attendant, and when the latter was elected Pope Pius XI, he continued as his personal secretary. He was appointed archbishop of L'Aquila in 1941. In 1950, he returned to Rome as secretary of the Sacred Congregation for Seminaries and Universities. Created a cardinal by John XXIII in 1958, he was appointed the following year to be archpriest of the Basilica of St. Mary Major. In 1961, he was appointed secretary of the Sacred Consistorial Congregation. He participated in the conclave of 1963. He attended the Second Vatican Council and the subsequent Synods of Bishops. In 1966, he was appointed pro-prefect of the Sacred Consistorial Congregation, and he was confirmed in that post in 1967, when he turned seventy-five. He was delegate president of the 1969 Extraordinary Synod of Bishops. In 1970, he added the presidency of the newly established Pontifical Commission for the Pastoral Care of Migration and Tourism to his posts. He resigned all his positions in 1973, when he turned eighty and lost his right to vote in the conclave. He nonetheless became sub-dean of the College of Cardinals in 1974 and its dean in 1977.

CONGAR, YVES-MARIE-JOSEPH (1904–1995), *cardinal.* Congar studied at the seminary of Rheims and the Institut Catholique of Paris, before joining the Order of Preachers (the Dominicans) in 1925 and making his profession the following year. After continuing his studies at the Dominican "Le Saulchoir" Seminary in Tournai, Belgium, he was ordained a priest in 1930. He joined the faculty at Le Saulchoir in 1931, remaining there until 1954, with the exception of the war years. From 1935, he was also secretary of the prestigious journal *Revue des sciences philosophiques et théologiques.* During the Second World War, he served as medical orderly in the French army, was taken prisoner by the Germans, escaped, and finished the war with the resistance. He was awarded the *Légion d'Honneur* and the *Croix de Guerre.* In 1954, because of his support for the "worker priest" movement, the Holy Office forbade him to teach, lecture, or publish, and the Vatican obliged his superiors to move him from one obscure post to another. Rehabilitated after the election of John XXIII, he served as a *peritus,* or official expert, at the Second Vatican Council and was subsequently named a member of the new International Theological Commission. He was created a cardinal by John Paul II in 1994.

CONSALVI, ERCOLE (1757–1824), *cardinal,* secretary of state and confidant of Pius VII (1800–1823). Consalvi was the scion of a noble Pisan family that had adopted the name of the Roman Consalvi clan when his grandfather came into that inheritance. After studies at the seminary of Frascati and the Pontifical Academy for Ecclesiastical Nobles, Consalvi, although not yet ordained, served Pope Pius VI (1775–1799) in various capacities from 1783 until the pope's deportation by the French in 1799. Prevented from following the pope, he moved to Venice, where he served as secretary of the conclave that elected Pius VII (1800–1823). The new pope created Consalvi a cardinal and appointed him secretary of state. He completed the negotiations for the pope's concordat with Napoleon and was ordained subdeacon and deacon by Pius VII in late 1801. He was never ordained to the priesthood. Forced out of his position by the French in 1806, he was subsequently imprisoned by Napoleon. Released in 1813, he was reappointed secretary of state in 1814. One of the greatest statesmen to ever serve the papacy, he participated in the Congress of Vienna and won the restoration of all the pre-revolutionary papal dominions except for the Avignon enclave.

COSTANTINI, CELSO BENIGNO LUIGI (1876–1958), *cardinal.* Costantini was ordained in 1899, after having earned doctorates in philosophy and theology. With the exception of service as a military chaplain with the Italian army during World War I, the first twenty years of his priesthood were spent in pastoral work in his native diocese of Concordia, where he dedicated his free time to cultivating his interest in Christian archaeology and art and founded the illustrated journal *Arte cristiana.* Appointed bishop in 1921, he was named by Pius XI to be the first apostolic delegate to China the following year. While he complained about the appointment, he came back more than a decade later—after serving not only as a diplomat but also as the bishop for Catholics in Harbin and having founded the Congregation of the Lord's Disciples, a Chinese religious order that soon spread to other Asian countries—totally enthralled with the Far East, furnishing his apartment with Chinese furniture and building a classical Chinese tomb for himself in his home town of Castions di Zoppola. Appointed secretary of the Sacred Congregation for the Propagation of the Faith in 1935, he became increasingly convinced of the future importance of the churches in the mission territories. Pope Pius XII created him a cardinal in 1953. The following year he was appointed chancellor of the Holy Roman Church. He died a week before the conclave of 1958, where his presence might have altered the course of events.

COTTIER, GEORGES MARIE MARTIN (born 1922), *cardinal*, theologian of the Papal Household. Born in Céligny, near Lausanne, Switzerland, Cottier joined the Order of Preachers (the Dominicans) in 1945. After studies at the University of Fribourg as well as in Rome, he was ordained a priest in 1951. He taught contemporary philosophy for many years at the Universities of Geneva and Fribourg and edited the journal *Nova et Vetera*. During the 1980s, he worked closely with Cardinal Joseph Ratzinger, prefect of the Congregation for the Doctrine of the Faith, and was instrumental in the doctrinal office's condemnation of the "theology of liberation." In 1989, he was appointed secretary of the International Theological Commission and, later that same year, theologian of the Papal Household, that is, the pope's personal theological advisor. Created a cardinal in 2003 by Pope John Paul II, he was ordained an archbishop the day before the consistory by his former student and fellow Dominican, Cardinal Christoph Schönborn of Vienna.

CRETONI, SERAFINO (1833–1909), *cardinal*. A native of Soriano, in the Diocese of Orte, Cretoni received a doctorate in theology from the Pontifical Roman Athenaeum of Sant'Apollinare and was ordained a priest in 1857. After a brief period as a professor of philosophy at the Pontifical Urbanian Athenaeum *de Propaganda Fide*, he entered the service of the Holy See and served in a variety of capacities in the Secretariat of State, the Oriental Section of the Sacred Congregation for the Propagation of the Faith, and the Supreme Sacred Congregation of the Holy Office. Appointed apostolic nuncio to Spain in 1893, he was elevated to the archiepiscopate. He was created a cardinal by Pope Leo XIII in 1896. In 1900, he was appointed camerlengo of the College of Cardinals and prefect of the Sacred Congregation of Indulgences and Relics. In 1903, he was transferred to the Sacred Congregation of Rites as its prefect. He participated in the conclave of 1903, where he gained some celebrity for casting null votes—writing *"neminem eligo"* ("I vote for no one") on his ballot papers—in protest after the announcement of the Emperor Franz Josef II's exclusionary veto against the candidacy of Cardinal Mariano Rampolla del Tindaro.

CSERNOCH, JÁNOS (1852–1927), *cardinal*. Born in what is now Slovakia, he was ordained a priest in 1874 after studies at the University of Vienna and the Pontifical Gregorian Uni-

versity in Rome. Csernoch was successively a seminary professor, an archdiocesan official, a cathedral canon, and a deputy in the Hungarian parliament (where he co-founded
the Catholic Party). Named bishop of Csanad in 1908, he was promoted to the
archbishopric of Kalocsa in 1911 and named, contemporaneously, a royal counselor.
The following year, he was promoted to the primatial see of Esztergom as archbishop
and prince-primate of Hungary. Created a cardinal by Pius X in the consistory of May
25, 1914, by ancient monarchical privilege, he received the red cardinal's biretta from the
hands of Archduke Franz Ferdinand, whose assassination in Sarajevo on June 14 precipi-
tated the chain of events leading to the outbreak of World War I. He participated in the
conclave of 1914. In 1916, Csernoch crowned Hungary's last king, the tragic Karl of
Habsburg, who was subsequently declared "Venerable" by Pope John Paul II in 2003.

DALLA COSTA, ELIA (1872–1961), *cardinal*. Ordained a priest in 1895, he worked in parishes and seminaries of his native diocese of Vicenza. He was appointed bishop of Padua
in 1923 and promoted to the archbishopric of Florence in 1931. He was created a cardinal by Pius XI in 1933. He participated in the conclaves of 1939 and 1958. The process for
his beatification was initiated in 1981.

DANTE, ENRICO (1884–1967), *cardinal*, longtime papal master of ceremonies. A native
Roman, he was ordained a priest in 1910, after studies at the Pontifical Gregorian University and the Studium of the Sacred Roman Rota. A long-time professor at the Pontifical Urbanian Athenaeum *de Propaganda Fide* as well as the holder of various offices of
the Roman Curia, he was appointed to the College of Pontifical Masters of Ceremonies
in 1914. In 1947, he was appointed prefect of the papal ceremonies, a charge he held
until his death, despite various other responsible secretariats. He was elevated to the
archbishopric by John XXIII in 1962 and created a cardinal by Paul VI in 1965. Dante's
somber and precise liturgical spirit shaped papal liturgies for more than half a century
and continues to influence the ceremonial for rare solemn occasions such as those associated with papal death and succession.

DE LAI, GAETANO (1853–1928), *cardinal*. Hailing from Malo, near Vicenza, De Lai was
ordained a priest in 1876 and spent almost his entire career at the Sacred Congregation
for the Council, entering its service as staff attaché in 1878 and rising to become its
secretary in 1903. Created a cardinal in 1907, he was named secretary of the Sacred
Consistorial Congregation the following year. He was ordained a bishop in 1911, when
he passed from the order of cardinal deacons to that of cardinal bishops. He became sub-
dean of the Sacred College in 1919. He participated in the conclaves of 1914 and 1922.

DELLA VOLPE, FRANCESCO SALESIO (1844–1916), *cardinal*. Born in Ravenna, he was ordained a priest in 1867 after studies at the Seminario Pio and the Pontifical Academy of
Noble Ecclesiastics. Della Volpe held a succession of curial offices under Leo XIII before
being created a cardinal *in pectore* in 1899 and published in 1901. At the time of the
conclave of 1914, he was camerlengo of the Holy Roman Church and archchancellor of
the Roman University. During the *sede vacante*, the camerlengo as "prince regent" of

the Church traditionally has coins struck bearing his coat of arms and titles. When the coins minted by Della Volpe came back with an error—the fox in the "canting" arms of Della Volpe (the name Volpe means "fox" in Italian) was in the wrong position—the camerlengo rejected the entire series and had the coinage minted fresh.

DULLES, AVERY ROBERT (born 1918), *cardinal*. The scion of one of America's great political families, Dulles is the son of Secretary of State John Foster Dulles and nephew of Allen Welsh Dulles, founding director of the Central Intelligence Agency. His great-grandfathers were Secretary of State John Watson Dulles and Speaker of the House of Representatives Theodore Medad Pomeroy. Raised a Presbyterian, he was a self-professed agnostic when he entered Harvard University in 1936, but he converted to Catholicism while in school, his conversion coming under the influence of then-Jesuit Father Leonard Feeney (1887–1978), an influential priest later excommunicated for his extreme interpretation of the doctrine of "no salvation outside the Church." After graduation, Dulles served in the United States Navy, working with intelligence liaison, for which he was awarded the *Croix de Guerre* by France. Joining the Society of Jesus in 1946, he was ordained in 1956. He taught at Fordham University in New York and the Catholic University of America in Washington as well as the Jesuit Faculty at Woodstock College. The author of over twenty books and nearly seven hundred scholarly articles, he has served as president of both the Catholic Theological Society of America and the American Theological Society, a predominantly Protestant group founded by the distinguished Presbyterian theologian Allen Macy Dulles, his grandfather. He was created a cardinal by Pope John Paul II in 2001.

DUVAL, LÉON-ETIENNE (1903–1996), *cardinal*. Duval studied at the seminary in his native Annecy as well as the Pontifical French Seminary in Rome before being ordained a priest in 1926. Until 1942, he was engaged in pastoral work and seminary teaching in Annecy. From 1942 to 1946, he served as vicar general of the Archdiocese of Algiers. In 1946, he was appointed bishop of Constantine, Algeria. He was promoted to be the archbishop of Algiers in 1954. He attended the Second Vatican Council and the subsequent Synods of Bishops. He was created a cardinal by Paul VI in 1965, and participated in the two conclaves of 1978. He resigned the pastoral governance of his archdiocese in 1988.

DZIWISZ, STANISLAW (born 1939), *archbishop*. Hailing from Raba Wylna, near Cracow, Dziwisz was ordained a priest in 1963 after studies at the diocesan seminary. After a brief pastoral stint, in 1966, he became the personal secretary of the then-cardinal archbishop of Cracow, Karol Wojtyla, a position he has maintained even as his mentor ascended to the papacy. In the 1981 assassination attempt on Pope John Paul II, it was Dziwisz who cradled the wounded pontiff as the "popemobile" sped away. Long one of the most influential figures in the Vatican—if not the most—due to his personal and physical (he shared the same apartment with the pontiff) proximity to John Paul II, Dziwisz was elevated to the episcopate in 1998 with the newly invented title of "adjunct prefect of the Papal Household." In 2003, he was promoted to the rank of archbishop. After the death of John Paul II, Pope Benedict XVI appoint Dziwisz archbishop of Cracow.

ENRIQUE Y TARANCÓN, VICENTE (1907–1994), *cardinal*. Enrique y Tarancón was educated in the seminary of his native diocese of Tortosa and the Pontifical Seminary of Valencia and ordained a priest in 1929. He carried out pastoral work in the diocese of Tortosa until 1946, with the exception of the period between 1933 and 1938, when he worked with Catholic Action in Madrid. Appointed bishop of Solsona in 1945, he was elected secretary of the Spanish Episcopate in 1953. He attended the Second Vatican Council as well as the subsequent Synods of Bishops. He was promoted to be archbishop of Oviedo in 1964 and transferred to the primatial see of Toledo in 1969. He was created a cardinal by Paul VI that same year. In 1971, he was named apostolic administrator of Madrid-Alcalá, and subsequently transferred as archbishop there. A moderate figure who gently, but firmly, called for the liberalization and democratization of the government of Generalissimo Francisco Franco, he attracted the ire of the Spanish right. At the 1973 funeral of the Spanish prime minister, Admiral Luis Carrero Blanco, who had been assassinated by the Basque terrorists of ETA, mourners shouted at the presiding cardinal: *"Tarancón al paredón!"* ("Tarancón against the [firing squad] wall!"). He participated in the two conclaves of 1978. He was named a member of the Real Academia de la Lengua Española. He resigned the pastoral governance of the Archdiocese of Madrid-Alcalá in 1983.

ETCHEGARAY, ROGER (born 1922), *cardinal*. Born in Espelette, near Bayonne, France, he studied at the seminary of Bayonne and the Pontifical Gregorian University in Rome and was ordained a priest in 1947. From 1947 to 1961, he worked in his home diocese of Bayonne as secretary to the bishop, secretary general of the diocesan section of Catholic Action, and vicar general. Moving to Paris in 1961, he became, successively, adjunct secretary (1961–1966) and secretary (1966–1970) of the French Episcopal Conference. In 1969, he was appointed auxiliary bishop of Paris. The following year, he was promoted to the archbishopric of Marseilles. From 1971 to 1979, he served as the first president of the European Episcopal Conference. In 1975, he added the office of prelate of the Mission de France to his responsibilities, serving in that capacity until 1982. He was created a cardinal by Pope John Paul II in 1979. Called to Rome in 1984, he was appointed president of the Pontifical Commission *Iustitia et Pax* and of the Pontifical Commission *Cor Unum*. He resigned his archbishopric the following year. Both commissions were later renamed "pontifical councils." He resigned the presidency of the Pontifical Council *Cor Unum* in 1995, and that of the Pontifical Council for Justice and Peace in 1998, to assume the presidency of the Central Committee for the Great Jubilee of the Year 2000. Retiring after the holy year, Etchegaray remained active as an *ad hoc* papal envoy to various trouble spots, including Jerusalem and Baghdad. After participating in the conclave of 2005, Etchegaray was elected vice dean of the College of Cardinals.

VON FAULHABER, MICHAEL (1869–1952), *cardinal*. After studies at the university in his native Würzburg, Faulhaber was ordained a priest in 1892. Following a brief interval in parish work, he taught at the seminary of Würzburg and then at the University of Strasbourg, then part of Germany. Appointed bishop of Speyer in 1911, he was promoted to be the archbishop of Munich and Freising in 1917. He was created a cardinal by Benedict XV in 1921 and was, at the time of his death, that pope's last surviving cardinal, having participated in the conclaves of 1922 and 1939. Seeing early on the direction that the Nazi regime was taking, he had the courage to challenge Hitler personally, on one occasion arguing one-on-one with the Führer for three hours. Realizing the uselessness of dialogue, he laid out the framework for Pope Pius XI's denunciation of Nazism by drafting the outlines of the encyclical *Mit brennender Sorge*. In the wake of the regime's reprisals after the publication of the papal document, Faulhaber stood firm: "Now is the time to speak out. I already see the flames . . . We shall remain Christians, Roman Catholics, committed Catholics, joyful Catholics."

FERRARI, *Blessed* ANDREA CARLO (1850–1921), *cardinal*. Born to a family of poor peasants in the Apennines near Parma, he was ordained a priest in 1873, after studies at the local seminary. Appointed bishop of Guastalla in 1890, he was promoted to be the 236th bishop of Milan, being named archbishop of the "Ambrosian Church" shortly after his cardinalate in 1894 and remaining there until his death. A zealous pastor much beloved by his people, during the pontificate of Pius X Ferrari fell under suspicion of modernism for his defense of professors at the seminary of Milan who were accused before the Holy Office for alleged doctrinal speculations. Confined to his bed from November 13, 1920, until his death on February 2, 1921, he had the doors of the archiepiscopal palace thrown open as thousands of ordinary Milanese filed past his simple iron bed to bid him a tearful farewell as he lay in agony (from January onward, he was able to take only sugared water). Even then, he kept his well-known humor. When Cardinal Pietro Maffi of Pisa, receiving a false report of his Milanese confrère's death, telegraphed his condolences to the vicar general of Milan, Monsignor Giovanni Rossi, the communication was mistakenly given to Ferrari's secretary, also named Giovanni Rossi, who absentmindedly passed it on to the dying cardinal. Ferrari telegraphed a response: "Eminence, am very grateful for the condolences that, with extraordinary solicitude, you were so kind to send to the Cathedral Chapter for my death. However, the Lord has not yet deigned to call me to the embrace of His arms. Awaiting that to happen, I commend myself to your prayers. With friendship forever, Ferrari." He was beatified by Pope John Paul II in 1987.

FERRATA, DOMENICO (1847–1914), *cardinal*. Hailing from Gradoli, near Montefiascone, he earned doctorates in theology, canon law, and civil law. After a brief sojourn as a seminary professor, he entered the diplomatic service of the Holy See, serving in France and Switzerland as well as in Rome. He was consecrated archbishop and appointed apostolic nuncio to Belgium in 1885 and was named apostolic nuncio to France in 1891. Created a cardinal in 1896, he served in a variety of curial offices. Appointed secretary of state in 1914 by Pope Benedict XV, he died after less than a month in office.

FISCHER, ANTON HUBERT (1840–1912), *cardinal*. Born to an extremely humble family, Fischer nonetheless acquired a first-rate education at the University of Bonn, the Akademia of Münster, the seminary in Cologne, and the University of Tübingen, where he received a doctorate in theology. Ordained a priest in 1863, he spent a distinguished twenty-five year career in academia before he was appointed auxiliary archbishop of Cologne in 1889. Elected archbishop by the canons of the metropolitan cathedral in 1902, he was confirmed by Leo XIII the following year. He was created a cardinal in 1903.

FOSSATI, MAURILIO (1876–1965), *cardinal.* Fossati was ordained a priest in 1898 after studies at the seminary of his native diocese of Novara. He served as the secretary of his bishop from 1901 to 1911, following the prelate when he was promoted to the archbishopric of Genoa. In 1911, Fossati joined the Oblates of SS. Gaudentius and Charles of Novara and did pastoral work until the outbreak of World War I. After serving as an Italian military chaplain during the conflict, he was the superior of the Oblates at Varallo Sessio. In 1924, he was appointed bishop of Nuora in Sardinia, adding, in 1925, the apostolic administration of the neighboring diocese of Ogliastra to his charge. In 1929, he was promoted to the metropolitan see of Sassari as archbishop. Transferred to the archbishopric of Turin in 1930, he was created a cardinal by Pius XI in 1933. A near legendary figure in the Italian Church of his time, Fossati was a dedicated pastor, even if sometimes an unwitting caricature of the Italian prelate. He once famously wrote a pastoral letter drawing various distinctions between "honest traditional dances" and "degenerate modern dances." Forever chomping on an Italian-style dry Toscano brand cigar, he declared that "there is nothing better than a good cigar."

DE FÜRSTENBERG, MAXIMILIEN (1904–1988), *cardinal.* Fürstenberg was born in the castle of Ter Worm near Heerlem in the Netherlands, the scion of the ancient noble family of Fürstenberg-Stammheim, his father being the Baron Adolf von Fürstenberg and his mother the Countess Elisabeth d'Oultremont. He studied at the college of the Abbey of Mardesous near Namur, the College of Saint-Louis in Brussels, the University of Louvain, the Pontifical Biblical Institute in Rome, and the Pontifical Gregorian University in Rome, where he received his doctorate in theology. Ordained a priest in 1931, he was incardinated in the Archdiocese of Mechlin (Malines). He served on the faculty of the diocesan College of Saint Jean Berchmans in Antwerp (1932–1934) and the seminary of Mechlin (1934–1946), before being named rector of the Pontifical Belgian College in Rome in 1946, where one of the students he took in was the young Polish priest Karol Wojtyla. In 1949, he was appointed apostolic delegate to Japan, and elevated to the rank of archbishop. In 1952, he became internuncio to Japan. In 1959, he was transferred as apostolic delegate to Australia, New Zealand, and Oceania. In 1962, he was appointed apostolic nuncio to Portugal. He attended the Second Vatican Council and several of the subsequent Synods of Bishops. Created a cardinal by Paul VI in 1967, he was appointed prefect of the Sacred Congregation for the Oriental Churches the following year. He resigned the prefecture in 1973 and was appointed Grand Master of the Equestrian Order of the Holy Sepulchre of Jerusalem, an order of chivalry under the protection of the Holy See. When he died in 1988, he was buried in the famous Franciscan Church, near Remagen, Germany, built by his great-grandfather Franz Egon von Fürstenberg-Stammheim.

VON GALEN, *Blessed* CLEMENS AUGUST (1878–1946), *cardinal,* bishop of Münster and hero of the anti-Nazi resistance. Von Galen was born in the family castle of Dinklage, near Oldenburg in the Diocese of Münster. Ordained a priest in 1904 after studies at Münster, Fribourg, and Innsbruck, he served in parishes in Berlin and Münster for three decades before being named bishop of his native diocese in 1933, the same year that Adolf Hitler came to power. The new bishop soon lived up to the motto he had adopted for his episcopal coat of arms: *"Nec laudibus nec timor"* ("[Motivated by] neither praise nor fear"). Denouncing Nazi policies long before many others took notice of them, Galen was such an irritant that Joseph Goebbels publicly swore that as soon as the war was won the bishop would be hung in the square of Münster. His internationally famous Lenten sermons against the regime so infuriated Hitler that his arrest was ordered, but the *Gauleiter* responded that such was his popularity that if the bishop were incarcerated the entire area would be useless to the German war effort. While others tried to be discreet in their relatively mild protests, the Bishop of Münster published his over the signature "Clemens August, Count von Galen, Bishop," employing his title of nobility, lest there be any doubt about who was protesting. When he was created a cardinal by Pius XII in 1946, the sixteen thousand faithful assembled in St. Peter's Basilica for the consistory rose in unprecedented applause as he approached the papal throne to receive his red hat. His return to Münster was a triumphal procession, greeted by sixty thousand people gathered in front of his cathedral. However, he was already too weary to address them and died shortly afterward. He was beatified by Pope Benedict XVI in 2005.

GANTIN, BERNARDIN (born 1922), *cardinal*, former dean of the College of Cardinals. Gantin studied at the seminary of Ouidah in his native Benin and was ordained a priest in 1951. After a brief stint in pastoral work in the Archdiocese of Cotonou, he was sent to Rome for graduate studies at the Pontifical Urbanian Athenaeum *de Propaganda Fide* in 1953. He was still in Rome wrapping up his studies when he was appointed auxiliary bishop of Cotonou in 1956 at the age of thirty-four. Three years later, he was promoted to be archbishop of Cotonou. He attended the Second Vatican Council and subsequent Synods of Bishops. In 1971, he resigned his see to come to Rome as adjunct secretary of the Sacred Congregation for the Evangelization of Peoples, as the Sacred Congregation *de Propaganda Fide* had been renamed after Vatican II. In 1973, he became secretary of the Sacred Congregation. In 1975, he was appointed vice-president of the Pontifical Commission *Iustitia et Pax*, becoming its pro-president the following year. He became its president and was created a cardinal by Paul VI in 1977, adding to his responsibilities the presidency of the Pontifical Council *Cor Unum*, overseeing Catholic relief and development agencies, in 1978. He resigned the presidencies of the two pontifical councils in 1984 to assume the offices of prefect of the Sacred Congregation for Bishops and president of the Pontifical Commission for Latin America. He was elected and confirmed dean of the College of Cardinals in 1993. In 1998, he resigned both the prefecture and the presidency. In 2002, he resigned as dean of the College of Cardinals, assuming the title of "dean emeritus," and returned to Benin.

GASPARRI, PIETRO (1852–1934), *cardinal*, secretary of state of Popes Benedict XV (1914–1922) and Pius XI (1922–1939). Ordained a priest in 1877, he served as the secretary of Cardinal Teodolfo Mertel before becoming a noted jurist in his own right, teaching in Rome and Paris. In 1898, Leo XIII appointed him archbishop and apostolic delegate in Peru, Ecuador, and Bolivia, but he was recalled by Pius X to undertake the codification of the vast corpus of canon law that had accumulated over the centuries, a project that took him thirteen years and resulted in the promulgation of the Code of Canon Law in 1917 (Gasparri later published a multivolume commentary on the sources he employed in the redaction of the Code). Created a cardinal in 1907, he was named secretary of state by Benedict XV in 1914. He was reappointed by Pius XI in 1922. He successfully negotiated the resolution of the "Roman Question" with the Italian government, signing the Lateran Treaty and Concordat with Benito Mussolini on February 11, 1929. Having thus crowned his career, he retired the following year to spend his last years writing. Among his less scientific, but by no means less influential, publications was a catechism long employed by Catholics in Italy. Despite his career, he always kept close to his rural roots in the mountains of Umbria, where he was ultimately buried in his native village. After the signing of the Lateran Treaty, Mussolini asked Gasparri what he desired for having reconciled Italy and the Holy See. The cardinal's reply was a rather simple request: "Oh, it would be nice if Ussita, my little hamlet of a native place, could conserve its communal autonomy." So it was that despite the Fascist era's consolidation of ancient communes into larger administrative districts, little Ussita, thanks to its most famous son, retained its local self-government.

Gasparri is also remembered for having picked a young priest, Eugenio Pacelli, to be his assistant in the project of the codification of canon law. Later, as secretary of state, he arranged for Pacelli's promotion to archbishop and nuncio first to Bavaria and then to all Germany. Created a cardinal in 1929, Pacelli was Gasparri's designated successor as secretary of state when he retired the following year. Pacelli, of course, became Pope Pius XII in 1939.

GIBBONS, JAMES (1834–1921), *cardinal*, archbishop of Baltimore. Born in Baltimore and educated in Maryland's St. Charles College and St. Mary's Seminary, he was ordained a priest in 1861. After a brief stint in pastoral work, he served as secretary to Baltimore's Archbishop Martin Spalding as well as assistant chancellor of the Second Plenary Council of Baltimore in 1866. Gibbons was appointed, successively, apostolic vicar of North Carolina in 1868, bishop of Richmond in 1872, coadjutor archbishop of Baltimore in 1877, and archbishop of Baltimore in 1877. As apostolic delegate, he convened the Third Plenary Council of Baltimore in 1884, the meeting that set the tenor for much of pre–Vatican II American Catholicism. He was created a cardinal in 1886. Pope Leo XIII addressed his condemnation of "Americanism," *Testem benevolentiae*, to Gibbons, although the cardinal denied that any such heresy ever existed. He was able to participate in the conclave of 1903, as he happened to be in Rome, but arrived too late to take part in the conclave of 1914.

GOTTI, GIROLAMO MARIA (1834–1916), *cardinal*. Gotti was born Giovanni Antonio Benedetto in Genoa and assumed the name Girolamo Maria when he joined the Discalced Carmelite order in 1850. Rising to superior general of his religious order, he was chosen as archbishop and internuncio to Bolivia by Leo XIII in 1892. Upon his return to Rome three years later, he was made a cardinal and held various curial offices. He participated in the conclaves of 1903 and 1914.

GOUYON, PAUL (1910–2000), *cardinal*. Gouyon was educated at the University of Bordeaux, the seminary of Bordeaux, the Seminary of Saint-Sulpice in Paris, the Pontifical Gregorian University, and the Institut Catholique in Paris and ordained a priest in 1937. He served briefly (1939–1940) in the French Army during the Second World War, before returning to pastoral work in the Archdiocese of Bordeaux. Appointed vicar general of the archdiocese in 1951, he was named bishop of Bayonne in 1957. Promoted to be coadjutor archbishop of Rennes in 1963, he succeeded to the see the following year. He attended the Second Vatican Council and the subsequent Synods of Bishops. He was created a cardinal by Paul VI in 1969, and participated in the two conclaves of 1978. Fervently committed to peace and justice issues, he was national president of the French association of Pax Christi. He resigned the pastoral governance of his see in 1985.

GRANITO PIGNATELLI DI BELMONTE, GENNARO (1851–1948), *cardinal*. The scion of a noble Neapolitan family that had given the Roman Church Pope Innocent XII (1691–1700) as well as countless other prelates, Granito Pignatelli di Belmonte was ordained a priest in 1879. After an early career in the administration of his native archdiocese, he entered the diplomatic service of the Holy See and was consecrated an archbishop in 1899, serving as nuncio to Belgium and Austria-Hungary as well as special papal envoy to Britain for the funeral of Queen Victoria and for the coronation of King George V. Created cardinal in 1911, he became sub-dean of the Sacred College in 1929 and its dean the following year. He participated in the conclaves of 1914, 1922, and 1939.

GROËR, HANS HERMANN (1919–2003), *cardinal*, archbishop of Vienna until he was forced to resign amid accusations of that he was a pedophile. Born in Vienna of Sudeten parents, Groër studied at the seminaries of Hollabrunn and Vienna, earning a doctorate in theology from the latter institution. Ordained a priest in 1942, he served as a military chaplain until 1946, when he was appointed to the staff of the minor seminary of Hollabrunn as prefect. From 1952 until 1974, while remaining on the faculty of Hollabrunn, Groër worked to restore the Marian shrine of Roggendorf, which had been secularized in 1790. In 1974, he joined the Order of St. Benedict, entering the abbey of Güttweig. He made his solemn profession as a monk in 1980. He was appointed archbishop of Vienna in 1986 and created a cardinal by Pope John Paul II in 1988. In 1995, amid accusations that he had sexually abused minors, he resigned the pastoral government of the Archdiocese of Vienna, although he refused to admit guilt. The following year, when an internal Church investigation—a state criminal prosecution was precluded by the statute of limitations in Austrian law—apparently verified the charges, he was asked by the pope to leave the country and refrain from the exercise of any of his ecclesiastical prerogatives. He eventually returned to Austria and retired to seclusion in a monastery.

VON HARTMANN, FELIX (1851–1919), *cardinal*. Ordained a priest in 1874 after studies at the seminary of Münster, he pursued advanced studies at the Pontifical Gregorian University and the Pontifical Athenaeum of Sant'Apollinare in Rome. Unlike many of his confrères in the Sacred College during that period, Hartmann had a pastoral career, serving successively as a chaplain, pastor, and cathedral canon, before being elected, in rapid succession, bishop of Münster (1911) and archbishop of Cologne (1912). He was created a cardinal in Pius X's last consistory in May 1914. Always pastoral, he also moved easily among the aristocracy, receiving the Grand Cross of the Equestrian Order of the Holy Sepulchre of Jerusalem and the Bailiff Grand Cross of the Sovereign Military Order of Malta, and being elected, in 1916, to the Prussian Chamber of Lords.

HARVEY, JAMES MICHAEL (born 1949), *archbishop*, prefect of the Papal Household. A native of Milwaukee, Harvey studied at the Pontifical North American College in Rome and was ordained a priest in 1975. After advanced studies at the Pontifical Ecclesiastical Academy, he entered the diplomatic service of the Holy See and served in various capacities in the Secretariat of State. In 1998, he was appointed prefect of the Papal Household and ordained a bishop by Pope John Paul II. In 2003, he was promoted to the rank of archbishop.

HINSLEY, ARTHUR (1865–1943), *cardinal*. Born in Selby, Hinsley was educated at Ushaw College, Durham, and, in Rome, at the Pontifical Gregorian University and the Pontifical Roman Academy of St. Thomas Aquinas. Ordained a priest in 1893, he served successively as a faculty member of Ushaw College (1893–1897), in pastoral work in the Archdiocese of Westminster (1898), as headmaster of St. Bede's Grammar School (1899–1904), and as rector of the Venerable English College in Rome (1917–1930). He was consecrated a titular bishop in 1926 and sent as apostolic visitor to British Africa the following year. In 1930, he was promoted to the rank of archbishop and sent as apostolic delegate to British missions in Africa not under the jurisdiction of the apostolic delegates in Egypt, the Belgian Congo, or South Africa. Returning to Rome in 1934, he was appointed a canon of the Vatican Basilica. In 1935, he was transferred to the metropolitan see of Westminster and, two years later, created a cardinal by Pope Pius XI. He participated in the conclave of 1943.

HÖFFNER, JOSEPH (1906–1987), *cardinal*. Born in Horhausen, near Trier, Germany, Höffner studied at the Theological Faculty of Freiburg im Breisgau and the Pontifical Gregorian University and was ordained a priest in 1932. He did pastoral work until 1945, when he began an academic career, teaching at the seminary of Trier (1945–1950), the Theological Faculty of Trier (1950–1951), and the University of Münster (1951–1962). He also founded the Institute of Christian Social Sciences in Munich, serving as its director from 1951 to 1961, during which period he also served as an advisor to several ministries of the Federal Republic of Germany. Appointed bishop of Münster in 1962, he attended all four sessions of the Second Vatican Council. In 1969, he was appointed coadjutor archbishop of Cologne, succeeding to the see shortly thereafter. Created a cardinal by Pope Paul VI that same year, he participated in the two conclaves of 1978. He resigned the pastoral governance of his archdiocese in 1987 and died less than a month later.

VON HORNIG, KÁROLY (1840–1917), *cardinal*. Scion of a noble Hungarian family, he was ordained a priest in 1862. Teaching at the Royal University of Budapest before accompanying the Hungarian bishops to the First Vatican Council (1869–1870), he returned from the assembly and was appointed rector of the seminary of Budapest. Hornig became bishop of Veszprém in 1888. He was created a cardinal by Pius X in 1912 and participated in the conclave of 1914. He participated in the coronation of the last Habsburg monarchs, Karl I and Zita, as king and queen of Hungary in 1916.

HUME, GEORGE BASIL (1923–1999), *cardinal*. Hume was born at Newcastle-on-Tyne. Educated at St. Lawrence Abbey, Ampleforth, Oxford University, and the University of Fribourg, he joined the Benedictine order and made his solemn profession as a monk in 1945. Ordained a priest in 1950, he was elected abbot of Ampleforth in 1963. He was appointed archbishop of Westminster in 1976, and created a cardinal by Paul VI that same year. A much-admired figure, shortly before his death he was appointed a member of the Order of Merit by Queen Elizabeth II.

INNITZER, THEODOR (1875–1955), *cardinal*. Born in Wipert, near Prague, then part of Austria-Hungary, Innitzer earned his doctorate from the University of Vienna and was ordained a priest in 1902. He was active in pastoral work and served as secretary of the Leo-Gesellschaft, a Catholic cultural society. He served as minister of social welfare in the cabinet of Chancellor Johann Schober from 1929 to 1930. Innitzer was appointed archbishop of Vienna in 1932 and created a cardinal by Pope Pius XI the following year. Although he initially welcomed the *Anschluss*, he eventually turned on the Nazis. He participated in the conclave of 1939.

JOAN, "POPE," a legendary female pope who never existed. From the mid-thirteenth through the mid-seventeenth century, the story that there had been a female pope, commonly, but not invariably, known as "Pope Joan," at some date in the ninth, tenth, or eleventh century, was almost universally accepted as historical fact. Even as late as the latter part of the nineteenth century, the tale continued to furnish ammunition to critics of the Roman Church in general and of the papal office in particular. Even now, at the beginning of the twenty-first century, a number of novels—all of which have been, without exception, flawed in some of the most basic historical detail despite pretenses to be works of *historical* fiction—the legend of the female pontiff continues to provide rich fare for the literary imagination.

   The story first appeared in the decade between 1240 and 1250, in the *Universal History of Metz*, attributed to the Dominican priest Jean de Mailly. According to the *Universal History*, Pope Victor III (1087) was succeeded on the papal throne by a talented woman who, disguised as a man, had obtained an education and then worked her way up in the Roman Curia as a notary, eventually being promoted to the rank of a cardinal. Elected pope after Victor's brief four-month pontificate, this woman was betrayed when, mounting her horse, she gave birth to a child, and was then ignominiously tied to the horse's tail, dragged around the city, and then stoned to death.

   Jean de Mailly's Dominican confrère Stephen de Bourbon (d. 1262) and the anonymous Franciscan friar who wrote the *Chronicon minor* around 1265 give roughly similar accounts, although they place the reign of the alleged "popess" around 1100 and 915, respectively. The tale was given its final form and widely diffused by the posthumous editions of the *Chronicle of Popes and Emperors* of the Polish Dominican friar Martin of Troppau (d. 1297). According to the account posthumously ascribed to Martin, Pope St. Leo IV (847–855) was succeeded by one John Anglicus, who reigned two years, seven months, and four days, and was, in fact, a woman. A native of Mainz, she supposedly went as a girl, dressed in a man's clothes but escorted by her lover, to Athens, had a brilliant student career there, and then settled in Rome, where her lectures were acclaimed by such distinguished audiences and her life so edifying—evidently, the lover made himself invisible—that she was unanimously elected pope. Her imposture was exposed when, riding in procession from St. Peter's Basilica to the Lateran Basilica, she gave birth to a child in a narrow street between the Coliseum and the Basilica of San Clemente. She died on the spot and was buried there. Because of this shameful episode, so went the tale, popes thereafter avoided traversing the street in question. The name "Pope Joan" derives from the feminine form of name that the *Chronicle* gave her, "John."

The story, often embellished with fantastic details, was accepted without question for centuries, in part because later generations were willing to believe almost anything about the period that came to be known as the "Dark Ages." It would probably have been forgotten had it not been perpetuated by early humanists like Petrarch (d. 1374) and Boccaccio (d. 1375), who kept its memory alive for their own propaganda purposes. Under their influence, it even influenced iconography: A bust of "Pope Joan" appears among the papal busts in the Siena Cathedral (the government of Siena, it should be recalled, being often at odds with the papacy at the time). The Bohemian precursor of the Protestant Reformation, John Hus (d. 1415), cited it in his defense when on trial for his life at the Council of Constance.

Although at the time of the Protestant Reformation some Catholic authors began to cast doubts on the story, ironically it was a French Protestant, David Blondel (1590–1655), who effectively demolished the legend's claims to historical veracity with a series of treatises published in Amsterdam between 1647 and 1657, the final studies being published after their author's death. As Blondel argued and subsequent historians have confirmed, not only is there no contemporary evidence for a female pope at any period in history, the known facts about the respective periods suggested for "Pope Joan" make it impossible to fit in her presumptive pontificate

The origin of the story, however, has never been satisfactorily explained—although its persistence is easy enough to attribute to an almost universal human temptation to a sort of historical gnosticism, a yearning for the "hidden truth" behind the conventional chronicle of events. (One could draw a contemporary parallel in the persistence in some fringe circles of ultra-conservative Catholicism of the belief that Pope Paul VI [1963–1978] was, at some point, substituted with a double.) The kernel of the story is generally taken to be an ancient Roman folktale—there are several that predate Christian times concerning talented women who, disguised as men, rose to the Senate or the command of the legions or became famous gladiators—that was blown up by a number of circumstances

needlessly taken to be suspicious, such as the deliberate avoidance of a certain street by
papal processions (perhaps because of the street's narrowness), the discovery of an enig-
matic statue taken to represent a woman suckling a child along with a puzzling inscription nearby that could be twisted to lend support to the legend, and the popular belief
that after his election a new pope had to undergo tests that he was really a male (a story
that grew out of the very strange shape of the papal throne in the old Lateran Palace—
a precious porphyry seat, lost since the 1527 sack of Rome by mutinous German soldiers from the imperial army, that, from its descriptions, may have had a different use in
its classical origins).

It is also possible that the recollection in the mid-thirteenth century that, sometime
during the tenth century, the papacy was indeed dominated by the three unscrupulous
women of the Theophylact clan—Theodora the Elder, Marozia, and Theodora the
Younger—gave currency to the legend. If this is the case, it is yet another example of the
old adage that truth is stranger than fiction.

DE JONG, JAN (1885–1955), *cardinal.* De Jong was ordained a priest in Rome in 1908,
pursuing advanced studies there after ordination. After a brief period in pastoral work in
his native archdiocese of Utrecht, he joined the faculty of the seminary of Rijsenburg,
where he remained until his appointment as coadjutor archbishop of Utrecht in 1935.
He succeeded to the see the following year. A leader of the Dutch resistance during the
Second World War, he was created cardinal by Pius XII in 1946. Ill health forced him to
leave the administration of his diocese to a coadjutor in 1951.

JOOS, GUSTAAF (1923-2004), *cardinal.* Born in Sint-Niklaas, near Gent, Belgium, to a pious family—three of his brothers became priests—he was ordained a priest in 1946 and
sent to pursue a doctorate in canon law at the Pontifical Gregorian University in Rome.
While studying in Rome, he lived at the Pontifical Belgian College, where he befriended
a young Polish priest who lodged there, Father Karol Wojtyla. After earning his doctorate, Joos returned to Belgium, where he taught at the diocesan seminary and served on
both the diocesan and national ecclesiastical tribunals. Created a cardinal in 2003 by his
old classmate, Pope John Paul II, he was ordained to the episcopate. The aged prelate
caused a bit of controversy after his sudden elevation with several intemperate remarks
about homosexuals.

KIM SOU-HWAN, STEPHEN (born 1922), *cardinal.* Following studies at the local seminary
and the Sophia Catholic University in Tokyo, Kim was ordained a priest of the apostolic
vicariate of Taeku (later the Archdiocese of Taegu), South Korea, in 1951. After serving
as a parish priest and secretary to the local bishop, he studied social sciences at the University of Münster from 1957 to 1964. Returning to South Korea, Kim was appointed
bishop of Masan by Pope Paul VI in 1966. Two years later, he was promoted to the
archbishopric of Seoul. He was created a cardinal by Pope Paul in 1969. Kim attended
several meetings of the Synod of Bishops and served as president-delegate of the Special

Assembly for Asia of the Synod of Bishops in 1998. He participated in the two conclaves of 1978. Upon the death of Austrian cardinal Franz König on March 13, 2004, Kim became the *cardinale primoprete*, the senior cardinal priest.

KÖNIG, FRANZ (1905–2004), *cardinal*. König was ordained a priest for his native diocese of Sankt Pölten in 1933, after studies at the Pontifical Gregorian University and the Pontifical Biblical Institute in Rome. After a brief period of pastoral work, he pursued further studies at the Catholic University of Lille, France (1936–1937). He then taught at the College of Krems, the University of Vienna, and the University of Salzburg. Appointed coadjutor bishop of Sankt Pölten in 1952, he never succeeded there, being promoted to archbishop of Vienna in 1956. Created a cardinal by John XXIII in 1958, the following year he was also appointed military vicar of Austria, a post he resigned in 1968. He attended the Second Vatican Council and the subsequent Synods of Bishops. In 1965, he was appointed president of the newly established Secretariat for Non-Believers, a post he held until 1980. He resigned the pastoral governance of the Archdiocese of Vienna in 1985. He participated in the conclave of 1963 and the two conclaves of 1978.

VON KOPP, GEORG (1837–1914), *cardinal*. Kopp was a former civil servant in the government of the German kingdom of Hanover before entering the seminary and being ordained a priest in 1862. After holding a succession of pastoral charges, he was appointed Bishop of Fulda in 1881. He was transferred to be prince-bishop of Breslau in 1887. Created a cardinal in 1893, he participated in the conclave of 1903.

KROL, JOHN JOSEPH (1910–1996), *cardinal*, archbishop of Philadelphia. Krol was born in Cleveland, Ohio, and educated at St. Mary's College in Orchard Lake, Michigan, St. Mary's Seminary in Cleveland, the Pontifical Gregorian University in Rome, and the Catholic University of America in Washington, D.C. Ordained a priest in 1937, he taught at St. Mary's Seminary in Cleveland and served successively as vice-chancellor and chancellor of the Diocese of Cleveland. In 1953, he was appointed auxiliary bishop of Cleveland. In 1961, he was promoted to be archbishop of Philadelphia. He attended the Second Vatican Council and several of the subsequent Synods of Bishops. He was created a cardinal by Paul VI in 1967. He was president of the National Conference of the Catholic Bishops/United States Catholic Conference from 1971 to 1974. In 1981, he was appointed to the Council of Cardinals for the Study of the Organizational and Economic Problems of the Holy See. He resigned the pastoral governance of the Archdiocese of Philadelphia in 1988.

KUNG PIN-MEI, IGNATIUS (1901–2000), *cardinal*. Kung was born into an old Catholic family in P'ou-tong, near Shanghai. Schooled in both Chinese classics and modern learning, he was ordained a priest in 1930, after studies at the seminary of Shanghai. He held a number of pastoral assignments in the Shanghai diocese and, although a diocesan priest, was appointed headmaster of the Jesuit-run Aurora High School and Gonzaga High School. In 1949, he was appointed bishop of Soochow. Transferred to be bishop of Shanghai the following year, he was appointed apostolic administrator of the dioceses of Soochow and Nanking. He spent the first years of his episcopate organizing the clerical and, most importantly, the lay structures of his dioceses for the persecution that he was certain would come with the new Communist regime. He was arrested in 1955 and sentenced to life in prison in 1960. His crime was apparently his refusal to break communion with the Holy See. He was released to house arrest in 1985. In 1988, he was allowed to come to the United States, where he had family, for medical treatment, and remained with them until his death. He was created a cardinal *in pectore* by Pope John Paul II in 1979, the nomination being published in 1991.

LA FONTAINE, PIETRO (1869–1935), *cardinal.* La Fontaine was ordained a priest in 1883. He did pastoral work in his native diocese of Viterbo and taught in its seminary from his ordination until 1906, when he was appointed bishop. Named secretary of the Sacred Congregation of Rites in 1910, he was promoted to the patriarchate of Venice in 1915, receiving the red hat of a cardinal the following year. After his death in 1935, his body was originally buried in a chapel of his own construction on the Lido of Venice dedicated to Mary Immaculate, surrounded by the tombs of Italian soldiers who died in the Piave campaign. The inscription he had inscribed on the tomb read simply: *"Petrus cardinalis La Fontaine, Venetiarum Patriarca, ad pedes Dominae Suae"* ("Pietro Cardinal La Fontaine, Patriarch of the Venetians, at the feet of his Lady"). While this monument is still there, the body was transferred in 1959 to the cathedral of Venice.

LAJOLO, GIOVANNI (born 1935), *archbishop,* secretary for relations with states. A native of Novara, he was ordained to the priesthood in 1960. After pastoral work in his diocese and earning a doctorate in canon law, he completed studies at the Pontifical Ecclesiastical Academy in Rome and entered the diplomatic service of the Holy See in 1970, serving at the apostolic nunciature in Bonn and in the Council for the Public Affairs of the Church (now the Second Section of the Secretariat of State, charged with the Vatican's foreign relations). In 1988, Pope John Paul II appointed him secretary of the Administration of the Patrimony of the Apostolic See and elevated him to the archiepiscopal rank. In 1995, he was appointed apostolic nuncio to Germany. In October 2003, when Archbishop Jean-Louis Tauran vacated the office upon being created a cardinal, Lajolo was promoted to be secretary for relations with states, effectively "foreign minister" of the Vatican.

LANDÁZURI RICKETTS, JUAN (1913–1997), *cardinal.* Born Guillermo Eduardo, Landázuri Ricketts adopted the name Juan when he joined the Franciscan order in 1933. Educated in the Colegio Nacional in his native Arequipa, Peru, and the Pontifical Athenaeum Antonianum in Rome, he was ordained a priest in 1939. After holding various posts in his order, he was appointed coadjutor archbishop of Lima in 1952, succeeding to the see in 1955. He was created a cardinal in 1962 by John XXIII and attended the Second Vatican Council and the subsequent Synods of Bishops. He participated in the two conclaves of 1978. He resigned the pastoral governance of his archdiocese in 1989.

LAURENTI, CAMILLO (1861–1938), *cardinal*. Ordained a priest in 1884 after studies at the Pontifical Gregorian University in Rome, Laurenti spent his entire early ecclesiastical career as a professor at the Pontifical Urbanian Athenaeum *de Propaganda Fide* and a staff attaché at the Sacred Congregation for the Propagation of the Faith, where he rose to the office of secretary. Created cardinal deacon in 1921, he was appointed prefect of the Sacred Congregation for Religious after the conclave of 1922 and subsequently that of the Sacred Congregation of Rites.

LAW, BERNARD FRANCIS (born 1931), *cardinal*, archbishop of Boston until public fallout from his mishandling of the clergy sexual abuse scandals forced his resignation in 2002. Born in Torreón, Mexico, to expatriate American parents, Law graduated from Harvard University before studying at St. Joseph's Seminary in St. Benedict, Louisiana, and the Pontifical College Josephinum in Worthington, Ohio. He was ordained a priest in 1961, for the Diocese of Natchez–Jackson, Mississippi. Director of the diocesan newspaper, he was active in the civil rights movement of the era. Pope Paul VI appointed him bishop of Springfield–Cape Girardeau, Missouri, in 1973. Pope John Paul II, while leaving him initially in that see, entrusted him with the administration of the "pastoral provision" for married Episcopal (Anglican) priests who converted to Catholicism and wanted to continue in ministry. In 1984, John Paul II promoted him to the archbishopric of Boston, creating him a cardinal the following year. It was at Law's suggestion, made during the extraordinary Synod of Bishops of 1985, that the *Catechism of the Catholic Church* was prepared. Amid the scandal of sexual abuse by priests of his archdiocese, a media furor led to Law's resignation as archbishop of Boston in 2002 and his temporary retirement to a convent in Maryland as its chaplain. In 2004, John Paul II brought him to Rome and appointed him Archpriest of the Patriarchal Liberian Basilica of St. Mary Major. Law took part in the conclave of 2005.

LEFEBVRE, MARCEL (1905–1991), *archbishop*, traditionalist prelate who led his follow-ers into schism in opposition to the reforms of Vatican II. Born to an intensely devout family—five of the eight children would enter religious life—Lefebvre was educated at the Pontifical French Seminary and the Pontifical Gregorian University in Rome. Or-dained a priest in 1929, he joined the Congregation of the Holy Spirit (Spiritans or Holy Ghost Fathers), a missionary religious community, and served as a missionary in French West Africa. Appointed apostolic vicar of Dakar and consecrated a bishop in 1947, he was promoted to the rank of archbishop the following year and appointed, while retain-ing his pastoral charge, apostolic delegate for an area of West Africa that would later become eighteen states. In 1955, he became the first archbishop of Dakar. In 1962, he resigned the See of Dakar in favor of a native African, the future Cardinal Hyacinthe Thiandoum, and became archbishop-bishop of Tulle in France. That same year, he was elected superior general of the Spiritan congregation. He participated in the Second Vatican Council, but resisted its changes, resigning both his diocese and his generalate in 1969. He then founded the Society of St. Pius X to preserve the old ways. He was excommunicated in 1988 for consecrating four traditionalist bishops without papal authorization.

LEHMANN, KARL (born 1936), *cardinal*, bishop of Mainz. Born in Sigmaringen, he studied at the diocesan seminary of Freiburg-im-Breisgau before earning doctorates in theology and philosophy from the Pontifical Gregorian University in Rome. He was ordained a priest in 1963. He served as Karl Rahner's assistant from 1964 until 1968, when he became professor of dogmatic theology at the University of Mainz. In 1971, he was appointed professor of dogmatic and ecumenical theology at the University of Freiburg, a position he retained until he was appointed bishop of Mainz in 1983. Elected vice-president of the German Episcopal Conference in 1985, he became its president in 1985, a position he still retains. He was created a cardinal by Pope John Paul II in 2001. A prolific writer, he is the only member of the College of Cardinals on whom a regularly updated academic bibliography is maintained (see http://www.theol.uni-freiburg.de/forsch/lehmann/lehmann1.htm). Lehmann took part in the conclave of 2005.

LERCARO, GIACOMO (1891–1976), *cardinal*. Lercaro was ordained a priest in 1914, having studied at the seminary of his native archdiocese of Genoa and the Pontifical Biblical Institute in Rome. After serving as a military chaplain with the Italian army during World War I, he returned to Genoa, where he taught in the seminary and did pastoral work until 1947, when he was appointed archbishop of Ravenna. He was transferred to the archbishopric of Bologna in 1952. He was created a cardinal by Pius XII in 1953 and participated in the conclaves of 1958 and 1963. During Vatican II, he served on the council's presidency and, after the council, was appointed to serve as president of the Consilium overseeing liturgical reforms (1966–1968). He resigned the pastoral governance of the archdiocese of Bologna in 1968.

VAN LIERDE, PETRUS CANISIUS JOHANNES (1907–1995), *bishop*, longtime vicar general of His Holiness for the Vatican. Born in Hasselt, Belgium, to an aristocratic Dutch family, he joined the Augustinian order and was ordained a priest in 1936. A gifted scholar and linguist, he subsequently earned doctorates in philosophy, theology, and Scripture and served as the rector of the Augustinian College of St. Monica in Rome. During the Second World War, he hid numerous refugees from the Nazis, including Jews, military officers, and government officials, in his college. Appointed vicar general of His Holiness for the Vatican and prefect of the Papal Sacristy by Pope Pius XII (1939–1958) in 1951, he was consecrated a bishop. He served in that capacity longer than any other incumbent, continuing under Pope John XXIII (1958–1963), Pope Paul VI (1963–1978), Pope John Paul I (1978), and Pope John Paul II. He administered the last rites to Pius XII and John XXIII and served as sacristan of the conclaves of 1958 and 1963, and the two conclaves of 1978. Retiring in 1991, he was given the title of "emeritus vicar general of His Holiness" and remained active, maintaining his quarters and offices in the heart of the medieval part of the Vatican Palace.

LOISY, ALFRED FIRMIN (1857–1940), French theologian, biblical scholar, and leader of the modernist movement. Born in Ambrires in French Lorraine to peasant parents, Loisy studied at the seminaries of St. Dizier and Chalôns-sur-Marne and was ordained a priest in 1879. After a brief stint as the pastor of two rural parishes in the Diocese of Chalôns, he was sent to the Institut Catholique in Paris, where he took a degree in theology, as well as the University of Paris, where, in 1890, he earned his doctorate with a dissertation on the development of the Old Testament canon. Loisy became a professor at the Catholic Institute, but he was dismissed in 1893 because of his then-novel critical approach to biblical studies. He subsequently taught at the Ecole des Hautes Etudes (1900–1904) and at the Collège de France (1909–1930). He became the one of the principal leaders of the modernist movement, which accepted the theories of higher criticism and developed a kind of liberal humanitarianism. His books were condemned severally and collectively by the Holy See, and in 1908 he was excommunicated. Thereafter he became increasingly opposed to the teachings of the church. His most influential works included *L'Evangile et l'église* ("The Gospel and the Church," 1902), *Le IVe Evangile* ("The Fourth Gospel," 1903), and *Les Evangiles synoptiques* ("The Synoptic Gospels," 1908).

LORSCHEIDER, ALOISI (born 1924), *cardinal*. Lorscheider joined the Franciscan order in 1942, studying at the Franciscan novitiate in Divinópolis before making his solemn profession in 1946 and being ordained a priest in 1948. He subsequently taught at the minor seminary of Taguari for two years before being sent for further studies at the Pontifical Athenaeum Antonianum in Rome (1950–1952). He then served in a variety of posts within the Franciscan order in Brazil (1952–1958) and in Rome (1958–1962). He was appointed bishop of Santo Angelo in 1962 and attended the Second Vatican Council and the subsequent Synods of Bishops. He was elected president of the Brazilian Episcopal Conference in 1971. He was promoted to be archbishop of Fortaleza in 1973. He was elected president of the Latin American Episcopal Conference (CELAM) in 1976, the same year he was created a cardinal by Paul VI. In an unprecedented demotion for a member of the College of Cardinals, Lorscheider was transferred by John Paul II in 1995 from the large archdiocese of Fortaleza (2.1 million Catholics, 78 parishes, 137 diocesan priests) to the minor archbishopric of Aparecida (198,000 Catholics, 15 parishes, 21 diocesan priests). He retired in 2004.

LUALDI, ALESSANDRO (1858–1927), *cardinal*. Ordained a priest in 1880, the Milanese prelate was named archbishop of Palermo in 1904 and created a cardinal by Pius X in 1907. He participated in the conclaves of 1914 and 1922.

DE LUBAC, HENRI-MARIE (1896–1991), *cardinal*. De Lubac joined the Society of Jesus at the age of seventeen. He was ordained a priest in 1927, after completing studies at the Jesuit centers of Jersey and Fourvière. He subsequently earned a doctorate in theology from the Pontifical Gregorian University in Rome. Teaching in Lyons, he co-founded, with fellow Jesuit and future cardinal Jean Daniélou, the patristic collection *Sources chrétiennes* in 1942. He was also director of the influential journal *Recerches de science religieuse*. During World War II, he was forced to flee Lyons and go into hiding because of his activities with the anti-Nazi resistance. His book *Surnaturel* (1946) attracted the suspicions of the Holy Office, and he was obligated to abandon all intellectual activities, although the French Academy of Moral and Political Sciences nonetheless elected him to membership in 1957. Rehabilitated after the election of John XXIII, he joined the faculty of the Institut Catholique in Paris and served as a *peritus*, or official expert, at the Second Vatican Council and was subsequently named a member of the new International Theological Commission. John Paul II created him a cardinal in 1983.

MACCHI, PASQUALE (born 1923), *archbishop*, private secretary of Pope Paul VI. A native of Varese in the Archdiocese of Milan, Macchi was ordained a priest in 1946 and served as Paul VI's private secretary both during the then-Archbishop Montini's tenure in Milan and during his pontificate. He was appointed papal delegate for the Shrine of the Holy House of Loreto in succession to Pope John XXIII's former private secretary, Loris Capovilla, in 1988 and ordained an archbishop in 1989. He retired in 1996.

MAFFI, PIETRO (1858–1931), *cardinal*. Ordained a priest in 1881 after earning a doctorate in theology from the seminary of his native Pavia, Maffi was a noted student of both faith and science. He founded the meteorological observatory of Pavia and, for many years, edited the leading Italian scientific journal, the *Rivista di scienze fisiche e matematiche* ("Review of physical and mathematical sciences"). He became auxiliary bishop of Ravenna in 1902 and was promoted to archbishop of Pisa the following year. He was created a cardinal in 1907 and participated in the conclaves of 1914 and 1922. In 1930, he celebrated the marriage between Crown Prince Umberto of Italy and Princess Marie-José of Belgium, who were destined to be Italy's last sovereigns.

MAGLIONE, LUIGI (1877–1944), *cardinal*, secretary of state of Pope Pius XII from 1939 until his death. Hailing from Casoria, near Naples, Maglione was ordained a priest in 1901, after studies at the Capranica College in Rome, and returned to several years of pastoral work in his native archdiocese of Naples. He then went on to earn doctorates in philosophy and theology from the Jesuit-run Gregorian University before finishing his training at the Pontifical Academy of Noble Ecclesiastics. He entered the diplomatic service of the Holy See and worked on the staff of the Secretariat of State. In 1918, Benedict XV appointed him as the special papal envoy to Switzerland and entrusted him with the diplomatic brief of serving as the provisional papal representative to the League of Nations. Appointed the first resident nuncio in Switzerland in centuries, he was elevated to the rank of archbishop in 1920. In 1926, he was appointed apostolic nuncio to France, where he cultivated his personal historical interest in the Napoleonic campaigns as well as helping to rebuild the French Church after the privations of the unilateral separation of Church and state two decades earlier. Recalled to Rome in 1935, he was created a cardinal by Pius XI and appointed prefect of the Sacred Congregation of the Council. After the conclave of 1939, he was appointed secretary of state.

MALULA, JOSEPH-ALBERT (1917–1989), *cardinal*. Malula was born in Leopoldville (now Kinhasa). After studies at the minor seminaries of Mbata Kiela and Bolongo (Lisale) and the major seminary of Christ-Roi in Kabwe, he was ordained a priest in 1946. He served successively on the faculty of the minor seminary of Bokoro, as vicar of the parish of Saint-Pierre, Leopoldville, and vicar and then pastor of the parish of Christ-Roi, Leopoldville. Appointed auxiliary bishop of Leopoldville in 1959, he attended the Second Vatican Council and several of the subsequent Synods of Bishops. He became archbishop of Leopoldville in 1964. The name of his archdiocese was changed to Kinhasa the following year. In the wake of the liturgical reforms of Vatican II, he led the way in introducing African cultural expressions into the liturgy, obtaining provisional approval of the so-called Zaire Rite, of which he was the principal creator. He was created a cardinal by Paul VI in 1969. He participated in the two conclaves of 1978.

MARCHISANO, FRANCESCO (born 1929), *cardinal*, archpriest of the Vatican Basilica. A native of Racconigi, near Turin, Marchisano was ordained a priest in 1952. After advanced studies at the Pontifical Lombard Seminary in Rome, he entered the service of the Holy See at the Sacred Congregation for the Council (now the Congregation for the Clergy) as the protégé of the future Cardinal Carlo Confalonieri. He has served his entire career in the Roman Curia. Elevated to the episcopate in 1989, he was promoted to the archiepiscopal dignity in 1994. Presently, in addition to being the archpriest of the Vatican Basilica and vicar general of His Holiness for Vatican City, he is president of the Pontifical Commissions for the Cultural Goods of the Church and for Sacred Archaeology and president of the Pontifical Commission for the Reverend Fabric of St. Peter's. He was created a cardinal by Pope John Paul II in 2003 and took part in the conclave of 2005.

MARINI, PIERO (born 1942), *archbishop*, master of papal liturgical celebrations. A native of Valverde, in the Diocese of Piacenza-Bobbio, Marini was ordained a priest in 1965. A longtime papal master of ceremonies, he was elevated to the episcopate in 1998. In 2003, he was promoted to the rank of archbishop.

MARTIN, JACQUES (1908–1992), *cardinal*, long-time prefect of the Papal Household. Martin was born in Amiens. After studies at the University of Strasbourg, the Pontifical French Seminary in Rome, and the Pontifical Gregorian University, where he earned a doctorate in theology, he was ordained a priest in 1934. Continuing at the Pontifical Ecclesiastical Academy (formerly the Pontifical Academy of Noble Ecclesiastics) and the Pontifical Lateran University, he earned a doctorate in canon law before entering the service of the Secretariat of State in 1938. That same year, he accompanied the legate *a latere*, the then-Cardinal Eugenio Pacelli, on his mission to Budapest. In 1954, he was the special envoy of the Holy See to the celebration of the silver jubilee of the coronation of the Ethiopian emperor Haile Selaissie. John XXIII appointed him a canon of the Patriarchal Vatican Basilica. In 1964, he accompanied Paul VI on the pilgrimage to the Holy Land and was appointed a bishop by the pope onboard ship on the Sea of Galilee— another one of Paul's gestures. In 1969, Paul appointed him prefect of the Papal Household. He served as prefect under three popes, retiring in 1986 and being elevated to the rank of archbishop. He was created a cardinal by John Paul II in 1988.

MARTÍNEZ SOMALO, EDUARDO (born 1927), *cardinal*, camerlengo of the Holy Roman Church. He studied at the seminary in Logroño, the Pontifical Gregorian University (where he earned licentiate degrees in theology and canon law), the Pontifical Lateran University (where he received his doctorate in canon law), and the Pontifical Ecclesiastical Academy. Ordained a priest in 1950, he joined the diplomatic service of the Holy See upon the completion of his graduate studies, serving in the Secretariat of State. Appointed apostolic nuncio to Colombia in 1970, he was elevated to the rank of archbishop. In 1979, he was recalled to Rome to serve as substitute of the Secretariat of State. Created a cardinal by Pope John Paul II in 1988, he was appointed prefect of the Congregation for Divine Worship and the Discipline of the Sacraments. In 1992, he was transferred as prefect to the Congregation for Institutes of Consecrated Life and Societies of Apostolic Life, the dicastery in charge of religious orders and their members, an office he held until 2004. In 1993, John Paul II appointed him camerlengo of the Holy Roman Church. After the pontiff's death, he oversaw the interregnum and participated in the conclave of 2005.

MARTINI, CARLO MARIA (born 1927), *cardinal*, archbishop emeritus of Milan. A native of Turin, Martini joined the Society of Jesus at the age of seventeen in 1944, pursuing his studies in various institutes of the Jesuit order before obtaining his doctorate in theology from the Pontifical Gregorian University with a dissertation on the historical problem of the Resurrection in recent studies. After post-graduate studies at the Pontifical Biblical Institute, he taught briefly at the Theological Faculty in Chieri before joining the faculty of the Pontifical Biblical Institute. He was appointed rector of the Pontifical Biblical Institute in 1969. In 1978, he was appointed rector of the Pontifical Gregorian University. That same year, Pope Paul VI invited him to give the annual Lenten retreat in the Vatican. Appointed archbishop of Milan in 1979, he was created a cardinal in 1983 by Pope John Paul II. Despite a prodigious pastoral activity, he maintained a prolific publishing schedule, although his emphasis was more pastoral and spiritual, rather than academic, in recent years. He retired in 2002. He took part in the conclave of 2005.

MASELLA, BENEDETTO ALOISI (1879–1970), *cardinal*. Masella was the nephew of Cardinal Gaetano Aloisi Masella (1826–1902), longtime datary and financial administrator of the Holy See under Leo XIII. Educated at the seminary of his native Ferentino, the Pontifical Gregorian University, the Pontifical Roman Athenaeum of Sant'Apollinare, and the Pontifical Academy of Noble Ecclesiastics, he was ordained a priest in 1902. He served as his uncle's secretary until the latter's death, then entered the service of the Secretariat of State. Appointed secretary of the apostolic nunciature in Portugal in 1908, he served as *chargé d'affaires* from 1910–1919, during the upheavals of the Portuguese revolution. Appointed nuncio to Chile in 1919, he was consecrated an archbishop. In 1927, he was transferred as nuncio to Brazil. Created a cardinal by Pius XII in 1946, he became archpriest of the Lateran Archbasilica and prefect of the Sacred Congregation for the Discipline of the

Sacraments in 1954. When Pius XII died with the office of camerlengo vacant, the cardinals present in Rome elected him to fill the office. He participated in the conclaves of 1958 and 1963. He attended the Second Vatican Council. In 1969, he retired from his prefecture.

MARTY, FRANÇOIS (1904–1994), *cardinal*. Marty was baptized with the names Gabriel François, but during his early schooling he switched to being called François to avoid confusion with a classmate also named Gabriel Marty. He was ordained a priest in 1930, after studies at the seminary of his native diocese of Rodez and the Catholic Institute of Toulouse, and carried out pastoral work in the diocese. In 1951, he was appointed vicar general of the Diocese of Rodez. The following year, he was appointed bishop of Saint-Flour. In 1959, he was promoted to be coadjutor archbishop of Reims, succeeding to the see the following year. He attended the Second Vatican Council and the subsequent Synods of Bishops. From 1965 to 1968 (and briefly again in 1975), he was also "prelate *nullius*" of the Mission de France, the jurisdiction set up to give a canonical status to the "worker priests." He was transferred to be archbishop of Paris in 1968, was created a cardinal by Paul VI in 1969, and participated in the two conclaves of 1978. He resigned the pastoral governance of his archdiocese in 1981 and died in a car and train accident in 1994.

MATHIEU, FRANÇOIS-DÉSIRÉ (1839–1908), *cardinal*. After studies at the seminary of his native diocese of Nancy, he was ordained a priest in 1863 and held a succession of pastoral and academic offices. He earned a doctorate in letters from the University of Nancy in 1878. Appointed bishop of Angers in 1893, he was promoted to the archbishopric of Toulouse in 1896. Created a cardinal in 1899 by Leo XIII, he was brought to Rome and entrusted with various curial posts. Because of his position in the curia, he was the *de facto* leader of the French-speaking bloc at the conclave of 1903. In 1907, he was elected a member of the Académie Française.

MERCIER, DÉSIRÉ-FÉLICIEN-FRANÇOIS-JOSEPH (1851–1926), *cardinal*, one of the great figures in the neo-scholastic revival of the late nineteenth and early twentieth centuries. After studies at the seminary of Mechlin and the University of Louvain, he was ordained a priest in 1874. He also pursued advanced studies in psychology in Paris at the Charcot Clinic. For many years a professor at the University of Louvain and editor of the influential *Revue Néoscholastique*, he became archbishop of Mechlin (Malines) in 1906, and a cardinal the following year. After World War I, he organized the famous "Malines Conversations" with leaders of the Anglican Communion with a view toward a reunion of the Churches. He participated in the conclaves of 1914 and 1922.

MERRY DEL VAL Y ZULUETA, RAFAEL (1865–1930), *cardinal*, secretary of state of Pope St. Pius X (1903–1914) and one of the most fascinating figures in modern ecclesiastical history. Born in London, the son of the Spanish ambassador to the Court of St. James, Merry del Val's career was meteoric, even for a young man with his connections. Before he was even a priest, he was named secretary of the special pontifical mission sent to the celebrations of Queen Victoria's fiftieth anniversary, with the title of "monsignor" although he was only twenty-two years old. Ordained a priest in 1888, at the age of twenty-three, without having attended a seminary—Leo XIII placed him directly in the postgraduate Pontifical Academy of Noble Ecclesiastics—he became a privy chamberlain at age twenty-six, secretary of the Pontifical Commission to Study the Validity of Anglican Orders at twenty-nine, apostolic delegate to Canada at thirty, and president of the Pontifical Academy of Noble Ecclesiastics and archbishop in 1900, when he was thirty-four years-old. After the conclave of 1903, he became secretary of state at thirty-seven, adding, a few months at later at barely thirty-eight, to that high office the dignity of the cardinalate and the prefecture of the Apostolic Palace. Following his retirement from the Secretariat of State after the election of Benedict XV in 1914, he became archpriest of the Vatican Basilica and secretary of the Supreme Sacred Congregation of the Holy Office. In addition to his high ecclesiastical offices, he was the chaplain (and, it was later found out, chief financial benefactor) of a refuge for poor juveniles in the slums of the Trastevere section of Rome. He was also a noted composer of music, both choral and instrumental, as well as an avid sportsman. Even his ecclesiastical critics—and there were many—admitted that while he was frustratingly zealous in his political intrigues, especially during the reign of Pius X, he was also a personal ascetic who regularly recited a "litany of humility" of his own composition, wore a penitential cilice, and was given to self-flagellation. He died on February 26, 1930, not yet sixty-five years of age. In 1953, the process for his beatification was opened. His body rests in a magnificent tomb in the crypt of St. Peter's Basilica, next to that of Pope Pius XI, where, in accord with his wishes, the only inscription aside from his name is his motto: *"Da mihi animas, coetera tolle"* ("Give me souls, take the rest").

MERTEL, TEODOLFO (1806–1899), *cardinal,* last member of the College of Cardinals who was not a priest. A brilliant legal mind, Mertel obtained doctorates in canon and civil law at the age of twenty-two. He held a number of judicial appointments and was active in the *pro bono* defense of the poor. In 1847, he was appointed an auditor (judge) of the Sacred Roman Rota by Pope Pius IX (1846–1878), the last layman to ever be appointed to that tribunal. He served as secretary of the commission charged with preparing a constitution for the Papal States and was subsequently appointed, in 1850, a minister without portfolio in the civil government of the papal dominions. In 1853, he was appointed minister of the interior and of grace and justice. Created a cardinal by Pius IX on March 15, 1858, he was appointed president of the Supreme Council for Internal Affairs of State. He was ordained a deacon the following day and, on March 18, took possession of his diaconal title, Sant'Eustachio, near the Pantheon. In 1860, he was appointed prefect of economics for the Sacred Congregation for the Propagation of the Faith. In 1863, he was appointed president of the Supreme Council of State for the Papal States. He participated in the First Vatican Council. After the loss of the Papal States, he was appointed prefect of the Tribunal of the Signatura of Justice in 1877. The following year, he took part in the conclave that elected Leo XIII, who, in 1884, appointed him vice-chancellor of the Holy Roman Church, a post he held until his death.

MINDSZENTY, JÓZSEF (1892–1975), *cardinal.* Mindszenty was ordained in 1915, after studies at the seminary in his native diocese of Szombathely. He was arrested by Communists during the abortive revolt of Bela Kun in 1919, narrowly missing summary execution. After a long career in pastoral work, he was appointed bishop of Veszprém in 1944. However, his episcopal ministry was cut short by his arrest by the Nazis, who imprisoned him until 1945. Shortly after his release, he was promoted to the primatial see of Esztergom as archbishop and prince-primate. He was created a cardinal by Pius XII in 1946. Arrested and tortured by the newly installed Communist regime, he was condemned to life imprisonment after a show trial in 1949. During the 1956 anti-Soviet uprising, he was sprung from his prison and took refuge in the United States legation, where he remained until 1971, when he was allowed to leave Hungary. Although he resigned neither his see nor his primatial title, Pope Paul VI, considering the pastoral problems of the archdiocese, declared the see vacant and appointed an apostolic administrator in 1974, a move Mindszenty bitterly resented and lamented in his *Memoirs* (New York: Macmillan, 1974). When he died in 1975, his body was temporarily buried in the Hungarian chapel of the Marian shrine of Mariazell in Austria. The body was found to be incorrupt when the tomb was opened in 1991 to transfer the remains back to a now-liberated Hungary. The process for his beatification was started in 1996.

MOONEY, EDWARD ALOYSIUS (1882–1958), *cardinal,* archbishop of Detroit. A native of Mount Savage, Maryland, Mooney was ordained a priest in 1909. He served on the faculty of St. Mary's Seminary in Cleveland and principal of that city's Cathedral Latin School. Appointed spiritual director of the Pontifical North American College in Rome in 1923, he attracted the attention of the Roman Curia and was appointed apostolic delegate in the East Indies in 1926, and elevated at the same time to a titular archbishopric. In 1931, he was appointed apostolic delegate to Japan. Transferred to the Diocese of Rochester, New York, in 1933, he was promoted to the archbishopric of Detroit five years later. He was created a cardinal by Pius XII in 1946, in part out of recognition for his having founded and directed the War Relief Service that supplied thousands of tons of humanitarian supplies during and after the Second World War. He died an hour before the opening of the conclave of 1958.

MURRAY, JOHN COURTNEY (1904–1967), American Jesuit priest and theologian. Murray was editor, from 1942 until his death in 1967, of *Theological Studies.* Suspicions about his pioneering work on religious pluralism led him to be silenced between 1955 and 1962. As an official consultant at the Second Vatican Council, however, he helped reconcile secular doctrines of separation of Church and state and freedom of conscience with the theological tradition of the Catholic Church, his influence being particularly noticeable in the articulation of the council's landmark declaration on religious liberty, *Dignitatis humanae.*

NAGY, STANISLAW KAZIMIERZ (born 1921), *cardinal.* Born in near Wadowice in the Archdiocese of Cracow, Poland, Nagy joined the Congregation of the Priests of the Sacred Heart of Jesus (the Dehonians) and was ordained a priest in 1945. For many years he taught fundamental theology at the Catholic University of Lublin, where the young Father Karol Wojtyla taught moral theology. At the invitation of his former colleague, then the pope, he attended the 1985 and 1991 Synods of Bishops. Created a cardinal in 2003 by Pope John Paul II, he was ordained to the episcopate a week before the consistory.

NEVES, LUCAS MOREIRA (1925–2002), *cardinal*, prefect of the Congregation of Bishops and, until his death, a leading *papabile*. Born in São João del Rey, Brazil, he joined the Order of Preachers (the Dominicans) after studies in the minor seminary of Mariana. After studies at Dominican institutes in São Paulo, Brazil, and Toulon, France, he was ordained a priest in 1950. Following an intensive period of pastoral ministry to students, intellectuals, and artists, he was appointed auxiliary bishop of São Paulo in 1967. From 1971 to 1974, he served as president of the Brazilian National Caritas relief agency. Called to Rome in 1974, he was appointed vice-president of the Pontifical Council for the Laity. In 1979, he was promoted to the archiepiscopal rank and appointed secretary of the Congregation for Bishops. In 1987, he returned home as archbishop of São Salvador da Bahia and primate of Brazil. He was created a cardinal in 1988 by Pope John Paul II. In 1998, he was called back to Rome to serve as prefect of the Congregation for Bishops and president of the Pontifical Commission for Latin America. Many thought he was eminently *papabile*, but he became stricken with cancer, which complicated his diabetes. He resigned his offices in 2000.

NGUYÊN VAN THUÂN, FRANÇOIS-XAVIER (1928–2002), *cardinal*, president of the Pontifical Council for Justice and Peace and, until his death, a leading *papabile*. Born in the Vietnamese imperial capital of Huê, Nguyên van Thuân was the scion of one of country's most prominent families; his uncles included the nationalist Ngo dinh Diem, first president of the Republic of Vietnam, and Pierre-Martin Ngo dinh Thuc, archbishop of Huê. He was ordained a priest in 1953, after studies at the seminary of Huê. After a brief stint in pastoral ministry, he was sent to Rome for advanced studies, eventually earning a doctorate in canon law from the Pontifical Urbanian Athenaeum *de Propaganda Fide*. Returning to Huê, he served successively as professor and rector of the seminary and vicar general of the archdiocese. In 1967, he was appointed bishop of Nha Trang. In 1975, shortly before the Communist takeover of South Vietnam, he was appointed titular archbishop of Vadesi and coadjutor archbishop with the right of succession to the metropolitan see of Saigon (presently renamed Ho Chi Minh City). He was imprisoned by the Communist regime without trial, and his fate was unknown until he was released in 1988. It was later learned that he spent over nine years in an underground isolation cell. Impeded from returning to his see, he lived under house arrest in north Vietnam until late 1991 when he was expelled from the country as *persona non grata*. He resigned his see in 1994 when Pope John Paul II appointed him vice-president of the Pontifical Council for Justice and Peace. In 1998, he became its president. The pope invited him to preach the Lenten retreat in the Vatican for the Jubilee Year 2000. Created a cardinal by John Paul II in 2001, he was considered a leading candidate for the papal office on account of his unique story as well as his extensive travels after he was exiled and his linguistic abilities (he spoke nearly a dozen languages fluently), but he died after a brief battle with cancer in 2002.[2]

O'BRIEN, KEITH MICHAEL PATRICK (born 1938), *cardinal*, archbishop of St. Andrews and Edinburgh. Born in Ballycastle, in the Irish diocese of Down and Connor, O'Brien was a child when his parents emigrated to Scotland. After earning a degree in science from the University of Edinburgh in 1959, he entered the diocesan seminary there and was ordained a priest in 1965. He served in a succession of parochial assignments until 1978, when he was appointed spiritual director of St. Andrew's College, Drygrange. In 1980, he was appointed rector of St. Mary's College, Blairs. Pope John Paul II appointed him archbishop of Saint Andrews and Edinburgh in 1985 and created him a cardinal in 2003. O'Brien caused a stir when, the day after his appointment to the College of Cardinals, he spoke favorably of a more open attitude toward married priests, homosexual priests, and contraception. He was forced to retract his statements a week later. He took part in the conclave of 2005.

O'CONNELL, WILLIAM HENRY (1859–1944), *cardinal*, archbishop of Boston. Ordained a priest in 1884 after studies at Boston College and the Pontifical Urbanian Athenaeum *de Propaganda Fide*, he served in his native archdiocese of Boston for a decade before becoming rector of the Pontifical North American College in Rome in 1895. Appointed bishop of Portland, Maine, in 1901, he served as a special papal envoy to Japan in 1905. He was promoted to be coadjutor of Boston in 1906 and succeeded to that see the following year. Created a cardinal in 1911, he arrived late for the conclaves of 1914 and 1922 but lived long enough to participate in the conclave of 1939.

OREGLIA DI SANTO STEFANO, LUIGI (1828–1913), *cardinal*, dean of the Sacred College of Cardinals and camerlengo of the Holy Roman Church at the turn of the twentieth century. Oreglia di Santo Stefano was born to a noble family that had befriended and assisted St. John Bosco, who visited the house frequently. After finishing his training as a diplomat at the Pontifical Academy for Ecclesiastical Nobles, he served as a referendary (judge consultor) of the Supreme Tribunal of the Apostolic Signatura for several years before being named internuncio to the Netherlands in 1863. Consecrated archbishop in 1866, he served successively as apostolic nuncio in Belgium and Portugal before being created a cardinal by Pius IX (1846–1878) in 1873. Thereafter, he served in a variety of curial offices, becoming camerlengo of the Holy Roman Church and archchancellor of the Roman University in 1885; he held both offices until his death. Sub-dean of the Sacred College from 1889, he became its dean in 1896.

---

[2]His principal spiritual work is *The Road of Hope: Thoughts of Light from a Prison Cell*, edited and translated with introduction by the present author (London: New City Press, 1997). His memoirs, *Five Loaves and Two Fish*, likewise edited with introduction by the present author (Washington, D.C.: Morley Books, 2001), had the unique distinction of carrying a dust-jacket endorsement from no less a figure than Pope John Paul II.

OTTAVIANI, ALFREDO (1890–1979), *cardinal*, longtime stalwart of the pre–Vatican II orthodoxy. One of thirteen children of a humble baker from the tenements of the Trastevere neighborhood in Rome, Ottaviani was ordained a priest in 1916 after studies at the Pontifical Roman Seminary. After ordination, he served as a faculty member of the Pontifical Urbanian Athenaeum *de Propaganda Fide* and the Pontifical Roman Athenaeum of Sant'Apollinare as well as doing pastoral work. Even as he rose to the highest ranks of the Roman Church, he was to maintain a lifelong commitment to his apostolate among the rough youths of his native quarter. After a brief stint as rector of the Pontifical Bohemian College in Rome, he was appointed secretary of the Holy See's "foreign office," the Sacred Congregation for Extraordinary Ecclesiastical Affairs, in 1928. The following year, he was appointed substitute of the Secretariat of State. In 1935, he was appointed assessor of the Supreme Sacred Congregation of the Holy Office. In this role, he was instrumental in enacting the automatic excommunication against Catholics who belonged to the Communist Party. He was also dreaded for the investigations he launched against theologians whose orthodoxy he suspected, including the future cardinals Henri de Lubac and Yves-Marie Congar. Pius XII created him a cardinal in 1953, promoting him to the office of pro-secretary of the Holy Office. He became the secretary of the same Supreme Sacred Congregation of the Holy Office in 1959. He was consecrated to the episcopate by John XXIII in 1962 and attended the Second Vatican Council. After the Ecumenical Council, his dicastery was rebaptized the Sacred Congregation for the Doctrine of the Faith in 1966, and he was appointed its pro-prefect. He retired in 1968 and received the title of prefect emeritus of the Sacred Congregation for the Doctrine of the Faith. He lost the right to vote in 1971 as he was older than eighty years of age, having previously participated in the conclaves of 1958 and 1963. He was buried in the chapel of San Salvatore *in ossibus* in the Vatican, a church attached to his old bureau in the Palace of the Holy Office. The motto Ottaviani adopted for his coat of arms, *"Semper Idem"* ("Always the same"), announced his theological vision.

PAPPALARDO, SALVATORE (born 1918), *cardinal*. A native of Villafranca Sicula (near Agrigento in Sicily), Pappalardo was ordained a priest in 1941, after studies at the Pontifical Roman Seminary and the Pontifical Gregorian University. Passing to the Pontifical Ecclesiastical Academy, he finished his studies at the Pontifical Lateran Athenaeum. Entering the diplomatic service of the Holy See in 1947, he served in the Secretariat of State and also taught at the Pontifical Ecclesiastical Academy and the Pontifical Lateran University from 1959 to 1965. He was appointed apostolic pro-nuncio to Indonesia in 1965, and elevated to the rank of archbishop. In 1969, he was recalled to Rome as president of the Pontifical Ecclesiastical Academy. The following year, he was appointed archbishop of Palermo. He was created a cardinal by Paul VI in 1973 and participated in the two conclaves of 1978. Pappalardo was noted for being a nonconformist, both as a priest and as a Sicilian. With regard to the latter, his anti-Mafia campaigns from the pulpit stood out during an era when *omertà* was still the rule. He resigned the pastoral governance of his see in 1996.

PERRAUD, ADOLPHE-LOUISE-ALBERT (1828–1906), *cardinal*. Born in Lyons, he studied at the Ecole Normale there and was a professor of history at the Lyceum of Angers, joining the Congregation of the Oratory of Paris in 1852. Ordained a priest two years later, he taught at the seminary of Coutances and the Sorbonne. He was appointed bishop of Autun in 1874. He also served as superior general of the Oratory from 1884 to 1901. A noted scholar, he was elected a member of the Académie Française in 1882. He was created a cardinal in 1895 and participated in the conclave of 1903.

PETRUCCI, ALFONSO (1490–1517), *cardinal*, executed for his part in a plot against the life of Pope Leo X. Son of Pandolfo Petrucci, lord of Siena, he was installed as bishop of Sovana in 1498. Through his father's intervention, he was created cardinal by Julius II in 1511. Angered that Leo X had deposed his brother Borghese Petrucci as lord of Siena with a view to subjecting the town to the rule of the pope's Medici relatives in Florence, Petrucci conspired with the papal physician, Battista Vercelli, to poison the pontiff. The plot was discovered because of the clumsiness of Petrucci's secretary, Marcantonio Nino, who was detained and tortured. Petrucci was arrested, deposed from his cardinalate on June 22, 1517, and strangled in the dungeon of Castel Sant'Angelo on July 6.

PIFFL, FRIEDRICH GUSTAV (1864–1932), *cardinal*. Born in Bohemia, he joined the Canons Regular of the Austrian Lateran Congregation in 1883 and was ordained a priest in 1888. After twenty-five years of pastoral work, he was picked by the Emperor Franz Josef as the prince-archbishop of Vienna in 1913. The following year, Pius X elevated him to the Sacred College. As the pope died after publishing Piffl's name but before giving him his red hat, Piffl has the unusual distinction of being named by one pope (Pius X) and receiving his hat from another (Benedict XV). He participated in the conclaves of 1914 and 1922.

PIZZARDO, GIUSEPPE (1877–1970), *cardinal*. Pizzardo was ordained a priest in 1903 after studies at the seminary in his native Savona and at the Pontifical Gregorian University in Rome. After continuing studies at the Pontifical Athenaeum of Sant'Apollinare and the Pontifical Academy of Noble Ecclesiastics, he entered the service of the Secretariat of State, serving at the nunciature in Bavaria and in the Sacred Congregation for Extraordinary Ecclesiastical Affairs (i.e., the "foreign ministry" of the Vatican), rising to be the substitute and later the secretary of the congregation. Ordained an archbishop in 1930, he was appointed president of the Pontifical Commission for Russia in 1934. In 1937, he was the special envoy to the coronation of King George VI in London. Created a cardinal by Pope Pius XI in 1937, he was named prefect of the Sacred Congregation for Seminaries and Universities in 1939. From 1951 to 1959, he served as secretary of the Supreme Sacred Congregation of the Holy Office. He participated in the conclaves of 1939, 1958, and 1963. He became sub-dean of the Sacred College in 1965.

POGGI, LUIGI (born 1917), *cardinal*, proto-deacon of the Holy Roman Church. A native of Piacenza, he studied at the Alberoni College in that city and was ordained a priest in 1940. After a brief stint in pastoral work, he was sent to further studies in Rome, where he earned a doctorate in canon and civil law from the Pontifical Athenaeum of

Sant'Apollinare and completed his studies at the Pontifical Ecclesiastical Academy. Entering the diplomatic service of the Holy See, he held various offices in the Secretariat of State and, in 1963–1964, successfully negotiated the *modus vivendi* between the Church and the Tunisian government. Appointed apostolic delegate to Central Africa (Cameroon, Chad, Congo-Brazzaville, Gabon, and the Central African Republic) in 1965, he was elevated to the archbishopric. In the subsequent years, with the independence of the countries, he became apostolic pro-nuncio. In 1969, he was transferred as apostolic nuncio to Peru. In 1973, he was named nuncio with the special charge to improve relations with Poland, Hungary, Czechoslovakia, Rumania, and Bulgaria. He was appointed nuncio to Italy in 1986. In 1992, he was appointed pro-librarian and pro-archivist of the Holy Roman Church. Created a cardinal by Pope John Paul II in 1994, he became librarian and archivist of the Holy Roman Church. He lost the right to participate in the conclave with his eightieth birthday in 1997 and retired the following year. In 2002, he became the senior cardinal of the order of deacons.

POLETTO, SEVERINO (born 1933), *cardinal*, archbishop of Turin. The youngest of eleven children, Poletto was born in Salgareda, near Treviso, and studied at the seminaries of Treviso and Casale Monferrato before earning a licentiate in moral theology from the Accademia Alfonsiana of the Pontifical Lateran University in Rome. Ordained a priest in 1957, he served in a succession of pastoral ministries before being appointed coadjutor bishop of Fossano in 1980. He succeeded to the see shortly thereafter. In 1989, he was transferred to the bishopric of Asti. Promoted to the archbishopric of Turin in 1999, he was created a cardinal by Pope John Paul II in 2001. Poletto took part in the conclave of 2005.

POMPILJ, BASILIO (1858–1931), *cardinal*. A native of Spoleto in southern Italy, he was ordained a priest in 1888. After a brief pastoral service, he held various curial offices before being named a cardinal in 1911. In 1913, he was appointed vicar general of the pope for Rome and archpriest of the Lateran Archbasilica and consecrated a bishop. He participated in the conclaves of 1914 and 1922.

VON PREYSING LICHTENEGG-MOOS, KONRAD (1880–1950), *cardinal*. Born in his family's castle, Kronwinkel, near Munich and ordained a priest in 1912 after studies in at Munich, Würzburg, and Innsbruck, Preysing served as secretary to the cardinal archbishop of Munich and Freising and did pastoral work before his appointment in 1932 as Bishop of Eichstätt. Transferred to Berlin in 1935, he was a strong opponent of the Nazi regime. After the war, he lived the pathos of being the bishop of a divided city under occupation, spending all his resources to relieve suffering. When he was created a cardinal by Pius XII in 1946, the apostolic nuncio in Paris, Angelo Roncalli, had to lend him money for the trip to Rome. Despite the difficulties of his mission, he was not without his wry humor. At the 1946 consistory, one of the other new cardinals tried to make small talk by remarking to Preysing that when they died, their red hats would be suspended from the ceilings of their respective cathedrals, to which the German, thinking of his bombed-out cathedral, replied, "Your Eminence forgets that I have no roof."

PUZYNA KNIAZ (PRINCE) DE KOSIELSKO, JAN (1842–1911), *cardinal*, best remembered for being the bearer of the Emperor Franz Josef II's veto against the election of Cardinal Mariano Rampolla del Tindaro to the papacy in the conclave of 1903. The scion of Russian-Polish nobility, he arrived at his vocation later than most of his contemporaries. After receiving a doctorate in law and working for a number of years in the Austrian imperial administration, he entered the seminary at Przemysl. Ordained at the age of thirty-six, he became auxiliary bishop of Leopolis (present-day Lviv) of the Latins only seven years later, in 1886. Promoted to prince-bishop of Cracow in 1895, he was created a cardinal in 1901. For his service to the empire during the conclave of 1903, the Emperor Franz Josef II awarded him the Grand Cross of the Austrian Order of St. Stephen the following year.

RAHNER, KARL (1904–1984), Jesuit theologian who was one of the most influential figures in Catholic intellectual life in the twentieth century. Born in Freiburg-im-Breisgau, Rahner joined the Society of Jesus in 1922. After studies in Jesuit institutions in Austria, Germany, and the Netherlands, he was ordained a priest in 1932. After four semesters of graduate philosophy studies under Martin Heidegger at Freiburg, he completed his doctorate and *Habilitation* degrees in theology from the theological faculty at Innsbruck. He taught at Innsbruck until the Jesuits were expelled by the Nazis in 1939. Rahner spent the war years in pastoral work, returning to teaching afterward at Pullach (1945–1948) and Innsbruck (1948–1964). A *peritus,* or official theological expert, at the Second Vatican Council, he played an influential role in formulating several of the conciliar documents. In 1964, he succeeded Romano Guardini in the chair of Christianity and the Philosophy of Religion at the University of Munich. In 1967, he became professor of dogmatic theology at the University of Münster, a position he held until his retirement in 1981. He served from 1967 until 1974 on the International Theological Commission. His influence on post–Vatican II Catholic theology, chiefly through the diffusion of his thought by his former students and readers who became influential in their own countries, cannot be underestimated. Toward the end of his life, however, he found that his theological vision, especially the notion of the "anonymous Christian," had fallen out of favor in many official circles and in his last works he complained of a "winter" that choked the "spring" of the Council.

RAMPOLLA DEL TINDARO, MARIANO (1843–1913), *cardinal*, secretary of state of Pope Leo XIII (1878–1903). Born to a noble family in Polizzi, near Cefalù, in Sicily, Rampolla studied at Capranica College and the Gregorian University in Rome, where he earned doctorates in canon and civil law. Ordained a priest in 1866, he finished his studies at the Pontifical Academy of Noble Ecclesiastics. He was a career Vatican diplomat with a wide experience of the Eastern Churches and the missions as well as a stint at the apostolic nunciature in Spain before becoming, in 1882, apostolic nuncio to Spain and elevated to the archbishopric. In 1887, Leo XIII recalled him to Rome, where he was created a cardinal and appointed secretary of state. Quickly becoming the pope's principal collaborator, he accumulated the additional responsibilities of the presidency of the Council for the Administration of the Wealth of the Apostolic See (1887), the office of camerlengo (treasurer) of the College of Cardinals (1893), that of archpriest of the Vatican Basilica and president of the Reverend Fabric of St. Peter's (1894), that of the grand prior of the Sovereign Military Order of Malta (1896), and the presidency of the Pontifical Biblical Commission (1902). Both admirers and detractors gave him considerable credit for the relatively progressive policies of Leo's pontificate, although more politically conservative Catholics questioned his "francophile" tendencies. After the election of Pius X, he was relieved of many of his offices, becoming successively secretary of the Supreme Sacred Congregation of the Holy Office (1908), president of the Roman Academy of St. Thomas Aquinas (1910), and librarian of the Holy Roman Church (1912), before dying on December 16, 1913. When he died, it was said that his papers were removed even before his body was, the allegation being that it was feared that his bitter opposition to the conservative policies of Pius X and his secretary of state, Cardinal Rafael Merry del Val, would be revealed. As a result, his last will and testament was never found.

RE, GIOVANNI BATTISTA (born 1934), *cardinal*, prefect of the Congregation for Bishops. Born in Brescia, he studied at the diocesan seminary there before transferring to the Pontifical French Seminary in Rome to continue his schooling. Ordained a priest in 1957, he earned a doctorate in canon law at the Pontifical Gregorian University and, after a brief pastoral stint in Brescia, finished his studies at the Pontifical Ecclesiastical Academy. Joining the diplomatic service of the Holy See in 1963, he served successively at the apostolic nunciatures in Panama and Iran, before returning to Rome to serve as the secretary to the then-*sostituto*, Giovanni Benelli. In 1979, he was appointed assessor of the Secretariat of State. In 1987, he was appointed secretary of the Congregation for Bishops and elevated to the rank of archbishop. In 1989, he returned to the Secretariat of State as *sostituto*. In 2000, he was appointed prefect of the Congregation for Bishops and president of the Pontifical Commission for Latin America. He was created a cardinal by Pope John Paul II in 2001 and took part in the conclave of 2005.

RICHELMY, AGOSTINO (1850–1923), *cardinal*. Born in Turin, he earned a doctorate in theology from the seminary there before being ordained a priest in 1873. After a career as a seminary professor, he was appointed bishop of Ivrea in 1886 and was promoted to be archbishop of Turin in 1897, serving there until his death. He was created a cardinal by Leo XIII in 1899 and participated in the conclaves of 1903, 1914, and 1922.

RIZZATO, OSCAR (born 1929), *archbishop*, almoner of His Holiness. A native of San Giorgio delle Pertiche, near Padua, he was ordained a priest in 1954. After completing studies at the Pontifical Ecclesiastical Academy, he entered the diplomatic service of the Holy See and held various offices in the Secretariat of State. Appointed to head the office of the Apostolic Almoner at the end of 1989, he was ordained an archbishop the following January.

RUGAMBWA, LAUREAN (1912–1997), *cardinal*, first African appointed to the Sacred College. Born in Bukongo near Bukoba in the then-German East Africa, Rugambwa was
baptized by missionaries at the age of nine. After studies at the Regional Major Seminary of Katigondo, Uganda, he was ordained a priest in 1943. From 1944 to 1949, he
served as a missionary in West Africa, then pursued advanced studies at the Pontifical
Urban Athenaeum in Rome from 1949 to 1951. In 1951, he was consecrated a titular
bishop and appointed apostolic vicar of Lower Rugera. Two years later, he was transferred to the residential diocese of Rutabo, Taganyika. Created a cardinal by Pope John
XXIII in 1960, he was transferred to his home diocese of Bukoba that same year. In 1968,
he was promoted to the new metropolitan see of Dar-es-Salaam as its archbishop.
Rugambwa participated in the Second Vatican Council and in the conclave of 1963 and
the two conclaves of 1978. He resigned the pastoral governance of his archdiocese in 1992.

RUINI, CAMILLO (born 1931), *cardinal*, vicar general of His Holiness for the Diocese of
Rome. From Sassuolo, near Reggio Emilia, Ruini was educated in the seminary of Reggio
Emilia and the Pontifical Gregorian University in Rome, where he earned a doctorate in
theology. Ordained a priest in 1954, he served on the faculty of the seminary in Reggio
Emilia from 1957 until 1968, when it merged to become the Inter-Diocesan Theological
Seminary of Modena-Reggio Emilia, which he served as the director of from 1968 until
1977. From 1977 until 1983, he taught at the Theological Faculty in Bologna. In 1983, he
was appointed auxiliary bishop of Reggio Emilia. In 1986, he became secretary general
of the Italian Episcopal Conference. Promoted to archbishop in 1991, he was appointed
pro-vicar general of the Diocese of Rome and president of the Italian Episcopal Conference. Created a cardinal by John Paul II in 1991, he was appointed Vicar General of His
Holiness for the Diocese of Rome and archpriest of the Lateran Archbasilica. He took
part in the conclave of 2005.

VAN ROSSUM, WILLEM MARINUS (1854–1932), *cardinal.* Joining the Congregation of the
Most Holy Redeemer in 1873, he was ordained a priest in 1879 and held various offices
in his order. Created cardinal in 1911, he was only the second member of his Redemptorist
religious congregation to receive the red hat, the other being the nineteenth-century
archbishop of Mechlin (Malines), Victor Dechamps (1810–1883). He served as president
of the Pontifical Biblical Commission and major penitentiary of the Holy Roman Church,
before becoming prefect of the Congregation *de Propaganda Fide* and being consecrated
bishop in 1918. Known for his rigor and severity, even as a cardinal, he dressed in the
simple black habit of his order, allowing only a narrow strip of red at the collar to indicate his rank.

SALIÈGE, JULES-GÉRAUD (1870–1956), *cardinal.* Saliège was ordained a priest in 1870. Except for a period as a military chaplain during World War I, his entire priestly career was
spent in the minor seminary of Pleaux and the seminary of Saint-Flour. Appointed bishop
of Gap in 1925, he was promoted to the archbishopric of Toulouse in 1928. He was
created a cardinal by Pius XII in 1946.

SANDRI, LEONARDO (born 1943), *archbishop*, substitute of the Secretariat of State. Born in Buenos Aires of Italian émigré parents, Sandri was ordained a priest in 1967. After advanced studies at the Pontifical Ecclesiastical Academy in Rome, he entered the diplomatic service of the Holy See and held various offices in the Secretariat of State as well as the Papal Household. In 1997, he was appointed apostolic nuncio to Venezuela and ordained an archbishop. He served briefly as apostolic nuncio to Mexico in 2000, before being recalled to Rome and appointed substitute (*sostituto*) of the Secretariat of State.

SAPIEHA, ADAM STEFAN STANISLAW BONIFATIUSZ JÓZEF (1867–1951), *cardinal*, archbishop of Cracow and mentor to the future Pope John Paul II, Sapieha was born to a princely Polish-Lithuanian family. Ordained in Rome in 1893 after studies at the Pontifical Gregorian University, he did pastoral work in the Diocese of Lemberg (now Lviv, Ukraine) and taught in its seminary. Appointed prince-bishop of Cracow in 1911 as the successor of the unfortunate veto-bearing Cardinal Jan Puzyna de Kosielsko, he was consecrated bishop by Pope Pius X. He became archbishop when Cracow was raised to a metropolitan see in 1925. During the Nazi occupation of Poland, he remained in his see. Numerous stories are told of his courage under literal siege—the cathedral and episcopal residence of Cracow share Wawel Castle with the royal residence where the German governor-general Hans Frank, later hanged for war crimes, installed himself. Although he tried to avoid receiving the occupiers, he was finally compelled to entertain the Nazi governor-general, to whom he served, with the exquisite china inherited from his noble forebears, black bread and *ersatz* coffee, explaining that such was the diet of Poles under occupation. He was created a cardinal by Pius XII in 1946.

SCHEFFCZYK, LEO (born 1920), *cardinal*. Scheffczyk studied at the University of Breslau, the Philosophical-Theological Faculty of Freising, and the University of Munich, earning a doctorate in theology as well as the German postdoctoral degree of the *Habilitation*. He was ordained a priest in 1947. After a brief stint in pastoral work, he taught in the Philosophical-Theological Faculty of Königstein. He was subsequently a professor of dogmatic theology at the University of Tübingen and the University of Munich. He was appointed a member of the Bayerische Akademie der Wissenschaften as well as the Pontifical International Marian Academy and the Pontifical Roman Theological Academy. He was created a cardinal by Pope John Paul II in 2001.

VON SCHÖNBORN, CHRISTOPH MARIA MICHAEL HUGO DAMIAN PETER ADALBERT (born 1945), *cardinal*, archbishop of Vienna. Born Graf (Count) von Schönborn at the family estate of Skalsko in what is now the Czech Republic, he entered the Order of Preachers (the Domicans) in 1963. After studies in Dominican institutions in Germany and France, he earned a doctorate in theology and pursued post-graduate studies at the University of Paris-Sorbonne and the Institut Catholique in Paris. He was ordained a priest in 1970. After a brief period as a university chaplain in Graz, Austria, he was appointed professor of theology at the University of Fribourg, Switzerland. From 1987 to 1992, he served as the secretary of the commission of the Congregation for the Doctrine of the Faith charged with editing the *Catechism of the Catholic Church*. In 1991, he was appointed auxiliary bishop of Vienna, becoming coadjutor archbishop in 1995. He succeeded to the see in 1996. He was elected president of the Austrian Episcopal Conference in 1998 and was created a cardinal by Pope John Paul II that same year. He took part in the conclave of 2005.

SCHRÖFFER, JOSEPH (1903–1983), cardinal. A native of Ingolstadt, Germany, he was educated at the seminary of Eichstätt and the Pontifical Gregorian University in Rome. Ordained a priest in 1928, he did pastoral work in Eichstätt and taught at the Superior School of Philosophy and Theology (now the University of Eichstätt) until he was appointed vicar general of the diocese in 1941. In 1948, he was appointed bishop of Eichstätt. He attended the four sessions of the Second Vatican Council. In 1967, he was called to Rome, raised to the archiepiscopal rank, and appointed secretary of the Sacred Congregation of Seminaries and Universities (later the Congregation for Catholic Education). He was created a cardinal by Pope Paul VI in 1976 and participated in the two conclaves of 1978.

SCOLA, ANGELO (born 1941), cardinal, patriarch of Venice. A native of Malgrate, near Milan, Scola earned a doctorate in philosophy from the Catholic University of the Sacred Heart in Milan before entering, successively, the seminaries of Saronno and Venegono. He was ordained a priest in 1970 for the Diocese of Teramo. He subsequently earned a doctorate in theology from the University of Fribourg and pursued advanced studies at Munich and Paris. He held a succession of academic posts at the University of Fribourg, the John Paul II Institute for Studies of Marriage and the Family in Rome, and the Pontifical Lateran University in Rome, as well as the editorship of the Italian edition of the international theological review Communio. Appointed bishop of Grosseto in 1991, he resigned the see when he was appointed rector of the Lateran University in 1995. Promoted to the patriarchate of Venice in 2002, he was created a cardinal by Pope John Paul II in 2003. He took part in the conclave of 2005.

SEPE, CRESCENZIO (born 1943), cardinal, prefect of the Congregation for the Evangelization of Peoples. Born in Carinaro in southern Italy, Sepe studied at the Seminary of Aversa, the Pontifical Regional Seminary of Salerno, and the Pontifical Roman Seminary before being ordained a priest in 1967. He earned a doctorate in theology and a licentiate in canon law from the Pontifical Lateran University and then taught at that institution and the Pontifical Urban University while earning a doctorate in philosophy from the University of Rome "La Sapienza." After advanced studies at the Pontifical Ecclesiastical Academy, he entered the diplomatic service of the Holy See and served as secretary of the nunciature in Brazil from 1972 to 1975, when he returned to work at the Secretariat of State. In 1987, he was appointed assessor for general affairs of the Secretariat of State. In 1992, he was appointed Secretary of the Congregation for the Clergy and consecrated an archbishop by Pope John Paul II. In 1997, he was appointed secretary general of the Committee for the Great Jubilee of the Year 2000. Created a cardinal by John Paul II in 2001, he was appointed prefect of the Congregation for the Evangelization of Peoples. Sepe participated in the conclave of 2005.

SERAFINI, DOMENICO (1852–1918), *cardinal*. A native Roman, he became a Benedictine monk at the abbey of Subiaco in 1874 and was ordained a priest in 1877. Subsequently, he was abbot of his monastery and abbot general of his monastic Cassinese Benedictine Congregation, before being appointed archbishop of Spoleto in 1900. Sent by Pius X as apostolic delegate to Mexico in 1904, he returned to Rome and was appointed assessor of the Supreme Sacred Congregation of the Holy Office in 1911, just as the anti-modernist campaign was coming into full swing. He was named a cardinal in 1914 and participated in the conclave of that year. Later he served as prefect of the Sacred Congregation for Religious and then prefect of the Sacred Congregation for the Propagation of the Faith.

SILVA HENRÍQUEZ, RAÚL (1907–1999), *cardinal*. Silva Henríquez earned a doctorate in civil law from the Catholic University of Santiago de Chile before joining the Salesians of Don Bosco in 1930. After studies at the Salesian philosophical faculty in Santiago and the Pontifical Salesian Athenaeum in Turin, Italy, where he earned doctorates in theology and canon law, he was ordained a priest in 1938. He taught in different Chilean schools and universities from 1938 to 1959, when he was appointed bishop of Valparaíso. Promoted to be archbishop of Santiago in 1961, he was created a cardinal by Pope John XXIII in 1962. Already noted for his human rights work (he had received the Human Rights Prize of the Latin American Jewish Congress in 1971), during the political-military crisis in Chile in the early 1970s he established a Committee of Cooperation for Peace in Chile, followed by a "Vicariate of Solidarity" to defend human rights. He participated in the conclaves of 1978. He received the United Nations Human Rights Prize in 1978 and the Bruno Kreisky Prize the following year. Resigning the pastoral governance of his archdiocese in 1983, he founded the Blas Cañas University.

SINCERO, LUIGI (1870–1936), *cardinal*. Ordained a priest in 1892, Sincero, a canonist and theologian, was successively a seminary professor, auditor (judge) on the Tribunal of the Roman Rota, secretary of the Pontifical Commission for the Authentic Interpretation of the Code of Canon Law, and, contemporaneously, secretary of the College of Cardinals and assessor of the Sacred Consistorial Congregation. Created cardinal deacon in 1923, he became secretary of the Sacred Congregation for the Oriental Churches. He was consecrated bishop in 1929 and promoted to the order of cardinal bishops in 1933. In 1934, he became president of the Pontifical Commission for the Codification of Oriental Canon Law as well as president of the Pontifical Commission for the Authentic Interpretation of the Code of Canon Law.

SIRI, GIUSEPPE (1906–1989), *cardinal*. A native of Genoa, Siri was ordained a priest in 1928, after studies in the local seminary. Following graduate studies at the Pontifical Gregorian University in Rome, he returned to the Ligurian city to teach at its seminary and to collaborate in pastoral activities. Appointed auxiliary bishop of Genoa in 1944, he was promoted to the archbishopric two years later when the saintly Cardinal Pietro Boetto died. Created a cardinal by Pius XII in 1953, he was considered a contender in every subsequent conclave in which he participated (1958, 1963, and the two conclaves of 1978) and was nearly elected in the second conclave of 1978. A bastion of traditional orthodoxy who was noted for his sharp critique of the excesses of the progressive elements, especially in the wake of the Second Vatican Council, he was nonetheless noted for his pastoral zeal and much beloved by the people of the diocese he served his entire life. He lost the right to vote in the conclaves when he turned eighty in 1986 and resigned the pastoral government of his archdiocese the following year.

DE SKRBENSKY Z HRISTE, LEV (1863–1938), *cardinal*, arguably the most mysterious historical figure to belong to the College of Cardinals in the twentieth century. An officer in the Sixth Regiment of the Imperial Dragoons, he abruptly resigned his commission, entered the seminary in Olomouc, went on to earn a doctorate in canon law from Rome's Gregorian University, and was ordained a priest—all before he was twenty-six years old. In 1899, when he was thirty-six, he was named prince-archbishop of Prague by the Emperor Franz Josef. Barely a year later, he was created a cardinal by Leo XIII at the insistence of the Austrian emperor, from whom he received the cardinal's biretta. He thus became the youngest cardinal of the twentieth century, being two months shy of his thirty-eighth birthday. He participated in the conclaves of 1903 and 1914. In 1916, he was transferred to Olomouc as prince-archbishop, but, in the upheavals of the breakup of the Habsburg monarchy, he resigned the pastoral governance of his archdiocese in 1920 and retired to a monastery of the Teutonic order. In February and March 1922, instead of coming to the conclave where he was expected, he disappeared. When he died on Christmas Eve 1938, he was the senior cardinal priest and the last surviving creation of Leo XIII. It has long been speculated that he was the illegitimate son of the Emperor Franz Josef, who had promoted his career, and that, following the collapse of the dual monarchy, certain quarters in the Vatican wanted him to likewise "disappear."

SODANO, ANGELO (born 1927), *cardinal*, secretary of state and dean of the College of Cardinals. Sodano hails from near Asti; his father was a deputy in the Italian parliament. He studied at the seminary in Asti and was ordained a priest in 1950, then worked in pastoral assignments in his native diocese, including teaching at its seminary. Pursuing graduate studies in Rome, he studied at the Pontifical Gregorian University, the Pontifical Lateran University, and the Pontifical Ecclesiastical Academy, the postgraduate institute for training the Vatican's diplomats, earning doctorates in theology and canon law. Entering the diplomatic service of the Holy See, he served at the apostolic nunciatures in Ecuador, Uruguay, and Chile, as well as the Council for Public Affairs of the Church, as the Vatican's "foreign office" was called at the time. In 1977, he was appointed apostolic nuncio to Chile and elevated to the rank of archbishop. In 1988, he was recalled to Rome as secretary of the Council for the Public Affairs of the Church, which, after the curial reorganization the following year, became known as the Section for Relations with States of the Secretariat of State. In 1990, he was appointed pro-secretary of state. Created a cardinal by Pope John Paul II in 1991, he was appointed secretary of state. He was elected vice-dean of the College of Cardinals in 2002. After taking part in the conclave of 2005, Sodano was elected dean of the College of Cardinals in succession to new Pope Benedict XVI.

SPELLMAN, FRANCIS JOSEPH (1889–1967), *cardinal*, archbishop of New York and, in his heyday, the most powerful churchman in the Catholic Church in the United States. Son of a druggist from Whitman, Massachusetts, Spellman studied at Fordham College and the North American College in Rome before being ordained in 1916. After several years of pastoral work in Boston, he managed to get himself appointed as the first American attaché in the Secretariat of State in 1925. There he caught the attention of then-Cardinal Pacelli, whose protégé and friend he became. Appointed titular bishop of Sila and auxiliary to the archbishop of Boston, he was consecrated a bishop by Pacelli himself in St. Peter's Basilica in 1932. One of the first American appointments made by Pacelli, then the newly elected Pius XII, was to promote Spellman to the archbishopric of New York, to which office was added the charge of military vicar of the United States Armed Forces. Created a cardinal in 1946, he was given Pacelli's former title, Santi Giovanni e Paolo. He served as papal legate on a number of occasions in the 1950s and attended the Second Vatican Council, serving on the council's presidency, but his influence waned with the death of his patron and the changing times in the American church.

STAFFORD, JAMES FRANCIS (born 1932), *cardinal*, major penitentiary of the Holy Roman Church. A native of Baltimore, Maryland, he attended Loyola College and St. Mary's Seminary in that city before being sent to complete his education at the Pontifical North American College in Rome, where he earned a licentiate in theology from the Pontifical Gregorian University. Ordained a priest in 1957, he returned to his home diocese, where he held several pastoral assignments before being sent to the Catholic University of America in Washington, D.C., where he earned a master's degree in social work in 1964. Returning once more to Baltimore, he served as director of Catholic Charities until 1976, when he was appointed auxiliary bishop of Baltimore by Pope Paul VI. He was transferred to Memphis, Tennessee, as bishop in 1982. In 1986, he was promoted by Pope John Paul II to the archbishopric of Denver, Colorado. In 1993, he successfully hosted the World Youth Day. Summoned to the Vatican in 1996, he was appointed president of the Pontifical Council for the Laity. He was created a cardinal by Pope John Paul II in 1998. In 2003, he was transferred to the Apostolic Penitentiary as major penitentiary of the Holy Roman Church. Stafford took part in the conclave of 2005.

STEPINAC, *Blessed* ALOJZIJE (1898–1960), *cardinal*. Stepinac studied agriculture before entering the seminary. After studies at the Pontifical Gregorian University in Rome, he was ordained in 1930 and returned home to pastoral work in his native archdiocese of Zagreb. Appointed coadjutor archbishop of Zagreb in 1934, he succeeded to the see in 1937. During the Second World War, he condemned the racist policies of both the Nazis and their Croatian puppets, declaring in an October 25, 1942, sermon in his cathedral: "Every nation and every race on the earth has the right to a life worthy of a person and to treatment worthy of a person. All without differentiation, whether members of the Gypsy race or any others, whether black or distinguished Europeans, despised Jews or haughty Aryans, have the same right to say: 'Our Father who art in Heaven!' And if God has granted this right to all, what human authorities can negate it?" He was arrested by

the Communist regime of Marshal Tito in 1946 and condemned after a show trial, endured five years in the harsh prison of Lepoglava, and eventually was imprisoned in his
home village under strict house arrest. He was created a cardinal by Pius XII in 1953 but
never actually received his red hat or biretta. He was beatified by Pope John Paul II in 1996.

SUENENS, LEO-JOZEF (1904–1996), *cardinal.* Suenens was ordained a priest in 1927, after
studies at the Episcopal College of Saint-Marie in Mechlin and the Pontifical Gregorian
University in Rome. He then served on the faculty of the seminary of Mechlin until
1940, when he was appointed vice-rector of the University of Louvain. He served as
acting rector of the university during the Nazi occupation of Belgium (1941–1945). He
was appointed auxiliary bishop of Mechlin in 1945, becoming archbishop in 1961. At
that time, the name of the archdiocese was changed to Mechlin-Brussels (Malines-
Bruxelles). In 1962, he was created a cardinal by John XXIII and named to the additional
charge of military vicar for Belgium. He participated in the conclave of 1963 and the
two conclaves of 1978. An active participant at Vatican II and the subsequent Synods of
Bishops, he resigned the pastoral governance of his see in 1979.

TAPPOUNI, IGNACE-GABRIEL I (1879–1968), *cardinal,* patriarch of the Syrian Catholic
Church. Born in Mosul, now Iraq, with the original name of Léon-Gabriel Tappouni, he
was educated at the Syro-Chaldean Seminary run by the Dominicans in his hometown,
he was ordained a priest in 1902. After ordination, he served on the faculty of his alma
mater until 1908, when he became secretary of the apostolic delegation for Mesopotamia.
In 1912, he was appointed bishop and patriarchal vicar in Mardin and took the name of
Théophile-Gabriel at the time of his episcopal ordination. During the Turkish persecutions of the Armenians, Syrians, and other non-Muslim minorities, in 1918, he was arrested and imprisoned, being freed only when the Austrian empress Zita intervened.
Transferred as patriarchal vicar to Aleppo, he became bishop of Aleppo when a separate
Syrian eparchy (diocese) was established there. In May 1929, he became apostolic administrator of the Syrian Catholic Patriarchate and was elected by the Synod of Syrian
Catholic Bishops as patriarch of Antioch of the Syrians and head of the Syrian Catholic
Church on June 24, 1929, assuming the style of "Ignace-Gabriel I." Papal confirmation
of the election was granted on July 15, 1929. In 1935, Pius XI created him cardinal, the
first Eastern Rite hierarch appointed to the Sacred College since Andon-Bedros (Antoine)
IX Hassoun (1809–1884), patriarch of Cilicia of the Armenians, was created a cardinal by
Leo XIII in 1880. He participated in the conclaves of 1958 and 1963.

TARDINI, DOMENICO (1888–1961), *cardinal,* pro-secretary of state of Pope Pius XII (1939–
1958) and secretary of state of Pope John XXIII (1958–1963). Tardini was ordained a
priest in 1912 and served on the faculty of his alma mater, the Pontifical Roman Seminary, as well as that of the Pontifical Urbanian Athenaeum *de Propaganda Fide.* Joining
the Sacred Congregation of Extraordinary Ecclesiastical Affairs (i.e., the "foreign ministry" section of the Secretariat of State) in 1921, he became its undersecretary in 1929. He
was appointed substitute of the Secretariat of State (i.e., "interior minister") in 1935 and

then secretary of the Sacred Congregation for Extraordinary Ecclesiastical Affairs in 1937. Pius XII gave him the title of "pro-secretary of state for extraordinary ecclesiastical affairs" in 1952. After his election, Pope John XXIII appointed Tardini secretary of state and prefect of the Sacred Congregation for Extraordinary Ecclesiastical Affairs as well as archpriest of the Vatican Basilica, creating him a cardinal and ordaining him a bishop.

TAURAN, JEAN-LOUIS (born 1943), *cardinal*, librarian and archivist of the Holy Roman Church, formerly secretary for relations with states. A native of Bordeaux, he was ordained a priest in 1969, after studies at the Pontifical French Seminary and the Pontifical Gregorian University in Rome. After completing advanced studies at the Pontifical Ecclesiastical Academy, he entered the diplomatic service of the Holy See and held various offices in the Secretariat of State. He was appointed secretary for relations with states in 1990 and was ordained an archbishop the following year. Serving effectively as the Vatican foreign minister, he was one of the principal architects of the redirection of the Holy See's diplomatic activity after the collapse of Communism in Central and Eastern Europe. He was created a cardinal by Pope John Paul II in 2003 and appointed librarian and archivist of the Holy Roman Church. Tauran took part in the conclave of 2005.

TEDESCHINI, FEDERICO (1873–1959), *cardinal*. Of scholarly bent, Tedeschini held earned doctorates in philosophy, theology, canon law, and civil law. Ordained a priest in 1896, he entered the service of the Secretariat of State in 1900, where he worked for Monsignor Giacomo della Chiesa, later Pope Benedict XV. Because of his talents as a classical Latinist, he was named chancellor of apostolic briefs in 1903 and made responsible for the composition of official papal documents. With the election of Benedict XV, he was named substitute of the Secretariat of State (i.e., "interior minister" of the Holy See) in 1914. Appointed apostolic nuncio to Spain in 1922, he was elevated to the rank of archbishop. His work in the turbulent Spanish context of the time was appreciated by all: When he left Spain in 1933, the republican government of the time, a regime not noted for friendliness to the Church, awarded him the Grand Cross of the Order of Isabella the Catholic. He was created cardinal *in pectore* by Pius XI in 1933; his nomination was published in 1935, when he was appointed apostolic datary (i.e., placed in charge of the papal appointments). Pius XII appointed Tedeschini to succeed him as archpriest of the Vatican Basilica.

TESTA, GUSTAVO (1886–1969), *cardinal*. A native of Boltierre, in the same diocese of Bergamo from which Pope John XXIII hailed, Testa grew up on a farm only a few miles from the holdings of the Roncalli family. He was ordained a priest in 1910 after studies at the Pontifical Lateran Athenaeum, the Pontifical Roman Athenaeum of Sant'Apollinare, and the Pontifical Biblical Institute. After a number of years of pastoral ministry in Bergamo, he entered the service of the Secretariat of State in 1920, serving in Austria, Germany, and Peru, as well as in Rome. Appointed apostolic delegate in Egypt, Arabia, Eritrea, Abyssinia, and Palestine, he was consecrated an archbishop in 1934. In 1953, he was transferred as apostolic nuncio to Switzerland. John XXIII called him back to Rome in 1959, creating him a cardinal. He was entrusted with various commissions and was appointed secretary of the Sacred Congregation for the Oriental Churches in 1962. He participated in the conclave of 1963 as well as the Second Vatican Council and the first Synod of Bishops, before retiring in 1968. Testa is perhaps best remembered for his unconventional coat of arms: a plain shield inscribed with the words *"Sola gratia tua"* ("Thanks to you alone") and surrounded by a scroll inscribed with the motto *"et patria et cor"* ("and homeland and heart"), both clear references to his ties to John XXIII, to which the cardinal attributed his elevation.

TETTAMANZI, DIONIGI (born 1934), *cardinal*, archbishop of Milan. Born in Renate, near Milan, Tettamanzi studied at the minor seminary of Seveso and the major seminary of Venegono Inferiore before he was ordained a priest in 1957. He subsequently earned a doctorate in theology from the Pontifical Gregorian University. Returning to the Archdiocese of Milan in 1960, he embarked on an academic career, teaching at the seminaries of Masnago, Seveso San Pietro, and Venegono, as well as the Lombard Pastoral Institute, and publishing some two dozen works. He was called to the Vatican to participate in the Synods of Bishops of 1980 and 1987 as a theological expert and was appointed rector of the Pontifical Lombard Seminary in Rome in 1987. He was appointed archbishop of Ancona-Osimo in 1989 but resigned two years later to become secretary general of the Italian Episcopal Conference. In 1995, he was appointed archbishop of Genoa and elected vice-president of the Italian Episcopal Conference. Created a cardinal in 1998 by Pope John Paul II, he was transferred to Milan as archbishop in 2002. Tettamanzi participated in the conclave of 2005 and was considered by many a possible candidate.

THIANDOUM, HYACINTHE (1921–2004), *cardinal*. Thiandoum was ordained the first native Senegalese priest in 1949, after studying at the regional seminary of Dakar, by the then–apostolic delegate for French West Africa, Archbishop Marcel Lefebvre, who was to later lead what became the traditionalist schism in the aftermath of Vatican II. After four years of pastoral work, he was sent to further studies at the Pontifical Gregorian University in Rome. Returning to Senegal 1955, he was appointed vicar general of Dakar by Lefebvre, who was then the first Archbishop of Dakar as well as apostolic delegate. When Lefebvre returned to France in 1962, he recommended Thiandoum as his successor. Thus Thiandoum was appointed archbishop of Dakar in 1962. He attended the Second Vatican Council and the subsequent Synods of Bishops. Created a cardinal by Paul VI in 1976, he tried, unsuccessfully, to mediate the widening rift between his old mentor and the Vatican. Although traditionalist himself—he has advocated the creation of an "African canonical order" distinct from the "Western Tridentine model"—he described Lefebvre's excommunication for consecrating four traditionalist bishops without papal mandate in 1988 as one of the saddest days of his life. He resigned the pastoral governance of his archdiocese in 2000.

TISSERANT, EUGÈNE-GABRIEL-GERVAIS-LAURENT (1884–1972), *cardinal*, one of the most colorful characters in the twentieth-century history of the Sacred College of which he was for many years the dean. Ordained a priest in 1907, after studies at the seminary of his native Nancy as well as the Institut Catholique of Paris and the Pontifical Biblical Institute in Jerusalem, he was a first-class Orientalist, completely conversant in the ancient Hebrew, Aramaic, Chaldean, and other languages as well as classical and modern Arabic. Appointed professor of Assyrian at the Pontifical Athenaeum of Sant'Apollinare and a curator of the Vatican Library in 1908, he resigned in 1914 to enlist in the French army—and not as chaplain. Rising to the rank of colonel, he served in the French expedition to the Middle East. At the end of the Great War, he returned to the Vatican Library, where he was appointed assistant librarian in 1919. In 1930, he became pro-prefect of the library. Created a cardinal by his former superior in the library, then Pope Pius XI, in 1936, he was appointed secretary of the Sacred Congregation for the Oriental Church. The following year he received episcopal consecration at the hands of the then–secretary of state, Cardinal Eugenio Pacelli. Becoming sub-dean of the Sacred College in 1948, he acceded to the office of dean in 1951, the same year he became prefect of the Sacred Ceremonial Congregation. In 1957, he was appointed librarian and archivist of the Holy Roman Church. In 1959, he resigned the secretariat of the Oriental Congregation, becoming the following year grand master of the Equestrian Order of the Holy Sepulchre of Jerusalem. In 1962, he was elected a member of the Académie Française. During the Second Vatican Council, he served on the council's presidency. Much to his ill-disguised chagrin, he lost the right to vote in the conclave and was forced to resign as librarian and archivist of the Holy Roman Church when he reached the age of eighty in 1971. He participated in the conclaves of 1939, 1958, and 1963.

DE LA TORRE, CARLOS MARÍA (1873–1968), *cardinal.* Ordained in 1896 after studies in the seminary of Quito and the Pontifical Gregorian University, he held various pastoral, academic, and administrative posts in the Archdiocese of Quito until his appointment, in 1911, as bishop of Loja. Transferred to the Diocese of Guayaquil in 1926, he was promoted to the archbishopric of Quito in 1933. Created a cardinal in 1953 by Pius XII, he participated in the conclave of 1958 but was too ill to take part in that of 1963. Nonetheless he recovered sufficiently to attend the Second Vatican Council. He resigned the pastoral governance of his archdiocese in 1967.

TRAGLIA, LUIGI (1895–1977), *cardinal.* Traglia was ordained a priest in 1917 after studies at the Pontifical Lateran Athenaeum. After further studies at the Pontifical Gregorian University, he joined the faculty of the Pontifical Urbanian Athenaeum *de Propaganda Fide,* where he taught until 1936. In 1927, he joined the staff of the Sacred Congregation for the Propagation of the Faith. In September 1936, he was appointed an auditor (judge) of the Sacred Roman Rota, but he had barely entered into office when, in December 1936, he was appointed archbishop and vice-gerent of the Diocese of Rome. Created a cardinal by John XXIII in 1960, he was appointed pro-vicar general of Rome. In 1965, he became vicar general of Rome but resigned the vicariate in 1968 to become the last chancellor of the Holy Roman Church (the office was abolished when he resigned in 1973). He was elected and confirmed sub-dean of the College of Cardinals in 1972 and its dean in 1974.

TUCCI, ROBERTO (born 1921), *cardinal.* Tucci joined the Society of Jesus (the Jesuits) in 1936. After studies at the various Jesuit houses of study as well as the University of Louvain and the Pontifical Gregorian University in Rome, he was ordained a priest in 1950. He taught at the Theological Faculty of San Luigi in Naples, where he founded and directed the journals *Digest religioso* and *Rassegna di Teologia*, until he was named to the writers' board of the influential journal *La Civiltà Cattolica* in 1956. He became the director of the latter publication in 1959. He served on various commissions at the Second Vatican Council as well as being secretary general of the Italian province of the Jesuits from 1967 to 1969. He was a member for several years of the editorial board of the progressive journal *Concilium* and was active in various journalistic endeavors. In 1973, he joined Vatican Radio and served as its director general until 1989. Until almost the end of the pontificate, he managed all of Pope John Paul II's international travels and accompanied the pope on all but two of his pilgrimages outside Italy. John Paul created him a cardinal in 2001.

TYRRELL, GEORGE (1861–1909), theologian and leader of the modernist movement. Tyrrell was born in Dublin to a Protestant Anglo-Irish family noted for its intellectual distinction in 1861. He was educated at Rathmines School and entered Trinity College in 1878. He was greatly influenced by the writings of Cardinal Newman, and early in 1879 he converted to Catholicism. In 1880 he joined the Society of Jesus and passed his novitiate at Manresa and other houses of the order. Ordained a priest, he became a teacher of philosophy at Stonyhurst but was dismissed soon thereafter because of his views on papal infallibility and the intellectual element in revelation. He was excommunicated in 1908. His most influential works included *External Religion: Its Use and Abuse* (1901), *The Faith of Millions* (1902), *The Church and the Future* (1903), *The Programme of Modernism* (1908), and *Christianity at the Crossroads* (1909).

URBANI, GIOVANNI (1900–1969), *cardinal.* A native Venetian, Urbani was ordained a priest in 1922, after studies at the Patriarchal Seminary of Venice. After a period of pastoral work in Venice as well as graduate studies, he taught in the Patriarchal Seminary from 1927 until 1946, when he was appointed secretary and national counselor of the Central Committee of Italian Catholic Action, elevated at the same time to the episcopate. At Catholic Action, he played a significant role in the defeat of the Communist-dominated left in Italy's first postwar elections that ensured the predominance of the Christian Democrats. For his success, he was elevated, in 1948, to the rank of archbishop by Pius XII. Appointed to the See of Verona in 1955, he was chosen by John XXIII to succeed him in Venice in 1958. He was created a cardinal by John that same year. He participated in the conclave of 1963.

VALERI, VALERIO (1883–1963), *cardinal.* A native of Santa Fiore near Città della Pieve, Valeri was educated at the Pio-Roman Seminary and the Pontifical Roman Athenaeum of Sant'Apollinare and ordained a priest in 1907. He served on the faculty of the Pontifical

Regional Seminary of Fano (1907–1909) and that of his alma mater, the Pontfical Roman Athenaeum of Sant'Apollinare (1909–1920), with a break during World War I to serve as an Italian military chaplain. In 1920, he joined the staff of the Secretariat of State, serving at the reopened nunciature in Paris from 1921 to 1927. Appointed apostolic delegate in Egypt and Arabia in 1927, he was elevated to the rank of archbishop. He was transferred to Romania in 1933 as apostolic nuncio. In 1936, he was appointed apostolic nuncio to France. Following the French surrender, with the rest of the diplomatic corps accredited to the government of Marshal Pétain, he moved to Vichy. After the liberation of Paris by the Allies in 1944, as a matter of policy, the provisional government established by the Free French demanded the recall of all diplomatic envoys who had gone to Vichy. However, to demonstrate that there was no rancor against the departing nuncio, General Charles de Gaulle decorated him with the Grand Cross of the *Légion d'Honneur*. Valeri then served in the Sacred Congregation for Extraordinary Ecclesiastical Affairs (i.e., the Holy See's "foreign ministry") until 1948, when he was named assessor of the Sacred Congregation for the Oriental Church and president of the organizing committee for the Holy Year of 1950. In 1953, he was created a cardinal by Pius XII and appointed prefect of the Sacred Congregation for Religious.

VANNUTELLI, SERAFINO (1834–1915), *cardinal.* Born in Genazzano, near Palestrina, in the Roman countryside, he was ordained a priest in 1860 after studies at the Capranica College and the Collegio Romano, where he earned doctorates in canon and civil law. A career Vatican diplomat with extensive experience in Latin America (Mexico, Ecuador, Peru, Colombia, Venezuela, El Salvador, Guatemala, Costa Rica, Honduras, and Nicaragua) as well as Germany, Belgium, and Austria-Hungary, he was consecrated an archbishop in 1869. Created a cardinal in 1887, he served in various curial posts, including that of secretary of the Supreme Sacred Congregation of the Holy Office (1903–1908). Longtime sub-dean of the Sacred College, he became dean in 1913.

VANNUTELLI, VINCENZO (1836–1930), *cardinal.* Born in Palestrina, he studied at the Gregorian University and the Pontifical Athenaeum of Sant'Apollinare. Ordained a priest in 1860 the day after his older brother's ordination, he followed his sibling's path as career Vatican diplomat, albeit one whose international experience was limited to a long tour at the nunciature in Brussels, a brief sojourn at the Sublime Porte in Constantinople, and a tour as nuncio in Lisbon. Consecrated an archbishop in 1880 and created a cardinal in 1889 (although reserved *in pectore* until the following year), he returned to Rome to serve as archpriest of the Basilica of St. Mary Major as well as in some minor curial posts before being named prefect of the Supreme Tribunal of the Apostolic Signatura in 1908. He succeeded his brother as Dean of the Sacred College when the latter died in 1915.

VASZARY, KOLOS FERENC (1832–1915), *cardinal.* Entering the Benedictine order as a monk in 1847, he was ordained a priest in 1856. He was elected abbot of Pannonhalma in 1885. He became archbishop of Esztergom and prince-primate of Hungary in 1893 and was created a cardinal the following year. He participated in the conclave of 1903. He resigned his pastoral office in 1912 because of ill health and did not participate in the conclave of 1914.

VERDIER, JEAN (1864–1940), *cardinal*. A member of the Society of St. Sulpice, a congregation of diocesan priests dedicated to the education of seminarians, Verdier was ordained a priest in 1887. Superior general of the Sulpicians, he was tapped to be vicar general of the Archdiocese of Paris. At the suggestion of Luigi Maglione, then nuncio in Paris, he was appointed archbishop of the French capital in 1929 and created a cardinal the same year. During his episcopate, he built over one hundred churches to minister to the working-class neighborhoods that had sprung up around Paris. An advocate of social justice, he regularly denounced racism—making pointed reference to Nazi Germany—from the pulpit of his cathedral and often slipped away from his office to work in a soup kitchen run by the Little Sisters of Paris.

VIDAL I BARRAQUER, FRANCISCO DE ASÍS (1868–1943), *cardinal*. Born in Cambrils, near Tarragona, Spain, to a family of rural landowners and liberal professionals, Vidal I Barraquer was educated in the Jesuit school at Manresa and the Seminary of Barcelona. While at Barcelona, he also earned a licentiate in civil law from the faculty of that city (he eventually received a doctorate in civil law from the University of Madrid) and practiced law for a year before finishing his theological studies at the Seminary of Tarragona. Ordained a priest in 1899, he earned doctorates in theology and canon law from the Pontifical Faculty at Tarragona. He held different posts in the archdiocesan curia of Tarragona. In 1907, he was appointed a canon of the cathedral; in 1911, he was elected vicar capitular upon the death of the incumbent archbishop. In 1913, he was appointed apostolic administrator of the Diocese of Solsona and consecrated a titular bishop. From 1914 to 1916, he served as a senator of the Spanish kingdom from the province of Tarragona. In 1919, he was promoted to the metropolitan see of Tarragona as archbishop. Two years later, he was created a cardinal by Pope Benedict XV. During his episcopate, he defended both the rights of the Church and those of the Catalan language. With the proclamation of the republic in 1931, his friendship with President Alcalá Zamora and his ties to Catalan nationalists contributed to the mitigation in Catalonia of the abuses suffered by the Church elsewhere in Spain. When his auxiliary bishop was assassinated, he moved to Barcelona; in 1936, he was forced to take refuge in Italy. For his refusal to sign the collective letter of the Spanish episcopate of July 1, 1937, in favor of Generalissimo Francisco Franco, he was not allowed to return home after the civil war. He spent the rest of his life in exile in monasteries of the Carthusian order while his archdiocese, which he refused to resign, was governed in his name by successive vicars general. He participated in the conclaves of 1922 and 1939.

VILLENEUVE, JEAN-MARIE-RODRIGUE (1883–1947), *cardinal*. Born in Montréal, Canada, he joined the Oblates of Mary Immaculate in 1901 and made his profession the following year. After stuies at various institutes of the Oblate congregation and the University of

Ottawa, he was ordained a priest in 1907. He served as a faculty member of the Catholic University of Ottawa from 1907 until 1919 and as superior of the Oblate Scholasticate in Ottawa from 1920 until 1930, when he was appointed bishop of Gravelbourg. The following year, he was promoted to the metropolitan see of Québec as archbishop. He was created a cardinal by Pope Pius XI in 1933. He participated in the conclave of 1939.

VILLOT, JEAN (1905–1979), *cardinal*, secretary of state of Pope Paul VI (1963–1978), Pope John Paul I (1978), and, briefly, Pope John Paul II. Villot was ordained a priest in 1930, after studies at the seminary of the Institut Catholique of Paris and the Pontifical Athenaeum Angelicum in Rome. After further studies, he joined the faculties of the seminary in his native diocese of Clermont-Ferrand and the Catholic University of Lyons in 1934. He became vice-rector of the Catholic University of Lyons in 1942. In 1950, he was appointed director of the secretariat of the French Episcopal Conference. He was appointed auxiliary bishop of Paris in 1954. In 1959, he was promoted to be coadjutor archbishop of Lyons, succeeding to the see in 1965. He attended the Second Vatican Council and the subsequent Synods of Bishops. Created a cardinal by Paul VI in 1965, he became the first non-diplomat to be appointed to the positions when Pope Paul nominated him secretary of state, prefect of the Council for the Public Affairs of the Church (formerly the Sacred Congregation for Extraordinary Ecclesiastical Affairs, i.e., the Holy See's "foreign office"), president of the Pontifical Commission for the Vatican City State, and president of the Administration of the Patrimony of the Holy See in 1969. He was appointed camerlengo of the Holy Roman Church in 1970 and president of the new Pontifical Council *Cor Unum*, established to oversee Catholic relief and development organizations, in 1971. He is buried in the Roman Church of Trinità dei Monti at the top of the so-called Spanish Steps.

VIVES Y TUTÓ, JOSÉ DE CALASANZ FÉLIX SANTIAGO (1854–1913), *cardinal*. Born near Barcelona, he joined the Capuchins, the most austere of the three principal Franciscan orders, at the age of fifteen in 1869. Ordained a priest in 1877, he enjoyed a reputation for sanctity among his confrères. Pope Leo XIII brought him into the service of the Holy See, entrusting him with various offices. He was created a cardinal in 1899. He assisted Leo XIII on his deathbed and was later the confessor of Pius X. A prolific author, he published over one hundred titles.

WILLEBRANDS, JOHANNES (born 1909), *cardinal*. Willebrands was educated at the seminary of Warmond and the Pontifical Athenaeum Angelicum. After his priestly ordination in 1934, he worked in his native diocese of Haarlem and taught at the seminary of Warmond, serving as its rector from 1945 until 1960. In 1960, he was appointed secretary of the newly established Secretariat for Christian Unity, in which capacity he attended the Second Vatican Council as an official expert. In 1964, he was ordained a bishop. In 1969, he was appointed president of the Secretariat for Christian Unity and created a cardinal by Paul VI. He attended many of the post–Vatican II Synods of Bishops. In 1975, he was appointed Archbishop of Utrecht and military vicar of the Netherlands, retaining, however, the presidency of the Secretariat for Christian Unity. He participated in the two conclaves of 1978. In 1982, he resigned the military vicariate, and resigned the archbishopric of Utrecht the following year. In 1988, the Secretariat for Christian Unity became the Pontifical Council for the Promotion of Christian Unity, and Willebrands was confirmed as its president. He resigned the presidency and became president emeritus in 1989, when he reached the age of eighty.

WRIGHT, JOHN JOSEPH (1909–1979), *cardinal,* onetime bishop of Pittsburgh. Wright was born in Boston and attended Boston College, St. John's Seminary in Brighton, Massachusetts, and the Pontifical Gregorian University in Rome before being ordained a priest in 1935. After further studies (1935–1939), he returned to teach at St. John's Seminary (1939–1943), before serving as secretary to then-Archbishop Richard Cushing of Boston (1944–1947). Appointed auxiliary bishop of Boston in 1947, he was transferred to be bishop of Wooster, Massachusetts, in 1950. He was transferred again to be bishop of Pittsburgh, Pennsylvania, in 1959. He attended the Second Vatican Council as well as several of the subsequent Synods of Bishops. Created cardinal by Paul VI in 1969, he was called to Rome and appointed prefect of the Sacred Congregation for the Clergy (formerly the Sacred Congregation for the Council). He recovered from illness sufficiently to participate in the second conclave of 1978 but died the following year. He is buried in his family plot in Brookline, Massachusetts.

WYSZÝNSKI, STEFAN (1901–1981), *cardinal,* longtime primate of Poland. Wyszýnski was born in Zuzela, near Lomza, Poland, and was educated at the seminary of Wloclawek and the University of Lublin. Ordained a priest in 1924, he did pastoral work in the Diocese of Lomza and taught at the seminary of Wloclawek as well as editing a review for the clergy. During World War II, he did clandestine pastoral work. Appointed bishop of Lublin in 1946, he was promoted to the primatial archdiocese of Gniezno with the Archdiocese of Warsaw entrusted to him *ad personam* in 1948. He was imprisoned by the Communists from 1946 to 1956. While he was imprisoned, he was created a cardinal in 1953 by Pius XII. He attended the Second Vatican Council but was prevented by the Communist authorities from attending the first Ordinary Synod of Bishops in 1967. He was subsequently able to attend every other synodal meeting. He participated in the conclaves of 1958 and 1963, as well as the two conclaves of 1978.

Appendix 5

A GLOSSARY OF SELECT TERMS

The following is a brief glossary of ecclesiastical terms employed in and pertinent to the text. Other terms have been adequately defined within the text. For more complete information, see the newly revised *New Catholic Encyclopedia* (Washington: Catholic University of America Press, 2002) or any of several one-volume dictionaries, including Wolfgang Beinert, Francis Schussler Fiorenza, and Elizabeth Schussler Fiorenza, eds., *The Handbook of Catholic Theology* (New York: Crossroad, 1995); and Richard P. McBrien, ed., *The HarperCollins Encyclopedia of Catholicism* (San Francisco: HarperCollins, 1995). For more details on questions of historical theological doctrines and issues, see Trevor A. Hart, ed., *The Dictionary of Historical Theology* (Grand Rapids, Michigan: Wm. B. Eerdmans, 2000); and, for a more popular reference written treating the material in very general terms, Matthew Bunson, *Encyclopedia of Catholic History* (Huntington, Indiana: Our Sunday Visitor, 1995).

AD LIMINA VISIT. From the Latin phrase *ad limina Apostolorum* ("to the threshold of the Apostles"), the visit that each diocesan bishop or equivalent must make every five years to Rome (the "threshold of the Apostles" Peter and Paul) to report to the pope and officials of the Roman Curia on the state of his diocese. In addition to the reports, the bishops are expected to make pilgrimages to the tombs of the two apostles at St. Peter's Basilica in the Vatican and the Ostian Basilica of St. Paul-outside-the-Walls. The custom began during the pontificate of Pope Benedict VII (974–983), although it only became more generalized with the advent of modern transportation.

ALBIGENSIANISM. A medieval heresy holding that all things material were the creation of evil while all things spiritual alone emanated from God. Flourishing in southern France and nearby remote parts of Italy and Switzerland, in its extreme form the heresy implied a rejection of civil social order. The Order of Preachers (the Dominicans) was originally founded to combat this heresy, which eventually succumbed to a crusade authorized by Pope Innocent III (1198–1216).

ALLOCUTION. Technical term for an address given by the pope.

ALMONER, APOSTOLIC. The office, headed by an archbishop, the "almoner of His Holiness," that administers the pope's personal charities; some of the funds it raises by selling parchments attesting to apostolic blessings given to individuals or institutions. The archbishop almoner participates in papal ceremonies, walking behind the pope alongside the prefect (and adjunct prefect) of the Papal Household.

AMERICANISM. A nineteenth-century movement to adapt Catholicism to American polity and culture that was condemned by Pope Leo XIII in his apostolic letter *Testem benevolentiae* (1899), addressed to the senior hierarch, Cardinal James Gibbons, archbishop of Baltimore. Leo defined "Americanism" as a complex of opinions, the underlying principle of which was "that in order to more easily attract those who differ from her, the Church should shape her teachings more in accord with the spirit of the age and relax some of her ancient severity and make some concessions to new opinions. Many think that these concessions should be made not only in regard to ways of living, but even in regard to doctrines which belong to the deposit of the faith. They contend that it would be opportune, in order to gain those who differ from us, to omit certain points of her teaching which are of lesser importance, and to tone down the meaning which the Church has always attached to them." Gibbons, interestingly, denied that such a doctrine existed.

ANTIPOPE. A false claimant to the papal office in opposition to the incumbent canonically elected or recognized. The *Annuario Pontificio* takes notice of some thirty-seven such pretenders, while historian J.N.D. Kelly, in his *Oxford Dictionary of Popes* (Oxford: Oxford University Press, 1986), and theologian Richard McBrien, in his *Lives of the Popes: The Pontiffs from St. Peter to John Paul II* (San Francisco: HarperSanFrancisco, 1997), both list thirty-nine antipopes. Historically, the first antipope was St. Hippolytus (217–235); the last was Felix V (1439–1449). In modern times, a number of disturbed individuals have put themselves forward as "the true pope," but none has garnered anything approaching the level of popular support enjoyed by some of the historical antipopes.

APOSTOLIC DELEGATE. A cleric, in the modern period usually of archiepiscopal rank, who acts as the papal representative in a particular country or region where the Holy See does not maintain formal diplomatic relations. In the latter case, the representative is usually designated as an "apostolic nuncio." There was an apostolic delegate to the United States until, during the presidency of Ronald Reagan, formal bilateral diplomatic relations were established between the Holy See and the United States, at which time the apostolic delegate, then-Archbishop Pio Laghi, was formally accredited as a diplomatic envoy to the American government. In recent times, however, most apostolic delegates have become nuncios, as the Holy See has established diplomatic relations at the ambassadorial level with some 172 countries as well as with the European Union and the Sovereign Military Order of Malta, in addition to what are described as "diplomatic relations of a special nature" with the Russian Federation and the Palestinian Liberation Organization.

APOSTOLIC NUNCIO. A cleric, almost always of archiepiscopal rank, who acts as the papal representative to the Church in a particular country or group of countries as well as the Holy See's official diplomatic representative to the government or governments. According to the 1961 Vienna Convention on Diplomatic Relations, nuncios are ranked as ambassadors in diplomatic protocol. Many countries, some but not all traditionally Catholic, maintain the custom of the papal representative being *ex ufficio* the dean of the diplomatic corps in their capital of residence. Formerly, the Holy See maintained the distinction between "apostolic nuncios" and "apostolic pro-nuncios," the former being the ambassadors whose prerogative to the deanship *de iure* was recognized. This distinction was abolished in 1992. The embassy of the apostolic nuncio is referred to as the "apostolic nunciature."

ARIANISM. The first of the major doctrinal heresies to upset the Church after the peace of Constantine. In brief, the heresy denied the divinity of Jesus Christ, considering him just the greatest of creatures. Although its origins antedate him, the doctrine was developed and propagated by an Alexandrian priest, Arius. He described the Son as a second, or inferior, God, standing midway between the "first cause" (the Father) and creatures; himself made out of nothing, yet as making all things else; as existing before the worlds of the ages; and as arrayed in all divine perfections except the one which was their stay and foundation. God alone was without beginning, unoriginated; the Son was originated, and once had not existed. For all that has origin must begin to be. In Greek terms, Arianism denies that the Son is of one essence, nature, or substance with God; He is not consubstantial (*homoousios*) with the Father, and therefore not like Him, or equal in dignity, or co-eternal, or within the real sphere of Deity. Arianism was condemned by the first Ecumenical Council, the First Council of Nicaea, in 325. Despite its condemnation, the heresy continue to divide the Church until it was definitively anathematized by the second Ecumenical Council, the First Council of Constantinople, in 381, through the theological and pastoral efforts of St. Athanasius, St. Basil the Great, St. Gregory of Nazianzus, and St. Gregory of Nyssa.

BENEFICE. An income-producing ecclesiastical office. In modern times, most of these have been replaced by the payment of modest stipends to those who provide ecclesiastical services.

BIRETTA. A square cap with three ridges or peaks worn by clerics in choral vesture at certain liturgical functions. With the exception of the biretta of cardinals, the biretta is usually topped with a tassel. The color and material of the biretta matches that of the dignity of its wearer: A cardinal wears a scarlet (in Italian, *ponzò*) watered-silk biretta, a papal nuncio wears a violet (in Italian, *paonazza*) biretta, an archbishop or bishop wears a violet (*paonazza*) biretta in plain material, certain prelates may wear a black biretta in plain material topped with a red or violet tassel, and all other clerics wear a plain black biretta. Holders of ecclesiastical doctorates may wear, as part of their academic attire, a biretta with four ridges or peaks, trimmed with colors appropriate to their respective faculties and disciplines. The imposition of the scarlet biretta is the principal rite of the ceremonial investiture of a new cardinal by the pope who created him.

BLESSING, APOSTOLIC. A blessing given by the pope, most solemnly in the form *Urbi et Orbi* ("to the City [of Rome] and to the World"), that carries with it a plenary indulgence to the recipients. Before 1870, the apostolic blessing was imparted with great parsimony, traditionally from the *loggia*, or balcony, of St. Peter's Basilica on Holy Thursday and Easter Sunday, that of the Lateran Archbasilica on Ascension Thursday, and that of the Basilica of St. Mary Major on the Feast of the Assumption (August 15). Nowadays, the pope imparts it with greater frequency, and bishops may also impart it in the name of the pontiff on certain occasions.

BRIEF, PAPAL (OR APOSTOLIC). A papal document, less solemn than a bull. Briefs are issued with a direct form of address and sealed with the seal of the Fisherman's Ring. They are employed for ordinary administrative matters.

BULL, PAPAL. The most solemn form of papal document issued for the most important of circumstances, including the conferral of titles or offices on bishops, the canonization of saints, and the proclamation of a "Holy Year." The "bull" is so called because it is authenticated by the circular lead seal (Latin, *bulla*) attached to the parchment document by either silk (in the case of documents granting favors) or hemp (in the case of disciplinary documents) cords. The seal bears the portrait of the apostles Peter and Paul on one side and the name of the reigning pope on the reverse side. Bulls are issued in the third person and begin with the name of the reigning pope and his title in Latin, for example *"Ioannes Paulus PP. II, Episcopus, Servus Servorum Dei"* ("John Paul, Father of Fathers, II, Bishop, Servant of the Servants of God"). A recent example of a papal bull was the bull of indiction for the Great Jubilee of the Year 2000, *Incarnationis Mysterium*, promulgated by Pope John Paul II on November 29, 1998.

CANON LAW. The law of the Church. The canons were first codified by Cardinal Pietro Gasparri in a Code of Canon Law, promulgated by Pope Benedict XV in 1917. This codification was superseded by a new Code, promulgated by Pope John Paul II in 1983. In 1990, John Paul II also promulgated a Code of Canons of the Eastern Churches for the Catholic communities belonging to the ancient Eastern liturgical traditions. The Codes are collections, by no means exhaustive, of ecclesiastical laws and serve as a basis for juridical processes in the Church.

CONCILIARISM. A doctrine developed by canon lawyers and theologians influenced by them in the late medieval period that held that Ecumenical Councils constitute the highest authority in the Church, even over the Roman pontiff. Propagated at the Council of Constance (1415), the doctrine reached its apogee during the Council of Basel (1431–1449).

CONCORDAT. A formal agreement, having all the characteristics of an international treaty, between the Holy See and a civil government, generally to regulate matters of mutual interest in countries where there is not complete separation of Church and state.

CONGREGATION, CURIAL. A department of the Roman Curia. They were formerly called "sacred congregations." The name derives from the collegial nature of their structure. While they have permanent staffs like any governmental agency, authority is formally vested in the members of the congregation, cardinals and bishops appointed by the pope to deliberate with the cardinal prefect of the congregation over all matters within the competency of the department. The day-to-day operations of the staff are supervised by an archbishop who, as the secretary of the congregation, carries out functions equivalent to that of a permanent secretary in the ministries of most parliamentary democracies.

There are presently nine congregations in the Roman Curia: the Congregation for the Doctrine of the Faith, formerly the Holy Office, which oversees doctrinal questions; the Congregation for the Oriental Churches, which oversees the Eastern Rite Churches in communion with the Roman See; the Congregation for Divine Worship and the Discipline of the Sacraments, which has jurisdiction over liturgical and sacramental matters; the Congregation for the Causes of Saints, which deals with canonizations and beatifications; the Congregation for Bishops, which oversees the appointment of bishops and dioceses in developed regions; the Congregation for the Evangelization of Peoples, which oversees the Church in missionary areas; the Congregation for the Clergy, which has jurisdiction over members of the clergy as well as catechetical matters and matters of ecclesiastical property; the Congregation for Institutes of Consecrated Life and for the Societies of Apostolic Life, which oversees religious communities; and the Congregation for Catholic Education, which supervises Catholic universities and seminaries.

CONSISTORY. A formal meeting of cardinals, convened and presided over by the Roman pontiff. In modern times, they have been held principally for the purposes of the creation of new cardinals and to ratify causes of canonization and beatification.

CONSTITUTION, APOSTOLIC. A type of papal document that generally establishes disciplinary or legislative provisions. Pope John Paul II's legislation of papal elections, *Universi Dominici gregis*, promulgated February 22, 1996, is an example of this type of document.

COUNCIL. A lawfully convened assembly of ecclesiastical dignitaries and theological experts for the purpose of discussing and regulating matters of church doctrine and discipline, usually in response to some challenge. The terms *council* and *synod* are synonymous, especially in their official Latin and Greek texts, although in some classical Christian literature the ordinary meetings for worship are also called "synods." In general, for purposes of the present study, councils (or synods) are understood to be legally convened meetings of members of the hierarchy, for the purpose of carrying out their judicial and doctrinal functions, by means of deliberation in common resulting in regulations and decrees invested with the authority of the whole assembly.

Ecumenical Councils are those to which bishops and other hierarchs entitled to vote are convoked from the whole world (Greek, *oikoumene*). The Catholic tradition has added that Ecumenical Councils must meet under the presidency of the pope or his legates and that their decrees, having received papal confirmation, bind all Christians. A council, ecumenical in its convocation, may fail to secure the approbation of the whole Church or of the pope, and thus not rank in authority with Ecumenical Councils. Such was the case with the so-called Robber Synod (*Latrocinium Ephesinum*) of 449, the Synod of Pisa in 1409, and in part with the Councils of Constance and Basel. In the second rank after the Ecumenical Councils are the *general synods* of the Eastern or Western Church, constituted by one-half of the episcopate. The Synod of Constantinople (381) was originally only an Eastern general synod, at which were present the four patriarchs of the East (i.e., those of Constantinople, Alexandria, Antioch, and Jerusalem), with many metropolitans and bishops. It ranks as ecumenical because its decrees were ultimately received in the West.

Traditionally, the Eastern (Orthodox) and Western (Catholic) Churches have been unanimous in accepting the seven Ecumenical Councils: Nicaea I (325), Constantinople I (381), Ephesus (431), Chalcedon (451), Constantinople II (553), Constantinople III (680–681), and Nicaea II (787). The Western (Catholic) tradition also counts fourteen other councils as ecumenical on the thesis that papal convocation and approval were sufficient to ensure their "universal" character, whereas the Eastern (Orthodox) view is that these meetings were only general synods of the Western Church: Constantinople IV (869–870), Lateran I (1123), Lateran II (1139), Lateran III (1179), Lateran IV (1215), Lyons I (1245), Lyons II (1274), Vienne (1311–1312), Constance (1414–1418), Basel-Ferrara-Florence (1431–1445), Lateran V (1512–1517), Trent (1545–1563), Vatican I (1869–1870), and Vatican II (1962–1965).

COUNCIL, PONTIFICAL. A department of the Roman Curia, structured like a congregation but created in the wake of the Second Vatican Council's opening of the Church to new initiatives and concerns. The head of a pontifical council is referred to as a "president" rather than a "prefect."

Presently there are eleven pontifical councils: the Pontifical Council for the Laity, which handles concerns of the laity as such within the Church as well as lay movements; the Pontifical Council for the Promotion of Christian Unity, which promotes ecumenism with other Christian Churches as well as religious dialogue with Judaism; the Pontifical Council for the Family, which promotes family-related concerns; the Pontifical Council for Justice and Peace, which oversees Catholic social doctrine as well as the Holy See's concerns for political, human, economic, and social rights issues; the Pontifical Council *Cor Unum*, which oversees Catholic relief and development agencies; the Pontifical Council for the Pastoral Care of Migrants and Itinerants, which supervises the pastoral care of refugees and migrant peoples; the Pontifical Council for the Healthcare Apostolate, which promotes reflections on bioethical concerns; the Pontifical Council for Legislative Texts, which oversees the "authentic interpretation" of canon laws; the Pontifical Council for Inter-Religious Dialogue, which conducts discussions and promotes understanding with non-Christian religions other than Judaism; the Pontifical Council for

Culture, which represents the Church's interests in the cultural sphere; and the Pontifical Council for Social Communications, which has interests in media communications of the Church's message.

CURIA. The network of offices and administrative agencies that assist a bishop in the government of his local Church or, in the case of the Roman pontiff and his Roman Curia, that assist the pope in the government of the Universal Church.

DICASTERY. Generic term for any office or department of the Roman Curia.

EASTERN CHURCHES. Christian Churches whose origins hark back to the eastern half of the Roman Empire. From the fifth century, various theological controversies led to the splintering of some of these bodies from the Great Church; these breakaway groups became what are today known as the "Ancient (or Oriental) Orthodox" Churches. In 1054, a schism occurred between the main group of Eastern Churches, centered in Constantinople, and the Western (Latin) Church when the legates of Pope Leo IX excommunicated Patriarch Michael Cerularius and his followers and were, in turn, excommunicated by the ecumenical patriarch and his synod. This led to the formation of the "Orthodox" Churches in the East and the Western Church's transformation into the "Catholic" Church.

In addition to the Eastern Orthodox Churches, there are also Eastern Catholic Churches, which, while in communion with the See of Rome, retain their own distinctive liturgical and theological traditions ("rites") as well as great autonomy of government. Many of these "Eastern Catholic Churches" either did not break communion with the Roman Church at the time of the 1054 schism between Rome and Constantinople or restored communion during the seventeenth and eighteenth centuries.

ENCYCLICAL. A papal document in the form of a circular letter addressed to a group of bishops, clergy, or laity, or even to the entire world, expounding on some spiritual or pastoral concern. Encyclicals are perhaps the best-known modern papal documents. The best-known, and perhaps most controversial, example of a modern encyclical is *Humanae vitae*, issued by Paul VI (1963–1968) on July 25, 1968, which declared that every act of sexual intercourse within marriage must be open to the transmission of life and condemned "artificial" means of contraception.

EXCOMMUNICATION. The most severe ecclesiastical sanction, it excludes the one excommunicated from communion with the Church and its members. While the excommunicated person does not cease to be a Christian, he or she is considered "exiled" from ecclesiastical society and forbidden access to the Eucharist or other sacraments until the excommunication has been lifted. Under present canon law, excommunications can either be decreed (*ferendae sententiae*) or automatic upon the commission of certain prohibited acts (*latae sententiae*), such as participation in willful abortion.

FISHERMAN'S RING. The papal signet ring engraved with the image of St. Peter fishing from a boat and encircled with the name and title of the reigning pope. The ring is actually not worn by the pope but simply used to seal apostolic briefs and certain other documents. Its use dates back to at least the reign of Clement IV (1265–1268). The ring that the pope actually wears is a matter of personal choice and taste. The Fisherman's Ring is destroyed on the death of the pope.

GALLICANISM. From the Latin *Gallia* ("Gaul"), the historical geographic designation for the territory of modern-day France, the term refers to a movement that sought to assert the independence of the French Church from papal interventions. The four basic articles of Gallicanism were asserted in the famous "Declaration of the Clergy of France" in 1682: (1) St. Peter and his papal successors—and the Church itself—received the authority of God only over spiritual matters, not over temporal or civil matters; (2) the decrees of the Council of Constance (1414–1418) regarding the authority of general councils, accepted at the time of the Great Schism by the Holy See, retain their validity; (3) rules, customs, and constitutions of nations and national churches—specifically those of the French kingdom and the Gallican church—having been accepted in the past by the papacy, retain their force; and (4) papal decisions are neither infallible nor irreformable until they receive the consent of the Church. While the movement disappeared amid the chaos of the French Revolution, the decrees of the First Vatican Council (1869–1870) on papal infallibility were, at least in part, a response to Gallican tendencies.

HERESY. The denial of a defined dogma of the Church's faith. Heresy is contrasted with schism, the latter being a denial of authority rather than doctrine.

HOLY SEE. Derived from the Latin *sancta sedes* ("holy seat" or "holy chair"), the term originally referred to the pope enthroned on the chair of the Apostle St. Peter and then expanded to include his government in the same manner that the term "the Crown" referred originally to the British sovereign and, by implication, his or her government. Juridically, the term "Holy See" refers to the pope, the Roman Curia, and the entire central government of the Catholic Church as a subject of international law and is constituted by both the spiritual and diplomatic-political authority of the Roman pontiff. The Holy See is distinguished from the Vatican City State, the geographical territory and political entity on which the Holy See is physically located and which guarantees its independence. However, nations enter diplomatic relations with the Holy See and not with the Vatican City State, as evidenced by the fact that after the takeover of Rome by the forces of Italian unification in 1870 and before the creation of the Vatican City State by the Lateran Treaty in 1929, the Holy See as such remained an actor on the international stage. The diplomatic representation of the papacy on the international stage is carried out in the name of the "Holy See" as opposed to the "Vatican City State," the former representing the latter in cases that pertain strictly to the material functions of the little statelet.

HOLY SEPULCHRE, KNIGHTS OF THE. The Equestrian Order of the Holy Sepulchre of Jerusalem is an order of chivalry under the protection of the Holy See. Tracing its origins to the First Crusade and the military company organized to defend the liberated holy places, the order was reorganized by Blessed Pope Pius IX in 1847 and 1868. Pio Nono's successors continued to update the order, its present statutes being approved by Pope John Paul II in 1994. The order has a cardinal as its grand master and is entrusted with the preservation of the Christian presence in the Holy Land. The white mantles of the knights and the black mantles of the dames, both signed with the red "Cross of Jerusalem," are a common sight at many ecclesiastical ceremonies.

HOUSEHOLD, PREFECTURE OF THE PAPAL. In Italian, *Prefettura della Casa Pontificia*. The office in the Holy See, directed by a bishop (currently an archbishop) as its prefect (who is presently seconded by another archbishop as its adjunct prefect), that oversees the Papal Household, formerly the "Papal Court," including all matters of furnishings, maintenance, and personnel. The prefecture also supervises papal audiences and ceremonies, except for the strictly liturgical parts, including protocol, tickets, and admission.

ICONOCLASM. From the Greek term *eikonoklasmos* ("image-breaking"); refers to the heresy that shook the Eastern Churches during the eighth century. Inspired in part by the Muslim onslaught that destroyed images in many areas that fell under the banner of Islam, the controversy over the reverence to be given to images by Christians became the proxy for various struggles within the Eastern Churches. The controversy was initiated by the Byzantine emperor Leo III the Isaurian (716–741), who concluded that the icons venerated by the Eastern Christians were the principal hindrance to the conversion of Jews and Muslims and a source of superstition. In 726, the emperor decreed the destruction of images in all the churches of the empire, provoking disturbances and the resistance of the monastic orders. Leo then persecuted the orthodox believers, many of whom found refuge with the papacy in Rome. Receiving the appeal of Patriarch Germanus of Constantinople, Pope Gregory II (713–731) condemned the iconoclasts. The dispute continued for a number of years, often engendering violent actions. The Second Ecumenical Council of Nicaea (787) decreed the resolution of the controversy by declaring: "We define with all certainty and care that both the figure of the sacred and life-giving Cross, as also the venerable and holy images, whether made in colors or mosaic or other materials, are to be placed suitably in the holy churches of God, on sacred vessels and vestments, on walls and pictures, in houses and by roads; that is to say, the images of our Lord God and Savior Jesus Christ, of our immaculate Lady the holy Mother of God, of the honorable angels and all saints and holy men. For as often as they are seen in their pictorial representations, people who look at them are ardently lifted up to the memory and love of the originals and induced to give them respect and worshipful honor but not real adoration which according to our faith is due only to the Divine Nature. So that offerings of incense and lights are to be given to these as to the figure of the sacred and life-giving Cross, to the holy Gospel-books and other sacred objects in order to do them honor, as was the pious custom of ancient times. For honor paid to an image passes on to its prototype; he who worships an image worships the reality of him who is painted in it." During the ninth century, there was a brief outburst of iconoclasm anew that inspired the writings of St. John of Damascus.

INDULGENCES. Latin, *indulgentia*, from *indulgeo* ("to be kind or tender"); refers in theology to the "remission of the temporal punishment due to sin, the guilt for which has been forgiven and which the faithful Christian who is duly disposed gains under certain prescribed conditions through the action of the Church which, as the minister of redemption, dispenses and applies with authority the treasury of the satisfactions of Christ and the saints" (*Catechism of the Catholic Church*, n. 1471). An indulgence is "partial" or "plenary" according to whether it removes part or all of the temporal punishment due to sin. Indulgences may be applied to the living or the dead

INFALLIBILITY. The supernatural prerogative by which the Church founded by Christ is, by a special divine assistance, preserved from error in matters of faith and morals when the teaching is declared to be definitive and to be held by the entire Church. Traditionally, theologians have held that the Church is considered infallible in her objective definitive teaching regarding faith and morals, not that believers are infallible in their subjective interpretation of her teaching. The consensus of the Catholic doctrinal and theological tradition, confirmed by the First Vatican Council, is that the pope is infallible when he solemnly and explicitly defines a matter of faith or morals *ex cathedra*, that is, by virtue of his apostolic authority as successor to St. Peter and head of the Church. An Ecumenical Council, acting together with the pope would, under the same conditions, enjoy the same prerogative. Subject to greater nuance—and thus more controverted—is understanding infallibility to be attributed to the constant teaching of the bishops of the world, in union with the pope, known as the Church's "ordinary Magisterium." The *Catechism of the Catholic Church* articulates the doctrine in the following manner: "'The Roman Pontiff, head of the college of bishops, enjoys this infallibility in virtue of his office, when, as supreme pastor and teacher of all the faithful—who confirms his brethren in the faith he proclaims by a definitive act a doctrine pertaining to faith or morals . . . The infallibility promised to the Church is also present in the body of bishops when, together with Peter's successor, they exercise the supreme Magisterium,' above all in an Ecumenical Council. When the Church through its supreme Magisterium proposes a doctrine 'for belief as being divinely revealed,' and as the teaching of Christ, the definitions 'must be adhered to with the obedience of faith.' This infallibility extends as far as the deposit of divine Revelation itself. Divine assistance is also given to the successors of the apostles, teaching in communion with the successor of Peter, and, in a particular way, to the bishop of Rome, pastor of the whole Church, when, without arriving at an infallible definition and without pronouncing in a 'definitive manner,' they propose in the exercise of the ordinary Magisterium a teaching that leads to better understanding of Revelation in matters of faith and morals. To this ordinary teaching the faithful 'are to adhere to it with religious assent' which, though distinct from the assent of faith, is nonetheless an extension of it" (n. 891–892).

INTERDICT. A prohibition excluding a member of the faithful or all the faithful belonging to a censured group, or residing in a territory under ban, from participation in certain holy things, usually the sacraments or liturgical rites. The prohibition varies according to the circumstances. The effect is not unlike that of an embargo. The most famous interdict is perhaps the one that Pope Innocent III (1198–1216) decreed against the entire kingdom of England in 1208 when King John Lackland refused to accept the canonical election of Stephen Langton as archbishop of Canterbury. Until the king capitulated and the sentence was lifted in 1213, no ecclesiastical rites could be celebrated in the realm. The most recent public interdict of a place was the one that Pope St. Pius X (1903–1914) decreed against the Italian town of Adria on September 30, 1909, which eventually lasted fifteen days. The residents of Adria had physically attacked their bishop in an effort to prevent him from moving his residence to the town of Rovigo, where that see is now located. During those fifteen days, the celebration of Mass and all other public liturgical ceremonies was prohibited, as was the ringing of bells, the public celebration of the sacraments, and solemn Christian burial of the dead.

INVESTITURE CONTROVERSY. German, *Investiturstreit;* refers to the conflict between the popes and German monarchs during the period approximately between 1075 and 1122, ostensibly over the early medieval practice whereby bishops and abbots were appointed to and installed ("invested") in their offices by the lay ruler, who presented the prelate with the ring and crosier (or pastoral staff) that were the symbols of his ecclesiastical office after the churchman had paid homage to the ruler as feudal overlord. The controversy is not without its ongoing implications for the history of the Church, not least because the memories of the conflict continue to influence the reaction of the Catholic hierarchy to lay involvement in decision making, including such recent cases as those concerning the supervision and discipline of clergy accused of sexual abuse.

Although the conflict eventually became a battle over whether the papal or the imperial power was to be supreme in Christendom, it began as a question of how to properly install clergy, who were chosen for spiritual offices that nonetheless held very material rights and obligations. For the papacy, it was an issue of protecting the Church's clergy from any undue pressure coming from the laity, especially rulers, in purely ecclesiastical matters. For rulers, on the other hand, given the economic and military power of the feudal territories that had become attached to bishoprics and abbeys, it was a question of control over the state itself.

JANSENISM. A Catholic reform movement that originated from the posthumously published commentary on the theology of St. Augustine by Cornelius Jansen (1585–1638), bishop of Ypres in the Spanish Netherlands. Propagated by an able group of French intellectuals (including Antoine Arnauld and Blaise Pascal), eventually centered at Port-Royal, a monastery of Cistercian nuns with houses in Paris and in the countryside outside the French capital, the movement's ideas spread throughout France, the Low Countries, and Italy. While the doctrines of Jansenism are controverted—its adherents claimed that they never espoused the propositions contained in a series of papal condemnations—its spirit was pessimistic in its view of human nature and its practice emphasized asceticism. The movement also opposed the centralization of the Catholic Counter-Reformation as well as the absolutist tendencies of the French monarchy. While censured as early as 1641 by Pope Urban VIII in his bull *In eminenti* and solemnly condemned by Innocent X with the bull *Cum occasione* (1653), Jansenism did not disappear as a coherent movement until the destruction of the abbey of Port-Royal des Champs in 1709 and the death in 1729 of the sympathetic Cardinal de Noailles, archbishop of Paris. Relics of Jansenism persist in the rigorist theological spirit taught in French seminaries and French-influenced seminaries into the twentieth century as well as a schism in the Netherlands that, in 1723, led to the establishment of the Old Catholic Church of Utrecht.

LETTER, APOSTOLIC. A form of papal document drawn up in the name of the pope to address a specific case or to expound on a principle. Traditionally, apostolic letters were categorized as either "chirographs" (*chirographa*) or "simple" (*semplices*), depending on whether the reigning pontiff physically signed them or not. This distinction has been lost in recent years as Pope John Paul II has tended to sign all documents issued by his direct authority. A recent example of an apostolic letter is John Paul II's October 16, 2002, apostolic letter *Rosarium Virginis Mariae*, marking the beginning of the twenty-fifth year of his pontificate by instituting five new mysteries (the "Luminous Mysteries") to the traditional rosary devotion.

MAGISTERIUM. From the Latin *magister* ("teacher"), the term refers to the teaching office and authority of the Church. While it is invested, under different aspects, in both the hierarchy and in theologians, the usage of the term in contemporary times has been generally reserved to the official teaching of the hierarchy.

MALTA, KNIGHTS OF. The Knights of the "Sovereign Military and Hospitaller Order of St. John of Jerusalem, of Rhodes, and of Malta," today commonly known as the "Sovereign Military Order of Malta" or the "Knights of Malta," constitute a lay religious order of the Roman Catholic Church dating back to the Crusades, being founded in 1099. Consequently, the Order of Malta is the fourth oldest religious order of the Church, preceded only by the Augustinians, Benedictines, and Basilians. The origin of the Order was a hospice for pilgrims, founded in Jerusalem by Blessed Gerard about 1070. After the First Crusade took Jerusalem in 1099, many of the crusaders joined Gerard in the constitution of a lay religious hospitaller order to continue his work with the sick and the poor. A large hospital was founded in Jerusalem, and other hospices were later founded along the important pilgrimage routes of Europe and the Middle East. Many of those who joined this new order were from European noble families, often with great power and wealth, who forsook their personal fortunes to serve the poor. The motto of the order has, since 1099, been *"Tuitio Fidei et Obsequium Pauperum"* ("The defense of the faith and service to the poor"). Gradually the first objective took precedence as the Knights took on a military function and became one of the most advanced fighting and naval forces in the world. Their battles defending the island of Rhodes and later the island of

Malta are legendary. However, the second objective was never completely eclipsed and the Order was responsible for a number of medical innovations. Following the Order's loss of Malta to Napoleon in 1798, its work with the sick and the poor once again became its primary purpose, its military function being relegated to assisting the casualties of war. The order was founded as a "lay" order, that is, the members were not clerics or priests, although there have always been priest chaplains. Through the first seven hundred years of its history, most members were lay religious who did take the religious vows of obedience, poverty, and chastity. After the departure from Malta, the composition of the membership changed so that within a few years most members were lay persons without religious vows. Today there remain approximately fifty knights and chaplains in religious vows, the other members of the order being lay associates who are not religious. The religious superior of the order, the grand master, enjoys the style of "Most Eminent Highness" and is the only non-cleric Catholic accorded equality of rank with members of the College of Cardinals. He also enjoys the rank in international protocol of a sovereign prince. The order, interestingly, has maintained through the vicissitudes of history its international recognition and presently has diplomatic relations with ninety countries and an ambassador accredited as its permanent observer at the United Nations General Assembly. The modern-day order employs its unique international character in a wide network of charitable and relief functions, much in accord with its hospitaller origins.

MENDICANTS. From the Latin *mendicare* ("to beg"), the term refers to the members of the religious orders—originally the Franciscans and Dominicans—who were given the privilege of begging alms for their livelihood since they initially worked as itinerant preachers rather than deriving their living from landed property like the older monastic orders.

METROPOLITAN. As a noun or as an adjective, the term refers to the chief local Church in a region (the ecclesiastical "province") and its bishop, the metropolitan archbishop.

MITER. The miter is a kind of folding hat worn in liturgical functions by the pope, cardinals, archbishops, and bishops, as well as certain prelates, such as abbots, who have received the privilege of its use. It consists of two like parts, each stiffened by a lining and rising to a peak. These two pieces are sewn together on the sides and are joined above by a piece of material that can fold together. Two *infulae*, or flaps, trimmed on the ends with fringe hang down from the back.

  Some scholars believe that the miter descended from the headgear of the Jewish high priests, which it resembles, but others dispute this provenance, suggesting a Hellenic origin. In the classic Roman tradition, there are three kinds of mitres: the *mitra preciosa* ("precious miter"), richly embroidered and often set with gemstones and reserved for the most solemn occasions; the *mitra auriphrygiata* ("golden, orphreyed miter"), in gold or white silk and occasionally decorated with orphreys; and the *mitra simplex* ("simple miter"), in pure white, damasked silk for cardinals and linen for other prelates. The recent use by some prelates of colored mitrer, often matching the liturgical vestments of the prelate, is an affectation without historical or liturgical precedence.

MODERNISM. A term for the complex of liberalizing intellectual movements condemned *en bloc* by Pope St. Pius X, who branded it as "the synthesis of all heresies" in his encyclical *Pascendi Dominici gregis* (September 8, 1907) and imposed on the clergy an oath explicitly disavowing its tenets with the decree *Sacrorum antistitum* (September 1, 1910). The doctrines condemned were listed in sixty-five ambiguous propositions contained in a decree of the Supreme Sacred Congregation of the Holy Office, *Lamentabili sane exitu,* published on July 3, 1907, and included "the Church has no right to pass judgment on the assertions of the human sciences" (n. 5) and "the organic constitution of the Church is not immutable; like human society, Christian society is subject to a perpetual evolution" (n. 53). A secret network, the Sodalitium Pianum, was set up to report suspected modernists to ecclesiastical authorities in Rome. The entire crisis, despite the efforts of Pope Benedict XV to bring it to an end, had a dampening effect on Catholic scholarship until the Second Vatican Council.

MONOPHYSITISM. A heresy that arose in a reaction against Nestorianism, which taught that in Christ there is a human *hypostasis,* or person, as well as a Divine, and was condemned by the Council of Ephesus (431), the third Ecumenical Council. In contrast to the Nestorians, the Monophysites held that Jesus Christ had only a divine nature and did not possess a human nature. With the backing of Pope St. Leo I, who addressed his famous *Tome* to Patriarch Flavian of Constantinople on the subject, the fourth Ecumenical Council, Chalcedon, condemned Monophysitism in 451 and articulated the orthodox doctrine that Jesus Christ is one person with two natures, human and divine. The condemnation of the Monophysite doctrine, combined with political factors, led to the schism of the Coptic, Syrian, and Armenian Churches from the Great Church.

MONOTHELITISM. A heresy that was propagated after the Council of Chalcedon (451), the fourth Ecumenical Council, condemned the Monophysites, who had held that Christ was one person with one nature in contrast to the orthodox doctrine of one person with two natures, human and divine. The Monothelites tried to conciliate the Monophysites by holding that while Christ was one person with two natures, he had only one will, a mixture of the divine and human. The orthodox counterargument is that the faculty of willing is an integral part of human nature: Therefore if the Son took on a perfect human nature, he must have a perfect human will alongside his divine will, which is numerically one with that of the Father and the Holy Spirit. It is therefore necessary to acknowledge two wills in Christ. The Monothelite heresy was condemned by the Third Council of Constantinople (680–681).

MOTU PROPRIO. The Latin phrase *motu proprio* ("of his own accord") designates a type of papal document whose provisions were decided on by the pope personally, that is, not on the advice of the cardinals or others but for reasons that he himself deemed sufficient. In form, it is signed personally by the pope and is neither sealed nor countersigned. It usually begins by stating the reasons inducing the pontiff to act, followed by the provision being stipulated. A notable example of a *motu proprio* was the decree of

Paul VI (1963–1978), *Pontificalis Domus*, issued March 28, 1968, whereby the pope formally abolished the "Papal Court" as such, substituting for it a much-reduced "Papal Household."

MOZZETTA. The short shoulder cape, closed in front with a row of silk buttons, worn by prelates. The color of the mozzetta matches the color of the formal choral cassock of the wearer (scarlet for cardinals, violet for archbishops and bishops, etc.), except for the pope, whose mozzetta is, within the bounds noted in Chapter 5, of "imperial" ("papal") red (*purpora*). Traditionally, the garment was a symbol of jurisdiction, but Pope Paul VI changed it to a symbol of dignity.

NESTORIANISM. A heresy named after Patriarch Nestorius of Constantinople, who articulated its doctrine that in Jesus Christ there were two persons, one divine and one human. A consequence of this doctrine was that Mary was the mother of only the human person and not of the divine person and thus should be hailed as *Christokos* ("Christ-bearer") and not as *Theotokos* ("God-bearer" or "Mother of God"). The heresy was condemned by the third Ecumenical Council, the Council of Ephesus, in 431.

NOBLE GUARD. Until abolished by Pope Paul VI in 1969, the Noble Guard constituted an elite corps that appeared mainly at ceremonial functions. To receive a commission as a Noble Guard—all the members of the Guard were commissioned as officers—the candidate had to prove that he was in possession of at least a century of noble ancestry as well as sufficient personal income to maintain himself in Rome in a decorous manner. Before the Lateran Treaty of 1929 settled the "Roman Question," only those candidates coming from the former territories of the Papal States were considered. After the accord, the Guard was opened to members of the nobility from throughout the kingdom of Italy, although a request by King Alfonso XIII of Spain that the privilege be extended to all Catholic noblemen was rebuffed. Members of the Noble Guard entered and left public functions with the Roman pontiff. The Noble Guard was commanded by a "captain commander" with the military rank of lieutenant general, usually chosen from a Roman nobleman of princely rank.

ORDINARY. From the Latin *ordinarius*, meaning "judge," a term designating any person possessing or exercising ordinary jurisdiction, that is, governing authority connected permanently or at least in a stable manner with an office, regardless of whether this connection derives from divine ordinance (as in the case of the pope and bishops) or from positive church law (as in the case of other offices). Ordinary jurisdiction is contrasted with delegated jurisdiction, a temporary grant of authority made by a superior to an inferior who exercises it in the name of his superior. A person may be an ordinary within his own sphere and at the same time have delegated powers for certain acts or the exercise of special authority. The jurisdiction that constitutes an ordinary is real and full jurisdiction in the external forum, comprising the power of legislating, adjudicating, and governing. Jurisdiction in the internal forum, being partial and exercised only in private matters, does not constitute an ordinary. Parish priests, for example, are not ordinaries, although they exercise authority in the internal forum of conscience, since they do not have jurisdiction in the external forum, being incapable of legislating and acting as judges on their own right. The term "ordinary" is commonly used to designate diocesan bishops and those equivalent to them in the hierarchy.

PALATINE GUARD. Until the Palatine Guard was abolished by Pope Paul VI in 1969, it constituted the military corps charged, as the name implied, with protecting the papal palaces. During the Second World War, with the German occupation of Rome, Pope Pius XII increased the strength of the Palatine Guard to over four thousand men for the duration of the conflict and armed them with modern weapons, entrusting them with the protection of the numerous Jews, escaped Allied prisoners of war, and other refugees who had taken shelter on papal properties. Any Catholic who met the requirements of age, height, general physical fitness, and moral character was eligible to enlist in the Palatine Guard.

PALLIUM. A woolen vestment, consisting of a narrow band of unbleached lamb's wool marked with six dark crosses, worn about the neck as a symbol of the pastoral authority of a metropolitan archbishop. Derived from imperial insignia, since the ninth century it has been the exclusive prerogative of the pope to confer it on new metropolitan archbishops. In recent times, the conferral has taken place on the feast of SS. Peter and Paul (June 29), to reiterate the ties with the Roman See. In lieu of the coronation with the tiara, Pope John Paul I and Pope John Paul II have adopted the reception of their pallia as archbishop and metropolitan of the Roman province as the symbol of their investiture in the papal office. Pope Benedict XVI adopted a distinctive historical form of the pallium.

PAPABILE. Plural, *papabili*, a term derived from the Italian colloquialism meaning, literally, "pope-able." The term is never used officially but is popular with the press and other observers to designate credible candidates for the papal office.

PATRIARCH. From the Greek *patriarches* and the Latin *patriarchas*, meaning "father (or chief) of a nation," the term came to be used to designate the chief bishop who had authority over the metropolitan archbishops of an autonomous Church. Originally, the early Church recognized the bishops of Rome, Alexandria, and Antioch as "patriarchs." The bishop of Constantinople, the imperial capital that was thought of as "New Rome," was recognized as a patriarch by the second Ecumenical Council, the Council of Constantinople in 381, and assigned the place of precedence after the pope, the Patriarch of the West, based in "Old Rome." The fourth Ecumenical Council, the Council of Chalcedon in 451, elevated the bishop of Jerusalem to the patriarchal dignity, ranking him as the fifth of the traditional patriarchs. Later, other prelates such as the chief hierarch of the Russian Orthodox Church, who bears the title of "patriarch of Moscow and All the Russias," assumed the patriarchal title, but only the original five have the sanction of the Ecumenical Councils.

In the Catholic Church, in addition to the pope, who is "patriarch of the West," there are six patriarchs of the Eastern Rites who head of ancient Churches, traditionally of apostolic origin, in communion with the See of Rome but retaining their own distinctive liturgical and theological traditions ("rites") as well as great autonomy of government. Many of these "Eastern Catholic Churches" either did not break communion with the Roman Church at the time of the 1054 schism between Rome and Constantinople or restored communion during the seventeenth and eighteenth centuries. The six Eastern Catholic patriarchs are the Coptic Rite patriarch of Alexandria; the Syrian Rite patriarch of Antioch; the Greek Melkite Rite patriarch of Antioch, Alexandria, and Jerusalem; the Maronite Rite patriarch of Antioch; the Chaldean Rite patriarch of Babylon; and the Armenian Rite patriarch of Cilicia. In addition, within the Latin Rite, the archbishops of Jerusalem, Venice, Lisbon, and Goa enjoy the honorary title of "patriarch"—the latter as "patriarch of the East Indies," a title dating back to the Portuguese colonial period—without any authority beyond that enjoyed by other archbishops but with honorary precedence.

PRELATE. The incumbent of a "prelature," that is, of an ecclesiastical office with jurisdiction (bishops, holders of curial offices, etc.). There are also honorary prelates who enjoy the distinctions of ecclesiastical dignity without any corresponding office. Traditionally, all prelates enjoy the use, according to carefully legislated conventions, of the color purple (or violet) and the title of "monsignor" (from the Italian for "my lord").

PRINCE ASSISTANTS AT THE THRONE. Members of the highest Roman nobility who were traditionally allowed to take part in papal ceremonies along with the highest ecclesiastical dignitaries. Because of the rivalries between the leading Roman families, Pope Julius II, in a decision confirmed by Popes Sixtus V and Clement XI, limited the honor to the heads of the princely houses of Orsini and Colonna. Pope Benedict XIII stipulated that only the senior of the two prince assistants would actually serve in ceremonies, standing next to the cardinal deacon at the pope's right, while the other would be his alternate. With the abolition of the papal court by Pope Paul VI, the serving prince assistant only functions during state visits by heads of state and may process behind the pope in liturgical processions, immediately behind the prefect (and adjunct prefect) of the Papal Household and the papal almoner. Presently, the Prince Assistant at the Throne is Prince Don Alessandro Torlonia, prince of Fucino and heir to the Orsini. The alternate Prince Assistant at the Throne is Prince Don Marcantonio Colonna, prince-duke of Paliano, duke of Mariano.

ROMAN QUESTION. The so-called Roman Question arose when the newly unified Italian kingdom absorbed even the last remnant of the temporal sovereignty of the papacy by occupying Rome on September 20, 1870, after the withdrawal of the French garrison. Blessed Pope Pius IX (1846–1878) and his successors refused to recognize the usurpation and consequently refused diplomatic recognition of the Italian government. The government subsequently passed a "Law of Guarantees," offering the papacy immunity within certain precincts and an indemnity for the domain that had been absorbed into the new kingdom, but the act, being unilateral, was spurned and the indemnity never claimed. Pius IX and his successors declared themselves "prisoners of the Vatican," since to go out into territory controlled by the Italian government would be an implicit recognition of its legitimacy. Aggravating the conflict was the Vatican's prohibition against Catholics participating in the new Italian government, a step that left the regime in the overwhelmingly Catholic nation in the hands of a small non-Catholic (if not outright anti-Catholic) minority. The impasse was resolved with the Lateran Treaty of February 11, 1929, signed by Cardinal Pietro Gasparri on behalf of Pope Pius XI (1922–1939) and Benito Mussolini on behalf of King Victor Emmanuel III. The Holy See recognized the Italian kingdom with Rome as its capital, while Italy indemnified the Holy See for the loss of its temporal domains. The Vatican City State was created as an independent, neutral state to guarantee the territorial independence of the pope. Annexed to the treaty was the Lateran Concordat, which settled social and religious questions, declaring Roman Catholicism the state religion of Italy. The concordat was renegotiated in 1985, the agreement being amended to remove Catholicism's status as the official state religion, end mandatory (but not voluntary) religious instruction in public schools, and end the Italian state's payment of the salaries of the clergy.

SCHISM. A term, derived from the Greek *schisma* ("tear"), used to designate a rupture in Church unity in contrast to heresy, which is a break with the Church's faith. Unlike heresy, schism's object is the authority of the Church's hierarchy rather than the belief of the ecclesiastical community. The most famous schisms in ecclesiastical history were the 1054 rupture between the Eastern and Western Churches and the Western Schism of 1378–1417 between the competing popes and antipopes in Western Europe.

SEE. From the Latin *sedes* ("seat"), referring to the bishop's throne as symbol of his authority, the term is used to designate any diocese or territorial church equivalent.

SIMONY. Term derived from the name of Simon Magus, whose unsuccessful attempt to buy miraculous powers from the Apostle Peter is recorded in the Acts of the Apostles (8:18–24) and classically defined as the purchase, sale, or other exchange of "spiritual goods" for temporal or material gain. The "spiritual goods" include not only intangible objects conducive to the supernatural benefit of the soul but also ecclesiastical offices and spiritual authority. Pope St. Gregory I distinguished three types of temporal or material prices that fall under his strict ban against simony: (1) *munus a manu* ("material advantage"), including money, all movable and immovable property, and all rights appreciable in pecuniary value; (2) *munus a lingua* ("oral advantage"), including oral commendation, public expressions of approval, and moral support in high places; and (3) *munus ab obsequio* ("homage"), which consists in subservience and the rendering of undue services. Pope Julius II declared papal elections obtained through simony invalid, an enactment that was, oddly enough, rescinded by Pope St. Pius X in his 1904 apostolic constitution *Vacante Sede Apostolica*.

SUBURBICARIAN SEES. From the Latin term *suburbicarius,* used in Roman law to describe the districts adjacent to "the City [of Rome]," the *Urbs*, the term designates the seven dioceses neighboring the Diocese of Rome: Ostia, Albano, Frascati (historically, Tusculum), Palestrina, Porto-Santa-Rufina, Sabina-Poggio Mirteto, and Velletri-Segni. The titular bishops of these sees constitute, along with any Eastern patriarchs who are also cardinals, the order of bishops within the College of Cardinals. Since the *motu proprio* decree *Edita a Nobis* of Pope St. Pius X (1914), the dean of the College of Cardinals holds the title to the Diocese of Ostia in addition to the see he held previously. Pius X also stipulated, in his apostolic constitution *Apostolicae Romanorum* (1910), that each of the suburbicarian sees would be governed by its own resident bishop as suffragan of the cardinal titular, with the exception of Ostia, which has been subsumed into the pastoral ministry of the Diocese of Rome. Blessed Pope John XXIII, with his *motu proprio* decree *Suburbicariis sedibus* of 1962, ended any jurisdiction of the cardinal bishops over their sees, raising the suffragans to ordinary jurisdiction and leaving the cardinal bishops with only a titular connection to their sees.

SWISS GUARD. The military corps recruited from Switzerland and entrusted with the direct protection of the person of the pope, established by Pope Julius II. The first 150 Swiss Guards took up duty in 1506. During the Sack of Rome (May 6, 1527, a date still commemorated by the Guard with the swearing-in ceremony of new recruits), 147 of the Swiss Guards were slaughtered protecting Pope Clement VII's escape into Castel Sant'Angelo with the surviving 42 members of the Guard. The complement of Swiss Guard, fixed presently at between 100 and 110 members, all dressed in the picturesque blue, yellow, and red uniforms, is commanded by a "captain commandant" with the military rank of colonel. The plumes on the helmets of members of the Guard distinguish their rank: white for the commandant and sergeant-major, purple for the lieutenants, red for the halberdiers, and yellow-and-black for the drummers. The Guard is always present when the person of the pope is and also has custody of the papal antechambers, the papal palaces, and the entrances to the Vatican City. Recruits must be Swiss citizens of the Catholic faith, at least nineteen years of age and no more than thirty years of age, and at least 175 centimeters (five feet, nine inches) tall and in excellent physical health, and they must have letters of recommendation from former members of the Guard, their parish priest, and Swiss government and police officials. The Swiss Guard is the only exception to the ban on mercenary service now enforced by the Federal Government of the Swiss Confederation. Members of the Guard enlist for two-year stints and may not marry until after they reach the rank of corporal, usually during the second tour. Despite their colorful appearance, the members of the Swiss Guard are trained not only in the use of their medieval halberds, lances, and swords but also in martial arts, firearms, and other modern armaments. The oath sworn by a member of the Swiss Guard declares: "I swear to serve faithfully, loyally, and honorably the person of the Sovereign Pontiff, His Holiness Pope [Name], and his legitimate successors canonically elected, as well as to dedicate myself to them with all my strength by sacrificing, should it become necessary, even my own life in their defense. I likewise assume this promise toward the members of the Sacred College during the period of the 'Sede Vacante.' Furthermore, I pledge to the Commandant and to my superiors, respect, obedience, and fidelity. By this I swear. May almighty God and His Saints protect me."

SYLLABUS OF ERRORS. A document attached to Blessed Pope Pius IX's encyclical letter *Quanta cura*, promulgated on December 8, 1864, listing, under ten headings, eighty theses that had been previously condemned. Among the "errors" anathematized were freedom of religion and the proposition that "the Roman Pontiff can, and ought to, reconcile himself, and come to terms with progress, liberalism and modern civilization."

TE DEUM. The ancient hymn of thanksgiving, so called because of the first words of the Latin text: "*Te Deum laudamus* . . . We praise thee, O God." Also known as the "Ambrosian Hymn" from its putative authorship by St. Ambrose of Milan (or St. Ambrose with St. Augustine of Hippo), the hymn dates from at least the fifth century. The hymn exists in one plain-chant melody, albeit distinguished musicologically in two forms (*tonus solemnis* and *iuxta morum romanum*). Over the centuries, numerous composers have written settings for the hymn, including Palestrina, Handel, Mozart, and Berlioz.

TIARA. The papal crown, a costly covering for the head, ornamented with precious stones and pearls, which is shaped like a beehive, has a small cross at its highest point, and is also adorned, since beginning of the fourteenth century, with three royal diadems, on account of which it is sometimes called the "triregnum." The tiara is a non-liturgical ornament, worn only for non-liturgical ceremonies, ceremonial processions, and at solemn acts of jurisdiction such as solemn dogmatic decisions. The pope, like the bishops, wears a miter at pontifical liturgical functions. Since the coronation of Pope Paul VI in 1963, the tiara has not been worn by a pope, although it has not been abolished and still figures in the official heraldry of the pope and the Holy See.

VETO, EXCLUSIONARY. Latin, *ius exclusivae* ("right of exclusion"), the right asserted by the principal Catholic powers—Austria, France, and Spain—to indicate the candidates to the papal office whose election they opposed. Although the "veto" was informally exercised earlier, being communicated by a cardinal entrusted with that mission by his sovereign, it was first formally applied in the conclave of 1644 when King Philip III of Spain formally opposed the candidacy of Cardinal Giulio Sacchetti. The veto was last exercised in the conclave of 1903, when the Austrian emperor Franz Josef II opposed the candidacy of the progressive Cardinal Mariano Rampolla del Tindaro. Pope St. Pius X formally abolished all pretense to a right of veto with his apostolic constitution *Commissum Nobis* in 1904. Whether the *ius exclusivae* was a valid right or not, it is nonetheless true that, during the centuries of its existence, no cardinal against whom the exclusionary veto has been invoked has ever been elected to the papacy.

ZUCCHETTO. The skullcap worn by the pope, cardinals, bishops, and other prelates. The pope wears a white watered-silk zucchetto, a cardinal wears a scarlet (in Italian, *ponzo*) watered-silk zucchetto, a papal nuncio weara a violet (in Italian, *paonazza*) zucchetto, an archbishop or bishop wears a violet (*paonazza*) zucchetto in plain silk, and other prelates may wear a black zucchetto.

LAST WILL AND TESTAMENT OF
BLESSED POPE JOHN XXIII[1]

On the point of presenting myself before the One and Triune Lord who created me, redeemed me, chose me to be his priest and bishop, and covered me with unending graces, I entrust my poor soul to His mercy; I humbly ask pardon for my sins and deficiencies. I offer Him the little good, although petty and imperfect, that with His aid I have succeeded in doing, for His glory, for the service of Holy Church, for the edification of my brethren, begging Him finally to receive me, like a good and kind father, with His Saints into eternal happiness.

I profess once again with all my heart my entire Christian and Catholic faith, my adherence and subjection to the Holy Apostolic and Roman Church, and my complete devotion and obedience to her August Head, the Supreme Pontiff, whom it was my great honor to represent for long years in various regions of the East and West, who at the end chose to have me come to Venice as Cardinal and Patriarch, and whom I have always followed with sincere affection, aside from and above and beyond any dignity conferred upon me. The sense of my own littleness and nothingness has always been my good companion, keeping me humble and calm, and making me employ myself to the best of my ability in a constant exercise of obedience and charity for souls and for the interests of the Kingdom of Jesus, my Lord and my all. To Him be all glory; for me and for my merit. His mercy. *Meritum meum miseratio Domini. Domine, tu omnia nosti: tu scis quia amo Te.*[2] This alone is enough for me.

I ask pardon of those whom I have unwittingly offended, of all to whom I have not been a source of edification. I feel that I have nothing to forgive anyone, for all who have known and dealt with me—including those who have offended me, scorned me, held

---

[1]The text was written in Italian with the exception of the lines the pontiff wrote in Latin.

[2]Latin, "My merit is the mercy of the Lord. Lord thou hast known all things. Thou knowest that I love Thee." The quote is taken from one of the forms suggested for the Rite of the Sacrament of Penance that was traditionally popular in the pre–Vatican II devotional practice.

me in bad esteem (with good reason, for that matter), or have been a source of affliction to me—I regard solely as brothers and benefactors, to whom I am grateful and for whom I pray and always will pray.

Born poor, but of honorable and humble people, I am particularly happy to die poor, having given away, in accordance with the various demands and circumstances of my simple and modest life, for the benefit of the poor and of the Holy Church that had nurtured me, all that came into my hands—which was little enough, as a matter of fact—during the years of my priesthood and episcopacy. Outward appearances of ease and comfort often veiled hidden thorns of distressing poverty and kept me from giving with all the largesse I would have liked. I thank God for this grace of poverty, which I vowed in my youth, poverty of spirit as a priest of the Sacred Heart, and real poverty. This grace has sustained me in never asking for anything, neither positions, nor money, nor favors—never, not for myself, nor for my relatives or friends.

To my beloved family *secundum sanguinem*[3]—from whom, in fact, I have received no material wealth—I can leave only a whole-hearted and most special blessing, inviting it to maintain that fear of God that always made it so dear and beloved to me, simple and modest as it was, without my ever feeling ashamed of it: this is its true title to honor. I have also helped it at times in its more serious needs, as one poor man with the other poor, but without ever removing it from the honorable poverty with which it was content. I pray and always will pray for its prosperity; I am happy to see in its new, vigorous offshoots that strength and loyalty to their fathers' religious tradition which will always be its fortune. My most fervent wish is that none of my relatives and dear ones may miss the joy of that last eternal reunion.

Departing, as I trust, for the roads of Heaven, I salute and thank and bless the many who formed my spiritual family at Bergamo, at Rome, in the East, in France, and at Venice, and who were my fellow townsmen, benefactors, colleagues, students, aides, friends and acquaintances, priests and laymen. Brothers and Sisters, and for whom, by the disposition of Providence, I was, no matter how unworthy, a colleague, a father, or a pastor.

The goodness directed toward my poor person by all whom I met along my path made my life serene. As I face death, I recall each and every one—those who have preceded me in taking the final step, those who will survive me and who will follow me. May they pray for me. I will repay them from Purgatory or from Paradise, where I hope to be received, I repeat it once again, not because of my merits, but because of the mercy of my Lord.

I remember all and will pray for all. But my children of Venice—the last ones the Lord placed around me, as a final consolation and joy for my priestly life—I want especially to mention as a sign of my admiration, my gratitude, my very special tenderness. I embrace them all in spirit, clergy and laity without exception, as I have loved them without exception as members of the same family, the object of one paternal and priestly care and love. *Pater sancte, serva eos in nomine tuo quos dedisti mihi: ut sint unum sicut et nos.*[4]

---

[3]Latin, "by blood."

[4]Latin, "Holy Father, keep them in thy name whom thou hast given me; that they may be one, as we also are" (John 17:11).

At the moment for saying farewell, or better still, *arrivederci*,[5] I once more remind everyone of what counts most in life: blessed Jesus Christ, His Holy Church, His Gospel; and in the Gospel, above all, the *Pater noster*,[6] in the spirit and heart of Jesus and the Gospel, the truth and goodness, the goodness meek and kind, active and patient, victorious and unbowed.

My children, my brethren, *arrivederci*. In the name of the Father, of the Son, of the Holy Spirit. In the name of Jesus, our love; of Mary, our and His most sweet Mother; of St. Joseph, my first and specially loved Protector. In the name of St. Peter, St. John the Baptist, St. Mark, St. Lawrence Justinian, and St. Pius X. Amen.

Venice, June 29, 1954.

(*signed*) Cardinal Angelo Giuseppe Roncalli, Patriarch

★ ★ ★

The following two additions to the text were made in his own handwriting:

The pages that I have written are valid, as an attestation of my absolute will in case of my sudden death.

Venice, September 17, 1957.

Angelo Giuseppe Cardinal Roncalli

★ ★ ★

And they are valid also as a spiritual testament to be added to the provisions of the will joined here under the date of April 30, 1959.

Rome, December 4, 1959.

IOANNES PP. XXIII

Under the dear and trusting auspices of Mary, my heavenly Mother, to whose name is dedicated today's liturgy, and in the eightieth year of my age, I hereby lay down and renew my testament, annulling every other declaration concerning my will made and written prior to this a number of times.

I await and will accept with simplicity and joy the arrival of sister death in all the circumstances with which it will please the Lord to send her to me.

First of all, I ask forgiveness of the Father of mercies *pro innumerabilibus peccatis, offensionibus et negligentiis meis*,[7] as I have so often said and repeated in offering my daily Sacrifice.

---

[5] The Italian salute equivalent to "good-bye"; the expression literally means "until we see each other again."

[6] Latin, "Our Father," referring to the Lord's Prayer.

[7] Latin, "for my countless sins, offenses, and omissions." The text is taken from the Roman Missal.

For this first grace of Jesus's pardon for all my faults, and of my soul's introduction into blessed and eternal Paradise, I recommend myself to the prayers of all who have followed me and known me during the whole of my life as priest, bishop, and most humble and unworthy Servant of the Servants of the Lord.

Next, my heart leaps with joy to make a fervent, whole-hearted renewal of my profession of Catholic, apostolic, and Roman faith. Among the various forms and symbols with which the faith is usually expressed, I prefer the priestly and pontifical *Credo* of the Mass because of its more vast, more sonorous elevation as in union with the universal Church of every rite, of every age, of every region—from the *"Credo in unum Deum, patrem omnipotentem"*[8] to the *"et vitam venturi saeculi."*[9]

Castel Gandolfo, September 12, 1961.

IOANNES PP. XXIII

---

[8]Latin, "I believe in one God, the Father almighty."
[9]Latin, "and in the life of the age to come."

Appendix 7

LAST WILL AND TESTAMENT OF POPE PAUL VI[1]

In nómine Patris, et Fílii, et Spíritus Sancti. Amen.[2]

1. I fix my gaze on the mystery of death, and on what follows it, in the light of Christ that alone can brighten it, and for this reason with simple and serene trust. I recognize the truth, which for me has always reflected on present life regarding this mystery, and I bless the victor over death for having escaped its shadows and unveiled the light.

Thus before death, in total and definitive separation from the present life, I feel the duty to celebrate the gift, the good fortune, the beauty, the destiny of this very fleeting existence. Lord, I thank you that you have called me to life, and still more that, by making me a Christian, you have regenerated and destined me for the fullness of life.

Likewise I feel the duty to thank and to bless those who were mediators for me of the gifts of life bestowed on me by you, O Lord: those who brought me to life (Oh! May my most worthy parents be blessed!), those who educated me, wished me well, were kind to me, helped me and surrounded me with good example, attention, affection, trust, kindness, courtesy, friendship, faithfulness, respect. I am thinking with thanks about the natural and spiritual relationships that have given origin, aid, comfort and significance to my humble existence. How many gifts, how many beautiful and noble things, how much hope have I received in this world!

Now that the day is setting, and all is finishing and this stupendous, dramatic temporal and earthly scene is disappearing, how again can I thank you, O Lord, for the gift of faith and of grace, higher than the gift of natural life, in which at the end my being takes refuge?

How can I worthily celebrate your kindness, O Lord, for having been included just as I entered into this world, in the ineffable world of the Catholic Church? For having been called and initiated into the priesthood of Christ? For having the joy and mission of

---

[1]The text was written in Italian with the exception of the lines the pontiff wrote in Latin.

[2]Latin, "In the name of the Father and of the Son and of the Holy Spirit. Amen."

serving souls, brothers, youth, the poor, the people of God, and for having the unmerited honor of being a minister of the holy Church, in Rome especially, next to the Pope, then in Milan as archbishop on a throne too exalted for me, the most venerable throne of Sts. Ambrose and Charles, and finally on that supreme, most formidable and most holy throne of St. Peter? *In aeternum Domini misericordias cantabo.*[3]

May all those whom I have met on my earthly pilgrimage be blessed and saluted: those who were my collaborators, counselors, and friends—and they were many, such good people, generous and dear! Blessed be those who welcomed my ministry and were my sons and brothers in Our Lord!

To you, Ludovico and Francesco, brothers in blood and spirit, and to all you dear ones of my home, who never asked anything of me, and never had from me any earthly favor, and who always gave me an example of human and Christian virtues, you who understood me with so much discretion and cordiality and who above all helped me to seek in the present life the life of the future—my peace and my benediction be with you.

The mind turns back and its horizons broaden around me, and I know well that this farewell would not be a happy one, were I not to remember to ask pardon of those I've offended, failed to serve or failed to love enough, and to ask pardon of anyone who desires it of me. May the Lord's peace be with you.

I feel that the Church surrounds me. O holy Church, one, catholic and apostolic, receive my supreme act of love with a salute and blessing.

To you, Rome, diocese of St. Peter and of the vicar of Christ, most beloved to this last servant of the servants of God, I give my most paternal and full blessing so that you, city of the world, will be always mindful of your mysterious vocation and with human virtue and Christian faith, know how to respond to your spiritual and universal mission, however long will be the world's history.

And to all of you venerated brothers in the episcopate, my cordial and reverent greeting. I am with you in the one faith, in service together to the Gospel, for the building up of the Church of Christ and for the salvation of all humanity.

To all priests, to men and women religious, to students in our seminaries, to militant and faithful Catholics, to youth, to the suffering, the poor, seekers of the truth and justice, to all, the benediction of the Pope who is dying.

And thus, with special reverence and recognition for the Lord Cardinals and for all the Roman Curia: Before you who surrounded me most closely, I profess solemnly our faith, I declare our hope, I celebrate our charity which does not die by accepting humbly from divine will the death which is my destiny, invoking the great mercy of the Lord, imploring the clement intercession of most holy Mary, of the angels and saints, and recommending my soul to the remembrance of the good.

2. I name the Holy See my universal heir: I owe it duty, gratitude, love. Except for the dispositions otherwise indicated in the following paragraphs.

---

[3]Latin, "I will sing out the Lord's mercies forever" (Psalm 88:2).

3. My private secretary[4] is to be executor of my testament. He will want to take counsel with the Secretariat of State and conform to the juridical norms in force and to good Church custom.

4. Concerning the things of this world: I have decided to die poor and thus simplify any question in this regard.

As for possessions and properties that I still have from my family, my brothers Ludovico and Francesco are to dispose of them freely; I beg of them some remembrance for my soul and for those of our dead. May they bestow some alms on needy persons and good causes. May they keep for themselves, and give to those who merit and desire it, some memento from among the possessions, religious objects or books belonging to me.

My notes, notebooks, and correspondence, as well as my personal writings should be destroyed.

Concerning the other things which can be considered my own: My personal secretary is to dispose of them, as executor, keeping some mementos for himself and giving some small object as a memory to my best friends. I would like manuscripts and notes written in my own hand to be destroyed; and may the correspondence received of a spiritual and confidential nature, which was not intended to be shown to others, be burnt.

If the executor cannot see to this, the Secretary of State should take charge.

5. I strongly urge my possessions be disposed of for proper remembrances and as generous contributions, as much as possible.

About the funeral: May it be pious and simple. (The catafalque now in use for pontifical funeral rites should be replaced by a humble and decorous contrivance.)

The tomb: I would like to be in real earth, with a humble marker indicating the place and asking for Christian mercy. No monument for me.

6. And concerning what counts most, my departure from this world's scene and my journey to meet the judgment and mercy of God: I would have so many, many things to say.

On the state of the Church: May she listen to a few of our words, uttered with seriousness and love for her.

Concerning the Council: May it be brought to a good climax and be executed faithfully. Regarding ecumenism: May the work of bringing together separated brothers proceed with much understanding, patience and great love, but without defecting from true Catholic doctrine.

Concerning the world: Do not think the Church can help it by assuming its thoughts, customs, tastes, but rather by studying it, loving it, serving it.

I close my eyes upon this sad, dramatic and magnificent earth calling once again still on divine kindness. I again bless everyone. Especially Rome, Milan, Brescia. A special blessing and greeting to the Holy Land, the land of Jesus, where I was a pilgrim of faith and peace.

And to the Church, to the most beloved Catholic Church, and to the whole of humanity, my apostolic blessing.

---

[4]Paul VI's private secretary was Monsignor Pasquale Macchi, later archbishop-prelate of the Shrine of the Holy House of Loreto.

Then: *In manus tua, Domine, commendo spiritum meum.*[5]

Given in Rome, near St. Peter, June 30, 1965, third year of our pontificate.

PAULUS PP. VII

★ ★ ★

The following two additions to the text were made in his own handwriting:

Complementary Note to My Testament

In manus tua, Domine, commendo spiritum meum.[6] *Magnificat anima mea Dominum.*[7] *Maria! Credo. Spero. Amo. In pax.*[8]

I thank those who have done good to me. I ask pardon of those to whom I have not done good.

I give peace to all in the Lord.

I greet my dearest brother Ludovico and all my relatives and friends, and those who have welcomed my ministry.

To all collaborators, thank you. Especially to the Secretariat of State.

I bless Brescia, Milan, Rome, and the whole Church with special charity. *Quam dilecta tabernacula tua, Domine!*[9]

May dear Don Pasquale Macchi, my private secretary, see to providing for some remembrances and benefices and giving some memento among my books and objects to dear ones.

I do not want a special tomb.

Some prayers that God may be merciful.

In te, Domine, speravi.[10] Amen, alleluia.

To all my blessing, in the name of the Lord.

Castel Gandolfo, September 16, 1972, 7:30 a.m.

PAULUS PP. VI

★ ★ ★

Addition to the Dispositions of My Testament

I want my funeral to be very simple and I do not want any special monument. Some remembrances (alms and prayers).

July 14, 1973.

PAULUS PP. VI

---

[5]Latin, "Into your hands, O Lord, I commend my spirit" (Luke 23:46 paraphrase).

[6]Latin, "Into your hands, O Lord, I commend my spirit" (Luke 23:46 paraphrase).

[7]Latin, "My soul magnifies the Lord" (Luke 1:46).

[8]Latin, "I believe. I hope. I love. In peace."

[9]Latin, "How lovely is your dwelling place, O Lord!" (Psalm 83:2).

[10]Latin, "In you, O Lord, have I placed my hope" (Psalm 70:1 etc.).

Appendix 8

LAST WILL AND TESTAMENT OF POPE JOHN PAUL II[1]

Totus tuus ero sum.[2]
In the Name of the Most Holy Trinity. Amen.

"Watch, therefore, for you do not know on what day your Lord is coming" (cf. Matthew 24: 42)—these words remind me of the last call that will come at whatever time the Lord desires. I want to follow Him and I want all that is part of my earthly life to prepare me for this moment. I do not know when it will come but I place this moment, like all other things, in the hands of the Mother of my Master: *Totus Tuus*. In these same maternal hands I leave everything and everyone to whom my life and my vocation brought me into contact with. In these hands I leave, above all, the Church, as well as my Nation and all mankind. I thank everyone. I ask forgiveness of everyone. I also ask for prayers, so that the Mercy of God may prove greater than my own weakness and unworthiness.

During the spiritual exercises I reread the testament of the Holy Father Paul VI. This reading led me to write this testament.

I leave no possessions that require disposal. With regard to the things I use every day, I ask that they be distributed as shall be deemed opportune. My personal notes should be burned. I ask that Father Stanislaw[3] see to this, and I thank him for his collaboration and

---

[1] The text was written in Polish with the exception of the lines the pontiff wrote in Latin. The English translation given here is from those excerpts of the Italian translation released by the Secretariat of State and officially communicated to the Holy See's diplomatic missions in *Bollettino per le Rappresentanze Pontificie* 6, no. 97 (April 7, 2005): 2-5.

[2] Latin, "I am all yours" (a variant on the pope's episcopal motto, *Totus Tuus*).

[3] Archbishop Stanislaw Dziwisz, the pontiff's longtime personal secretary and now Archbishop of Cracow. Dziwisz subsequently disobeyed this directive—the "first time he ever disobeyed the pope" according to the Polish prelate's admirers—and declared two months after John Paul's death that "nothing has been burnt, nothing is fit for burning, everything should be preserved and kept for history for future generations—every single sentence." However, Dziwisz did not elaborate on the modality of access to the papers.

service, so comprehensive and prolonged over the years. On the other hand, I leave all my other thanks in my heart, before God Himself, because it is difficult to express them.

With regard to my funeral, I repeat the instructions that were given by the Holy Father Paul VI. [*Notation by the Secretariat of State:* Here a note in the margin reads: "Burial in the ground and not in a sarcophagus, March 13, 1992."]

Apud Dominum misericordia et copiosa apud Eum redemptio.[4]

IOANNES PAULUS PP. II

Rome, March 6, 1979
[*Notation by the Secretariat of State:* Here a note in the margin reads: "After my death, I ask for Holy Masses and prayers, March 5, 1990."]

* * *

Undated Page

I express the most profound trust that, in spite of all my weakness, the Lord will grant me every grace necessary to face, in accordance with His will, any task, test or suffering that He sees fit to ask of His servant during the course of life. I am also confident that He will never permit me through some attitude I may have—words, deeds or omissions—fail in my duties to this holy Petrine See.

* * *

February 24-March 1, 1980

Also during these spiritual exercises I reflected on the truth of the Priesthood of Christ in the perspective of that Passing for each one of us which is the moment of death. The Resurrection of Christ is an eloquent [*Notation by the Secretariat of State:* Here a note added above reads: "decisive"] sign of the departure from this world for rebirth in the other, future world.

I therefore read the draft of my testament last year, also written during the spiritual exercises—I have compared it with the testament of my great Predecessor and Father, Paul VI, with his sublime witness on the death of a Christian and a Pope—and I reminded myself of the matters mentioned in the draft of March 6, 1979, prepared by me (in a rather provisional manner).

Today, I would like to add only this: that everyone keep in mind the prospect of death. And be ready to go before the Lord and Judge—who is, at the same time, Redeemer and Father. So I keep this continuously in my mind, entrusting that decisive moment to the Mother of Christ and of the Church—to the Mother of my hope.

The times we are living in are indescribably difficult and troubling. The Church's journey, characteristic of these times, has also become difficult and stressful—for Faithful as well as for the Pastors. In some Countries (as, for example, those I read about

---

[4] Latin, "With the Lord there is mercy, and with Him is plenteous redemption" (Psalm 129/130:7).

during the spiritual exercises), the Church finds herself in a period of persecution that is not less evil than those of her early centuries; indeed it is worse, because of the degree of ruthlessness and hatred. *Sanguis martyrum—semen christianorum.*[5] And in addition to this, so many innocent people disappear, even in this country in which we live. . . .

I desire once more to entrust myself entirely to the Lord's grace. He Himself will decide when and how I am to end my earthly life and my pastoral ministry. In life and in death [I am] *Totus Tuus* through the Immaculate [Mary]. I hope, in already accepting my death now, that Christ will give me the grace I need for the final journey, that is, [my] Passover. I also hope that He will make it useful to the important cause I seek to serve: the salvation of mankind, the preservation of the human family and, within in it, all the nations and peoples (among which, I refer particularly to my earthly Homeland), useful for the persons that He has specially entrusted to me, for the matter of the Church, and for the glory of God Himself.

I do not wish to add anything to what I wrote a year ago—except to express this readiness and, at the same time, this trust, which these spiritual exercises have once again inspired in me.

IOANNES PAULUS PP. II

★ ★ ★

March 5, 1982

Totus Tuus ego sum.[6]

In the course of this year's spiritual exercises I read (several times) the text of my testament of March 6, 1979. Although I still consider it as provisional (not definitive), I am leaving it in its present form. I am not (for now) changing anything, nor am I adding anything, with regard to the arrangements contained therein.

The attempt on my life on May 13, 1981, in some ways has confirmed the exactness of the words I wrote during the spiritual exercises in 1980 (February 24-March 1).

All the more profoundly I feel that I am totally in the Hands of God's—and I remain constantly at the disposition of my Lord, entrusting myself to Him through His Immaculate Mother *(Totus Tuus*[7]*)*.

IOANNES PAULUS PP. II

★ ★ ★

---

[5] Latin, "the blood of the martyrs [is] the seed of Christians," a line from the writings of the influential Christian writer Tertullian (ca. 150-ca. 230).

[6] Latin, "I am all yours" (a variant on the pope's episcopal motto, *Totus Tuus*).

[7] Latin, "all yours."

March 5, 1982

With respect to the last sentence of my testament of March 6, 1979 ("Let the College of Cardinals and my Compatriots decide on the place—that is, the place of the funeral"[8])—I clarify that I have in mind: the Metropolitan of Cracow or the General Council of the Polish Episcopate—I ask the College of Cardinals, in the meantime, to satisfy to the extent possible requests of those listed above.

* * *

March 1, 1985 (during the spiritual exercises)

Once again—with regard to the expression "the College of Cardinals and my Compatriots": the "College of Cardinals" is not obliged to consult "my Compatriots" on this question; it may, however, do so, if for some reason it should deem it appropriate.

JPII

* * *

The spiritual exercises in the Jubilee Year 2000
(March 12-18)

For the testament

1. When, on October 16, 1978, the Conclave of Cardinals chose John Paul II, the Primate of Poland, Cardinal Stefan Wyszyński, told me: "*The task of the new Pope* will be *to lead the Church into the Third Millennium.*" I do not know if I am repeating the sentence exactly as he said it, but this was at least the sense of what I heard him say at the time. These words were spoken by the Man who went down in history as the Primate of the Millennium: a great Primate. I was a witness of his mission, his total confidence. Of his struggles and of his triumph. "Victory, when it comes, will be a victory through Mary"—the Primate of the Millennium was fond of repeating these words of his Predecessor, Cardinal August Hlond.

In this manner I was in some way prepared for the task that that day, October 16, 1978, presented me with. In the moment on which I write these words, *the Great Jubilee of the Year 2000* is already a reality that is taking place. On the night of December 24, 1999, the symbolic Great Jubilee Door in the Basilica of Saint Peter was opened, and subsequently that of Saint John Lateran, then that of Saint Mary Major (on New Year's

---

[8] The sentence quoted by the pope does not appear in the text of his will published by the Holy See after his death. This omission, along with the fact that copies of the original papers were never made available, has led to some speculation that the documents may have been edited by Vatican officials to ensure that John Paul II was buried in Rome. If such was the case, it would not be the first time in recent history that the Roman Curia has tampered with the dispositions of its just deceased master. During the process leading up to the beatification of Pope John XXIII in 2000, for example, it was revealed that the pope's request to buried in the Lateran Basilica was suppressed.

Day), and on January 19, the Door of the Basilica of Saint Paul "Outside-the-Walls." This last event, because of its ecumenical character, has remained engraved in memory in a particular way.

2. As the Jubilee Year 2000 continues, day by day the twentieth century closes behind us and the twenty-first century opens. In accordance with the designs of Providence, I have been granted to live in the difficult century that is passing, and now in the year in which I have reach my eighties ("*octogesima adveniens*"[9]), I must ask myself *whether the time has come to say with Simeon of the Bible, "Nunc dimittis."*[10]

On May 13, 1981, the day of the attack on the Pope during the General Audience in Saint Peter's Square, Divine Providence miraculously saved me from death. He who is the one Lord of life and death Himself extended this life of mine, and, in a certain way, gave it to me anew. Ever since that moment it has belonged even more to Him. I hope He will help me recognize how long I must continue this service to which he called me on October 16, 1978. I ask him to deign to call me to Himself whenever he wishes. "In life and in death we belong to the Lord... we are the Lord's" (cf. Romans 14:8). I also hope that as long as I am granted to carry out the Petrine service in the Church, the Mercy of God will grant me the necessary strength for this service.

3. As I do every year during the spiritual exercises, I have read my testament of March 6, 1979. I continue to maintain the dispositions contained therein. What was added then and during the subsequent spiritual retreats reflects the difficult and tense general situation that marked the 1980s. After autumn of the year 1989, this situation changed. The final decade of the last century was free of the previous tensions; this does not mean that it did not bring new problems and difficulties. In a special way *may Divine Providence be praised for this*, that the period known as the "Cold War" ended *without violent nuclear conflict*, the danger of which weighed heavily on the world in the preceding period.

4. As I stand on the threshold of the Third Millennium "*in medio Ecclesiae,*"[11] I would like once again to express my *gratitude to the Holy Spirit* for *the great gift of the Second Vatican Council,* to which, together with the whole Church—and especially with the whole Episcopate—I feel indebted. I am convinced that it will long be granted to the new generations to draw from the treasures that this 20th century Council has lavished upon us. As a bishop who took part in the Conciliar event from the first to the last day, I

---

[9] Latin, "coming eightieth." John Paul is clearly making a pun, referring also to the title of a well-known apostolic letter of Pope Paul VI, issued under that title in 1971.

[10] Latin, "now let" (Luke 2:29). The allusion is to the full verse, *Nunc dimittis servum tuum Domine secundum verbum tuum in pace* ("Lord, now let your servant depart in peace, according to your word"), the opening line of the prayer of the prophet Simeon having fulfilled his vocation of seeing arrival of the messiah. In the Roman liturgy, the canticle is also the last biblical passage of the last divine office of the day, Compline.

[11] Latin, "in the midst of the assembly [the Church]" (Psalm 91:2). The allusion is to the full verse, *In medio Ecclesiae aperuit os eius: et implevit eum Dominus spiritu sapientiae, et intellectus: stolam gloriae induit eum* ("In the midst of the Church the Lord opened his mouth: and filled him with the spirit of wisdom and understanding: He clothed him with a robe of glory").

desire to entrust this great patrimony to all who are and will be called in the future to put it into practice. For my part, I thank the eternal Pastor who has enabled me to serve this very great cause in the course of all the years of my Pontificate.

"*In medio Ecclesiae*" . . . from the very first years of my service as a Bishop—precisely thanks to the Council—I was granted to *experience the fraternal communion of the Episcopate*. As a priest of the Archdiocese of Cracow, I was granted to experience the fraternal communion of the presbyterate—the Council opened a new dimension of this experience.

5. *How many people* I should list here! The Lord God has probably called the majority of them to Himself—as for those who are still here, may the words of this testament recall them, everyone and everywhere, wherever they may happen to be.

In the course of the more than twenty years since I have been carrying out the Petrine service "*in medio Ecclesiae,*" *I have experienced the benevolent and most especially the fruitful collaboration of so many* Cardinals, Archbishops, and Bishops, so many priests and so many consecrated persons—Brothers and Sisters—finally, of a great many lay people, in the Curial ambiance, in the Vicariate of the Diocese of Rome, as well as outside these settings.

How could I not embrace with grateful memories all the Episcopal Conferences in the world, which I met in the course of their visits *ad limina Apostolorum!*[12] Besides, how could I fail to remember all the Christian Brethren—non-Catholics! And the Rabbi of Rome as well as all the numerous representatives of non-Christian religions! And how many representatives of the worlds of culture, science, politics, and means of social communication!

6. As the end of my earthly life draws close, I think back to its beginning, to my Parents, to my Brother, and to my Sister (whom I never knew, for she died before my birth), to the Parish of Wadowice where I was baptized, to that city of my love, to my peers, my companions of both sexes in elementary school, in high school, at university, until the time of the Occupation when I worked as a laborer, and, later, to the Parish of Niegowiæ, to that of Saint Florian's Parish in Cracow, to the pastoral work of academics, to the setting . . . to all the settings . . . to Cracow and to Rome . . . to the persons who were especially entrusted to me by the Lord.

I want to say just one thing to them all: "May God reward you!"

In manus Tuas, Domine, commendo spiritum meum.[13]

March 17, 2000 A.D.

---

[12] Latin, "to the threshold of the Apostles." See "ad limina visit" in Appendix 5.

[13] Latin, "Into your hands, O Lord, I commend my spirit" (Luke 23:46, paraphrase).

NOTES

Preface to the Original Edition

1. Italian term meaning "substitute," used in the Roman Curia to designate the second-ranking official of a dicastery, or office, who enjoys delegated full power to act for the titular of the office in the exercise of the authority of the office. While in the past there have been many *sostituti*, each attached to a different dicastery, presently the only official with the title is the substitute of the Secretariat of State. Exceptionally, Giovanni Battista Montini, who was *sostituto* of the Secretariat of State from 1937 until his appointment as archbishop of Milan in 1954, held the title for some ten years (1944–1954) despite the vacancy in the office of the secretary of state following the death of Cardinal Luigi Maglione on August 22, 1944. In effect, he was the "substitute" for a nonexistent incumbent.
2. Charles de Gaulle, *Mémoires de guerre. L'Unité 1942–1944* (Paris: Plon, 1956), 233–234.
3. Paul Gray, "Empire of the Spirit," *Time* 144/20 (December 26, 1994): 20.
4. There has been some confusion, even among official sources at the Vatican, as to the number of popes in the line of succession accepted as legitimate. The number most commonly cited, 264, is based on counting the number of *pontificates*— including that of the Prince of the Apostles—chronicled in the official yearbook of the Holy See, the *Annuario Pontificio*. Consequently, this number is taken without closer scrutiny to represent the number of popes and repeated on numerous occasions: Even the programs handed out at the twenty-fifth anniversary of Pope John Paul II's election to the papacy refer to him as the "263rd successor to St. Peter." However, while the pope's pontificate is the 263rd since that of Simon Peter, he is *not* the 264th man to hold the office of bishop of Rome but the 262nd. In the eleventh century, Benedict IX held the papal office on three separate occasions: August/September 1032 to September 1044; March 10, 1045, to May 1, 1045; and October 1047 to July 1048. Consequently, while there have been 263 *pontificates* since the time of Peter, there have only been 261 *popes*.

5. Latin term meaning "vacant see" or "vacant throne"; it refers to the interregnum between the death of one pope and the election of his successor. During the *sede vacante*, the hierarchy of the Catholic Church is officially "on hold," awaiting the selection of its next pontiff.

Introduction

1. The dean is the *primus inter pares*, the first among equals, of the members of the College of Cardinals. Historically, the office fell to the senior-ranked cardinal among the six cardinal bishops who hold title to the suburbicarian sees, dioceses immediately surrounding the Roman diocese and historically closely linked with it. More recently, the dean has been elected by the cardinal bishops, subject to confirmation by the reigning pope. The dean presides over meetings of the cardinals and normally over the funeral rites for the deceased pope.
2. Later, in keeping with ancient custom, the cypress casket was sealed inside a zinc coffin, which was placed inside another wooden coffin.
3. This famous anecdote is vouchsafed for by no less than Winston Churchill; see Winston Churchill, *The Second World War*, vol. 1, *The Gathering Storm* (Boston: Houghton Mifflin, 1948), 134–135.
4. The pope's personal literary production since his election to the papacy included *Crossing the Threshold of Hope*, edited by Vittorio Messori (New York: Random House, 1994); *Gift and Mystery: On the Fiftieth Anniversary of My Priestly Ordination* (New York: Doubleday, 1997); *Rise, Let Us Be on Our Way* (New York: Warner Books, 2004); and *Memory and Identity: Conversations at the Dawn of a Millennium* (New York: Rizzoli, 2005).
5. Papal documents are usually referred to by the first two or three words of their official Latin text. Hence, the papal chancery has always been careful to avoid using the same words to begin different documents—an amazing feat given the number of documents produced over the centuries. There are two modern exceptions to this rule in that Pope Pius XI (1922–1939) issued his encyclical letters critiquing Italian Fascism and German Nazism in those respective languages in order that there would be no mistaking his meaning. Hence those documents, published in 1931 and 1937, respectively, were entitled *Non abbiamo bisogno* and *Mit brennender Sorge*.
6. In addition, the pope confirmed the centuries-old but unofficial *cultus* of seven other *beati*, whom popular devotion had venerated.
7. Ultimately, two of the eligible electors, Cardinal Jaime Lachica Sin, archbishop emeritus of Manila, and Cardinal Adolfo Suarez Rivera, archbishop emeritus of Monterrey, did not participate in the conclave due to health reasons.
8. The countries with which the Holy See forged or reestablished full diplomatic relations during the pontificate of John Paul II and the respective years of the accords are Grenada, Barbados, Greece, Jamaica, Bahamas, and Mali (1979); Zimbabwe

(1980); Togo, Singapore, Dominica, and Equatorial Guinea (1981); Great Britain, Monaco, Denmark, Norway, and Sweden (1982); Belize and Nepal (1983); the United States of America, the Solomon Islands, the Seychelles, Santa Lucia, and São Tomé and Principe (1984); Liechtenstein (1985); San Marino, Guinea, Guinea-Bissau, and Antigua and Barbuda (1986); Chad (1988); Poland (1989); Hungary, Saint Vincent and Grenadine, Romania, and Bulgaria (1990); Albania, Lithuania, Latvia, and Estonia (1991); Croatia, Slovenia, Ukraine, Swaziland, Mongolia, Armenia, Azerbaijan, Georgia, Moldava, Nauru, Bosnia-Herzegovina, Kyrghyzstan, Mexico, Kazakhstan, Uzbekistan, and Byelorussia (1992); Czech Republic, Slovakia, and the Marshall Islands (1993); Micronesia, Surinam, Jordan, South Africa, Cambodia, Samoa, Israel, Vanuatu, Tonga, and the former Yugoslav Republic of Macedonia (1994); Kiribati, Andorra, Eritrea, Namibia, and Mozambique (1995); Tadjikistan, Turkemistan, and Sierra Leone (1996); Libya, Guyana, and Angola (1997); Yemen and Palau (1998); the Cook Islands and Saints Kitts and Nevis (1999); Bahrain and Djibouti (2000); and East Timor and Qatar (2002). In addition, the diplomatic legation of the Sovereign Military Order of Malta was raised to an embassy in 1983.

9. For a complete list, see Chapter 4, note 37.

10. For a discussion of the impact of John Paul II's travels, see Margaret B. Melady, *The Rhetoric of John Paul II: The Pastoral Visit as the New Vocabulary of the Sacred* (Westport, Connecticut/London: Praeger Publishers, 1999). The author, formerly president of the American University of Rome, is the wife of Thomas Patrick Melady, United States ambassador to the Holy See from 1989 to 1993.

11. Albania, Angola, Argentina, Armenia, Australia, Austria, Azerbaijan, the Bahamas, Bangladesh, Belgium, Belize, Benin, Bolivia, Bosnia-Herzegovina, Botswana, Brazil, Bulgaria, Burkina Faso, Burundi, Cameroon, Canada, Capo Verde, the Central African Republic, Chad, Chile, Colombia, the Democratic Republic of Congo (Zaire), Congo (Brazzaville), Costa Rica, Côte d'Ivoire, Croatia, Cuba, Curaçao, the Czech Republic, Denmark, Dominican Republic, East Timor, Ecuador, Egypt, El Salvador, Equatorial Guinea, Estonia, Fiji, Finland, France, Gabon, The Gambia, Georgia, Germany, Ghana, Great Britain, Greece, Guam, Guatemala, Guinea, Guinea-Bissau, Haiti, Honduras, Hungary, Iceland, India, Indonesia, Ireland, Israel, Jamaica, Japan, Jerusalem, Jordan, Kazakhstan, Kenya, Latvia, Lebanon, Lesotho, Liechtenstein, Lithuania, Madagascar, Malawi, Mali, Malta, Mauritius, Mexico, Morocco, Mozambique, New Zealand, Nicaragua, Nigeria, Norway, Pakistan, Panama, Papua New Guinea, Paraguay, Peru, the Philippines, Poland, Portugal, Puerto Rico, Réunion, Romania, Rwanda, San Marino, Santa Lucia, São Tomé and Principe, Senegal, the Seychelles, Singapore, Slovakia, Slovenia, Solomon Islands, South Africa, South Korea, Spain, Sri Lanka, Sudan, Swaziland, Sweden, Switzerland, Syria, Tanzania, Thailand, Togo, Trinidad and Tabago, Tunisia, Turkey, Ukraine, Uruguay, Uganda, the United States of America, Venezuela, West Bank (Palestinian Authority Territories), Zambia, and Zimbabwe.

12. John Paul II, *Crossing the Threshold of Hope,* 11.

13. Peter Steinfels, *A People Adrift: The Crisis of the Roman Catholic Church in America* (New York: Simon & Schuster, 2003), 1.

14. The communication was contained in a special addendum to the daily *Bollettino per le Rappresentanze Pontificie* ("Bulletin for the Pontifical Representations") on October 12, 2003.

15. Uwe Siemon-Netto, "The Next Pope," *National Interest* 74 (Winter 2003–2004): 109.

16. Churchill, *The Second World War*, vol. 1, *The Gathering Storm*, 135.

Chapter One

1. Alexander VII was born Fabio Chigi, a scion of the princely Chigi family, on February 13, 1599, in Siena. Popes are often referred to in historical and other narratives, but never in official documents, by their surnames. To this day, for example, Italians still refer to "Papa Roncalli" when speaking or writing about Blessed Pope John XXIII (1958–1963), who was born Angelo Giuseppe Roncalli.

2. The conventional everyday designation of the Roman pontiff as the "pope" (*il Papa* in Italian) is derived from the ecclesiastical Latin title *papa* that is itself a derivation of the Greek *pappas*, or "father." At one time, the title was used with great latitude. In the Christian East, it has often been used to designate any priest, although the Coptic Orthodox Church reserves it for its head, who is entitled the "Patriarch of Alexandria and Pope of the See of St. Mark." In the West, however, at least by the time of the ecclesiastical controversialist Tertullian in the second century, the use of the title "pope" was limited to bishops. By the fifth century, its use in the West was almost exclusively the prerogative of the bishop of Rome, who was referred to as *"Summus Pontifex et Universalis Papa"* ("Supreme Pontiff and Universal Pope").

3. "Lay investiture" refers to the early medieval practice whereby bishops and abbots were appointed to and installed ("invested") in their offices by the lay ruler, who presented the prelate with the ring and crosier (or pastoral staff) that were the symbols of his ecclesiastical office after the churchman had paid homage to the ruler as feudal overlord. See Appendix 5 for a more detailed explanation of this controversy, whose memory continues to influence, however subconsciously, the Church's institutional response to certain challenges.

4. It should be recalled that for most of the Church's history, the men elected to the papacy were not bishops, being only priests or deacons, if not laymen. In fact, the early Church censured the practice of a bishop transferring to another see, as evidenced by the posthumous controversy over the validity of the election of Formosus, bishop of Porto, as Pope Formosus (891–896), the first case of someone already a bishop being elevated to the papacy. Even after it became accepted that bishops could be transferred, many popes were elected from cardinals who, while priests or deacons, had not yet been consecrated bishops. The last pope elected who was not a bishop was Gregory XVI (1831–1846). A Benedictine monk, he was the abbot of San Gregorio al Monte Celio, having twice turned down the

offer of residential bishoprics. Pope Leo XII (1823–1829) had created him a cardinal and appointed him prefect of the Sacred Congregation for the Propagation of the Faith. Elected pope on February 2, 1831, he was ordained a bishop in the Vatican Basilica on February 6 by Cardinal Bartolomeo Pacca, dean of the College of Cardinals, and then crowned pope by Cardinal Giuseppe Albani, proto-deacon of the Roman Church.

5. An "antipope" is a false claimant to the papal office in opposition to the incumbent canonically elected or recognized. The *Annuario Pontificio* takes notice of some thirty-seven such pretenders, while historian J.N.D. Kelly, in his *Oxford Dictionary of Popes* (Oxford: Oxford University Press, 1986), and theologian Richard McBrien, in his *Lives of the Popes: The Pontiffs from St. Peter to John Paul II* (San Francisco: HarperSanFrancisco, 1997), both list thirty-nine antipopes.

6. The "Patriarchal Lateran Archbasilica of Our Savior and of SS. John the Baptist and John the Evangelist" is the oldest of the four "patriarchal" basilicas of Rome, the others being the Vatican Basilica of St. Peter, the Ostian Basilica of St. Paul-outside-the-Walls, and the Liberian Basilica of St. Mary Major. It is called "Lateran" because it occupies land where the palace of the noble Roman Laterani family once stood. The property was given over to the Roman Church by the Emperor Constantine the Great, and the church was built that became the cathedral church of the bishops of Rome. The Lateran Basilica remains the cathedral church of the popes, hence the boast inscribed on its façade: "Mother and Head of all the churches of the City and the World." Adjacent to the basilica is the Lateran Palace, for many centuries the principal residence of the popes.

7. The cardinal secretary of state is effectively the papal prime minister. The Secretariat of State, over which he presides, is divided into two sections. The "First Section," headed by an archbishop with the title of "substitute" (*sostituto*), coordinates the work of the Roman Curia. The "Second Section," headed by an archbishop with the title of "secretary for relations with states," is effectively the foreign ministry of the Holy See.

8. The cardinal camerlengo (or chamberlain) presides over the Apostolic Camera (or Chamber). The principal charge of this office is to keep custody of the temporal rights of the Holy See during the vacancy between the death of one pope and the election of his successor, effectively serving as a council of regency for the papal monarchy.

9. The cardinal major penitentiary handles absolution from censures, dispensations, indulgences, and other spiritual matters that, by canon law, are reserved to the Roman pontiff. He is assisted by an office known as the Apostolic Penitentiary. For the good of souls, his authority, unlike that of most papal officials, is not suspended by the death of a pope.

10. As of the beginning of 2004, the College of Prelates of the Camera had three members: its dean, Monsignor Karel Kasteel, a Dutch prelate who is the secretary of the Pontifical Council *Cor Unum*, and two prelates, Monsignors Antonio Macculi and Vincenzo Ferrara, both Italians.

11. It is exceedingly doubtful whether the present vice-camerlengo, Italian archbishop Ettore Cunial, will actually carry out any functions should a vacancy in the papal office occur in the near future. The prelate is rather frail at at his advanced age—he was born in 1905—and is reputed to be rather absentminded, to put it charitably.

12. The master of papal liturgical celebrations presides over the Office for the Liturgical Celebrations of the Supreme Pontiff, successor to the former Sacred Congregation for Ceremonies, the dicastery charged with organizing the liturgical and other sacred ceremonies at which the pope presides or assists or which some other prelate conducts in the name of the pontiff. The office also supervises liturgical and other services during the period between the death of a pope and the election of his successor.

13. The papal apartment of Pope John Paul II is shared with Polish archbishop Stanislaw Dziwisz, adjunct prefect of the Papal Household and the pontiff's personal secretary since John Paul's tenure as archbishop of Cracow, several personal assistants, and a group of Polish nuns who handle the domestic arrangements.

14. The cardinal vicar for Rome is formally known as the "vicar general of His Holiness for the Diocese of Rome."

15. Castel Gandolfo, the papal summer residence, is located outside Rome on the shores of the volcanic Alban Lake on the site of Alba Longa, the citadel considered by the ancient Romans to be the mother of all Latin cities, including Rome itself. By the provisions of the Lateran Treaty of 1929, its seventy hectares (approximately 173 acres) are considered extraterritorial property of the Holy See and exempt from the jurisdiction of the Italian state. The original property, prime villa real estate since the Roman imperial period, was acquired by the Apostolic Camera in 1596 from the heirs of the Savelli family. In 1626, Pope Urban VIII (1623–1644) had Carlo Maderno erect the present papal palace, which was decorated by the Baroque artists Bartolomeo Breccioli and Domenico Castelli. In 1773, the neighboring Villa Cybo was added to the property. In the Lateran Treaty, Mussolini gave the Holy See the adjoining Villa Barberini, with its magnificent ruins dating from the Emperor Domitian; the historical irony of giving the papacy title to the summer residence where, according to some historians, the Roman emperor signed his edict of persecution against the early Church did not escape the Italian dictator. Castel Gandolfo also houses the Vatican Observatory, although, because of nighttime glare from the lights of encroaching urbanization, most of the scientific work of the institute has moved to Mount Graham, Arizona.

16. At the beginning of 2004, the senior cardinal of the order of bishops is German cardinal Joseph Ratzinger, dean of the College of Cardinals. The senior cardinal priest is Korean cardinal Stephen Kim Sou-hwan, archbishop emeritus of Seoul, while the senior cardinal deacon is Italian cardinal Luigi Poggi, former librarian and archivist of the Holy Roman Church.

17. More detailed historical information follows in the subsequent chapters for those popes who figure prominently in the development of this story.

18. Councils are lawfully convened assemblies of ecclesiastical dignitaries and theological experts for the purpose of discussing and regulating matters of church
doctrine and discipline, usually in response to some challenge. Ecumenical Councils are those to which bishops and other hierarchs entitled to vote are convoked
from the whole world (Greek, *oikoumene*). The Catholic tradition has added that
Ecumenical Councils must meet under the presidency of the pope or his legates
and that their decrees, having received papal confirmation, bind all Christians.
Traditionally, the Eastern (Orthodox) and Western (Catholic) Churches have been
unanimous in accepting the seven Ecumenical Councils: Nicaea I (325),
Constantinople I (381), Ephesus (431), Chalcedon (451), Constantinople II (553),
Constantinople III (680–681), and Nicaea II (787). The Western (Catholic) tradition also counts fourteen other councils, including the reforming Vatican II (1962–
1965), as ecumenical on the thesis that papal convocation and approval were
sufficient to ensure their "universal" character.

19. The distinction between the personal theological inquiry of a pope and his official teaching office is a difficult one to make given the claims of papal infallibility.
John XXII's successors managed it by refraining from personal theological opinions and limiting their doctrinal pronouncements to official declarations. John
Paul II, however, has once more reopened the question with his considerable theological work, expressed in the "catechisms" he delivers at his weekly Wednesday
general audiences as well as in the books he has published since his election to the
papacy, some of which have sparked controversy.

20. More on Leo XIII's remarkable pontificate is found in the chapter on the electoral
conclaves of the twentieth century.

21. The Great Western Schism (1378–1417) was a period when the papal office was
contested among several claimants, each backed by different countries. The schism
will be discussed in greater detail in the third chapter.

22. Originally established in 1551 by St. Ignatius Loyola as a training school for the
priests of the order he founded, the Society of Jesus (the Jesuits), the "Roman
College" soon attracted non-Jesuit students as its fame spread. In 1584, Pope Gre-
gory XIII took the institution under his protection. Since then, the Pontifical
Gregorian University has been the alma mater of fourteen popes and hundreds of
cardinals, archbishops, and bishops, as well as twenty saints and thirty-nine *beati*.
For more on this institution, see Philip Caraman, *University of the Nations: The
Story of the Gregorian University of Rome from 1551 to Vatican II* (New York/Ramsey,
New Jersey: Paulist Press, 1981).

23. Gian Lorenzo Bernini created a magnificent funerary monument for his patron,
Urban VIII, near his famous *Gloria*. The tomb of the Barberini pope features in its
iconography a book ingeniously sculpted in black marble with the pope's name
written on it. One page, however, is not entirely turned, and on it is visible the
initial of Urban's predecessor, Gregory XV (1621–1623). The Roman populace of
the time were not quite so impressed. Composing a sarcastic epitaph that referred
to the bees emblazoned on the Barberini family's coat of arms, they complained

of the heavy taxation they paid to enrich the nepotistic pontiff's kinsmen: *"Pauca haec Urbani sint verba incisa sepulcro—Quam bene pavit apes, tam male pavit oves"* ("There are few words written on the tomb of Urban—But how well he looks after the bees and how badly after his flock").

24. As Clement XIV's tomb is located just steps away from the Jesuit-run Pontifical Gregorian University and Pontifical Biblical Institute, it has become a tradition among students at those institutions to conclude their ostensibly rigorous studies by laying flowers at the magnificent monument to the pope created by Antonio Canova.

25. Thus Dante depicted Nicholas III:

> *Ché dopo lui verrà di più laida opra*
> *di ver' ponente, un pastor sanza legge,*
> *tal che convien che lui e me ricuopra.*
> *Novo Iasón sarà, di cui si legge*
> *Ne' Maccabei; e come a quel fu molle*
> *su re, così fia lui chi Francia regge.*
> *Io non so s'i mi fui qui troppo folle,*
> *Ch'i pur rispuosi lui a questo metro:*
> *Deh, or mi dì: quanto tesoro volle*
> *Nostro Segnore in prima da san Pietro*
> *Ch'ei ponesse le chiavi in sua balìa?*
> *Certo non chiese se non Viemmi retro.*
> *Né Pier né li altri tolsero a Matia*
> *oro od argento, quando fu sortito*
> *al loco che perdé l'anima ria.*
> *Però ti sta, ché tu se' ben punito;*
> *e guarda ben la mal tolta moneta*
> *che ti fece contra Carlo ardito.*
> *E se non fosse ch'ancor lo mi vieta*
> *la reverenza delle somme chiavi*
> *che tu tenesti ne la vita lieta,*
> *io userei parole ancor più gravi;*
> *ché la vostra avarizia il mondo attrista.*
> *calcando i buoni e sollevando i pravi.*

> For after him shall come of fouler deed
> From tow'rds the west a Pastor without law,
> Such as befits to cover him and me.
> New Jason will he be, of whom we read
> in Maccabees; and as his king was pliant,
> So he who governs France shall be to this one.
> I do not know if I were here too bold,
> That him I answered only in thus metre:

I pray thee tell me now how great a treasure
Our Lord demanded of Saint Peter first,
Before he put the keys into his keeping?
Truly he nothing asked but "Follow me."
Nor Peter nor the rest asked of Matthias
Silver or gold, when he by lot was chosen
Unto the place the guilty soul had lost.
Therefore stay here, for thou art justly punished,
And keep safe guard o'er the ill-gotten money,
Which caused thee to be valiant against Charles.
And were it not that still forbids it me
The reverence for the keys superlative
Thou hadst in keeping the gladsome life,
I would make use of words more grievous still;
Because your avarice afflicts the world,
Trampling the good and lifting the depraved.

[tr. Henry Wadsworth Longfellow]

26. David Yallop, *In God's Name: An Investigation into the Murder of Pope John Paul I* (London: J. Cape, 1984). For a more balanced account, which concludes that more likely the pope died of medical neglect and that exposes the chain of poor decisions that created the appearance of wrongdoing, see John Cornwell, *A Thief in the Night: Life and Death in the Vatican* (1989; New York: Penguin, 2001).

27. Thus Dante elegized John XXI:

Ma per amore de la verace manna
i picciol tempo gran dottor se feo;
tal che si mise a circuir la vigna
che tosto imbianca, se 'l vignaio è reo.

But through his longing after the true manna,
He in short time became so great a teacher,
That he began to go about the vineyard,
Which fadeth soon, if faithless be the dresser.

[tr. Henry Wadsworth Longfellow]

28. The official yearbook of the Holy See, the *Annuario Pontificio*, has, for many years, given the date of Martin I's death as September 16, 655, while noting the start of the pontificate of his successor, St. Eugenius I (654–657), as August 10, 654. This gives rise to an interesting question. As Richard McBrien, in his *Lives of the Popes*, has commented: "Martin's situation in exile was exacerbated by the lack of support he received from the church in Rome. Not only did it not come to his aid, but it even elected a successor while he was still alive . . . Was his successor, Eugenius I, a legitimate pope? Can the Church have two popes at the same time? These are

the kinds of questions that challenge much mistaken popular belief about the papacy, even today . . . His successor, Eugenius I, accepted election while Martin I was still alive, but only after the Roman clergy had waited more than a year, all the while resisting pressure from the emperor Constans II to replace Martin. Eugenius and the other Roman clergy probably concluded that Martin would never return to Rome and that if they waited any longer, the emperor would impose a Monothelite pope on the Church. It may have been a matter of choosing the lesser of two evils. However, a month or so before Eugenius was elected, Martin sent a letter to a friend in Constantinople in which he mentioned three ecclesiastical officials who were acting as his deputies in governing the Roman church. And just before his death on September 16, 655, he sent another letter to his friend, mentioning he prayed especially 'for the one who is now ruling over the Church.' Was this a tacit acquiescence or approval of Eugenius's election? We do not know. Accordingly, even though the official *Annuario Pontificio* begins Eugenius's pontificate in 654, he cannot be considered incontestably to have been pope until after Martin's death a year later. (Ideally, Martin should have resigned in order to remove all ambiguity about Eugenius's election during his imprisonment in exile.) One wonders, in the meantime, why the *Annuario Pontificio* lists the end of Martin's pontificate as September 16, 655, and the beginning of Eugenius I's as August 10, 654. Does the Vatican wish to affirm that the Catholic Church at one time had two legitimately elected and consecrated popes serving concurrently? That would be an extraordinary assertion indeed. But that is exactly what the Vatican's official list of popes implies" (106–107).

29. While not allowing a surgical autopsy, the College of Cardinals did permit the leading anatomist of the period, Bernardino Speroni, and a group of physicians to examine Leo X's body. Their report, according to papers left by Paolo Giovio Nucerini, a titular bishop attached to the papal court, concluded that the pope had been a victim of poisoning.

30. In May 2003, Pope John Paul II gave the Church of St. Vincent and St. Anastasius to the Bulgarian Orthodox Patriarch Maxim for the use of the small Bulgarian Orthodox Christian community resident in Rome, which had been without a place of worship.

31. The papal vestments are described in the chapter on the newly elected pontiff.

32. Canons are priests, usually prelates or other ecclesiastical dignitaries, who form a chapter, or collegiate body, attached to cathedrals or other churches of great significance. They assure the liturgical and pastoral services in that church and receive an income from the endowed funds attached to the chapter of canons. By ancient tradition, the chapters of the four patriarchal basilicas of Rome enjoy the patronage of the four major powers: France (St. John Lateran), Austria (St. Peter's), Spain (St. Mary Major), and England (St. Paul-outside-the-Walls). The French head of state enjoys the distinction of being "first canon" of the Lateran Archbasilica. Shortly after his election to the French presidency in 1995, Jacques Chirac paid a state visit to the Vatican and then proceeded to have himself installed as a titular canon of the Lateran Chapter on January 22, 1996.

33. The Scala Regia, which connect the medieval part of the Vatican Palace to the colonnade of St. Peter's Square, were built by Gian Lorenzo Bernini on orders from Pope Alexander VII (1655–1667). Interestingly, Bernini considered them his greatest architectural achievement. According to the late Cardinal Jacques Martin, longtime prefect of the Papal Household under Popes Paul VI, John Paul I, and John Paul II, Bernini thought that the talent of a great artist should not be judged by works that he could create without obstacles and restrictions—that is, in cases where he had total freedom to express himself—but by those works he undertook when his freedom of space and movement were restricted. Such, the late cardinal contended, was the case of Bernini's transformation of the narrow, dark and asymmetric corridor that leads from the basilica to the Sala Regia and the Sistine Chapel.

34. The Chapel of the Blessed Sacrament (Cappella del Santissimo Sacramento) was completed by Gian Lorenzo Bernini's younger brother, Luigi (1612–1681), at the behest of Pope Clement XI (1700–1721).

35. Acting as camerlengo *ad interim*, the dean of the Sacred College, Cardinal Eugène Tisserant, arranged for a taller than normal catafalque to be erected and crowd barriers to be set back, explaining these steps as necessary to facilitate the quick passage of the expected crowds. However, the tears and nasal discharges—both symptomatic of the irritation caused by the bizarre embalming procedures— suffered by the members of the Noble Guard who stood watch close to the papal remains gave away to those in the know the real motivation.

36. The Chapel of the Canons of the Vatican Basilica (Cappella del Coro dei Canonici Vaticani) was decorated by Gian Lorenzo Bernini for Pope Urban VIII (1623–1644), whose family arms (the Barberini bees) adorn it. The pope had the ashes of Countess Mathilda of Tuscany, Gregory VII's great supporter against Henry IV, brought to Rome and enshrined in front of it. Inside the chapel is the simple funerary monument of Pope Clement XI with the inscription *"Clemens XI P.M – huius Basilicae – olim vicarius – postea canonicus – sibi vivens poni iussit – orate pro eo"* ("Clement X – Supreme Pontiff – first vicar – later canon of this Basilica – ordered this stone to be laid down while he was still alive – Pray for him").

37. See John XXIII's testamentary dispositions in Appendix 6.

38. In May 2001, the mummified body of John XXIII was transferred to be displayed in a glass case at a side altar on the main level of St. Peter's Basilica.

39. See Paul VI's last will and testament in Appendix 7.

40. The Fontana delle Fiumi was itself commissioned by Innocent X, whose coat of arms adorns it. The pope also commissioned Bernini to line the then-bare stone pillars of the nave of St. Peter's Basilica with marble and decorate them in time for the Holy Year of 1650. Visitors to the basilica can still see the dove with the olive branch in various medallions along the nave, the image being the principal heraldic charge in the coat of arms of the pontiff's Pamphilj family. Innocent also commissioned Gian Lorenzo Bernini's brother, Luigi, to sculpt the cherubs that adorn many of the cornices in the Vatican Basilica.

Chapter Two

1. The Council of Chalcedon, the fourth ecumenical council, was convened by the Emperor Leo I in 451, during the pontificate of Leo I (440–461), who sent legates to it and subsequently ratified its acts. The assembly, consisting primarily of Eastern bishops, defined that the person of Christ contained two natures, human and divine, "without confusion, without change, without division, without separation."

2. The bishop of Rome was represented at Nicaea by Bishop Hosius of Cordoba and two Roman priests, Vitus and Vitale. Of the total assembly of about 250 bishops, only five were from the West. Most of the early councils were predominantly Eastern affairs.

3. The mutual excommunications were finally annulled on December 7, 1965, by a joint declaration of Pope Paul VI (1963–1978) and the Ecumenical Patriarch Athenagoras I of Constantinople.

Chapter Three

1. The camerlengo, or chamberlain, of the College of Cardinals is the official, usually a prelate, charged with the adminstration of the goods that the College holds as a corporate body. This official, called the "camerlengo of the College of Cardinals," should not be confused with the "camerlengo of the Holy Roman Church," the cardinal charged with the "regency" during the *sede vacante*.

2. Patriarchs of Eastern Rite Catholic Churches who are appointed to the College of Cardinals do not receive a Roman "title" since that would turn them into members of the clergy of the Roman diocese.

3. The last cardinal to not have been ordained a priest was the distinguished canonist Teodolfo Mertel (1806–1899), who was ordained a deacon the day after he was created a cardinal by Pope Pius IX (1846–1878) in 1858 but was never ordained to the priesthood.

4. Another relative of the Stuarts, Rinaldo d'Este, brother-in-law of King James II, is remembered for resigning his cardinalate in order to become sovereign of the then-independent Duchy of Modena. He was created a cardinal by Pope Innocent XI in the consistory of September 2, 1686. In 1694, the pope gave him permission to succeed to the sovereignty of Modena after the death of his childless nephew Duke Francesco II. When his last surviving male relative died shortly thereafter, the pope, to prevent the extinction of the House of Este, permitted him to resign from the Sacred College and be laicized on March 21, 1695. On November 18 of the same year, the cardinal-turned-duke married Carlotta Felicita of Brunswick. He died in 1737.

5. As for Celestine, now styled "Brother Pietro" at his own request, he had hoped to return to his cave on Mount Morrone. His successor, however, feared that the naive former pope could easily be a rallying point for a potential schism if he fell in with the wrong company. Boniface thus kept his predecessor under guard. The

former pope, however, despite his age, managed to escape and lived for several months in hiding in the wilderness before he was recaptured and placed in confinement in the tower of Castel Fumone, near Ferentino. He died on May 19, 1296, of an infection caused by an abscess and was canonized seventeen years later as St. Peter Celestine.

The hapless Celestine V had as little peace in death as he had had in life. Originally buried in Ferrentino, he was exhumed in 1327, his remains being taken to L'Aquila to the church of Santa Maria di Collemaggio, an edifice he himself had caused to be erected. His remains were finally laid to rest in 1517 in a marble mausoleum by the Lombard Renaissance master Girolamo da Vicenza. However, the relics were twice pillaged: in 1528, when soldiers under the command of the Prince of Orange stole the saint's remains along with the silver reliquary by the School of Sulmona, and again in 1799, when the soldiers of revolutionary France stole the eighteenth-century replacement urn. Today, what remains of the poor man were recovered after the two sacks can be viewed in the church, where the relics are dressed up in pontifical vestments and laid out in a crystal and silver casket by Luigi Cardilli.

6. Before "Papa Luna," Benedict XIII, died on May 23, 1423, he made his four remaining cardinals swear to elect a successor. The three who were available met in conclave at the castle of Peñiscola on June 10, 1423, and chose one of their number, Gil Sanchez Muñoz, who adopted the style "Clement VIII" in commemoration of the first pope of the Avignon line, Robert of Geneva (Clement VII). Blockaded inside his castle by the royal forces of Queen Maria of Aragon, acting as regent for Alfonso V, Clement presided over a papal court in miniature, creating two additional cardinals. Securely installed in Rome, Martin V viewed the comedy being played out at Peñiscola with a certain bemusement and instructed a commission of Aragonese bishops, consisting of the archbishop of Tarragona and the bishops of Tortosa and Barcelona, to deal gently with the misguided prelates provided they came to their senses. Clement VIII responded gracefully and abdicated on July 29, 1429. He and his four cardinals then proceeded to elect "Oddo Colonna" (Martin V) as pope. Martin subsequently appointed Clement bishop of Majorca, which office he held until his death in 1446.

As for the deceased Papa Luna, the subsequent travails of his mortal remains, although not included in the chapter on papal death and burial since he is considered an antipope, deserve recounting. Shortly after his death, Aragonese peasants began to gather around his tomb in the "papal chapel" of the castle of Peñiscola, attracted by a delicate perfume said to emanate from it. After the blockade of the fortress was lifted following the abdication of Clement VIII, Papa Luna's nephew Juan de Luna obtained permission from King Alfonso V to remove the remains to the Luna ancestral castle at Illueca. The mummified corpse was put on display in a crystal case in the room in which Papa Luna was born, transformed for the purpose into a chapel. The chapel was a local pilgrimage site for over a century until, in 1537, a visiting Italian prelate, scandalized that votive candles were lit in front of the tomb of an antipope, smashed the crystal coffin with his walking stick, provoking rioting by the local peasantry. The archbishop of Zaragoza, in whose territory the shrine was located, then ordered the chapel sealed to prevent further disturbances. Thus things remained until the beginning of the eighteenth century when the Luna family backed the Archduke Carlos against Philip of Anjou, later Philip V of Spain, during the War of the Spanish Succession. The castle was besieged and sacked by French troops, who decapitated the mummy and paraded about with Papa Luna's head. Afterward, only the mummified head was recovered— the body was reportedly torn to pieces—and placed in a reliquary, decorated with the papal coat of arms, in the Sabiñán Palace of the Counts of Morata, not far from Illueca. As late as the early-20th century, visitors noted the remarkable state in which the presumptive relic was preserved. In 1936, during the Spanish Civil War, the head was buried to prevent it from being vandalized by the Republican forces that had carried out various outrages against ecclesiastics and other religious, living and deceased. After the conflict, the head was restored to its display in the Sabiñán Palace, although the effects of the burial caused it to decay. Today, only the right eye remains preserved inside a dried skull.

The fourth of Papa Luna's cardinals, Jean Carrier, who was the vicar general, was away on business in Armagnac when his colleagues held their conclave. Upon his return, he judged the election held in his absence invalid because of simony and other irregularities. On November 25, 1425, he took it upon himself to hold an election with himself as the only elector, choosing a certain Bernard Garnier, sacristan of the parish church in Rodez, and consecrating him under the style of "Benedict XIV." This "pontiff" disappeared from history, although chroniclers as late as 1467 reported fanatics in the region of Armagnac holding out for "Pope Benedict XIV."

7. During the conclave of 1655, the Spanish Jesuit Cardinal Juan de Lugo (1583–1660) wrote a learned treatise, subsequently never published, entitled *Memorie del conclave d'Innocenzo X: Riposta al discorso . . . che le corone hanno jus d'eschiudere li cardinali del Pontificato*, defending the Spanish crown's *ius exclusivae*.

8. For the complete text of the apostolic constitution, see Appendix 2.

9. As noted previously, the Fisherman's Ring is so called because it depicts the image of St. Peter casting his net into the sea. The ring bears, in Latin, the pope's name and title. The ring is in fact not worn by the pope, but simply used to seal certain documents. Its use dates back to at least the reign of Clement IV (1265–1268). The ring that the pope actually wears is a matter of personal choice and taste. Pope Pius IX wore a ring that contained over one hundred diamonds, while Pope John XXIII preferred a simple cameo. Pope John Paul II seems to prefer a simple band of hammered gold.

10. Ironically, the improvement of communications and transportation, coupled with the now-extended interval between the death of one pope and the beginning of the conclave for the election of his successor, risks leaving the cardinals *too much* time. Adding to this the media coverage that will undoubtedly follow the events raises serious concerns—thus far unaddressed—about pressures on the electors.

11. The patriarchs are the heads of ancient Churches, traditionally of apostolic origin, in communion with the See of Rome, but retaining their own distinctive liturgical and theological traditions ("rites") as well as great autonomy of government. Many of these "Eastern Catholic Churches" either did not break communion with the Roman Church at the time of the 1054 schism between Rome and Constantinople when the legates of Pope Leo IX excommunicated the Patriarch Michael Cerularius and his followers and were, in turn, excommunicated by the ecumenical patriarch and his synod, or restored communion during the seventeenth and eighteenth centuries. The six Eastern Catholic patriarchs are the Coptic Rite patriarch of Alexandria; the Syrian Rite patriarch of Antioch; the Greek Melkite Rite patriarch of Antioch, Alexandria, and Jerusalem; the Maronite Rite patriarch of Antioch; the Chaldean Rite patriarch of Babylon; and the Armenian Rite patriarch of Cilicia.

12. The irony of the exclusion of cardinals over the age of eighty is that, while originally intended primarily to exclude presumably more conservative electors named by Pius XII, its retention in John Paul II's apostolic constitution has the reverse effect of ensuring that the electors in the next conclave will almost all be the presumably more conservative nominees of John Paul II. Of the 135 cardinals eligible to vote as of the consistory of October 21, 2003, only five created by Paul VI (Pio Taofinu'u, Jaime Sin, William Wakefield Baum, Alois Lorscheider, and Joseph Ratzinger) are not creations of John Paul II. See Appendix 3 for the complete list of cardinals presently eligible to participate in a conclave.

13. Since the late Middle Ages the Papal Sacristy has been entrusted to the care of the religious of the Order of St. Augustine. Until 1991, the prefect of the Papal Sacristy was contemporaneously the Vicar General of His Holiness for the Vatican. The last incumbent in that office was the Dutch bishop Peter Canisius Johannes van Lierde, who died in 1995; he held the twin offices for over forty years through the pontificates of five popes: Pius XII, John XXIII, Paul VI, John Paul I, and John Paul II.

14. Thomas Jefferson learned about the *rote* in a description of the conclave of 1774–1775 that he read while serving as the United States representative in France from 1783 to 1789. Returning to America, he had one built into his dining room wall at Monticello so that he and his guests could dine without the intrusion of servants.

15. During the period before the two 1978 conclaves, the camerlengo, French cardinal Jean Villot, gave the discourses himself. Perhaps he was apprehensive about a repeat of the shocking performance, given in 1963, after the death of Pope John XXIII, when the conservative orator, Monsignor Amleto Tondini, launched into a tirade against the upheavals unleashed by the late pope's tentative opening to the world and not too subtly attacked the memory of the deceased.

16. The requirement of a two-thirds majority was the standard through the conclave of 1939, with the provision that the one elected did not vote for himself. Consequently, if the election was by a precise two-thirds majority, the ballots had to be examined to ascertain that a cardinal was not elected pope thanks to his own vote. Pope Pius XII changed the requirement to two-thirds plus one, but eliminated by that change the ban against voting for oneself, the argument being that if a candi-

date achieved a majority of two-thirds plus one, even if he had voted for himself, he was nonetheless the choice of the clear majority of the electors. Thus, the election of Pope John XXIII in 1958 required a majority of at least two-thirds of the electors plus one. John then eliminated the requirement for the additional vote above the two-thirds majority, so that the election of Pope Paul VI in 1963 required just the two-thirds majority. Paul, in turn, restored the requirement for the additional vote, which was thus necessary for the election in 1978 of Pope John Paul I and Pope John Paul II.

17. These provisions are, no doubt, to prevent the violation of the secrecy of the conclave by the heirs or executors of long-deceased cardinals who kept their own papers, some of which were published and others of which have been made available to well-connected scholars. John XXIII tried to arrange that all the papers from the conclave that followed his death would be kept somewhere in the Vatican Archives, but the collection efforts in 1963 were, according to well-informed sources, haphazard, and there is some confusion as to where the papers that were collected ended up. Paul VI ordered the destruction of all notes taken in subsequent conclaves, a decree confirmed by John Paul II.

18. Theoretically, any male Catholic could be elected, although the last time the College of Cardinals reached outside of its own membership was in 1378, when, under pressure from the Roman mob, the elected the Italian archbishop Bartolomeo Prignano of Bari as Urban VI. Under the present circumstances of a large electoral college consisting of cardinals from throughout the world, it is difficult to imagine the conditions in which such a body could arrive at a name outside its membership. In any event, both the Code of Canon Law and the apostolic constitution provide for the possibility of such an election, stipulating that if the newly elected pope is not already a bishop, the dean of the College of Cardinals or, in his absence, the sub-dean, or the next senior cardinal bishop, shall ordain him one before the announcement of his election is made. Interestingly, this theoretical procedure departs from the ancient tradition wherein most of the popes in the first twelve centuries were not bishops at the time of their election and their solemn episcopal consecration by the dean was part of their enthronement. As mentioned previously, the last time this took place was when Cardinal Bartolomeo Alberto Mauro Cappellari was elected Gregory XVI in 1831. He was consecrated four days after his election by the dean of the Sacred College, Cardinal Bartolomeo Pacca.

19. A notable (and eccentric) exception to this rule was Paul II (1464–1471). At the time of his election to the papacy, Cardinal Pietro Barbo, who was noted for both his good looks and the vanity that stemmed from his own knowledge of his physical attributes, had already acquired a reputation for his taste for magnificence as illustrated by his construction of the lavish Palazzo San Marco (now the Palazzo di Venezia) as his private residence. Even centuries later the palace was admired for its grandeur; the Italian dictator Benito Mussolini adopted it as his official headquarters. In any event, the new pope assumed the style of "Formusus II," the

name meaning "handsome" in Latin. However, met by a flurry of scorn from the cardinals as well as ridicule from historians who recalled the only other Pope Formusus (the craven character who was responsible for the ghastly posthumous "trial" of his predecessor's corpse), he quickly took the style of "Paul II."

Chapter Four

1. Among his many works, De Agostini is the author of a fascinatingly chatty book of anecdotes about some of the cardinals he has known, *Eminenti e Eminentissimi. Tutto quello che si dovrebbe sapere sui Cardinali del '900* (Casale Monferrato: Edizioni PIEMME, 2000).

2. At the conclave following Leo XIII's death, of the sixty-two cardinals present (two others were absent), only the dean of the Sacred College, Italian cardinal Luigi Oreglia di Santo Stefano, had been present at the conclave of 1878. All the other electors of 1878 had died, and, with the exception of its dean, the entire electoral college of 1903 was the creation of Pope Leo.

3. There are many sources of information for the conclave of 1903, the most authoritative being the dossiers and accounts collected and published shortly after the events by the Italian author Giovanni Berthelet in his book *Storia e rivelazioni sul conclave del 1903. L'elezione di Pio X* (Turin / Rome: Casa Editrice Nazionale, 1903).

4. Not far from Piazza Navona is an ancient statue dubbed *"Il Pasquino"* by the Romans. From times immemorial it has been a gathering place for the declamations and postings of mocking verses, each of which is duly dubbed a *"pasquinata."*

5. Giuseppe Melchiorre Sarto (1835–1914) hailed from a humble family in Riese, in the upper Venetian region. After studies at the seminary of Padua, he was ordained a priest in 1858. He spent the first nine years of his priesthood as a curate, followed by eight years as pastor, in rural Salzano. In 1875, he was appointed chancellor of his home diocese of Treviso and spiritual director of its seminary. In 1884, he was appointed bishop of Mantua. In 1893, Pope Leo XIII promoted him to the patriarchate of Venice and created him a cardinal. In both his dioceses, he was known to be a hardworking shepherd who steered clear of politics, concentrating on doctrinal matters, a predilection that he would preserve as pontiff.

6. Cardinal Ferrari's detailed diary of the conclave, the contents of which were published for the most part in the second volume, *I tempi di Pio X*, of Carlo Snider's definitive biography of the Milanese archbishop, *L'episcopato del cardinale Andrea C. Ferrara* (Vicenza: Neri Pozza Editore, 1982), is a precious source for reconstructing the events surrounding Cardinal Puzyna's announcement of the imperial veto, giving an almost journalistic chronicle.

7. Protesting unified Italy's takeover of its territory, the Holy See could not very well recognize the same government's despoiling of the other monarchies of pre-unification Italy, especially a state such as the Kingdom of the Two Sicilies, which

had, for a millennium, been juridically a fief held under the suzerainty of the pope. Thus, after the death in 1894 of the exiled King Francesco II, the Holy See recognized the rights of and received an ambassador from his brother and heir, Prince Alfonso of Bourbon, Count of Caserta, who maintained a modest court in exile at Nice.

8. Cretoni (1833–1909) was identified as the culprit since the electoral rules of the time required the cardinals to sign their ballots and to seal them in red wax with their signet rings.

9. Cardinal Piffl took copious notes of his observations during the two conclaves he participated in, jotting down events and conversations in little notebooks, which he diligently labeled: "Secrets of the Conclave: To be burned after my death." The notebooks, however, were not burned, and their contents were transcribed and published in the July–August 1963 issue of *La nouvelle revue*.

10. Giacomo della Chiesa (1854–1922), scion of an aristocratic family with a long tradition of public service (his father was a distinguished magistrate, while his brother was an admiral in the Italian navy), earned a doctorate in civil law from the University of Genoa at the age of twenty-one before beginning studies for the priesthood. Following abbreviated studies at the Capranica College and the Pontifical Gregorian University in Rome, he was ordained a priest in 1878. After ordination he trained for the diplomatic service of the Holy See at the Pontifical Academy of Noble Ecclesiastics. Upon completing his studies, he joined the staff of the Secretariat of State. From 1883 to 1887, he served as deputy to then-Archbishop Mariano Rampolla del Tindaro at the nunciature in Madrid, during which period the papacy mediated the dispute between Spain and Germany over the Carolinas. When Rampolla del Tindaro received the cardinal's hat in 1887 and was appointed secretary of state, he brought his protégé with him back to Rome as his undersecretary. He continued in the Secretariat of State after Rampolla del Tindaro was replaced by Cardinal Rafael Merry del Val after the conclave of 1907, but his reserve over the anti-modernist condemnations aroused the suspicions of the new regime. In 1907, he was removed from the diplomatic service and sent to Bologna as archbishop, but without the traditional red hat, which was conferred only months before the conclave of 1914. Because of trauma at his birth, della Chiesa presented a physically unimpressive figure: One eye, one ear, and one shoulder were noticeably higher than the other; in addition, he was short and stoop-shouldered and walked with a distinct limp.

11. It should be noted that Benedict patiently laid the foundations for a breakthrough in the diplomatic impasse. Despite being excluded from the Versailles Conference, he gave general support to the League of Nations and worked to construct Church-state relations with the new states that emerged in the aftermath of the war. His reign saw the rise in the number of countries accrediting resident diplomatic missions to the Holy See despite the still-unresolved dispute with Italy over the territorial sovereignty of the papacy. At his election in 1914, there were fourteen missions; when he died in 1922, the number had risen to twenty-seven, including Great Britain, which in 1915 accredited a minister to the papal court for

the first time since the seventeenth century, and France, which in 1921 resumed the diplomatic relations broken during the pontificate of Pius X by accrediting an ambassador. He also put out feelers to the Italian government, signaling his readiness to arrive at an honorable settlement and abolishing both the ban on Catholic participation in Italian national political life and the prohibition on official visits by Catholic heads of state to the Quirinal (once the residence of the popes but since 1870 the official residence of the kings of Italy).

12. Particularly frustrating for the individual concerned was the case of Cardinal William Henry O'Connell (1859–1944), archbishop of Boston from 1907 until his death, created cardinal by Pius X in 1911. Distance meant that he raced across the Atlantic only to arrive too late for the conclave twice (1914, 1922). The second time, he arrived while the conclave was still in session, but upon being admitted to the Sistine, he discovered that the election had just taken place. It was largely due to his insistence with Pius XI that a longer interval was prescribed between the death of a pope and the election of his successor. O'Connell lived long enough to benefit from the change, participating in the conclave of 1939.

13. A former Imperial Dragoon in the Austrian army, Lev de Skrbensky z Hriste was only thirty-six years old when he was appointed prince-archbishop of Prague in 1899 by the Emperor Franz Josef, who was reputed to have been his natural father. Barely a year later, he was created a cardinal by Leo XIII at the insistence of the Austrian sovereign, from whom he received the cardinal's biretta. He thus became the youngest cardinal of the twentieth century, being two months shy of his thirty-eighth birthday. He participated in the conclaves of 1903 and 1914. In 1916, he was transferred to Olomouc as prince-archbishop, but, in the upheavals of the breakup of the Habsburg monarchy, he resigned the pastoral governance of his archdiocese in 1920 and retired to a monastery of the Teutonic order. In February and March 1922, instead of coming to the conclave where he was expected, he disappeared for a time. When he died on Christmas Eve 1938, he was the senior cardinal priest and the last surviving creation of Leo XIII. It has long been speculated that, after the collapse of the dual monarchy, certain quarters in the Vatican found him an embarrassing reminder of the Holy See's close ties with the *ancien régime* and did not want his appearance to resurrect presumably settled questions.

14. Ambrogio Damiano Achille Ratti (1857–1939), son of a silk-factory manager from near Milan, was ordained in 1879. After earning three doctorates, he was a seminary professor and librarian, first at the Ambrosian Library in Milan and then at the Vatican Library. An expert paleographer, he published extensively. However, he was not completely a bookworm: In his spare time, he was a champion mountaineer. Ratti, after being named archbishop, was sent to newly reconstituted Poland as apostolic visitor and then nuncio; his impartiality became the target of Polish nationalist sentiment, and he was recalled. Created a cardinal in June 1921, he was named archbishop of Milan contemporaneously. He was destined to emerge from the conclave as Pope Pius XI (1922–1939).

15. Gasparri's memoirs, which he never had the opportunity to edit, remained unpublished for nearly four decades after his death. They were brought to light in *Il Cardinale Gasparri e la questione romana (Con brani delle memorie inedite)*, edited by Giovanni Spadolini (Florence: Le Monnier, 1973).

16. Eugenio Maria Giuseppe Giovanni Pacelli (1876–1958) was the scion of a noble Roman family long in the service of the papacy. His grandfather had been Pope Pius IX's interior minister in the last days of the papal monarchy and his father was a consistorial advocate, while his brother was the Holy See's principal legal advisor during the negotiations leading up to the Lateran Treaty. After ordination to the priesthood (1899) and further studies, then-Archbishop Pietro Gasparri brought him into the service of the Holy See, first as his personal assistant and then, successively, as under-secretary and secretary of the Sacred Congregation for Extraordinary Ecclesiastical Affairs (i.e., the Holy See's "foreign ministry"). Appointed archbishop and apostolic nuncio to Bavaria in 1917, he was the bearer to Germany of Benedict XV's failed peace initiative. In 1920, he became nuncio to all Germany. Created a cardinal by Pius XI in 1929, he succeeded Gasparri (at the latter's recommendation) as secretary of state the following year, when he was also named archpriest of the Vatican Basilica. He was also appointed camerlengo of the Holy Roman Church, in 1935. Repeatedly sent abroad as Pius XI's legate, he was to succeed him as Pope Pius XII in 1939.

17. A legate *a latere* (Latin, "from the side") is, in modern times, an exceptionally rare form of envoy, employed exclusively by the pope. The legate *a latere* represents the very person of the pontiff as his alter ego. In the ecclesiastical context, the legate *a latere* takes precedence over all other church dignitaries and presides in the name of the pope. Under international law, the legate *a latere* enjoys all the immunities and privileges of the sovereign he represents and is received with the same diplomatic protocol and honors due to that sovereign in the state to which he is sent as well as in any he travels through en route to the destination. Thus, Pius XI's decision to send Pacelli abroad as a legate *a latere* was a not so subtle hint to both ecclesiastics and statesmen.

18. The conclave of 1939 did not have a Cardinal Gustav Piffl, whose indiscreet but detailed diaries gave a play-by-play chronicle. The most reliable reconstructions of the events have been the ones attempted by Pius XII's Italian biographer, Antonio Spinosa in his *Pio XII, l'ultimo papa* (Milan: Mondadori, 1992), and the Italian historian of the papacy Gianfranco Zizola, *Il conclave: Storia e segreti. L'elezione papale da San Pietro a Giovanni Paolo II* (Rome: Newton Compton Editori, 1993), based on their privileged access to the papers and private correspondence of some of the participants.

19. The hereditary office of governor of the conclave, until it was abolished by Pope Paul VI in his post–Vatican II simplifications of the papal court, belonged since the thirteenth century to the Savelli family, to whom it was given in gratitude for the role members of the family played in protecting the conclave of 1268–1271. Later, when the Savelli line died out, it was inherited by their Chigi heirs. Interestingly,

during the conclave of 1939, the office was held by Prince Ludovico Chigi Albano della Rovere, who was, as the seventy-sixth grand master of the Sovereign Military Order of Malta from 1931 to his death in 1951, also a professed lay religious *and* a sovereign prince.

20. The precise vote is known because immediately after the conclave the rumor made the rounds that the new pope had been elected by near unanimity, receiving every vote but his own, which allegedly went to Dalla Costa. A religious journalist interviewing French cardinal Alfred Baudrillart congratulated him on the reported unanimity of the Sacred College. "What unanimity?" asked the cardinal. When told that Pacelli had received sixty-one votes, Baudrillart replied, "More like forty-eight."

21. Karol Wojtyla (born 1922) is the present pope, John Paul II. He entered the clandestine seminary run by Adam Sapieha during the Second World War and was ordained a priest on November 1, 1946. After advanced studies in Rome he eventually earned doctorates in theology and philosophy; he served in parishes of the Cracow archdiocese as well as teaching university courses. Appointed titular bishop of Ombi and auxiliary to the apostolic administrator of Cracow in 1958, he was promoted to the archbishopric in 1964. Paul VI created him cardinal in 1967. He was elected pope in the second conclave of 1978.

     An exhaustive, if at times all too adulatory, account of Wojtyla's life and thought, and the influences upon him, can be found in George Weigel's semi-official *Witness to Hope: The Biography of Pope John Paul II* (New York: HarperCollins, 1999).

22. The story of former Chief Rabbi Zolli's conversion to Catholicism is told in an autobiographical account originally published in 1953. See Eugenio (Israel) Zolli, *Why I Became a Catholic* (Fort Collins, Colorado: Roman Catholic Books, 1996).

23. Giovanni Battista Enrico Antonio Maria Montini (1897–1978) was the son of a prosperous lawyer who was also a newspaper editor and parliamentary deputy. Of frail health, he attended the diocesan seminary of Brescia while living at home and, after his ordination in 1920, pursued graduate studies in Rome at the Pontifical Gregorian University, the University of Rome, and the Pontifical Academy for Ecclesiastical Nobles. Joining the diplomatic service of the Holy See, he was sent to the nunciature in Poland, but health reasons necessitated his recall after only a few months. Working in the Secretariat of State, he was also a faculty member of the diplomatic academy and national chaplain of the Federation of Italian Catholic University Students (FUCI). Many of his protégés among the FUCI members later rose to prominence in post–World War II Italian politics, including prime ministers Aldo Moro and Giulio Andreotti. He was appointed substitute of the Secretariat of State in 1937 and given the title "pro-secretary of state for ordinary ecclesiastical affairs" by Pope Pius XII in 1952. He somehow fell out with Pius and was exiled to Milan as archbishop in 1954, although he was not given the cardinal's hat that had, for centuries, gone with that nomination. He was created a cardinal by John XXIII in 1958, who purposely made him the first of his creations. Elected pope in 1963, he took the name Paul VI. To him fell the difficult task of bringing the Second Vatican Council to a conclusion and implementing its reforms. His cause for beatification was begun in 1993.

24. In contrast to the well-documented first half of the twentieth century, the record of the ballot-by-ballot returns of the conclaves of the second half are not consistent. In what follows for the four conclaves between 1958 and 1978, the firsthand confidences of witnesses, some of whom are now deceased, is relied upon to reconstruct the course of events.

25. Angelo Giuseppe Roncalli (1881–1963), the son of peasants from Sotto-il-Monte (now renamed Sotto-il-Monte-Giovanni XXIII in his honor by the Italian government) near Bergamo, he was ordained a priest in 1904 after studies at the seminary of Bergamo and the Pontifical Roman Seminary. From 1905 to 1914, he served as the secretary of the saintly bishop of Bergamo, Giacomo Maria Radini Tedeschi. During the First World War, he served as a military chaplain with the Italian army and was assigned to the medical corps along the front with Austria. Returning from the conflict, he was appointed spiritual director of the Bergamo seminary. In 1921, however, Benedict XV brought him to Rome as president of the Italian Society for the Propagation of the Faith. In 1925, he was appointed apostolic visitor in Bulgaria and raised to the archiepiscopal dignity. In 1931, he was appointed apostolic delegate. In 1935, he was transferred to Istanbul with the charge of apostolic delegate to Turkey and Greece. When the Second World War broke out he was in Greece, where his selfless humanitarian efforts did much to soften the long-hostile attitude of the Greek Orthodox Church toward the Roman Church. He also assisted many Jews to escape by issuing "transit visas" from the apostolic delegation. In December 1944, Pius XII appointed him nuncio to France. Created a cardinal by Pius XII in 1953, he was appointed to the patriarchate of Venice. Elected pope by the conclave of 1958, he took the name John XXIII. His pontificate, which lasted less than five years, changed the course of Catholicism as he opened the Church to the modern world, both by his personal charisma and by summoning the Second Vatican Council, which he opened but the conclusion of which he left to his successor. He was beatified by John Paul II in 2000.

26. Although not all of the conservatives seem to have appreciated the fact that, as a historical and sociological phenomenon, the council had taken on a life of its own. In the traditional pre-conclave Latin discourse *"pro eligendo Pontifice"* surveying the needs of the Church, the secretary for briefs to princes, Monsignor Amleto Tondini, had launched into an unprecedented critique of the preceding pontificate. "Doubt should be cast," the prelate thundered at the shocked cardinals, "on the enthusiastic applause received by the 'pope of peace,' and it is to be wondered whether this enthusiasm came from people who were true believers, who accepted all the dogmatic and moral teachings of the Church." According to Tondini's logic, if John XXIII had been applauded by Communists and other non-believers, then he was obviously not "true."

27. Maintaining the close ties to the Vatican establishment that he has assiduously cultivated over the decades, Andreotti, now an Italian senator-for-life, edits an influential Catholic monthly, *30 Giorni,* that is translated into several languages and has written a number of books in which, beneath his lengthy prose, he reveals a significant amount of "insider" information on the Holy See. Most relevant to

the present subject is *A ogni morte di papa. I papi che ho conosciuto* (Milan: Biblioteca Universale Rizzoli, 1982).

28. Lercaro would have cause to lament that fate did not treat him kindly. Taking enthusiastically to the reforms of the Second Vatican Council, he moved energetically to implement a progressive agenda in his archdiocese of Bologna, perhaps proceeding at a pace that caused discomfort to the other Italian hierarchs. On the morning of February 12, 1968, he opened his copy of *L'Osservatore Romano* to read that Paul VI had "kindly accepted his resignation for reasons of advanced age and ill health." Deprived of his see—but, obviously, not of his health, the official Vatican newspaper notwithstanding—Lercaro lived until 1976.

29. With his *motu proprio* of November 21, 1970, *Ingravescentem aetatem*, Pope Paul VI excluded those cardinals who reached the age of eighty from having a vote in the conclave. While the official motive given was to spare their years the rigors of the electoral enclosure, most commentators noted that the pontiff feared that, in the event of his untimely death, the conservative faction within the College of Cardinals (presumably roughly identical with the older members of the college) would elect a pope who would undo his reforms.

30. Albino Luciani (1912–1978) was born in Forno di Canale d'Agrodo, near Belluno in northern Italy, to a poor family of migrant workers. After an education at the minor seminary of Feltre, the seminary of Belluno, and the Pontifical Gregorian University in Rome, he was ordained a priest in 1935. He taught in the seminary of Belluno and assisted in parishes until 1948, when he was appointed pro-vicar general of the diocese. He became vicar general in 1954. In 1958, he was appointed bishop of Vittorio Veneto. He attended the Second Vatican Council. In 1969, he was appointed patriarch of Venice. In 1972, he hosted Paul VI during a visit to the city. During the visit, in one of his famous impromptu gestures, the pope removed his stole and placed it on the patriarch's shoulders. The photo of the occasion was later cited by pundits to indicate some sort of special favor. He was created a cardinal by Pope Paul in 1973. Although conservative in his personal theology and devotion, he defended the rights of conscience with regard to Paul VI's ruling on birth control and had no use for displays of pomp, encouraging his priests to sell precious articles for the benefit of the poor and proposing a sort of tax on churches in wealthy countries to support churches in the developing world. Elected John Paul I in the first conclave of 1978, he died after barely a month on the papal throne.

31. Cardinal Jacques Martin was the prefect of the Papal Household under three popes (Paul VI, John Paul I, and John Paul II) and, prior to that, an official in the Secretariat of State. His posthumously published memoirs, *Oltre il portone di bronzo (Appunti di un cardinale vissuto a fianco di 6 papi)* (Milan: Edizioni Paoline, 1996), constitute a precious source of anecdotes on the modern papacy.

32. This conspiratorial thesis, based on a series of improbabilities, was synthesized in a fascinating but ludicrous account by British journalist David A. Yallop in his book *In God's Name: An Investigation into the Murder of Pope John Paul I* (London: J. Cape, 1984). A more balanced account, which concludes that more likely the pope

died of medical neglect and exposes the chain of poor decisions that created the appearance of wrong-doing, is John Cornwell's *A Thief in the Night: Life and Death in the Vatican* (1989; New York: Penguin, 2001).

33. In his book, *Il Papa non eletto. Giuseppe Siri, cardinale di Santa Romana Chiesa* (Bari: Laterza, 1993), journalist Benny Lai reconstructs this strange episode in detail and lays the blame both for the broken journalistic promise and for the attempt to exploit it against Siri's candidacy at the door of several curial prelates close to Cardinal Giovanni Benelli.

34. An English translation was published in 1981 by Franciscan Herald Press, Chicago.

35. John Paul II recounts a number of anecdotes of milestones in his life in his book *Gift and Mystery: On the Fiftieth Anniversary of My Priestly Ordination* (New York: Doubleday, 1997).

36. The anecdote and other details are related in Mario Grone, *Accanto al "mio" Cardinal Siri* (Genoa: Marietti, 1996).

37. Recall that as of John Paul II's twenty-fifth anniversary on the papal throne, October 16, 2003, the Holy See maintained bilateral diplomatic relations at the ambassadorial level with 174 countries as well as with the European Union and the Sovereign Military Order of Malta, in addition to what is described as "diplomatic relations of a special nature" with the Russian Federation and the Palestinian Liberation Organization, with the permanent exchange of "envoys on special mission with the personal rank of ambassador" in the case of the former. The 174 countries are Albania, Algeria, Andorra, Angola, Antigua and Barbuda, Argentina, Armenia, Australia, Austria, Azerbaijan, Bahamas, Bahrain, Bangladesh, Barbados, Belgium, Belize, Benin, Bolivia, Bosnia-Herzegovina, Brazil, Bulgaria, Burkina Faso, Burundi, Byelorussia, Cambodia, Cameroon, Canada, Cape Verde, the Central African Republic, Chad, Chile, China (the Republic of China on Taiwan), Colombia, Congo (Brazzaville), the Democratic Republic of Congo, Cook Islands, Costa Rica, Côte d'Ivoire, Croatia, Cuba, Cyprus, the Czech Republic, Denmark, Djibouti, Dominica, the Dominican Republic, East Timor, Ecuador, Egypt, El Salvador, Equatorial Guinea, Eritrea, Estonia, Ethiopia, Fiji, Finland, France, Gabon, The Gambia, Georgia, Germany, Ghana, Great Britain, Greece, Grenada, Guatemala, Guinea, Guinea-Bissau, Guyana, Haiti, Honduras, Hungary, Iceland, India, Indonesia, Iran, Iraq, Ireland, Israel, Italy, Jamaica, Japan, Jordan, Kazakhstan, Kenya, Kiribati, the Republic of Korea, Kuwait, Kyrgyzstan, Latvia, Lebanon, Lesotho, Liberia, Libya, Liechtenstein, Lithuania, Luxembourg, the ex-Yugoslav Republic of Macedonia, Madagascar, Malawi, Mali, Malta, Marshall Islands, Mauritius, Mexico, Micronesia, Moldova, Monaco, Mongolia, Morocco, Mozambique, Namibia, Nauru, Nepal, the Netherlands, New Zealand, Nicaragua, Niger, Nigeria, Norway, Pakistan, Palau, Panama, Papua New Guinea, Paraguay, Peru, the Philippines, Poland, Portugal, Qatar, Romania, Rwanda, Saint Kitts and Nevis, Saint Vincent and Grenadine, Samoa, San Marino, Santa Lucia, São Tomé and Principe, Senegal, Serbia and Montenegro, Seychelles, Sierra Leone,

Singapore, Syria, Slovakia, Slovenia, Solomon Islands, South Africa, Spain, Sri Lanka, Sudan, Surinam, Swaziland, Sweden, Switzerland, Tadjikistan, Tanzania, Thailand, Togo, Tonga, Trinidad and Tobago, Tunisia, Turkey, Turkmenistan, Ukraine, Uganda, the United States of America, Uruguay, Uzbekistan, Vanuatu, Venezuela, Yemen, Zambia, and Zimbabwe. In addition, the Holy See maintains permanent observers, usually with the rank of apostolic nuncio (that is, at the ambassadorial level), at the United Nations in New York, the United Nations Specialized Agencies in Geneva, the United Nations Organizations for the Environment (UN Habitat) in Nairobi, the United Nations Food and Agricultural Organizations (FAO, IFAD, WFP) in Rome, the World Trade Organization in Geneva, the Organization of American States in Washington, the Organization of the Arab League in Cairo, and the African Union in Addis Ababa. Permanent observers are also accredited to the International Atomic Energy Agency in Vienna, the Office of Specialized United Nations Agencies in Vienna, the United Nations Organization for Industrial Development in Vienna, the United Nations Educational, Scientific, and Cultural Organization (UNESCO) in Paris, the Council of Europe in Strasbourg, the Organization for Security and Cooperation in Europe (OSCE) in Vienna, and the World Tourism Organization in Madrid.

Chapter Five

1. The origin of the custom of vesting the popes in white is much discussed. Officially, the papal color is the distinctive reddish hue known in Latin as *purpura* (Italian, *porpora*), or imperial red. Whatever the historicity of the claims that it was bestowed by the Emperor Constantine the Great on Pope St. Sylvester I (314–335) in recognition of the spiritual sovereignty of the bishop of Rome, the color was emblematic of authority in the Roman cultural milieu: Senators bordered their tunics with it, while the emperor alone was allowed to robe himself in a mantle of the color. Certainly, during the period of the investiture controversy, the medieval pontiffs jealously and explicitly defended their rights to use robes of *purpora*. Even in the present day, after the simplifications introduced into Catholic rituals following Vatican II, the pope still reserves to himself alone the use of a *purpora*-colored cape and a similarly-colored mozzetta, or buttoned shoulder cape. And the color for papal funerals and mourning has never been the black (or, more recently, violet or white) utilized for the offices for other Catholics but that same distinctive reddish hue.

    Whatever the specific origin of the papal use of the imperial red, its employ is ancient, as seen in numerous frescoes and mosaics dating back to the fifth century. In those same artistic monuments, the only white that appeared in papal vesture was the common white tunic that everyone wore under his external vesture. Only with the election of popes from religious orders that traditionally wore white habits—especially the Cistercians and Dominicans—did popes principally vest themselves entirely in white. Consequently, the papal use of white is usually attributed to Pope St. Pius V (1566–1572), who continued, even during his pontificate, to dress ordinarily in his simple white Dominican habit. But, as noted above, even since then, the *purpora* remains the official distinctive papal color, and other churchmen, especially in tropical countries, also wear a white cassock.

2. While traditionally tight-sleeved and lace-decorated, since the pontificate of Pope Paul VI, the popes themselves and other prelates have favored wider-sleeved rochets made of fabrics that are easier to maintain, although the older form of the vestment has never been officially altered. Pope John Paul II has preferred a very simple design, discreetly decorated by gray-colored embroidery and hand knotting, made in Valencia, Spain, by Manantial/Sorgente, a cooperative run by a lay religious institute of women.

3. Pope John Paul II has worn exclusively the simple red model traditionally known as the "summer mozzetta." Earlier pontiffs used this garment from Pentecost to the onset of cold weather. During the cold months they used the "winter mozzetta," made of red velvet and trimmed with white ermine. From Easter until Pentecost, the mozzetta was traditionally white damask trimmed with white ermine. For "imperial red," see note 1 above.

4. Traditionally, the papal zucchetto is presented to the new pontiff by the secretary of the conclave, to whom the pope gives the red cardinal's skullcap he previously used, as a sign of the man being elevated to the College of Cardinals to take the place of one elected pope as well as to reward him for his services during the *sede vacante*. Leo XIII (1878–1903) put an end to this centuries-old custom when he simply pocketed his red cardinal's hat. John XXIII, a noted lover of old customs despite his progressive spirit, placed his own red skullcap on the head of the kneeling secretary of the conclave, Monsignor Alberto di Jorio, naming him cardinal deacon. Interestingly, John also restored the use of the papal *camauro*, a soft hat made of imperial ("papal") red velvet and lined with white ermine, as an occasional substitute for the white skullcap, becoming the first pope to use that headgear since the Renaissance.

   Until the pontificate of John Paul II, who prefers ordinary (brownish-colored) loafers, the popes wore red silk slippers trimmed with gold cord and embroidered in gold thread with a cross that indicated the place on the papal foot that supplicants were expected to kiss.

5. The hymn is often called the "Ambrosian Hymn" for its legendary origins in the baptism of the newly converted St. Augustine by St. Ambrose, the Bishop of Milan. According to this account, the first line of the *Te Deum* was intoned by Ambrose in thanksgiving. The newly baptized Augustine responded with the second line. Whatever the truth of the legend, the hymn is of extremely ancient origin and is traditionally sung by two choirs, alternating the stanzas. Over the centuries, the hymn, both in its hauntingly melodic original chant form and in the various settings that classical composers have been inspired to compose for it, has been sung on numerous solemn historical occasions.

6. After the fall of Rome to the armies of the Italian unification under the Savoy monarchy in 1870, Pope Leo XIII, Pope St. Pius X, and Pope Benedict XV did not appear on the external balcony, which faced into the city that they regarded as illegally occupied against them. After the announcement of their election, there was a momentary pause while the crowd filed into St. Peter's Basilica to greet the pope, who appeared on an internal balcony, also accessed from the Hall of Benedictions. The appearance of Pope Pius XI (1922–1939) on the external balcony was an early indication of his commitment to reaching a settlement with the Italian state, as he himself explained to the astonished cardinals: "I desire to add one word. I protest in the presence of the members of the Sacred College that it is my heart's desire to safeguard and defend all the rights of the Church and all the prerogatives of the Holy See, and, having said that, I wish that my first blessing should go forth as a symbol of that peace to which humanity aspires, not only to Rome and to Italy, but to all the Church and to the whole world. I will give my blessing from the outer balcony of St. Peter's."

7. The Mass for the coronation of the pope had another particular rite. Three times during the entrance, the procession would halt and a master of ceremonies would approach the pope carrying a rod with a ball of flax mounted at the end. Holding the ball before the pope, the master of ceremonies would light it on fire, quickly reducing it to ashes. During this fiery display, the master of ceremonies would intone the formula *"Pater Sancte, sic transit gloria mundi!"* ("Holy Father, thus passes the world's glory!"). It was as if the new pope, in the midst of his earthly exaltation, would need reminding that it was all transitory.

8. Thomas Babington Macaulay, *Critical and Historical Essays*, vol. 2 (London: J.M. Dent & Sons, 1907), 38–39. The essay was originally published in *The Edinburgh Review* 72 (October 1840): 227–228.

Chapter Six

1. ABC News perhaps took the prize for prematurity with the revision of its in-house *Papal Handbook* in early 1996. The preceding year saw the publication of Peter Hebblethwaite's *The Next Pope* (San Francisco: Harper-San Francisco, 1995). After Hebblethwaite's death, his widow, Margaret, published a revised edition in 2000. Ironically, not only did Hebblethwaite predecease Pope John Paul II, but several of veteran Vatican observer's "top picks" to succeed the pontiff have died awaiting their chance as *papabili*. On May 11, 1998, *U.S. News & World Report* featured as its cover story "The Next Pope"; again, John Paul ended up presiding at funeral services for several of the "leading contenders" mentioned by the newsmagazine.

2. On February 1, 2005, immediately before Pope John Paul II's first hospitalization, the director of the Press Office of the Holy See, Dr. Joaquin Navarro Valls—a physician by training, no less—claimed that the pontiff was merely suffering from

a bout of the flu. When the pope was hospitalized the second time, on February 25, Vatican officials circulated the text of a letter he allegedly dictated while en route to the Gemelli Hospital—a rather prodigious feat considering that the medical condition that necessitated his hospitalization led his physicians to carry out a tracheotomy.

3. The formal certification noted the proximate medical causes of death were "septic shock and cardiac arrest" and officially acknowledged for the first time what many had long suspected, that the late pontiff had suffered from Parkinson's disease.

4. A third eligible Pauline cardinal, Jaime Sin, archbishop emeritus of Manila, was excused due to health reasons as was one creation of John Paul II, Cardinal Adolfo Suarez Rivera, archbishop emeritus of Monterrey.

5. Contrary to the popular notion, the Second Vatican Council did not abolish the use of Latin in the Catholic Church. Rather the council permitted the introduction of modern languages into the liturgy, while retaining Latin as the official liturgical language of the Roman ("Latin") Rite as well as the official language of the Roman Curia. However, the introduction of the vernacular has in fact come at the expense of the Latin language. During one meeting of the Synod of Bishops attended by the author, when the participants broke into discussion groups, only two people showed up for the Latin group: the author as the appointed secretary and an elderly Eastern European bishop who spoke none of the other principal languages offered. See my study on the demise of Latin in the Church: "Latin in the Liturgy Today: Theological, Canonical, and Pastoral Reflections," *Sacred Music* 125, no. 3 (Fall 1998): 10–18.

6. The nadir to which Latin has fallen was evidenced to all during Pope John Paul II's penultimate consistory for the creation of cardinals. During the concelebrated Mass in St. Peter's Square on February 23, 2001, one of the newly created cardinals, Bernard Agré, archbishop of Abidjan, Côte d'Ivoire, when called upon to read aloud part of the eucharistic prayer, proceeded to read the instructions telling the celebrant how to read the text—the instructions were printed in Latin in the Latin-language missal on the papal altar—totally oblivious to what he was reading out.

7. Others, in contrast, made great efforts to speak up precisely to prove their linguistic skills as they not so subtly promoted their own candidacies.

8. In Pope John Paul's legislation on the conclave, he opened the door to the possibility of a pope selected by a simple majority, pushing aside a bar first set by Alexander III (1159–1181) with his 1179 constitution, *Licet de vitanda*. Specifically, the apostolic constitution *Universi Dominici gregis* stipulated:

> 74. In the event that the Cardinal electors find it difficult to agree on the person to be elected, after balloting has been carried out for three days in the form described above (in Nos. 62ff) without result, voting is to be suspended for a maximum of one day in order to allow a pause for prayer, informal discussion among the voters, and a brief spiritual exhortation given by the senior Cardinal in the Order of Deacons. Voting is then resumed in the usual manner, and after seven ballots, if the election has not taken place, there is another

pause for prayer, discussion and an exhortation given by the senior Cardinal in the Order of Priests. Another series of seven ballots is then held and, if there has still been no election, this is followed by a further pause for prayer, discussion and an exhortation given by the senior Cardinal in the Order of Bishops. Voting is then resumed in the usual manner and, unless the election occurs, it is to continue for seven ballots.

75. If the balloting does not result in an election, even after the provisions of No. 74 have been fulfilled, the Cardinal electors shall be invited by the Camerlengo to express an opinion about the manner of proceeding. The election will then proceed in accordance with what the absolute majority of the electors decides.

Nevertheless, there can be no waiving of the requirement that a valid election takes place only by an absolute majority of the votes or else by voting only on the two names which in the ballot immediately preceding have received the greatest number of votes; also in this second case only an absolute majority is required.

9. In perspective, part of the resentment may have been due to Martini's very effective communications department: Not only were his comments on many issues professionally distributed, but almost all his sermons and speeches were recorded and published, not only in Italian but in all the major European languages as well.

10. The precise number of John Paul II's cardinalatial creations is subject to debate. There were to have been twenty-five new cardinals created in the consistory of June 28, 1988—which was announced on May 29—but one of the prelates, Swiss theologian Hans Urs von Balthasar, died unexpectedly on June 26. The list for the consistory of February 21, 1998, had twenty-three names, but Archbishop Giuseppe Uhác died the morning of the public announcement, January 18, after being informed of his elevation, but before its publication. The consistory of October 21, 2003, included the nomination of a cardinal *in pectore*, whose name was not made public. Under the former canonical legislation, it was clear that a prelate did not become a member of the College of Cardinals until after the ceremonies of the consistory. The present legislation is uncertain on the point, but internal references seem to indicate that membership in the college takes effect with the announcement of the name, even before the formal consistorial rites.

11. Italian for the French *dauphin*, the heir to the throne. In modern ecclesiastical historiography, the term has been used twice to designate a cardinal whom an incumbent pontiff desired as his successor: for Cardinal Eugenio Pacelli, later Pope Pius XII (1939–1958), during the later years of Pope Pius XI (1922–1939), and for Cardinal Giovanni Benelli under Pope Paul VI (1963–1978).

12. The future Pope Paul VI's immediate superior in the Secretariat of State, the future Cardinal Alfredo Ottaviani, who was the *sostituto* at the time, arranged for the young Monsignor Montini to be sent to the seaside resort of Nettuno for complete rest, paying his stipend in full—a rare kindness in the Roman Curia of the time. Paul repaid Ottaviani's kindness by forcing the old cardinal, by then blind but still mentally sharp, into involuntary retirement in 1968.

13. See Giovanni Reale and Tadeusz Styczen, eds., *Metafisica della persona. Tutte le opera filosofiche e saggi integratividi Karol Wojtyla* (Rome: Bompiani, 2003).

14. Zimbabwean president Robert G. Mugabe, a Roman Catholic, used his attendance at the funeral as a diplomatic loophole to evade European Union sanctions that would have otherwise barred him from traveling to any of the union's member states because of his regime's appalling human rights record.

15. Cardinal Nguyên van Thuân's principal spiritual work is *The Road of Hope: Thoughts of Light from a Prison Cell*, edited and translated with introduction by the present author (London: New City Press, 1997). Editions of this work, which the cardinal wrote and smuggled from prison, have been translated into some two dozen languages. His memoirs, *Five Loaves and Two Fish*, likewise edited with an introduction by the present author (Washington, D.C.: Morley Books, 2001), had the unique distinction of carrying a dust-jacket endorsement from no less a figure than Pope John Paul II.

16. Marco Damilano, "Prove di conclave. La frenetica campagna del cardinale Tettamanzi," *Espresso*, October 10, 2003.

17. See Angelo Scola, *Hans Urs von Balthasar: A Theological Style* (Grand Rapids, Michigan: William B. Eerdmans Publishing, 1995).

18. At the time of his death in 2002, Cardinal François-Xavier Nguyên van Thuân was the only cardinal in the Roman Curia to descend from a family of the hereditary nobility; in his case, his heroic story and personal simplicity, as well as the fact that Far Eastern aristocracy is not well known in Rome, played in his favor. In contrast, until as recently as the time of the Second Vatican Council, the papal court had cardinals bearing historic names like Caccia Dominioni, Canali, Fürstenberg, Granito Pignatelli di Belmonte, and Nasalli Rocca di Corneliano.

19. Although one incident does not a trend make, the conclave of 2005 suggests that John Paul II's changes to the electoral system, should they be maintained, might over time entirely change the dynamics of electing a Roman Pontiff.

20. See John R. Quinn, *The Reform of the Papacy: The Costly Call to Christian Unity* (New York: Crossroad/Herder & Herder, 1999).

21. See Avery Dulles, "The Reform of the Papacy," *First Things* 104 (June/July 2000): 62–64.

22. Adding up the various figures reported in the *Annuario Pontificio* 2005—for some reason, the official yearbook of the Holy See gives data by individual diocese or religious order, but no global, regional, or national composites—there are 405,058 priests worldwide, of whom 267,344 were diocesan priests and 137,724 were priests who are members of religious communities. The yearbook also reported the ordinations of 9,317 new priests in the preceding year. Worldwide, there were 112,373 seminarians preparing for ordination, although that number includes students ranging from those who just had finished their secondary education to ordained transitional deacons completing graduate theological studies.

23. These data and other indices were compiled as part of a national Seminary Assessment Project directed by the present author for the Morley Institute in the

1990s. For a summary report see "Seminaries and Seminarians: A Profile," *Crisis* 16, no. 11 (December 1998): 20–23.

24. For more details, see the present author's report "America's Seminaries: A House Built on Sand," *Crisis* 16, no. 10 (November 1998): 14–19.

25. See Richard John Neuhaus, "Scandal Time (Continued)," *First Things* 124 (June/ July 2002): 75–100.

26. Although clerical celibacy in the Latin Church is an ecclesiastical discipline rather than a matter of theological faith, it has been defended with a fervor usually re- served for the latter. Giving the lie to the Second Vatican Council's affirmation that "the Catholic Church holds in high esteem the institutions, liturgical rites, ecclesiastical traditions and the established standards of the Christian life of the Eastern Churches…distinguished as they are for their venerable antiquity" (*Orientalium Ecclesiarum*, n. 1), the Vatican seems to fear that the married priests of the Eastern Catholic Churches might somehow "infect" the Western Church. After all, if they can legitimately marry, why can't priests of the Latin Rite? As late as the summer of 2003, the Italian Episcopal Conference asked the Catholic bish- ops of Ukraine to stop sending married priests to Italy to minister to their immi- grant confrères, declaring that the married clergy "create confusion among our faithful." In the United States, a special prohibition on the ordination of married priests for Eastern Churches is still officially in place, although the Ukrainian and Greek Melkite hierarchs have been honoring it in the breach.

27. See John T. Noonan Jr., *Contraception: A History of Its Treatment by Catholic Theologians and Canonists* (Cambridge: Harvard University Press, 1966).

28. See, for example, Ralph M. McInerny, *What Went Wrong with Vatican II: The Catholic Crisis Explained* (Manchester, New Hampshire: Sophia Institute Press, 1998); and George Weigel, *The Courage to Be Catholic: Crisis, Reform, and the Future of the Church* (New York: Basic Books, 2002). Both authors are among those who attribute the "crisis of dissent" and other woes in the contemporary Catholic Church to the failure to enforce adherence to the moral doctrine of *Humanae vitae* and other official teachings on sexual matters.

29. See, for example, Garry Wills, *Papal Sins: Structures of Deceit* (New York: Doubleday, 2000); and John Cornwell, *Breaking Faith: Can the Catholic Church Save Itself?* (New York: Penguin, 2002). Both authors are among those who point to the Church's teachings on contraception as examples of its "disconnect" with modernity.

30. Although the document bore the traditional formula "Given at the Vatican . . . ," Pope John Paul II was in Rome's Gemelli Clinic recovering from a complete re- placement of his right hip (the pontiff had a complete trans-cervical fracture of his right femur following a fall on April 28, 1994) and did not return to the Vatican until May 29, 1994.

31. New York: Pantheon Books, 1997. For a more dispassionate, but nonetheless criti- cal, account of the phenomenon of annulments, see Robert H. Vasoli, *What God Has Joined Together: The Annulment Crisis in American Catholicism* (New York:

Oxford University Press, 1998). Vasoli is a retired professor of sociology at the University of Notre Dame.

32. In fairness to ecclesiastical tribunals in the United States, it should be noted that they are not alone in their lackadaisical approach. Vasoli, *What God Has Joined Together*, 228, cites Vatican statistics that show Canadian tribunals being equally permissive.

33. See Vasoli, *What God Has Joined Together*, 160.

34. David Van Biema, "The Political Fallout of an Annulment: Should Annulments Be So Easy?" *Time*, May 12, 1997.

35. For a complete list, see note 17 to Chapter 4.

36. The unbalanced nature of the Holy See's official diplomatic position was troubling to a number of insiders. An official position paper (N. 1756/03, dated February 28, 2003) prepared by the Section for Relations with States of the Secretariat of State (the Holy See's "foreign ministry") and circulated in the form of a *pro memoria* to the heads of the Holy See's diplomatic missions around the world categorically "rejecte[d] the notion of 'pre-emptive war,' which the Holy See judges an error" and declared that "only the [United Nations] Security Council can determine if there is a threat to peace." The document, which passed over in silence any mention of the grave human rights and other abuses by Saddam Hussein, went on to adopt the extraordinary position that "priority should be given to resolving the ongoing grave conflict in the Holy Land" before addressing the Iraqi situation. Given that the Holy See's position did not differ substantially from the line espoused by French diplomacy, a few diplomats noted that the then-secretary for relations with states, Archbishop Jean-Louis Tauran, was himself a Frenchman and attempted to ascribe a certain causal relationship between the two observations. While such a thesis cannot be excluded *a priori*, it fails to account for the consistently *pacifistic* position that the Holy See espoused during John Paul II's pontificate.

37. Concerning his experience, Bernhard Häring once wrote to the present author: "Remember whoever loves the Church must also be prepared to suffer in the Church, with the Church, through the Church, and for the Church!" (Letter, April 7, 1994).

38. Hilaire Belloc, *Europe and the Faith* (New York: Paulist Press, 1920), ix.

39. This estimate is based on projections in David B. Barrett, George T. Kurian, and Todd M. Johnson, eds., *World Christian Encyclopedia*, 2d ed. (New York: Oxford University Press, 2001), 12.

40. Philip Jenkins, *The Next Christendom: The Coming of Global Christianity* (New York: Oxford University Press, 2002), 195.

41. See Bruce Bawer, "Mendacity and the Magisterium," *Hudson Review* 56, no. 2 (Summer 2003).

42. While there was much talk following John Paul II's death about the possibility of his successor coming from the global south, with the deaths of the two likely standard bearers mentioned above, this author found the prospect rather unlikely. See the op-ed published the day of conclave's opening, "Is America Really Ready for a Third World Pope?" *Wall Street Journal* (April 18, 2005): A18.

43. The *Annuario Pontificio 2005* claims 1,086,000,000 baptized Catholics, representing 17.3 percent of a global population of 6.3 billion. The distribution of the world's Catholics puts just under 50 percent in the Americas, 25.7 percent in Europe, 13.2 percent in Africa, 10.3 percent in Asia, and 0.8 percent in Oceania. With respect to the entire population, Catholics represent 62.5 percent of the inhabitants of the Americas, 39.5 percent of Europeans, 26.4 percent of the inhabitants of Oceania, 16.7 percent of Africans, and 2.9 percent of Asians.

SELECT BIBLIOGRAPHY

Principal Official Documents of the Modern Period Relevant to the "Sede Vacante" and the Election of the Roman Pontiff[1]

Pius IX. Apostolic Constitution *In hac sublime* (August 21, 1871).

———. Apostolic Constitution *Licet per apostolicas* (September 8, 1874).

———. Apostolic Constitution *Consulturi* (October 10, 1877).

Pius X. Apostolic Constitution *Commissum Nobis* (January 20, 1904).

———. Apostolic Constitution *Vacante Sede Apostolica* (December 25, 1904).

Pius XI. Motu Proprio *Cum proxime* (March 1, 1922).

Pius XII. Apostolic Constitution *Vacantis Apostolicae Sedis* (December 8, 1945).

John XXIII. Motu Proprio *Regimini Ecclesiae Universae* (August 15, 1967).

Paul VI. Motu Proprio *Ingravescentem aetatem* (November 21, 1970).

———. Apostolic Constitution *Romano Pontifici eligendo* (October 1, 1975).

John Paul II. Apostolic Constitution *Pastor Bonus* (June 28, 1988).

———. Apostolic Constitution *Universi Dominici gregis* (February 22, 1996).

Code of Canon Law (1983), especially canons 330–359.

Other Sources

Accatoli, Luigi. *Karol Wojtýa. L'uomo di fine millennio*. Milan: Edizioni San Paolo, 1998.

Alberigo, Giuseppe, and Andrea Riccardi. *Chiesa e papato nel mondo contemporaneo*. Rome/Bari: Editori Laterza, 1990.

---

[1] These and other official documents of the Holy See are published in its official gazettes: *Acta Sanctae Sedis* (1900–1907) and *Acta Apostolicae Sedis* (1908–present).

Alvarez, David. *Spies in the Vatican: Espionage and Intrigue from Napoleon to the Holocaust.* Lawrence, Kansas: University Press of Kansas, 2002.

Alvarez, David, and Robert A. Graham. *Nothing Sacred: Nazi Espionage against the Vatican, 1939–1945.* London/Portland, Oregon: Frank Cass Publishers, 1997.

Andreotti, Giulio. *Visti da vicino.* Milan: Edizioni Rizzoli, 1992.

———. *A ogni morte di papa. I papi che ho conosciuto.* Milan: Biblioteca Universale Rizzoli, 1982.

Arborio Mella di Sant'Elia, Alberto. *Istanee inedited degli ultimi 4 Papi.* Modena: Edizioni Paoline, 1956.

Baldan, Sergio. *Il conclave di Venezia e l'elezione di Pio VII, 1 dicembre 1799–14 marzo 1800.* Venice: Marsilio/Regione di Venezia, 2000.

Barrett, David B., George T. Kurian, and Todd M. Johnson, eds. *World Christian Encyclopedia,* 2d ed. New York: Oxford University Press, 2001.

Beinert, Wolfgang, Francis Schussler Fiorenza, and Elizabeth Schussler Fiorenza, eds. *The Handbook of Catholic Theology.* New York: Crossroad, 1995.

Bernstein, Carl, and Marco Politi. *His Holiness: John Paul II and the Hidden History of Our Time.* New York: Doubleday, 1996.

Berthelet, Giovanni. *La elezione del papa. Storia e documenti.* Rome: Forzani e C. Tipografi Editori, 1903.

———. *Storia e rivelazioni sul conclave del 1903.* Turin/Rome: Casa Editrice Nazionale, 1904.

Biffi, Monica M. *Mons. Cesare Orsenigo. Nunzio Apostolico in Germania (1930–1946).* Milan: NED, 1997.

Bihlmeyer, Karl, with Hermann Tüchle. *Church History,* 3 vols. 13th edition. Trans. Victor E. Mills and Francis J. Muller. Westminster, Maryland: Newman Press, 1966–1968.

Blet, Pierre. *Pius XII and the Second World War.* Trans. Lawrence J. Johnson. New York: Paulist Press, 1999.

Brandmüller, Walter. *Papst und Konzil im Grossen Schism (1378–1431): Studien und Quellen.* Paderborn: F. Schöningh, 1990.

Bunson, Matthew. *Encyclopedia of Catholic History.* Huntington, Indiana: Our Sunday Visitor, 1995.

Caraman, Philip. *University of the Nations: The Story of the Gregorian University of Rome from 1551 to Vatican II.* New York/Ramsey, New Jersey: Paulist Press, 1981.

Cardinale, Hyginus Eugene. *The Holy See and the International Order.* Gerrards Cross: Colin Smythe, 1976.

Casaroli, Agostino. *Il martirio della pazienza. La Santa Sede e i paesi comunisti, 1963–1989.* Ed. Carlo Felice Casula and Giovanni Maria Vann. Turin: Einaudi, 2000.

Cavaterra, Emilio. *Il prefetto del Sant'Uffizio. Le opere e i giorni del cardinale Ottaviani.* Milan: Edizioni Mursia, 1990.

Cenci, Pio. *Il cardinale Merry del Val.* Rome/Turin: Roberto Berruti e C. Editori, 1955.

Cerreti, Alfonso. *La politica dei papi nel medioevo da Giovanni I ad Innocenzo III.* Messina: A. Sessa Editore, 1950.

Chadwick, Owen. *Britain and the Vatican during the Second World War.* Cambridge: Cambridge University Press, 1986.

————. *A History of the Popes, 1830–1914.* Oxford: Clarendon Press, 1998.

Chelini, Jean. *La vita quotidiana in Vaticano sotto Giovanni Paolo II.* Milan: Biblioteca Universale Rizzoli, 1986.

Confalonieri, Carlo. *Pio XI visto da vicino.* Rev. ed. Ed. Giuseppe Frasso. Cinisello Balsamo: Edizioni Paoline, 1993.

Consalvi, Ercole. *Mémoires du cardinal Consalvi,* 2 vols. Rev. ed. Ed. with introduction by J. Crétineau-Joly. Paris: H. Plon, 1866.

Coppa, Frank J. *The Modern Papacy since 1789.* London/New York: Pearson Longman, 1998.

————. *Controversial Concordats: The Vatican's Relations with Napoleon, Mussolini, and Hitler.* Washington, D.C.: Catholic University of America Press, 1999.

Coppa, Frank J. (ed.). *Encyclopedia of the Vatican and the Papacy.* Westport, Connecticut: Greenwood Press, 1999.

Cornwell, John. *Breaking Faith: Can the Catholic Church Save Itself?* New York: Penguin, 2002.

————. *Hitler's Pope: The Secret History of Pius XII.* New York: Viking, 1999.

————. *A Thief in the Night: Life and Death in the Vatican.* 1989; New York: Penguin, 2001.

Corral Salvador, Carlos. *La relacción entre la Iglesia y la comunidad política.* Madrid: Biblioteca de Autores Cristianos, 2003.

Davis, Raymond, trans. and ed. *The Book of Pontiffs (Liber Pontificalis): The Ancient Biographies of the First Ninety Roman Bishops to A.D. 715.* Rev. ed. Liverpool: Liverpool University Press, 2000.

De Agostini, Cesare. *Eminenti e Eminentissimi. Tutto quello che dovrebbe sapere sui cardinali del '900.* Casale Monferrato: Edizioni PIEMME, 2002.

————. *Segregati da Dio. Tutti I conclave del '900.* Casale Monferrato: Edizioni PIEMME, 2002.

Duffy, Eamon. *Saints and Sinners: A History of the Popes.* Rev. ed. New Haven: Yale University Press, 2002.

Feldkamp, Martin F. *La diplomatie pontificale de Sylvestre Ier à Jean-Paul II. Une vue d'ensemble.* Paris: Paris: Editions du Cerf, 2001.

Franchi, Antonino. *Il conclave di Viterbo (1268–1271) e le sue origini. Saggio con documenti inediti.* Ascoli Piceno: Edizioni Porziuncola, 1993.

Frossard, André. *Le monde de Jean-Paul II.* Paris: Editions Fayard, 1991.

————. *"N'ayez pas peur!" André Frossard dialogue avec Jean-Paul II.* Paris: Editions Robert Laffront, 1982.

Garuti, Adriano. *Primato del vescovo di Roma e dialogo ecumenico.* Rome: Pontificio Ateneo "Antonianum," 2000.

Gligora, Francesco, and Biagia Catanzaro, eds. *Storia dei papi e degli antipapi da San Pietro a Giovanni Paolo II,* 2 vols. Padua: Edizioni Panda, 1989.

Graham, Robert A. *The Vatican and Communism in World War II: What Really Happened?* San Francisco: Ignatius Press, 1996.

————. *Vatican Diplomacy: A Study of Church and State on the International Plane.* Princeton: Princeton University Press, 1959.

Greeley, Andrew M. *The Making of the Popes, 1978: The Politics of Intrigue in the Vatican.* Kansas City: Andrews & McMeel, 1979.

Grone, Mario. *Accanto al "mio" Cardinal Siri.* Genoa: Casa Editrice Marietti, 1996.

Guitton, Jean. *Dialogues avec Paul VI.* Paris: Editions Fayard, 1967.

Hart, Trevor A., ed. *The Dictionary of Historical Theology.* Grand Rapids, Michigan: Wm. B. Eerdmans, 2000.

Hebblethwaite, Peter. *John XXIII: Pope of the Council.* Revised edition. London: Fount/Collins, 1994.

———. *The Next Pope: A Behind-the-Scenes Look at How the Successor to John Paul II Will Be Elected and Where He Will Lead the Church.* Rev. ed. Rev. and updated by Margaret Hebblethwaite. San Francisco: HarperSanFrancisco, 2000.

———. *Paul VI: The First Modern Pope.* London: HarperCollins, 1993.

———. *The Year of Three Popes.* London: Fount/Collins, 1978.

Heim, Bruno Bernhard. *Heraldry in the Catholic Church: Its Origins, Customs, and Laws.* Rev. ed. Gerrards Cross: Van Duren Publishers, 1981.

Hughes, John Jay. *Pontiffs: Popes Who Shaped History.* Huntington, Indiana: Our Sunday Visitor Press, 1994.

Jaki, Stanley L. *And On This Rock: The Witness of One Land and Two Covenants.* 2d ed. Manassas, Virginia: Trinity Communications, 1987.

———. *Keys of the Kingdom: A Tool's Witness to Truth.* Chicago: Franciscan Herald Press, 1987.

Jedin, Hubert, ed. *Handbuch der Kirchengeschichte.* Freiburg: Herder, 1999.

Jenkins, Philip. *The Next Christendom: The Coming of Global Christianity.* New York: Oxford University Press, 2002.

John XXIII. *Journal of a Soul: The Autobiography of John XXIII.* Trans. Dorothy White with introduction by Loris Capovilla. New York: McGraw-Hill, 1965.

John Paul II. *Crossing the Threshold of Hope.* Edited by Vittorio Messori. New York: Alfred A. Knopf, 1994.

———. *Gift and Mystery: On the Fiftieth Anniversary of My Priestly Ordination.* New York: Doubleday, 1997.

Kelly, J.N.D. *The Oxford Dictionary of Popes.* Oxford and New York: Oxford University Press, 1986.

Kennedy, Sheila Rauch. *Shattered Faith: A Woman's Struggle to Stop the Catholic Church from Annulling Her Marriage.* New York: Pantheon Books, 1997.

Lai, Benny. *Il papa non eletto. Giuseppe Siri, cardinale di Santa Romana Chiesa.* Bari: Editori Laterza, 1993.

———. *I segreti del Vaticano da Pio XII a papa Wojtyla.* Rome/Bari: Editori Laterza, 1984.

Lector, Lucius.[2] *Le conclave. Origines, histoire, organisation, législation ancienne et moderne.* Paris: Editions P. Lethielleux, 1894.

---

[2]"Lucius Lector," the pseudonym under which this valuable reference work—as well as its shorter predecessor volume (1878)—was published, was a French prelate, Monsignor Joseph Guthlin.

Lefebvre, Marcel. *I Accuse the Council*. Kansas City, Missouri: Angelus Press, 1982.

Levillain, Philippe, ed. *Dictionnaire historique de la papauté*. Paris: Editions Fayard, 1994.

van Lierde, Petrus Canisius Johannes. *The Holy See at Work: How the Church is Governed*. Trans. James Tucek. New York: Hawthorn Books, 1962.

van Lierde, Petrus Canisius Johannes, with A. Giraud. *What Is a Cardinal?* Trans. A. Manson. *Twentieth-Century Encyclopedia of Catholicism*, vol. 84. New York: Hawthorn Books, 1964.

Luidprand of Cremona. *The Embassy to Constantinople and Other Writings*. Trans. F. A. Wright. Ed. John Julius Norwich. London/Portland, Vermont: J. M. Denton/Charles E. Tuttle Company, 1993.

McBrien, Richard P. *Lives of the Popes*. San Francisco: HarperSanFrancisco, 1997.

———, ed. *The HarperCollins Encyclopedia of Catholicism*. San Francisco: HarperCollins, 1995.

McInerny, Ralph M. *What Went Wrong with Vatican II: The Catholic Crisis Explained*. Manchester, New Hampshire: Sophia Institute Press, 1998.

Malinski, Mieczyslaw. *Pope John Paul II: The Life of Karol Wojtyla*. New York: Seabury Press, 1979.

Martin, Jacques. *Heraldry in the Vatican*. Ed. with introduction by Peter Bander van Duren. Gerrards Cross: Van Duren Publishers, 1987.

———. *Oltre il portone di bronzo (Appunti di un cardinale vissuto a fianco di 6 papi)*. Milan: Edizioni Paoline, 1996.

Martin, Victor. *Les cardinaux et la curie. Tribunaux et offices. La vacance du Siège apostolique*. Paris: Blond & Gay, 1930.

Mathieu, François-Desiré. *Le concordat de 1801. Ses origines—son histoire d'après des documents inédits*. Paris: Perrin et Cie., 1903.

Melady, Margaret B. *The Rhetoric of John Paul II: The Pastoral Visit as the New Vocabulary of the Sacred*. Westport, Connecticut/London: Praeger Publishers, 1999.

Melady, Thomas Patrick. *The Ambassador's Story: The United States and the Vatican in World Affairs*. Huntington, Indiana: Our Sunday Visitor Press, 1994.

Mondin, Battista. *Dizionario enciclopedico dei papi*. Rome: Città Nuova Editrice, 1995.

Montini, Giovanni Battista (Paul VI). *La "Responsio super nuntiaturis" di papa Pio VI. Appunti delle lezioni. Pontificio Istituto "Utriusque Iuris" S. Apollinare, Anno accademico 1936–1937*. Rome: Editrice Studium, 1936.

Nasalli Rocca di Corneliano, Mario. *Accanto ai Papi*. Vatican City: Libreria Editrice Vaticana, 1976.

Nguyên van Thuân, François-Xavier. *Five Loaves and Two Fish: Spiritual Memoirs of a Prisoner for Christ*. Ed. with introduction by John-Peter Pham. Washington, D.C.: Morley Books, 2000.

———. *The Road of Hope: Thoughts of Light from a Prison Cell*. Trans. and ed. with introduction by John-Peter Pham. London: New City Press, 1997.

Noonan, John T., Jr. *Contraception: A History of Its Treatment by Catholic Theologians and Canonists*. Cambridge: Harvard University Press, 1966.

Oddi, Silvio. *Il tenero mastino di Dio. Memorie del Cardinale Silvio Oddi.* Rome: Museali Editori, 1995.

d'Onorio, Joël-Benoît. *La nomination des évêques. Procédures canoniques et conventions diplomatiques.* Revised edition. Paris: Tardy, 2003.

———. *Plaidoyer pour Jean-Paul II.* Paris: J.-C. Lattès, 1996.

———. *Le Saint-Siège dans les relations internationales.* Paris: Editions du Cerf, 1989.

———, ed. *La diplomatie de Jean-Paul II.* Paris: Editions du Cerf, 2000.

von Pastor, Ludwig. *The History of the Popes from the Close of the Middle Ages, Drawn from the Secret Archives of the Vatican and Other Sources.* 40 vols. Saint Louis: B. Herder, 1899–1933.

Pelikan, Jaroslav. *The Christian Tradition: A History of the Development of Doctrine,* 5 vols. Chicago: University of Chicago Press, 1971–1989.

Peyrefitte, Roger. *Les secrets des conclaves.* Paris: Editions Flammarion, 1964.

Pham, John-Peter. *A Primer for the Catechism of the Catholic Church.* Rev. ed. Chicago: Midwest Theological Forum, 1997.

———. *I primi martiri cristiani. Lineamenti tentativi di una nuova valutazioni critica delle fonti.* Rome: Pontificio Istituto di Archaeologia Cristiana, 1994.

———. *The Sacrament of Penance in the Teachings of the Last Five Popes.* Chicago: Midwest Theological Forum, 1996.

———, ed. *Centesimus Annus: Assessment and Perspectives for the Future of Catholic Social Doctrine.* Vatican City: Libreria Editrice Vaticana, 1998.

Pirie, Valérie. *The Triple Crown: An Account of the Papal Conclaves from the Fifteenth Century to the Present Day.* London: Sidgwick & Jackson, 1935.

Plock, Herbert. *Das "ius exclusivae" der Staaten bei der Papstwahl und sein Verbot durch die päpstliche Bulle "Commissum nobis."* Göttingen: Hofer-Verlag, 1910.

Pollard, John F. *The Unknown Pope: Benedict XV (1914–1922) and the Pursuit of Peace.* London: Geoffrey Chapman, 1999.

Quinn, John R. *The Reform of the Papacy: The Costly Call to Christian Unity.* New York: Crossroad/Herder & Herder, 1999.

von Ranke, Leopold. *History of the Papacy: Political and Ecclesiastical in the Sixteenth and Seventeenth Centuries,* 2 vols. Trans. with introduction by Jean-Henri Merle d'Aubigné. Glasgow: Blackie & Son, 1863.

Reese, Thomas J. *Inside the Vatican: The Politics and Organization of the Catholic Church.* Cambridge: Harvard University Press, 1996.

Rhodes, Anthony. *The Vatican in the Age of Dictators.* New York: Holt, Rinehart & Winston, 1973.

Roncalli, Marco. *Giovanni XXIII. Nel ricordo del segretario Loris F. Capovilla.* Milan: Edizioni San Paolo, 1994.

Saba, Agostino, and Carlo Castiglioni. *Storia dei papi,* 2 vols. Turin: Unione Tipografico-Editrice Torinese, 1957.

Santolaria de Puey y Cruells, José-Apeles. *El Papa ha muerto ¡Viva el Papa!* Barcelona: Plaza Janés Editores, 1997.

Schatz, Klaus. *Papal Primacy: From Its Origins to the Present.* Trans. John A. Otto and Linda M. Maloney. Collegeville, Minnesota: Michael Glazier Books/Liturgical Press, 1996.

Schimmelpfennig, Bernhard. *The Papacy.* Trans. James Sievert. New York: Columbia University Press, 1992.

Seppelt, Franz Xavier. *Geschichte der Päpste von den Anfängen bis zur Mitte des zwanzigsten Jahrhunderts,* 5 vols. Munich: Kösel-Verlag, 1954–1959.

———. *Studien zum pontifikat papst Coelestins V.* Berlin: W. Rothschild, 1910.

Siri, Giuseppe. *Gethsemane: Reflections on the Contemporary Theological Movement.* Chicago: Franciscan Herald Press, 1981.

Snider, Carlo. *L'episcopato del cardinale Andrea C. Ferrara.* Vicenza: Neri Pozza Editore, 1982.

Spadolini, Giovanni, ed. *Il Cardinale Gasparri e la questione romana (Con brani delle memorie inedite).* Florence: Le Monnier, 1973.

Spinosa, Antonio. *Pio XII, l'ultimo papa.* Milan: Mondadori, 1992.

Tillard, Jean-Marie-Roger. *The Bishop of Rome.* Wilmington, Delaware: Michael Glazier, 1983.

Vasoli, Robert H. *What God Has Joined Together: The Annulment Crisis in American Catholicism.* New York: Oxford University Press, 1998.

Vercruysse, Jos. *Fidelis Populus.* "Institut für Europäische Geschichte" Series 48. Wiesbaden: F. Steinger, 1968.

Weigel, George. *The Courage to Be Catholic: Crisis, Reform and the Future of the Church.* New York: Basic Books, 2002.

———. *Witness to Hope: The Biography of Pope John Paul II.* New York: HarperCollins, 1999.

Williamson, Benedict. *The Treaty of the Lateran.* London: Burns, Oates & Washbourne, 1929.

Wills, Garry. *Papal Sin: Structures of Deceit.* New York: Doubleday, 2000.

Wolfe, Alan. *The Transformation of American Religion: How We Actually Live Our Faith.* New York: Free Press, 2003.

Wright, A. D. *The Early Modern Papacy: From the Council of Trent to the French Revolution, 1564–1789.* London/New York: Pearson Longman, 2000.

Yallop, David A. *In God's Name: An Investigation into the Murder of Pope John Paul I.* London: J. Cape, 1984.

Zambarbieri, Annibale. *Il nuovo papato. Sviluppi dell'universalism della Santa Sede dal 1870 ad oggi.* Milan: Edizioni San Paolo, 2001.

Zizola, Gianfranco. *Il conclave: Storia e segreti. L'elezione papale da San Pietro a Giovanni Paolo II.* Rome: Newton Compton Editori, 1993.

———. *Quale papa? Analisi delle strutture elettorali e governative del papato romano.* Rome: Edizioni Borla, 1977.

Zolli, Eugenio (Israel). *Why I Became a Catholic.* Fort Collins, Colorado: Roman Catholic Books, 1996.

INDEX